Fish into Wine

Fish

THE NEWFOUNDLAND
PLANTATION IN THE
SEVENTEENTH CENTURY

PETER E. POPE

The voiage for Bristoll

Published for the Omohundro Institute

of Early American History and

Culture, Williamsburg, Virginia, by the

University of North Carolina Press,

Chapel Hill and London

into Wine

Ne vynes from bordeaux but for goulde

Il bringe goulde from England for vynes

Goulde

The Omohundro Institute of Early American History and Culture is sponsored jointly by the College of William and Mary and the Colonial Williamsburg Foundation. On November 15, 1996, the Institute adopted the present name in honor of a bequest from Malvern H. Omohundro, Jr.

Library of Congress
Cataloging-in-Publication Data
Pope, Peter Edward, 1946–
Fish into wine : the Newfoundland plantation in the
seventeenth century / Peter E. Pope.
    p. cm.
Includes bibliographical references and index.
ISBN 0-8078-2910-2 (alk. paper) —
ISBN 0-8078-5576-6 (pbk. : alk. paper)
1. Newfoundland and Labrador—Social life and customs—
17th century.   2. Newfoundland and Labrador—Economic
conditions—17th century.   3. Plantation life—Newfoundland
and Labrador—History—17th century.   4. Frontier and
pioneer life—Newfoundland and Labrador.   5. English—
Newfoundland and Labrador—History—17th century.
6. Cod fisheries—Newfoundland and Labrador—History—
17th century.   7. Land settlement—Newfoundland and
Labrador—History—17th century.   8. Newfoundland and
Labrador—Emigration and immigration—History—17th
century.   9. England—Emigration and immigration—
History—17th century.   I. Omohundro Institute of Early
American History & Culture.   II. Title.
F1123.P66   2004
971.8′01—dc22
2004002521

This volume received indirect support from an
unrestricted book publication grant awarded to the
Institute by the L. J. Skaggs and Mary C. Skaggs
Foundation of Oakland, California.

cloth   08 07 06 05 04   5 4 3 2 1
paper   08 07 06 05 04   5 4 3 2 1

PREFACE

It is tempting to write several forewords. American readers certainly deserve one to whet their demonstrated appetite for alternative colonial histories: a meal of northern cod to complement the banquet already set by researchers over the last few decades along the eastern seaboard and beyond. The prudent Newfoundlander will write a more diffident foreword for Canadians, reminding them (again) that the history of northern settlement before the British conquest of 1763 is more than the history of New France. That claim will resonate more clearly in Acadia or Quebec than in Upper Canada, for Newfoundland's past is intricately interconnected with the history of its neighbors, whereas central Canadians have an impressive capacity to acknowledge the existence of Atlantic Canada without paying it much sustained attention. In mythic terms, Canada for them is the result of a historic engagement between Britain and France in the mid-eighteenth century, and the existence of earlier English settlements on the Atlantic fringe often seems no more than an inconsistent detail. The colorful story of the Newfoundland fishery will be familiar to British readers, or at least to those with an interest in the West Country or Ireland. Given that a presumed conflict of economic interests between fisher and settler remains the default assumption when English historians turn to the subject of early Newfoundland, they are likely to take the present volume as a piece of revisionism. Newfoundlanders themselves may well read it as a parti pris in a continuing debate over our foundation myth: the supposed illegality of settlement. This is a key feature of our traditional historiography, popularized a century ago by the accomplished regional historian Judge Prowse, in which powerful West Country commercial interests supposedly impeded settlement. This mythology remains influential, although scholars have begun to agree that paper regulation has been overinterpreted as a practical attempt to eliminate settlement. European readers and others familiar with the long and complex history of the Breton, Norman, and Basque transatlantic fisheries will know how much is left as background in this study in order to focus attention on one aspect of North Atlantic history.[1] In the end, I can

1. For alternative colonial histories, see Daniel Vickers, ed., *A Companion to Colonial America* (Malden, Mass., 2003); and Margaret R. Conrad and James K. Hiller, *Atlantic Canada: A Region in the Making* (Don Mills, Ont., 2001). For a tra-

only hope that readers, whatever their point of view, will find the story as interesting as I do.

⟨⟨ The origins of this book lie almost twenty years ago, in my frustration as a student of historical archaeology, when I went to the library to find a social history of the English settlements of seventeenth-century Newfoundland. Not that I came back empty-handed. Gillian Cell's book, *English Enterprise in Newfoundland, 1577–1660*, and C. Grant Head's geographer's perspective in *Eighteenth Century Newfoundland* turned out to be invaluable guides to the periods before and after the one I was trying to understand, roughly 1630–1700. The late Keith Matthew's seminal "Fence-building" essay helped make sense of the existing secondary literature, which seemed curiously selective in its attention to the documentary record. The prejudices of some contemporary visitors to seventeenth-century Newfoundland had prevented them from recognizing in its tiny fishing hamlets a level of social organization that they could accept as a civil society. An eighteenth-century perception that migratory fishers and settlers were inevitably in conflict over the issue of local government evolved into the nineteenth-century idea that they were actually in conflict over settlement itself. Reinforced by the mythology of illegal settlement, this theory of "retarded development" misled many twentieth-century historians into the unsupportable assumption that there was no continuous European presence worth speaking of in seventeenth-century Newfoundland. Given how pervasive this point of view was only a few years ago, that no one thought it worth trying to parse the socioeconomic structure of early settlement is hardly surprising.[2]

This book, then, is an attempt to record the way of life that developed between three and four centuries ago in the part of North America first exploited by Europeans. Although Newfoundland and its fishery were once of great importance to Europe, the colonies that developed here were small and of less importance economically and politically than the

---

ditional view, see Prowse, *History*. On paper regulation versus practice, see Keith Matthews, "Historical Fence Building: A Critique of the Historiography of Newfoundland," *Newfoundland Studies*, XVII (2001), 143–165; and Jerry Bannister, "Whigs and Nationalists: The Legacy of Judge Prowse's *History of Newfoundland*," *Acadiensis*, XXXII, no. 1 (2002), 84–109.

2. Cell, *English Enterprise*; Head, *Newfoundland*; Matthews, "Historical Fence Building," *Newfoundland Studies*, XVII (2001), 143–165.

industry they served. They are, though, an instructive case, as an example of how capitalism scattered Europeans across the Atlantic. These colonies came to play an important cultural role in the fishery, and another aim of this book is to explain how Newfoundland settlement served this industry in what seems to me a peculiarly modern way. This was a cash or at least a credit economy in which the accidents of geography limited the possibilities for agricultural self-sufficiency, while the riches of the fishery encouraged ordinary folk to earn and spend. In their precocious consumerism, fishers and their hosts in Newfoundland were experimenting with a new kind of economy.

In the interests of elucidating this burgeoning economic activity, I sometimes offer approximate present-day U.S. dollar equivalents for seventeenth-century monetary figures. This practice, which will offend many historians, who are strongly convinced that such estimates are misleading, is worth some discussion—the more so, if it will also serve to introduce one of the central themes of the book, the early development *One central theme of the book* of a modern consumer economy. Although it may be true that the calculation of monetary equivalents across centuries is misleading to some degree, it may be even more misleading to let early modern monetary values stand without some attempt at translation into modern figures. The difficult question thus arises of how to compare the value of currencies over time. Since we have prices for certain key goods, notably bread and beer, over many centuries, this is not, on the face of it, an insuperable technical problem. Interpretative issues certainly lurk here, but they are not peculiar to the attempt to compare two economies historically.

The central problem that arises in any attempt to define a rate of exchange between any two separate economies is that it is meaningful to compare prices only for goods available in the markets of both economies. If either twenty dollars in U.S. dollars or thirty dollars Canadian will buy a barrel of oil, the Canadian dollar will be worth something like sixty-seven cents U.S. The determination of historical exchange rates over centuries is not, however, very much like comparing U.S. and Canadian currencies, which are used in similar markets by populations with similar consumption habits, choosing from similar baskets of goods. The central problem raised by historical exchange rates is much more like the problem of expressing monetary equivalents between an advanced Western economy, whether Britain, the United States, or Canada, and a smaller developing economy like Thailand or even an underdeveloped economy like Zambia. The official exchange rate determined by international markets in such cases partakes of the same arbitrariness that can justly be decried in the attempt to define historical exchange rates. Consider an adjustment in the international rates: suppose the Zambian *kwacha* falls by 10 percent against the U.S. dollar. Such a drop will surely mean that trucks or video cameras or, indeed, barrels of oil will become 10 percent more expensive there. But, if few people have trucks or video cameras, if most of the economy is not dependent on oil imports, if most people spend most of their money on food and housing, most of it locally produced, the Zambian standard of living will not fall by 10 percent. The international exchange rate is only vaguely indicative of the value of the respective currencies within their own economies.

The problem with comparing the currencies of economies at different stages of development is the difficulty in accounting for differences in the basket of goods consumed in the relevant markets. Thanks to the patient work of an earlier generation of economic historians we can confidently compare the prices of bread and beer over time. The pint of beer that cost a seventeenth-century fisherman a few pence in a Dartmouth alehouse the night before he set sail to Newfoundland in 1620 would cost something approaching two pounds sterling or four U.S. dollars today. Less easily accounted for is that present-day Newfoundland fishers have many other uses for their incomes. The average fisherman will run a pickup truck, his wife may well expect to use a computer worth a thousand dollars to keep their tax records, and the family will certainly own a refrigerator, a washing machine, a television set, perhaps a snowmobile, and so on. It is a safe bet that beer will once more be part of the annual budget, but beer and bread (and, indeed, fish and wine) play a much smaller part in modern economies than they once did.[3]

Any estimate of the present value of one pound sterling 350 years ago elides this central difficulty and must therefore be interpreted with circumspection. This concern does not mean that the estimate is not worth making. We must use the same circumspection when we make estimates of the annual income of a Zambian farm laborer. Estimates that cross the boundaries of economic cultures have much to tell us, even if what they tell us needs more interpretation than we might at first suppose.[4]

3. E. H. Phelps Brown and Sheila V. Hopkins, "Seven Centuries of the Prices of Consumables, Compared with Builders' Wage-Rates," *Economica*, XXIII (1956), 296–314.

4. Cf. Jan de Vries, "Between Purchasing Power and the World of Goods: Understanding the Household Economy in Early Modern Europe," in John

Opening our eyes to changes in monetary values over time is important precisely because social historians so often tactfully avert their gaze from this messy issue. A look at historical sources on price inflation to about 1950 indicates that seventeenth-century England suffered significant price fluctuations and the steep price inflation that characterized the later sixteenth century carried on into the first quarter of the seventeenth, but there was very little change through the rest of the century, short-term fluctuations apart. For interpretative purposes, we can consider monetary values for the period from about 1620 to be roughly typical of the rest of the century, and we can estimate inflation over the following 250 years to 1950 to be in the order of 600 percent. Comparison with official estimates of inflation since 1950 will soon suggest a staggering fact: the second half of the twentieth century saw inflation of about twice this amount—that is, not another 5 or 600 percent, but another 1,100 percent between 1950 and 2000. What cost about £1 in 1620 (a new coat?) might have cost £6 in 1950 and would probably cost about £65, or U.S. $130, when this book was written. In other words, by far the greatest part of the historical price inflation, about 90 percent of present values, has happened within the lifetime of many of the historians and archaeologists for whom this should be an issue. Interpretative caveats are needed, of course, even to compare values in 1950 with values fifty years later: in some peripheral areas, the economy of 1950 might have resembled that of 1650 as much as that of the present.

This approach provides a means of appreciating the large amounts of money (in the order of present millions) invested by certain patrons of development in early modern Newfoundland. It also permits a rough estimate of seventeenth-century fishermen's incomes in modern terms. A skilled fishing servant who expected to clear twenty pounds in a season was earning something like twenty-five hundred dollars today—not a great deal, by North American standards, but an excellent income compared with Third World figures in our own day. This is a more relevant standard if we wish to discount for the absence of trucks, video cameras, and so on from these economies and to focus instead on bread and beer and, especially, on fish and wine.

Brewer and Roy Porter, eds., *Consumption and the World of Goods* (London, 1993), 85–132; John J. McCusker, "How Much Is That in Real Money?: A Historical Price Index for Use as a Deflator of Money Values in the Economy of the United States," American Antiquarian Society, *Proceedings*, CI, pt. 2 (1991), 297–368 (esp. 337–350, table B1).

ACKNOWLEDGMENTS

Over the years, many people helped me in my research, too many now to acknowledge individually. I would, though, particularly thank James Tuck, Daniel Vickers, and the late Ralph Pastore for their help at the formative stage and my editor, Fredrika Teute, for advice at later stages as well as Virginia Montijo for her patient copy editing. Special thanks are due the archivists and librarians of various institutions where I was fortunate enough to work, particularly those at the British Library, London; the Centre for Newfoundland Studies and the Maritime History Archives at Memorial University of Newfoundland; the Devon Record Office, Exeter, and the West Devon Record Office, Plymouth; the Essex Institute, Salem, Mass.; the Public Record Office, Kew, and especially the staff of the Round Room in the old PRO at Chancery Lane. An extended project of this sort depends on the patient support of family and friends, and I would particularly thank my daughters, Molly and Laura, as well as Sharon Gray and Geneviève Duguay. The Department of Anthropology at Memorial has provided me with a wonderfully supportive environment for interdisciplinary work within the Archaeology Unit, and I thank Memorial's academic and professional staff and our graduate students for their interest and advice. Earlier versions of certain sections appeared in *Avalon Chronicles, Histoire sociale / Social History, International Journal of Maritime History, Newfoundland Studies, Northern Mariner, Northern Seas Yearbook*, and *Studia Atlantica*, and I acknowledge, with thanks, not only permission to present material from these journals but also the many useful comments made by editors and readers, anonymous and otherwise. The faults remaining are my own.

My research was supported by the Social Sciences and Humanities Research Council of Canada, the Province of Newfoundland and Labrador, Memorial University's Institute for Social and Economic Research, its Office of Research, and its Maritime Studies Research Unit. I am very thankful for this support, which has been a great encouragement. I also acknowledge with thanks support from the Publication Subvention Program of Memorial University of Newfoundland for reproduction of illustrations.

CONTENTS

ILLUSTRATIONS

TABLES

ABBREVIATIONS & SHORT TITLES

Add MS
Additional Manuscript, British Library, London
ADM
Admiralty Papers, Public Record Office, London
Annales: ESC
Annales: Économies, Sociétés, Civilisations
APC: Colonial
W. L. Grant, James Munro, and Almeric W. Fitzroy, eds., *Acts of the Privy Council of England*, Colonial Series, I, *A.D. 1613–1680* (London, 1908)
Archaeology Nfld
Archaeology in Newfoundland and Labrador, 1980–1986, Annual Reports nos. 1–7, Newfoundland Museum (St. John's, 1981–1989)
Aspinwall Records
A Volume Relating to the Early History of Boston Containing the Aspinwall Notarial Records from 1644 to 1651, Report of the Record Commissioners of the City of Boston, no. 32 (Boston, 1903)
Baxter MSS, IV, VI
James Phinney Baxter, ed., *Documentary History of the State of Maine*, IV, *The Baxter Manuscripts* (Portland, Maine, 1889), and VI, *The Baxter Manuscripts* (Portland, Maine, 1900)
Bristol Depositions, I, II
H. E. Nott, ed., *Deposition Books of Bristol*, I, *1643–1647*, Bristol Record Society, VI (Bristol, 1935), and II, *1650–1654*, Bristol Record Society, XIII (Bristol, 1948)
Cell, *English Enterprise*
Gillian T. Cell, *English Enterprise in Newfoundland, 1577–1660* (Toronto, 1969)
Cell, *Newfoundland Discovered*
Gillian T. Cell, ed., *Newfoundland Discovered: English Attempts at Colonization, 1610–1630*, Hakluyt Society, 2d Ser., CLX (London, 1982)
CHR
Canadian Historical Review

CO
Colonial Office, Public Record Office, London
CSP: Colonial
Great Britain, Public Record Office, *Calendar of State Papers*,
Colonial Series, *America and West Indies*, ed. W. Noel Sainsbury
et al., V, *1661-1668*, VII, *1669-1674*, IX, *1675-1676* and *Addenda*,
1574-1674, X, *1677-1680*, XI, *1681-1685*, XII, *1685-1688* (London,
1880-1899)
CSP: Domestic
Great Britain, Public Record Office, *Calendar of State Papers*,
Domestic Series, *Of the Reign of Charles I*, ed. John Bruce
(London, 1858-1897); *Calendar of State Papers*, Domestic Series,
1649-[1660], ed. Mary Anne Everett Green (London, 1875-1886);
Calendar of State Papers, Domestic Series, *Of the Reign of
Charles II*, ed. Green et al. (London, 1860-1909)
CTP
Committee for Trade and Plantations
DCB
George W. Brown and Marcel Trudel, eds., *Dictionary of Canadian
Biography*, I, *1000 to 1700* (Toronto, 1966)
Denys, *Histoire naturelle*
Nicholas Denys, *Histoire naturelle des peuples, des animaux, des
arbres et plantes de l'Amérique septentrionale, et de ses divers
climats*, II [1672], in William F. Ganong, ed., *The Description and
Natural History of the Coasts of North America (Acadia) by Nicholas
Denys* (1908; rpt. New York, 1968)
DNB
Leslie Stephen and Sidney Lee, eds., *The Dictionary of National
Biography* . . . (London, 1917)
DNE
G. M. Story, W. J. Kirwin, and J. D. A. Widdowson, eds.,
Dictionary of Newfoundland English (Toronto, 1982)
DRO Exeter
Devon Record Office, Exeter
E
Exchequer, Public Record Office, London
EHR
Economic History Review
GA Amsterdam NA
Gemeente Archief Amsterdam, Notarial Archives, in Jan Kupp,

"Dutch Documents Taken from the Notarial Archives of Holland Relating to the Fur Trade and Cod Fisheries of North America," National Archives of Canada, Ottawa, MG 18 O12

Handcock, *Origins*
W. Gordon Handcock, *Soe Longe as There Comes Noe Women: Origins of English Settlement in Newfoundland* (St. John's, 1989)

HCA
High Court of Admiralty, Public Record Office, London

Head, *Newfoundland*
C. Grant Head, *Eighteenth Century Newfoundland: A Geographer's Perspective* (Toronto, 1976)

Historical Atlas of Canada, I
R. Cole Harris and Geoffrey J. Matthews, *Historical Atlas of Canada*, I, *From the Beginning to 1800* (Toronto, 1987)

HMC
Historical Manuscripts Commission, London

IJMH
International Journal of Maritime History

IND
Index, Public Record Office, London

Innis, *Cod Fisheries*
Harold A. Innis, *The Cod Fisheries: The History of an International Economy*, rev. ed. (1954; rpt. Toronto, 1978)

Josselyn, *Voyages*
Paul J. Lindholdt, ed., *John Josselyn, Colonial Traveller: A Critical Edition of Two Voyages to New-England* (Hanover, N.H., 1988)

Maritime History of Devon, I
Michael Duffy et al., eds., *New Maritime History of Devon*, I, *From Early Times to the Late Eighteenth Century* (London, 1992)

Matthews, *Constitutional Laws*
Keith Matthews, ed., *Collection and Commentary on the Constitutional Laws of Seventeenth Century Newfoundland* (St. John's, 1975)

Matthews, "Fisheries"
Keith Matthews, "A History of the West of England–Newfoundland Fisheries" (D.Phil. diss., Oxford, 1968)

Md. HS
Maryland Historical Society, Baltimore

MHS
Massachusetts Historical Society

MUN
  Memorial University of Newfoundland, St. John's
NAC
  National Archives of Canada, Ottawa
NDRO Barnstaple
  North Devon Record Office, Barnstaple
OED
  Oxford English Dictionary, 20 vols., 2d ed. (Oxford, 1989)
Paige, *Letters*
  George F. Steckley, ed., *The Letters of John Paige, London Merchant, 1648–1658* (London, 1984)
PANL
  Provincial Archives of Newfoundland and Labrador
Pope, "South Avalon"
  Peter E. Pope, "The South Avalon Planters, 1630 to 1700: Residence, Labour, Demand, and Exchange in Seventeenth-Century Newfoundland" (Ph.D. diss., Memorial University of Newfoundland, 1992)
PRO
  Great Britain, Public Record Office, London. Numbers in parentheses in Colonial Office citations are those assigned to early PRO papers by W. Noel Sainsbury and later editors of the *Calendar of State Papers*
PROB
  Prerogative Court of Canterbury, Public Record Office, London
Prowse, *History*
  D. W. Prowse, *A History of Newfoundland from the English, Colonial, and Foreign Records* (1895; rpt. Belleville, Ont., 1972)
Quinn, *New American World*, I, IV
  David B. Quinn, ed., *New American World: A Documentary History of North America to 1612*, I, *America from Concept to Discovery: Early Exploration of North America*, and IV, *Newfoundland from Fishery to Colony: Northwest Passage Searches* (New York, 1979)
RFQC Essex Co.
  [George F. Dow and Mary G. Thresher, eds.], *Records and Files of the Quarterly Court of Essex County, Massachusetts*, 9 vols. (Salem, Mass., 1911–1975)
RHAF
  Revue d'Histoire de l'Amérique française

RT Devon
    *Report and Transactions of the Devonshire Association for the
    Advancement of Science, Literature, and Art*
Scisco, "Testimony"
    Louis D. Scisco, "Testimony Taken at Newfoundland in 1652,"
    Canadian Historical Review, IX (1928), 239–251
Southampton Examinations, 1601–1602, and I–IV
    R. C. Anderson, ed., *Book of Examinations, 1601–1602*,
    Southampton Record Society, XXVI (Southampton, 1926);
    Anderson, ed., *Book of Examinations and Depositions, 1622–1644*,
    I, *1622–1627*, II, *1627–1634*, III, *1634–1639*, IV, *1639–1644*,
    Southampton Record Society, XXIX, XXXI, XXXIV, XXXVI
    (Southampton, 1929–1936)
SP
    State Papers, Public Record Office, London
Stock, *Debates*
    Leo Francis Stock, ed., *Proceedings and Debates of the British
    Parliaments respecting North America*, I, *1542–1688* (Washington,
    D.C., 1924)
Suffolk Records
    Allyn Bailey Forbes, ed., *Records of the Suffolk County Court, 1671–
    1680*, Colonial Society of Massachusetts, *Publications*, XXIX,
    Collections (Boston, 1933)
Trelawny Papers
    James Phinney Baxter, ed., *Documentary History of the State of
    Maine*, III, *The Trelawny Papers* (Portland, Maine, 1884)
TRHS
    Transactions of the Royal Historical Society
Vickers, *Farmers and Fishermen*
    Daniel Vickers, *Farmers and Fishermen: Two Centuries of Work in
    Essex County, Massachusetts, 1630–1850* (Chapel Hill, N.C., 1994)
WDRO Plymouth
    West Devon Record Office, Plymouth
Whitbourne, *Discourse*
    Richard Whitbourne, *A Discourse and Discovery of New-Found-
    Land* (1622), in Gillian T. Cell, ed., *Newfoundland Discovered:
    English Attempts at Colonization, 1610–1630*, Hakluyt Society,
    2d Ser., CLX (London, 1982), 101–206
Winthrop Papers
    Samuel Eliot Morison et al., eds., *Winthrop Papers* (Boston, 1929–)

WMQ
  William and Mary Quarterly
Yonge, *Journal*
  James Yonge, "Journall," Plymouth [Devon] Athenaeum, in
  F. N. L. Poynter, ed., *The Journal of James Yonge [1647-1721]:*
  Plymouth Surgeon (London, 1963)

METHODOLOGY

Documents are cited by author, title, and date as well as the archival or published source. In references, names of authors are spelled as in the document, hence they will sometimes be inconsistent. A single version is used in the text. Dates for English documents are cited in the Old Style Julian calendar, except that the year is taken to have begun on January 1, rather than March 25. In the seventeenth century, the Julian calendar was ten days behind the modern Gregorian calendar, then already in use in France, so that April 1 in an English document was what we or a French writer of the time would call April 10. Transcription of documents follows the principles set out by Giles E. Dawson and Laetitia Kennedy-Skipton (*Elizabethan Handwriting, 1500–1650: A Manual* [1966; rpt. London, 1981]). Several modernizations are regularly employed in this system of transcription. The modern *th* is substituted for the thorn that resembles the modern *y* and was used in early modern times to represent the sound *th* (for example, in "ye" for "the"). The modern capital *F* is used for *ff*, when the doubled letter is used as a capital (for example, in "fferryland" for "Ferryland"). The interchangeable early modern *u* and *v* are rendered as the appropriate letter in modern spelling, and common contractions and ampersands are expanded. Otherwise, early modern spelling is retained. Punctuation and capitalization have been modernized in quotations; extensive emendations are noted. For weights and measures, the study relies throughout on Lester A. Ross's work (*Archaeological Metrology: English, French, American, and Canadian Systems of Weights and Measures for North American Historical Archaeology* [Ottawa, 1983]), and, for international exchange rates, on John J. McCusker's study (*Money and Exchange in Europe and America, 1600–1775: A Handbook* [Chapel Hill, N.C., 1978]). Monetary equivalents over time are more problematic. Approximate present-day equivalents are sometimes supplied and are intended as rough approximations for the year 2000 in U.S. dollars, to use a convenient contemporary unit of account. A defense of this practice, to which some historians object, can be found in the Preface.

Fish into Wine

Nulle société ne peut exister sans échange . . .

—*Jean-Jacques Rousseau,* Emile

INTRODUCTION ఇ౿ THE
NEWFOUNDLAND PLANTATION

There is besides a colony of English upon the eastern coast of
Newfoundland without government ecclesiastical or civil who live
by catching fish.
—"An Account of His Majesties Plantations in America," circa 1680

Today the term "plantation" has a particular connotation, redolent of
southern monoculture. Seventeenth-century English usage was different: "plantation" was equivalent simply to "colony," metaphorically emphasizing that people and, perhaps, societies could be transplanted. In
Newfoundland, "plantation" came to mean the waterfront premises from
which the fishery was conducted, a narrowing of sense that paralleled
the southern evolution of the term but with a very different connotation.
Nor did "planter," the word normally used for the European settlers of
Newfoundland, bear a scent of magnolias. In eighteenth-century Newfoundland, "planter" began to denote a certain class of settlers, those who
owned boats and plantations (in the narrow sense) and employed other
men. This meaning was implicit in the previous century, embedded in a
convention that servants did not count as economic or political individuals but were incorporated in the personality of their masters or, occasionally, mistresses. There were inhabitants of seventeenth-century Newfoundland who did not own boats and employ others, but, because they
lacked a distinct economic personality, they were rarely named in censuses of planters. We therefore know much less about them as individuals than we do about their employers—a situation paralleled in other
colonies. In seventeenth-century Ulster, "planter" meant one who contracted to plant colonists and develop an infrastructure. In a similar vein,
a planter in seventeenth-century Newfoundland was not simply an inhabitant but a settler who counted as an economic personality.[1]

1. "Plantation" and "colony" were used interchangeably with "dominion," reflecting the assumption that colonized regions were dependencies; see M. I. Finley,
"Colonies—An Attempt at a Typology," *TRHS*, 5th Ser., XXVI (London, 1976),
167-188. On the narrow meaning of "plantation," see Jack P. Greene, *Periph-*
eries and Center: Constitutional Development in the Extended Polities of the British

In the later seventeenth century, English bureaucrats exhibited some uncertainty about whether "planter" and "plantation" were appropriate terms for Newfoundland. When the Commissioners of Customs expressed the view that "Newfoundland is not to be taken or accompted a plantation," they were implicitly questioning the legitimacy of settlement in a place "being under noe government or other regulation as all his Majesty's plantations are." Delicacy in diction thus reflected a political issue. Were the planters of Newfoundland genuine colonists, there by royal invitation in a colony that had been founded with a series of royal patents, as they themselves argued? Or were they squatters, like those on unenclosed woodlands in Britain itself, whose settlements had no right to be where they were?[2]

Literate middle-class observers often criticized Newfoundland settlers in much the same terms applied to contemporary vagrants and woodland squatters. In 1650, the Merchant Adventurers of Plymouth found the Newfoundland planters "rude, prophane, and athisticall." The merchant gentry of the West Country ports described them in 1675 as "some looser sort of people and ill-governed men" and argued, "Such is the barreness of that island (it affordeth neither foode nor cloathing) and the inhabitants for the most part poore and debauched, that their poverty and debauchery putts them upon committing of all vice and mischeife." Others took a less-jaundiced view. The naval officers who conducted censuses

---

Empire and the United States, 1607-1788 (Athens, Ga., 1986), 10-13; *DNE*, s.v. "plantation"; *OED*, s.v. "planter" (meaning seven is in error: the word has been in Newfoundland since the seventeenth century, and the proposed nineteenth-century derivation from fishing "plant" is incorrect; cf. *DNE*, s.v. "planter"). On early modern masters and servants, see Christopher Hill, "The Poor and the People in Seventeenth-Century England," in Frederick Krantz, ed., *History from Below: Studies in Popular Protest and Popular Ideology in Honour of George Rudé* (Montreal, 1985), 75-93. Occasionally, census lists acknowledge omissions, for example, Richard Holdsworth, "Report," May 13, 1701, CO 194/2 (39). Cf. David Cressy, *Coming Over: Migration and Communication between England and New England in the Seventeenth Century* (New York, 1987), 37, 52-63. Note Captain Robert Robinson's distinction in "An Account of . . . St. John's and Baye of Bulls . . . ," Sept. 16, 1680, CO 1/46 (8iii), 23.

2. T. Chudleigh et al. to Edmond Andros, Jan. 12, 1687, *Baxter MSS*, VI, 226-229 (quotation). The summary in *CSP*: Colonial uses the phrase "Newfoundland is not a plantation like other of the King's plantations," but this is a nineteenth-century gloss. For the planters' view, see Inhabitants of Newfoundland, Petition to Charles II, Dec. 19, 1677, CO 1/41 (128), 290 (quoted below, Chapter 6).

late in the century often avoided the political issue of the planters' right to be where they were by using the more neutral term "inhabitants" for the people they found living in about thirty harbors along the English Shore. These people raised difficult issues, whether they were described as "planters," with implied property rights, or simply as "inhabitants," thus leaving unspecified whether they were proprietors, or servants, or even masterless men.[3]

Uncertainty about early settlement survives as an unresolved tension in the history of Newfoundland. The first attempts at sponsored colonization, in the early seventeenth century, can be described as failures. Yet the censuses of later-seventeenth-century Newfoundland leave little doubt that by 1700 approximately two thousand fisherfolk overwintered along what was by then known as the English Shore. This disparity between the failure of early officially recognized colonies and the later reality of a small but significant settled population can be resolved by emphasizing unorganized casual incremental growth as the basis of seventeenth-century settlement. Another way of resolving the issue is to minimize permanent settlement by assuming that neither the Newfoundland planters nor their servants were really permanent inhabitants.[4]

3. Petition of the Merchant Adventurers of Plymouth, England, to the Council of State, ca. 1650, *Winthrop Papers*, VI, 4-6; Gentry of Western Parts of England Trading to Newfoundland, and Merchants, Owners, and Masters of Ships Concerned in the Fishing Trade of Newfoundland, Petitions to Charles II, both in Mar. 25, 1675, CO 1/65 (25), 100, 101. Even some of those who defended the planters perceived them as living "like bruits"; see "Reasons for the Settlement of Newfoundland . . . under Government," ca. 1668, CO 1/22 (69), 115-116. Cf. Paul A. Slack, "Vagrants and Vagrancy in England, 1598-1664," *EHR*, 2d Ser., XXVII (1974), 360-379; Alan Everitt, "Farm Labourers," in Joan Thirsk, ed., *The Agrarian History of England and Wales*, IV, *1500-1640* (London, 1967-), 396-465 (esp. 409-412), in H. P. R. Finberg, gen. ed., *The Agrarian History of England and Wales*.

4. Cell, *English Enterprise*, 96; Head, *Newfoundland*, 35; Kenneth R. Andrews, *Trade, Plunder, and Settlement: Maritime Enterprise and the Genesis of the British Empire, 1480-1630* (Cambridge, 1984), 337-338. Cell, *Newfoundland Discovered*, 56-57, accepts that some of Calvert's colonists remained but ends her seminal collection of documents with a report on the failure of colonization (302). Cf. Handcock, *Origins*, 44; Cole Harris, "European Beginnings in the Northwest Atlantic: A Comparative View," in David D. Hall and David Grayson Allen, eds., *Seventeenth-Century New England: A Conference Held by the Colonial Society of Massachusetts, June 18 and 19, 1982*, Colonial Society of Massachusetts, *Publica-*

A different view is proposed here. Seen within the context of the population mobility characteristic of the period, the extent and permanence of early settlement in Newfoundland has been underestimated. Furthermore, even failed proprietary colonies did, to some degree, facilitate long-term settlement, outlasting a single generation of settlers. This ancestral role is particularly evident in Conception Bay and along the south Avalon, that is, the east coast of Newfoundland south of St. John's, a region dominated in the seventeenth century by Ferryland, the site of the most successful of the proprietary schemes (Map 1). Most of the English settlements in Newfoundland were eclipsed during the wars with France at the end of the century, but the censuses of the preceding decades report a population of planters and their servants, between Trepassey in the south and Bonavista in the north, about a quarter of them in the south Avalon area. Henry Southwood's map, *A New Chart of the Trading Part of New Found Land*, shows the extensive occupation of the English Shore achieved by 1675 (Map 2).[5]

Ferryland has been continuously inhabited since its founding as the centerpiece of the Province of Avalon in 1621, when James I granted a proprietary patent to his secretary of state, Sir George Calvert, later Lord Baltimore. After a year's residence in the late 1620s, Calvert lost interest in Newfoundland. In 1629, when he wrote off his investment, most of his colonists (although not all) were gone. Ferryland remained the most important of the south Avalon settlements and, considered with nearby Caplin Bay, one of the larger settlements on Newfoundland's English Shore—ranking with Carbonear, Bay de Verde, and Old Perlican—after St. John's. Calvert's decision to abandon this fishery-based settlement marks the end of an early era of organized attempts at proprietary colonization. On the other hand, his effort in the 1620s to set up a settlement-based fishery was the foundation upon which a self-sustaining European population would, in time, develop.[6]

---

tions, LXIII, *Collections* (Boston, 1984), 119–152; Keith M. Matthews, *Lectures on the History of Newfoundland, 1500–1830* (St. John's, 1988), 19–20, 83–88.

5. Henry Southwood published two maps of the English Shore at this time, which were incorporated as a single map, *A New Chart of the Trading Part of New Found Land*, in William Fisher and John Thornton, *The English Pilot*, bk. 4, ed. Coolie Verner (1689; rpt. Amsterdam, 1967), 13; see Fabian O'Dea, *The Seventeenth Century Cartography of Newfoundland*, Cartographica, monograph no. 1 (Toronto, 1971), 34–35.

6. Ferryland's inhabitants were removed by the French to Devon and Plaisance

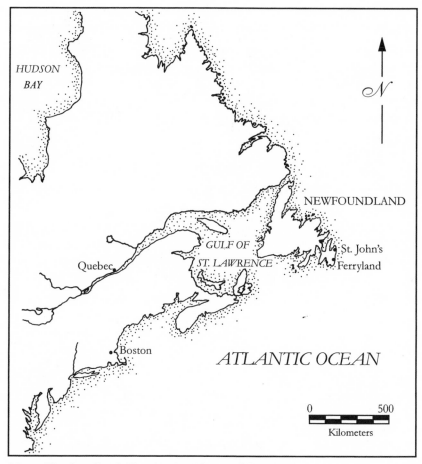

Map 1. Newfoundland, Showing St. John's and Ferryland.
Drawn by Ed Eastaugh

Archaeological research at Calvert's Avalon colony at Ferryland attests to the importance of his underlying contribution, at least in the most literal of senses. Here Sir David Kirke, and later his widow Sara and their sons, developed the infrastructure of an important resident fishery on

---

during the war year 1697. Because Ferryland and Caplin Bay are not consistently distinguished in the records, it is convenient to consider them together. The Royal Navy officer Francis Wheler calls them "Ferryland South" and "Ferryland North" in "English Planters Inhabiting the Easterne Coast of Newfound Land . . . ," Oct. 27, 1684, CO 1/55 (56vii), 257. On Calvert's Avalon colony, see Cell, *English Enterprise*, 92–96; and Cell, *Newfoundland Discovered*, 45–59, 250–302.

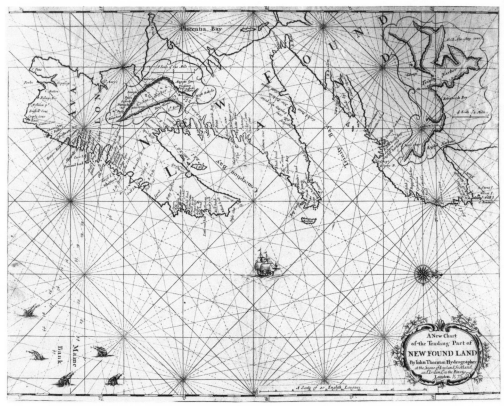

Map 2. A New Chart of the Trading Part of New Found Land. *By Henry Southwood, circa 1677. Published by John Thornton, in William Fisher and Thornton,* The English Pilot, *bk. 4 (London, 1689). North is to the right. Courtesy, Centre for Newfoundland Studies, Memorial University of Newfoundland, St. John's*

and around the foundations that had been laid by Calvert, or rather his on-site manager, Captain Edward Wynne. Although the Calverts went on to secure the proprietorship of Maryland, George's son Cecil, second Lord Baltimore, made persistent attempts to recover control of the northern colony from the heirs of Sir David Kirke, who expropriated Ferryland in 1638 under a patent for a Newfoundland Plantation, granted by Charles I to Kirke and a group of court favorites. Ferryland became a kind of colonial capital in the mid-seventeenth century, during the heyday of the Newfoundland Plantation. Sir David died in 1654, but his wife Sara and his four sons remained in Newfoundland, operating large fishing plantations in the south Avalon area around Ferryland until these were devastated by the French in the winter of 1697.[7]

The *English Pilot* of 1689 advised mariners that in Ferryland they would find "the *Pool* which is a place on the larbord-side (going in) within a point of *Beach*, where you ride in 12 foot water at low-water, and there the admiral ship generally rides"—the *admiral* being the first migratory vessel to reach a fishing station each season—and added, "The stages being near, several planters inhabitants live in this place." This was the site of Calvert's establishment, which Kirke appropriated and which became known as the Pool Plantation (Map 3). The archaeological remains of this well-established settlement, together with the relatively rich documentation resulting from the legal tug-of-war between the Calverts and the Kirkes, make Ferryland a useful focus for a study of the seventeenth-century English settlement of Newfoundland.[8]

Sir David Kirke and his family personally settled and remained in Ferryland much longer than the Calverts: about sixty years, as opposed to one or two. The career of this family, in documentary and archaeological context, will therefore shed far more light on settlement than the career of the Calverts, celebrated as the latter may be for their other achievements, including foundation of the Province of Avalon. The Kirkes were, without doubt, unusually well connected: they were literate and litigious, relatively wealthy and rather long-lived (when not incarcerated). They cannot be taken, by any stretch of the imagination, as representative Newfoundland planters. On the other hand, these distinctions also mean we know more about them than we do about other planters. Their lives are at the center of this study, as they must have been at the center of the economic and social experience of those who once dwelt on Newfoundland's English Shore.

Focus on Kirke family ↓ center of economic & social experience ↓ Ferryland

When officers of the Royal Navy took the first censuses of English Newfoundland in the 1670s, Ferryland itself consisted of about a dozen planter households, and adjacent Caplin Bay generally had one or two plantations. The number of planters' boats reported suggests a flourish-

---

7. Charles I, "A Grant of Newfoundland," Nov. 13, 1637, CO 195/1 (2), 11–27, in Matthews, *Constitutional Laws*, 77–116; Barry Gaulton, "Seventeenth-Century Stone Construction at Ferryland, Newfoundland (Area C)," *Avalon Chronicles*, II (1997), 1–43.

8. Southwood, *New Chart of the Trading Part of New Found Land*, in Fisher and Thornton, *The English Pilot*, bk. 4, ed. Verner, 13.

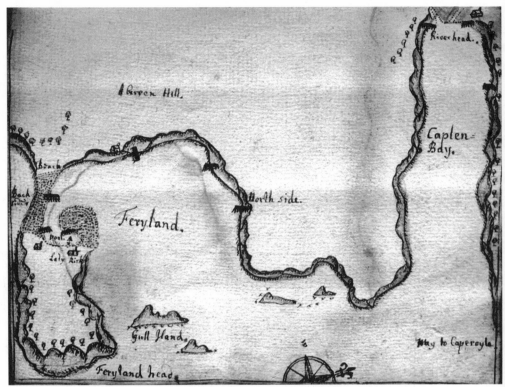

Map 3. Ferryland. By James Yonge, circa 1663. Shows the premises of "Lady Kirk" beside the Ferryland Pool. Courtesy, Plymouth Athenaeum

ing fishery in the later 1670s, followed by a crisis in the early 1680s, which was accompanied by a decline in the number of households. The population, if not the fishery, had recovered by 1696, when a force from the French settlement of Plaisance, on the south coast, drove the residents from their homes. The French chaplain, Father Jean Baudoin, recorded fourteen planters operating eighteen boats. Two years after the French attack, Commodore John Norris found only seven households and ten boats, but, as in other Newfoundland communities, the resident English population rebounded in the early eighteenth century.[9]

The carefully laid seventeenth-century stone foundations, still standing near the Pool at Ferryland, are not the traces of temporary cabins, knocked together for a seasonal migratory venture; they are the remnants of the infrastructure of a well-capitalized resident industry. The

9. For census figures, see Chapters 2 and 6, below.

Plate 1. The Ferryland Waterfront, circa 1625, with a Masonry Quayside Bounding One Side of the Pool and an Adjacent Warehouse. Painting by David Webber. Reconstructed on the basis of archaeological research. Courtesy, Colony of Avalon Foundation

light construction of the wooden shore structures normally used in the Atlantic coastal fishery and the frequency with which they were recycled means that they usually have poor archaeological visibility and are therefore difficult to identify and to interpret. The permanent stone features at Ferryland have marked the site for posterity, facilitating the recovery of more than a million artifacts, since James A. Tuck, of the Memorial University of Newfoundland Archaeology Unit, began investigating these largely undisturbed archaeological remains in the 1980s (Plate 1). Investigations at Ferryland, Cupids, St. John's, Renews, Placentia, and other archaeological sites on the English and French Shores of Newfoundland provide material evidence of the early modern European occupation of the island. Historical archaeologists have, in effect, reminded historians that there was a colony of English upon the eastern coast of Newfoundland who lived by catching fish. The documents tell us that this was a society "without government, ecclesiastical or civil," an observation in need of some qualification, perhaps, but one that suggests that there are no simple answers to the questions archaeology has raised about Newfoundland settlement, about the cod fishery, and about the business of turning fish into wine.[10]

10. Gaulton, "Stone Construction," *Avalon Chronicles*, II (1997), 1–43; James A. Tuck, "Archaeology at Ferryland, Newfoundland," *Newfoundland Studies*, IX (1993), 294–310; Tuck, "Archaeology at Ferryland, Newfoundland, 1936–1995," *Avalon Chronicles*, I (1996), 21–42; Tuck, "The Forgotten Colonies: Seventeenth-Century English Settlement in Newfoundland, Canada," *Review of Archaeology*, XVII, no. 2 (1996), 28–32; Matthew Carter, Barry Gaulton, and Tuck, "Archaeology at Ferryland, Newfoundland—1997," *Avalon Chronicles*, III (1998), 49–62; Tuck and Gaulton, "Archaeology of Ferryland, 1998–2000," ibid., VI (2001), 89–106. Cf. Alaric Faulkner, "Archaeology of the Cod Fishery: Damariscove Island," *Historical Archaeology*, XIX, no. 2 (1985), 57–86.

I ⚜ THE EARLY FISHERY

The sea there is swarming with fish. . . . I have heard this
Messer Zoane [Cabot] state so much. . . . These same English,
his companions, say that they could bring so many fish that this
kingdom would have no further need of Iceland, from which there
comes a very great quantity of the fish called stockfish.
—Raimondo de Soncino to the duke of Milan, Dec. 18, 1497

The practice of catching and transforming cod into a dried food suitable for ocean transport to distant markets is much older than the Newfoundland fishery. Stockfish, as wind-dried cod and ling were called in
medieval times, was the first mass-produced food commodity: a stable,
light, and eminently transportable source of protein. From about 1100,
Norway exported commercial quantities of stockfish to the European
continent. By 1350, stockfish had become Iceland's staple export commodity. English merchants, among others, brought grain, salt, and wine
to trade for stockfish, but Icelandic fishermen could not keep up with
European demand. Thus, after 1400, the English developed their own
migratory fishery at Iceland, carried on at seasonal fishing stations. Bristol participated in this industry, but the North Sea port of Hull became
a more significant player. English customs accounts of the 1470s record
imports of several kinds of Icelandic fish, including "salt fish" valued at
twice the price of the unsalted wind-dried stockfish. Who developed the
lightly salted dry cure for cod is now forgotten, but the same method was
used by Breton fishermen to process hake, a related fish, in late-medieval
times. It was such salt-dried fish that the English would later produce
in Newfoundland.[1]

1. Jón Th. Thór, "Foreign Fisheries off Iceland, c. 1400–1800," in Juliette Rod-
ing and Lex Heerma van Voss, eds., *The North Sea and Culture (1550–1800): Pro-*
ceedings of the International Conference Held at Leiden 21–22 April 1995 (Hilver-
sum, Neth., 1996), 124–134; Thór, "Icelandic Fishing History: A Survey," and Pal
Christensen and Alf Ragnar Nielssen, "Norwegian Fisheries, 1100–1970: Main
Developments," both in Poul Holm, David J. Starkey, and Thór, eds., *The North*
Atlantic Fisheries, 1100–1976: National Perspectives on a Common Resource (Reykjavik, 1996), 13–27, 145–167; Helge Sorheim, "The Origin of Commercial Fisheries and the Trade of Stockfish in the Northern Part of Western Norway," in Guy

The fishing industry of England's West Country expanded rapidly after about 1400. The numbers of ships fishing and carrying fish grew rapidly in the fifteenth century, so that Devon and Cornwall together exported more fish, both by volume and value, than any other English region. A growth in home demand for fish, itself an expression of late-medieval prosperity, was probably a key factor in contemporary expansion of fisheries and in technological advances in salt processing. Devon and Cornwall were able to take advantage of this potential for growth, because their merchants had capital to invest in shipping and in the fish trade and because the West Country had easy access to cheap salt in the Bay of Biscay and Iberia, regions that also proved to be lucrative markets. Cornwall and the south Devon ports of Plymouth and Dartmouth developed export fisheries prosecuted far from their home waters, although the Dorset and north Devon fisheries remained, at this time, largely local. In the second half of the fifteenth century, south Devon crews began to fish in the English Channel, building seasonal camps in Kent, Sussex, and East Anglia. Some fishers from Devon and Cornwall took part in the Icelandic fishery, but by 1500 Devon fishers were much more involved in a new seasonal fishery on the west coast of Ireland, where they produced salt fish at shore camps, as they would do a century later in Newfoundland. The southwestern industry was not highly regulated, compared to the trade on England's east coast; this situation facilitated the rapid development of these new fisheries. In brief, the merchants and fishers of the West Country were well prepared to exploit the waters of Atlantic Canada when these waters appeared on Europe's horizon.[2]

de Boe and F. Verhaeghe, eds., *Exchange and Trade in Medieval Europe* (Zellik, Belg., 1997); Wendy Childs, "England's Icelandic Trade in the Fifteenth Century: The Role of the Port of Hull," in Holm, Olaf Janzen, and Thór, eds., *Northern Seas, 1995: Yearbook of the Association for the History of the Northern Seas* (St. John's, 1995), 11–31; Evan Jones, "England's Icelandic Fisheries in the Early Modern Period," in Starkey, Chris Reid, and Neil Ashcroft, eds., *England's Sea Fisheries: The Commercial Sea Fisheries of England and Wales since 1300* (London, 2000), 36–45; Laurier Turgeon, "Le temps des pêches lointaines: permanences et transformations (vers 1500–vers 1850)," in Michel Mollat, ed., *Histoire des pêches maritimes en France* (Toulouse, 1987), 134–181 (esp. 138); Turgeon, "Pour redécouvrir notre 16e siècle: les pêches à Terre-neuve d'après les archives notariales de Bordeaux," *RHAF*, XXXIX (1986), 523–549 (esp. 534).

2. Maryanne Kowaleski, "The Expansion of the South-Western Fisheries in Late Medieval England," *EHR*, 2d Ser., LIII (2000), 429–454.

At the end of the fifteenth century, the obscure Venetian navigator, Zuan Cabotto, whom we remember as John Cabot, explored the eastern coast of Newfoundland, as far north as Labrador, for the English king, Henry VII, and a syndicate of Bristol merchants. Certain documents suggest obliquely that fishermen from that western port might already have been frequenting these waters for some decades, as had Native peoples since the end of the last Ice Age. There is evidence, at least, that English fishers had reached as far as Greenland. In its own terms, Cabot's voyage was nonetheless a voyage of discovery, for this expedition made a "new land" known to his European contemporaries. He was followed westward in the early 1500s by a series of exploratory voyages to Newfoundland, Labrador, and Greenland sponsored by Bristol merchants and Azorean Portuguese captains, sometimes in cooperation. These early attempts at finding a northwest passage to the Far East indicate that Europeans had realized they had not found Tartary, to be coasted southward to Japan, but something else between Europe and Asia. Cabot's voyage also had the effect of publicizing the immense marine resources of the northwest Atlantic.[3]

The Gulf of St. Lawrence, including Newfoundland, is close to Europe, relative to the rest of North America. Geography itself implies that this region would be one of the first parts of the New World exploited by Europeans, who soon identified economically valuable commodities in fish, whale oil, and furs. By the later sixteenth century, European commercial activity in Atlantic Canada exceeded, in volume and value, European trade with the Gulf of Mexico, which is usually treated as the American center of gravity of early transatlantic commerce. The cod fishery was by far the most important component of European commer-

3. On the original form of John Cabot's name, see Edoardo Giuffrida, "New Documents on Giovanni Caboto," trans. Paula C. Clarke, in Rosella Mamoli Zorzi, ed., *Attraversare gli oceani: da Giovanni Caboto al Canada multiculturale* (Venice, 1999), 61-72. On early voyages, see David B. Quinn, *North America from Earliest Discovery to First Settlements: The Norse Voyages to 1612* (New York, 1977), 60-64; Kirsten A. Seaver, *The Frozen Echo: Greenland and the Exploration of North America, ca. A.D. 1000-1500* (Stanford, Calif., 1996), 159-253; Peter E. Pope, *The Many Landfalls of John Cabot* (Toronto, 1997), 40-42. On marine resources, see Johanna J. (Sheila) Heymans and Tony J. Pitcher, "A Picasso-esque View of the Marine Ecosystem of Newfoundland and Southern Labrador: Models for the Time Periods 1450 and 1900," Fisheries Centre, University of British Columbia, *Research Reports*, X, no. 5 (2002), 44-74.

cial activity in northern North America, and it would remain for centuries much more important than the trade in furs.[4]

The dry salt cure worked well in the temperate climate of Atlantic Canada and produced a very stable product, well suited for export to Iberian and Mediterranean markets. Production of lightly salted dry fish was not, however, confined to the English. The Breton fishermen of northern France used many of the same techniques, the men of Saint-Malo, in particular, often employing the lightly salted air-dried cure on the Petit Nord, Newfoundland's Great Northern Peninsula. The Basques, who fished in Placentia and Trinity Bays, preferred this method to a green cure, in which fish are heavily salted and left wet. The Normans used the green cure in their offshore fishery on the Grand Banks but were also familiar with the land-based dry cure and used it when fishing inshore. (Inshore fisheries are prosecuted from shore in day-to-day voyages by open boats on fishing grounds close to the coast; offshore fisheries are prosecuted from ships voyaging for weeks at a time to fishing banks, which may be days or even weeks sailing from dry land.)[5]

Although the British Isles lacked major supplies of salt, the international market in this commodity made it easy for West Country supply ships to obtain suitable salt in southwest France or Portugal. A transatlantic itinerary via Saintonge or Setubal was not the inefficient detour it appears to the modern eye, given that vessels sailing westward across

4. On furs, see Bernard Allaire, *Pelleteries, manchons et chapeaux de castor: les fourrures nord-américaines à Paris, 1500–1632* (Quebec, 1999). On trade, see Laurier Turgeon, "French Fishers, Fur Traders, and Amerindians during the Sixteenth Century: History and Archaeology," *WMQ*, 3d Ser., LV (1998), 585–610 (esp. 592). For emphasis on bullion, see Andre Gunder Frank, *Dependent Accumulation and Underdevelopment* (New York, 1979), 44. Robert Brenner, *Merchants and Revolution: Commercial Change, Political Conflict, and London's Overseas Traders, 1550–1653* (Princeton, N.J., 1993), 117, assumes the fur trade was more important; but see Peter E. Pope, "Comparisons: Atlantic Canada," in Daniel Vickers, ed., *A Companion to Colonial America* (Malden, Mass., 2003), 489–507.

5. On cures, see Mark Eliot Ferguson, "Making Fish: Salt-Cod Processing on the East Coast of Newfoundland: A Study in Historic Occupational Folklife" (master's thesis, MUN, 1996), 197–204; Charles de La Morandière, *Histoire de la pêche française de la morue dans l'Amérique septentrionale*, 3 vols. (Paris, 1962–1966), I, 244, 252–258, 308–311; Denys, *Histoire naturelle*, 526. Innis, *Cod Fisheries*, 26–28, underestimates the European dry fishery, following Anthony Parkhurst to Richard Hakluyt, Sr., Nov. 13, 1578, in Quinn, *New American World*, IV, 7–10.

the Atlantic in midlatitudes have to set a course tending northward or southward in order to make headway into prevailing winds. In short, salt for the fishery was neither difficult to obtain nor particularly costly to ship to Newfoundland; indeed, in 1677 salt was cheaper on the English Shore than it was in France. Thus, dependence on imported salt is not a plausible explanation for West Country reliance on the dry cure, with its conveniently light requirement for salt. The technological choice was a consequence of consumer habits in England's markets: the southern ports to which the West Country shipped Newfoundland fish were not much interested in wet fish, most of which was consumed in the relatively cooler climes of northern France.[6]

⁂ The Sixteenth-Century European Migratory Fishery

In 1502, the *Gabriel* of Bristol brought home the first recorded cargo of North American cod: thirty-six tons of salt fish, worth £180 to the merchant Hugh Elyot, an early and persistent transatlantic investor. By 1510, European crews were seasonally fishing the waters of Atlantic Canada, known then indiscriminately as "the new found land," "terre neuve," or "terra do bacalhau"—the land of the cod. Given that Newfoundland and its marine resources were discovered for Europe by an English expedition, the extent of early English participation in the transatlantic cod fishery historically has been easy to exaggerate. In fact, French and Iberian records of the middle decades of the sixteenth century suggest a scale of effort by Bretons, Normans, and Basques unmatched, until the 1570s, by the few English ports that occasionally took part in the early industry, notably Southampton and Plymouth. As the seventeenth-century

6. On salt, see Robert P. Multhauf, *Neptune's Gift: A History of Common Salt* (Baltimore, 1978); Whitbourne, *Discourse*, 142; William Poole, "Answers to the Severall Heads of Inquiry . . . ," Sept. 10, 1677, CO 1/41 (62i), 149–152. On sailing routes, see Ian K. Steele, *The English Atlantic, 1675-1740: An Exploration of Communication and Community* (Oxford, 1986), 78–93. Innis, *Cod Fisheries*, 10, 486, and Cell, *Newfoundland Discovered*, 41, accept a supposed lack of salt as an explanation for the English dry cure. On the market for wet fish, see Laurier Turgeon, "Consommation de morue et sensibilité alimentaire en France au xviiie siècle," Canadian Historical Association, *Historical Papers / Communications historiques* (1984), 21–41; and Turgeon, "Le temps des pêches lointaines," in Mollat, ed., *Histoire des pêches*, 134–181 (esp. 153–166).

history *The English Empire in America* admitted, the Newfoundland trade had been "laid aside many years." Breton, Norman, and French Basque crews dominated the nascent transatlantic cod fishery, and their activities grew dramatically in the 1540s. Crews from the Basque coast of Spain had joined the fishery by this time, and, until about 1610, the merchants of San Sebastián and the other Guipúzcoan towns also financed a shore-based whale hunt in the Strait of Belle Isle, between Newfoundland and Labrador. Despite the early Anglo-Azorean voyages, the Portuguese did not become major participants in the migratory fishery. Even in the second half of the sixteenth century, when the port of Viana, in particular, sent ships regularly to Newfoundland, they did not commit themselves as seriously as the French already had or as the English would. In the summer of 1527, an English visitor to St. John's found only two Portuguese ships among the fourteen fishing there; the rest were French. Portugal had other fish to fry—not simply in the sense that it had its own new fisheries off Madeira and the Azores but also in the sense that this relatively small nation had staked widespread claims in Brazil, Africa, and the Indian Ocean. The English in the sixteenth century had few imperial commitments beyond Ireland, so it is more difficult to explain why their intermittent efforts in Newfoundland expanded only after 1565.[7]

7. Board of Trade to earl of Dartmouth, Jan. 13, 1713, British Library, Add MS 35913, 4; A. Anderson, *An Historical and Chronological Deduction of the Origin of Commerce, from the Earliest Accounts to the Present Time; Containing, an History of the Great Commercial Interests of the British Empire . . . ,* 4 vols. (London, 1764), I, 347, 379, 417; Quinn, *North America,* 353–357; La Morandière, *Histoire de la pêche,* I, 215–270; Réné Bélanger, *Les Basques dans l'estuaire du Saint-Laurent, 1535–1635* (Montreal, 1971); Laurier Turgeon, "Bordeaux and the Newfoundland Trade during the Sixteenth Century," *IJMH,* IX (1997), 1–28; Robert Robinson, "Certaine Arguments or Reasons for a Settled Government . . . ," 1670, CO 1/25 (111), 278–279; Cell, *English Enterprise,* 22; Todd Gray, "Devon's Fisheries and Early Stuart Northern New England," *Maritime History of Devon,* I, 139–144; Gray, "Fishing and the Commercial World of Early Stuart Dartmouth," in Gray, Margery Rowe, and Audrey Erskine, eds., *Tudor and Stuart Devon: The Common Estate and Government: Essays Presented to Joyce Youings* (Exeter, 1992), 173–199; R. B. [Nathaniel Crouch], *The English Empire in America . . . ,* 5th ed. (London, 1711), 60; Turgeon, "Le temps des pêches lointaines," in Mollat, ed., *Histoire de pêches,* 134–181 (esp. 136–142); Selma [Barkham] Huxley, "Los vascos y las pesquerias transatlanticas, 1517–1713," in Huxley, ed., *Itsasoa,* III, *Los vascos en el marco Atlántico Norte, siglos XVI y XVII* (San Sebastián, 1986), 27–210; James A. Tuck and Robert Grenier, *Red Bay, Labrador: World Whaling Capital,*

Through the mid-sixteenth century, England was often, in effect, a client state of Spain. In the 1550s, the English even had a Habsburg king: before Philip became king of Spain in 1556, he shared the English throne briefly with his wife, Queen Mary. Mary's death in 1558 marks an important turning point in European history, together with the treaty of Câteau-Cambrésis between France and Spain, signed the following year. Until then, England had to operate within the diplomatic reality of the struggle between Habsburg Spain and Valois France. After reconciliation of the two major Catholic powers in 1559, conflict emerged between Catholic, Mediterranean Spain and the newly Protestant north. Over the following half-century, while Portuguese and Guipúzcoan Basque participation in the transatlantic fishery collapsed under the onerous weight of the Spanish crown, the English West Country counties of Devon and Dorset became serious competitors of western France in this trade. In the late sixteenth century, the English did not merely expand their own small Newfoundland fishery; they displaced the Iberian industry there.[8]

How did a few Devon and Dorset outports elbow their way into such a potentially lucrative economic niche? This rapid expansion might be explained, at least in part, by Spain's declining international clout. Bernard Drake, one of Elizabeth I's privateering "sea-dogs," disrupted the Spanish Basque and Portuguese fisheries with an attack on their Newfoundland ships in 1585. Philip of Spain, who had by this time ascended to the throne of Portugal as well, pressed Basque and Portuguese fishing and whaling vessels into the service of his great Armada of 1588, while others hired on as freighters. Subsequent losses must have dimmed the prospects of both fishers and whalers. Iberian decline was not, how-

---

A.D. 1550–1600 (St. John's, 1989); Jean-Pierre Proulx, *Basque Whaling in Labrador in the Sixteenth Century* (Ottawa, 1993); John Rut to Henry VIII, 1527, in Quinn, *New American World*, I, 189–190; Darlene Abreu-Ferreira, "Terra Nova through the Iberian Looking Glass: The Portuguese-Newfoundland Cod Fishery in the Sixteenth Century," *CHR*, LXXIX (1998), 100–115. On late-medieval Portuguese overseas fisheries, see Peter Russell, *Prince Henry "the Navigator": A Life* (New Haven, Conn., 2000), 87, 98, 102. The notion of pre-Columbian Basque fishers in Newfoundland waters is a recurring fantasy of writers with more interest in a good story than in the evidence; see, for example, Mark Kurlansky, *Cod: A Biography of the Fish That Changed the World* (New York, 1997), 17–29.

8. Kenneth R. Andrews, *Trade, Plunder, and Settlement: Maritime Enterprise and the Genesis of the British Empire, 1480–1630* (Cambridge, 1984), 223–225; C[harles] R. Boxer, *The Dutch Seaborne Empire, 1600–1800* (1965; rpt. London, 1988), 1–33; Innis, *Cod Fisheries*, 30–51.

ever, simply military. The Spanish crown also weakened the commercial strength of the Basque region with new taxes, and the depletion of its oak forests undercut its shipbuilding and iron industries. At a macro-economic level, the inflationary pressure of precious metals from South and Central America drove a price-wage spiral that left the Iberian transatlantic fishery less and less competitive. Within a few years, Basque outfitting for the fishery at Bordeaux was in a serious slump. Whether cause or effect of the expansion of the English inshore fishery, this decline is unlikely to be a simple coincidence. The eclipse of the Iberian ports involved in the early transatlantic fishery was part of a long-term trend that saw an initially diffuse industry, spread over many European ports, increasingly concentrated in a few.[9]

Although European crises affected migratory fisheries at Newfoundland and elsewhere, the industry was rarely used as an effective instrument of foreign policy, for its lack of centralization made it hard to control. In 1580, the Danes began to tax English ships at Iceland, but this maneuver probably had little impact on the nascent West Country fishery at Newfoundland. It was primarily England's east coast ports that were involved in Iceland; besides, England's fishery there, far from collapsing, flourished well into the second half of the seventeenth century. The late-

9. On the rise of the Devon ports, see Alison Grant, "Breaking the Mould: North Devon Maritime Enterprise, 1560–1640," and Gray, "Early Stuart Dartmouth," in Gray, Rowe, and Erskine, eds., *Tudor and Stuart Devon*, 119–140, 173–199. On Spanish decline, see Steaven Damiskette et al., Libel, Sept. 20, 1585, British Library, Add MS 11405, 243–246; Michael Barkham, "Spanish Ships and Shipping," in M. J. Rodríguez-Salgado, ed., *Armada, 1588–1988* (London, 1988), 151–163; Jean-Pierre Proulx, *Whaling in the North Atlantic from Earliest Times to the Mid-Nineteenth Century* (Ottawa, 1986), 22–25; Harold A. Innis, "The Rise and Fall of the Spanish Fishery in Newfoundland," in Innis, *Essays in Canadian Economic History*, ed. Mary Q. Innis (Toronto, 1956), 43–61. In 1613, the English turned back fifteen Basque whaling ships en route to Labrador; see John Sanford to William Trumbull, ca. 1614, in HMC, "Report on the Manuscripts of the Marquess of Downshire . . . ," in *Eighteenth Report of the Royal Commission on Historical Manuscripts*, IV (London, 1940), 197. See Matthews, "Fisheries," 49, for other examples. On Bordeaux, see Turgeon, "French Fishers," *WMQ*, 3d Ser., LV (1998), 585–610 (esp. 593). [John Downing et al.], "An Account of the Colony and Fishery of Newfoundland," Sept. 10, 1677, British Library, Add MS 13972, 15–31, notes: "There are some few and inconsiderable ships from Biscay and Portugal that use this trade and keep their stations on the north coast of Newfoundland and upon the bank."

sixteenth-century expansion of England's cod fishery at Newfoundland was part of a general rise in English maritime activity at this time, which was, in turn, an aspect of a shift in the economic center of the European world economy from the Mediterranean to the North Sea. France, preoccupied with a religious civil war, maintained a share in the New World fisheries but was not as successful as England in opening new markets in southern Europe. In the second half of the sixteenth century, the French developed an offshore banks fishery, which must have reduced competition on the traditional inshore fishing grounds. Perhaps the expansion in West Country trade awaited the appropriate political climate, following the end of the alliance with Spain in 1559; perhaps it simply required the spread of new navigational skills among northern fishing masters. English shipmasters were better prepared to pilot their own vessels across the Atlantic and back in Drake's day than they were in Cabot's. Fishermen would go where they were able to fill their holds, and, for West Country crews, Newfoundland was a natural extension of the Irish fishery.[10]

Although the English were well established within the Newfoundland industry by the end of the sixteenth century, France's transatlantic fishery was still at least twice its size and would remain so through the following century. In 1578, Anthony Parkhurst estimated about 50 English, 50 Portuguese, 100 Basque, and 150 Norman or Breton vessels engaged in the transatlantic cod fishery. If we trust Parkhurst's rough figures, reading him as a participant and not as a lobbyist, we might suppose that these 350 European ships imported salt cod processed from

10. On Iceland, compare Innis, *Cod Fisheries*, 49, and Cell, *English Enterprise*, 23, with Childs, "England's Icelandic Trade," in Holm, Janzen, and Thór, eds., *Northern Seas, 1995*, 11–31, and Jones, "England's Icelandic Fishery," in Starkey, Reid, and Ashcroft, eds., *England's Sea Fisheries*, 36–45. On the rise of English trade, see Ralph Davis, "England and the Mediterranean, 1570–1670," in F. J. Fisher, ed., *Essays in the Economic and Social History of Tudor and Stuart England, in Honour of R. H. Tawney* (Cambridge, 1961), 117–137; Davis, *The Rise of the English Shipping Industry in the Seventeenth and Eighteenth Centuries* (London, 1962), 1–21. On the banks fishery, see Innis, *Cod Fisheries*, 25; Turgeon, "Le temps des pêches lointaines," in Mollat, ed., *Histoire des pêches*, 134–181 (esp. 138). On navigation, see D. W. Waters, "The English Pilot: English Sailing Directions and Charts and the Rise of English Shipping, Sixteenth to Eighteenth Centuries," *Journal of Navigation*, XLII (1989), 317–354. On the West Country fishers, see Todd Gray, "Devon's Coastal and Overseas Fisheries and New England Migration, 1597–1642" (Ph.D. diss., University of Exeter, 1988), 123–132.

a transatlantic live catch of about 75,000 tonnes. (The metric ton is used here for estimates of biomass.) Such a figure might even underestimate the size of the industry, however, for the archives of Bordeaux, Rouen, and La Rochelle suggest that, by midcentury, these ports alone were often provisioning 150 vessels annually for the transatlantic fishery. Hence, the Elizabethan pamphleteer Robert Hitchcock might not have been exaggerating when he put the total French transatlantic fleet at 500 vessels in 1580. French ships involved in the fishery in the later sixteenth century were about 100 tons burthen; English vessels were often only half that size. Altogether, European live catches might have been as much as 200,000 tonnes a season—approximately the total catch at Newfoundland implied by early administrative statistics collected by France and England in the 1660s, 1670s, and 1680s and already in the same order of magnitude as catches of northern cod in the late nineteenth and early twentieth century. The early modern fishery at Newfoundland was an enormous industry for its time, and even for our own.[11]

11. Parkhurst to Hakluyt, Nov. 13, 1578, in Quinn, *New American World*, IV, 7–10. Parkhurst may overestimate the number of Spanish Basque vessels, although he also seems to underestimate their tonnage; see Selma Barkham, "The Documentary Evidence for Basque Whaling Ships in the Strait of Belle Isle," in G. M. Story, ed., *Early European Settlement and Exploitation in Atlantic Canada* (St. John's, 1982), 53–96. J. D. Rogers, *A Historical Geography of the British Colonies*, V, pt. 4, *Newfoundland* (Oxford, 1911), 25, takes Parkhurst's figures as exaggerations, as others have done. On the French, see Turgeon, "French Fishers," *WMQ*, 3d Ser., LV (1998), 585–610 (esp. 592); Robert Hitchcock, *A Pollitique Platt for the Honour of the Prince* . . . (1580), in R. H. Tawney and Eileen Power, eds., *Tudor Economic Documents*, III (1924; rpt. London, 1953), 239–256. On the size of vessels, see Turgeon, "Le temps des pêches lointaines," in Mollat, ed., *Histoire des pêches*, 134–181 (esp. 138); Cell, *English Enterprise*, 130, table 12. A *ton* of 2,240 pounds was a traditional unit of weight for salt fish and also for the displacement of a ship. In the second sense, a *ton* was originally the space taken to stow a *tun* of wine, a large staved container holding 925 liters. A *tonne* is a metric ton of 1,000 kilograms, or about 2,205 pounds, and is used here for estimates of the biomass of fish caught. The French *tonneau de mer* was slightly larger than the English freight *ton*, but, since contemporary estimates of ships' burthen were only approximate, this discrepancy can be ignored here (see Glossary, below). For nineteenth-century catches, see Jeffrey A. Hutchings, "Spatial and Temporal Variation in the Exploitation of Northern Cod, *Gadus Morhua*: A Historical Perspective from 1500 to Present," in *Maritime Resources and Human Societies in the North Atlantic since 1500*, ISER Conference Paper, no. 5 (St. John's, 1997), 43–85. For an argument that this time series underestimates early catches, see Peter Pope, "Early

Like most early modern industries, the migratory cod fishery at New-foundland was constrained by natural forces to an annual cycle no less than to long-term change in the climatic, economic, and diplomatic environments. This web is too complex to untangle with one tug, but we can begin by tracing its seasonal patterns. In early-seventeenth-century England, April 1 was the official date for setting out on the Newfoundland voyage, and ships in fact often sailed for the fishery about this date. As the century wore on, ships tended to leave earlier for Newfoundland, probably as a result of competition for shore space. By the 1670s, the official sailing date was March 1, and ships were sometimes setting sail in February. The voyage usually took about five weeks, so that ships arrived in Newfoundland in April or May. Ships going via Saintonge, Portugal, or the Cape Verde Islands for salt or via the Canaries or the Azores for wine left earlier. The *sack ships*, which were trading vessels that went to Newfoundland primarily to pick up salt cod and to take it to market rather than to prosecute the fishery themselves, did not expect ladings of dried fish until July or August and so could afford later departures.[12]

Estimates: Assessment of Catches in the Newfoundland Cod Fishery, 1660–1690," ibid., 9–40.

12. The days and months discussed here are in the Old Style, Julian calendar, about ten days behind the New Style, modern Gregorian calendar (Apr. 1, for example, is, today, Apr. 11). On the annual cycle, see B. A. Holderness, *Pre-Industrial England: Economy and Society, 1500-1750* (London, 1976), 1–4; Steele, *English Atlantic*, 78–85; cf. Privy Council, "Orders to Devon, Cornwall, and Western Ports," Feb. 28, 1628, in *APC*: Colonial; John Cull, Deposition Taken at Totnes, Nov. 27, 1667, WDRO Plymouth, W360/74. Ships sometimes left as much as a month early, as in Oliver Wheeler, Peter Enough, and Roger Wheeler, Deposition, Sept. 23, 1630, *Southampton Examinations*, II, 66–67; Henry Hatsell to Admiralty, Mar. 30, 1660, James Blackborne to James Hickes, Feb. 26, Mar. 17, 1671, William Hurt to Joseph Williamson, Feb. 4, 1678, Ambrose Mudd to Williamson, Feb. 5, 1678, all in *CSP*: Domestic; Merchants Trading to America, Petition, Mar. 1, 1667, SP 29/193 (2, 2i), 2–4; William Downing, Petition, Apr. 2, 1679, CO 1/43 (40), 64; Symon Salvement and Cornelis Jacobsen, Charter Party, Dec. 31, 1609, GA Amsterdam NA 118, 66–67, NAC MG 18 012/13; George Haresonep, Examination, July 16, 1651, HCA 13/65, n.p. On salt and sack ships, see Elizeas Ricart, Simon Farwell, and John Bunne, Depositions, June 3, 1640, *Southampton Examinations*, IV, 9–10; Sir David Kirke, Petition, May 5, 1652, Md. HS, Calvert MSS 174/199, in Louis Dow Scisco, "Kirke's Memorial on Newfoundland," *CHR*,

Although Parkhurst, Hitchcock, and later visitors to Newfoundland often attempted to quantify the industry in terms of the number of ships involved, the English migratory fishery was an inshore industry, prosecuted from boats rather than from the ships that brought fishermen from the West Country. As Lewes Roberts explained in his *Merchants Mappe of Commerce* of 1638, they would "unrigge their shippes, set up boothes and cabanets on the shore in divers creekes and harbours, and there, with fishing provisions and salt, begin their fishing in shallops and boates." Augustine Fitzhugh depicted this practice in a map of 1693 by contrasting French crews on the Grand Banks with English boats fishing inshore off the coast of Newfoundland (Map 4). Shore-based crews had to row as much as three or four miles out and back daily from their fishing grounds, where they moored their boats as much as a half-mile offshore in water to forty fathoms deep. It was only after 1713 that vessels flying the Union Jack began to engage in the offshore Grand Banks fishery, which ships from Normandy, in particular, had pursued for a century and a half.[13]

Every spring, when the crews of these so-called fishing ships arrived in Newfoundland, they faced weeks of work ashore. It might take a month to repair or reproduce the boats, the *stages* for landing fish, and the wooden flakes for drying them, besides the cookrooms and cabins to which the fishers resorted in their off-hours. These various constructions they used intensively each summer and then abandoned every fall to the elements and to the ingenuity of Newfoundland's Native people, who often then dismantled the wooden infrastructure of the fishery in order to extract the iron that held it together. Parallel tasks awaited fishing crews in late summer, at the end of the season. They would load their tackle aboard ship, along with a cargo of fish if they were going to mar-

VII (1926), 47–51; Francis Bellott to Williamson, July 1, 8, 1678, SP 29/405 (5, 56), in *CSP*: Domestic.

13. Lewes Roberts, *The Merchants Mappe of Commerce* (London, 1638), 57; Rogers, *Historical Geography of the British Colonies*, V, pt. 4, *Newfoundland*, 117; Head, *Newfoundland*, 63. This key point, that the early English fishery was shore-based and not a bank fishery far offshore, is sometimes ignored or even denied; see, for example, K. G. Davies, *The North Atlantic World in the Seventeenth Century* (Minneapolis, Minn., 1974), 156–168; Glanville James Davies, "England and Newfoundland: Policy and Trade, 1660–1783" (Ph.D. diss., University of Southampton, 1980), Introduction and 12, 250, 270; Grant, "North Devon Maritime Enterprise," in Gray, Rowe, and Erskine, eds., *Tudor and Stuart Devon*, 119–140 (esp. 122). For emphasized terms, see *DNE*.

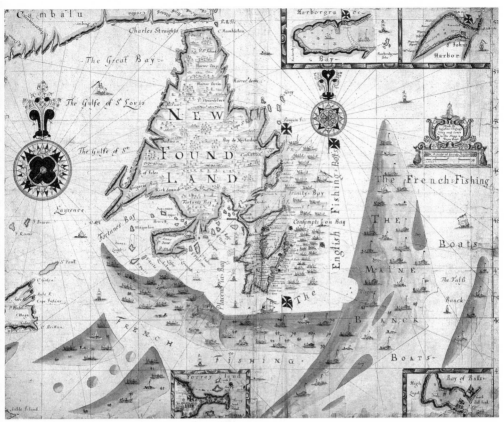

Map 4. New Found Land. *By Augustine Fitzhugh, 1693. Add MSS 5415, 30. Detail showing French crews on the Grand Banks and English boats fishing inshore. Permission of British Library, London*

ket, and, if time permitted, recycle suitable shore structures as firewood for the return journey, or even for export to England. In the intervening eight to ten weeks, a crew of five was expected to catch and cure something like two hundred quintals of salt cod, or ten traditional long tons—well in excess of twenty thousand fish.[14]

14. On the technology of the dry fishery, see John Downing, "The Maner of Catching and Makeing Drie Fishe in Newland," 1676, British Library, Egerton MS 2395, 565-566; Yonge, *Journal*, 54-60; Roberts, *Merchants Mappe*, 57-58; John Collins, *Salt and Fishery . . .* (London, 1682), 93-101; Denys, *Histoire naturelle*, 517-562; Marc Lescarbot, *Histoire de la Nouvelle-France*, III (1618), in H. P. Biggar, ed., *The History of New France by Marc Lescarbot*, 3 vols., trans. W. L. Grant (1909-1914; rpt. New York, 1968), 430-434; André Dommergues, "La

Fishing itself, no less than curing and marketing, required skills, including small-boat seamanship and familiarity with the habits of the codfish, preferably on a particular stretch of shore. *Gadus morhua* occupies an ecological niche near the top of the marine food chain, preying on crustaceans and capelin or other small fish, which graze in turn on plankton. Plankton bloom around upwellings of cold, nutrient-rich waters. Hence, summer concentrations of cod occur where the southward-trending Labrador Current encounters Newfoundland's promontories, shoals, and islands and exactly where the fishing stations and settlements of the seventeenth and eighteenth centuries were located. In the 1660s, for example, the fishermen of Barnstaple, in north Devon, preferred to fish at Fermeuse, just south of Ferryland Head. The inshore fishing boats would cluster on particularly productive grounds. A naval chaplain who visited Newfoundland in 1680 drew a vivid picture: "In St. John's harbour, unto which belongs 300 boats and upwards, which will be seen to cover the sea near the shoar when they are fishing in a pleasant maner, thick and near one another, as a great drift of cattle may be seen in a fair field depasturing."[15]

The Plymouth ship's surgeon, James Yonge, who worked on the English Shore in the 1660s, tells us that boats were manned by three men: the boatmaster, his midshipman, or mate, and the foreshipman. He adds that the "boats' masters, generally, are able men, the midshipman next,

---

peche à la morue au xviie siècle d'après le témoignage de Nicholas Denys," *Études Canadiennes/Canadian Studies*, XII (1982), 15–24; and Alaric Faulkner, "Archaeology of the Cod Fishery: Damariscove Island," *Historical Archaeology*, XIX, no. 2 (1985), 57–86. For impact, see James E. Candow, "The Evolution and Impact of European Fishing Stations in the Northwest Atlantic," in Poul Holm and David J. Starkey, eds., *Technological Change in the North Atlantic Fisheries, Studia Atlantica*, III (2000), 9–33. For structures, see Chapter 9, below. On firewood, see John Berry to Williamson, July 24, 1675, CO 1/34 (118), 240–241.

15. W. B. Scott and M. G. Scott, *Atlantic Fishes of Canada* (Toronto, 1988), xxiv–xxvi, 266–270; Head, *Newfoundland*, 21–24 (see fig. 1.4); Ransom A. Myers, "Testing Ecological Models: The Influence of Catch Rates on Settlement of Fishermen in Newfoundland, 1710–1833," in Poul Holm, Tim D. Smith, and David J. Starkey, eds., *The Exploited Seas: New Directions for Marine Environmental History*, Research in Maritime History no. 21 (St. John's, 2001), 13–30; Yonge, *Journal*, 56; John Thomas, Letter from Bay Bulls, Sept. 15, 1680, Codrington Library, All Souls College, Oxford University, Wynne Collection, MS 239, 229–230, in Peter Pope, "*A True and Faithful Account*: Newfoundland in 1680," *Newfoundland Studies*, XII (1996), 32–49 (esp. 40).

and the foreshipmen are generally striplings." In other words, although every man did not have to be fully skilled, every crew did. In typical early modern fashion, the passing on of skills was built into the employment structure of the industry, and every crew included a certain proportion of *youngsters*, or *green men*. (Yonge himself was only sixteen when he made his first voyage to Newfoundland.)[16]

Whether green men or seasoned hands, fishers went to work at dawn and, as Yonge reported, "row hard and fish all day." Each fisherman baited a pair of hooks on two or three weighted lines and lowered them over the side, hoping to tempt the cod, which normally feed near the bottom. The technology was medieval: the eyeless wrought-iron fishhooks and simple cast lead weights recovered from seventeenth-century archaeological contexts at Ferryland and Renews are identical to examples recovered from medieval English waterfront sites. Simple wooden hand-frames for winding in handlines seem to have been an early modern invention, coming into use about the time the Newfoundland industry developed. Archaeological examples from the English Shore differ in no important respect from those still used for handlines in the twentieth century (Plate 2). If fishing was good, the crews would head for their fishing rooms in late afternoon, each boat with as many as one thousand or twelve hundred fish, weighing altogether several tonnes. Given that it often must have taken an hour or two to return from the fishing berth, fishermen had a long working day. The Acadian fishing merchant Nicholas Denys tells us that French crews fished until about four in the afternoon in order to return to their fishing rooms to unload their catch about six. There, while the young foreshipman boiled up a supper for the crew, the boatmaster and his mate would offload the catch, which was now the responsibility of the shoremen.[17]

The shore crews began the task of making fish right on the *stage*

16. Yonge, *Journal*, 57; Handcock, *Origins*, 61–63.

17. J. M. Steane and M. Foreman, "The Archaeology of Medieval Fishing Tackle," in G. L. Good, R. H. Jones, and M. W. Ponsford, eds., *Waterfront Archaeology: Proceedings of the Third International Conference on Waterfront Archaeology Held at Bristol, 23–26 September 1988*, CBA Research Report no. 74 (London, 1991), 88–101. The introduction of the cod trap, in the later nineteenth century, displaced handlining, which was then relegated to a casual subsistence or recreational activity. On the working day, see Lescarbot, *Histoire*, in Biggar, ed., *History of New France*, 433; Yonge, *Journal*, 57, 60; Denys, *Histoire naturelle*, 544, 548. Among French crews, the surgeon was the cook.

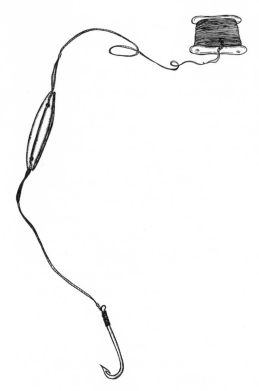

Plate 2. Cod's-Eye View of Fishing Equipment: Wrought Iron Fish Hook and Lead Sinker on Handline with Wooden Line Frame. Hook and sinker about eight centimeters; line frame about twenty-five centimeters. Drawn by Talva Jacobson, based on artifacts from Ferryland (CgAf-2) and Renews (CfAf-5)

head, the combination wharf and processing plant where the fish was unloaded. A boy would lay the fish on a table for the *header*, who gutted and then decapitated the fish "with notable dexterity and suddenness," as Yonge put it. (Later accounts give the first step of slitting the belly of the fish to the *cut-throat*.) The cod livers were set aside and dumped into a *train vat*, where the oil rendered in the sun. The header pushed the gutted fish across the table to the *splitter*, who opened the fish and removed the spine. "There are some that will split incredibly swift," Yonge observed, as many as "24 score in half an hour"—which is a fish split every four seconds, or better. (Good splitters can, in fact, work at this rate.) Two shoremen could handle the catch of a three-man boat, so that, when numbers of men and boats are reported for the dry fishery, they usually occur in a ratio of about five to one. Shore crew specialists were skilled, but the youngsters who assisted them were not. Untrained boys moved the split fish in handbarrows and piled it up for an initial wet-salting. This salting required experience and judgment, as Yonge stressed: "A salter is a skilful officer, for too much salt burns the fish and makes it break, and wet, too little makes it redshanks, that is, look red when dried, and so is not merchantable." (*Merchantable fish* was a premium grade; *not merchantable*, or *refuse, fish* was, in fact, salable, but of a cheaper grade.)[18]

This initial wet-salting played an interesting role in the technical evolution of the industry, because, by prolonging this phase of the cure, fish could be held for future air-drying, with some loss of quality. As noted, southern markets preferred dry fish, but they did import small quantities of green-cured wet fish, with the intention of air-drying it—a traditional practice, which makes absolute generalizations about import patterns problematic. Wet-cured *corfish*, as it was called, turned up in southern ports because crews producing dry fish also marketed small quantities of this wet fish at a discount. They did so because virtually all inshore crews produced some wet fish when the season was too late for the dry cure. Beginning in late-seventeenth-century New England, the technique of recuring fish after a prolonged initial wet-salting became increasingly important in the New World. (Similar processes had long been in use on the other side of the Atlantic.) Eighteenth-century fishers at both Île Royale (Cape Breton Island) and Newfoundland added this technique to their repertoires, permitting small schooners to make voyages of several days to offshore banks, where the fishers wet-salted their catch; later, on return to a shore station, they would air-dry the wet fish. Limited inshore stocks forced Île Royale fishers offshore; in Newfoundland, resident fishers used delayed air-drying to expand their catches by entering the Grand Banks fishery for the first time in the peace that followed the Treaty of Utrecht in 1713. Inevitably, this delayed cure produced an inferior product—but one cheap enough to compete as provisions for enslaved Africans in the expanding Caribbean market of the eighteenth century. In the century preceding, however, neither the combination cure nor the New World market was typical in Newfoundland.[19]

18. Gerald L. Pocius, "The House That Poor-Jack Built: Architectural Stages in the Newfoundland Fishery," in Larry McCann and Carrie MacMillan, eds., *The Sea and Culture of Atlantic Canada: A Multidisciplinary Sampler* (Sackville, N.B., 1992), 63–105 (esp. 84–101); Whitbourne, *Discourse*, 179; Tobias Burr, "Account of the Several Harbours," Mar. 3, 1675, CO 1/34 (191), 37. Quotations from Yonge, *Journal*, 57. On "cut-throat" and "merchantable," see *DNE*; and Josselyn, *Voyages*, 144.

19. Darlene Abreu-Ferreira, "The Portuguese in Newfoundland: Documentary Evidence Examined," *Portuguese Studies Review*, IV (1995), 11–33 (esp. 13); Kowaleski, "South-Western Fisheries," *EHR*, 2d Ser., LIII (2000), 439; B. A.

Earlier fishers made better fish with a more timely cure. After a few days in salt, the shore crews would rinse the fish in seawater and pile it on a platform of beach stones, called a *horse*, for a day or two before spreading it out to dry on a cobble beach or on *flakes*, rough wooden platforms covered with fir boughs or birch bark. As a contemporary tract *Salt and Fishery* observed, "A temperate windy season is best," and such conditions are typical of summers on the original English Shore, the east coast of Newfoundland's Avalon Peninsula. At night and in wet weather, the fish being processed had to be turned skin side up or collected in protected heaps. After four or five days of good weather, it was ready to be stored in carefully layered larger piles containing about fifteen hundred fish, like a haystack, as the St. John's merchant John Downing put it. Anyone who has participated in the unsuccessful salting of fish knows that the work of *making* fish was skilled. Nevertheless, the output of a competitively priced product—and, indeed, the reproduction of the whole system—also required the employment of untrained apprentices.[20]

A few specialized workers handled other tasks, notably carpenters, smiths, and surgeons, but most additional work fell to the fishermen themselves. Throughout the fishing season, they caught smaller species as bait, typically herring or capelin. For this they used *seines*, which were nets deployed like a curtain around a school of fish to trap them when the bottom was pulled together to form a bag. Yonge reported crews working herring seines every second night. Downing estimated that 15 men in two or three boats could keep thirty boats and 150 men supplied with capelin in this way. His example suggests a cooperative effort by the crews fishing from a particular harbor. At the end of the season, if the ship fishing was itself going to market, it would have to be loaded with the processed catch, including a few quintals of late-season, wet-cured corfish and barrels of a profitable by-product of the fishery rendered from cod livers, known as *train oil* (because it was used to lubri-

---

Balcom, *The Cod Fishery of Isle Royale, 1713–58* (Ottawa, 1984), 31–48; Head, *Newfoundland*, 72–74.

20. Collins says the fish were kept one day in salt (*Salt and Fishery*, 93); Downing, "Makeing Fishe," Egerton MS 2395, 565, says they were kept two days or more "as weather serveth." On rinsing, see Collins, *Salt and Fishery*, 93; and Denys, *Histoire naturelle*, 554. Cf. Colin C. Banfield, "The Climatic Environment of Newfoundland," in Alan G. Macpherson and Joyce Brown Macpherson, eds., *The Natural Environment of Newfoundland, Past and Present* (St. John's, 1981), 83–153.

cate heavy mechanisms, or "trains," in early modern parlance). From the early seventeenth century, the trading vessels known as sack ships called late in the season to take fish to market, but the crews of these vessels normally loaded their own cargoes.[21]

In the early seventeenth century, the catching of fish, if not the salt cure, seems to have been over by the end of July. Later, the season lasted somewhat longer, though even in 1684 Captain Francis Wheler thought "the best of the sport is over the twentieth of August." The sack ships and whichever fishing ships were going to market sailed a few at a time or, if seriously threatened by war, together under naval convoy in August or early September. The first ships to reach the Iberian and Mediterranean ports with cargoes of merchantable salt fish got the best prices and would, as one seventeenth-century participant in the business put it, "venture all to get the first market" in late September or October. The ships that had taken fish to a European market could be home in England by late November or December. Many ships did not go to market but returned directly home to England, carrying their own fishing crews, additional migratory fishermen (as passengers), sometimes fish, sometimes firewood, and often train oil. A direct voyage home from Newfoundland for these ships could take as little as three weeks; in the West Country, the Newfoundland men were expected in late September and early October.[22]

The seasonal rhythm of the early modern fishery was an essential as-

21. On carpenters, see W. Hammon et al., Protest, Jan. 11, 1614, GA Amsterdam NA 512, 56–57, NAC MG 18 012/94; William Clarcke, Examination, in *Pickering and Taylor v. Waringe and Grafton*, Apr. 3, 1638, HCA 13/53, 594; Denys, *Histoire naturelle*, 531. On surgeons, see Yonge, *Journal*, 56–60; Denys, *Histoire naturelle*, 528, 536. On sack lading, see Jan Oort and Hendrick Schram, "Charterparty re *de Coninck David*," Apr. 1, 1624, GA Amsterdam NA 631, 68–70, NAC MG 18 012/35; and Edward Milbery, Deposition, Nov. 22, 1630, *Southampton Examinations*, II, 72–75.

22. Cull, Deposition, Nov. 27, 1667, WDRO Plymouth, W360/74; Francis Wheler, "Answers to the Heads of Inquirys . . . ," Oct. 27, 1684, CO 1/55 (56), 239–246; Wheeler, Enough, and Wheeler, Deposition, Sept. 23, 1630, *Southampton Examinations*, II, 66–67; Elizeas Ricart, Simon Farwell, and John Bunne, Depositions, June 3, 1640, *Southampton Examinations*, IV, 9–10; [W. Davies], Letter [to Mr. Wren], Sept. 16, 1671, CO 1/27 (27), 74; Robert Blake to Admiralty, Oct. 25, 1655, Thomas Allin to Williamson, Oct. 23, 1669, Merchants, Petition, Sept. 20, 1672, William Wakeman to Hickes, Nov. 29, 1672, all in *CSP: Domestic*. On the east-bound voyage, see Steele, *English Atlantic*, 82.

pect of a *vernacular industry*. The term is used here to draw attention to the local and traditional character of this and many other industries in which labor and capital markets were narrowly circumscribed. The transatlantic fishing industry was, to be sure, an international economy, in the sense that markets were often distant from the ports mounting fishing voyages. On the other hand, these markets had specific local preferences regarding the cure and preferred source of the fish they imported. Ship, crew, and victuals might be marshaled in different ports; yet these three elements of the fishing voyage were each the product of the collective experience of a geographically bounded local community. The ability of early modern communities to transmit skills from one generation to another, irrespective of literacy, through informal apprenticeship systems was crucial to the reproduction of these vernacular industries. In fact, the breakdown of the traditional system of training fishermen would eventually be an important aspect of the decline of the migratory Newfoundland fishery in the watershed of the Napoleonic Wars.[23]

Vernacular industry can be contrasted with *directed industry*. The directed industry is conceived, often by a board of directors, before it physically exists and is a project, closely controlled in many particulars, not by custom, but by directive. The ability to transmit information as text using standardized terms is decisive. Capital and labor are treated initially as abstractions and may be sought anywhere, regional or even national boundaries notwithstanding. The distinction proposed, between vernacular and directed industries, parallels the distinction between vernacular and professional architecture or between a vernacular and a national language. Historically, vernacular industries have generally preceded directed industries, just as merchant capitalism or "commercialism" generally preceded industrial capitalism. The vernacular-directed distinction is not logically equivalent, however, to the distinction between merchant and industrial capitalism and is, in fact, intended to

23. Joan Thirsk, *Economic Policy and Projects: The Development of a Consumer Society in Early Modern England* (Oxford, 1978), 106–132; Vickers, *Farmers and Fishermen*, 88–89; Immanuel Wallerstein, "Introduction," *Commodity Chains in the World-Economy, 1590–1790*, Fernand Braudel Center, *Review*, XXIII, no. 1 (2000), 1–13 (esp. 1–5); Peter E. Pope, "The Sixteenth-Century Fishing Voyage," in James E. Candow and Carol Corbin, eds., *How Deep Is the Ocean? Historical Essays on Canada's Atlantic Fishery* (Sidney, N.S., 1997), 15–30; Keith Matthews, *Lectures on the History of Newfoundland, 1500–1830* (St. John's, 1988), 143. *An International Economy* is the subtitle of Innis, *Cod Fisheries*.

address some of the analytic shortcomings of "merchant capitalism" as an adequate description of the economic context of early modern industry. Most industries, even in early modern times, have both vernacular and directed characteristics. The analytic question, in the case of any particular industry, is where it belongs on a vernacular-directed continuum. The sixteenth-century Basque whaling industry, for example, operated toward the vernacular end of this spectrum, the much less successful seventeenth-century English whaling industry toward the directed end.[24]

We might well ask why vernacular industries were more efficient in the early modern period than directed industries, which have subsequently predominated. Literacy and industrial work discipline are important conditions of successful textually directed industry. These preconditions were only nascent in the early modern period, although they were developing. A more fundamental factor might have been the absence of modern mass markets. Vernacular industries, like the early modern cod fishery on Newfoundland's English Shore, were well adapted to the "flexible specialization" that characterized production for markets with regionally varying tastes, in this case the southern European market for lightly salted dry cod. As the inquisitive, late-seventeenth-century colonial bureaucrat Sir Joseph Williamson noted to himself: "Some sorts of fish are for some places and go off better, others at others." Vernacular industries suited vernacular markets.[25]

24. On the unplanned character of many early modern industries, see Thirsk, *Economic Policy and Projects*, 171. In applying the word "vernacular" to economies and contrasting it to the term "industrial," Ivan Illich, "Vernacular Values," *Coevolution Quarterly*, XXVI (1980), 22–49, has emphasized the self-sustaining aspect of the vernacular economy as opposed to the commodity orientation of the industrial economy, which is not the point here. For an exploration of the vernacular character of early whaling, see Brad Loewen, "Les barriques de Red Bay et l'espace atlantique septentrional, vers 1565" (Ph.D. diss., Université Laval, 1999); cf. J. T. Jenkins, *A History of the Whale Fisheries: From the Basque Fisheries of the Tenth Century to the Hunting of the Finner Whale at the Present Date* (London, 1921), 70–118.

25. E. P. Thompson, "Time, Work-Discipline, and Industrial Capitalism," *Past and Present*, no. 38 (December 1967), 56–97 (esp. 79–97); E. J. Hobsbawm, "The General Crisis of the European Economy in the Seventeenth Century," *Past and Present*, no. 5 (May 1954), 33–53, and Hobsbawm, "The Crisis of the Seventeenth Century—II," no. 6 (November 1954), 44–65; Maxine Berg, "Markets, Trade, and European Manufacture," in Berg, ed., *Markets and Manufacture in Early*

Late Elizabethan and early Stuart England saw the rise (and fall) of a variety of commercial projects consciously intended to build new and distinctly nonvernacular industries. Newfoundland was not immune to the "projectors," as they were called. (Today we would call them "developers.") The London and Bristol-based Newfoundland Company underwrote the first European settlement in Newfoundland at Cupids Cove, deep in Conception Bay, in 1610. This settlement was one of a number of contemporary commercial North American colonization projects and might have been, in part, a stratagem for local monopolization of the fishery. The slightly later Province of Avalon, sponsored in the 1620s by Sir George Calvert, Lord Baltimore, was centered at the well-established fishing station of Ferryland, on the southeast coast of the Avalon Peninsula. What Calvert had in mind was, without doubt, a fishery project. Sir David Kirke, who expropriated Calvert's establishment at Ferryland in the 1630s, had a royal patent specifically permitting his syndicate to centralize the fish trade. Such fishery projects, which boomed from 1610 to 1640 in both Newfoundland and New England, were directed companies, typical of southern England's outward-looking, innovative economy. In Newfoundland, as elsewhere, most of the the projected monopolies did not succeed; the West Country ports persisted in their local endeavors, and the transatlantic fishery remained vernacular. Kirke's project succeeded precisely to the degree to which he accommodated his proprietorship to the essentially vernacular growth of a planter fishery. The grant of the first "Western Charter" in 1634 to the English ports involved severally in the Newfoundland trade legitimized the traditional right of the West Country outports—notably the Devon towns of Topsham, Dartmouth, Plymouth, Bideford, and Barnstaple, and the Dorset ports of Poole and Weymouth—to order their own affairs in Newfoundland, according to specified vernacular customs, which were reiterated in the second and third Charters of 1661 and 1676.[26]

Industrial Europe (London, 1991), 3–25; Joseph Williamson, "Newfoundland," 1675, CO 1/34 (16), 24–57, 69–73 (transcription in *CSP: Colonial*, 1675–1676, Addenda, 1574–1674, 156–163).

26. Thirsk, *Economic Policy and Projects*, 24–105; Cell, *English Enterprise*, 56; Theodore K. Rabb, *Enterprise and Empire: Merchant and Gentry Investment in the Expansion of England, 1575–1630* (Cambridge, Mass., 1967); K. R. Andrews, *Ships, Money, and Politics: Seafaring and Naval Enterprise in the Reign of Charles I* (Cambridge, 1991); Brenner, *Merchants and Revolution*, 184–193. For charters, see Matthews, *Constitutional Laws*, 65–75, 127–131, 167–180.

The English fishery at Newfoundland enjoyed a boom in the late sixteenth century, which lasted into the 1620s. The rest of the seventeenth century saw stabilization at best, rather than secular growth. In fact, later lobbyists and pamphleteers tended to look back on the first decades of the century as the golden age of the migratory fishery. The size of this early maximum is difficult to fix. When a member of Parliament talked of ten thousand men in the West Country fishery at Newfoundland in 1621, he was probably just suggesting an order of magnitude by echoing commercial propaganda. During negotiations with France in 1614, a British diplomat claimed six thousand English fishermen were employed at Newfoundland, which is a more likely figure. In his contemporary *Discourse of Newfoundland*, Richard Whitbourne estimated that there were more than 250 English ships there in 1615, employing at least five thousand men and producing about 300,000 quintals of dry fish. A quintal represented 112 pounds, which Whitbourne took to average 120 fish, dry. These figures imply annual live catches by English fishermen at Newfoundland in the early seventeenth century of seventy-five thousand tonnes. Such a catch was exceeded later in the century only once, at least in the handful of years for which we have evidence.[27]

Cod stocks have always been subject to fluctuation. Cod were scarce at Newfoundland in 1592 and 1621, and the very bad season of 1592 coincided with scarcity in both the Cornish and Irish fisheries. When the Scottish east coast fishery collapsed about this time, the legal scholar William Welwod blamed overfishing by the Dutch. Modern scholars are more apt to relate such fluctuations, in the early modern period at least, to climate change. The seventeenth century was the coldest in the last millennium. New England weather records suggest two major climate

27. Cell, *English Enterprise*, 22–33, 100–106; William Nyell, MP, Commons Debate, Apr. 25, 1621, in Stock, *Debates*, I, 36; cf. Treasurer and Company of the Plantations in Newfoundland, Petition to James I, Mar. 16, 1620, CO 1/1 (54); Mr. Winwood, "Answer to the French Complaints," 1614, in *CSP: Colonial, 1675–1676, Addenda, 1574–1674*, 53–54; Whitbourne, *Discourse*, 124. The weight conversion assumes a ratio of 1:4.9 dry to live weight, that is, 1 quintal dry to 0.25 tonnes live catch. This calculation ignores the small proportion of fish that English fishermen shipped "wet," or "green," generally less than 10 percent of their catch. Assuming a 10 percent catch of such wet "corfish," the conversion ratio would be about 1 quintal cured fish shipped to 0.24 tonnes live catch; see Pope, "Early Estimates," in *Maritime Resources and Human Societies*, 9–40 (esp. 30, table 2).

fluctuations in northeastern North America at this time: a warming in the late 1650s from the cold winters of the preceding decades, followed by a cooling in the mid-1670s and the extremely harsh winters of the 1680s and 1690s. Visitors to Newfoundland in the 1670s reported wet summers and extensive sea ice. The European evidence also supports the New England data: temperatures in Iceland, the Faeroes, and Scotland fell in the 1670s and remained very cold until the early 1700s, provoking a complete failure in the Icelandic, Norwegian, and Faeroese cod fisheries in the late seventeenth century. Cooling at Newfoundland would not necessarily have had the same effect, since the island is not at the northern limit of the cod's range. Ocean temperature changes do, however, affect reproduction, recruitment, and local distribution of stocks, as the fishers of present-day Newfoundland have become vividly aware following late-twentieth-century overfishing, collapse of the stocks in the 1980s, and an administrative moratorium on the cod fishery in the 1990s, which continued into the new century.[28]

An inspection of eighteenth-century catch rates for specific areas of Newfoundland suggests that catches could fluctuate from less than half to almost twice the expected two hundred quintals per boat and that poor seasons often occurred in runs, for example, 1723–1725 or 1753–1755. When catches were depressed, they were often depressed over a

28. For an overview, see Henry Lear, "History of the Fisheries in the Northwest Atlantic: The Five-Hundred-Year Perspective," *Journal of Northwest Atlantic Fishery Science*, XXIII (1998), 41–73. For details, see Gray, "Devon's Fisheries," *Maritime History of Devon*, I, 139–144; William Welwod, *An Abridgement of All Sea-Lawes* . . . (London, 1613), 72; J. Jónsson, "Fisheries off Iceland, 1600–1900," and V. Oiestad, "Historic Changes in Cod Stocks and Cod Fisheries: Northeast Arctic Cod," both in Jakob Jakobsson, ed., *Cod and Climate Change: Proceedings of a Symposium Held in Reykjavík, 23–27 August 1993*, International Council for the Exploration of the Sea Marine Science Symposia, CXCVIII (Copenhagen, 1994), 3–16 (esp. 9, table 3), 17–30; John Pocock to Hickes, Sept. 17, 1670, [William Hurt] to Hickes, Nov. 4, 1672, [?] Page to [Williamson?], Sept. 20, 1675, all in *CSP*: Domestic; H. H. Lamb, *Climate History and the Modern World* (London, 1982), 201–231 (esp. 207, 210, 214, 221). For background, see D. H. Cushing, *Climate and Fisheries* (London, 1982); Karen Ordahl Kupperman, "Climate and Mastery of the Wildernesss in Seventeenth-Century New England," in David D. Hall and David Grayson Allen, eds., *Seventeenth-Century New England: A Conference Held by the Colonial Society of Massachusetts, June 18 and 19, 1982*, Colonial Society of Massachusetts, *Publications*, LXIII, *Collections* (Boston, 1984), 3–37.

wide area. Both periods cited saw the major Breton fishing port of Saint-Malo withdraw from the Labrador fishery to the Gaspé Peninsula, on the south of the Gulf of St. Lawrence, possibly for climatic reasons. Periods of transition to new climate patterns are typically characterized by increased weather variability, and variability is as risky for fishermen as it is for other predators. Fishermen, of course, expected short-term fluctuations in their catches. Sir Joseph Williamson observed: "It happens that some months are better fish and more than in another; for none knows when it will be a good or a bad year till the time be quite over, and being in different bays they know not where it is good, where bad." Gerard Malynes, commenting on the Dutch fishery, declared: "Of mine owne knowledge . . . they are contented to have one good yeare for fishing in seven." A depression in fish stocks that lasted decades, rather than a few years, would, however, precipitate a crisis in any fishery. Those involved in the West Country trade at Newfoundland agreed that the Interregnum (1649–1659) and the war with Spain (1655–1660), in particular, saw a serious decline in the migratory fishery. Lobbyists were still complaining about this decline as late as 1675. At this time, some migratory fishing interests blamed the continued crisis on the contemporary growth of a resident fishery. A review of what we know of catch rates in the second half of the century suggests that such critics of the resident fishery might have been ignoring a larger biological context, just as Welwod had, when he blamed an earlier crisis on the Dutch.[29]

To comprehend failure in the fishery we must understand success in that industry; we recognize bad years only in the context of better. A hasty survey of reported success at various fishing stations might easily misrepresent the relative availability of cod. In other words, such evaluations have to be interpreted. Several factors besides the catch affected

29. R. Forsey and W. H. Lear, *Historical Catches and Catch Rates of Atlantic Cod at Newfoundland during 1677–1833*, Canadian Data Report of Fisheries and Aquatic Sciences, no. 622 (Ottawa, 1987), table 18; cf. Head, *Newfoundland*, 65–66; Laurier Turgeon, "Pour une histoire de la pêche: le marché de la morue à Marseille au XVIIIe siècle," *Histoire sociale / Social History*, XIV (1981), 295–322; Jean-Francois Brière, *La pêche française en Amérique du nord au XVIIIe siècle* (Saint-Laurent, Quebec, 1990), 161–193; Lamb, *Climate History*, 256–260; Williamson, "Newfoundland," 1675, CO 1/34 (16), 24–57; Gerard Malynes, *Consuetudo, vel, Lex Mercatoria; or, The Antient Law-Merchant . . .*, 2d ed. (London, 1636), 170 (quotation). On reaction to declining stocks, see Matthews, "Fisheries," 146, 197–239.

seasonal success, in particular, prices and weather. In 1672, catches were good at Bonavista, at the north of the English Shore, but wet weather interfered with curing the fish. Catches were "indifferent" (that is, average) in Conception Bay in 1676, but fishermen made "good voyages," because prices were high. The most historically accessible biological evaluation is the number of quintals taken per boat, an estimate made often enough, even before total catches were recorded. Other documents give a more impressionistic evaluation of catches but nevertheless shed light on catch rates, indicating that inshore fish stocks were considerably depressed on the English Shore between 1657 and 1675, when poor or bad years are frequently recorded, and reported catch rates generally range between 100 and 140 quintals per boat, or only 50–70 percent of the normative catch (Table 1). Cod stocks along the English Shore rebounded in the last quarter of the century, although war continued to disrupt the fishery every few decades. Catch rates between 1675 and 1684 were generally considered "indifferent" to "very good," and the statistical evidence indicates catch rates were just short of the 200 quintals expected in a good year. There were several exceptionally productive seasons, biologically speaking, in the 1690s, when catches reached 425 quintals per boat in 1693 and 350 in 1698, before falling back, in 1701, to 218.[30]

An industry like the cod fishery operates in a complex context, of which the natural environment is but one aspect. In the postmedieval world, individuals, communities, and even whole industries were at the mercy of a larger economy. In early modern Newfoundland, the economic climate was most vividly reflected in the price of fish. The available evidence indicates that the price of cod at Newfoundland was reasonably stable through most of the seventeenth century, or at least that there was no secular trend in price after the late 1630s, until a decline late in the century (Table 2). The low prices reported at Newfoundland in the 1620s and early 1630s probably represent a trough, since the European

30. Nathaniel Osborne to Hickes, Oct. 5, 1672, Anthony Thorold to Williamson, Oct. 7, 1676, both in *CSP*: Domestic. Cf. Jónsson, "Fisheries off Iceland," in Jakobsson, ed., *Cod and Climate Change*, 3–16 (esp. 7–10). On the English Shore after 1657, see Table 37, below, and Pope, "Early Estimates," in *Maritime Resources and Human Societies*, 9–40 (esp. 29, table 1). The year 1668 saw, reportedly, an "excellent" season, although even two hundred quintals per boat might have seemed excellent in the context of the poor catches of the decade. The bait fishery for capelin failed between 1655 and 1675; see Downing, "Makeing Fishe," British Library, Egerton MS 2395, 565–566.

Table 1. *Catch Rates, English Shore, circa 1615–1701*

Year	Quintals per Boat	Contemporary Descriptive Comment
ca. 1615	>200	usual
1657	—	poor, low
1659	—	poor
1663	<130	poor (at Renews)
1664	130	very bad (at Bay Bulls)
1668	—	excellent
1669	>140	bad, owing to storms and bad weather
1670	140	bad, though early season good
1671	140	very bad (but 200 quintals in Conception Bay)
1672	100–120	very bad (but good at Bonavista)
1675	—	good
1676	188	average
1677	194	average or very good
1678	—	good
1680	180	—
1682	150	poor
1684	195	—
1692	350	—
1693	425	—
1698	285	—
1701	218	—

Note: A catch of 200 quintals was considered normal. "Indifferent" is reported here as "average." Catch rates for 1676, 1677, and 1684–1701 are calculated from adjusted catch and participation statistics. A quintal is 112 pounds.

Source: Peter Pope, "Early Estimates: Assessment of Catches in the Newfoundland Cod Fishery, 1660–1690," in *Maritime Resources and Human Societies in the North Atlantic since 1500*, ISER Conference Paper, no. 5 (St. John's, 1997), 9–40.

price of cod fell about 13 percent from 1602 to 1623, before rising to new highs in the 1630s. The price of fish delivered at Newfoundland, set early each season in England to facilitate forward contracts, reflected current European market conditions, although catch rates during the ensuing season would affect the spot market at Newfoundland itself. The price of fish at Newfoundland was generally a shade higher than the New England price, which probably reflects proximity to Europe rather than any

Table 2. *Prices of Cod, 1609-1702*

Shillings per Quintal

Year	Newfoundland Merchantable Cod	New England Spring Merchantable Cod
1609	8.0	—
1612	7.0	—
1623	7.2	—
1630	7.0	—
1633	8.9	—
1638	12.0	—
1639	10.0	—
1650	11.7	—
1655	12.5	—
1657	8.9	—
1659	12.8	—
1663	14.0	13.9
1672	12.9	12.4
1675	15.3	—
1676	13.6	11.6
1677	11.8	12.5
1679	13.5	11.7
1680	11.9	—
1681	11.5	11.0
1684	10.9	10.4
1689	11.1	—
1691	12.0	—
1693	10.8	9.6
1699	13.5	—
1701	9.0	—
1702	7.8	—

Note: Figures are expressed in shillings and decimal parts of a shilling sterling. Where two figures are available, their mean is used. The price in Spain was higher, 36 reals per quintal in 1638, for example.

Sources: The Newfoundland figures are documented in Pope, "South Avalon," 24 (table 1.1). The Massachusetts figures are from Daniel Vickers, "'A Knowen and Staple Commoditie': Codfish Prices in Essex Country, Massachusetts, 1640-1775," Essex Institute, *Historical Collections*, CXXIV (1988), 186-203.

perceived difference in quality. Long-term price stability for cod through most of the seventeenth century is striking, in the context of falling prices for other American regional staples like wheat, sugar, and tobacco, and may suggest the maturity of the cod fishery both as a trade and as an industry. The low prices at Newfoundland noted for 1657 and 1702 were typical of war years. As the London merchant John Paige put it at the outbreak of war in 1655: "Men being afraid of wars . . . will not adventure upon such a perishing commodity in such uncertain times." France and Britain were at war with each other from 1627 to 1629, 1689 to 1697, and 1701 to 1713, and these conflicts certainly reduced fishing effort, particularly by France. British participation was also very low in some years, including the biologically abundant season of 1693.[31]

𝕆 The Seventeenth-Century Resident Fishery

In more peaceful times, during the pleasant summer of 1620, the Dutch skipper David de Vries visited Newfoundland to buy fish. He found migratory English crews fishing on what he called "the middle coast," roughly the eastern shore of the Avalon Peninsula. Their Breton, Norman, and Basque competitors exploited the south and northeast coasts of Newfoundland, the adjacent coast of Labrador to the north, and fishing grounds in the Gulf of St. Lawrence and off Cape Breton Island, which they had frequented for more than a century. In the early seventeenth century, the European occupation of Newfoundland diverged

31. John Coq and Martin Bishart, Examination, Oct. 14, 1602, *Southampton Examinations, 1601-1602*, 45-46; Richard Newall to John Plumleigh and Mr. Wills, July 26, Oct. 24, 1623, Bodleian Library, Oxford University, Malone MSS, 2, 4, 6; Thomas Hollis, Examination, in *Kirke v. Jennings*, Aug. 4, 1638, HCA 13/71, 210; John Paige to William Clerke, Dec. 14, 1654, Feb. 3, June 8, Sept. 28, 1655, in Paige, *Letters*, documents 93, 95, 104, 108; F. P. Braudel and F. Spooner, "Prices in Europe from 1450 to 1750," in E. E. Rich and C. H. Wilson, eds., *The Cambridge Economic History of Europe*, IV, *The Economy of Expanding Europe in the Sixteenth and Seventeenth Centuries* (Cambridge, 1967), 374-485 (esp. 464, fig. 11); Richard S. Dunn, *Sugar and Slaves: The Rise of the Planter Class in the English West Indies, 1624-1713* (Chapel Hill, N.C., 1972), 203; Russell R. Menard, "The Tobacco Industry in the Chesapeake Colonies, 1617-1730: An Interpretation," *Research in Economic History*, V (1980), 109-177; Paige to Clerke, Apr. 14, 1655, in Paige, *Letters*, document 99a (quotation). He was wrong about the final price in 1655, which was kept to the normal level by a poor catch.

from this well-established pattern of seasonal migration. English proprietors began to settle colonists, at first with hopes of economic diversification and soon enough with more practical aims closely related to the fishery. The economic contraction of the later 1620s and 1630s made such proprietary investment look doubtful, but the later 1630s and 1640s nevertheless saw a continued transformation of the English fishery at Newfoundland, as interloping London merchants challenged the existing commercial network of the Devon and Dorset *Western Adventurers.* These West Country merchants were, perhaps, absorbed with the political conflict that culminated in the English Civil War (1642–1648). That the permanent settlement of Newfoundland, previously the preserve of migratory fishermen and a few sponsored colonists, began in earnest in the 1640s is surely no coincidence. The Civil War cast populations adrift, and turmoil in the metropolis created opportunity for initiative at the periphery. By 1660, resident fisherfolk were well established on the English Shore, and by 1680 they were catching and processing about a third of the fish exported by the British fishery at Newfoundland. In 1677, the planters operated 337 boats. The resident fishery on the English Shore was, by then, comparable in scale to the contemporary New England inshore fishery, for which 440 boats were reported in 1675.[32]

Major planters, like Sir David Kirke, who settled in Newfoundland in 1638, operated on the same scale as the West Country merchants who provisioned and manned ships with boat crews. Such planters owned or freighted ships bringing crews and supplies to Newfoundland and owned permanent fishing premises and fleets of fishing boats. In 1675, Sir David's widow, Lady Sara Kirke, and their son Phillip each operated five boats at Ferryland. That summer, the ships *True Love, Dimond,* and *Lyon,* all of Bideford in north Devon, manned four, five, and six boats, respectively, at nearby Caplin Bay. In other words, a large plantation employed about as many men and boats as the average ship fishing. The various branches of the Kirke family at Ferryland manned seventeen boats with crews totaling eighty-one men at this time. The largest ship

32. David Peterszoon de Vries, *Short Historical and Journal Notes of Several Voyages Made in the Four Parts of the World, Namely, Europe, Africa, Asia, and America* (1655), trans. Henry C. Murphy, New-York Historical Society, *Collections,* 2d Ser., III, pt. 1 (New York, 1857), 7. Compare John Berry, "Observations . . . in Relation to the Trade and Inhabitants of Newfoundland," Aug. 18, 1676, CO 1/35 (81), 325–326; and "The Account of New England," 1675, British Library, Egerton MS 2395, 522.

operations in 1675 were those of the *Real Friend* of Plymouth at Witless Bay and the *Darius* of Dartmouth at St. John's, each with nineteen boats. In the early 1650s, David Kirke had operated a minimum of thirty boats, and George Calvert manned at least as many in the late 1620s. Planters operating on this scale were, in effect, Newfoundland-based merchants, with kin and commercial ties to trading houses in London or the West Country.[33]

Smaller operations emerged as well. Precisely because the seventeenth-century fishery at Newfoundland was an inshore fishery, the owner of just one or two boats could enter it, employing a few other men and relying on sack ships to buy the catch. Most Newfoundland planters operated two boats, and Captain Charles Talbot observed in 1679 that "few of the colony keepe above 3 boats." A few planters did not own their own boats, like "one poore woman" of Petty Harbour in 1677, "which cannot follow the fishery but lets out her house and stage for yearly rent." With a few such exceptions, all planters kept boats, and these proprietors and their families were the people enumerated by the naval censuses of the period. Individual fishing servants were economically beneath official notice in this respect, although an estimate was usually made of their numbers and sometimes of what proportion intended to overwinter or return to England.[34]

Most of the small-scale employers were inhabitants, but some, known as *by-boat-keepers*, took passage out and back on ships fishing, that is, engaged in the fishery, and left their boats in Newfoundland every winter under the care of cooperative planters. This mode of production developed in the 1660s, particularly around St. John's, and by-boats ac-

33. John Berry, "A List of the Planters Names . . . ," and Berry, "A List of Ships Makinge Fishinge Voyages; with Boatkeepers . . . ," Sept. 12, 1675, CO 1/35 (17i, ii), 136–148, 150–156; "Upon the Severall Petitions . . . ," Apr. 24, 1654, CO 1/12 (20), 59; John Slaughter, "The Examination and Deposition . . . ," Aug. 31, 1652, Amy Taylor, "The Examinations and Depositions . . . ," Aug. 24, 1652, Md. HS, Calvert MSS 174/200, in Scisco, "Testimony."

34. Charles Talbot, "Answers to the Enquiries . . . ," Sept. 15, 1679, CO 1/43 (121), 214–217. The distribution of boats is discussed in Chapter 8, below. On the "poor woman," see William Poole, "A Particular Accompt of All the Inhabitants and Planters," Sept. 10, 1677, CO 1/41 (62iv, vi, vii), 157–166. Nonboatkeeping inhabitants reported range between five in 1677 and eleven in 1681; cf. Berry, "Planters," Sept. 12, 1675, CO 1/35 (17ii), 149–156; James Story, "An Account of What Fishing Shipps, Sack Shipps, Planters, etc., Boat Keepers . . . ," Sept. 1, 1681, CO 1/47 (52i), 113–121.

Table 3. *Boats and Servants Employed by Planters and By-Boat-Keepers,*
Newfoundland, English Shore, 1675

	Production Units	Mean No. of Boats	Mean No. of Servants
Planters	116	2.4	10.8
By-boat-keepers	28	2.2	9.8

Sources: John Berry, "A List of the Planters Names . . . ," and Berry, "A List of Ships Makinge Fishinge Voyages; with Boatkeepers . . . ," Sept. 12, 1675, CO 1/35 (17i, ii), 136–148, 150–156.

counted for an increasing proportion of catches. Contemporaries often considered by-boat-men and planters in the same breath and sometimes even put them together under the rubric of *boatkeeper*, a useful term that embraces both types of employers. The average by-boat-keeper operated on the same scale as the average planter (Table 3). It is not difficult to see how by-boat-keepers found an economic niche in the competitive world of the fishery. The ships fishing came to Newfoundland more or less in ballast, and the emergence of sack ship market transports meant many fishing ships would return to England without fish but laden only with relatively small cargoes of train oil. Fishing masters thus had space to carry *passengers* at competitive rates. In the 1670s, each one-way passenger paid about two pounds. The sack ships made it possible for by-boats to dispose of their catches in Newfoundland. If sacks competed with fishing ships in the carrying trade, at least the latter could profit by carrying their by-boat competitors to Newfoundland. Meanwhile, the by-boat-keepers thus escaped the unpredictable shipping overheads of the ship-based fishery or paid a fraction of this overhead in the predictable form of passage money. This sector of the fishery therefore attracted those with moderate capital. James Yonge perceived by-boat-keepers as newcomers in the 1660s and first reported them at St. John's in 1669. Both he and others refer to them at this time as "interlopers." In the censuses of the 1670s and 1680s, by-boat-keeping is limited almost entirely to the St. John's area. Many independent units of production competed with one another among the ships fishing and by-boat-keepers in that major harbor. The marginal cost in reduced catches to any one ship of introducing yet another by-boat competitor was probably smaller than the profit earned from passage money. In the smaller harbors of the south Avalon or north of St. John's in Conception and Trinity Bays, these trade-offs were likely assessed differently. In 1699, Commodore Andrew Leake reported 115 by-boats on the English Shore, of which 92 were at St. John's, a few at Bonavista and Port de Grave, and 10 in the Aquaforte-Ferryland area. The spread of by-boat-keeping to the south Avalon at the end of the century resulted, possibly, from wartime disturbance to planters.[35]

Not long after they established themselves in Newfoundland, planters and by-boat-keepers found themselves sensitive topics, politically contested in England. Following the Restoration of Charles II in 1660, many of those involved in the fishery were preoccupied with a return to normality. The crucial question among those with an interest in Newfoundland was the character of the norm to which the English Shore was to be returned. Was the fishery better off with few settlers and customary Newfoundland law under the informal control of the Western ports, as had been the case until the 1620s? Or did normality now imply acceptance of the relatively new resident fishery and a resident governor, with the powers exercised by Sir David Kirke between 1638 and 1651? Many identified the 1650s as a period of decline in the migratory fishery, and, by ignoring the larger environmental and economic context, some found

35. Matthews, "Fisheries," 162–171; Berry to Williamson, July 24, 1675, CO 1/34 (118), 240–241; Yonge, *Journal*, 55, 119–120; Talbot, "Answers," Sept. 15, 1679, CO 1/43 (121), 214–217; Andrew Leake, "Answere to the Inquiries," Sept. 17, 1699, CO 194/1 (150), 334–345. A hull might cost only six pounds, but fitting out each boat with salt, lines, etc., would cost sixty to seventy pounds, plus wages; see William Poole, "Answers," Sept. 10, 1677, CO 1/41 (62i), 149–152; Francis Wheler, "The Charge for Fitting Out Two Boats . . . according to the Custome of the Inhabitants . . . ," Oct. 27, 1684, CO 1/55 (56iii), 251–252. In 1671, the mayors of the West Country ports dated the intrusion of by-boat-men to the Dutch War of 1664–1667; see Mayor of Exeter et al., Petition to Charles II in Council, Dec. 23, 1670, CO 389/5, 18–19. It has been claimed that by-boat-keeping was introduced by Sir David Kirke; see Ralph Greenlee Lounsbury, *The British Fishery at Newfoundland, 1634–1763* (1934; rpt. Hamden, Conn., 1969), 110. No contemporary evidence for this speculation exists, and Kirke's commercial practice suggests it is mistaken, despite the vague assertions of the eighteenth-century CTP, alluded to in Handcock, *Origins*, 26–27 n. 18. For a contemporary view, see [James Yonge], *Some Considerations Touching the Present Debate between Owners, etc., and Fishermen, Relating to the New-Found-Land Trade . . .* (Oxford, 1671). I am indebted to Keith D. Mercer, "The Rise of the Newfoundland Bye-Boat Fishery, 1660–1684" (master's thesis, MUN, 2002), for drawing this pamphlet to my attention and for identifying its author.

the origins of this decline either in Kirke's governorship during the Civil War of the 1640s or in the contemporary growth in the resident fishery. John Parrett, a lobbyist for a so-minded faction of West Country merchants, cited "the disadvantages to this kingdome by inhabitants" as he saw them in 1675: "By reason of inhabitants and bye boats, which carry away all our choice men, we have not one third of the number of ships on this employment as formerly." Parrett exaggerated the impact of these new modes of production, but his unease about these changes was typical of senior merchants and bureaucrats of the period. The planter and by-boat fisheries of the later seventeenth century were vernacular developments. They grew as small local initiatives and were not directed projects like the colonial and commercial schemes of Calvert and Kirke and their predecessors in the first half of the century. The early proprietors had tried, in various ways with their grants and patents, to turn the Newfoundland trade into a directed industry, but their efforts turned out to have been aberrations. The Newfoundland fishery developed during the seventeenth century, but the significant developments were unplanned and undirected, that is, they were vernacular. By 1675, the economic geography of the fishery was changing, under the very noses of the Western Adventurers who invested in the traditional migratory fishery, as West Country fisherfolk made the decision either to settle in Newfoundland or at least to keep a boat there.[36]

36. Thomas Horwood (mayor of Barnstaple) et al., Petition to Council of State, ca. 1653, Anthony Thorold to Williamson, Oct. 15, 1677, both in *CSP*: Domestic; James Houblon to Robert Southwell, Mar. 20, 1675, CO 1/65 (23), 97–n.p.; John Parrett, "The Great Advantages to This Kingdom . . . [of] Fishing Ships," Mar. 25, 1675, CO 1/65 (27), 103. See Chapter 6, below.

Haveing bene imployed for severall yeares in a newe plantation,
I have seryously studyed which way that yet imperfect busines might
be improved to His Majesties and his subjects best advantage. . . .
You shall finde it a busines honorable, profitable, feasable, facill,
and oportune.
—*Robert Hayman, "A Proposition of Profitt and Honor," 1628*

Although Newfoundland lies in the same latitudes as France and southern England, its climate is subarctic, its shores washed by the Labrador Current rather than the Gulf Stream. The island was almost completely glaciated by the Laurentide ice sheet until about thirteen thousand years ago. Most of its soils are therefore youthful and shallow because they have not had much time to develop in the cool maritime climate. Where Newfoundland's soils are derived from glacial materials, they are deeper, but such soils are limited in extent. Newfoundland's cool climate and poor soils restrict biomass, and the accidents of insular geography have set the scene for a relatively simple ecosystem. Only fourteen mammals are indigenous to the island, nine of which are carnivores. This small ecosystem, top-heavy with predators and perturbed by erratic weather, produces boom-and-bust cycles in populations of prey, for example, caribou.[1]

Such biogeographic instability has had fatal potential for human beings as well. The Maritime Archaic Amerindians, who arrived in Labrador as the glaciers retreated nine thousand years ago, colonized the island of Newfoundland from the north at least five thousand years ago, flour-

---

1. Colin E. Banfield, "Climate," and Bruce A. Roberts, "Soils," in G. Robin South, ed., *Biogeography and Ecology of the Island of Newfoundland* (The Hague, 1983), 37–106, 107–163; Arthur S. Dyke and Victor K. Prest, "Late Wisconsinan and Holocene History of the Laurentide Ice Sheet," *Géographie physique et quaternaire*, XLI, no. 2 (1987), 237–263, map 1702A; Robert J. Mednis, "Indigenous Plants and Animals of Newfoundland: Their Geographical Affinities and Distributions," in Alan G. Macpherson and Joyce Brown Macpherson, eds., *The Natural Environment of Newfoundland, Past and Present* (St. John's, 1981), 218–250; Arthur T. Bergerud, "Prey Switching in a Simple Ecosystem," *Scientific American*, CCXLIX, no. 6 (December 1983), 130–141.

ished on the island for about two thousand years, but then disappeared. A little later, Paleoeskimo bands of the Dorset and related cultures re-populated the island, but they, too, disappear from the archaeological record, in this case by about 800 C.E. Another Amerindian group, whom archaeologists call Recent Indians, appeared on the island about the year 200 C.E. They were probably descendants of the Labrador Maritime Archaic and ancestors of the historic Beothuk, the people Europeans found in Newfoundland at the turn of the sixteenth century. Shanawdithit, the last known Beothuk, died in St. John's of tuberculosis in 1829. Her demise and that of her people occurred within the framework of European expansion, but the extinction of her predecessors on the island of Newfoundland is not as easily explained by ethnic competition.[2]

At least two well-established early Native cultures disappeared from Newfoundland, likely the victims of the constraints of island biogeography. As small populations, isolated from all but a trickle of immigration, dependent on a handful of prey species, the odds were never in their favor. Hunter-gatherers arriving in Newfoundland joined the nine indigenous carnivores to become the tenth predator in a small and unstable ecosystem. It is therefore not surprising that human populations came and went, extinguished or at best banished when prey populations collapsed, as they periodically did. A band might survive a mild spring when harp seals whelped too far offshore to hunt; the stronger members might survive an ensuing summer when, for some reason, salmon or seabirds were scarce; but, if such bad luck was followed by a crash in the caribou population, a hunting people would then face extinction. The same environmental trap would await any inhabitants of the island who depended on terrestrial resources, even if extended by agriculture. The limitations of climate and soil effectively restrict economic production to livestock, vegetables, and the hardiest of grains; even these are subject to severe weather fluctuation, so that historically they have been supplements to local subsistence, rather than staples.[3]

Europeans were attracted, not by Newfoundland's agricultural poten-

2. James A. Tuck, *Newfoundland and Labrador Prehistory* (Toronto, 1976); Ingeborg Marshall, *A History and Ethnography of the Beothuk* (Montreal, 1996), 201–223.

3. Robert H. MacArthur and Edward O. Wilson, *The Theory of Island Biogeography* (Princeton, N.J., 1967); James A. Tuck and Ralph T. Pastore, "A Nice Place to Visit, but . . . Prehistoric Human Extinction on the Island of Newfoundland," *Canadian Journal of Archaeology*, IX (1985), 69–80.

tial, however, but by Atlantic cod. They could exploit this relatively stable resource, whereas the Native people of the island did not, because the newcomers had hooks and lines, had developed a method of preserving cod with salt, and could rely on distant markets to transform catches of a single species of fish into the various goods they perceived as necessary for the life they expected to live. To do so, they did not, however, need to settle in Newfoundland—or, at least, this perception was common among merchants in the later seventeenth century and is still prevalent in historical analysis. The earliest documented European settlements in Newfoundland were proprietary colonies. They were probably doomed to failure, in the sense that there was not enough profit in the fishery to support fishers, on the one hand, and to satisfy investors, on the other. Yet, between about 1620 and 1680, West Country fisherfolk did settle the English Shore as part of a vernacular diversification of the original migratory fishery. To these later immigrants, the financial failure of the proprietary colonies was largely irrelevant, except for the benefit derived from the groundwork laid by the earlier attempts at colonization.[4]

⁊ℵ Early Proprietary Colonies

Before 1600, Europeans rarely overwintered in northern North America. If they did, it was for a year at a time, as in the case of the skeleton crews of Basque whalers who occasionally risked a winter in Labrador in the later decades of the sixteenth century. They did so either because the ice closed in before the regular December departure for their home ports in the Bay of Biscay or to free valuable hull space for a particularly ample cargo of oil. That English fishing ships also left winter crews behind at this time is, however, unlikely.[5]

From the time of Elizabeth I, a series of writers advocated the settlement of Newfoundland. Four are distinguished by their extensive firsthand knowledge of the island: Anthony Parkhurst, Edward Hayes, John

4. Gillian T. Cell, "The Cupids Cove Settlement: A Case Study of the Problems of Early Colonisation," in George M. Story, ed., *Early European Settlement and Exploitation in Atlantic Canada* (St. John's, 1982), 97–114.

5. James A. Tuck and Robert Grenier, *Red Bay, Labrador: World Whaling Capital, A.D. 1550–1600* (St. John's, 1989), 56–63; Jean-Pierre Proulx, *Basque Whaling in Labrador in the Sixteenth Century* (Ottawa, 1993), 64.

Mason, and Richard Whitbourne. Parkhurst's plantation scheme of 1577 came to nothing. Hayes was inspired by a stopover at St. John's in 1583 with Sir Humphrey Gilbert. This visit is sometimes misunderstood as an effort at Newfoundland colonization, but it was not. Gilbert had plans to exploit "Norumbega," that is, the coast of Maine; St. John's was just a port where he could supplement his lean provisions by bullying the European fishermen he found there. Newfoundland introduced both Gilbert and his companion Hayes to the possibilities of northern settlement, but within a few weeks a storm off Sable Island had dispersed the expedition en route to the proposed southern colony, and Sir Humphrey went down with his beloved *Squirrel*, histrionic to the end, proclaiming that he was as near heaven by sea as by land. Hayes, who survived to sail another day, lacked the capital to finance a colony and could do little more than publicize the possibilities as he saw them, as Mason and Whitbourne would do a few decades later. These early-seventeenth-century promoters of English settlement had years of experience at Newfoundland from 1574 on; they report enthusiastically on John Guy's Cupids Cove colony of 1610 as well as subsequent settlement experiments (Map 5). Yet, they make no mention of earlier attempts to overwinter. These keen observers, no less than their predecessors, would have made much of any attempts at year-round occupation, so regular overwintering before the documented colonization ventures of the 1610s and 1620s is not likely.[6]

The early proponents of Newfoundland settlement offered various grandiose justifications for their schemes, but the most relevant advantages of the island were those related to the fishery. Whitbourne, for example, in his *Discourse and Discovery of Newfoundland* (1620; rev. ed., 1622), defended colonization of the island with most of the contemporary rationales for English settlement abroad—from "converting the Inhabitants to Christianitie" to disburdening England of its "super-

---

6. Anthony Parkhurst [to Edward Dyer?], "Commodities to Growe by Frequenting of Traficq to New Found Land," 1577, and Parkhurst to Richard Hakluyt the elder, Nov. 13, 1578, in Quinn, *New American World*, IV, 5–7, 7–10; Edward Hayes, Narrative, [Oct. 1583?], in David Beers Quinn, ed., *The Voyages and Colonising Enterprises of Sir Humphrey Gilbert*, Hakluyt Society, 2d Ser., I, II, nos. 83–84 (London, 1940), 385–423 (and see the editor's discussion, 1–104); John Mason, *A Briefe Discourse of the New-Found-Land* (Edinburgh, 1620), in Cell, *Newfoundland Discovered*, 89–99; Whitbourne, *Discourse*. A possible overwintering in 1609 is noted, below.

Area Shown

BONAVISTA BAY

Bonavista

Trinity
Trouty
English Harbour
Bonaventure

TRINITY BAY

Old Perlican
Bay de Verde

Scilly Cove
New Perlican
Heart's Content

CONCEPTION BAY

Carbonear
Harbour Grace
Mosquito
Bryants Cove
Torbay

Bay Roberts
Port de Grave
Cupids
St. John's

Brigus

Harbour Main
Petty Harbour

AVALON
PENINSULA
Bay Bulls

Witless Bay

Plaisance
Toad's Cove
Bauline South
Isles of Spear

PLACENTIA BAY
Brigus South

Cape Broyle
Caplin Bay
Aquafort
Ferryland

Renews
Fermeuse

ST. MARY'S BAY
Trepassey

N

0   50

Kilometers

*Map 5. Permanently Inhabited English Fishing Harbors in Newfoundland,
1675–1684. Drawn by Ed Eastaugh*

abounding multitudes"—but he presented in greatest detail the case that settlement would permit a more efficient fishery. He also suggested that overwintering crews could preempt fishing rooms, raising the possibility of establishing a monopoly on the dry fishery. Such an outcome might have been a disguised part of the strategy of the Newfoundland Company, which backed John Guy's colony at Cupids Cove in 1610. The aims of the Bristol and London merchants who set up the Newfoundland Company were practical. They had no doubt about the main value of settlement at Newfoundland: the company charter states that the investors were intending "to secure and make safe the trade of fishing." The early 1600s saw the emergence of various European joint-stock companies set up to exploit trading zones in distant lands. Many of the English schemes were designed to underwrite the plantation of colonists, among them the Londonderry, Virginia, Bermuda, and Newfoundland Companies, all incorporated at this time. The investors in these enterprises overlapped, and the organizers of the Newfoundland venture probably drew lessons from Virginia—hence, perhaps, the businesslike aim to exploit the fishery.[7]

Thirty-nine colonists set out from Bristol in 1610 under John Guy, an experienced merchant. The settlers had detailed instructions to fortify Cupids, or "Cupers," Cove in Conception Bay, experiment with farming, cut spars and planks, make salt, potash, and glass, collect samples of ore, and, last but not least, to fish and trade in cured fish and train oil. The first two winters were mild, the death rate was low, and the colonists were able to carry out most of their instructions. In 1612, Guy brought over sixteen women, which marked a turning point toward the self-replicating European settlement of Newfoundland and, indeed, North America. There were, however, problems. Soil and climate were not as good as hoped: the colonists succeeded in raising vegetables, but their goats ate their barley, and the fodder they managed to harvest could not keep their livestock through the hard winter of 1613. The pirate Peter Easton harassed the settlement and forced the colonists to pay protection in the form of these precious animals. Guy quarreled with the company

7. Whitbourne, *Discourse*, esp. 125; Newfoundland Company Charter, British Library, Harleian MS 589, 8, in Prowse, *History*, 122–125; Gillian T. Cell, "The Newfoundland Company: A Study of Subscribers to a Colonizing Venture," *WMQ*, 3d Ser., XXII (1965), 611–625; Cell, *English Enterprise*, esp. 55; Theodore K. Rabb, *Enterprise and Empire: Merchant and Gentry Investment in the Expansion of England, 1575–1630* (Cambridge, Mass., 1967), 106–109.

about property that he expected for himself and about wages due his men. When he withdrew from the company in 1615, he probably took the other Bristol investors with him, for they soon established the offshoot colony of Bristol's Hope at Harbour Grace.[8]

The Newfoundland Company eventually replaced Guy with the capable mariner John Mason, who was probably chosen for a perceived ability to deal with the pirates. Unfortunately, he was not especially attentive to the fishery, and this inattention undercut the colony's economic stability. Their interim leader, Henry Crout, thought the colonists never exploited the fishery as fully as they might have, there being too many who "scorned to torne a fish," as he put it. Some West Country fishing interests nevertheless perceived the settlers as serious competition, and, by 1618, they were at odds with them. Mason moved on to New England in 1621. Because Cupids is not well documented after this time, historians have tended to assume that the colony withered away, but archaeological work suggests that settlers occupied at least one of the structures erected for Guy's original colony until it was destroyed by fire about 1665.[9]

The Cupids plantation did not produce the profits that investors in the Newfoundland Company had hoped for. The merchants involved eventually did what most businessmen would do: they liquidated their investments by subdividing the original grant into several lots and reselling regional proprietorships. Several of these successor proprietors organized colonies, among them Sir William Vaughan at Renews, Sir George Calvert, Lord Baltimore, at Ferryland, and William Payne and others at St. John's. Although Cupids was a business failure, it was successful in a different sense: English colonists were planted in a new and some-

8. Cell, *English Enterprise*, esp. 61; Newfoundland Company, "Instructions . . . to John Guy," 1610, British Library, Cotton MSS, Otho E VIII, 3, in Prowse, *History*, 94–96. A fuller version survives in the Middleton MSS at the University of Nottingham; see Cell, *Newfoundland Discovered*, 6. The modern Bristol's Hope was known in the seventeenth century as "Mosquito."

9. Henry Crout to Percival Willoughby, Aug. 20, 1612, cited in Cell, "Cupids Cove Settlement," in Story, ed., *Early European Settlement*, 97–144 (esp. 105). On the fate of Cupids, compare Cell, *Newfoundland Discovered*, 14, and William Gilbert, "Looking for Cupers Cove: Initial Archaeological Survey and Excavations at Cupids, Newfoundland," *Avalon Chronicles*, I (1996), 67–96. See also "Finding Cupers Cove, Archaeological Excavations at Cupids, 1995–1999," Bacclieu Trail Heritage Corporation, report on file, Culture and Heritage Division, Newfoundland, 2000.

what inhospitable territory. Significant settlement took hold elsewhere in Conception Bay rather than at the original Cupids colony, but Nicholas Guy and his family, who prospered at Harbour Grace and later at nearby Carbonear, had begun their lives in the new-found land at Cupids. The plantation in Conception Bay was not only the first English settlement in Newfoundland; it was ancestral to subsequent settlements both in its personnel and in the succession of its patent rights.[10]

In 1616, the Welsh intellectual Sir William Vaughan purchased the Newfoundland Company's grant for the Avalon Peninsula, south of Ferryland, an area he rechristened "New Cambriol." The following year, he sent a few ill-prepared colonists to the harbor of Aquaforte, where they spent the winter in the rough cabins built by migratory fishermen for their summers' work on the coast. In 1618, Vaughan hired the experienced fishing master Richard Whitbourne to bring colonists and provisions to the precarious settlement. Whitbourne did his best to reorganize the colony by moving it to better quarters in Renews, a few miles to the south. Unfortunately, he had to deal with a piratical attack on one of his ships by deserters from Sir Walter Raleigh's Guiana fleet. In the end, only six colonists spent the winter of 1619 at Renews, and they abandoned the settlement the following year. Besides supporting a brief attempt at colonization, Vaughan also promoted Newfoundland settlement in a series of fanciful books, notably *Cambrensium Caroleia* (1625), *The Golden Fleece* (1626), and *The Newlanders Cure* (1630). Vaughan purports to have written the second in Newfoundland itself, although it is doubtful that he himself was ever there. In the end, the Welsh poet was less prolific of settlement than of publication, including not only his own euphuistic exercises but also, indirectly, Whitbourne's invaluable *Discourse*, which examines Newfoundland and its fishery as well as the justifications and prospects for settlement. Vaughan retained his property south of Renews, after selling off the Ferryland area to Sir George Calvert and the Fermeuse lot to Henry Cary, Lord Falkland.[11]

Cary obtained control over two of the subdivided Newfoundland lots: "South Falkland," which included Fermeuse and part of the harbor of Renews, and "North Falkland," or the Bonavista Peninsula. In 1622, James I named Falkland lord deputy of Ireland; Irish and Newfound-

10. Cell, *English Enterprise*, 69–96.

11. Cell, *English Enterprise*, 81–86; Cell, *Newfoundland Discovered*, 19–26; Cell, "Vaughan, Sir William," *DCB*. Prowse, *History*, 110–111, misidentifies Vaughan's original colony as Trepassey.

land colonial schemes thus intersected, as they did in Lord Baltimore's career. Falkland's colonial promoters made generous offers of land to those who would settle and work in the fishery. No one attempted to colonize Falkland's grant in Trinity Bay in this period, but, according to Vaughan's *Newlanders Cure*, in 1623 Sir Francis Tanfield founded a colony at Fermeuse. We do not know who the settlers were, nor exactly how long the colony lasted as a sponsored settlement—probably only a few years. Yet settlement in the Fermeuse-Renews area seems to have been continuous from this period, and, if it was, South Falkland was not a complete failure as a colonial effort, even if it did not turn a profit for its aristocratic backer.[12]

St. John's, the most important of the migratory fishing stations, is also among the more obscure successor colonies of the 1620s. It was "the principall prime and chief lot in all the country," according to one of its key shareholders, William Payne. The St. John's lot included the fishing stations of Petty Harbour and Torbay as well as the then-unoccupied southeast side of Conception Bay. In the mid-1620s, St. John's had "plantations" and "some howses allreddy built." These might have dated to the preceding decade: the later-seventeenth-century St. John's planter Thomas Oxford maintained that his ancestors had owned stages and houses there since about 1610. By the 1670s, when Royal Navy officers began to take censuses, St. John's was by far the largest settlement on the English Shore. The intervening decades are, unfortunately, thinly documented, although archaeological research has confirmed the presence of substantial planters in the mid-seventeenth century, and it has yielded evidence of investment in harbor improvement by about 1665. Although the impact of proprietary colonization on settlement there is uncertain, St. John's remains an important case and always worth comparison when the data are available. For the period up to 1670, however, it cannot provide anything like the thick context, archaeological and documentary, that has survived for the south Avalon community of Ferryland.[13]

12. Whitbourne promoted these areas for colonization in the second edition of his *Discourse* (1622), and another colonial propagandist, identifying himself as "T. C.," did the same in *A Short Discourse of the New-Found-Land*, published in Dublin in 1623. The author of the latter was probably Viscount Falkland's kinsman Thomas Cary; see Cell, *Newfoundland Discovered*, 36–45, 228n.

13. William Payne to Lady Katherine Conway, Nov. 2, 1627, and John Slany to Willoughby, Feb. 13, 1625, quoted in Cell, *English Enterprise*, 78; Thomas Oxford, "Humble Petition," Apr. 2, 1679, CO 1/43 (41), 67; Peter E. Pope, "1998 Excava-

Sir George Calvert's plantation of 1621 made Ferryland one of the earliest permanent European settlements in northeastern North America and among the best capitalized, for James I's secretary of state was an influential and wealthy man. The grant of the Province of Avalon that James made to Calvert in 1623 recognized the transfer of the Ferryland lot from his predecessor Vaughan and gave Calvert title to much of the Avalon Peninsula south of St. John's. Initially, he hired managers to administer his Ferryland project, notably the Welshman Captain Edward Wynne and Sir Arthur Aston, who replaced Wynne in 1625. By this time, Calvert had declared his reversion to Roman Catholicism, had retired from politics, and had been made first baron of Baltimore in Ireland. In the summer of 1627, Lord Baltimore himself visited his colony in Newfoundland. He returned to Ferryland the following year, with his baronial household of forty (family members and servants), to inhabit the Mansion House that Wynne had built for him. Possibly, some of these colonists came from Ireland, where the family had been living for several years. In the end, Calvert was dissatisfied with his first North American province, and he began to lobby for another in the Chesapeake, after he departed Newfoundland in 1629. The thirty or so fisherfolk he left behind included men, women, and children who were among the earliest English settlers of what is now Canada.[14]

It has been suggested that even substantial proprietorships like Calvert's at Ferryland or the Newfoundland Company's early colony at Cupids were doomed from the start because they could not provide returns large enough to satisfy shareholders and to support a corporate colony at the same time. (Corporate colonies, in this sense, were formed, subsidized, and directed by proprietors who owned the colony outright.) This blunt explanation of financial failure is not without subtlety, for it implies that settlements not beholden to investors might support themselves precariously, which in fact began to happen in the 1620s, in Conception Bay and St. John's. The internal economy of Calvert's establishment at Ferryland is obscure, but the tenor of his correspondence with Captain Wynne, including the enumeration of colonists and the priority given

tions at 327 Water Street, St. John's, CjAe-08," report on file, Culture and Heritage Division, Newfoundland and Labrador, 1999.

14. Allan M. Fraser, "Calvert, Sir George," *DCB*; Cell, *English Enterprise*, 92–96; Cell, *Newfoundland Discovered*, 45–56, 272n; James I, "Grant of the Province of Avalon," Apr. 7, 1623, CO 195/1 (1), 1–10, in Matthews, *Constitutional Laws*, 39–63; Calvert to Charles I, Aug. 19, 1629, CO 1/5 (27), 75.

construction of a brewhouse, bakehouse, and smithy, suggests that he was willing, at least for a while, to subsidize a corporate colony. Sir David Kirke's Newfoundland Plantation of the late 1630s was a different sort of proprietorship. The Newfoundland Plantation was more sophisticated economically, envisaging as it did dominance of local markets and other developing epiphenomena of the existing fishery, in particular vernacular diversification into resident boatkeeping. Kirke set out to establish a profitable node in a trading network, not to sponsor a corporate colony.[15]

The traditional mercantilist assumption that exploitation of the fishery did not require the settlement of Newfoundland might have merit as an economic analysis, but, as a contribution to demography, it has been beside the point since 1610. There were many possible motives for migration in the seventeenth century. For those without an inheritance, one of the most important was the hope of becoming householders in their own right. If settlement was slow to expand at corporate colonies like Cupids, the proprietors' reluctance to allot premises to servants was likely as significant a factor as the colony's profitability. To the extent that we are now able to identify families who established themselves on the early English Shore, they were those who had appropriated their own fishing rooms and were set up where they could rely on the transatlantic commercial connections of a resident merchant. David Kirke might not have sponsored colonists as John Guy and George Calvert did in their day, but, in the end, he had more to do with the permanent English occupation of Newfoundland than either of his predecessors.

Ꝑꞓ Early Population Growth

In 1621, John Guy, by then a member of Parliament for Bristol, told the Commons that there were "but three real plantations in Newfoundland." He probably meant Cupids, Harbour Grace/Carbonear, and St.

15. Cell, "Cupids Cove Settlement," in Story, ed., *Early European Settlement*, 97–144 (esp. 111); Cole Harris, "European Beginnings in the Northwest Atlantic: A Comparative View," in David D. Hall and David Grayson Allen, eds., *Seventeenth-Century New England: A Conference Held by the Colonial Society of Massachusetts, June 18 and 19, 1982*, Colonial Society of Massachusetts, *Publications*, LXII, *Collections* (Boston, 1984), 119–152 (see 128–132 on the hunger for land); Karen Ordahl Kupperman, *Providence Island, 1630-1641: The Other Puritan Colony* (Cambridge, 1993).

John's. These settlements would have consisted, largely, of single males like Gabriell Viddomas, a longtime Carbonear fishing servant, who later recalled that, in the 1620s, "there inhabited in all the Newfoundland nott above five families." Viddomas was using "family" in its original sense of those who served a householder, that is, he was recalling fishing plantations, not kin groups, perhaps adding Ferryland and Renews or Fermeuse to Guy's earlier estimate. "Families" in this earlier sense did not exclude women, and Viddomas himself worked for a female planter, Joan Clay. Women were present on the English Shore from its early days, living lives that paralleled those led by their rural sisters elsewhere, which is another way of saying that fishing plantations were often run by married couples and sometimes by widows. Men outnumbered women, even within planter households, because fishing servants were almost invariably male. The original Cupids settlement started out with seven boats; Calvert's enterprise based at Ferryland involved at least thirty, suggesting that the early plantations would have employed 30–150 fishing servants each, some of whom would have overwintered with early householders. By 1625, 100 people lived in Calvert's corporate colony at Ferryland, of whom 30–35 remained in an unsponsored settlement in 1630. The total Newfoundland European winter population at this time might have been 200 souls.[16]

One or two lists of personnel apart, we have nothing resembling a count of the early population in corporate colonies nor of the informally settled communities of the English Shore until the early 1660s, when the surgeon James Yonge took notes on Renews, Fermeuse, and Ferryland. On the other hand, creditors' accounts, tenants' agreements, and petitions have survived, and named individuals also signed receipts and gave or were the subject of depositions. Scant as such documentation for Newfoundland is, the south Avalon is best recorded. An evaluation of surviving documents shows that by 1680 a number of south Avalon families had been established for decades. Some surname recurrences undoubt-

16. Guy, "Commons Journal," Dec. 1, 1621, in Stock, *Debates*, I, 55; Gabriell Viddomas, Deposition, Nov. 27, 1667, WDRO Plymouth, W360/74; Cell, *English Enterprise*, 93; "An Inventorie of . . . the English Coloni in Cupies Cove," Aug. 26, 1611, in Cell, *Newfoundland Discovered*, 65-67; John Slaughter, "The Examination and Deposition . . . ," Aug. 31, 1652, in Scisco, "Testimony"; Simon Stock to Propaganda Fide, Jan. 1, 1631, in Luca Codignola, *The Coldest Harbour in the Land: Simon Stock and Lord Baltimore's Colony in Newfoundland, 1621-1649* (Montreal and Kingston, 1988), 121-122.

edly reflect the complex residential behavior of what have been aptly termed "transatlantic extended families": particular West Country families with Newfoundland experience who were prone to send individuals overseas to work for a time there. Some members of a transatlantic extended family might be planters, that is, resident proprietors of fishing plantations, but complex family links with Newfoundland typically implied continuing involvement with the migratory fishery rather than generational succession in Newfoundland. The Perrimans of Trepassey or the Cruses of Bay Bulls are good examples of transatlantic extended families with complex links to Newfoundland, turning up at various times as planters, seasonal by-boat-keepers, and even as shipmasters. Many other surnames turn up so often in reference to south Avalon planters that a simpler explanation of nominal reiteration is more likely to apply—that is, the establishment of a lineage resident in the region. The Kirkes themselves are the best known of these planter families (Figure 1). There are others as well. At least twenty-four south Avalon families appear to have reproduced themselves in Newfoundland before 1670.[17]

Five of these families had origins in Sir George Calvert's Province of Avalon. Founding members of the Davies, Lee, Love (Lowe), Poole, and Taylor families were among Ferryland colonists circa 1629, and these names survived on the south Avalon until the 1670s. Three were women: Philis Davies, Anne Love, and Amy Taylor. A fourth founding female, the wife of William Poole, gave birth to a son (Richard?) at Ferryland in 1628. These four might have been among the handful of Roman Catholic women who stayed behind on the departure of Calvert in 1629, perhaps because of personal attachments that crystallized into marriage. A number of complex transatlantic extended family links might also have originated in this period: the names Bayly, Bennett, Hacker, Hill, Stevens, and Waymouth recur intermittently with south Avalon connections but without evidence of a planter lineage. John Slaughter was established as

17. Individuals recorded in the miscellany of noncensus sources were indexed and cross-checked with planters in the censuses of 1675 to 1681. See Pope, "South Avalon," appendix C. The term "lineage" is used here, not "patriline," since, in some cases, the original female partner is the earliest identifiable memeber of a kin group. Cf. E. R. Seary, *Family Names of the Island of Newfoundland*, ed. William Kirwin (St. John's, 1998), which includes some of the seventeenth-century planters. See Handcock, *Origins*, 34, for an alternate view, finding "very limited generational succession" before the last quarter of the seventeenth century, and 46–47, for transatlantic extended families.

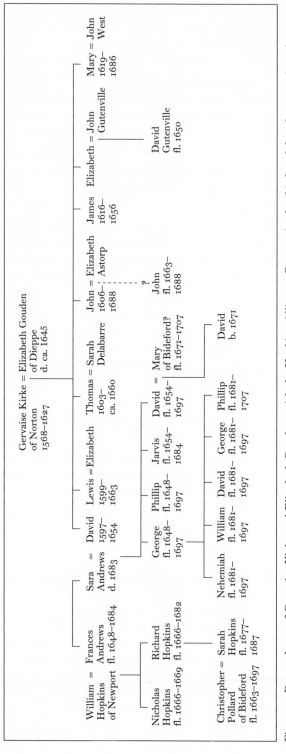

Figure 1. *Descendants of Gervaise Kirke and Elizabeth Gouden, with the Hopkins Alliance. Persons in the third and fourth generations (except David Gutenville) were Newfoundland planters*

a planter at Ferryland about 1628–1652 but probably moved on to Salem, Massachusetts, before 1663.[18]

The decade following Calvert's departure in 1629 was much less significant for south Avalon settlement. At the time of Kirke's arrival in 1638, the contemporary assumption was that the planters already there remained from the earlier proprietary colony. This perception was probably accurate: only a few arrivals in the early 1630s are documented. William and Amy Wrixon established themselves at Ferryland in 1631 and remained in the area until at least the 1660s, but, if they raised children in Newfoundland, the evidence has not survived. No south Avalon lineages are, on present evidence, traceable to the period 1630–1637. The tenure of Thomas Cruse as a tavern-keeping planter at Bay Bulls from 1635 to 1653 seems to mark the beginning of a complex family link with that harbor, but, again, Cruse did not establish a family there.[19]

The Kirkes' appropriation of Ferryland in 1638 marked the establishment of a planter family that would dominate the south Avalon for more than half a century. Of the five other planter lineages traceable to the period following, three were founded by associates of Sir David Kirke. The elder John Downing arrived in 1641 as a representative of Kirke's fellow proprietors. John Mathews was allied with Kirke in complex litigation circa 1650 and might have been one of the thirty servants Kirke was said to have brought with him. Lady Frances Hopkins, who arrived with her family in 1649, was a political refugee who arrived in Newfoundland with Charles I's personal plea to Sir David Kirke for her protection: "I thought good to desire you, whether by your advice in the business of that country, or otherwise in any kind, as her occasion shall require, to afforde her your best assistance . . . althoughe I make noe question, but this would have bin don, in regard of the neere alliance that is betwixt you." Charles refers to her as Kirke's "sister," but he was using a loose seventeenth-century sense of the term to mean sister-in-law. Frances Andrews Hopkins and Sir David's wife, Sara Andrews Kirke, were the sisters. Lady Frances was the wife of

18. Stock to Propaganda Fide, Jan. 1, 1631, in Codignola, *The Coldest Harbour in the Land*, 121–122. Unfortunately, we know only the married names of the Ferryland women. Unmarried women in early Newfoundland are discussed further in Chapter 6, below.

19. On the existing planters of 1638, see P. Vincent, "True Relation of the Late Battell . . ." (1638), MHS, *Colls.*, 3d Ser., VI (Boston, 1837), 29–43; Thomas Cruse, Deposition, Nov. 27, 1667, WDRO Plymouth, W360/74.

Sir William Hopkins, headmaster of the Newport Grammar School and King Charles's host during the tense months of house arrest on the Isle of Wight in late 1648, before his imprisonment, trial, and execution. Sir William did not accompany his wife to Newfoundland and, apparently, died about this time. Kirke's associates Downing and Mathews also might have had political cause, if less spectacular, for remaining in Newfoundland, as, perhaps, did Robert Dench, who arrived in 1650, just after the end of the Civil War. Trustrum Dodridge was already in Newfoundland by 1647, perhaps one of the civilians displaced when royalist forces slighted the pro-parliamentary West Country port towns like Barnstaple and Dartmouth. A number of transatlantic extended family links date to this period: Boones, Cookes, and Willicotts began to frequent Newfoundland and might have seen the island as a refuge from the turmoil of the Civil War—but they did not establish planter lineages at this time.[20]

Interregnum data are almost completely lacking, but a tenants' agreement with the Calverts in 1663, when they were, for a time, restored to their proprietorship, gives Codner, Coombe, Dale, Gilder, Moon (Mooney), Mintor, Oliver, Pollard, Roberts (Robbins), and Wallis as planter names between Aquaforte and Witless Bay. Eight of these eleven surnames survive into the census period of the last quarter of the century, as does that of the "Mr. Matthews," who was recalled from St. Mary's Bay in 1662. Ezekial and George Mintor passed their time in Newfoundland without issue, but the names Oliver and Wallis survived among an assortment of later by-boat-keepers and servants, suggesting possible continuing complex transatlantic family links originating before the restoration of the Calverts in the early 1660s but seeming to rule out early planter lineages among these two families. Between 1663 and 1670, five new planter surnames turn up in scattered sources relating to the south

20. Charles I to Sir David Kirke, Nov. 11, 1648, British Library, Egerton MS 2395, 36. Lady Hopkins is referred to as Sara Kirke's sister in Richard Hartnoll et al., Deposition, Sept. 15, 1707, CO 194/4 (77ix), 316. On "sister" as sister-in-law, see *OED*. On Charles and Lady Hopkins, see Charles I to William Hopkins, Aug. 20, 1628, in [Thomas Wagstaffe], *A Vindication of King Charles the Martyr* . . . , 2d ed. (London, 1711), 154; George Hillier, *A Narrative of the Attempted Escapes of Charles the First from Carisbrook Castle, and of His Detention in the Isle of Wight* (London, 1852), 251–253; C. V. Wedgwood, *The Trial of Charles I* (London, 1964), 15; Charles Carlton, *Charles I: The Personal Monarch* (London, 1983), 332–336.

Table 4. *South Avalon Planter Surnames, 1621–1670*

Foundation Period	Possible Family Lineages	Possible Complex Links	Childless Persons and Couples	Total
1621–1629	5	6	1	12
1630–1637	0	1	1	2
1638–1651	6	3	0	9
1652–1662	8	2	1	11
1663–1670	5	2	1	8
Total	24	14	4	42

Note: The table reports repeated occurrences of surnames in the records, not necessarily households, much less individuals. Names were included only if two planters so named lived in Newfoundland in at least two different years up to 1682. "Complex Links" lists surnames of transatlantic extended families that had a repeated connection with Newfoundland, including at least one planter, but for which there is no evidence for establishment of a lineage in Newfoundland before 1675.

Source: Pope, "South Avalon," appendix C. Administrators without their own plantations, like Wynne, Treworgy, and Rayner, are excluded.

Avalon: Collins, Pearce (Piercey), Toms, White, and Wood. The recurrence of these surnames in later censuses suggests that these families did establish planter lineages. The Hilliards and Prowses, who also occur in these later-seventeenth-century censuses, were more likely restricted to transatlantic extended family links in the 1660s. An individual planter without known progeny, Richard Maynard, also appeared at this time.

These data yield some simple conclusions about the timing of settlement on the south Avalon (Table 4). Settlement was fairly evenly spread, with one exception, over the half-century in question, 1620–1670. The two periods of active proprietorship, 1621–1629 and 1638–1651, were at least as important in establishing planter lineages as the later period, 1663–1670, which was best documented. The 1630s were insignificant for settlement until the arrival of the Kirkes in 1638, whereas the Interregnum period of the 1650s was important. If possible complex transatlantic extended family links and childless couples and individuals are tallied as well, the picture does not significantly change. Note that the surnames analyzed represent only the tip of the iceberg: some thirty to thirty-five individuals inhabited Ferryland in 1630, yet we know the names of a half-dozen at most. The lack of such information must, obviously, limit our ability to study continuity of settlement. Nevertheless, a cross-checking of documented south Avalon planter surnames indicates significant continuity through the early period of informal settlement. There are no obvious reasons to suppose that the situation was much different in the original settlement area of Conception Bay or at St. John's. Between 1630 and 1675, an unplanned process of small-scale informal settlement populated the traditional fishing harbors of the English Shore with resident fisherfolk. Kirke's proprietorship, between 1638 and 1651, was certainly an important period for settlement, at least on the south Avalon. Although he brought his own servants from England, he is not known to have sponsored the immigration of planters, except perhaps for his sister-in-law Lady Hopkins. Migration to Newfoundland was— like the evolution of the fishery—predominantly vernacular. The rapid increase in the number of plantations reported in naval censuses between 1675 and 1681 indicates that the overwintering population continued to grow into the 1680s. Contemporary complaints voiced by some of the wealthier Western Adventurers suggest that migration remained a vernacular phenomenon.[21]

How many people were scattered in these coastal hamlets along the English Shore? The seasonality of the cod fishery and the interlocking residence patterns associated with the several sectors of the industry complicate this question. Again, the seventeenth-century British fishery at Newfoundland was an inshore fishery prosecuted in daily voyages in open boats. The amount of time any man spent ashore in the particular harbor from which his employer sent out fishing boats depended, not on whether the employer was migratory fishing master, by-boat-keeper, or planter, but rather on the particular job the employee had been hired to do. The summer population of Newfoundland fishing stations did not consist merely of planters, with their kin and the servants they employed fishing. These inhabitants of fishing plantations were joined every summer by thousands of servants engaged in the two migratory sectors of the fishery, that is, the so-called fishing ships and the by-boats. Contemporary estimates of summer populations of about six thousand in the first

21. There are difficulties in assessing the chronological distribution of these reiterated south Avalon surnames. In many cases, we have evidence for presence in a particular year, but the date of arrival remains conjectural. Furthermore, documentation is uneven: later periods are better documented. Finally, the periods are not of equal duration but are artifacts of political history and the available evidence. See Chapter 4, below, for a discussion of St. John's.

half of the century are probably more reliable than retrospective figures ranging up to ten thousand, offered by later lobbyists.[22]

In 1660, the London civil servant Thomas Povey wrote a report on Newfoundland that provides the basis for an informed estimate of the winter population at that time. He estimated that there were 180 "families" on the island, meaning planter households, including servants, which suggests a summer population of two thousand or more in planter households, of whom perhaps fifteen hundred would overwinter. Estimating how many people overwintered in the seventeenth century is a tricky question. Planters or their families occasionally revisited England, but they were normally permanent residents, in Newfoundland winter and summer. The same cannot be assumed for their servants: some were, in effect, also inhabitants, also overwintering on the island, but some were not.[23]

The winter servant population was normally much smaller than the summer population, for fishing servants did not necessarily remain in Newfoundland at the end of the season. The proportion who did was affected by catches and markets as well as by war or the threat of war. In a tract of 1680, John Collins complained that the migratory English fishery in Newfoundland had been undermined not only by the fishermen of France and New England but also by "1000 of our own seamen that stay'd there on shore in 1665 to avoid the service against the *Dutch*," implying that fishing servants had settled in Newfoundland, thus fostering the resident fishery, to avoid the threat of impressment on return to their home ports in the West Country. Only rarely did census takers give the actual number of servants overwintering, but figures for 1680 suggest that 65 percent of planters' servants stayed that winter in Newfoundland. This rate of overwintering was probably typical, for prices and catches

22. The figures for summer populations given in Robert V. Wells, *The Population of the British Colonies in America before 1776: A Survey of Census Data* (Princeton, N.J., 1975), 47, table II-1, are only 20–25 percent of probable total summer populations. For lobbyists' overestimates, see John Parrett, "The Great Advantages to This Kingdom . . . [of] Fishing Ships," Mar. 25, 1675, CO 1/65 (27), 102–103; William Davies, "Reasons of the Decay of the Trade . . . ," 1672, CO 1/29 (78), 206–207. Such participation was achieved in the eighteenth century; see Head, *Newfoundland*, 54–62.

23. Thomas Povey, "True State of Affairs in Newfoundland," 1660, British Library, Egerton MS 2395, 264. Cell, *Newfoundland Discovered*, 57, reports Povey's figure as "about 150," but my reading of 180 is confirmed by the NAC transcription. Dependency rates are discussed in Chapter 6, below.

were average, and the economic and social outlook was unaffected by the threat of war. Some 1,130 of 1,718 planters' servants overwintered in 1680–1681. Thus, with 562 planters, wives, and children in the household reported, about 1,700 persons inhabited the English Shore in the winter of 1681. To put this total winter population in another perspective, it was only a little more than a quarter of the total summer population, including fishermen employed by ships fishing and by-boats as well as the 2,280 persons in planter households, in the summer of 1680.[24]

A rule of thumb implying that about two of three planters' servants overwintered would be consistent with typical residence of three summers and two winters in Newfoundland. French *habitants-pêcheurs* (resident fishers) usually hired their servants for three years. Although few indentures relating to service in the British seventeenth-century resident fishery have survived, one of these, made in the 1640s for Newfoundland and Maine, is for a three-year term. By chance we happen to know that Anthony Gay served Phillip Kirke at Ferryland for three years, 1688–1690. Many men hired themselves to planters by the season, just as they hired themselves to migratory ships. They might, nevertheless, remain in Newfoundland for a quarter of a century, as did Gabriell Viddomas, who worked at Carbonear between 1627 and 1651.[25]

24. Quotation from John Collins, *A Plea for the Bringing in of Irish Cattel, and Keeping out of Fish Caught by Foreigners* . . . (London, 1680), 21. [John Wyborn], "The Names of the English Inhabitants . . . ," Dec. 7, 1676, CO 1/38 (89), 239–242, observes that "about half" the planters' servants returned to England every year. For exact figures, see "Planters and Inhabitants in the English Ports, etc., in Newfoundland," 1680, British Library, Add MS 15898, 133; cf. John Norris, "Planters," and Norris, "Shipps," Sept. 27, 1698, CO 194/1 (125i, ii), 262, 264. Keith Matthews, *Lectures on the History of Newfoundland, 1500–1830* (St. John's, 1988), 85; Matthews, *Fisheries*, 173; and Handcock, *Origins*, 26, find lower rates for planters' servants by extrapolating from a reference to ship fishermen in Francis Wheler, "Answers to the Heads of Inquirys . . . ," and Wheler, "Account of Inhabitants . . . ," Oct. 27, 1684, CO 1/55 (56, 56vii), 237–246, 257. For another comparison of winter and summer populations, on a different basis, see Wells, *Population*, 47, table II-1. Overwintering rates might well have been lower in the eighteenth century.

25. On length of service, see Peter Moogk, "Manon's Fellow Exiles: Emigration from France to North America before 1763," in Nicholas Canny, ed., *Europeans on the Move: Studies on European Migration, 1500–1800* (Oxford, 1994), 236–260; George Spry and Paul Mitchell, Indenture of Paul Mitchell, Apr. 6, 1643, *Trelawny Papers*, 342–343. Other indentures are also for three years. Cf. Todd

Thomas Povey's report of 1660 is an early example of bureaucratic attention to Newfoundland prompted by an increasingly bitter debate over the desirability of settlement. The growing chorus of complaints about boatkeepers in general and planters in particular was a symptom of the political difficulties faced by these men and women, but it is also a testimony to their increasingly important role within what had once been an entirely migratory industry. There were obvious economic attractions to boatkeeping for migratory fishing masters with limited capital. Like by-boat-keepers, most planters avoided unpredictable shipping overheads by bringing in their boat crews as passengers on ships engaged in the migratory fishery and by exporting their dried catches of cod on sack ships. The planters, however, also had to shoulder the cost of overwintering, not only for themselves but also for many of their servants. The economic niche occupied by the planter and servant inhabitants of seventeenth-century Newfoundland is, in this sense, less obvious than the smaller niche occupied by their cousins, the by-boat-keepers and their migratory crews. If the proprietors failed to plant more than a few hundred men and women in the new-found land by 1630, what was the economic function of the much larger unsubsidized overwintering population of about seventeen hundred people established on the eastern coast of Newfoundland by 1680? Was it really true that the seventeenth-century Newfoundland fishery did not require settlement?[26]

?⅚ The Economic Logic of Newfoundland Settlement

After the Restoration of 1660, the Newfoundland planters faced a new challenge, not merely to settled government but to settlement itself. Some West Country merchants accused them of preempting the best shore space, destroying their competitors' stages and cookrooms, and enticing fishing servants to remain in Newfoundland. In the mid-1670s, marauding migratory crews attacked plantations in the St. John's area,

---

Gray, "Devon's Fisheries and Early Stuart Northern New England," *Maritime History of Devon*, I, 139–144; Anthony Gay, Deposition, Oct. 16, 1707, CO 194/4 (51), 187; Wheler, "Answers," Oct. 27, 1684, CO 1/55 (56), 237–246; Robert Alward, Libel, in *Alward v. Kirke*, 1650, HCA 24/111 (4); Gabriell Viddomas, Deposition, Nov. 27, 1667, WDRO Plymouth, W360/74.

26. Povey, "True State of Affairs," 1660, British Library, Egerton MS 2395, 264.

and, in 1675, the Committee for Trade and Plantations instructed the planters to leave. Sir John Berry, the judicious and humane naval commodore sent to implement this harsh policy, found it impractical and eloquently defended Newfoundland settlement:

> I have to the best of my judgment made diligent inquiry into all those things layd to the planters charge by the merchant adventurers and found most of them to be false . . . by which you have reason to see those planters are not soe bad as the merchants makes them to his Majesty. Some selfe ended persons have a mind to engage all into their own hands and especially if the planters be gone. . . . The opinion of experienced commanders that have used this trade, [is] that in case those people should be removed out of this country, his Majesty's selfe in a few years would find the ill effects of itt.

Besides, he argued, many of Newfoundland's inhabitants were too poor to pay their own passage and would inevitably become charitable charges on the English parishes to which they were sent. Perhaps the Committee for Trade and Plantations saw the wisdom of Berry's doubts; at any rate, after years of fence straddling, it soon accepted settlement as a fait accompli. The arguments of the vocal antiplanter faction among the West Country fishing interests during the 1670s have, nevertheless, enjoyed a rhetorical afterlife. Distinguished historians have argued that successful exploitation of the Newfoundland fishery did not require settlement and that the fishery had no place for a settled population. Some disinterested contemporaries thought otherwise.[27]

The planters themselves and several naval officers as well as certain West Country merchants, fishing masters, and lobbyists pressed the prosettlement position from the 1660s on. Besides Sir John Berry, who

27. Matthews, "Fisheries," 200–239; Cell, "Cupids Cove Settlement," in Story, ed., *Early European Settlement*, 111; Gentry of Exeter, Dartmouth, Totnes Plymouth, etc., Petition to Charles II, Mar. 25, 1675, CO 1/65 (25), 100; Parrett, "Advantages [of] Fishing Ships," Mar. 25, 1675, CO 1/65 (27), 102–103; John Downing, "The Humble Petition" [to Charles II], Nov. 7, 1676, CO 1/38 (33), 69; CTP, Minutes, Apr. 8, 1675, CO 391/1, 17, 18; John Berry to Joseph Williamson, July 24, 1675, CO 1/34 (118), 240–241. For a discussion of how their class origins and profession might have constrained the impartiality of the gentlemen in command of the Royal Navy by alienating them from the world of trade, see John E. Crowley, "Empire versus Truck: the Official Interpretation of Debt and Labour in the Eighteenth-Century Newfoundland Fishery," *CHR*, LXX (1989), 311–336. The settlement debate is discussed further in Chapter 6, below.

defended settlement after his experience as naval commodore, a junior naval officer, rejoicing in the name Nehemiah Troute, made a cogent case for Newfoundland settlement. He was a Plymouth man, experienced in the migratory fishery, who returned to Newfoundland in 1675 as purser of Berry's HMS *Swann* and who was asked for his opinions by the Committee for Trade and Plantations in 1678. Troute was, as he put it, "a person indifferent," opposed to neither Merchant Adventurers nor inhabitants, although sympathetic to the latter. Troute and Berry agreed that the planter fishery was as useful to Britain as was the migratory West Country fishery: the resident fishery trained proportionately as did the migratory fishery and was thus also "a nursery of seamen." Furthermore, the inhabitants spent their earnings on English agricultural produce and manufactures no less than the migratory industry did. Both stressed the strategic importance of a British colony in Newfoundland. Here and in several other key respects, the arguments of Troute and Berry echoed those advanced in favor of settlement by Whitbourne and other early proponents of colonization. As Troute put it, the planters were "possessors of the country for his Majestie which if taken by the French, or any other enemy and possest would be very prejudiciall . . . an open gapp left which will tend to the ruin of our West India trade." The planters, he emphasized, were loyal subjects. During the Dutch attack on St. John's in 1665, despite "being reduced . . . to greate want, although courted by De Rutter to sayle with him, [they] swore the death of each other that would goe . . . or fight against his Majestie or Country." Nor were many tempted to move to the new French settlements in Placentia Bay, where they might "accept of the French King's offer . . . three yeares provision to every head that will come to him." A contemporary map of the "Province Avalonia" manifests English concerns about the "French trading to and from Plasentia Bay" (Map 6).[28]

28. "Reasons for the Settlement of Newfoundland . . . under Government," ca. 1668, CO 1/22 (69), 115–116; Newfoundland Planters, ". . . Reply to the West-Country Owners," ca. 1670, British Library, Egerton MS 2395, 668–669; John Gould to Robert Southwell, Mar. 3, 1675, CO 1/65 (22), 95; Berry to Williamson, July 24, 1675, CO 1/34 (118), 240–241; William Poole to CTP, Sept. 10, 1677, CO 1/41 (62), 147–148; Christopher Martin, Deposition, Jan. 28, 1678, CO 1/42 (20), 54; Charles Talbot, "Answers to the Enquiries . . . ," Sept. 15, 1679, CO 1/43 (121), 214–217; John Carter [mayor of Poole] et al., "Severall Reasons Offered for Not Removing the Planters . . . ," ca. 1680, CO 1/46 (77), 151; John Berry, "Observations . . . in Relation to the Trade and Inhabitants of Newfoundland," Aug. 18, 1676, CO 1/35 (81), 325–326; Nehemiah Troute, Deposition, Feb. 1, 1678, CO

As Berry had done, Troute refuted two of the charges most often made against the planters, that they destroyed fishing rooms in the off-season and that they preempted rooms that were needed by migratory fishermen. It was the migratory fishermen who destroyed fishing rooms, by selling off their own stages and shipping the timber home or by dismantling competitors' stages. Disputes over fishing rooms happened when the admiral, or first migratory master to arrive in each harbor, took excessive territory and appropriated or destroyed infrastructure to eliminate competitors—a problem Whitbourne had observed a half-century earlier. Like Captain Berry, Troute also stressed the various ways in which the inhabitants actually benefited the migratory fishery. In spring, ships sent boat crews ahead to claim fishing rooms, from as much as one hundred miles offshore, when ships might be caught in ice or delayed by westerly winds. Troute observed they would "travell to severall harbors and leave one man in each harbor to be possessor which mens' dependency is upon the inhabitants without whose relief his Majesties subjects would perish." Besides this, the inhabitants cut timber and prepared boards, oars, and boats for the migratory industry. In his call for settlement, Whitbourne had predicted that residents would improve the efficiency of the fishery through both accommodation of early crews and maintenance of infrastructure; half a century later, Troute validated these predictions.[29]

Troute also justified another of Whitbourne's predictions by observing that the inhabitants acted as caretakers for boats left to overwinter by migratory fishermen. The planters, he said, were "carefull in preserving the adventurers boates which, if destroyed, would prove ruinous to the voyage." He recalled that "for the value of 40 shillings I have given

---

1/42 (22), 58-59; cf. Whitbourne, *Discourse*, 126-128. In 1668, Troute delivered a petition for the planters; see John Scott, William Hill, John Hoyle, et al., "The Present Condition of Newfoundland Truly Stated," Jan. 8, 1668, CO 1/22 (5), 12. Troute's fascinating document rates only a one-line summary in *CSP*: Colonial. For the "nursery of seamen," see Gerald S. Graham, "Fisheries and Sea Power," in Canadian Historical Association, *Report of the Annual Meeting* (1941), 24-31; David J. Starkey, "The West Country-Newfoundland Fishery and the Manning of the Royal Navy," in R. Higham, ed., *Security and Defence in South-West England before 1800* (Exeter, 1987), 93-101.

29. Whitbourne, *Discourse*, 131-133, 160. On ice, see John Downing, "A Breif Narrative concerning Newfoundland," Nov. 24, 1676, British Library, Egerton MS 2395, 560-563. On winds, see William Poole to CTP, Sept. 10, 1677, CO 1/41 (62), 147-148.

Map 6. An Exact Mapp of Newfoundland Soe Far as the English and French
Fishing Trade Is Concerned. *By Robert Robinson, 1669. MS Rawlinson A 183,
fol. 101. A map that manifests contemporary English concerns about "the French
trading to and from Plasentia Bay." Permission of Bodleian Library,
Oxford University*

the inhabitant (and been thanked by my imployer) they have given a full
and just account of every thing committed to their charge, as 20 boates,
etc., which cannot be built under £6 per boate." Troute omitted two arguments sometimes used to justify settlement. Berry had raised a public health issue: "The inhabitants cure yearly many hundred fishermen
of the scurvy, an art they have which is not understood, nor can bee

done by the masters or chirurgeons, and is such a raging distemper, as would discourage men from going thither, did they not find so speedy a remedy upon the place." Finally, the prosettlement West Country merchant James Houblon argued that the inhabitants could produce fish cheaper and of better quality than the migratory fishermen. The latter was a questionable argument. Most proponents of settlement admitted that the costs of overwintering at least matched the transit costs of the ships fishing, unless the inhabitants could be kept fishing most of the year.[30]

The positive justifications for Newfoundland settlement were those Troute and Berry stressed: accommodation of early or marooned crews, access to timber for boats and other wood products, caretaking of boats and rooms, and, last, but not least, protection of British sovereignty. Hospitality or lumber might have become important components of the planter economy, but one doubts that their marginal benefits could have themselves triggered settlement. Management of scurvy was critical to the industry, but James Yonge's experience suggests that surgeons could learn the relevant cures from the planters. The two remaining arguments, micro and macro versions of a single rationale, convincingly explain why the settlement of Newfoundland was, in the words of Robert Hayman—an early governor of Harbour Grace—"a business honorable, profitable, feasible, facile, and opportune." From the earliest proposals for settlement to the protracted late-seventeenth-century debate on the need for government, the settlement of Newfoundland was justified, in great part, as a means of protecting the infrastructure of the British fishery. Why was such protection necessary?[31]

30. Yonge, *Journal*, 58–59; James Houblon to CTP, Mar. 20, 1675, CO 1/65 (23), esp. 97; "Some Modest Observations," Mar. 25, 1675, CO 1/34 (32), 69–72; cf. William Poole, "Answers to the Severall Heads of Inquiry . . . ," Sept. 10, 1677, CO 1/41 (62i), 149–152; Wheler, "Answers," Oct. 27, 1684, CO 1/55 (56), 237–246. The Plymouth surgeon, James Yonge, noted that scurvy in Newfoundland at this time was "a disease not curable by all the medicines which can be carried there, but easily by a few vegitives of the country." Along with "scurvy leaves" and other herbs, he mentions spruce beer, which indeed had become a standard beverage among the planters by the later seventeenth century, although the recipe was hardly secret.

31. Robert Hayman, "A Proposition of Profitt and Honor," ca. 1620, British Library, Egerton MS 2541, 162–169; Parkhurst to [Dyer?], "Traficq to New Found Land," 1577, in Quinn, *New American World*, IV, 7–10; Whitbourne, *Discourse*, 132; [Edward Wynne], "The Brittish India," ca. 1628, British Library,

Seventeenth-century arguments about Newfoundland suggest an economic logic to settlement implicit in the open-access character of the industry. The fishery is, notoriously, a common-property resource, that is, one difficult to enclose. Consequently, the territories of fishermen are not protected from interlopers by conventional property rights. Extralegal competition among fishermen over access to the resource was, therefore, as common in the seventeenth-century fishery as it is today. There is a vein of Newfoundland historiography rich with conflicts between migratory and settled fishermen. Seventeenth-century observers often saw such conflicts as examples of a wider phenomenon: competition typical of fisherman in general. Troute described this kind of extralegal competition vividly: "The great greivance of fishing is from the masters difference betweene themselves, who robb each others stages and roomes to the merchants great losse, for where each roome is for 12 boates, the admirall (if but 6 boats) will and doth secure that roome, besides pull upp other stages and houses halfe a mile from them. They have done it in one harbour to cary to another." Whitbourne had already observed the same problem in his years as a fishing master in the early seventeenth century, "by which unfit disorders of some first arrivers . . . the voyages of the after-commers there are often greatly hindred and prolonged." Nor was such conflict peculiar to the English Shore. The French on the south and north coasts had to deal with like problems. Similar incidents were widespread in coastal Maine and Massachusetts. The unruly behavior of West Country immigrants to Gloucester and Marblehead has been ascribed to cultural incompatibilities, but the confrontational culture of these particular immigrants was rooted in the economics of a specific industry. Fishing crews were quite capable of destroying each other's stages or stealing each other's boats and train vats, as the reiteration of regulations against such practices suggests. The economic logic of competition for an open-access resource led fishermen to do such things.[32]

Royal MSS 17 A LVII, 3–36; Sir David Kirke to Privy Council, Sept. 12, 1640, CO 1/10 (77), 196. On Hayman, see David Galloway, "Robert Hayman (1575–1629): Some Material for the Life of a Colonial Governor and First 'Canadian' Author," *WMQ*, 3d Ser., XXIV (1967), 75–87.

32. H. Scott Gordon, "The Economic Theory of a Common-Property Resource: The Fishery," *Journal of Political Economy*, LXII (1954), 124–142; Rosemary E. Ommer, "'All the Fish of the Post': Property Resource Rights and Development in a Nineteenth-Century Inshore Fishery," *Acadiensis*, X, no. 2 (1981), 107–123. For the conflict model, see Prowse, *History*, for example, 138–139, 186–197; Charles

A migratory master who could depend on a resident to protect his boats, reserve his fishing rooms, and preserve his stages and vats would have a competitive advantage, even if he had to pay for it. Payment often took the form of rent during Sir David Kirke's administration of the south Avalon in the 1640s, and the practice continued there and around St. John's. Once one fishing master in an area had a winter caretaker, such caretakers became necessary for his competitors, because fishermen whose equipment was unprotected were then at the mercy of those whose boats and rooms were secure. Even the relationship between French and English fishermen in Newfoundland can be seen in this light. If the French were to continue fishing in proximity to the permanent English settlements that developed in the mid-seventeenth century, they would have to set up their own colony of resident fishermen to protect their seasonal stations, as they did at Plaisance in 1662. Conversely, the existence of French settlement became a strong argument for the maintenance of the English fishing settlements. After the Treaty of Utrecht in 1713 banned French settlement, France's metropolitan fishermen continued to regard English settlement as a significant competitive advan-

---

Burnet Judah, *The North American Fisheries and British Policy to 1713* (Urbana, Ill., 1933), 78–79, 104–105; Cell, *English Enterprise*, 108–125. For a critique, see Keith Matthews, "Historical Fence Building: A Critique of the Historiography of Newfoundland," *Newfoundland Studies*, XVII (2001), 143–165. For contemporary views, see Poole, "Answers," Sept. 10, 1677, CO 1/41 (62i), 149–152; Troute, Deposition, Feb. 1, 1678, CO 1/42 (22), 58–59 (quotation on 58); Talbot, "Answers," Sept. 15, 1679, CO 1/43 (121), 214–217; John Collins, *Salt and Fishery* . . . (London, 1682), 96; Whitbourne, *Discourse*, 131 (quotation). On the French legislation of 1613 designed to control the destruction of stages, see Henry P. Biggar, *The Early Trading Companies of New France: A Contribution to the History of Commerce and Discovery in North America* (1901; rpt. St. Clair Shores, Mich., 1972), 198. On New England, see Christine Leigh Heyrman, *Commerce and Culture: The Maritime Communities of Colonial Massachusetts, 1690–1750* (New York, 1984), esp. 36, 214; Charles E. Clark, *The Eastern Frontier: The Settlement of Northern New England, 1610–1763* (1970; rpt. Hanover, N.H., 1983), esp. 29; Daniel Vickers, "Work and Life on the Fishing Periphery of Essex County, Massachusetts, 1630–1675," in Hall and Allen, eds., *Seventeenth-Century New England*, 83–117. On regulations, see Prowse, *History*, 99n; Charles I in Council, Charter, Feb. 10, 1634, DRO, Exeter, DO 62571; Council of State, "Laws, Rules, and Ordinances . . . ," June 3, 1653, CO 1/38 (33iii), 74–75; Charles II in Council, Charter, Jan. 26, 1661, CO 1/15 (3). The charters are in Matthews, *Constitutional Laws*, 71–75, 123–126, 131.

tage, which they sought to limit. Meanwhile, some French refugees from the British occupation of Plaisance in the early eighteenth century simply moved to clandestine settlements on the west coast of the island.[33]

Initial informal settlement was encouraged by an economic pressure on the Newfoundland fishery exerted by Newfoundland's Native people, the Beothuk, who treated fishing premises as stores of iron. They were particularly interested in nails and fishhooks, which were easily reworked into useful tools, like the well-fashioned projectile points, scrapers, and awls recovered from a late-seventeenth-century Native encampment at Boyd's Cove, Notre Dame Bay (Plate 3). Informal trade with French fishermen and the early Cupids colonists gave the Beothuk some access to desirable goods, but the easiest way to obtain iron was to burn seasonally abandoned equipment. Each fishing boat would contain about twelve hundred nails plus other ironwork; a fishing stage would use thousands of nails. Before European contact, the Beothuk had not regularly exploited the Avalon Peninsula south of Conception Bay. The recovery of worked stone tools of Beothuk design in aboriginal contexts sandwiched between sixteenth-century European deposits at Ferryland indicates that the Beothuk had expanded their range in this period. European fishers and the new materials they brought with them prompted the Natives to scavenge for iron at seasonal stations like Ferryland, as they did a century later in the Notre Dame Bay no-man's-land between the English and French Shores, which would become their northern refugium. Beothuk pilfering thus annually threatened the infrastructure of the fishery, even during the fishing season. In the early seventeenth

33. Richard Parker, Deposition, Nov. 27, 1667, WDRO Plymouth, W360/74; William Swanley et al., "An Act Made by the Tenants of Avalon," Aug. 30, 1663, Md. HS, Calvert MSS 174/210; Wheler, "Answers," Oct. 27, 1684, CO 1/55 (56), 240; John Cull, Nicholas Luce, Thomas Pitcher, Depositions, Nov. 27, 1667, WDRO Plymouth, W360/74; Richard Hooper and Thomas Gearing, "Answer from the Mayors [of Barnstaple and Bideford]," Mar. 30, 1675, CO 1/34 (38), 87–88; Martin, Deposition, Jan. 28, 1678, CO 1/42 (20), 54; Jean-François Brière, *La pêche française en Amérique du nord au XVIIIe siècle* (Saint-Laurent, Quebec, 1990), 219–246; Olaf Uwe Janzen, "'Une grande liaison': French Fishermen from Île Royale on the Coast of Southwestern Newfoundland, 1714-1766—A Preliminary Survey," *Newfoundland Studies*, III (1987), 183–200; Janzen, "'Une Petite Republique' in Southwestern Newfoundland: The Limits of Imperial Authority in a Remote Maritime Environment," in Lewis R. Fischer and Walter E. Minchinton, eds., *People of the Northern Seas*, International Maritime Economic History Association, Research in Maritime History, no. 3 (St. John's, 1992), 1–33.

Plate 3. Beothuk Reworked Iron Tools: Projectile Points, Scrapers, and Awls, Cold-Worked from European Nails and Fish Hooks. Recovered from a late-seventeenth-century Beothuk encampment at Boyd's Cove, Notre Dame Bay (DiAp-3). Photograph from Ralph Pastore Collection. Courtesy, Centre for Newfoundland Studies, Memorial University of Newfoundland, St. John's

century, Richard Whitbourne had observed "the savage people of [Bona-vista Bay] . . . secretly every yeere, come into *Trinity* Bay and Harbour, in the night time, purposely to steale sailes, lines, hatchets, hookes, knives, and such like." Such behavior was bound to lead to open conflict with fishermen, as David Kirke concluded, in 1639. The deterioration of economic relations between the Beothuk and English fishermen may explain, at least in part, why early friendly contacts were forgotten and why, by 1680, the Natives were said to "bear a deadly fewd and hatred to the English."[34]

34. Ralph T. Pastore, "Fishermen, Furriers, and Beothuks: The Economy of Extinction," *Man in the Northeast*, XXXIII (1987), 47–62 (esp. 55), 66; Pastore, "The Spatial Distribution of Late Paleo-Eskimo Sites on the Island of Newfound-

Beothuk scavenging constituted a significant incentive for overwintering. A record in the Rashleigh account books of what sounds like overwintering in Conception Bay in 1609 may be an echo of an early experiment with caretaking, a year before the proprietary colonization of Cupids, when the Beothuk still frequented this area. According to Whitbourne and Kirke, English fishers in Trinity Bay in the 1620s and 1630s found the Natives to be "badd neighbours." Given the limited stress northern woodland peoples put on property rights together with the failure of reciprocal economic relations between the Beothuk and the English, Natives had no reason to refrain from picking over seasonally abandoned fishing premises. Such scavenging must have been a significant factor in the destruction of fisheries equipment left unattended within the Beothuk fall and winter range. Whether or not the perpetrators were correctly identified, the migratory owners of damaged equipment regarded such acts as outrages. The obvious solution to the problem was the stationing of overwintering caretakers, as Whitbourne had argued in the early days of settlement: "If such pinnaces, and such stages and houses may be there maintained and kept in such readinesse yeerely, it would bee the most pleasant, profitable, and commodious trade of fishing." The threat of Native pilfering remained an inducement to overwinter, as the settlement frontier moved northward. In 1680, the mayor of Poole, in Dorset, recognized aboriginal scavenging at Bonavista as one of the "reasons for not removing the planters," just when his constituents were beginning to settle the area and fish the bay to the north: "The

land," in *Paleo-Eskimo Cultures in Newfoundland, Labrador and Ungava*, Reports in Archaeology, no. 1 (St. John's, 1986), 125-134; Laurie Allan MacLean, "The Beothuk Adoption of Iron Technology" (master's thesis, MUN, 1989); James A. Tuck, "Archaeology at Ferryland, Newfoundland," *Newfoundland Studies*, IX (1993), 294-310; William Gilbert, "'Divers Places': The Beothuk Indians and John Guy's Voyage into Trinity Bay in 1612," ibid., VI (1990), 147-167; "'... great good Done': Beothuk-European Relations in Trinity Bay," *Newfoundland Quarterly*, LXXXIII, no. 3 (1992), 2-10; John Downing, "Newfoundland, an Account concerning the Following Perticulars ...," Dec. 14, 1676, British Library, Egerton MS 2395, 564; Whitbourne, *Discourse*, 118, 149, 174; Sir David Kirke, "Reply to the Answeare to the Description of Newfoundland," Sept. 29, 1639, CO 1/10 (38), 97-114. Quotation from John Thomas to Sir Richard [?], Sept. 15, 1680, Codrington Library, All Soul's College, Oxford University, Wynne Collection, MS 239, 229-230, in Peter Pope, *"A True and Faithful Account*: Newfoundland in 1680," *Newfoundland Studies*, XII (1996), 32-49.

Indians having beene so bold this last yeare, as to come into our harbor and doe mischeife."[35]

After about 1620, the Beothuk avoided trade or other interaction with Europeans. This strategy served them well for several generations, but it left their small bands open to eventual economic eclipse in the eighteenth century, when English planters appropriated the northeast coast. By then, the newcomers had little stake in the continued well-being of the Natives. The Beothuk practice of scavenging at seasonally abandoned fishing stations accelerated this dismal scenario by precipitating a particularly fateful feedback loop. Intense competition among fishermen meant that the arrival of one resident in an area created an economic incentive for further settlement. Other factors contributed to growth and persistence, which eventually drove the Beothuk inland, away from the diverse coastal resources upon which their survival had for centuries depended. Seen in this light, the idea that Newfoundland settlement was not economically necessary is mistaken. Such an assumption abstracts the fishery from the human context into which it had intruded and from the harsh realities of competition in an open-access, capitalist industry, based on a common-property resource, operating outside the effective jurisdiction of a distant and often uninterested bureaucracy. The informal settlement of Newfoundland in fact benefited the migratory fishery, as Whitbourne had predicted.[36]

35. John Scantlebury, "John Rashleigh of Fowey and the Newfoundland Cod Fishery, 1608–20," *Royal Institution of Cornwall Journal*, N.S., VIII (1978–1981), 61–71. On Native concepts of property, see Alfred Goldsworthy Bailey, *The Conflict of European and Eastern Algonkian Cultures, 1504–1700* (1937; rpt. Toronto, 1969), xix–xxii; T. J. Brasser, "Early Indian-European Contacts," in William T. Sturtevant, gen. ed., *Handbook of North American Indians*, XV, Bruce G. Trigger, ed., *Northeast* (Washington, D.C., 1978), 78–88. On reaction to pilfering, see William Parfay, Deposition, in *Cherie et al. v. Baker*, ca. 1595, HCA 24/63, 23, in Quinn, *New American World*, IV, 119. Quotations from Kirke, "Reply to the Answeare," Sept. 29, 1639, CO 1/10 (38), 97–114; Whitbourne, *Discourse*, 132; and Carter et al., "Reasons for Planters," ca. 1680, CO 1/46 (77), 151. Cf. Wheler, "Answers," Oct. 27, 1684, CO 1/55 (56), 244; Whitbourne, *Discourse*, 158–164; and Gerard Malynes, *Consuetudo, vel, Lex Mercatoria; or, The Antient Law-Merchant . . .* , 2d ed. (London, 1636), 167. John Carter's son was a planter at Old Perlican; see Matthews, *Lectures*, 70. The French, fishing farther north in Notre Dame Bay, faced similar problems; see Wheler, "Answers," Oct. 27, 1684, CO 1/55 (56), 239–246 (esp. 244).

36. Pastore, "Economy of Extinction," *Man in the Northeast*, XXXIII (1987),

The planters profited from the Beothuk withdrawal from the Avalon Peninsula to their ancestral territories to the north and west. The Avalon south of Conception Bay played no essential part in traditional Native subsistence strategies, despite its function in the later sixteenth century as one of several potential sources of exotic raw materials. For the Beothuk, there was thus no great cost attached to withdrawal—as long as seasonal fishing stations elsewhere remained accessible for off-season scavenging. The Beothuk and their cousins the Montagnais of Labrador were, in the first place, "tractable (being well used)," as Whitbourne put it. By the time the Natives became restless, the English were well established. The Beothuk themselves were not well armed; their economic isolation precluded the adoption of European weapons. Newfoundland's Native people did not facilitate European settlement, in the sense that their distant cousins the Mi'kmaq did by assisting the early Acadian colonists; but they did not seriously impede settlement.[37]

The European colonization of Newfoundland developed within the matrix of the migratory fishery. Early settlements could hardly have survived, and would certainly not have taken the form they did, without the annual summer visit of hundreds of ships, bringing supplies and fishing servants. These ships set out from England heavily ballasted; hence the cost of shipping goods to Newfoundland was low, subsidized by the need for a high volume of shipping to carry the relatively light and bulky cargo of salt cod back to Europe. Ships fishing carried the victuals and equipment that their own boat crews would need for a season of shore-based fishing, but plenty of room was left to bring supplies for the inhabitants and to carry passengers. The planters depended on ships fishing to bring men and women to serve in their resident fishery. Newfoundland would not have a native-born population sufficient for the demands of the fishery until the late eighteenth century, when, not coincidentally, the English migratory fishery began its final decline. Until then, migratory fishermen and resident fisherfolk sometimes competed over fish or fishing rooms, but they were, in the last analysis, interdependent.[38]

47–62; Ralph Pastore, "The Collapse of the Beothuk World," *Acadiensis*, XIX, no. 1 (1989), 52–71 (esp. 67).

37. Whitbourne, *Discourse*, 117. He also calls them "ingenuous" (117). On weapons, see Marshall, *The Beothuk*, 61, 74, 91.

38. Head, *Newfoundland*, 217–229; Shannon Ryan, "Fishery to Colony: A Newfoundland Watershed, 1793–1815," in P. A. Buckner, Gail Grace Campbell,

Finally, the Newfoundland plantation was utterly dependent on the commercial practice, still new in the early seventeenth century, of sending sack ships to Newfoundland to buy, rather than to catch, cod. Although ships fishing could afford to carry men and materials besides their own to the fishery, cargo space on the return voyage to Europe was often at a premium. The sack ships removed this bottleneck and, in doing so, gave the planters a market for fish in Newfoundland itself, an essential condition for their economic survival. Settlement and sacks did not, however, constitute some kind of system that can be analytically opposed to the West Country migratory fishery. The Newfoundland fishery, the Newfoundland sack ships, and the Newfoundland plantation of the seventeenth century together composed an intricate and evolving system.[39]

The operations of the London merchants Kirke, Barkeley, and company exemplify the increasingly important role of the sack ships in the fishing trade at Newfoundland and as a factor precipitating permanent settlement. Sir David Kirke, the last of Newfoundland's colonial proprietors, was also one of the first resident fish merchants. His connection with Newfoundland did not begin when he sailed into Ferryland, guns ablaze, in the summer of 1638: he and his extended family were already involved in the cod trade, as owners and freighters of Newfoundland sack ships.

---

and David Frank, eds., *Atlantic Canada before Confederation: The Acadiensis Reader*, 3d ed. (Fredericton, N.B., 1998), 130–148.

39. I. K. Steele, "Instructing the Master of a Newfoundland Sack Ship, 1715," *Mariner's Mirror*, LXIII (1977), 191–193; Matthews, "Historical Fence Building," *Newfoundland Studies*, XVII (2001), 143–165. The latter is the locus classicus for interdependence of the migratory and resident sectors. Cf. Peter E. Pope, "Introduction: The New Early Modern Newfoundland: The Eighteenth Century," ibid., 139–142.

3 ❧ ADVENTURES IN THE SACK TRADE

He also complained of the insupportable arrogance of his General [David Kirke], as a wine merchant, which he used to be at Bordeaux and Cognac, known to be ignorant of the sea, who didn't understand what it was to navigate, never having made any but these two voyages.
—*Samuel de Champlain,* Voyages, *1632*

Samuel de Champlain's doubts about David Kirke's seamanship might have been justified: his young English competitor was a merchant, not a mariner. That Champlain recalled such gossip is telling, for it suggests what a small place the seventeenth-century North Atlantic was. Champlain knew Kirke personally—they were adversaries at Quebec, but they also spent time together hunting. The Kirkes and the Calverts, to take a more obvious example, spent years in the Court of Admiralty suing one another. Ships bound for Ferryland, the Newfoundland settlement they would argue over, avoided a royal stay on shipping in 1625, thanks to a compromise brokered for George Calvert by John Mason, sometime governor of the earlier English colony at Cupids and founder of a later settlement at Piscataqua, Maine. Mason's Amerindian companion at Cupids, Squantum, ended his days back in his native territory, now Massachusetts, assisting the Pilgrim fathers. In the spring of 1630, Kirke and the Massachusetts colony's governor, John Winthrop, literally bumped into each other while becalmed at sea: they spoke, and their companions exchanged presents. Seventeenth-century North Americans were dispersed but not disconnected, either from one another or from their kin and creditors in the Old World.[1]

---

1. H. P. Biggar, ed., *The Works of Samuel de Champlain*, VI, *Second Part of the Voyages of the Sieur de Champlain: Book III* (1632) (1936; rpt. Toronto, 1971), 142 (Biggar's translation differs slightly from mine); Cell, *Newfoundland Discovered*, 52–53; Lincoln N. Kinnicutt, "The Plymouth Settlement and Tisquantum," MHS, *Proceedings*, XLVIII (Boston, 1914–1915), 108–113; Lynn Ceci, "Squanto and the Pilgrims," *Society*, XXVII, no. 4 (May–June 1990), 40–44; John Winthrop, Journal, Apr. 26–30, 1630, *Winthrop Papers*, II, 249–251; Horace E. Ware, "An Incident in Winthrop's Voyage to New England," Colonial Society of Massachusetts, *Publications*, XII, *Transactions* (Boston, 1911), 101–113.

In this respect, Newfoundland was neither isolated nor peripheral; it was a central node in an international network. In part, this role followed from the geography of ocean wind and current, which made the Avalon Peninsula a natural watering stop for transatlantic voyagers. What is more, the migratory rhythm of the fishery had the effect of subsidizing communications, for ships from both sides of the Atlantic met at Newfoundland fishing stations, where they exchanged news as well as more tangible commodities. Finally, the trade in salt cod was part of a complex commercial web that linked Newfoundland not only with the West Country but also with London, Iberia, the Mediterranean, the Atlantic islands, the Netherlands, New England, and even New France.[2]

The origins of the business that Sir David Kirke and his family developed at Newfoundland, after the expropriation of Ferryland from the Calverts in 1638, are a cameo illustration of the value of seeing cod, not in isolation, but as the complement of a trade in southern products, particularly wine. The Kirkes were, as Champlain pointed out, wine merchants long before they became interlopers in the new North Atlantic trades. Given the trading practices of the owners and freighters of the sack ships, which carried out a multilateral trade in fish and wine, the Kirkes' investment in a Newfoundland fishing plantation was no accident. This was but one of the strategies adopted by London merchants in the 1630s and 1640s to enter a profitable trade, hitherto dominated by the Dutch. The sack trade was an essential part of the commercial context in which a Newfoundland plantation would take root, and, in the end, this trade did at least as much to facilitate settlement as the early proprietary investment schemes.

⅋ Kirke, Barkeley, and Company

The business that David Kirke developed at Ferryland in the 1640s exemplifies an important generalization about early modern trade: its links were normally kin-based. In the late sixteenth century, David's father Gervaise had been an English merchant at Dieppe, where he took a French wife, Elizabeth Goudon. David, their eldest son, was born in 1597. He and his younger brothers Lewis, Thomas, John, and James

2. Ian K. Steele, *The English Atlantic, 1675–1740: An Exploration of Communication and Community* (Oxford, 1986), 78–85.

each played a role in the family business, by their time based in London, although Lewis and Thomas drifted into military careers. Their mother Elizabeth traded on her own account, as a London wine merchant in the 1630s, after the death of her husband. David's own sons, notably George, later traded wines with New England through their Newfoundland establishment.[3]

Although wine was the core of the Kirkes' business for decades, they demonstrated an adaptive willingness to interest themselves in other matters. As a rule, early modern merchants had to be flexible in their commitment to particular trades. Commercial information, let alone security, was uncertain; and it therefore made sense to avoid the concentration of risk that followed rigid specialization. The London wine merchants Gervaise Kirke and William Barkeley made such a choice when they set up the Company of Adventurers to Canada in 1627. These opportunists turned a war with France to advantage by obtaining letters of marque, permitting their vessels to mount a privateering raid on the "River of Canada." Their aim was to force their way into the lucrative fur trade the French had developed with the Native peoples of Acadia and the St. Lawrence River. The attempt to broaden their interests was an astute business move, since there was a glut of wine on the London market. With several large well-armed ships under their command, a certain amount of luck, and the help of the Montagnais people of the north shore of the St. Lawrence, Kirke's three eldest sons, David, Lewis, and Thomas, defeated a squadron of French ships and, thus, isolated the French trading post at Quebec, taking it in 1629. For Champlain, at least,

3. Bernard Bailyn, *The New England Merchants in the Seventeenth Century* (1955; rpt. Cambridge, Mass., 1982), 35; Richard Grassby, "Social Mobility and Business Enterprise in Seventeenth-Century England," in Donald Pennington and Keith Thomas, eds., *Puritans and Revolutionaries: Essays in Seventeenth-Century History Presented to Christopher Hill* (Oxford, 1978), 355–381; Jacob M. Price, *Perry of London: A Family and a Firm on the Seaborne Frontier, 1615–1753* (Cambridge, Mass., 1992); Henry Kirke, *The First English Conquest of Canada* (London, 1871), 27–28; Guildhall Library, London, "Boyd's Citizens of London," file 9799, "Kirk, Gervase"; John S. Moir, "Kirke, Sir David," "Kirke, Lewis," and "Kirke, Thomas," *DCB*; David Kirke and Nicholas Shapley, "Invoyce of Goods Shipped Abord the *David* of Ferryland . . . ," Sept. 8, 1648, *Baxter MSS*, VI, 2–4. By the eighteenth century, kin links might have become somewhat less important; see David Hancock, *Citizens of the World: London Merchants and the Integration of the British Atlantic Community, 1735–1785* (Cambridge, 1995), 106.

the English success was a surprise, given the limited maritime experience of their "general," David Kirke.[4]

Unfortunately for the Kirkes and their coadventurers, the war had ended before they took Quebec. Under the terms of the Treaty of Saint-Germain-en-Laye (1632), Britain was to restore both Quebec and Port Royal, in Nova Scotia, to France. The Kirkes surrendered Quebec and returned to London, but not empty-handed; they brought with them six thousand beaver pelts. Emery de Caen and the other Quebec merchants sued for these and other damages in Admiralty Court and were awarded £14,330. Although Kirke, Barkeley, and company paid this substantial sum, the equivalent of roughly $1.5 million today, they probably suffered no absolute loss, since the furs were worth £10,000–£12,000, and the ships they had taken as prizes were worth another £6,000. Gervaise Kirke had died in 1629, and his sons were now in partnership with Barkeley. The surviving partners never accepted the justice of the damages they were forced to pay the French, and they continued, for more than half a century, to press a series of unsuccessful counterclaims. Nor did they accept their exclusion from the fur trade: the Kirkes and Barkeley continued to send ships to Quebec and Acadia. At least two of these voyages ended in serious setbacks, however. In 1633, the French seized the *Mary Fortune* and its cargo at Tadoussac. In 1644, William Barkeley's son Isaac attempted to take their ship, the *Gilleflower*, to Charles La Tour's post on the St. John River in Acadia. The younger Barkeley had the misfortune of sailing into a civil war between La Tour and the other major Acadian proprietor, Charles d'Aulnay. When the *Gilleflower* made for Boston, La Tour's wife brought a highly politicized and successful suit, which ended with her wholesaling the ship's London cargo there.

4. W. T. Baxter, *The House of Hancock: Business in Boston, 1724-1775* (1945; rpt. New York, 1965), 298–300; William Robert Scott, *The Constitution and Finance of English, Scottish, and Irish Joint-Stock Companies to 1720*, II, *Companies for Foreign Trade, Colonization, Fishing, and Mining* (1912; rpt. New York, 1951), 320; Privy Council, Letters of Marque to Jervase Kirke et al., Dec. 17, 1627, to David and Thomas Kirke, Mar. 13, 1629, to David Kirke et al., Mar. 19, 1630, all in *CSP*: Domestic; Henry P. Biggar, *The Early Trading Companies of New France: A Contribution to the History of Commerce and Discovery in North America* (1901; rpt. St. Clair Shores, Mich., 1972), 51–131; Bruce G. Trigger, *Natives and Newcomers: Canada's "Heroic Age" Reconsidered* (Kingston, 1985), 164–225; André L. Simon, *The History of the Wine Trade in England*, III (1907; rpt. London, 1964), 34. On Gervaise Kirke, see Kirke, *English Conquest*, 27; and Guildhall Library, London, "Boyd's Citizens of London," file 9799, "Kirk, Gervase."

In the end, La Tour in Acadia and the Cent Associés (the French merchants investing in Quebec) forced Kirke, Barkeley, and company from the fur trade in the River of Canada.[5]

While Thomas and Lewis accepted naval commands, their elder brother preferred to remain in partnership with William Barkeley and to pursue commercial adventures with his younger brothers, John and James. King Charles knighted David Kirke in 1631, in recognition of his success at Quebec, already celebrated in Martin Parker's broadside ballad, *Englands Honour Revived by the Valiant Exploytes of Captain Kirke* (Plate 4). The London-based operations of Kirke, Barkeley, and company flourished. The use of the term "company" for the merchants associated with the younger Kirkes and William Barkeley is not intended to imply that they operated either as a regulated or a joint-stock company. David, John, James, and Barkeley were, nevertheless, partners in various ventures and were often referred to in this style. To learn something of their connections is to understand how the trade in fish and wine tied Newfoundland to a wider world.[6]

5. Charles I to Isaac Wake, 1632, British Library, Harleian MS 1760 (5), 10–12; Samuell Peirce, Examination, 1632, CO 1/6 (33); David Kirke et al., "An Answere Made by the Adventurers to Canada," ca. July 1632, CO 1/6 (66); "A Briefe Declaration of . . . Beaver Skinnes," ca. 1632, CO 1/6 (12), in Charles-Honoré Cauchon Laverdière, ed., *Oeuvres de Champlain*, 2d ed. (1870; rpt. Montreal, 1972), VI, 27–31. On the sale of the prize ships, see Thomas Wannerton, Examination, Aug. 13, 1633, HCA 13/50, 386; David Kirke et al., Interrogatories, in *Kirke et al. v. Delabarre*, ca. 1634, HCA 23/11 (299); Lewis Kirke et al., "A Memoriall of the Kirkes . . . ," April 1654, CO 1/12 (191), 50–51; Lewis Kirke and John Kirke, "Representation . . . Concern. Accadie," ca. 1660, *Baxter MSS*, IV, 232–240; Hudson's Bay Company, "The Case of the Adventurers of England Tradeing into Hudson's Bay in Reference to the French," May 6, 1687, CO 134/1, 165–168, in E. E. Rich, ed., *Copy-Book of Letters Outward, etc.* (Toronto, 1948), 222–226 (Rich, 224n, notes two other such documents ca. 1683 in CO 1/66, [108], 111). On the *Mary Fortune*, see Moir, "Kirke, Lewis," *DCB*; and David Kirke et al., Interrogatories, ca. 1638, HCA 23/11 (134). On the *Gilleflower*, see William Barkeley, Interrogatories, ca. 1646, HCA 23/14 (346), and Parliamentary Debates, May 5, 1645, in Stock, *Debates*, I, 160. See also M. A. MacDonald, *Fortune and La Tour: The Civil War in Acadia* (Toronto, 1983), 122–150; John G. Reid, *Acadia, Maine, and New Scotland: Marginal Colonies in the Seventeenth Century* (Toronto, 1982), 47–49, 88–102.

6. Moir, "Kirke, Lewis," and "Kirke, Thomas," *DCB*; Charles I, Grant of arms to David Kirke, Dec. 1, 1631, *CSP: Domestic*; M. P. [Martin Parker], "Englands

Plate 4. Attack on Quebec by Captain Kirke. *By Maximilian Van der Gucht*
(fl. 1650) or Michiel Van der Gucht (1660–1725). A fanciful later-seventeenth-
century view, very much in the spirit of Martin Parker's ballad, Englands
Honour Revived by the Valiant Exploytes of Captain Kirke, *circa 1630.*
Reproduced from Henry Kirke, The First English Conquest of Canada *(London,*
1871). Courtesy, Centre for Newfoundland Studies, Memorial University of
Newfoundland, St. John's

William Barkeley was born around 1586, making him about a decade older than David Kirke, who turned forty in 1637. This substantial merchant of St. Helen's, Bishopsgate, was probably the senior partner in both senses, at least after the death of Gervaise Kirke. Besides the sack and Canada trades carried on with the Kirkes, Barkeley was involved with Sir William Alexander's New Scotland Project to colonize Nova Scotia as well as with trade to Virginia, Bermuda, Greenland, and New England. He was typical of the new merchants of London in the first half of the seventeenth century. Often of obscure socioeconomic background, they pursued colonial North American commerce after the wealthier, established, company-organized city merchants had abandoned the region as unprofitable—a characterization that fits Barkeley's partners David, James, and John Kirke as well. These new, interloping colonial merchants played a key role in the "Independent" London leadership of the English Revolution of the 1640s. Barkeley became active in politics as a London alderman and from 1642 served on the revolutionary militia committee. From 1643, Alderman Barkeley served on the Customs Commission, which gave crucial support to the parliamentary navy and, from 1649, held Commonwealth appointments both to the Commission for the Navy and Customs and to the Prize Goods Commission.[7]

Honour Revived by the Valiant Exploytes of Captaine Kirke," ca. 1629, in J. S. Cox, ed., *News from Canada, 1628* (Beaminster, 1964). On regulated and joint-stock companies, see Theodore K. Rabb, *Enterprise and Empire: Merchant and Gentry Investment in the Expansion of England, 1575-1630* (Cambridge, Mass., 1967), 26-35; and Barry Supple, "The Nature of Enterprise," in E. E. Rich and C. H. Wilson, eds., *The Cambridge Economic History of Europe*, V, *The Economic Organization of Early Modern Europe* (Cambridge, 1977), 393-461. On David Kirke's attitude toward commerce, see Chapter 8, below.

7. Barkeley was also identified as William Barkly, Bartly, Berkeley, etc. In 1638, he paid an annual rent of thirty-four pounds in Bishopsgate, where he was still living in the 1640s; see William Barklye, Examination, Jan. 10, 1639, HCA 13/54, 413; W. J. Harvey, ed., *List of the Principal Inhabitants of the City of London, 1640, from Returns Made by the Aldermen of the Several Wards* (London, 1886), 3; T. C. Dale, *The Inhabitants of London in 1638, Edited from MS.272 in the Lambeth Palace Library* (London, 1931), 131a; Dale, "Citizens of London 1641-1643 from the State Papers," 1936, Guildhall Library, London. On his trading interests, see Robert Brenner, *Merchants and Revolution: Commercial Change, Political Conflict, and London's Overseas Traders, 1550-1653* (Princeton, N.J., 1993), 123, 189, 191; on new merchants, see 111-114; on "Independent" as a factional label, see

These activities should have brought him into conflict with his some-time partner, Sir David Kirke, who took a consistently royalist position throughout the Civil War. Whatever the political distance that developed between the original senior partners of Kirke, Barkeley, and company, the London alderman was still in partnership with John Kirke in the early 1650s. Barkeley's trading activities at this time led Parliament's police, the Keepers of the Liberty of England, to question his "affection to this Parliament and Commonwealth," which suggests that his commitment to the Good Old Cause might not have been as complete as his public political activities implied. In the end, Barkeley managed to evade the issue, until he died early in 1653.[8]

James Kirke seems to have remained a bachelor in the comfortable London household of his mother, Elizabeth, who survived into the 1640s. She was a parishioner of St. Andrew Undershaft, with which John and James continued to be connected after her death, and was one of the few substantial householders of tiny Limestreet Ward, near Bishopsgate. The wealth of the family is suggested by the four thousand pounds in recognizances posted in 1650 by Lewis, James, and their sister Mary's husband, John West, to guarantee that Lewis would do nothing "prejudiciall to the Commonwealth" if he went to Newfoundland. James died in 1656.[9]

460–465; on colonial merchants, see 326, 397, 399n, 430n; on political activities, see 371, 423, 484n, 511, 513, 553–556, 587; and C. H. Firth and R. S. Rait, eds., *Acts and Ordinances of the Interregnum, 1642–1660*, I (London, 1911), 5, 104, 990, 1257. On New Scotland, see Reid, *Acadia, Maine, and New Scotland*, 21–33.

8. William Barkley, John Kirke, and company, Interrogatories to the company of the *St. John* of Oleron, ca. 1649, and Interrogatories, in *Kirke, Berkeley, and company v. Spinosa et al.*, ca. 1649, HCA 23/16 (39), (43). On trading to Portugal and Holland, see HCA 13/252. See also Keepers of the Liberty of England, Interrogatories, in *Keepers v. Berkeley et al.*, ca. 1649, HCA 23/17 (53), which asks the libeled merchants: "Hath they any way expressed theire good affection to this Parliament and Commonwealth of England?"—a curious question to put to a commissioner of the navy. There were a number of contemporary William Barkeleys, but John Paige's correspondence makes the identity in question certain; see John Paige to George Paynter and William Clerke, Mar. 1, 1653, in Paige, *Letters*, document 68a. The political divergence between two merchants with similar class backgrounds and economic interests raises an apparent counterexample to Brenner's thesis in *Merchants and Revolution*—but one with an explanation, discussed in Chapter 4, below.

9. In 1638, Elizabeth Kirke paid thirty pounds in rent; see Dale, *Inhabitants*

John Kirke married in 1633 and was a substantial London house-holder in 1638. He and James prospered as overseas merchants before the Civil War. In 1664, after the Restoration, John inherited a court sinecure from his brother Lewis and could have retired from commerce (he was then fifty-eight). Instead, he returned to the fur trade, invest-ing three hundred pounds in the original stock of the Hudson's Bay Company in 1667, which became another family venture. About 1672, his daughter Elizabeth married Pierre Radisson, the celebrated Cana-dian *coureur de bois*, who explored Rupert's Land for the Company. The Kirkes were thus active participants in the three major commercial arenas of seventeenth-century Canada: the St. Lawrence fur trade, the Newfoundland fishery, and, finally, the new fur trade of Hudson Bay. In 1687, the elderly surviving brother, now Sir John, was conscious that his family fortunes had been consistently tied to the part of North America that is now Canada, arguing that the French could not claim the trading posts they had recently seized in Hudson Bay for several reasons, one which harked back to the early days in the River of Canada, when the Kirkes

about fifty yeares since held Quebeck . . . until they were comanded by King Charles the First to deliver the same to the French upon pay-ment of a great summe of money, which was by treaty betwixt the two crownes stipulated to be paid in consideration thereof, after which the said towne and country was delivered but noe part of the money was ever paid, by which it appears that the French have noe just title to Quebeck it selfe at this day.[10]

---

of London in 1638, 54. On Limestreet Ward, see Harvey, *Principal Inhabitants of 1640*, 15–16; cf. John Stow, *A Survey of London*, 2d ed. (1603; rpt. Lon-don, 1987), 136–148. Henry Vesey, curate of St. Andrew Undershaft, certified that John and James Kirke were "diligent resorters to the church"; see Feb. 23, 1641, HMC, "The Manuscripts of the House of Lords," in *Fourth Report of the Royal Commission on Historical Manuscripts* (London, 1874), 44. On merchant wealth, see Richard Grassby, "The Personal Wealth of the Business Community in Seventeenth-Century England," *EHR*, 2d Ser., XXIII (1970), 220–234. For the Kirkes, see Council of State, Account of Recognizance, May 25, 1650, SP 25/120 (26); Probate of James Kirke, Nov. 25, 1656, PROB 11/259, 88.

10. In 1638, John paid an annual rent of twenty pounds in the parish of St. Michael le Querne; see Dale, *Inhabitants of London in 1638*, 264. See also Guild-hall Library, London, "Citizens of London," file 42981, "Kirk, John"; Lewis Kirke, Will, Aug. 21, 1663, PROB 11/312, 131–132; Charles II, Grant to John Kirke,

Through the 1630s, the Kirkes, trading separately, severally, or as Kirke, Barkeley, and company, pursued the wine trade, a commercial preoccupation evident in the handful of London Port Books surviving from the period. Elizabeth Kirke imported thirty tuns of French wine to London on the *Lilly* in 1632 and another forty-two tuns on the *Comfort* in 1633. The same year, John Kirke received 77 butts of Malaga wine from a large cargo arriving in London on the *Amitie*, suggesting that Kirke, Barkeley, and company were shifting their trade from France to Spain. Because English law did not require the notarization of commercial documents, few remain from this period except those in court records. Consequently, surviving commercial records tend to be limited to disputed transactions. Fortunately, from the historical point of view, Kirke, Barkeley, and company were litigious—even exceptionally litigious—merchants. There might have been other areas of their overseas trade that proceeded smoothly and that were therefore undocumented, but the records of the High Court of Admiralty suggest that in the 1630s the Kirkes were breaking into the trade in Spanish wines and, thus, almost inevitably, into the Newfoundland trade. In 1636, James Kirke disputed an average, or distribution of a loss, resulting from the grounding of the *Neptune* of Ipswich, which was carrying a cargo of Malaga wine. In another case, William Barkeley complained that a lighter had been too slow in unloading wine from the *Red Lyon* when it sank about 1638. Kirke, Barkeley, and company had already, as part-owners, let the *St. George* of London to freight for a voyage to Barcelona and "other parts beyond the seas." This undertaking was in part a Newfoundland sack voyage, and the freighter was another prominent London wine merchant and sometime investor in the Canada trade, John Delabarre (circa 1599–1664).[11]

July 1664, in *CSP*: Domestic; Hudson's Bay Company, Ledger Accounts, 1667, HBC A.14/1, 53–54, in E. E. Rich, ed., *Minutes of the Hudson's Bay Company, 1671–1674*, I (Toronto, 1942), 172–175; G. L. Nute, "Radisson, Pierre-Esprit," in George W. Brown and Marcel Trudel, eds., *Dictionary of Canadian Biography*, II, *1701 to 1740* (Toronto, 1969); Martin Fournier, *Pierre-Esprit Radisson, aventurier et commerçant* (Quebec, 2001), 175–176, 193–209; Hudson's Bay Company, "Case of the Adventurers," May 6, 1687, CO 134/1, 165–168, in Rich, ed., *Copy-Book of Letters*, 222–226; Will of John Kirke, June 16, 1688, PROB 11/392, 71.

11. London Surveyor, Port Books, Dec. 31, 1632, Nov. 26, 1633, E 190/37/4. A tun of wine was 924 litres; London Surveyor, Port Books, Dec. 17, 1633, E 190/37/4. A butt was half a tun, so John's shipment was about the same size as his mother's. He appears here as "John de Kirke." See also James Kirke et al., Inter-

As the son of a Huguenot refugee, Delabarre also had French connections, like Gervaise and Elizabeth Goudon Kirke. If the Thomas Kirke who was made a freeman of the Fishmongers Company in 1649 was their son, then the families were bound as kin in 1652, when Thomas married John Delabarre's daughter Sarah. At any rate, Kirke, Barkeley, and company were deeply involved with Delabarre before the Civil War. Besides the *St. George*, in 1634 he freighted their 240-ton ship, the *Faith* of London, for a voyage to Newfoundland, thence to Cartagena and home.[12]

Kirke, Barkeley, and company let other ships to freight on the Newfoundland voyage in this period, for example, the *Hector* in 1637. Whether they themselves freighted sack ships on the triangular voyage to Newfoundland, Spain, and back to London before Sir David Kirke's move to Ferryland in 1638 is not certain. There are reasons to suspect that they had already entered the fish trade. They had use of the right ships at the right time—for example, the 1636 voyage of the *Neptune* to Malaga, a key market for salt cod. They presumed a knowledge of the trade in 1637, when the Kirkes alluded with confidence to "common use and custome" when "merchants freight a shippe to goe for Newfoundland." In the seventeenth century, merchant owners of a ship often let it to freight and simultaneously took another ship on charter to carry their own merchandise as a simple way of spreading the risks of commerce. In the mid-1630s, however, litigation in the Court of Admiralty suggests

------

rogatories regarding the *Neptune*, 1636, HCA 23/12 (241), William Allen, Nicholas Hopkin, and Joseph Hiscocke, Examinations, Aug. 28, Nov. 1, 1639, Feb. 6, 1640, HCA 13/55, 231, 327, 463, and William Berkely, Interrogatories, 1640, HCA 23/13 (35), all in *Barkley v. Foster*; David Keark et al. and William Barkley et al., Interrogatories, ca. 1636, 1637, HCA 23/11 (98), (326); David Kirke et al., Libel, in *Kirke et al. v. Delabarre*, ca. 1634, HCA 24/90 (195); John Delabarr, Interrogatories, in *Kirke et al. v. Delabarre*, ca. 1636, HCA 23/11 (282); Thomas Bredcake, Examination, in *Kirke v. Delabarre*, June 22, 1635, HCA 13/52, 23–24. On maritime "average," see Charles Molloy, *De Jure Maritimo et Navali; or, A Treatise of Affairs Maritime and of Commerce* (1676), 6th ed. (London, 1707), 273–286. On Delabarre's trade, see John Delabarre, Libel, in *Dellabarre v. Harbourne*, 1633, HCA 24/96 (334); Account Book, 1622, 1637, HCA 30/635; Simon, *Wine Trade*, III, 27; Kenneth R. Andrews, *Ships, Money, and Politics: Seafaring and Naval Enterprise in the Reign of Charles I* (Cambridge, 1991), 57; Brenner, *Merchants and Revolution*, 124n.

12. Andrews, *Ships, Money, and Politics*, 53; Guildhall Library, London, "Boyd's Citizens of London," file 26392, "Kirk, Thomas"; David Kirke et al., Interrogatories, in *Kirke et al. v. Delabarre*, ca. 1635, HCA 23/11 (217).

Kirke, Barkeley, and company had their capital invested mostly in the "fixed" form of ships, rather than in the circulating form of cargoes. In this respect, they differed from competitors like John Delabarre, who was both shipowner and active freighter.[13]

After 1638, the shoe was often on the other foot, and Kirke, Barkeley, and company appear in court as freighters of ships in the Spanish and Newfoundland trades. James Kirke freighted the *Robert Bonadventure* from its master in 1642, suffering damages to fruit shipped at Malaga through the vessel's "insufficiencie and leakiness." Since Kirke had taken the ship to freight for nine months in May, returning from Malaga in February 1643, this was, likely, a Newfoundland voyage. The very names of vessels owned in this period by the Kirkes and their associates suggest that these ships were designated for their own ventures, under the patronage of their fellow Newfoundland patentees, Marquis Hamilton and the earls of Pembroke and Holland: the *John*, the *John and Thomas*, the *James*, the *Pembrooke*, the *Hamilton* (all, probably, of London), the *David*, and the *Lady* (both of Ferryland). By 1640, Kirke, Barkeley, and company were in the Newfoundland sack trade with a vengeance; in fact, they had become major producers of fish. A closer look at the sack ship business will clarify why Sir David Kirke and his associates invested in a Newfoundland plantation.[14]

13. Kirke et al., Libel, in *Kirke et al. v. Jennings et al.*, Jan. 7, 1639, HCA 24/97 (232); Cell, *English Enterprise*, 10, 21; Andrews, *Ships, Money, and Politics*, 55.

14. James Kirke and G. Granger, Libels, in *Copeland v. Kirke and Granger*, Feb. 14, 1643, HCA 24/106 [box 105 in 1989], 82, 131. Cf. W. Copeland, Petition to House of Lords, Oct. 16, 1644, in HMC, "The Manuscripts of the Duke of Northumberland," in *Sixth Report of the Royal Commission on Historical Manuscripts* (London, 1877), 107. The Kirkes were in court in this period about another leaky vessel, the *Unity*, which John Kirke had freighted for Newfoundland in 1643; see John Kirke, Libel, in *Kirke v. Fletcher and Tylor*, Feb. 19, 1644, HCA 24/107 [box 106 in 1989] (67). This case is discussed in detail in Chapter 4, below. On ships' names, see James Pratt, Examination, in *Baltimore v. Kirke*, Mar. 12, 1652, HCA 13/65, n.p.; Richard Allward, Examination, in *Baltimore v. Kirke*, Mar. 29, 1652, HCA 13/65, n.p.; Privy Council, Minutes, Nov. 29, 1639, in *APC: Colonial*; James Kirke et al. and earl of Pembroke, Libels, in *Kirke et al. v. Brandt*, October 1640, Oct. 14, 1640, HCA 24/102 (211, 281); Kirke and Shapley, "Invoyce of Goods Shipped," Sept. 8, 1648, *Baxter MSS*, VI, 2–4; Dartmouth Searcher, Port Books, 1647, E 190/952/3; James Marquis Hamilton et al., Petition to Charles I, Jan. 25, 1640, SP 16/403, 78.

$\mathscr{e}\hspace{-2pt}\mathbb{S}$ Fish into Wine: Wine Merchants into Fish Merchants

The oft-made and oft-challenged assertion that the cod fishery was a multilateral trade is not a claim about the geographic path of every ship venturing from Newfoundland with a cargo of dried fish; it is an economic analysis of the flow of goods. Whatever the itineraries of individual ships, the trade was essentially triangular. Mediterranean and Iberian ports imported Newfoundland cod. These southern markets exported wine and fruit to English and Dutch ports. England, in its turn, exported labor and supplies to Newfoundland, but the ships venturing to the fishery were normally not heavily laden, either in tonnage or in value. In other words, if the Newfoundland trade was a triangular flow, it was a flow with two steady streams and one trickle. The wealth extracted from the sea and the value added in making fish returned to England from southern Europe, whether in specie or in the form of wine, fruit, oil, cork, or other goods. Only a fraction of these returns were redirected to Newfoundland.[15]

From the English point of view, the Newfoundland cod fishery solved a balance-of-payments problem. In the late sixteenth century, England's imports of wine, then primarily from France, were not balanced by exports to the wine-producing regions. In his *Pollitique Platt* of 1580, Robert Hitchcock argued that the trade in fish was "the best (and of lightest coste that can bee founde) to countervaile" this imbalance. Hitchcock emphasized the potential of North Sea herring and Newfoundland cod in this respect, stressing strong Iberian demand for well-cured fish. His prescient argument was that the English could trade fish for wine, as the Netherlanders had done for more than a century (Plate 5). The proposed

---

15. On multilateral trade, see Innis, *Cod Fisheries*; Ralph Davis, *The Rise of the English Shipping Industry in the Seventeenth and Eighteenth Centuries* (1962; rpt. London, 1972), 228–255; Matthews, "Fisheries," 60–98; Cell, *English Enterprise*, 2–21; and, for a later period, see Rosemary Ommer, *From Outpost to Outport: A Structural Analysis of the Jersey-Gaspé Cod Fishery, 1767–1886* (Montreal and Kingston, 1991), 68–104. For emphasis on shuttle voyages, see James F. Shepherd and Gary M. Walton, *Shipping, Maritime Trade, and the Economic Development of Colonial North America* (Cambridge, 1972), 49–71. Brenner, *Merchants and Revolution*, 110, assumes merchants sought returns for fish "from the Spanish empire." Although there was a flow of American silver from Spain into England, wine was consistently the most important return. On the import of specie, see Davis, *English Shipping*, 230; Pauline Croft, "English Mariners Trading to Spain and Portugal, 1558–1625," *Mariner's Mirror*, LXIX (1983), 251–268.

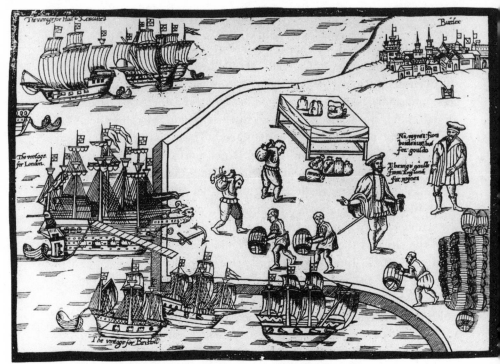

Plate 5. A Vision of the Late-Sixteenth-Century Balance of Payments Problem. From Robert Hitchcock, A Pollitique Platt for the Honour of the Prince . . . *(London, 1580). The French vintner (right) tells the merchant from London, "No wynes from Bordeaux but for goulde"; the buyer replies, "I bringe goulde from England for wynes." Courtesy, Queen Elizabeth II Library, Memorial University of Newfoundland, St. John's*

trade did, in fact, develop, but, since France maintained its own fisheries at Newfoundland, Spain, Portugal, Italy, and the Atlantic islands would be the primary markets where England would turn fish into wine.[16]

Early multilateral Newfoundland trade remains obscure, but its origin is clear enough: it was a development of the late-sixteenth-century

16. On wine imports into England, see A. D. Francis, *The Wine Trade* (London, 1972), 45; Simon, *Wine Trade*, esp. III, 253; Robert Hitchcock, *A Pollitique Platt for the Honour of the Prince* . . . (1580), in R. H. Tawney and Eileen Power, eds., *Tudor Economic Documents*, III (1924; rpt. London, 1953), 239–256 (esp. 254); Jan Craeybeckx, *Un grand commerce d'importation: les vins de France aux anciens Pays-Bas, XIIIe–XVIe siècle* (Paris, 1958), 273–275 (cf. 159 on commerce in wine as a "mother trade").

trade in fish between the West Country and southern Europe. Port books surviving from that period record extensive exports of Newfoundland fish from Dartmouth and Plymouth, with smaller quantities sent from Southampton, Exeter, Bristol, and Barnstaple, bound for France, Italy, and the Channel Islands. From 1600 to 1630, Exeter, Poole, and Weymouth competed with Dartmouth and Plymouth as major centers for this reexport of Newfoundland fish. The direction of the trade shifted in the second quarter of the century. Spain and Portugal became more important markets than France, while fish went to Madeira, the Canaries, the Azores, and the Netherlands as well. Dutch and English ships were still pursuing this trade at midcentury: *de Baak*, for example, went to Plymouth to load Newfoundland fish for Viana in 1643, and the *Mary* of Dartmouth went for Aveiro with fish from its home port in 1652. In 1675, the sack ship *Lyon* of Plymouth made its home port its intended market, and several others indicated that they would return to England. In 1684, a few sacks returned directly to Bristol and to the North Devon ports of Bideford and Barnstaple. Clearly, some Newfoundland fish was still marketed from the West Country late in the seventeenth century.[17]

By this time, however, most Newfoundland fish went directly to southern markets, and most ships involved in the trade either carried fishing crews to Newfoundland or fish to southern Europe (Maps 7 and 8). The multilateral voyage was a natural development from the inefficient system of reexport from England. The earliest recorded multilateral Newfoundland voyage dates to 1584. That Elizabeth I thought it necessary, in 1585, to send Bernard Drake to Newfoundland to warn English ships about the dangers of going to Spanish ports suggests both that the triangular voyage had already begun to replace exports from West Country ports and that fishing ships themselves were the first to pursue this

17. Cell, *English Enterprise*, 133–135 (tables 5–10), 137–140 (tables 12–19); Gysbert van Raaphorst and Abraham de Hartoch, Charter Party, Sept. 25, 1643, GA Amsterdam NA 1269, 47, NAC MG 18 012/508; Lawrence Wheeler and company, Interrogatories, 1652, HCA 23/17 (335); John Berry, "A List of Ships Makinge Fishinge Voyages; with Boatkeepers . . . ," Sept. 12, 1675, CO 1/35 (17i), 136–148; Francis Wheler, "An Account of Sack Shipps . . . ," Oct. 27, 1684, CO 1/55 (56v), 255. The Channel Islands probably reexported fish; see John C. Appleby, "Neutrality, Trade, and Privateering, 1500–1689," in A. G. Jamieson, ed., *A People of the Sea: The Maritime History of the Channel Islands* (London, 1986), 57–105 (esp. 76). On the Devon outports in this period, see Alison Grant, "Devon Shipping, Trade, and Ports, 1600–1689," *Maritime History of Devon*, I, 130–138.

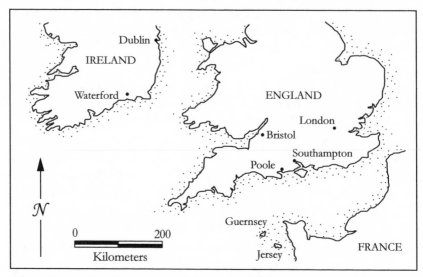

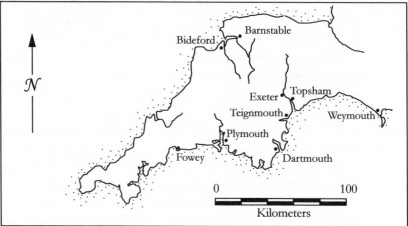

Map 7. British Ports Sending Sack Ships or Ships Fishing to Newfoundland, 1675-1684. Omits Brixham, Limerick, Lyme Regis, Shoreham, Swansea, and Yarmouth, each of which had only one ship at Newfoundland in this period. Drawn by Ed Eastaugh

new itinerary. By the beginning of the seventeenth century, sack ships, dedicated solely to freighting, had entered this business.[18]

English trade with Spain and Portugal rose rapidly in the first half of the seventeenth century, particularly during the shipping boom of

18. Cell, *English Enterprise*, 5; Elizabeth I, Commission to Bernard Drake, June 1585, in *CSP*: Colonial, 1675-1676, Addenda, 1574-1674, 28.

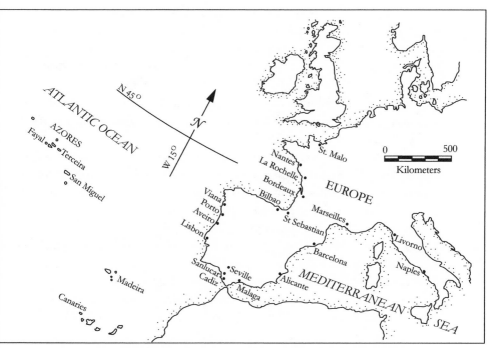

Map 8. European Markets for Dried Cod, Exported from the English Shore, 1675–1684. Drawn by Ed Eastaugh

the 1630s. Wine, much of it from Malaga, was a major import to England in this growing Iberian trade, although raisins and olive oil were also significant. The trade in these goods was no less seasonal than the trade in cod. Their respective commercial cycles meshed perfectly: raisins reached market in August; the vintage was shipped in September, October, and November; and olive oil was traded in the winter. Commercial efficiency dictated that the sack ships carrying Malaga and other Spanish wines to Britain were, in the main, ships that had arrived from Newfoundland with fish. The very name of these ships suggests the importance of sack, or wine, in this multilateral trade. "Sack" derives from *vino de sacca*, or wine set aside for export, rather than from *vino secco*, or dry wine. The wines in question were, in fact, sweet and strong rather than dry, which suited the English palate as well as enhancing their shipping qualities. (They were not, however, fortified with distilled spirits, a practice rare before the later seventeenth century.)[19]

19. Croft, "English Mariners Trading to Spain," *Mariner's Mirror*, LXIX (1983), 251–268; Andrews, *Ships, Money, and Politics*, 22–24; Brenner, *Mer-*

The southern vertex of the sack voyage was not always Iberian or even Mediterranean. A similar trade developed with the Atlantic islands (Madeira, the Canaries, and the Azores). The *Blessinge* of Southampton had called at Madeira with Newfoundland fish and was en route to the Canaries when it was taken by "Turks" in November 1635. The London records of the Canary wine merchant John Paige suggest that between 1648 and 1656 fully one-third of the goods imported by his trading partner in Tenerife consisted of Newfoundland fish. The Azores lie directly on one of the most practical sailing passages to Newfoundland from Europe, and Horta on the island of Fayal became not only a watering stop but a market for fish and a source of wine and brandy. The Dutch experimented with taking Newfoundland fish to southern markets in the New World, but voyages like that of *de Cooninck* to Pernambuco, Brazil, in 1636 were not common. English ships trading with Virginia sometimes carried fish from Newfoundland, and by the 1670s a few New England ships carried Newfoundland fish to the West Indies, like the sixty-ton *Nicholas*, which went to Barbados from Renews in 1677. These were still unusual voyages, however. Newfoundland's normal seventeenth-century trade linked the island with the wine-producing regions of southern Europe, at the opening of the century typically France and after 1620 typically Spain or one of the Atlantic islands.[20]

------

chants and Revolution, 30, 43, 89; W. B. Stephens, "English Wine Imports, c. 1603–40, with Special Reference to the Devon Ports," in Todd Gray, Margery Rowe, and Audrey Erskine, eds., *Tudor and Stuart Devon: The Common Estate and Government: Essays Presented to Joyce Youings* (Exeter, 1992), 141–172; Davis, *English Shipping*, 228–231; T. Bentley Duncan, *Atlantic Islands: Madeira, the Azores, and the Cape Verdes in Seventeenth-Century Commerce and Navigation* (Chicago, 1972), 38–39; Tim Unwin, *Wine and the Vine: An Historical Geography of Viticulture and the Wine Trade* (London, 1991), 222, 253–254, 263; Simon, *Wine Trade*, III, 18; Francis, *Wine Trade*, 50–51. Simon, *Wine Trade*, III, 339, underestimates imports from Malaga. Innis, *Cod Fisheries*, 54 n. 6, and Simon, *Wine Trade*, III, 322, propose derivation of "sack" from *sec*, or "dry."

20. William Stanley, Deposition, May 17, 1636, *Southampton Examinations*, III, 4–5; Simon van der Does et al., Protest, Oct. 16, 1638, GA Amsterdam NA 696, NAC MG 18 012/507; West India Company and Jacob Touteloop, Charter Party, June 8, 1642, Rotterdam City Archive, Notarial, Jan van Aller, 296–297, NAC MG 18 012/325; William Douglas et al., Depositions, Aug. 9, 1626, *Southampton Examinations*, I, 73–74; William Poole, "Account of Fishing and Sackships from Trepassy to Cape Broyle," Sept. 10, 1677, CO 1/41 (62viii), 168–169. On the Canary trade, see George F. Steckley, "The Wine Economy of Tene-

Although some London vessels made the voyage to buy fish in the early seventeenth century, and a few merchants in Barnstaple, Dartmouth, Weymouth, and, particularly, Southampton occasionally freighted Newfoundland sacks, English merchants played, as yet, a minor role in this sector of the trade. In 1620, Richard Whitbourne noted "divers Dutch and French ships" buying fish at Newfoundland. His *Discourse of Newfoundland* is, in part, an exposition of how English merchants might displace the Dutch from the sack trade. In the early 1630s, Trinity House, the guild of master mariners, complained that something like twenty-eight "strangers ships" were annually freighting fish at Newfoundland. Few English sack ships went to Newfoundland until the late 1630s, and until then Dutch sack ships were more common. Hector Pieters sailed from Carbonear in 1634, in convoy "with our eleven Dutch and two or three English ships." Relatively low costs might have given the Dutch a competitive advantage, at least before 1638, when Sir David Kirke began to apply a 5 percent tax on fish taken from Newfoundland in foreign bottoms. Dutch participation in the Newfoundland sack trade revived in the 1650s. A crucial consideration for the Dutch was peace with Spain, which they had enjoyed between 1609 and 1618 and which they finally achieved again in 1648. Ships from the Netherlands were active at Newfoundland during the Interregnum (1649-1659). The return of Dutch competition threatened English trade with Iberia, a situation exacerbated after 1655 by the Anglo-Spanish war. The Dutch Newfoundland trade predates this period of intense activity, however, by decades.[21]

---

rife in the Seventeenth Century: Anglo-Spanish Partnership in a Luxury Trade," *EHR*, 2d Ser., XXXIII (1980), 335-350; Steckley, "Introduction," in Paige, *Letters*, xx, table 2. On the other hand, Paige listed only three Newfoundland sacks among the forty ships he expected to be trading for wine at Tenerife in 1649, making up about 4.3 percent by tonnage (see appendix A). On Fayal, see Duncan, *Atlantic Islands*, 154-155. On routes, see Steele, *English Atlantic*, 78-93.

21. On early English sack ventures, see Matthews, "Fisheries," 68–69, 83; Davis, *English Shipping*, 228-229; Cell, *English Enterprise*, 5-21. On the minor role of the English in this period, see Davis, *English Shipping*, 236n. On the Dutch, see Whitbourne, *Discourse*, 128, 140-146; Trinity House, Petition to Privy Council, ca. 1633, SP 16/257 (29); Hector Pieterss to Dirck Joosten, Sept. 17, 1633, GA Amsterdam NA 694, 94, NAC MG 18 012/20. The early sack trade is conventionally supposed to have been dominated by London merchants; see, for example, Innis, *Cod Fisheries*, 54; W. B. Stephens, "The West Country Ports and the Struggle for the Newfoundland Fisheries in the Seventeenth Century," *RT Devon*,

On June 10, 1620, David de Vries set sail for Newfoundland from Texel, at the mouth of the Netherlands' inland sea, in a ship freighted by two Amsterdam merchants. He stopped at Weymouth, in Dorset, where he bought three guns for the ship and picked up letters of credit for purchase of fish in Newfoundland. On June 18, he called at Plymouth, Devon, to buy more guns. After a month at sea, he made land in Placentia Bay, on the south coast of Newfoundland, "where the Basques fish." Tentatively coasting east and north from his landfall, de Vries arrived August 4 at "Ferrelandt . . . in Cappelinge Bay." Here he found the fishing masters from whom he was supposed to buy fish. They were, unfortunately, sold out. De Vries managed to obtain a cargo elsewhere, and on September 10 he set sail, in convoy with four other Dutch ships, for Genoa. A chance encounter with another Netherlands vessel suggests that others were trading at Newfoundland at this time.[22]

The Dutch sack trade to Newfoundland dates as early as 1589. Sir Walter Raleigh complained of it to the House of Commons in 1593. Al-

---

LXXXVIII (1956), 90–101 (esp. 94); David J. Starkey, "Devonians and the Newfoundland Trade," *Maritime History of Devon*, I, 163–171. Cf. the earlier discussions analyzed in Keith Matthews, "Historical Fence Building: A Critique of the Historiography of Newfoundland," *Newfoundland Studies*, XVII (2001), 143–165. Matthews concluded, from a reading of the English administrative records, that the Dutch were important participants in the sack trade ca. 1620–1630; see Matthews, "Fisheries," 76. Cell, *English Enterprise*, 105, emphasizes England's early triangular trade, but this trade did not necessarily involve sack ships. On war and competition, see Violet Barbour, "Dutch and English Merchant Shipping in the Seventeenth Century," *EHR*, II (1930), 261–290; Brenner, *Merchants and Revolution*, 46–47, 599, 682. The idea that the Dutch competed effectively during the Civil War (1642–1648) is probably mistaken; cf. Dicky Glerum-Laurentius, "A History of Dutch Activity in the Newfoundland Fish Trade from about 1590 till about 1680" (master's thesis, MUN, 1960), 38–48.

22. Quotations from David Peterszoon de Vries, *Short Historical and Journal Notes of Several Voyages Made in the Four Parts of the World, Namely, Europe, Africa, Asia, and America* (1655), trans. Henry C. Murphy, New-York Historical Society, *Collections*, 2d Ser., III, pt. 1 (New York, 1857), 3–10 (quotations on 6), in light of the valuable readings in Glerum-Laurentius, "Dutch in Newfoundland," 22–25. The Murphy translation is neither reliable nor complete. Charles McKew Parr, *The Voyages of David de Vries: Navigator and Adventurer* (New York, 1969) is, unfortunately, a paraphrase.

though Dutch ships were regularly making the Newfoundland voyage by the turn of the seventeenth century, the trade must have remained relatively undeveloped for some time, since experienced masters were still in short supply in 1618. By the 1620s, however, the Newfoundland voyage was a regular one for Dutch ships and remained so until challenged by David Kirke and his associates in the late 1630s. After some interruption in the 1640s, Dutch activity at Newfoundland revived through the 1650s. *De Profeet Daniel* of Amsterdam went to Newfoundland and thence to Italy in 1656 on a voyage organized much as de Vries's had been in 1620.[23]

The Dutch took fish from Newfoundland to Genoa, Civita Vecchia, Naples, Lisbon, Oporto, and Cadiz as well as Bordeaux and other French ports. Some of these voyages were rather complex, like that of the *Sint Pieter*, which in 1627 sailed from the Netherlands to Newfoundland, to Bordeaux, thence to London with wines, to Topsham in Devon, and back to Newfoundland. These Dutch vessels were often large and well armed, like the 240-ton *St. Michiel*, which sailed from Enkhuizen in 1623 armed with ten guns, four pederos, handguns, muskets, firelocks, pikes, and "ammunition in proportion." The 300-ton *'t Vliegende Hart* carried sixteen guns when it went to Newfoundland in 1651. Not all Dutch sacks were this large, but they were rarely under 150 tons, and their size and armament are usually stressed in the charter parties. The Newfoundland harbors at which fish were laded by the Dutch are rarely specified. Scattered references to specific harbors suggest that Netherlands ships traded primarily on the south Avalon, at St. John's, and in Conception

23. Raleigh, Mar. 23, 1593, in Stock, *Debates*, I, 7; Pieter Wiltraet and Jan t'Herdt, Charter Party, June 19, 1601, GA Amsterdam NA 90, 4–5, NAC MG 18 012/6; Hendrick Lonck et al., Depositions, Dec. 4, 1606, GA Amsterdam NA 196, 85–86, NAC MG 18 012/69; Bartolotti et al. and Laurens Freissen, Agreement, Apr. 26, 1618, GA Amsterdam NA 152, 81–82, NAC MG 18 012/33; Everard Schott and Piter Naadt, Charter Party, June 12, 1656, GA Amsterdam NA 2117, 89–91, NAC MG 18 012/196. Jan Kupp, "Dutch Documents Taken from Notarial Archives of Holland Relating to the Fur Trade and Cod Fisheries of North America," NAC MG 18 012, vols. 1–18, are transcripts and translations providing many details about the Dutch Newfoundland trade not recorded in English administrative records. On these notarial records, see P. C. Van Royen, "Manning the Merchant Marine: The Dutch Maritime Labour Market about 1700," *IJMH*, I (1989), 1–28. On chronology, see Jan Kupp, "Le développement de l'intérêt hollandais dans la pêcherie de la morue de Terre-Neuve . . . ," *RHAF*, XXVII (1974), 565–569.

Bay. Depositions for an insurance claim indicate that *de Hoop* took on fish at St. John's, Witless Bay, Cape Broyle, and Aquaforte in 1626. The pilot refused to go on to Trinity Bay, regarding it as "too dangerous . . . with so much expensive fish." Factors' letters from Cupids in 1633 list purchases of fish there as well as at Carbonear and Bay Bulls. De Vries had called for fish in Ferryland in 1620, and *de Vreede* tarried at nearby Caplin Bay in 1659.[24]

Normal practice for Dutch ships was, originally, to call at a West Country port en route to the fishery, as de Vries had in 1620. Occasionally, English ports like Southampton or Dartmouth were involved, but Plymouth was by far the most commonly used: *de Luypaert* called there in 1658, as Dutch sack ships had in successive decades since the 1620s. There they would pick up a supercargo, or freighter's factor, who would bring with him "letters of credit, documents or money" for Newfoundland fish. Ritsert Heijnmers, a Dutch merchant living in Plymouth, was to contract for fish for the *St. Paulo* in 1629. *De Hoop* embarked a "pilot" at Plymouth in 1637, who would "enjoy free bread and living" on board, although the freighter was to pay his wages. This was a period when merchants from the Netherlands played an important role in West Country commerce. The Dutch needed regional contacts to negotiate in advance the purchase of Newfoundland fish, the normal arrangement in the early-seventeenth-century trade. Once their cargo was obtained in Newfoundland, they set out for their southern markets. This Dutch carrying trade was not precisely competition for the West Country, or at least not for those whose main business was fishing. London-based masters, like Whitbourne, were more likely to perceive the Dutch as competitors. Contacts with Dutch merchants probably gave Kirke, Barkeley, and

24. Jan Vrolyck, Declaration, Aug. 19, 1628, GA Amsterdam NA 693, 28, NAC MG 18 012/116; Jan Oort and Anthonis Jacobsen, Charter Party, Apr. 3, 1623, GA Amsterdam NA 738, 175-178, NAC MG 18 012/34; Everard Schot and Pieter Veen, Charter Party, May 9, 1651, GA Amsterdam NA 1574, 262, NAC MG 18 012/139; Jan Bastienss and Jan Pieterss, Deposition regarding *de Hope*, May 16, 1626, GA Amsterdam NA 256, 349 (Kupp transcribes Cape Broyle as "Taberevijl," but it appears on the manuscript to be "Caberijl") NAC MG 18 012/271; Hector Pieterss to Joosten, Sept. 17, 1633, GA Amsterdam NA 694, 94, NAC MG 18 012/20; Abraham Isaacq, Protest, Mar. 22, 1660, GA Amsterdam NA 2715, 509-511, NAC MG 18 012/221. Cf. Kupp, "L'intérêt hollandais," *RHAF*, XXVII (1974), 565-569 (esp. 567).

company exposure to the Newfoundland trade before their move to monopolize this business in the later 1630s.[25]

The "Grant of Newfoundland" to Sir David Kirke and his associates in 1637 did not exactly exclude "strangers" from either the fishing or the carrying trades, but it gave the Newfoundland patentees the right to levy a 5 percent tax on fish caught (primarily by the French) or carried (primarily by the Dutch). These fiscal rights quickly brought the Kirkes into a new relationship with their competitors. In 1638, Lewis Kirke taxed a 260-ton Basque vessel fishing at Trinity at 5 percent as well as wangling a shallop from the master. He also taxed a 140-ton Dutch sack ship fifty pounds at Bay Bulls. Both the Privy Council and the Kirkes presumed that these impositions would drive the Dutch out of the carrying trade from the English Shore. Whereas the French protested vociferously, the Netherlanders initially accepted the Kirkes' tax as a cost of doing business, then, as profits dropped, they temporarily reduced their interest in the Newfoundland trade. Companies trading "to the Plantations of Canada and New England" boasted in a 1639 petition to the Privy Council that they had "of late procured almost all the trade from Newfoundland from the Dutch."[26]

25. Philips Emanuels and Jan Jacobs, Charter Party, May 27, 1658, GA Amsterdam NA 1539, 187–188, NAC MG 18 012/206; William van Haesdonck and Bastien Lelij, Charter Party, Apr. 6, 1624, GA Amsterdam NA 170, 96–99, NAC MG 18 012/37; Jacques Thierry and Wijbrand Jonas, Charter Party, Apr. 26, 1634, GA Amsterdam NA 409, 352, NAC MG 18 012/84; West India Company and Touteloop, Charter Party, June 8, 1642, Rotterdam City Archives, Notarial, Jan van Aller, 296–297, NAC MG 18 012/325; Jochem Harmensz, Power of Attorney to Ritsert Heynmers, May 19, 1629, GA Amsterdam NA 239, 81–82, NAC MG 10 012/77; Paulus Timmerman and Gerritt Romyn, Charter Party, May 6, 1637, GA Amsterdam NA 674, 184–186, NAC MG 18 012/114; I. K. Steele, "Instructing the Master of a Newfoundland Sack Ship, 1715," *Mariner's Mirror*, LXIII (1977), 191–193. Kirke, Barkeley, and company let ships to Dutch freighters in this period. About 1635, Harman van Maerthuson freighted the *Mary* of London from John Kirke, which returned with wines; this enterprise might have been a Newfoundland sack voyage. See John Kirke, Interrogatories, in *[Kirke v. Delabarre?]*, ca. 1636, HCA 23/11 (318).

26. Charles I, "A Grant of Newfoundland," Nov. 13, 1637, CO 195/1 (2), 11–27, in Matthews, *Constitutional Laws*, 82–116 (esp. 108); William Hill, Examination, in *Lewis Kirke v. [?]*, Apr. 18, 1642, HCA 13/58, 9–10; Allward, Examination, in *Baltimore v. Kirke*, Mar. 12, 1652, HCA 13/65, n.p.; Privy Council, Min-

This willingness to skirmish with the Dutch had been typical of Stuart commercial policy since the 1620s, but it was not the coherent program of mercantilist exclusion that would be enacted with the Navigation Ordinances of the 1650s. The Newfoundland Patent of 1637 is better understood as an example of the kind of court patronage that particularly appealed to Charles I, who was promised a 10 percent share of the taxes collected. Traditional Dutch dependence on West Country supercargoes and trading houses probably explains the vehemence with which Plymouth interests, in particular, defended the Dutch sack trade against the impositions proposed by David Kirke's syndicate. Kirke, Barkeley, and company managed to co-opt other West Country merchants by emphasizing that the new regime would enable the West Country merchants and the patentees to engross, respectively, the fishing and the sack trade. The syndicate of Newfoundland patentees would fix the price of fish with the Western Adventurers, while the patentees agreed to buy and ship at least the average quantity sold to strangers in preceding years. Within a few years, the English Civil War would make these agreements moot, as tensions flared between a royalist governor in Newfoundland and the generally parliamentary western ports.[27]

Despite the Navigation Acts of 1650 and 1651, Dutch participation in the Newfoundland trade rebounded in the 1650s, since Interregnum governments exempted Newfoundland fish from the prohibition on export in foreign bottoms. The new stricter mercantilism announced by the acts was, nevertheless, the beginning of the end of the Dutch sack ship business. Although England and the Netherlands did not engage in open naval conflict at Newfoundland in the war that followed the Navigation Acts between 1652 and 1654, there is no doubt that the Dutch Newfoundland trade suffered. Sack ships were lost to the English on their way to market, and in 1653 the English navy simply prevented Dutch ships from setting out on the sack voyage. From about 1650, the destination specified in the Amsterdam charter parties was less often "English Newfoundland" and more often just "Newfoundland," sometimes explicitly indicating that ships were *not* to call in the West Country but were, like the *Coninck David* in 1651, to go "straight to English New-

utes, June 25, 1638, in *APC*: Colonial; John Coke to Francis Windebank, May 16, 1639, SP 16/421 (31); Privy Council, Minutes, Nov. 29, 1639, in *APC*: Colonial.

27. Charles Wilson, *England's Apprenticeship, 1603–1763*, 2d ed. (London, 1984), 52–65; Brenner, *Merchants and Revolution*, 659; Privy Council, Minutes, June 25, 1638, in *APC*: Colonial; Cell, *English Enterprise*, 115.

foundland." The itinerary of the *St. Jan Battisto* in 1653 was even more specific: "to the coast of Newfoundland to the French fisheries or there where the French fish." Dutch sack ships still carried supercargoes, but, by the 1650s, ships bound for French ports like Saint-Malo or Nantes were no doubt buying fish from French fishers and would have carried French factors. Some Dutch ships in the later 1650s took "nets, casks, salt and other necessities for the fishing in Newfoundland" but did so generally in cooperation with French merchants. There are few, if any, such indications of Dutch participation in the fishery itself on the English Shore. Commercial uncertainty during the Anglo-Spanish war between 1655 and 1660 led the Netherlands to require that masters going to Newfoundland declare "their intended actions or freighting" and obtain a pass before setting out. Vessels like *de Luypaert* still managed to carry on business at Plymouth and Newfoundland as late as 1658 and even returned in 1659 "to such English harbors as shall be ordered" when, significantly, the Dutch vessel augmented its armament. A few Dutch sacks continued to visit the English Shore into the 1660s, but Dutch participation was in decline and was extinct by 1670. By this time, a different kind of sack ship carried Newfoundland fish to market.[28]

28. Davis, *English Shipping*, 12; "An Act . . . for Transporting of Fish in Foreign Bottoms," ca. 1659, in C. H. Firth and R. S. Rait, eds., *Acts and Ordinances of the Interregnum, 1642-1660*, II (London, 1911), 1099-1100; Olivier Locquet, Deposition regarding the *Huis van Assendelft*, May 7, 1652, GA Amsterdam NA 1697, 1290, NAC MG 18 012/158; Cornelius Bloem, Declaration regarding *de Sonnenbloom*, Oct. 28, 1652, GA Amsterdam NA 1801, 801-802, NAC MG 18 012/165; Julien Lanson et al., Deposition regarding *de Elisabeth*, Mar. 20, 1655, GA Amsterdam NA 1703, 803, NAC MG 18 012/181; Jeronimo da Costa and Gerritt van Lynen, Charter Party, June 9, 1651, GA Amsterdam NA 1534, 277, NAC MG 18 012/154; Jacques Thierry et al. and Ariaen Jansz, Charter Party, June 20, 1653, GA Amsterdam NA 1664, 105-106, NAC MG 18 012/171; Guillaume Belin and Jan Kint, Charter Party, May 10, 1653, GA Amsterdam NA 2114, 993-994, NAC MG 18 012/167; Belin and Symon Vallom, Charter Party, May 17, 1653, GA Amsterdam NA 2114, 38-39, NAC MG 18 012/168; Jacques Thierry and Simon and Luis Rodrigues de Sousa, Charter Party, Apr. 1, 1655, GA Amsterdam NA 2116, 561-562, NAC MG 18 012/64; Everard Schott, Declaration, June 8, 1657, GA Amsterdam NA 2120, 282, NAC MG 18 012/200A; States General of the United Netherlands, "Regulations with Regard to the Newfoundland Trade," 1657, Ryks Archives, The Hague, Resolution of the Provincial States, Holland and West Friesland, 264-268, NAC MG 18 012/512; Emanuels and Jacobss, Charter Party, May 27, 1658, GA Amsterdam NA 1539, 187-188, NAC MG 18 012/206;

The Newfoundland sack ships, defined strictly as ships venturing solely to freight rather than to make fish, were not the only vessels taking fish to southern Europe and returning to England with cargoes of wine, fruit, oil, and so forth. Many fishing ships sailed with their own fish to market; in 1681, for example, they carried about 60 percent of the catch to market. The class of ships fishing and the class of ships trading in fish overlapped. In this situation lay an ambiguity: "sack ship" might mean either a ship freighted in Newfoundland with bought fish or a ship with a cargo of fish, whether made or bought. The narrower sense is intended here, but the wider sense was sometimes used in the seventeenth century. In 1684, for example, the naval commodore at Newfoundland, Captain Francis Wheler, listed a number of ships as both "Fishing Shipps" and "Sack Shipps." To confuse the issue even further, sack ship crews might participate in the making of fish to secure a full cargo quickly. In general, it was the crew that distinguished a so-called fishing ship from a sack ship: the former employed fishermen skilled in the inshore boat fishery; the latter, a relatively smaller deep-water company. The vessels themselves were largely interchangeable.[29]

In the eighteenth century, vessels on sack voyages were generally larger than vessels engaged in fishing, but, in the seventeenth century,

---

Pieter and Jan Meerman and Jan Verhoeck, Charter Party, June 14, 1659, GA Amsterdam NA 2988, 188–190, NAC MG 18 012/214. On the war and its aftermath, see J. R. Jones, *The Anglo-Dutch Wars of the Seventeenth Century* (London, 1996), 107–144; Glerum-Laurentius, "Dutch in Newfoundland," 48–86; and Kupp, "L'intérêt hollandais," *RHAF*, XXVII (1974), 565–569 (esp. 567–569). The English also lost fishing ships to the Dutch; see William Tozer, Deposition regarding the *Joseph* of Topsham, June 28, 1655, DRO Exeter, Moger, CC. 181/18/3.

29. "Abstract of the Accounts Returned from Newfoundland . . . ," Dec. 31, 1681, *CSP*: Colonial; *DNE*, s.v. "sack"; Francis Wheler, "An Account of Fishing Shipps . . . ," and Wheler, "Sack Shipps," Oct. 27, 1684, CO 1/55 (56iv, v), 254, 255; Thomas Read, Examination, in *Wheatley et al. v. Herringe et al.*, Jan. 10, 1639, HCA 13/54, 396–399; Jan Bastienss and Jan Pieterss, Deposition regarding *de Hoop*, May 16, 1626, GA Amsterdam NA 256, 349, NAC MG 18 012/79; Whitbourne, *Discourse*, 145; cf. John Mannion, "Victualling a Fishery: Newfoundland Diet and the Origins of the Irish Provisions Trade, 1675–1700," *IJMH*, XII (2000), 1–57 (esp. 50). The French "saque" had a different function: to carry crews, oil, and equipment back to France; see Jean-François Brière, *La pêche française en Amérique du nord au XVIIIe siècle* (Saint-Laurent, Quebec, 1990), 54.

Table 5. *Tonnage of Fishing and Sack Ships, with Boats per Ship,*
Newfoundland, 1675 and 1684

Activity	N	Tons	Mean Boats	Mean Boats per 100 Tons
			Sack Ships	
Carried no boats, 1675	69	76	0.0	0.0
Carried 1 or 2 boats, 1675	27	71	1.7	2.4
To a market, 1675	128	76	1.9	2.6
"Sack ship," 1684	67	69	—	—
			Fishing Ships	
Carried boats, 1675	105	84	6.0	7.1
Carried 3 or more boats, 1675	78	89	7.4	8.4
Back to England, 1675	30	100	9.3	9.3
"Fishing ship," 1684	42	90	6.6	7.3

Sources: John Berry, "A List of Ships Makinge Fishinge Voyages; with Boatkeepers . . . ," Sept. 12, 1675, CO 1/35 (17i), 136–148; Francis Wheler, "An Account of the Fishing Shipps . . . ," and Wheler, "An Account of Sack Shipps . . . ," Oct. 27, 1684, CO 1/55 (56iv, v), 254, 255. Cf. Peter E. Pope, "Sack Ships in the Seventeenth-Century Newfoundland Trade," in Poul Holm, Olaf Janzen, and Jón Thór, eds., *Northern Seas, 1999: Yearbook of the Association for the History of the Northern Seas* (St. John's, 1999), 33–46.

the opposite was the case. In 1608, when the Cornish merchant John Rashleigh wanted a sack for his fishing ship, the 100-ton *Success*, he sent a much smaller vessel, the *Tryfell* (of less than 50 tons), and this pattern endured, at least among British vessels. Compare, for example, Kirke, Barkeley, and company's 240-ton sack ship *Faith* and the three ships that were to supply it with fish in 1634: the 300-ton *Eagle*, the 120-ton *Ollive*, and the 250-ton *Desire*. These were unusually large ships, but the general point remains. Sack ships ranged in size from 20 tons to at least 250 tons, which was a large vessel, especially in the pre-Restoration period, but no larger than many fishing ships. In 1675, sack ships were, on the average, smaller than ships fishing (Table 5). The former averaged less than 75 tons, the latter almost 90. Fishing ships returning directly to England were even larger: more than 100 tons on average.[30]

Ships fishing grew larger over the century. Those returning directly to England averaged only fifty-five tons in the 1620s, eighty tons in the 1630s, but one hundred tons in 1675. Even the early-seventeenth-century ships fishing were already of greater burthen than the small vessels of only twenty to thirty-five tons that worked as sack ships at Newfoundland. The naval commodores' detailed replies to inquiries of the later seventeenth century permit statistical comparisons for that period (Table 6). The smallest vessels were, at that time, more likely to be sack ships than larger vessels. English-built ships of more than fifty tons were generally of a standard design: the armed merchantman, or "defensible ship," which the English had developed in the late sixteenth century to force their way into the Mediterranean trades (Plate 6). The smaller vessels in the Newfoundland trade, up to about fifty tons burthen, were the "ketches," or "barks," mentioned in contemporary documents (Plate 7). Such small vessels were vulnerable in the pirate-infested waters of southern Europe, but they must have been cost-effective, for there were many in the trade.[31]

30. On the eighteenth century, see Olaf Uwe Janzen, "'They Are Not Such Great Rogues as Some of Their Neighbours': A Scottish Supercargo in the Newfoundland Fish Trade, 1726," *Newfoundland Studies*, XVII (2001), 294–309. The conventional wisdom assumes seventeenth-century sack ships were larger than ships fishing; see Lewes Roberts, *The Merchants Mappe of Commerce* (London, 1638), 58; Matthews, "Fisheries," 71, 74; Cell, *English Enterprise*, 21. But see John Scantlebury, "John Rashleigh of Fowey and the Newfoundland Cod Fishery 1608–20," *Royal Institution of Cornwall Journal*, VIII (1978–1981), 61–71 (esp. 62); John Delabarre, "Memorandum for Master Thomas Breadcake," 1634, HCA 15/5, in Davis, *English Shipping*, 236–238; Berry, "List of Ships," Sept. 12, 1675, CO 1/35 (17i), 136–148. The estimate of the size of the *Tryfell* is based on its crew of five men. On tonnage measurements, see Glossary.

31. Cell, *English Enterprise*, 130, table 1 (using the mean of mean tonnages by port); Andrews, *Ships, Money, and Politics*, 26–28; Davis, *English Shipping*, 5–8; Brenner, *Merchants and Revolution*, 47; Edward Barlow, *Barlow's Journal . . . (1659–1703)*, ed. Basil Lubbock (London, 1934), I, 139–141. For further discussion of smaller ships, see Chapter 4, below. On piracy, see Todd Gray, "Turkish Piracy and Early Stuart Devon," *RT Devon*, CXXI (1989), 159–171; and Ralph Davis, "England and the Mediterranean, 1570–1670," in F. J. Fisher, ed., *Essays in the Economic and Social History of Tudor and Stuart England, in Honour of R. H. Tawney* (Cambridge, 1961), 117–137.

Table 6. *Ships by Activity and Tonnage, Newfoundland, 1675*

Activity	20–49 Tons	50–79 Tons	80–129 Tons	130–250 Tons	Total
			Number of Ships		
Sack Ships					
Sack voyage to a market	20	25	12	10	67
Sacklike voyage to a market	4	4	6	3	17
Sack or sacklike voyage to England	1	2	1	1	5
No data	0	2	0	0	2
Total	25	33	19	14	91
Fishing Ships					
Fishing voyage to a market	10	16	13	4	43
Fishing voyage back to England	1	8	11	5	25
No data	1	6	5	2	14
Total	12	30	29	11	82

Note: Ship activity has been counted as "sacklike" if the vessel operated only 1 or 2 boats or, in the case of vessels of less than 50 tons, only 1 boat.

Source: John Berry, "A List of Ships Makinge Fishinge Voyages; with Boatkeepers . . . ," Sept. 12, 1675, CO 1/35 (17i), 136–148.

The Newfoundland shipping censuses of the 1670s and 1680s indicate that many ships were not functionally specialized. Ships operating as sacks sometimes kept a few boats so that their crews could make a little fish, like the five hundred quintals made by the crew of the *Pelican* of Topsham in 1679. Some of these nonspecialized vessels were quite small, for example, the forty-ton *Blessing* of Kinsale, which came to Caplin Bay in 1676 to buy fish but kept a boat and was therefore able to make ninety quintals of dry fish, a hogshead of train oil, and three quintals of wet-salted corfish, worth sixty-six pounds to the ship, its master, and crew. Captain Sir William Poole's assessment of imports to Newfoundland in 1677 indicates that about 70 percent of sack ships brought goods and

Plate 6. The Real Friendship. *By Edward Barlow. Pen-and-ink drawing, circa 1669. This sack ship of 140 tons accidentally burned at Newfoundland in 1669. It mounted ten guns and could be sailed with a crew of sixteen. Permission of National Maritime Museum, Greenwich, London*

that the vessels importing goods were, typically, the smaller ones. Many brought wines or brandy. Captain John Berry's figures for ships importing alcohol in 1675 suggest that ships making mixed sacklike voyages were most likely to bring in wines and brandy. New England vessels imported provisions.[32]

32. John Cotton, Receipt, June 4, 1680, DRO Exeter, Chanter, 780 C, 157; John Wyborn, ". . . Sack Ships . . . between Trepasse and Bay Bulls," Dec. 7, 1676, CO 1/38 (87), 236, 232 *[sic]*; Poole, "Trepassey to Cape Broyle," and Poole, "Account of Fishing and Sackships from Balene to St. John's Harbour . . . ," Sept. 10, 1677, CO 1/41 (62viii, ix), 167–168, 168–170; Compare John Berry, "A List of Those That Have Furnisht . . . Brandy, Wines, etc. . . . ," Sept. 12, 1675, CO 1/35

Plate 7. A New England Ketch of the Mid-Seventeenth Century. Weighing about forty tons and fifty-three feet long. Reconstructed by William A. Baker. Reproduced by permission from Baker, The Mayflower and Other Colonial Vessels *(London, 1983), 143 (fig. 43)*

The 1675 data (Table 6) suggest that vessels of about 100 tons were most likely to be fishing ships, smaller vessels were more likely to be sack ships, and the few large vessels, 130–250 tons burthen or more, were evenly divided between sacks and ships fishing. The functions of the medium and larger vessels had probably not changed greatly since the 1630s, although British losses in the Spanish war (1655–1660) and second and third Dutch Wars (1664–1667, 1672–1674) might have affected the makeup of the Newfoundland fleet. In 1675, James Houblon offered a simple explanation for what was then perceived as a decline of the fish

(17iii), 157; and Berry, "List of Ships," Sept. 12, 1675, CO 1/35 (17i), 136–148. On corfish, see Chapter 1, above.

trade: "The infinite losses the English, who have driven that trade have in all times sustained by takings at sea, for want of protection (this trade being driven in smale vessels of little defence), but especially in the Spanish Warre, in anno 1657 to 1660, in which yeares were lost to the nation 1200 saile of ships, amongst which a greate number of fish ships." Just how small the "vessels of little defence" lost in these wars were remains an open question. We must, however, note Houblon's assumption that the sack trade had traditionally been carried on with relatively small vessels. Given the relatively low average tonnage of sacks, even in the 1670s, there is little reason to assume that most English sack ships in the 1630s had been large vessels like those Kirke, Barkeley, and company freighted to John Delabarre. Many were small, like John Rashleigh's *Tryfell* or the 26-ton bark that Lancelott Richards took, in 1633, from Barnstaple to Newfoundland for fish and thence to Cadiz for wines and fruit.[33]

The small transatlantic freighters involved in the sack trade, many not much larger than a good-sized modern yacht, were the trading equivalent of the Newfoundland planters and by-boat-keepers. They represent successful participation in the fish trade by merchants and masters of limited capital. In 1675, vessels of less than 50 tons accounted for more than 25 percent of British bottoms trading at Newfoundland, although, given their limited burthen, they probably moved less than 15 percent of fish exports. The 149 ships of less than 130 tons that Captain Berry found in the trade, at that time, together moved far more fish than the 25 larger ships. The importance of small vessels, however defined, is an indication of how dispersed the later-seventeenth-century sack trade was. Again, a resilient vernacular capitalism remained surprisingly persistent within an industry that had seen a century of projects meant to direct the trade toward centralization, if not actual monopoly.[34]

The businesses of catching and freighting fish complemented one another. Many voyages combined the two enterprises, and, when ships were devoted completely to one purpose, they depended on a working relationship with a ship or ships devoted to the other purpose. Not surprisingly, some West Country merchants followed John Rashleigh's example and operated both sacks and ships fishing. There were, however, regional differences in emphasis (Table 7). Most north Devon ships fished and went to market, whereas ships from the south Devon ports of Topsham

33. James Houblon to CTP, Mar. 20, 1675, CO 1/65 (23), 97–98; Lancelott Richards, Examination, Feb. 15, 1634, HCA 13/50, 608–609.

34. Berry, "List of Ships," Sept. 12, 1675, CO 1/35 (17i), 136–148.

Table 7. *Ships at Newfoundland, 1675, from English Ports*
by Activities and Itineraries

Number of Ships

Home Port (Total Ships)	Mean Tons	Sack to		Fishing to		No Data
		Market	England	Market	England	
Dartmouth (41)	120	20	0	4	15	2
Bideford (25)	74	3	2	16	0	4
London (21)	113	19	0	1	0	1
Plymouth (20)	93	10	2	4	3	1
Topsham (18)	52	13	0	2	3	0
Bristol (9)	59	8	0	0	0	1
Poole (8)	68	0	0	1	2	5
Weymouth (8)	76	4	0	2	1	1
Southampton (7)	98	2	0	4	0	1
Barnstaple (6)	86	2	0	4	0	0
Guernsey (5)	51	1	0	4	0	0
Teignmouth (2)	30	0	1	1	0	0
Brixham (1)	80	0	0	0	1	0
Falmouth (1)	120	1	0	0	0	0
Gosport (1)	50	1	0	0	0	0
Yarmouth (1)	120	1	0	0	0	0
Total (174)	81	85	5	43	25	16

Notes: "Sack Ships" are vessels carrying no boats, no more than 2 boats, or, in the case of vessels of less than 50 tons, only 1 boat.

Source: John Berry, "A List of Ships Makinge Fishinge Voyages; with Boatkeepers . . . ," Sept. 12, 1675, CO 1/35 (17i), 136–148.

and Plymouth were predominantly sacks. Dartmouth was heavily engaged in both aspects of the trade. London and Bristol freighted sack ships exclusively, although Bristol's were much smaller. If there were tensions between ships fishing and ships trading in this period, these were intramural West Country affairs as much as a struggle between the West and London. Whether the western ports had always controlled their own freighting is another question. For decades, the West Country had exported Newfoundland fish in Dutch bottoms. Eventually the business was dispersed, which was not quite what Kirke and his London associates had planned, but their short-lived attempt at a monopoly marks the point at which England began to exclude the Netherlands from the profits of the sack trade.[35]

⅗ Voyage of a Sack Ship: The Faith of London, 1634

Kirke, Barkeley, and company's shipping interests in the 1630s are an indication of their experience in Atlantic commerce before they committed themselves to the cod trade by appropriating the Newfoundland Plantation in 1638. The itineraries of particular vessels trace the trades in which Kirke, Barkeley, and company were involved. Charter parties, examinations of witnesses for the High Court of Admiralty, and instructions to the master have survived for the 1634 voyage of the 240-ton *Faith* of London, freighted by John Delabarre from Kirke, Barkeley, and company. These documents provide a vivid picture of the complex arrangements made for the voyage of a Newfoundland sack ship and suggest that the Kirkes' contacts with Newfoundland grew from their earlier Canada trade.[36]

Delabarre instructed Thomas Bredcake, master of the *Faith*, to "make all haste possible" to get to Newfoundland before late July. There he was to load four thousand quintals of "good merchantable drie Newfoundland fishe of 112 lbs. weight to the quintall" from three Dartmouth ships: the *Eagle*, the *Ollive*, and the *Desire*. Delabarre had arranged with Richard Lane, an experienced fish broker of Dittisham, near Dartmouth, for letters instructing the masters of these three ships to deliver fish at eleven shillings per quintal, which Bredcake was to pay with bills of exchange drawn on Delabarre in London. Presale of the fish and the ac-

35. Matthews, "Fisheries," 68–73; Stephens, "West Country Ports," *RT Devon*, LXXXVIII (1956), 90–101. The historiographic tradition that pits a sack ship interest against a fishing ship interest is no longer compelling; see Matthews, "Historical Fence Building," *Newfoundland Studies*, XVII (2001), 143–165. For late versions of the traditional view, see K. G. Davies, *The North Atlantic World in the Seventeenth Century* (Minneapolis, Minn., 1974), 156–168; and Glanville James Davies, "England and Newfoundland: Policy and Trade, 1660–1783" (Ph.D. diss., University of Southampton, 1980), 46.

36. The freighting and financing of sack ships in the first half of the seventeenth century are reasonably well understood; see Davis, *English Shipping*, 228–249, 338–346; Cell, *English Enterprise*, 18–21; Steele, "Instructing the Master," *Mariner's Mirror*, LXIII (1977), 191–193.

companying letters of credit were normal business practice in the New-foundland trade of the period. Delabarre's instructions touched on al-most every conceivable detail, even stowage and the possibility of default. What is not mentioned is where *Faith* would find *Desire* and her com-panions. Either Bredcake was expected to know where these ships would fish or was to find them promptly through word-of-mouth.[37]

The Newfoundland voyage went fairly smoothly. The *Faith* arrived July 22 and had soon taken on 3,784 quintals. One of the Dartmouth masters "fayled of his number of fish," as Bredcake later put it, but with the fish supplied and 1,000 quintals obtained from another fishing mas-ter, the ship had a good cargo. Once loaded, the *Faith* was not to delay "but [to] sail directly, and to be there one of the first, to Cartagena," and so it departed August 8. Delabarre emphasized: "It doth much concerne me to be first at markett, in the saille of my fishe." If delivered, the fish would have been worth about 127,000 reals, that is, £3,575. The *Faith* arrived at Cartagena on October 1, where Bredcake sold 1,635 quintals to the local factor for Delabarre's Spanish customer, John Romeno of Madrid. On October 22, Romeno's agent sent the *Faith* on to Barcelona, where another factor took most of the remaining cargo. Romeno's factors were to pay a freight deposit of 32,000 reals, that is, £900, on delivery, or to return Spanish goods for England. If the *Faith* was not reloaded at Cartagena, it was to go to Alicante, Majorca, or Malaga for freight. Dela-barre had specified that the *Faith* should unload within twenty days and reload within thirty. He had asked Bredcake "to be a good steward" and take "spetiall care that I runn in no daies of demurrage," that is, delay of the vessel in port beyond the time agreed with Kirke, Barkeley, and company, with a penalty of £5 per day.[38]

The execution of these instructions required a certain discretion. Dela-barre warned Bredcake, "By noe means lett not my factor know that I have your ship absolutely out and home," asking him to mislead the Spaniards by pretending that Delabarre had the ship for the voyage from Newfoundland to Spain and home to London at a flat rate of £5 10s. a ton

37. Delabarre, "Memorandum for Master Thomas Breadcake," 1634, HCA 15/5, in Davis, *English Shipping*, 236–238. On Lane, see Cell, *English Enter-prise*, 19.

38. Thomas Bredcake, Libel, in *Bredcake v. Kirke et al.*, Apr. 22, 1635, HCA 24/90 (165); Thomas Bredcake, Examination, in *Kirke v. Delabarre*, June 22, 1635, HCA 13/52, 23–24; David Kirke et al. and John De La Barre, Charter Party, May 1, 1634, HCA 15/5, n.p.; cf. Davis, *English Shipping*, 239.

for 240 tons—or £1,320. This rate would leave Delabarre in a position to claim costs of £420 on any cargo freighted in Spain for London. In fact, Delabarre had freighted the *Faith* from Kirke, Barkeley, and company for the Newfoundland-Spain and Spain-London legs of the voyage at £5 per ton, calculated on the Spanish cargo delivered to London. This rate for sack ships became standard in the 1630s, although the normal practice was to base the charges on the tonnage of fish on the Newfoundland-Spain leg of the voyage. Contracted separately, the freight on Newfoundland fish to Spain was about £4 per ton, and on Spanish goods to London it was £1 10s.–£2 per ton. The multilateral rate of £5 per ton remained stable through the rest of the century, suggesting that the industry had reached some kind of maturity by 1640.[39]

The problem that Kirke, Barkeley, and company faced in this particular case was that in late November 1634 a lieutenant general of the Spanish galleys "violentlie and passionattly" ordered *Faith*'s cables cut, so that the ship was lost at Barcelona and, therefore, could not return to London nor carry cargo homeward from Spain. Kirke, Barkeley, and company, naturally enough, wanted payment for freight to Spain and argued in the Court of Admiralty, against precedent, that the charges had been implied in their contract with Delabarre. But Admiralty law was clear on the issue: "When Ships are fraighted going and comming, there is nothing due for fraight until the whole Voyage be performed. So that if she perish, or be taken in the comming home, all is lost and nothing due unto her for any fraight outwards." Delabarre argued, of course, that he owed no freight, since *Faith* had not completed its voyage.[40]

The ensuing mare's nest of documents filed in this and a related case indicates that the Kirkes and their associates were not the owners of the *Faith* at all but that they had chartered it in mid-April 1634 from its

39. Kirke and Delabarre, Charter Party, May 1, 1634, HCA 15/5, n.p.; cf. David Kirke et al., Interrogatories, in *Kirke v. Delabarre*, ca. 1635, HCA 23/11 (217); Bredcake, Examination, in *Kirke v. Delabarre*, June 22, 1635, HCA 13/52, 23–24. On rates, see Davis, *English Shipping*, 236, 239. The Dutch sometimes used this tonnage system; see Guillelmo Bartolotti and Dirck Jonas, Charter Party regarding *den St. Joris*, May 20, 1634, GA Amsterdam NA 410, 53–54, NAC MG 18 012/55.

40. Bredcake, Libel, in *Bredcake v. Kirke et al.*, Apr. 22, 1635, HCA 24/90 (165); Bredcake, Examination, in *Kirke v. Delabarre*, June 22, 1635, HCA 13/52, 23–24; Kirke, Interrogatories, in *Kirke v. Delabarre*, ca. 1635, HCA 23/11 (217); Gerard Malynes, *Consuetudo, vel, Lex Mercatoria; or, The Antient Law-Merchant . . .* , 2d ed. (London, 1636), 98.

master and part-owner, Bredcake. They had the ship on a time charter, with a crew of thirty-seven men and two boys, for nine months at
£145 per month for a voyage "unto the Gulfe and river of Canada." A
provision in the charter party regarding the cost of gunpowder "spent
. . . in defence" suggests that both owners and freighters feared French
hostility. The *Faith* was then to sail to Newfoundland, for a "full lading
of fish," before proceeding to Spain for another cargo. Kirke, Barkeley,
and company promptly let the ship to freight to John Delabarre, for the
Newfoundland-Spain and Spain-London legs of the voyage, on the terms
described above.[41]

The Kirkes' involvement with Newfoundland came as an extension
of their efforts to participate in the Canada trade. The 1633 voyage of
the *St. George* had also been a combined Canada-Newfoundland venture,
which Kirke, Barkeley, and company had planned as a voyage into the
River of Canada, with Delabarre employing the vessel as a sack on the
return voyage from the New World. On May 17, 1634, the *St. George* set
sail for Canada again, under the command of Lewis Kirke, with Bredcake's *Faith* and another vessel, the *Aaron*, carrying hatchets, knives,
blankets, and other goods appropriate for the fur trade. Off the Cornish
coast, a storm broke the *Aaron*'s main and foremast. After his little convoy limped into Plymouth, Lewis sent his brother James to London with
the bad news, and James returned with instructions from David Kirke to
"give over his designe for Canada and proceed direct for Newfoundland."
The Kirkes' decision to call off the Canada voyage might have been dictated by delay or by fear that two ships could not achieve what they had
planned with three, recalling the loss of the *Mary Fortune* the previous
year.[42]

Whatever the reasons for their commercial disengagement from the
St. Lawrence, by the mid-1630s efficient deployment of their shipping

41. Thomas Bredcake and David Kirke et al., Charter Party, Apr. 18, 1634,
HCA 15/4, n.p.

42. Bredcake, Examination, in *Kirke v. Delabarre*, June 22, 1635, HCA 13/52,
23–24; Mr. Ford, "Winthrop in the London Port Books," MHS, *Proceedings*,
XLVII (Boston, 1913–1914), 178–190; Bredcake, Libel, in *Bredcake v. Kirke et al.*,
Apr. 22, 1635, HCA 24/90 (165). The itinerary for the *Faith* was more efficient
than the itinerary of the *Phoenix* of Yarmouth, which Kirke, Barkeley, and company had freighted to Newfoundland and, thence, to Canada ca. 1631; see Alexander Rice, Examination, in *Kirke et al. v. Allen and Simonds*, Aug. 10, 1632, HCA
13/50, 85.

had involved Kirke, Barkeley, and company in the Newfoundland sack trade. The Kirkes were not yet shipping their own fish but depended on those still-rare London merchants, like John Delabarre, with contacts in the trade. Within a few more years, the Kirkes became key players in the Newfoundland trade, not merely shipowners but proprietors of a major fishing plantation, in a successful effort to preempt the Dutch share of the carrying trade. Why did these London merchants invest in a permanent fishing station?

⅋⅋ The Rationale for Investment in Newfoundland

When John Delabarre freighted a vessel from Kirke, Barkeley, and company for a sack voyage, both parties could hope for substantial profits, if all went well. In the 1630s, a 250-ton freighter on a voyage from Newfoundland to Spain stood to earn something like £465, representing a profit of 14 percent on expenses of about £3,300, mostly for fish and freight (Table 8). Earnings from wine or other goods shipped to England from Spain would add to this return, without much affecting costs, because freight charges for the whole voyage were normally based on the tonnage of fish shipped: "The retorne from Spaine haveing fraight free," as a 1616 estimate of profits noted. Since this additional income could be earned by reinvestment of proceeds from the sale of fish, successful trade on this leg of a sack voyage might double the freighter's profits. Shipowners like Kirke, Barkeley, and company could also do well from such voyages. Against freighting income of about £1,000, they paid for wages, victualing, and annual repairs. Owners should also have set something aside for depreciation, even if not so conceptualized. If total annual costs were about £870, they stood to make £130 on the voyage, which was less than the freighter's profit but about the same rate of return that the freighter might expect on his cargo of fish.[43]

43. Ralph Davis, "Earnings of Capital in the English Shipping Industry, 1670–1730," *Journal of Economic History*, XVII (1957), 409–425; Davis, *English Shipping*, 338–346, 369–372; "Costs and Profits of a Newfoundland Voyage" (1616), in Cell, *English Enterprise*, appendix C. For profits in the French fishing trade, of up to 30 percent, see Robert Richard, "Comptes et profits de navires terreneuviers du Havre au XVIIe siècle (aspects économiques et sociaux)," *Revue d'Histoire Économique et Sociale*, LIV (1976), 476–509. Because the normal working life of early modern vessels is not agreed upon, rates of depreciation are uncertain. Davis, *En-*

Table 8. *Estimated Annual Earnings of a 250-Ton Newfoundland Sack Ship, 1630s*

	Freighter	Owner
Expenses		
Fish, 4,000 quintals @ 11s. per quintal	£2,200	
Freight, £5 per ton, 200 tons	1,000	
Pilotage, port charges, bribes	25	
Insurance on cargo, @ 4% of £2,200	90	
Wages, 36-man crew for 8 months		£380
Victualing, 36 men for 8 months		240
Annual repairs		150
Depreciation		100
(Subtotal to Spain	3,315	870)
Insurance on Spanish goods @ 4% of £2,200	90	
Total for triangular trade	£3,405	£870
Income		
4,480 Spanish quintals of fish @ 30 reals per quintal	£3,780	
Freight charges		£1,000
(Subtotal to Spain	3,780	1,000)
Net income on Iberian goods carried to England	575	
Total for triangular trade	£4,355	£1,000
Profit		
Voyage to Spain	£465	£130
Voyage to London	485	
Total	£950	£130
Rate of profit on voyage to Spain	14%	15%
Rate of profit on triangular voyage	28%	

Note: Profit on cargo from Spain should be regarded as a maximum.

Source: Peter Pope, "Adventures in the Sack Trade: London Merchants in the Canada and Newfoundland Trades, 1627–1648," *Northern Mariner*, VI (1996), 1–19 (esp. 10, table 1).

If such investments could be turned over once a year, a return of 15 percent for shipowners and up to twice that for freighters makes the sack trade sound attractive. Indeed, successful voyages were attractive propositions. The profits of one voyage, however, might easily be eaten up by losses on others. Vessel insurance was rare in the seventeenth century; owners gambled that their ships would not be lost to natural or human forces. The division of shipownership into shares spread this risk, but losses had to be made good from profits on successful voyages. Shipowning in the seventeenth century was not, apparently, itself a profitable enterprise. Average profitability was a remote and irrelevant concept for shipowners of the period, however; they paid more attention to the wide variability of profits and losses. Merchants must, nevertheless, have noticed the potential discrepancy between owners' and freighters' profits in the fish and wine trades, raising the question of why anyone would bother investing in a ship. The answer seems to be that major shareholders had some call on the use of the vessel. In other words, although shipownership itself might not have been profitable, it facilitated commercial adventures, like the Newfoundland sack trade, with high profit potential. This analysis is certainly consistent with the many owner-freighters in the sack trade, like the Delabarres and the Kirkes. Colonial merchants, which David Kirke would become, had additional reasons to commit themselves financially to the cost of shipownership: to assure dependable communications, supplies, and defense.[44]

The critical factors tending to profit or loss had different impacts on freighters and owners. In the Newfoundland sack trade, three considerations were of utmost importance for freighters: procurement of a full cargo of fish, a good price at market, and a reasonably full return cargo from southern Europe to London. These concerns are evident in Delabarre's instructions to Bredcake, in which he stressed the obligation of the Dartmouth masters to provide the *Faith* with fish, the importance of getting to market quickly, and Bredcake's duty to obtain a return cargo

---

glish *Shipping*, 376, suggests depreciation of 4 percent per annum, that is, one hundred pounds on a ship worth twenty-five hundred pounds, a ratio adopted here. Andrews, *Ships, Money, and Politics*, 32, suggests ships rarely survived more than fifteen years, implying somewhat higher depreciation.

44. Davis, *English Shipping*, 363–387; Davis, "Earnings of Capital," *Jour. Econ. Hist.*, XVII (1957), 409–425; W. Brulez, "Shipping Profits in the Early Modern Period," *Low Countries History Yearbook*, XVII (1981), 65–84; Andrews, *Ships, Money, and Politics*, 29–33.

from Spain. The normal system of tying freight charges for sack ships to the tonnage of cod taken to market meant owners were even more dependent than freighters on adequate cargoes. Consider the earnings for freighter and owner estimated above. If the freighter obtained only two-thirds of a cargo of fish, his costs would be proportionately reduced, and he would still make at least £275. For the shipowners, the voyage would result in a serious loss, since a reduced freight of only £670 would not even cover costs—hence the great stress those letting ships to freight put on the quantity of fish shipped.

Kirke, Barkeley, and company voiced this concern in a curious case involving the three-hundred-ton *Hector*, which had gone to Newfoundland about 1637, ballasted with relatively bulky rock rather than with lead. The Kirkes argued that when merchants freighted ships for the Newfoundland fishery they usually used lead for ballast, "in regard that Newfoundland fish is a light commoditie." The freighters of the *Hector*, they complained, had used stone ballast, reducing space in the hold for the cargo of fish by forty to sixty tons. At £4 or £5 per ton the shortfall in freight charges collected by Kirke, Barkeley, and company was about £250—more than their likely profit on the voyage. Ships in the Newfoundland trade did carry lead. John Rashleigh's small sack ship the *Tryfell* carried about a ton and a half of lead on its Newfoundland voyage of 1608. A surviving 1640 London Port Book records exports of "birdinge shott" and a ton of cast lead on the *Sarah Bonadventure* and two hundred "pigges" of lead on the *Judith*, both of London and bound for Newfoundland, and William Matthews took the *Marygold* of London to the Canaries carrying one hundred "small pigges of lead" for William Barkeley. Such records of lead exports in Port Books may well indicate the intention to carry a light cargo like dry fish, which was not subject to impost and which therefore passed through British ports without record.[45]

Disputes about ballast were less common, however, than litigation over good faith in securing an adequate cargo of fish. The unfortunate voyage of the *Thomasina* of London in 1637 was a case in point. It was on a time rather than a tonnage charter, which reversed the interests of freighter and owner vis-à-vis the size of the cargo. The critical impor-

45. Kirke et al., Libel, in *Kirke v. Jennings*, Jan. 7, 1639, 24/97 (232); Scantlebury, "John Rashleigh," *Royal Institution of Cornwall Journal*, VIII (1978–1981), 61–71 (esp. 66); London Searcher, Port Books (Exports of Denizens), 1640, E 190/44/1, 91–93. For another cargo of lead and dry fish, see William Bayley, Deposition, Feb. 4, 1653, *Bristol Depositions*, II, 139.

tance of an assured supply of fish in Newfoundland remains clear. Immediately on arrival in Newfoundland, the master, Thomas Shaftoe, had taken the ship to Fermeuse—but his designated suppliers "had no fish to lade abord her but had sould it away." Shaftoe therefore took the ship to Cape Broyle, where the planter Robert Gord was "consigned for part of his ladinge." Unfortunately, Gord was just loading a ship with fish, and the best he could promise was to make more fish "as soone as the weather would permitt." It took a month for the *Thomasina* to obtain six hundred quintals there. The ship then went to Carbonear, where it managed to get one thousand quintals immediately. At this point, Shaftoe warned the merchants' factor Walter Willimson that the *Thomasina's* time charter had expired and that they were due at market. Willimson objected that he had more fish to lade for his employer. At the factor's "earnest intreatie," Shaftoe took the time to go to Trinity, where they did manage to take on more fish before making a late departure for Portugal in September. Once finally at sea, the *Thomasina* met "an extraordinary great storme," which it only barely survived with the loss of the main mast.[46]

The sack trade was not without its risks, and a major one, besides those common to all deep-sea voyages, was that a full cargo of fish would not be obtained. As owners of ships let on tonnage charters for the Newfoundland sack voyage, Kirke, Barkeley, and company were dependent on the ability of their freighters to obtain full cargoes of fish. Merchants who managed to keep their vessels in particular trades did so by building the local relations that assured the good cargoes and quick turnarounds essential for regular profits. These relationships were particularly important in the Newfoundland trade. Metropolitan interlopers, whether based in Amsterdam or London, would have found it difficult to find assured cargoes without the assistance of West Country brokers like Richard Lane or Ritsert Heijnmers. The relationship between Kirke, Barkeley, and company and John Delabarre in the 1630s suggests that the latter had the experience and contacts to secure cargoes of fish that the former did not. From the Kirkes' point of view, this relationship would have been less than satisfactory, since the conditions of the tonnage charter left them, as shipowners, open to serious loss if the freighter's Newfoundland contacts failed him. Control of a Newfound-

46. Thomas Read, Examination, in *Wheatley et al. v. Herringe et al.*, Jan. 10, 1639, HCA 13/54, 396–399. For problems with freighting ships by the month from the freighter's point of view, see Paige to Paynter and Clerke, Feb. 16, 1652, in Paige, *Letters*, document 53.

land plantation was not the only way metropolitan merchants like the Kirkes could find a footing in the Newfoundland trade, but it might achieve this end if it would guarantee a supply of fish.[47]

47. For example, the *John and Ambrose*, ca. 1647; see Petter Milbery, Examination, May 8, 1648, HCA 13/61, 50–51. Cf. Jean Oort and Jan Schram, Charter Party regarding *de Coninck David*, Apr. 1, 1624, GA Amsterdam NA 631, 68–70, NAC MG 18 012/35; John Fletcher et al., Depositions, Jan. 21, 1631, *Southampton Examinations*, II, 77–78; Paige to Paynter and Clerke, Jan. 16, 1650, in Paige, *Letters*, document 11b; Davis, *English Shipping*, 345; Price, *Perry of London*, 28–51. The Kirkes sometimes let ships to freight on time charters, but the ships they freighted for the Newfoundland sack voyage in the 1630s were let on tonnage charters.

4 ⚘ PLANTING COUNTRIES

*In the case of planting countreys, as in that of planting woods,
you must account to lose almost twenty years profit and expect your
recompence in the end, it being necessary the province should first
find her self, and then enrich you.*
—David Lloyd, "Observations on the Life of Sir George Calvert,"
    1670

The seventeenth-century resident fishery on the English Shore south
of St. John's had its roots in Sir George Calvert's Province of Avalon, just
as settlement in Conception Bay had roots in the Newfoundland Company's colony at Cupids of 1610. In this sense, the better-organized early
proprietorships, despite their failure as investments, had some success
in promoting colonization of Newfoundland's English Shore. Calvert's
project was the best-capitalized of the proprietary plantations. Further
investment followed David Kirke's appropriation of Ferryland in 1638.
When the Royal Navy commodores took censuses of the Newfoundland
fishery in the 1670s and 1680s, Ferryland was one of the more populous
and stable Newfoundland settlements, characterized then by large plantations and a relatively strong commitment to agriculture. Four decades
after their arrival, the Kirkes still dominated this community: in 1677,
three generations of the extended family occupied five separate plantations. On the eve of the French invasion of 1696, three of David Kirke's
sons remained substantial planters in the south Avalon. Lord Baltimore
did not profit from his Newfoundland investments, but Sir David Kirke
and his heirs did. Furthermore, the tenacity of the Kirkes appears to
have fostered the persistence of other, less-well-connected planters. Merchants had compelling reasons to interest themselves in settlement, and
London merchants were not the only ones to do so.[1]

---

1. William Poole, "A Particular Accompt of All the Inhabitants and Plant-
ers . . . ," Sept. 10, 1677, CO 1/41 (61iv, vi, vii), 158–166; Richard Hartnoll et al.,
Deposition, Sept. 15, 1707, CO 194/4 (77ix), 316. For emphasis on failure, see
Innis, *Cod Fisheries*, 70; Cell, *Newfoundland Discovered*, 56, 302; Handcock, *Ori-
gins*, 33; David J. Starkey, "Devonians and the Newfoundland Trade," *Maritime
History of Devon*, I, 163–171.

The dependence of the Newfoundland Plantation's London promoters on West Country partners, evident in the record of their Newfoundland trade, underlines the enduring vernacular character of the West Country fishery at Newfoundland—despite involvement of these metropolitan merchant capitalists. Local connections between particular harbors on the English Shore and particular West Country ports were not, however, immutable. They shifted under the pressure of national and international tensions. In the mid-seventeenth century, Newfoundland's relationship with New England intensified as the continental colonies developed, a relationship that was given impetus by commercial disruption in the metropolis during the English Civil War (1642-1648). Of course, Ferryland and the Kirkes had their own particular commercial networks, which were paralleled, not duplicated, elsewhere on the English Shore.[2]

The original English colonization of the south Avalon was initiated by William Vaughan; Henry Cary, Lord Falkland; and George Calvert, Lord Baltimore—none of whom was, in anything but an incidental sense, a fish merchant. Settlement was, however, considerably reinvigorated after 1638 by the Kirkes, merchants with wide interests in the Newfoundland sack trade in fish and wine. This transition is an instance of a more general trend in the Atlantic world: the new colonial merchants of the period—like John, James, and David Kirke—developed trade in North America, where the large company merchants and the gentry had failed, because these latecomers accepted risks, profit margins, and methods of operation that their predecessors would not consider. Prior involvement in the Newfoundland sack trade was not the only reason David Kirke became one of the lords proprietor of Newfoundland. Sir David defended the plantation of Newfoundland with imperialistic braggadocio and made a convincing argument for the strategic value of Newfoundland to Britain. Such considerations did not, however, preclude commercial motivation, as he himself emphasized. Contrasting patterns of merchant and gentry participation in early imperial ventures suggest that merchant investors were primarily concerned with profits, whereas gentry investors tended to have some vision of national enterprise with respect to the expansion of sovereign territory. Although these conclusions verge on the self-evident (merchant capitalists sought profit, and landowners sought landownership), they are of analytic value in understanding how the investment Kirke, Barkeley, and company made in

2. Cf. Handcock, *Origins*, 46-52.

Newfoundland differed from that made by their predecessor, Sir George Calvert, first Baron Baltimore.[3]

⁊⁓ Metropolitan Investment at Ferryland: The Calverts

The grant of the Province of Avalon that James I made to George Calvert in 1623 is, among other things, title to a particular "portion of land"—a "lot" with specific bounds from Aquaforte, just south of Ferryland, to Petty Harbour, just south of St. John's, with all territory inland. Calvert had dominion over "ports, harbours, creeks and soyles, lands, woods, etc." as well as "fishing for all sorts of fish." He recognized that the fishery would be the main support of his plantation, and Ferryland remained, after its permanent settlement, a "fishing adventure." The Province was not created, however, so Lord Baltimore could go fishing; James I's secretary of state became involved in the fishery to further the development of his Newfoundland property. In 1629, when he petitioned for another North American province, he blamed this change of heart on the miserable weather he and his family had endured in Newfoundland in 1628–1629; but the economic climate was probably as much a factor as the "sadd face of winter." The fishery was in severe decline when Calvert withdrew from his Newfoundland adventure. In the late 1620s, wars with France and Spain, as well as economic troubles, reduced the trade to about a third of its level in the balmy days when the Province of Avalon had been planned. Calvert obtained another carefully bounded proprietorship in Chesapeake Bay, far to the south, and departed Newfoundland in 1629, satisfied "to committ this place to fishermen."[4]

3. Cell, *English Enterprise*, 81–96; Robert Brenner, *Merchants and Revolution: Commercial Change, Political Conflict, and London's Overseas Traders, 1550–1653* (Princeton, N.J., 1993), 107n, 112; David Kirke, "Narrative Made by the Latt Governor," ca. 1652, British Library, Egerton MS 2395, 259–261; David Kirke, "Reply to the Answeare to the Description of Newfoundland," Sept. 29, 1639, CO 1/10 (38), 97–114; Theodore K. Rabb, *Enterprise and Empire: Merchant and Gentry Investment in the Expansion of England, 1575–1630* (Cambridge, Mass., 1967), 41. Henry Kirke, *The First English Conquest of Canada* (London, 1871), 94–97, stresses his ancestor's strategic vision.

4. James I, "Grant of the Province of Avalon," Apr. 7, 1623, CO 195/1 (1), 1–10, in Matthews, *Constitutional Laws*, 39–63; George Cottington to John Finet, Apr. 7, 1628, British Library, Sloane MSS 3827, 124–125, in Cell, *Newfoundland Discovered*, 227–229; cf. Cecil Calvert, Libel, in *Baltimore v. Kirke*, HCA 24/110

Calvert's attitude to colonial investment probably differed from that of the later Newfoundland patentees. His Restoration biographer, David Lloyd, contrasted Calvert's efforts with Chief Justice Sir John Popham's backing of the Plymouth Company's short-lived Maine colony of 1607: "Judg Popham and Sir George Calvert agreed not more unanimously in the publick design of planting than they differed in the private. . . . [Popham] sent . . . the lewdest, [Calvert] the soberest people: the one was for present profit, the other for a reasonable expectation." By 1625, Calvert was said to "draw back yeerly some benefit," but he certainly did not recoup his substantial Newfoundland investment in the nine years of active proprietorship between 1621 and 1629. The extent of his investment supports his biographer's analysis; surely, he did not expect profit in the short term. He invested a significant part of his personal fortune in his Newfoundland plantation. Cecil Calvert, second Baron Baltimore, gave retrospective figures escalating from £20,000 in 1637 to £30,000 in 1660. Independent contemporary estimates ranged between £12,000 and £25,000. Some of George Calvert's colonists later gave figures of £17,000–£18,000, citing his own estimates.[5]

---

(329); George Calvert to Charles I, Aug. 19, 1629, CO 1/5 (27), 75; Cell, *English Enterprise*, 106–107. The idea that the Avalon colony was established as a Roman Catholic religious refuge has been discredited; see R. J. Lahey, "The Role of Religion in Lord Baltimore's Colonial Enterprise," *Maryland Historical Magazine*, LXXII (1977), 492–511; and Lahey, "Avalon: Lord Baltimore's Colony in Newfoundland," in G. M. Story, ed., *Early European Settlement and Exploitation in Atlantic Canada* (St. John's, 1982), 115–138; Cell, *Newfoundland Discovered*, 47–48. On Calvert's retirement from Newfoundland, see Cell, *English Enterprise*, 94–95; Cell, *Newfoundland Discovered*, 53–56.

5. David Lloyd, *State-Worthies; or, The States-Men and Favourites of England since the Reformation* . . . , 2d ed. (London, 1670), 750–752; William Alexander, *An Encouragement to Colonies* (London, 1624), 25; James Meddus to Katherine Conway, June 27, 1627, SP 16/108 (37), 80; Cecil Calvert, "Lord Baltimore's Case," Dec. 23, 1651, British Library, Egerton MS 2395, 310, in L. D. Scisco, "Calvert's Proceedings against Kirke," *CHR*, VIII (1927), 132–136; Cecil Calvert, Memorandum, February 1637, CO 1/9 (43), 108; Cecil Calvert, Petition to Charles II, June 17, 1660, CO 1/14 (9), 13; Philis Davies, "The Examination and Deposition . . . ," Aug. 24, 1652, Amy Taylor, "The Examinations and Depositions . . . ," Aug. 24, 1652, and John Slaughter, "The Examination and Deposition . . . ," Aug. 31, 1652, all in Md. HS, Calvert MSS 174/200, in Scisco, "Testimony"; cf. Peter E. Pope, "Baltimore vs. Kirke: Newfoundland Evidence in an Interregnum Lawsuit," *Avalon Chronicles*, III (1998), 63–98. Cell, *Newfoundland Discovered*,

Even if the first Lord Baltimore spent just seventeen thousand pounds on the Province of Avalon (something like one and a half million dollars today), what did this substantial investment buy? Early colonists recalled that Calvert provided "ships and boates for fishing." One suggested that Calvert kept thirty-two boats, probably at Ferryland itself; another that he kept as many as one hundred, probably within the bounds of his province, between Aquaforte and Bay Bulls. One hundred boats would have cost at least three thousand pounds outfitted—but the colony's fishing activity, surely, paid for itself. Shipping would have represented a more significant expense on Calvert's balance sheet. The *Anne*, which was built in the Province of Avalon itself, was probably the "barke of 60 tonnes" that Calvert sent in company with the *Benediction* of 360 tons to defend Cape Broyle against the French privateer Raymonde de La Rade in 1628. A ship of 60 tons was worth at most five hundred pounds, but a ship of 360 tons could be valued at three thousand pounds. Calvert could well have chartered the *Benediction*, however, as he chartered at various times the *Jonathan*, the *Peter Bonadventure*, and the *City of Poole*. He also had two ships at Dartmouth, bound for Ferryland in 1627, the 160-ton *Arke* of Avalon and the 140-ton *George* of Plymouth. These were probably the ships that Calvert owned with other investors in his Newfoundland "fishing adventure," an arrangement that went sour during his stay in Ireland, between 1625 and 1627. Calvert's shipping costs must have been considerable, whether for overhead on ships owned or freight charges on ships chartered. He claimed a loss of two thousand pounds for ships and servants employed in action in 1628, "thereby neglecting his plantation and fishinge to his prejudice." Only in peacetime would it have been possible to recover shipping costs by using his vessels as sack ships, which is how he used one of his French prizes, the *St. Claude*, in 1629. For too long, circumstance forced Calvert to use the ships at his disposal to protect the English fishery rather than to build the commerce on which his colony would have to depend, if he was ever to augment the credit side of his ledger.[6]

300–301, transcribes abstracts from the Calvert MSS, giving estimates of one-tenth the amounts in the full examinations. On Popham's Fort St. George, see David B. Quinn, *North America from Earliest Discovery to First Settlements: The Norse Voyages to 1612* (New York, 1977), 402–409.

6. Anne Love, "Examination and Deposition . . . ," Aug. 31, 1652, Slaughter, "Deposition," Aug. 31, 1652, and Taylor, "Depositions," Aug. 24, 1652, all in Md. HS, Calvert MSS 174/200, in Scisco, "Testimony"; George Calvert to the duke of

The major predictable costs for proprietors of any new colony were wages and victualing, while the colony could "find her self." By the winter of 1623, Calvert had thirty-two men and women at Ferryland and, after his own baronial household of forty persons joined the fishing plantation in 1628, his colony numbered more than one hundred. From year to year, the Calverts would have made money from their fishing crews; Cecil later claimed an annual profit of twenty to fifty pounds per boat. His father would not have recovered, in the short term, the wages and victualing costs of the quarrymen, stonelayers, smiths, and carpenters, who were equally numerous in the early days of the colony. Even if he victualed only twenty nonfishing personnel for the eight active years of his project, he would have spent something like two thousand pounds and at least as much on wages. Such expenditure, in the order of four thousand pounds, was essentially an investment in infrastructure, since these early colonists built the permanent settlement to which Calvert briefly removed himself, his family, and his entourage.[7]

Buckingham, Aug. 25, 1628, CO 1/4 (57), 141, "Relation of a Difference," December 1628, CO 1/4 (63), 151, George Calvert to John Coke, Mar. 15, 1625, George Calvert to Edward Nicholas, Apr. 7, 1627, CO 1/4 (19), all in Cell, *Newfoundland Discovered*, 270-272, 279-282, 288-289; Stephen Baker, Examination, Sept. 14, 1629, *Southampton Examinations*, II, 39-40; Cottington to Finet, Apr. 7, 1628, British Library, Sloane MSS 3827, 124-125, in Cell, *Newfoundland Discovered*, 277-279; Cell, *English Enterprise*, 94. The *Arke* and the *George* (at 220 tons and 180 tons) were at Dartmouth in October 1627 as Lord Baltimore's, but a year or so earlier they were in Plymouth (at 120 and 90 tons) as Sir James Bagg's, a probable investor in Calvert's "fishing adventure" (as well as the compiler of the list); see "A List of Ships Belonging to the Port of Dartmouth," Oct. 9, 1627, and "A List of Ships and Seamen in the Hundred of Roborough in Devon," ca. 1626, both in Todd Gray, ed., *Early-Stuart Mariners and Shipping: The Maritime Surveys of Devon and Cornwall, 1619-35* (Exeter, 1990), 84-90, 112.

7. Lloyd, *State-Worthies*, 750-752; George Calvert to Charles I, Aug. 19, 1628, CO 1/5 (27, 75); Erasmus Stourton, Examination, Oct. 9, 1628, CO 1/4 (59), 144, in Cell, *Newfoundland Discovered*, 284-285; Cecil Calvert, Libel, in *Baltimore v. Kirke*, Dec. 8, 1651, HCA 24/110 (329). Compare Baltimore's retinue with the forty-person household of a temporal lord in Gregory King, "Scheme of the Income and Expence of the Several Families of England" (ca. 1688), in Peter Laslett, *The World We Have Lost: Further Explored*, 3d ed. (London, 1983), 32-33, table 1. There were seven building craftsmen at Ferryland in 1622 and five boatmasters, fishermen, and coopers; see Edward Wynne to George Calvert, Aug. 17, 1622, in Cell, *Newfoundland Discovered*, 200-204.

Given the availability of slate and wood at Ferryland, in a period when forty pounds would build a good farmhouse, Calvert's employees were easily able to erect, within a year, not only a "strong and well contrived" house but many other structures. The archaeological evidence suggests that Calvert's Mansion House survived for at least thirty years, before being rebuilt about 1650. It was a large structure for the early Anglo-American New World: a two-story longhouse, fifteen by forty-four feet, probably of stone, partly roofed with boards, and partly with "sedge, flagges, and rushes." Under Edward Wynne's early stewardship, the colonists also built a stone kitchen, twelve by eighteen feet, with a large chimney and a "chamber" upstairs; a twelve-by-fourteen-foot "parlor" with "a lodging chamber over it"; a two-room storehouse of one and a half stories as well as a smithy, henhouse, unspecified "tenements," saltworks, and a brewhouse. Wynne also saw to the construction of an earthwork "face of defense" toward the water, a palisade around four acres of the plantation, and a wharf. Late in the summer of 1622, when Wynne already had three carpenters, a stonelayer, and a quarryman with him, he told Calvert the colony needed an additional six masons, four carpenters, two or three good quarrymen, a slater or two, and a limeburner (to prepare mortar). Captain Wynne, at least, believed the Avalon colony should be well built. Archaeological investigations indicate that he accomplished most of what he set out to do for his employer.[8]

George Calvert's most significant investments in the Province of Avalon were the "places of succour and defence for shipps," built at his expense between 1621 and 1628. Cecil Calvert subsequently claimed secure berths for fifty vessels. The best of these defended harbors was the Pool at Ferryland. Given Wynne's workforce and his preference for stone construction, the wharves and warehouses there were more solidly built than the temporary structures usual in the migratory fishery. Archaeological investigations have uncovered a seventeenth-century masonry quayside bounding one side of the Ferryland Pool and an adjacent warehouse, ex-

8. Wynne to George Calvert, July 28, Aug. 17, 1622, David Powell to George Calvert, July 28, 1622, in Cell, *Newfoundland Discovered*, 195–198, 198–200, 200–204; James A. Tuck, communication with author, July 1999; Barry Gaulton, "Seventeenth-Century Stone Construction at Ferryland, Newfoundland (Area C)," *Avalon Chronicles*, II (1997), 1–43. On building costs, see W. G. Hoskins, "The Rebuilding of Rural England, 1570–1640," *Past and Present*, no. 4 (November 1953), 44–59. Matthews, "Fisheries," 114, assumes that Wynne's reports were "fraudulent" but gives no evidence.

tended and modified through the century (Plate 1). By 1630, the Ferryland waterfront was beginning to resemble stone-built West Country ports like Dartmouth, in southwest Devon, as much as it did the wooden-built seasonal stations elsewhere on the English Shore (Map 9, Plate 8). So Calvert's biographer was probably right in saying that he built with "reasonable expectation" rather than "present profit" in mind. Unfortunately, as Charles I would point out, the "rugged and laborious beginnings" of new plantations demand "greater meanes in mannaging them then usually the power of one private subject." Furthermore, an investment strategy that accepts a high capital cost in expectation of low maintenance costs is practical only if the investor retains control over the infrastructure created.[9]

Calvert himself worried that he might lose his investments "for other men to build their fortunes upon." This fear was justified. If anyone profited from George Calvert's farsighted investment, it was Sir David Kirke. This outcome was not the result of some peculiar failing of the Calverts. Charles I habitually sold overlapping monopolies to competing interests, but George Calvert could hardly have foreseen this practice. Charles's commercialization of patronage was a departure from the exchange of favors typical of James I's court, with which Calvert was familiar. Nor could Calvert have foreseen that those coming late to colonial development would profit more than those who had committed early, nor that later metropolitan governments would rarely be able to enforce the rights of the heirs of original patentees. These patterns are evident elsewhere, for example, at Piscataqua, Maine, following John Mason's 1623 plantation. In 1675, Robert Mason was still unsuccessfully laying claim to the proprietorship of that colony, just as Cecil Calvert and his descendants continued to clamor for their rights in Newfoundland well into the eighteenth century.[10]

9. Love, "Deposition," Aug. 31, 1652, in Scisco, "Testimony"; Cecil Calvert, Interrogatories, in *Baltimore v. Kirke*, ca. 1651, HCA 23/16 (79); Gaulton, "Stone Construction," *Avalon Chronicles*, II (1997), 1–43; cf. Alaric Faulkner, "Archaeology of the Cod Fishery: Damariscove Island," *Historical Archaeology*, XIX, no. 2 (1985), 57–86; Charles I to George Calvert, Nov. 22, 1629, CO 1/5 (39), 99, in Cell, *Newfoundland Discovered*, 296–297.

10. George Calvert to Thomas Wentworth, May 21, 1627, in Cell, *Newfoundland Discovered*, 273–274; Robert Ashton, "Charles I and the City," in F. J. Fisher, ed., *Essays in the Economic and Social History of Tudor and Stuart England, in Honour of R. H. Tawney* (Cambridge, 1961), 138–163; Christopher Hill, *The Cen-*

Map 9. Plan of Dartmouth. *By Nicholas Townshend, 1619.*
Courtesy, Dartmouth Town Council and Devon Record Office, Exeter

Sir George Calvert, the original Baron Baltimore, planned a succession of plantations, first in Ireland, then in Newfoundland, and, finally, in the Chesapeake. Calvert had attained high office under James I but

---

tury of Revolution, 1603–1714 (London, 1969), 39–40; Linda Levy Peck, "'For a King Not to Be Bountiful Were a Fault': Perspectives on Court Patronage in Early Stuart England," *Journal of British Studies,* XXV (1986), 31–61; Nathaniel Adams, *Annals of Portsmouth* (Portsmouth, N.H., 1825), 9–58; John Frederick Martin, *Profits in the Wilderness: Entrepreneurship and the Founding of New England Towns in the Seventeenth Century* (Chapel Hill, N.C., 1991), 101–102; Robert Mason, ". . . Title and Case to the Province of New Hampshire . . . ," March 1675, CO 1/34 (46, 47), 103–104; Frederick Calvert, Petition, 1753, Md. HS, Calvert MSS, 174/507. The Calverts did manage to temporarily regain some rights over the south Avalon in the early 1660s.

Plate 8. Traditional Waterfront Structures in Dartmouth, Devon. Nineteenth century. Collection of Peter E. Pope

lost influence with the failure in 1623 of the Spanish plans, on which he had worked so assiduously, to marry Charles Stuart to the Infanta, Maria, daughter of Philip III, and, of course, a Roman Catholic. Retirement from court in 1625 meant Calvert could sell his office and give full attention to his plantation projects, which created a personal sphere in which he could enjoy not only the wealth he had amassed but also the status to which he had become accustomed. The charter of Avalon and the subsequent charter of Maryland gave him unusual and virtually absolute powers. Money seems to have been no object; what George Calvert sought was status as a landed proprietor.[11]

Calvert's decision to abandon Newfoundland as his family seat after a year there makes a good deal of sense, if we take these specific colonial aims into account. Several factors must have influenced his decision, including the misery of an unexpectedly severe winter, a decline in the economic cycle of the fishery, and the costs of protecting both resident and migratory fishers from French privateers. Calvert was certainly not driven out by competition from the West Country; in fact, migratory fishers assisted his colony and vice versa. This exchange, however, was not balanced: fishing masters provided his colonists with chickens and other small favors, whereas he provided them with naval protection. He rapidly learned that the costs of proprietorship in Newfoundland might be large. He must also have seen that the English Shore could not provide the landed status that he wanted for himself and his family. For this, Maryland was more promising terrain. By personally abandoning the Province of Avalon, Baltimore left the door open for others to appropriate his considerable investment at Ferryland, particularly if their operations already involved the deployment of defensible ships.[12]

?⁊ Metropolitan Investment at Ferryland: The Kirkes

Charles I's "Grant of Newfoundland" in 1637 to Marquis Hamilton, the earls of Pembroke and Holland, and Sir David Kirke was less

11. Cell, *Newfoundland Discovered*, 46–47; James I, "Grant of the Province of Avalon," Apr. 7, 1623, CO 195/1 (1), 1–10, in Matthews, *Constitutional Laws*, 39–63. On the Spanish marriage plan, see Glyn Redworth, *The Prince and the Infanta: The Cultural Politics of the Spanish Match* (New Haven, Conn., 2003).

12. Edward Winne to George Calvert, Aug. 26, 1621, in Cell, *Newfoundland Discovered*, 253–257.

a title to property than it was the grant of a commercial monopoly. It withheld property rights from the patentees in the only territory that mattered, the area near the coast: officially, they were not supposed to "plant or inhabite" within six miles of salt water. On the other hand, the patent gave Kirke and his associates administrative control of Newfoundland and permitted planters to fish, to cut wood, and "to build forts for the security of the fishing" along the shore between Cape Race and Bonavista, an exception that effectively nullified the paper ban on coastal settlement. Charles tacitly accepted Kirke's appropriation of Ferryland; and the Privy Council explicitly approved the right of the patentees to fishing rooms for their ships at three harbors clustered around the center of the English Shore (Petty Harbour, St. John's, and Torbay) and a fourth (Bay de Verde) strategically located between Conception and Trinity Bays.[13]

The patentees had rights to "the sole trade of the Newfoundland, the fishing excepted." Strangers would not be officially excluded from fishing or the sack trade on the English Shore, but the "Grant of Newfoundland" certainly discouraged them by empowering the patentees to collect a tax of 5 percent on their fish. This "impost of fish" would enable the patentees to engross the sack trade from the Dutch. Meanwhile, West Country merchants would benefit to the extent that the new tax discouraged their French competitors, who still frequented parts of the English Shore, particularly at its northern and southern limits. Together the patentees and the Western Adventurers agreed to fix the price of fish, and the patentees promised to buy and ship at least as much fish as had normally been exported by strangers (essentially the Dutch) in preceding years.[14]

13. Charles I, "A Grant of Newfoundland," Nov. 13, 1637, CO 195/1 (2), 11–27, in Matthews, *Constitutional Laws*, 77–116; Privy Council to Sir David Kirke, Mar. 11, 1640, in *APC*: Colonial. For further discussion, see Chapter 6, below. For a different interpretation of this patent, as "the most extensive grant of land made since 1610," see Cell, *English Enterprise*, 115–116.

14. Privy Council, Minutes, June 25, 1638, in *APC*: Colonial; James, Marquis Hamilton et al., Petition to Charles I, Jan. 25, 1640, SP 16/403, 78. Gillian T. Cell treats Kirke's activities as examples of a timeless struggle between "fishermen," whose interests she equates with those of West Country fish merchants and planters. For Cell, the real issue, even in *Baltimore v. Kirke*, was settlement versus the fishery; see Cell, *English Enterprise*, 114–125. The late Keith Matthews showed that the premise of inevitable conflict between fishermen and planters is not well founded and that, as an organizing principle for early modern Newfoundland his-

David Kirke's fellow patentees Henry Rich, earl of Holland (1590–1649), James Hamilton, marquis and duke of Hamilton (1606-1649), and Philip Herbert, earl of Pembroke (1584-1650) were influential policymakers and experienced colonial investors who made a considerable commitment to the project; they were not simply figureheads. Holland's family, the Riches, were among the great colonial entrepreneurs of the time, and Pembroke was one of the most influential aristocrats of the day. Hamilton was a key promoter of the wine contract of 1638, by which the London retail vintners were required to purchase a specified amount of wine at set prices from the wholesale wine importers—a scheme designed to benefit the crown, by way of taxes, as well as wine importers like Kirke, Barkeley, and company. The profit potential for a syndicate proposing to monopolize the Newfoundland sack trade in fish and wines is evident.[15]

The Patent of 1637 gave the partners in the Newfoundland Plantation some of the prerogatives of a chartered company. Since late-medieval times, the crown had granted privileges to certain merchants, independently capitalized but associated in regulated companies for the purposes of foreign trade. The Merchant Adventurers, the Eastland Company, the Russia Company, and the Levant Company were the major regulated companies of early modern England: monopolistic merchant associations to which admission was often difficult, except by inheritance. The sixteenth century saw the emergence of a more modern type of business organization, the joint-stock company, in which merchants held shares in a joint enterprise. This form of organization flourished among the smaller merchants excluded from the oligarchic regulated companies, but, confusingly, some of the grander joint-stock companies of the period also held monopolies on specific trades: the East India, Royal African, Greenland, and Hudson's Bay Companies. Joint-stock plantation companies, whether operating in Virginia, Bermuda, Massachusetts

---

tory, the fishermen-planter struggle is of limited value compared to a recognition of the interdependence of the various elements in the Newfoundland trade. Curiously, he did not apply his own generalization in this case and missed Kirke's dependence on secure West Country commercial relations. See Matthews, "Fisheries," 4-5 (abstract), 99, 136-157, 181.

15. *DNB*, s.v. "Hamilton, James," "Herbert, Philip," and "Rich, Henry"; David Kirke, "Narrative," ca. 1652, British Library, Egerton MS 2395, 259-261; Kirke, "Reply to the Answeare," Sept. 29, 1639, CO 1/10 (38), 97-114; Cell, *English Enterprise*, 114; Brenner, *Merchants and Revolution*, 111, 246-249, 284-285, 301.

Bay, or Newfoundland, claimed exclusive privileges as well. To further complicate matters, investors also formed partnerships without entering into a formal joint-stock arrangement, and such a continuing partnership might also be referred to as a "company"—for example, Kirke, Barkeley, and company.[16]

Sir David Kirke and the courtiers associated with him in the Grant of Newfoundland appear to have organized their venture as a partnership rather than as a joint-stock company: their patent specifically gives him "power to admitt merchants into their partnership." Kirke, Barkeley, and company were, from the beginning, "mannagers of the adventurers business in London." The interest of these merchants in the Newfoundland Plantation resulted from their interest in the fish trade, rather than the other way around. Their prior involvement in the region suggests that Sir David Kirke instigated the patent, finding investors who had the political connections to obtain a monopoly he wanted. This was the heyday of monopolies: inefficient as they were, Charles saw them as a source of revenue, when more traditional sources were drying up. As usual, the crown was promised its cut: a tenth of the tax on strangers shipping fish. Sir David Kirke's aristocratic associates, no less than Charles, certainly expected their share in the profits of the proposed monopoly. If this kind of predatory capitalism passed for normal in the late 1630s, the objections that the traditional West Country Adventurers trading to Newfoundland had to the Kirkes' subsequent exploitation of their trading monopoly were no less normal. When Parliament overturned many monopolies in the early 1640s, the Kirkes must have had to readjust their ambitions. Sir David's pivotal position at the intersection of the partners holding the patent with the company of merchants charged with making it profitable gave him the means and opportunity to redirect profits. By the end of the decade, the new regime, at least, was convinced that he had done so.[17]

Despite their alliance with a crown-sanctioned monopoly, Kirke,

16. William Robert Scott, *The Constitution and Finance of English, Scottish, and Irish Joint-Stock Companies to 1720*, I, *The General Development of the Joint-Stock System to 1720* (1912; rpt. New York, 1951), esp. 199–243; Perry Gauci, *The Politics of Trade: The Overseas Merchant in State and Society, 1660–1720* (Oxford, 2001), 112–137.

17. Charles I, "Grant of Newfoundland," Nov. 13, 1637, CO 195/1 (2), 11–27, in Matthews, *Constitutional Laws*, 77–116; James, Marquis Hamilton et al., Petition to Charles I, Jan. 25, 1640, SP 16/403, 78.

Barkeley, and company were typical of the interloping new merchants of the period in their personal involvement in the commercial innovation that characterized midcentury colonial projects. Since this London merchant house had patent rights in Newfoundland, at least indirectly, they were not interlopers in a legal sense, although the West Country merchants and the Calverts certainly saw them as such. Sir David Kirke's willingness to settle in Newfoundland itself, as he did in 1638, and his perseverance in the development of a circumatlantic trading network are nice examples of the kind of personal commitment typical of the new merchants. He and his brother John, in particular, were new merchants, no less than Alderman Barkeley, despite their political divergence from Barkeley in the 1640s. David Kirke's royalism was atypical of London's new merchants but consistent with his dependence on royal favor for his commercial rights. His royalism was a pattern of behavior more often seen among the privileged Merchant Adventurers and the Levant and French Company merchants but comprehensible in this case, given Kirke's particular circumstances as a "projector" with a royal patent. The Newfoundland Plantation exemplifies the alliance between colonially minded aristocrats and London's new merchants, with their connections among London retailers, ship captains, and tradesmen. The Janus-faced political allegiance of Kirke, Barkeley, and company to king and to Parliament suggests how politically complex these alliances could be.[18]

The investment made in Newfoundland by the patentees and their agents Kirke, Barkeley, and company must have been considerable, comprising not merely boats, wages, and victuals but also ordnance, commercial structures, and ships dedicated to serve the Newfoundland ter-

18. Brenner, *Merchants and Revolution*, 184–193, 281–290, 388, 643, 650, 685–686. Brenner does not consider Gervaise Kirke's sons in his analysis of the new-merchant leadership of the colonial interloping trades between 1616 and 1649 (table 4.2). Admittedly, they would complicate the analysis. To include at least one of the Kirkes in Brenner's analysis would double the royalist participation of London's new-merchant leadership from one case to two of eighty-five (table 7.1). It would slightly raise the percentage of armigerous colonial merchants and, more significant, increase the considerable majority born outside London (table 4.1). Robert Ashton has called the game of discovering royalist merchants a harmless pastime, provided that each discovery is not viewed as fresh evidence that economic interest did little to determine individual allegiance at the outbreak of the Civil War in 1642; see Ashton, "Charles I and the City," in Fisher, ed., *Tudor and Stuart England*, 146.

minus of their operations and to enforce the collection of the "impost of fish." Kirke later put initial expenses at ten thousand pounds "to sett forth shipps" and for "forthering a plantation." This sum is about half of what the Calverts claimed to have spent, although it would still represent roughly one million dollars today. In 1638, when David Kirke appropriated Ferryland, and specifically the Pool Plantation, it was no longer suitably equipped as a headquarters for a large commercial operation. Only one of Calvert's fishing boats remained, and it was "perished." Kirke and his family preempted the Mansion House from one William Hill, an agent of Cecil Calvert's, together with "six or seaven horses, 3 chaires, a table board, and an old bedstead." Apart from the house and perhaps the horses, these items were of little value. The Kirkes later claimed that Calvert's protected harbors and defenses had crumbled by this time. This assertion might have been true of the strictly military investments of the 1620s: archaeological excavations indicate that the defensive ditch and palisade erected for George Calvert by Captain Wynne were abandoned in the 1630s or 1640s. On the other hand, some of Wynne's commercial improvements survived into the 1640s, including the quayside itself, at least one warehouse, the cobbled street that ran through the community, and the smithy that he had boasted of building. Cleared gardens and pastures are also likely to have remained intact.[19]

The Kirkes added significantly to the substantial infrastructure they had appropriated. A letter to John Kirke in 1661 spoke of structures standing at Ferryland, "built by Sir David Kirke at his own proper cost and charge," and archaeologists have uncovered evidence of substantial rebuilding in the 1640s and 1650s. This shrewd and ruthless merchant family saw to a second phase of investment in Newfoundland on a scale comparable to that committed earlier to the Province of Avalon by

19. John Harrison, Jr., to John Winthrop, Aug. 11, 1639, *Winthrop Papers*, IV, 138; Kirke, "Reply to the Answeare," Sept. 29, 1639, CO 1/10 (38), 97–114; David Kirke, "Narrative," ca. 1652, British Library, Egerton MS 2395, 259–261; William Poole, "The Answere . . . upon the Interrogatories . . . ," Aug. 24, 1652, and John Slaughter, "The Answere . . . upon Interrogatories . . . ," Aug. 30, 1652, in Scisco, "Testimony"; John Pratt, Examination, in *Baltimore v. Kirke*, Mar. 12, 1652, HCA 13/65, n.p.; David Kirke, Libel, in *Baltimore v. Kirke*, Jan. 29, 1653, HCA 24/111 (120); Matthew Carter, Barry Gaulton, and James A. Tuck, "Archaeology at Ferryland, Newfoundland—1997," *Avalon Chronicles*, III (1998), 49–62, and Tuck, "Archaeology at Ferryland, Newfoundland, 1936–1995," I (1996), 21–42. The ordnance used to back up Ferryland's fortifications in the 1640s was mostly Kirke's, although some royal cannon might have remained in 1638 from the earlier colony.

George Calvert. Furthermore, this investment seems to have been profitable. Kirke, Barkeley, and company were in a position to engross much of the booming sack trade, by then well recovered from the slump of the 1620s, and there was much scope for other profits. Sir David appears to have manipulated the operations of the Newfoundland syndicate to benefit its merchant managers rather than his aristocratic fellow patentees. The patentees sent John Downing to investigate affairs in 1640, with instructions to send Sir David home. Kirke held on to his plantation in Ferryland, however, and Downing settled at St. John's, where his son (also John) would have a major plantation in the 1660s and 1670s. Although the Kirkes had aristocratic backing in the financing of their Newfoundland Plantation, profits were restricted to a closer, bourgeois circle. Nor did the crown ever receive the 10 percent share it had been promised from the patentees' impositions on strangers' fishing. Although the Kirkes were royalists, when it came to the remission of taxes political allegiance seems to have been tempered by the same commercial pragmatism that governed William Barkeley's respect for parliamentary trade ordinances.[20]

The victory of Parliament in 1648 and the trial and execution of Charles in 1649 did not bode well for Sir David Kirke. Within two years, he was under the scrutiny of a special commission appointed to look into his affairs in Newfoundland by the government of the newly proclaimed Commonwealth (1649–1653). Not entirely coincidentally, his coadventurers died early in the Interregnum. Holland and Hamilton were executed the same day, March 3, 1649; both had changed allegiance one too many times and were condemned by a Commonwealth committee, on which sat their erstwhile partner, William Barkeley. Pembroke, on

20. Charles Hill to John Kirke, Sept. 12, 1661, British Library, Egerton MS 2395, 308; Privy Council, Minutes, Nov. 29, 1639, in *APC*: Colonial; James, Marquis Hamilton et al., "Instructions for John Downing," June 20, 1640, CO 1/38 (3311), 72; John Downing II, Petition to Charles II, Nov. 7, 1676, CO 1/38 (33), 69; Council of State, Instructions to Walter Sikes et al., June 16, 1652, SP 25/29, 11–14. Barkeley himself was reputed to have left a "good estate" on his death in 1653, although it subsequently appeared that he had been bankrupted by a huge insurance loss of eight thousand pounds; see John Paige to William Clerke, Aug. 26, 1653, Apr. 25, Aug. 18, 1654, in Paige, *Letters*, documents 77a, 84b, 89e. On the 1620s slump and 1630s recovery in the fishery, see Todd Gray, "Fishing and the Commercial World of Early Stuart Dartmouth," in Gray, Margery Rowe, and Audrey Erskine, eds., *Tudor and Stuart Devon: The Common Estate and Government: Essays Presented to Joyce Youings* (Exeter, 1992), 173–199.

the other hand, supported Parliament from the outbreak of the Civil War and even represented the Good Old Cause in negotiation with the king. He passed away peacefully, however, early in 1650, leaving David Kirke not only as the sole surviving Newfoundland patentee but also as the one holding the bag, so to speak. Kirke's crimes were as much financial as political. He had been part of a royally sanctioned quasi monopoly together with three prewar grandees, whom he was reputed to have bilked of their profits. The revolutionary Council of State appointed a commission in 1651 to look into Kirke's operations at Newfoundland, with a view to recovering for the Commonwealth some of the profits he was assumed to have skimmed from his fellow patentees. The instructions to the Newfoundland commissioners and the testimony they recorded provide us with our best evidence about the profitability of the Newfoundland Plantation, although it is now impossible to be sure how much was diverted to Kirke's own pockets.[21]

The Council of State instructed their commissioners to examine witnesses on several key issues: exports to Newfoundland; the imposition on foreign ships; money received from planters for fishing, tavern licenses, and rents; the fur trade; and, finally, the profits of "fishing and buying and selling." The fur trade is not likely to have been significant: it is not even mentioned in Kirke's optimistic "Reply to the Answeare to the Description of Newfoundland" (1639). The Calverts later claimed that the 5 percent imposition on foreign fishermen and traders was worth five thousand pounds per annum, and Sir David Kirke himself once claimed ten thousand pounds, but these were overestimates, given the difficulties and costs of collection. Besides, the tax discouraged foreign ships and fishermen along the English Shore, as was probably intended. On the other hand, the "impost of fish" was often collected and, at a rate of about fifty pounds per ship, could easily have brought in hundreds or even a few thousand pounds a year in the form of "composition fish," paid in kind. In 1640, Kirke's fellow patentees had expected to obtain such composition fish, worth about three thousand pounds, although they complained that the London ship hired to enforce exactions from the French collected at least one thousand pounds less than it might have. Much depended on how many strangers' ships the Kirkes managed to tax. One merchant's estimate of thirty to forty French and Basque ships is probably closer to the mark than David Kirke's own claim of two hundred,

21. Brenner, *Merchants and Revolution*, 548; *DNB*, s.v. "Hamilton, James," "Herbert, Philip," and "Rich, Henry."

and that conservative estimate would put the annual value of the "impost," or "composition," collected closer to fifteen hundred or two thousand pounds.[22]

Kirke had other potential sources of income. Planters told the Newfoundland commissioners that he sought and obtained rents and license fees, charging, for example, £4 6s. 8d. "for a house and some ground" (presumably a fishing room) and £15 for a tavern license. He also rented fishing rooms to migratory crews. There were about three hundred fishing rooms between Renews and Bay Bulls. If Kirke collected rent for only two-thirds of these and licensed, say, twenty-five planter tippling houses, he might have collected more than £1,200 per annum from these exactions alone. Kirke was also later accused of engrossing key supplies like salt and of retailing them at high prices, and he was said to have monopolized the wholesale import of alcohol. These markets could easily have been as lucrative as licensing and rents. Although explicitly permitted by his patent, these practices clearly offended the customary expectations of some planters and many migratory fishermen. For the Council of State in the 1650s, each potential revenue source was more reason to believe that the profits of the Newfoundland Plantation in the 1630s and 1640s had remained in Kirke's hands.[23]

---

22. Council of State, "Articles for the Examining of Witnesses," Apr. 8, 1651, SP 25/65, 244; Cecil Calvert, Interrogatories, in *Baltimore v. Kirke*, ca. 1651, HCA 23/16 (79); Harrison to Winthrop, Aug. 11, 1639, *Winthrop Papers*, IV, 138; Hamilton et al., Petition to Charles I, Jan. 25, 1640, SP 16/403, 78; David Kirke, "Reply to the Answeare," Sept. 29, 1639, CO 1/10 (38), 107; cf. Cell, *English Enterprise*, 117. Lewis Kirke collected fifty pounds from a 140-ton Dutch ship in 1638 and 5 percent tax on the cargo of a 260-ton Basque ship in Trinity Bay; see Robert Allward, Examination, in *Baltimore v. Kirke*, Mar. 29, 1652, HCA 13/65, n.p.; and William Hill, Examination, in *Castmayle v. Lewis Kirke*, Apr. 16, 1642, HCA 13/58, 9–10. "Composition fish" was a term used in England's east coast Iceland fishery to refer to a toll that the crown took from the catch; see Evan Jones, "England's Icelandic Fisheries in the Early Modern Period," in David J. Starkey, Chris Reid, and Neil Ashcroft, eds., *England's Sea Fisheries: The Commercial Sea Fisheries of England and Wales since 1300* (London, 2000), 36–45. The Kirkes freighted the *Confident* from the new merchants Richard Cranley and Nathan Wright; see Brenner, *Merchants and Revolution*, 184–193, table 4.2.

23. Thomas Cruse, Richard Parker, and Gabriell Viddomas, Depositions, Nov. 27, 1667, WDRO Plymouth, W360/74; William Poole, "Account of Fishing and Sackships from Trepassy to Cape Broyle," and Poole, "Account of Fishing and Sackships from Balene to St. John's Harbour . . . ," Sept. 10, 1677, CO 1/41 (62viii,

Early in 1654, on his deathbed in London, where he had been recalled and imprisoned by the Commonwealth, David Kirke wrote a deceptively simple will, leaving the management of his whole estate to his youngest brother, James: "Deare brother . . . you knowe all my estate and how it stands. . . . I pray be carefull of [take care of] my wife and children. And what remaines thare I desire may goe to my wife and children." Yet Kirke was worth tens of thousands of pounds. Before coming to terms with the Commonwealth in 1652, he had posted a bond of forty thousand pounds. His elliptical will was probably drafted to avoid description of an estate that was very much in dispute, not within the family, but in the political arena. James, a bachelor, had already drafted a will in 1651, leaving land and houses in the home counties to David's eldest sons, Phillip and George. David may well have transferred some of his wealth, in life, to James, and he certainly made some such transfer to the second-eldest brother, Lewis. Lewis's deathbed will of 1663 restored "all the estate that their late father Sir David Kirke and their mother did give unto me" to his Newfoundland nephews George, David II, Phillip, and Jarvis.[24]

Why would Sir David Kirke have thus disguised his assets from the Commonwealth? Fears of confiscation would have been reasonable, for two reasons. First, he was, in the words of the pro-parliamentary merchants of Plymouth, "a knowne malignant and an inveterate enemye to this present state and government." His estates were therefore sequestrated by the Commonwealth in 1651. This loss, however, was not necessarily definitive. Royalists could compound for their estates, buying them back for a fine of 10–50 percent of their value. Sir Lewis Kirke, who fought ruthlessly for the king during the Civil War, suffered exactly such penalty but regained his estates (at 10 percent) and survived to claim a court sinecure on the restoration of Charles II. Sir David compounded,

ix), 167–168, 168–170; Poole, "Particular Accompt," Sept. 10, 1677, CO 1/41 (61iv, vi, vii), 158–166.

24. David Kirke, Will, Jan. 28, 1654, PROB 11/240, 177; David Kirke, Petition to Council of State, May 5, 1652, Md. HS, Calvert MSS 174/193, in L. D. Scisco, "Kirke's Memorial on Newfoundland," *CHR*, VII (1926), 46–51; James Kirke, Will, Mar. 24, 1651, PROB 11/259, 88; Lewis Kirke, Will, Aug. 21, 1663, PROB 11/312, 131–132. The second youngest brother, John, is mentioned in his brothers' wills, often as a life beneficiary, without indication of transfers of capital with David. When John died in 1688, age eighty-two, his estate went to his wife and children (John Kirke, Will, Nov. 20, 1685, PROB 11/392, 71).

in turn, for his estate, and sequestration on the Newfoundland Plantation was lifted in 1653. Cecil Calvert later claimed that about 1655 the Kirkes turned their patent over to Oliver Cromwell's son-in-law John Claypole and others, thus, perhaps, coming to terms with the Protectorate (1653–1659). Yet Kirke, Barkeley, and company never opened their books on the Newfoundland Plantation. The indications in the wills of Lewis and James Kirke that David had transferred some of his wealth to his brothers suggest a second reason for this reticence: Sir David Kirke and his family had done very well in Newfoundland.[25]

Neither Kirke, Barkeley, and company nor its heirs and successors were adverse to quoting figures to strengthen an argument, as in their successive petitions in the dispute with Emery de Caen over the Canada trade. After the Restoration of 1660, they found themselves in another serious dispute, this one over Ferryland, when Cecil Calvert asked to be restored to the proprietorship of the south Avalon. Charles II's chief legal officers, Sir Orlando Bridgeman and Heneage Finch, came down in favor of the second Lord Baltimore. The Kirkes now found themselves in the position the Calverts had been in for decades, attempting to reverse duly considered imperial policy. Yet few specific claims of expenditure on the Newfoundland Plantation by the Kirkes have survived to parallel the financial claims of the Calverts. Their reticence in this Restoration case might have resulted in part from a nonconfrontational strategy, successfully adopted by Kirke's widow Sara and their eldest son George, to deal with the Calverts' temporary success in reasserting their claims on the Avalon. Another reason might have been the family's reluctance to

25. Petition of the Merchant Adventurers of Plymouth, England, to the Council of State, ca. 1650, *Winthrop Papers*, VI, 4–6; Council of State, "Warrant for Seizing the Goods att Newfound Land," Apr. 8, 1651, CO 1/12 (20i), 53; J. P. Kenyon, ed., *The Stuart Constitution, 1603–1688: Documents and Commentary* (Cambridge, 1966), 273; Hill, *Century of Revolution*, 132; Eliot Warburton, *Memoirs of Prince Rupert, and the Cavaliers*, I (London, 1849), 503, 520–521; Kirke, *Conquest of Canada*, 172; Committee for Compounding, Orders, Feb. 2, Mar. 27, Apr. 21, 1648, in M. A. E. Green, ed., *Calendar of Proceedings of the Committee for Compounding, etc., 1643–1660*, V (London, 1892), 166, 194, 199; Charles II, Grant to Sir Lewis Kirke, November 1660, in *CSP*: Domestic. Cf. John S. Moir, "Kirke, Sir Lewis," *DCB*; Council of State, Minutes, June 3, 1653, SP 25/69, 197, 204; Calvert, Petition to Charles II, June 17, 1660, CO 1/14 (9), 13. On sequestration, see "An Ordinance for Sequestring," Mar. 27, 1643, in C. H. Firth and R. S. Rait, eds., *Acts and Ordinances of the Interregnum, 1642–1660* (London, 1911), I, 85–100.

discuss complex investments from which they had drawn much greater benefits than their business partners.[26]

Unlike the earlier proprietary colonies, the Newfoundland Plantation was not a commercial failure. Indeed, the Newfoundland Plantation was successful, in part, because it was not a proprietary colony in the early sense but rather a commercial monopoly, dependent on informal settlement. Kirke, Barkeley, and company made considerable profits from Newfoundland, quite apart from any that they might have expected from the making, buying, and selling of fish. Sir David Kirke's family remained among the most important in the region for six decades. At the same time, the colony grew, particularly the settlements in the south Avalon. Kirke's plans for the Newfoundland Plantation failed only in the sense that Parliament won the Civil War: another man without his royalist associations might have put settlement on an even firmer basis during the Interregnum. Instead, the Council of State's commissioners were given control of Newfoundland in 1651, when Sir David was forced to return to England as an enemy of the Commonwealth. He was able to bargain his way out of the charge of delinquency by compounding for his estate, but, at the suit of Cecil Calvert, second Baron Baltimore, Kirke was thrown in prison again, where he died in 1654. By this time, the Maine Puritan John Treworgy, a longtime commercial competitor, had control in Newfoundland. In any event, settlement was not impeded by the Interregnum commissioners, either on the south Avalon in general or in Ferryland in particular. Paradoxically, then, even Calvert's original proprietary plantation might be construed as a success of sorts, despite its financial failure. Whatever profits the Kirkes made in Newfoundland were bolstered by their initial appropriation of Ferryland. Although we cannot say precisely how important George Calvert's investments were to his successors, others built their fortunes on the foundations Lord Baltimore laid, as he had feared they would. In this sense, Calvert's investments paid off: his proprietary colony was the beginning of the first commercially successful resident fishery in the region.[27]

Calvert's investment in Ferryland was not, however, the only factor in the success of Kirke's subsequent Newfoundland Plantation. What

26. Orlando Bridgeman and Heneage Finch, "A Report to His Majestie," Feb. 28, 1661, CO 1/14 (9i), 15; Charles Hill to John Kirke, Sept. 12, 1661, British Library, Egerton MS 2395, 308.

27. Cell, *English Enterprise*, 120; Lahey, "Role of Religion," *Md. Hist. Mag.*, LXXII (1977), 492–511; Matthews, "Fisheries," 121.

David Kirke appropriated at Ferryland went beyond physical infrastructure. Ferryland had close connections with the West Country ports, which habitually sent their ships and men to the south Avalon. Part of what the Kirkes co-opted was a human infrastructure bridging the Atlantic.

ϑ҉ West Country Connections

In April 1643, the *Unity*, William Herkett master, set sail from Dartmouth with goods and passengers for Newfoundland. The ship's voyage had begun in London, and, curiously, this late clearance for the fishery was its second that year: it had already sailed from Dartmouth with other vessels bound for Newfoundland a month earlier. The *Unity*, however, had barely reached the Scilly Isles before proving "soe leaky that shee could nott proceede to finish her voyage." The ship's company agreed that the vessel would have to return to Dartmouth for refitting. When the job was done, the *Unity* was reloaded and set sail again, although not before Peter Wills, a Dartmouth notary, protested its unseaworthy condition on behalf of his "very good friend" John Kirke, the London merchant who had freighted the ship. This was an unusual Newfoundland voyage, but unusual only in the leakiness of the ship and its consequent return and redeparture. Ships going to Newfoundland commonly called in the West Country, whether or not they were owned or operated by merchants elsewhere; even Dutch sack ships picked up factors and letters of credit there. What is more, each West Country port had special connections with specific parts of Newfoundland's English Shore.[28]

The close commercial ties between particular West Country ports and particular Newfoundland fishing harbors in the seventeenth century can be traced by noting the home ports of British ships engaged in the fishery, recorded in naval censuses of 1675–1684 (Figure 2). Ships from Bideford and Barnstaple in north Devon dominated the southernmost part of the English Shore from Trepassey to Ferryland, and ships of Plymouth, Topsham, and Teignmouth in south Devon concentrated

28. John Kirke, Libel, Feb. 19, 1644, William Herkett, "Account of What Money I Have Payed Out," Apr. 8, 1644, and Peter Wills, Protest, Apr. 5, 1643, all in *Kirke v. Fletcher and Tylor*, HCA 24/106 (67). On the Dutch, see Chapter 3, above.

their efforts around St. John's. Dartmouth ships were active in St. John's and northward in Conception Bay as well, whereas they left Trinity Bay, by and large, to Dorset, Southampton, and Channel Island interests. Bristol was active almost exclusively at Harbour Grace.[29]

The voyage of the *Unity* is only one of several indications of a commercial relationship among Sir David Kirke in Newfoundland, Kirke, Barkeley, and company in London, and Dartmouth interests. Robert Alward, for example, an experienced fishing master of Kingswear (near Dartmouth), was hired in 1649 by David Gutenville, a nephew of the Kirke brothers, to organize fishing crews to work for Sir David Kirke at Ferryland. The twenty-four fishermen Alward hired at Dartmouth were only a fraction of the men the Kirkes hired that summer in Plymouth, Barnstaple, and other western ports, so we cannot assume that they manned their Newfoundland operation solely through this one port. Nevertheless, the surviving records and archaeological evidence from Ferryland suggest that Dartmouth was an essential link in their transatlantic operations. This dependence is striking within the context of hostility to the metropolitan operation on the part of other Dartmouth interests, including major merchant houses like the Holdsworths.[30]

By 1638, Dartmouth had connections with Ferryland that stretched back to the previous century. William Sayer of Dartmouth was fishing admiral at Ferryland in 1597. The Cupids Colony manager, Henry Crout, found Dartmouth and Plymouth fishing masters at Ferryland in 1613, and it was from Dartmouth that George Calvert sent supply ships in the 1620s. This established connection no doubt explains the hostility of some fishing merchants to the interloping Kirkes. Kirke, Barkeley, and company would be competitors for those whose profits came from shipping fish, while Kirke's own fishing crews were competition for the Dartmouth ships accustomed to fishing at Ferryland. These traditional connections may also account for the Kirkes' incorporation of

29. Matthews, "Fisheries," 181–186, 213–214; John Mannion and Gordon Handcock, "The Seventeenth Century Fishery," in *Historical Atlas of Canada*, I, plate 23; Handcock, *Origins*, 56, 58, 64–68; Starkey, "Devonians and the Newfoundland Trade," *Maritime History of Devon*, I, 163–171.

30. Robert Alward, Libel, in *Alward v. Kirke*, 1650, HCA 24/III (4); David Gutenville, Examination, in *Alward v. Kirke*, May 10, 1652, HCA 13/124, n.p.; Council of State, Order, Feb. 23, 1649, SP 25/94, 17; Council of State, Minutes, Feb. 11, 1651, SP 25/17 (65). On Gutenville, see James Kirke, Will, Mar. 24, 1651, PROB 11/259, 88. Handcock's useful analysis unfortunately omits Ferryland (see *Origins*, table 3.1).

Newfoundland Harbors
from North to South

English Ports
from Most Distant to Closest by Sea

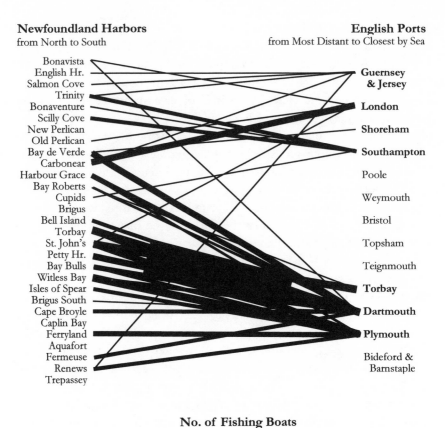

No. of Fishing Boats

< 5	————	5	▬▬▬
10	▬▬▬▬	20	██████
30	████████		and proportionately

The massive link of 86 boat crews from Dartmouth at St. John's is abbreviated here, to reveal some of the other strong connections between Torbay (Devon), Dartmouth, and Plymouth and the St. John's area.

Figure 2. Vernacular Links between West Country Ports and Newfoundland Fishing Stations, 1675. The thickness of the linking lines is proportional to the number of fishing boats operated by crews from each English port at each Newfoundland fishing station in 1675. Compiled from John Berry, "A List of the Ships Makinge Fishinge Voyages; with Boatkeepers . . . ," Sept. 12, 1675, CO 1/35 (17i), 137-148. Drawn by Peter E. Pope

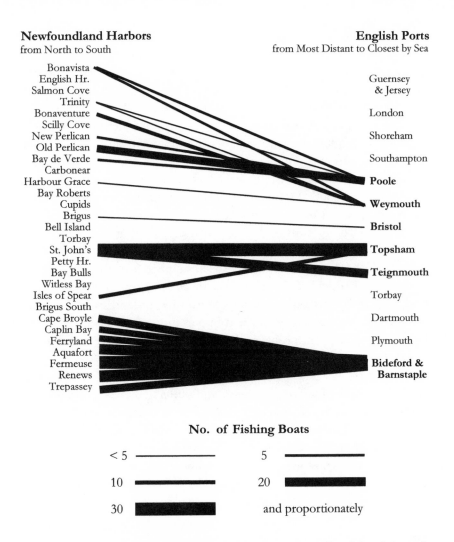

Newfoundland Harbors
from North to South

English Ports
from Most Distant to Closest by Sea

Bonavista
English Hr.
Salmon Cove
Trinity
Bonaventure
Scilly Cove
New Perlican
Old Perlican
Bay de Verde
Carbonear
Harbour Grace
Bay Roberts
Cupids
Brigus
Bell Island
Torbay
St. John's
Petty Hr.
Bay Bulls
Witless Bay
Isles of Spear
Brigus South
Cape Broyle
Caplin Bay
Ferryland
Aquafort
Fermeuse
Renews
Trepassey

Guernsey
& Jersey
London
Shoreham
Southampton
Poole
Weymouth
Bristol
Topsham
Teignmouth
Torbay
Dartmouth
Plymouth
**Bideford &
Barnstaple**

No. of Fishing Boats

< 5 ——— 5 ▬▬▬

10 ▬▬▬ 20 ▬▬▬

30 ▬▬▬ and proportionately

Dartmouth into their trading network. The accumulated local knowledge in Dartmouth and its hinterland of the area between St. John's and Ferryland and the personal transatlantic links between these regions were too useful for the Kirkes not to cultivate or, one might even say, parasitize. Although the entry of an active London trading house would threaten some interests, at the same time it presented opportunities for others. In the end, much of the opposition to Kirke was expressed in terms of the religious and cultural tensions of the Civil War.[31]

31. "The Voyage of M. Charles Leigh," 1597, in Quinn, *New American World,* IV, 68; Henry Crout to Percival Willoughby, Apr. 10, 1613, and George Calvert

Archaeological finds at Ferryland confirm the importance of south Devon commercial connections in the pre-Restoration period but suggest a shift about 1660 in the Devon region to which Ferryland looked as a commercial metropole. Coarse earthenware pottery manufactured at Totnes, near Dartmouth, has been recovered from the Ferryland excavations — the first examples of this distinctive ceramic ware identified in North America. Given its very restricted distribution in Britain itself, finds of Totnes ware strongly confirm the presence of fisherfolk from the communities along the Dart. Stylistic analysis of clay tobacco pipes has further confirmed south Devon connections, insofar as distinctive Exeter, Plymouth, Poole, London, and Dutch forms, common in the south Devon ports, make up most of the identified pipes dating before 1660. On the other hand, the relative representation of Barnstaple, Bristol, Wiltshire, and other forms, likely to have been supplied from the north Devon ports, roughly doubles after 1660. North Devon ships and planters had traditionally dominated the fishery south of Ferryland, whereas early-seventeenth-century Ferryland had important Dartmouth connections. By the late seventeenth century, Ferryland's planters were more closely linked to north Devon. Sir David Kirke's Newfoundland-born grandson, David III, was baptized, age five, at Bideford in 1676, and it was in Appledore, near Bideford, that Ferryland's inhabitants took refuge in the winter of 1697, after their settlement had been sacked by the French.[32]

The cause of this shift in transatlantic regional ties is unclear. Perhaps it was simply that Dartmouth, the dominant home port, could concentrate its activities on the English Shore wherever it chose, and St. John's had become more important than Ferryland. Perhaps Dartmouth's considerable losses in the Third Dutch War (1672–1674) reduced its ship-

to Nicholas, Apr. 7, 1627, CO 1/4 (19), in Cell, *Newfoundland Discovered*, 79–89, 272; Prowse, *History*, 159; W. B. Stephens, "The West Country Ports and the Struggle for the Newfoundland Fisheries in the Seventeenth Century," *RT Devon*, LXXXVIII (1956), 90–101.

32. Peter E. Pope, "Excavations at Ferryland," *Maritime History of Devon*, I, 172; J. P. Allan and Peter Pope, "A New Class of South-West English Pottery in North America," *Post-Medieval Archaeology*, XXIV (1990), 51–59; Pope, "South Avalon," appendix B; Bideford, Births and Baptisms (1653–1678), in "Parish Register III," Devon and Cornwall Record Society, transcript, microfilm on file at Maritime History Archive, MUN; John Clappe et al., Petition to William III, 1697, CO 194/1 (6), 14.

ping capacity to the extent that it had to consolidate its fishing efforts. In 1673, the Dutch captain Nicholas Boes and his fleet burned boats and shore facilities at Ferryland itself and nearby Caplin Bay, including those of Nicholas Neville and company of Dartmouth. Perhaps these local losses were enough to trigger a withdrawal northward toward the relative security of St. John's. Alternatively, the decline of the Dartmouth connection may reflect a withdrawal by John Kirke, the only surviving partner of Kirke, Barkeley, and company, from the Newfoundland trade. Although he was still concerned about the fate of the Newfoundland plantations of his kinfolk as late as 1661, in the following years the metropolitan connection seems to have weakened and with it, perhaps, the influence of his "good friends" at Dartmouth. Sir John survived until 1688, but his name is not evident in later Stuart documents relating either to the wine or the Newfoundland trades. We know that another John Kirke, perhaps a son, ran a plantation at Renews in the 1660s and 1670s. If the Kirkes in Newfoundland were doing business with London or Dartmouth in the 1670s, the records do not show it. The Kirkes now depended, like other Ferryland planters, on commercial ties with north Devon and, increasingly, New England.[33]

33. Stephens, "West Country Ports," *RT Devon*, LXXXVIII (1956), 90–101 (esp. 93); Dudley Lovelace, ". . . The Dutch Fleet upon the Coast . . . ," Mar. 29, 1675, CO 1/34 (37), 85; Hill to John Kirke, Sept. 12, 1661, British Library, Egerton MS 2395, 308; Yonge, *Journal*, 55; Robert Prowse et al., Petition to George Kirke, Mar. 18, 1667, British Library, Egerton MS 2395, 447; Poole, "Particular Accompt," Sept. 10, 1677, CO 1/41 (61iv, vi, vii); Lewis Kirke, Will, Aug. 21, 1663, PROB 11/312, 131–132. Dartmouth's losses at Newfoundland were said to have amounted to eight thousand pounds; see John Collins, *A Plea for the Bringing in of Irish Cattel, and Keeping out of Fish Caught by Foreigners* . . . (London, 1680), 21. Donald G. Shomette and Robert D. Haslach, *Raid on America: The Dutch Naval Campaign of 1672–1674* (Columbia, S.C., 1988), 203–204, asserts that the Dutch laid waste to Ferryland, but the extant documents do not support complete destruction, nor does the archaeological evidence. John Kirke did not import Spanish wine to London in 1664 or 1676; see London, Controller, Port Books, 1664, E 190/50/3, 1676, E 190/63/1. Nor was Kirke a litigant in the Court of Admiralty between 1660 and 1680; see Index to HCA Acts, IND 1/8977, IND 1/8978, IND 1/8979; Index to HCA Interrogatories and Libels, IND 1/8999, IND 1/9000, IND 1/9001. He was not signatory to the petition filed by supporters of settled government in 1667; see Merchants of London, Petition to Charles II, December 1667, SP 25/224 (56).

By the late eighteenth century, the North Atlantic littoral from Cape Cod to Newfoundland was linked economically into a greater New England. American historians have, naturally, tended to emphasize the ambitions and activities of their own merchants in the development of economic ties among the colonies and have sketched a vivid picture of Yankee trade at Newfoundland in the late seventeenth and early eighteenth centuries. This perspective is, however, inadequate for the pre-Restoration period. Newfoundland certainly traded with the American mainland at this time, but only part of this early trade was organized by colonial merchants to the south. The earliest British North American intercolonial commerce was an extension of international trade at Newfoundland, rather than the other way around. In its early years, the English colony of Virginia regularly imported fish from Newfoundland. After the Native uprising of 1622, supplies of fish from Newfoundland were needed desperately. English ships continued to trade cargoes of Newfoundland fish for tobacco at Virginia in the 1620s and 1630s, as did the good bark the *Swallow* of Virginia in 1638. Archaeological traces of this continuing connection are apparent at Ferryland, where a significant minority of excavated seventeenth-century tobacco pipes consist of the distinctive pink and beige clays of the Chesapeake. The archaeological record also suggests that Sir David Kirke himself was involved in this trade: excavators have recovered a number of decorated clay tobacco pipes, monogrammed "D. K.," in a distinctive style produced in the Chesapeake region in the 1640s (Plate 12, center). The rapid expansion of New England must have led to sharp competition from the northern continental colonies, given their locational advantages, but, as late as 1675, the sixty-five-ton *Loyalty* of Bideford went from Ferryland to Virginia with fish, where, presumably, it loaded tobacco, like so many other small north Devon vessels. Through the century, small north Devon vessels, owned by merchants like John Delbridge of Barnstaple, served in intercolonial trade along the North American littoral.[34]

34. John J. McCusker and Russell R. Menard, *The Economy of British America, 1607–1789* (Chapel Hill, N.C., 1985), 91–116; Ralph Greenlee Lounsbury, "Yankee Trade at Newfoundland," *New England Quarterly*, III (1930), 607–626; W. T. Baxter, *The House of Hancock: Business in Boston, 1724–1775* (1945; rpt. New York, 1965); Bernard Bailyn, *The New England Merchants in the Seventeenth Century* (1955; rpt. Cambridge, Mass., 1982), 129–131; Dephebus Canne to John

Newfoundland lies much closer to New England than to the Chesapeake. More important, it lies on the sailing route to Old England from New England. The rapid settlement of the northern colonies in the 1630s and 1640s strengthened shipping links with Newfoundland. Consider again the *Desire*, a vessel we have already met as a ship fishing at Newfoundland in 1636. The accident of a letter dated June 11, 1639, at Fermeuse, indicates that the *Desire* had stopped there en route from New England to the British Isles. It might have called into this south Avalon port for water or other supplies, or it might have been there to buy fish. Ships' passes, issued by the Privy Council in 1640, show that vessels taking passengers and goods to New England regularly called at Newfoundland on their eastern passage, and, in fact, a pass survives for the *Desire*. Other passes make it clear that such ships would often go thence to Spain or the Mediterranean, suggesting that they were carrying fish. Sometimes West Country ships engaged in the Maine fishery would go to Newfoundland to complete their cargoes, like the *Samuel*, which came from Richmond Island in 1638. On the other hand, ships sometimes left the Newfoundland fishery for Maine, as did the *Hercules* in 1641. In short, New England was linked from its very beginnings to Newfoundland, by location and by mutual interest in the fishery.[35]

The rapid economic growth and diversification of New England, well

Delbridge, July 2, 1623, CO 1/2 (36), 171-172; Edward Simmons, Deposition, May 17, 1644, *Bristol Depositions*, I, 63; cf. William Douglas et al., Depositions, Aug. 9, 1626, *Southampton Examinations*, I, 73-74; Walter Childes, Examination, July 24, 1637, HCA 13/53, 268-270, in Dorothy O. Shilton and Richard Holworthy, eds., *High Court of Admiralty Examinations (Ms. Volume 53), 1637-1638* (London, 1932), 127-128; James A. Tuck, "Archaeology at Ferryland, Newfoundland," *Newfoundland Studies*, IX (1993), 294-310; John Berry, "A List of Ships Makinge Fishinge Voyages; with Boatkeepers . . . ," Sept. 12, 1675, CO 1/35 (17i), 136-148; Alison Grant, *North Devon Pottery: The Seventeenth Century* (Exeter, 1983), 114-122; Grant, "Breaking the Mould: North Devon Maritime Enterprise, 1560-1640," in Gray, Rowe, and Erskine, eds., *Tudor and Stuart Devon*, 119-140. Archaeologists have also recovered Cheaspeake pipes from Renews, St. John's, and Cupids.

35. Ian K. Steele, *The English Atlantic, 1675-1740: An Exploration of Communication and Community* (London, 1986), 80, fig. 4; Chapter 3, above; Harrison to Winthrop, Aug. 11, 1639, *Winthrop Papers*, IV, 138; Privy Council, Orders, Jan. 17, 26, 1640, CO 1/10 (50, 51, 53), 135, 136, 138; John Winter to Robert Trelawny, July 1638, July 30, 1638, Trelawny to Winter, June 29, 1641, *Trelawny Papers*, 123-125, 134-142, 272-275.

under way before the disruptions of the English Civil War, made it an alternative source of vessels and commercial services for Newfoundland planters. West Country ports, although predominantly parliamentarian in sentiment, were hotly disputed, and it was sometimes unsafe for ships even to approach home. By 1649, Kirke, Barkeley, and company had removed at least some of their operations to France and the Netherlands. They shifted other operations from the West Country to the growing colonial port of Boston and developed a trade in European supplies to New England, a trade that grew in the matrix of Dartmouth's commercial network at Newfoundland and Maine. Kirke, Barkeley, and company had close relationships with John Bodington, a Boston merchant, and Nicholas Shapley, a Maine planter and shipmaster. Bodington was trading in fish at Newfoundland in the mid-1640s. A London brother worked for James Kirke, where he, too, dealt in fish. Shapley was the son of Alexander Shapley of Kingswear, a Dartmouth merchant active in both the Chesapeake and Newfoundland trades. In October 1646, David Kirke asked the New Englanders to obtain a ketch of forty or fifty tons and to charter another vessel of one hundred tons for a year or two. The tone of Kirke's "Orders" suggests his correspondents were employees or agents. The Kirkes certainly trusted Bodington, for in September 1646 Sir David gave him a draft for £50 on John and James Kirke and asked him to sell for them in New England dry fish worth about £300. The proceeds might have been intended as payment for the vessel David Kirke wanted to buy, because in November Bodington bought two vessels in Charlestown: the *Judith*, a twenty-five-ton ketch, for £40 and the *Hopewell*, a forty-ton bark, for £230.[36]

36. Inkerman Rogers, "Barnstaple, Bideford, and Torrington during the Civil War," *RT Devon*, XLIX (1927), 323–341; J. D. Davies, "Devon and the Navy in the Civil and Dutch Wars," *Maritime History of Devon*, I, 173–178; Keepers of the Liberty of England, Interrogatories, in *Keepers of Liberty v. Berkeley et al.*, ca. 1649, HCA 23/17 (53); John Kirke and company, Interrogatories regarding the *St. John* of Oleron, ca. 1649, HCA 23/16 (39); John Bodington, Receipt, Dec. 10, 1646 (published as 1640, but provenance and contents indicate a misreading for 1646), Richard Russell, Annotation on Receipt, Dec. 12, 1646, and Thomas Bushrode, Accounts regarding the *Susan*, Mar. 18, 1647, all in *Aspinwall Records*, 69, 205–206; Dartmouth Customer, Port Books, 1638, E 190/950/9; Gray, "Early Stuart Dartmouth," in Gray, Rowe, and Erskine, eds., *Tudor and Stuart Devon*, 173–199 (esp. 186); David Kirke, "Orders to John Bodington," Sept. 3, Oct. 1, 1646, and Richard Russell, Bill of Sale, Nov. 10, 1646, both in *Aspinwall Records*, 76–77. On the problems a ship from Newfoundland might have, consider the

Kirke, Barkeley, and company owned or freighted many ships. Most were London-based, but in the late 1640s David Kirke operated vessels from Ferryland itself. He shipped about twenty tons of goods to Boston on the *David* of Ferryland in 1648. He probably also owned the *Lady* of Ferryland, which delivered fourteen tons of train oil to Dartmouth in 1647. These eponymous vessels are among the earliest-known merchant vessels based in Newfoundland. Either the *David* or the *Lady* might have been the forty-ton "bark" Kirke had obtained in New England. In originally specifying a ketch, he probably did not mean a particular rig but a small, seaworthy, beamy, flush-decked, double-ended vessel: in effect, a protoschooner (Plate 6).[37]

The masters of the *Lady* and the *David*, John Maverick and Nicholas Shapley, also seem to have had New England connections. Maverick was probably related to Samuel Maverick of Noddles Island, near Boston. Shapley owned a fishing plantation at Piscataqua but was also an experienced transatlantic master, often away at sea in the 1630s and 1640s. Given his family connections in Dartmouth, he would have been a useful agent for David Kirke, on both sides of the Atlantic. In the bill of lading for the *David*'s September 1648 voyage from Ferryland, Shapley promises "to do my best indeaver for the selling of the said goods." His relationship with Kirke, Barkeley, and company was intricate. Shapley left the management of his Piscataqua plantation in the hands of a nephew, John Treworgy—but the latter withdrew from the partnership in 1647, when Shapley failed to send supplies, and spent at least part of the summer on a voyage to Newfoundland. The following year, Shapley sold

---

Elizabeth Constant of Dartmouth, discussed in Cell, *English Enterprise*, 119. Kirke was not the only merchant to seek vessels for the Newfoundland trade in New England about this time; see John Manning (of Boston) and Joseph Profitt (of London), Charter Party regarding the *Anne and Margarett*, May 20, 1650, *Aspinwall Records*, 302.

37. On Kirke, Barkeley, and company's ships, see Chapter 3, above; David Kirke and Nicholas Shapley, "Invoyce of Goods Shipped Abord the *David* of Ferryland . . . ," Sept. 8, 1648, *Baxter MSS*, VI, 2–4. A later dispute with David Yale suggests Boston was the destination; see John Marius, Protest, Nov. 8, 1650, *Aspinwall Records*, 388–389. On the *Lady*, see Dartmouth Searcher, Port Books, 1647, E 190/952/3. On ketches, see William Avery Baker, "Vessel Types of Colonial Massachusetts," in P. C. F. Smith, ed., *Seafaring in Colonial Massachusetts: A Conference Held by the Colonial Society of Massachusetts, November 21 and 22, 1975*, Colonial Society of Massachusetts, *Publications*, LII, *Collections* (Boston, 1980), 3–29 (esp. 12–13).

his Piscataqua premises, lock, stock, and barrel, to David Kirke's partner William Barkeley, for fifteen hundred pounds. Shapley returned to Maine during the Interregnum and remained an important planter there for many decades. Treworgy went on to become the senior commissioner at Newfoundland between 1651 and 1659. Such prior connections suggest that the Council of State's Newfoundland commissioners were not random appointments.[38]

With the exception of Virginia tobacco, the *David*'s 1648 cargo consisted entirely of transatlantic imports. Some of these goods might have been English, but most were not: the wines came from the Atlantic islands, and probably the sugar as well; the yard goods were Breton fabrics. The ship's cargo confirms that Kirke, Barkeley, and company had shifted their transatlantic commerce away from Britain. It is noteworthy that Kirke's sons are named on the bill of lading as the consignors of the goods, possibly indicating that Sir David Kirke was transferring assets to his sons, as he had done to his brothers. Perhaps he had seen the writing on the wall in Oliver Cromwell's rapid victories in the "Second Civil

38. Kirke and Maverick were anti-Puritan Anglicans, and both were associated with David Yale, a Boston merchant; see Bailyn, *New England Merchants*, 83, 107; David Kirke to Archbishop Laud, Oct. 2, 1639, CO 1/10 (40), 119; David Kirk, Bill of Exchange, Sept. 13, 1650, *Aspinwall Records*, 388. On Shapley and Maverick, see Thomas Turner to Samuel Maverick, Oct. 16, 1647, *Aspinwall Records*, 95–96. Shapley was master of the *George* on a voyage from Bristol to New England in 1635; see John Hull, "Diary," *Archaeologia Americana*, American Antiquarian Society, *Transactions and Collections*, III (Worcester, Mass., 1857), 142. For the 1640s, see Nicholas Shapley, Letter of Attorney, Nov. 6, 1644, John Treworgy, Declaration, June 12, 1649, both in *Aspinwall Records*, 222, 373–374. On Shapley, Kirke, and Treworgy, see Kirke and Shapley, "Invoyce of Goods Shipped," Sept. 8, 1648, *Baxter MSS*, VI, 2–4; Nicholas Shapley, Power of Attorney, Nov. 6, 1644, John Treworgy, Declarations, Apr. 15, June 12, 1649, Thomas Bushrode, Receipt to Alexander Shapley, Mar. 18, 1648, all in *Aspinwall Records*, 203, 206, 222–223; Edward Starbuke, Deposition, Mar. 14, 1650, *Baxter MSS*, VI, 5–6; Nicholas Shapleigh, Deed, June 26, 1648, *Baxter MSS*, IV, 9–10; Gillian T. Cell, "Treworgie, John," *DCB*. What Barkeley did with the Piscataqua purchase is not clear. It might not have been a wise investment: Shapley's boats had been abandoned in the late 1640s and "staved or torne to peices." See Humphrey Cadburne, Deposition, Apr. 5, 1653, *Baxter MSS*, VI, 10–11. Shapley is listed in "Inhabetanc of Cetterry," 1652, *Baxter MSS*, IV, 25, and was still in business with Treworgy after the Restoration; see *Shapleigh v. Clarke and Davis*, July 16, 1673, *Suffolk Records*, 289.

War" (1648) or simply in the blatant prejudice against his plantation, evident when Parliament passed a remission of colonial duties in 1647 but exempted Newfoundland, meaning that many goods bound there would still be dutiable.[39]

The invoice for the *David*'s cargo to Boston indicates that in 1648 Newfoundland was not simply a point of supply for fish or train oil; it was already an entrepôt for Old World goods, as it would be after the Restoration. Nor was this voyage an isolated instance, for the invoice also mentions debts due the Kirkes by New England merchants. In the 1680s, the Commissioners of Customs observed: "Under colour of trade to Newfoundland for fish, great quantities of wine brandy and other European goods are imported from thence to His Majesty's plantations (particularly New England) . . . to which purpose 'tis now become a magazine of all sorts of goods brought thither directly from France, Holland, Scottland, Ireland, and other places." It was not really Yankee trade at Newfoundland that was new in the second half of the seventeenth century; it was the legal situation, following the Navigation Acts. Trading links with the continental colonies were first forged, not in the 1650s, but in the 1620s, with the foundation of the first enduring settlements in Newfoundland, New England, and the Chesapeake. Newfoundland's trading connections with New England grew in the 1630s and 1640s, using Dartmouth's commercial network. The north Devon ports of Bideford and Barnstaple played a similar role in facilitating trade with the Chesapeake. By 1660, New England merchants had a well-developed Newfoundland market for provisions, lumber, sugar, molasses, and tobacco traded for specie, bills of exchange, fishing equipment, and European goods. That Newfoundland was governed during the Protectorate by the Maine merchant, John Treworgy, would probably not have hurt the trade. This official connection was hardly necessary, however: Treworgy himself had acted as a Newfoundland agent for his kinsman Alexander Shapley since the late 1630s. Newfoundland's intercolonial trade found its footing in the 1640s, during the Civil War, "New England having had of late great traffique with Newfoundland," as David Kirke noted

---

39. The shipment is further discussed in Chapter 10, below. Sir David personally took up a consequent legal dispute; see Marius, Protest, Nov. 8, 1650, *Aspinwall Records*, 388–389. On duties, see Council of State, "An Ordinance for Encouragement of Adventurers . . . ," Jan. 23, 1647, in Firth and Rait, eds., *Acts of the Interregnum*, I, 912.

in 1651. By this time, New England merchants, particularly those with Dartmouth connections, were no strangers to Newfoundland.⁴⁰

Several of the Newfoundland commissioners sent by the Commonwealth to investigate Sir David Kirke were not merely familiar with its intercolonial trade but were engaged in commercial disputes there, some with Kirke himself. These include William (alias Miles) Pyle, Nicholas Redwood, Walter Sikes, and John Treworgy. Pyle and Redwood were both experienced Dartmouth-Newfoundland masters. In 1649, Redwood became involved in a drawn-out court case with John Mathews, a sometime Newfoundland planter and associate of David Kirke. In 1650, the Dartmouth master Sikes sued Kirke in the Vice Admiralty Court of Devon over a financial default. Kirke was particularly vehement in the denunciation of Commissioner Sikes as a biased and interested party. Given that Nicholas Shapley had sold his Piscataqua plantation to William Barkeley and that Shapley and Treworgy were then in dispute about Treworgy's management of this property, the suspicion must be that Treworgy likewise came to Ferryland with his own ax to grind. The Interregnum was not so much the period in which Newfoundland's intercolonial trade developed but the period in which control was wrested from Newfoundland. The Commonwealth commissioners who oversaw this reorganization of intercolonial trade, including the New England merchant Treworgy, seem to have qualified for appointment as much by their grudges against Sir David Kirke as by anything else.⁴¹

40. T. Chudleigh et al. to Edmond Andros, Jan. 12, 1687, *Baxter MSS*, VI, 228–229; Lounsbury, "Yankee Trade," *NEQ*, III (1930), 607–626; Grant, "North Devon Maritime Enterprise," in Gray, Rowe, and Erskine, eds., *Tudor and Stuart Devon*, 119–140 (esp. 129–134); Prowse, *History*, 164; Bushrode, Account regarding the *Susan*, Mar. 18, 1647, *Aspinwall Records*, 205–206; David Kirke, "Narrative," ca. 1652, British Library, Egerton MS 2395, 261. Bailyn, *New England Merchants*, 120, 130, seems to think this trade was new in the 1650s.

41. Commissioners for 1651 were John Treworgy, Walter Sikes, John Littlebury, and three shipmasters; for 1652, Treworgy, Sikes, Robert Street, Nicholas Redwood, and William (alias Miles) Pyle; from 1653 to 1659, Treworgy. See Council of State, "Warrant," Apr. 8, 1651, CO 1/12 (20i), 53; Council of State, Instructions to Sikes et al., June 16, 1652, SP 25/29, 11–14; Council of State, "Minutes," May 27, 1653, SP 25/69 (160), 197; John Treworgey, Petition, April 1660, British Library, Egerton MS 2395, 262. On Pyle, see John Cherry, Examination regarding the *Jonas*, Mar. 14, 1649, HCA 13/61, 349–351; Miles Pyle, Examination regarding the *Palm Tree*, HCA 13/71 (129); Henry Johnson, Deposition, Dec. 26, 1646, *Bristol Depositions*, I, 173. He also appears frequently in Paige, *Letters*. On

There is no doubt, however, that New England supply became more important to the Newfoundland planters after 1660. This development might have been due, in part, to the willingness of Yankee merchants to extend credit to colonial customers. When the wealthy Salem, Massachusetts, merchant John Croad died in 1670, he held more than £1,500 in bills from about thirty Newfoundlanders. Among south Avalon planters, William Davis, Jr., and George Kirke owed Croad £50 and £94, respectively, and William Davis, Sr., owed almost £230. Some debts might have been of long standing, like the suspiciously round figure of £300 owed by John Treworgy, who is not known to have been in Newfoundland after 1660. Debts more likely to have been current ranged widely in size from hundreds of pounds down to the £1 10s. owed by a Ferryland servant, Christopher Browning. The substantial levels of certain accounts suggest some planters counted on Salem for annual supply, a pattern even more common in Joseph Buckley's accounts for a 1693 Salem-Newfoundland voyage.[42]

In the course of the seventeenth century, then, the geography of trade at Newfoundland had changed profoundly, as was inevitable with the development of European colonies in America. There were, to be sure, some constants: in the Old World, ships provisioned every spring for a summer fishery at Newfoundland; England's West Country ports spon-

Redwood, see Dartmouth Controller, Port Books, 1641, E 190/951/8; John Loveringe, Examination regarding the *Elizabeth Constant*, May 25, 1644, HCA 13/59, 269-270; Court of Admiralty, Devon, Acts, 1649, DRO Exeter, Chanter 780c, 9, in "Transcripts and Transactions" (MS transcript of Chanter 780, b-d), II, 21; High Court of Admiralty, Acts, 1650-1652, HCA 3/44, 38, HCA 3/45, 11; John Mathews, "Concerning the French . . . ," British Library, Egerton MS 2395, 471. On Sikes, see Court of Admiralty, Acts regarding *Sikes v. Kirke*, Oct. 11-Dec. 6, 1650, DRO Exeter, Chanter 780c, 76-84, in "Transcripts and Transactions" (MS transcript of Chanter 780, b-d), II, 50-56; David Kirke, Petition, May 5, 1652, Md. HS, Calvert MSS 174/193, in Scisco, "Kirke's Memorial," *CHR*, VII (1926), 46-51.

42. Veren Hilliard et al., Inventory of John Croad, June 1671, *RFQC Essex Co.*, IV, 401-403. The published source reads "George Kocke," but the manuscript reads "Kirke." See Essex Institute, Salem, Mass., Salem Quarterly Court, XXXVIII (box 17). To obtain sterling figures for Croad's accounts, deflate by a factor of 0.8. On Browning, see William Davies, Receipt, Sept. 26, 1647, *Aspinwall Records*, 126; Hartnoll et al., Deposition, Sept. 15, 1707, CO 194/4 (77ix), 316. On supply, see Joseph Buckley, "Leager 1693," Peabody Museum, Salem, Mass., Acc,16,100.

sored most of Britain's share of this industry; and ships from London, Bristol, and some of the western ports traded the dried product of the fishery to southern Europe and the Atlantic islands in return for southern goods carried home to northern Europe. This triangular trade was in effect a flywheel: an Atlantic turbine around which new trades developed like eddies. David Kirke was not just a hardier George Calvert; he was a merchant whose family firm was already implicated in the business of turning fish into wine and all the other goods that Europe produced and that America, or at least Euramericans, needed. The Kirkes' commercial network, once extended to Newfoundland, inevitably reached rapidly down the American littoral.

The early metropolitan proprietors of Ferryland depended on West Country contacts no less than the London investors in the Cupids colony had depended on John Guy and his Bristol connections. The Calverts and Kirkes both favored Dartmouth as a transatlantic portal. Their choice is comprehensible, given the extent of Dartmouth's involvement in early transatlantic trade. From one point of view, Newfoundland's incipient settlements were but dependencies of such British ports. Considering the whole Atlantic panorama, on the other hand, many of these dominant British ports were themselves only the maritime agents of more powerful communities trading inland. Dartmouth was the port of the older and much wealthier town of Totnes, and, as Dartmouth was to Totnes, so Appledore was to Bideford and Topsham to Exeter. Each of these western regions developed a special relationship with part or parts of Newfoundland's English Shore. Bristol had an interest in Conception Bay, traceable, perhaps, to the retrenchment of some of the early Cupids colonists in Harbour Grace. Poole would eventually have an economic empire in Trinity Bay, and Exeter-Topsham already had interests in and around St. John's, Dartmouth-Totnes had interests in St. John's and in Conception Bay to the north, and north Devon had an early relationship with Renews and Fermeuse, toward the south of the English Shore. Archaeological assemblages suggest that after 1660 north Devon extended its south Avalon realm to include Ferryland, just when Dartmouth withdrew northward toward St. John's. Given the Dartmouth connections of many of the early New Englanders commercially engaged with Newfoundland, the evident expansion of New England supply to the south Avalon might be seen as an old trade in a new guise.[43]

43. Grant, "North Devon Maritime Enterprise," and Gray, "Early Stuart Dartmouth," in Gray, Rowe, and Erskine, eds., *Tudor and Stuart Devon*, 119–140 (esp.

Newfoundland had key advantages as an entrepôt: its mid-Atlantic location and the annual arrival of ships of several nations, under cover of the fishery, many of which would otherwise sail in ballast. The fishery effectively subsidized the entrepôt trade, as it would eventually subsidize settlement. Low transport costs favored Newfoundland as an entrepôt, even after the Navigation Acts and subsequent legislation attempted to contain such leakage from national mercantile systems. Settlement of the island was not necessary for it to function as an entrepôt, licit or not, but having an establishment in Newfoundland was certainly useful for entrepreneurs like Sir David Kirke. His family trading house in London, with its well-established network, could sponsor intercolonial trade, and his docking facilities, secure berths, and warehousing at Ferryland permitted him to engage in the kind of transshipment carried by the *David* to Boston in 1648. The entrepôt trade certainly benefited settlement, bringing stability to supply and, eventually, competition, which must have helped to keep import prices down. Thus, the shipping subsidy, implied by the existence of a huge fishing industry that annually brought thousands of tons of shipping to Newfoundland in ballast, would benefit residents through low prices rather than simply profit suppliers. The entrepôt trade brought increased economic activity to Newfoundland ports, and others, besides merchant planters like the Kirkes, came to depend on this commercial expansion. Trade between Newfoundland and New England developed in the 1640s—that is to say, as soon as New England had been settled—a period when the political and cultural struggle of the Civil War created a favorable economic climate in the context of a wider trade vacuum. The resolution of that conflict in 1648 and the accidents of political history then gave New England merchants the chance to wrest control of intercolonial trade from the Kirkes. Whatever the occasion of this shift, New England was probably destined to dominate its trade with Newfoundland.[44]

New England was, from the beginning, far wealthier and far more populous than Newfoundland and enjoyed key resource advantages, not the least of which were the lumber and naval stores that permitted the rapid development of an efficient shipbuilding industry. The twenty-five-ton ketch and the forty-ton bark David Kirke purchased in Charlestown

119–120), 173–199; Keith Matthews, *Lectures on the History of Newfoundland, 1500–1830* (St. John's, 1988), 45–46.

44. On the Civil War trade vacuum, see Brenner, *Merchants and Revolution,* 586.

in 1646 were by no means the last vessels brought into Newfoundland service from New England. A parallel might be drawn to Iceland's relationship with Norway in the late Middle Ages. Ships built in Norway might be sold into Icelandic hands, but, in the long run, Iceland would always lack the advantage of being able to depend on its own vessels. There would eventually be a small shipbuilding industry in Newfoundland, but, given the slow growth of the local forest and the limited species at hand, it would never compete with the continental colonies. As the New England economy diversified, its comparative advantage with Newfoundland grew. By the end of the century, New England was producing more of the goods that Newfoundland needed, including barks and ketches.[45]

The interaction of demographic and commercial pressures in the continental colonies in the late seventeenth century and the expanding ambitions of American colonial merchants furthered the integration of Atlantic colonies, including Newfoundland, into a "greater New England." This model does not, however, apply to the first half of the century. Early trade between the south Avalon and New England was an extension of metropolitan investment in Newfoundland, grown in the matrix of a West Country commercial network. A general model of interaction between commercial development and population growth can, however, be applied to the English Shore, where the international economy of the fishery intersected the demographic tides that pulled European populations to the New World. These commercial and demographic pressures were mediated by the economic culture of the time and place—in Newfoundland, most crucially, by the practice of service in the fishery.[46]

45. Bruce E. Gelsinger, *Icelandic Enterprise: Commerce and Economy in the Middle Ages* (Columbia, S.C., 1981), 51, 176-177; Kirsten Hastrup, *Culture and History in Medieval Iceland: An Anthropological Analysis of Structure and Change* (Oxford, 1985), 224-225; Alan D. Cass, "The Schooner *Jenny*," *Mariner's Mirror*, LXXXII (1996), 325-335; Buckley, "Leager 1693," Peabody Museum, Acc,16,100, further discussed in Chapter 10, below. On the rise of New England shipbuilding, see Stephen Innes, *Creating the Commonwealth: The Economic Culture of Puritan New England* (New York, 1995), 271-307.

46. For "greater New England," see McCusker and Menard, *Economy of British America*, 114.

5 ❧ SERVICE IN THE FISHERY

*Everie fisherman can informe you that they come to Newfoundland,
not upon wages, but for their shares of the voyage. To some is a
quarter part of all the fishe that are taken and oyles that are made; to
others a third thereof, yet upon other conditions, so that if the voyage
be good, it is as good to the fisherman in their proportions as to the
adventurers. If otherwise, the losse is their owne as well as the
marchantes; and therefore the lesse feare of negligence on their
parte soe longe as the fishinge continues.*
— Sir David Kirke, "Reply to the Answeare to the Description of
   Newfoundland," Sept. 29, 1639

In the seventeenth century, most Newfoundland fishermen were paid
in shares. David Kirke was, by no means, the only witness to this practice, although few were as candid about the commercial advantages of
the share system as a form of labor discipline.[1] We can get some sense
of how merchants like the Kirkes recruited labor for fishing operations
in Newfoundland from a suit in the Court of Admiralty, brought against
Sir David in 1650 by Robert Alward, an experienced fishing master of
Kingswear (near Dartmouth in Devon). Documents filed in this case
suggest that shares were not the whole story and that merchants were
already offering fixed wages to at least some of the participants in the
fishery. The interesting questions are, How widespread was the practice
of paying wages, and when and how did the practice grow?[2]

Alward was hired in 1649 by David Gutenville, a nephew of Kirke,

1. Sir David Kirke, "Reply to the Answeare to the Description of Newfoundland," Sept. 29, 1639, CO 1/10 (38), 97–114 (esp. 98–99). The document is a re-
buttal of a West Country answer (now lost) to an earlier description of Newfoundland by Kirke (also now lost). My transcription assumes Kirke slipped and placed
the caret for an insertion of the word "not" in the first sentence, one line lower than
intended. The alternative reading is nonsensical: "Everie fishermen can informe
you that they come to Newfoundland upon wages, but for their shares of the voyage, not to some is a quarter part of all the fishe that are taken and oyles that are
made."

2. Robert Alward, Libel, in *Alward v. Kirke*, 1650, HCA 24/111 (4), n.p.; David
Gutenville, Answers to Allegations, in *Alward v. Kirke*, May 10, 1652, HCA 13/
124, n.p.

who acted as one of Kirke's London agents. Alward's job was to round up a crew of twenty-four fishermen, which was probably easy enough to do in the Dartmouth area in the spring of 1649. Food prices had soared after a series of bad harvests, the parliamentary navy was pressing men for service, and the Kirkes were offering what one contemporary report called "high wages." According to Alward, his men signed on for a voyage to Newfoundland, at various rates, and Gutenville promised him a wage of thirty pounds, with the further encouragement of five pounds to provision his crew, pending departure. Alward and his men set sail on the *John* of Plymouth, and, when they arrived at Ferryland, they presented themselves to Sir David "and shewed him a list of the perticuler mens names and of their perticular wages, and of his owne wages, all of which the said Sir David Kirke very well liked and approved of and promised payment." The fishing season went well, and Alward's crew worked "with all diligence and carefulnesse and did get and preserve great quantity of fish." Kirke paid the men but not Alward himself, with whom he had worked for years. The Newfoundland merchant not only refused the Devon master his wages but also seized personal goods to force repayment of the five pounds for provisions and, in a typical flourish, demanded an additional pound "for the adventure thereof." Kirke's motives for reneging on his agreement remain obscure, as do the details of the crew's "perticular wages," but Alward's assumptions about his service in the fishery are quite plain.[3]

As Alward made abundantly clear in court, he expected to be paid a fee for services—a common practice for the fishing masters who subcontracted to organize boat crews. As for the servants themselves, we must resist the temptation to assume that the term "wages," used here to describe their remuneration, carried our modern sense of an agreed price

3. Joan Thirsk, *Economic Policy and Projects: The Development of a Consumer Society in Early Modern England* (Oxford, 1978), 138; Alan Everitt, "The Marketing of Agricultural Produce," in Thirsk, ed., *Agrarian History of England and Wales*, IV, *1500-1640* (Cambridge, 1967), 466-592, in H. P. R. Finberg, gen. ed., *The Agrarian History of England and Wales*; Council of State, Order, Feb. 23, 1649, SP 25/94, 17. On Gutenville's relationship to the Kirkes, see James Kirke, Will, May 24, 1651, PROB 11/259, 88. Alward was master of the *Hamilton*, which collected the Kirkes' fishery imposition in 1638; see Robert Allward, Examination, in *Baltimore v. Kirke*, Mar. 29, 1652, HCA 13/65, n.p. Alward was litigious; see *Robert Alward v. Nicholas Tasker*, Mar. 28, 1644, and *Robert Allward v. William Jeffry*, May 11, 1649, in DRO Exeter, "Transcripts and Transactions" (MS transcript of Chanter 780, b-d), I, 69, II, 19.

at which a period of labor is sold. Confusingly, "wage" and "wages" are often used loosely in early modern documents, sometimes for what we would call a share. Hence, the "perticular wages" Alward negotiated on behalf of his men could well refer to shares or some complicated combination of shares and straight wages, of the sort often reported later in the seventeenth century. The use of the word "wages" does not require us to believe that David Kirke paid the fishing servants on a wage basis, or even that Kirke emphasized wages in a complex wage-share system. The case does underline the explicitly contractual character of the relationship between master and servant in the Newfoundland fishery. The relationship between Kirke and Alward himself was significantly less commercial and, in Gutenville's account, more reminiscent of the kind of patron-client relationships that typified relationships between merchants and planters in Newfoundland. When Gutenville told Alward that he could hire masters to assemble crews for less than the thirty pounds Alward proposed, Alward is supposed to have replied "that hee would stand to the courtesie of Sir David Kirke"—the response of a client maintaining his relationship with a patron, rather than that of a subcontractor negotiating a contract.[4]

🦋 Wages and Shares

The timing and manner in which wages, in the modern sense, appear in Newfoundland remain uncertain. As early as 1600, some Dartmouth fishermen expected wage payments, and the account books of the Cornish fish merchant John Rashleigh record some fixed wages paid for Newfoundland voyages between 1608 and 1620. The use of wage payments evolved with the share system through the seventeenth and into the eighteenth century. As late as 1700, most fishing servants were still employed partly on shares rather than solely on wages. One influential study of the British fishery at Newfoundland credits Kirke himself with making the Newfoundland fishery a capitalist enterprise "in the modern sense" by introducing wage labor and replacing the older system of fishing on shares. According to this interpretation, wage labor was particularly associated with the emerging planter and by-boat fisheries. This version of an important chapter in economic history is appealing in its

4. Cell, *English Enterprise*, 16; *OED*, s.v. "wage." On patronage, see Chapter 8, below.

simplicity and often accepted as authoritative. There is, however, no direct evidence that Kirke himself paid fishing servants on a wage basis, let alone that he introduced this mode of production to the Newfoundland fishery. A gradual shift to wages was certainly under way in the seventeenth century, but whether this transformation was a result of the development of the boatkeeping sectors of the fishery remains an open question. At a more theoretical level, we might also ask what the transition from shares to wages has to do with the rise of "modern," or "true," capitalism, to use the terms some historians of the fisheries have invoked.[5]

Questions about wages and shares are a way of asking about the relationship between masters and servants in the fishery. As we have seen, the documentary evidence does not always speak directly to these questions, because "wage" once had a wider and looser sense than it does today. The term "share" was also ambiguous, particularly as used in the fishery. A share in a voyage might represent two different kinds of participation. On the one hand, I might be part-owner of a boat, with a few others, perhaps my brothers or other kin. If we fished together, I would expect to receive a share of the catch after expenses. Suppose, on the

5. Todd Gray, "Devon's Coastal and Overseas Fisheries and New England Migration, 1597–1642" (Ph.D. diss., University of Exeter, 1988), 122; John Scantlebury, "John Rashleigh of Fowey and the Newfoundland Cod Fishery, 1608–20," *Royal Institution of Cornwall Journal*, N.S., VIII (1978–1981), 61–71 (esp. 64–65); Cell, *English Enterprise*, 16–17; Matthews, "Fisheries," 134. For the view that Kirke introduced wages, see Ralph Greenlee Lounsbury, *The British Fishery at Newfoundland, 1634–1763* (1935; rpt. Hamden, Conn., 1969), 89–90, 110. The argument is not, however, compelling; the only relevant document he cites is David Kirke's "Reply to the Answeare," Sept. 29, 1639, CO 1/10 (38), 97–114, which he seems to misread. If Lounsbury read Kirke to mean that gentlemen like himself paid wages, whereas the merchant backers of traditional migratory fishing voyages paid shares, then he was ignoring the wider sense "wages" could have in the period. Although Lounsbury associates the introduction of wages with an early resident fishery as well, later historians have noted and accepted only the association with by-boat-keeping, perhaps because Lounsbury argues (with no evidence) that this innovation in the fishery was also an innovation of Kirke's; see W. B. Stephens, "The West Country Ports and the Struggle for the Newfoundland Fisheries in the Seventeenth Century," *RT Devon*, LXXXVIII (1956), 90–101 (esp. 94); Matthews, "Fisheries," 163; David J. Starkey, "Devonians and the Newfoundland Trade," *Maritime History of Devon*, I, 163–171 (esp. 164); John E. Crowley, "Empire versus Truck: The Official Interpretation of Debt and Labour in the Eighteenth-Century Newfoundland Fishery," *CHR*, LXX (1989), 311–336.

other hand, that I did not own a share in a boat but worked as a crewman for others. If my employer was a typical English fishing ship, the owners would take one-third of the catch, the provisioning merchants would expect one-third, and the crew would receive one-third. With, say, twenty-five other crewmen, I could expect a share of about $1/25$ of $1/3$ of the catch. Differing skill levels would mean crew members would not receive equal shares. Actual shares received would, however, be expressed in terms of such a notional equal share. These two different situations, sometimes conflated under the rubric of "the share system," may be contrasted with one another and, in turn, with the wage system. In the latter case, the master of a ship fishing, a planter, or a by-boat-keeper would offer me a wage of, perhaps, ten pounds to work for a season. Others would share in the profits, after all expenses were paid, including wages promised crewmen like myself. What is in question at Newfoundland in the seventeenth century is the beginning of a shift from the second and more complex of these share systems to a system of fixed wages. Under the share system, fishing crews invested their labor in the enterprise; they did not get paid until the voyage was over. With a shift to wages, in this schematic history of the fishery the economic functions of entrepreneur and laborer were increasingly differentiated. The payment of wages sounds more modern; it is certainly more typical of industrial capitalism. But, practically speaking, how would this change in economic culture have affected merchants and crews?[6]

Today, fishers usually prefer wages to shares. For the working person, a wage means that income is predictable. Wages eliminate the risk of a bad voyage—a potential disaster for the individual, whereas an exceptional voyage is not proportionately advantageous. In the early modern period, a fixed wage might also have been easier to borrow against and would thereby have expedited payment. The mate and crew of the *Beginning* of Salem, Massachusetts, which fished at Caplin Cove, near

6. Thomas F. Nemec, "I Fish with My Brother: The Structure and Behavior of Agnatic-Based Fishing Crews in a Newfoundland Irish Outport," in Raoul Andersen and Cato Wadel, eds., *North Atlantic Fishermen: Anthropological Essays on Modern Fishing* (St. John's, 1972), 9–34; Todd Gray, "Fishing and the Commercial World of Early Stuart Dartmouth," in Gray, Margery Rowe, and Audrey Erskine, eds., *Tudor and Stuart Devon: The Common Estate and Government: Essays Presented to Joyce Youings* (Exeter, 1992), 173–199 (esp. 186). J. D. Rogers, *A Historical Geography of the British Colonies*, V, pt. 4, *Newfoundland* (Oxford, 1911), 118, appears to conflate different senses of "share."

Ferryland, in 1708, did not expect to be paid until the end of their voyage, but they were prepared to strike to insist on their right to be allowed advances in alcohol and tobacco against wages expected. Whatever the final outcome of the voyage, these New England crewmen would enjoy some of the fruits of their labors, unlike George Bennet of Exeter, Devon, who had fished at Newfoundland a century earlier and who died in 1609, leaving an estate of eleven pounds that consisted largely of his maps and cross-staff and eight pounds due him for "his voyage for the Newfoundland." The date and size of the credit to Bennet indicate that it was almost certainly a share, which was generally not determined until the fish were sold, although advances might be made to "Wifes or other relations."[7]

From a strictly economic point of view, then, fishermen might prefer wages to share agreements. We must balance this economic rationale, however, with the aversion early modern workers had to wage labor, "pottage for freeborn Englishmen," in Christopher Hill's memorable phrase. To become dependent on wages amounted to a loss of status as a free individual. Wage laborers in the seventeenth century were generally impoverished, often separated from a stable community, and sometimes even segregated from other workers by industrial specialization. Even seamen, who suffered such social discrimination anyway, preferred to avoid complete dependency on wages. Newfoundland fishermen were unlikely, therefore, to have freely sought straight wage agreements, although they might have accepted a wage component in their remuneration.[8]

7. John Elletson, Veren Parkman, and Samuel Tapley, Deposition, in *Marston v. Holmes*, Jan. 15, 1709, Essex Institute, Salem, Mass., Court of Common Pleas, 3530.F.14; William Symons and George Ryder, Inventory of George Bennet, Dec. 1, 1609, DRO Exeter, 48/13/2/3/2, 144; Francis Wheler, "Answers to the Heads of Inquirys . . . ," Oct. 27, 1684, CO 1/55 (56i), 239–245 (esp. 242). On advances, see Edward Hickman and William Brooking, Response to Allegations, in *Cotton et al. of the Pellican of Topsham v. Hickman and Brooking*, Sept. 27, 1681, DRO Exeter, Moger, CC 181/18/8.

8. Christopher Hill, "Pottage for Freeborn Englishmen: Attitudes to Wage-labour," in Hill, *Change and Continuity in Seventeenth-Century England* (London, 1974), 219–238. See also Hill's comment on Keith Thomas, "Work and Leisure in Pre-Industrial Society: Conference Paper," *Past and Present*, no. 29 (December 1964), 50–66; and Hill, "The Poor and the People in Seventeenth-Century England," in Frederick Krantz, ed., *History from Below: Studies in Popular Protest*

We might also ask why employers, whether large or small, based in the West Country or in Newfoundland, would favor wage payments. One possible rationale depended on Britain's growing naval standing in international waters. The fishing ships that took crews to Newfoundland often also carried their catches to market in southern Europe. Shipmasters had a strong interest in reducing crews on the Mediterranean leg of their voyages, since fishing and processing required many more hands than delivering fish, unless the ship had to be defended. As Humfrey Slanye wrote in his instructions for the Newfoundland voyage of the *Luke* of London in 1623, "A good man is better than 3 others, and we desire to go with so small company as conveniently we may to save chardges." The end of the war with France in 1629 meant that British shipping in southern waters was safer than it had been since open conflict with Spain broke out in the 1580s. The Spanish war of the later 1650s put English shipping to the Straits at risk again, but the war and its concomitant dangers were over by the Restoration of 1660. The containment of Algerian pirates after 1670 further enhanced regional stability. Peace in the Mediterranean made reduction of crews feasible without undue risk. For the Western Adventurers, wage agreements facilitated the timely layoff of part of their crews, even in Newfoundland itself, if that was mutually agreeable. Fishermen often chose to stay behind in Newfoundland, sometimes to use the island as a stepping-stone to mainland North America. Security in the Mediterranean and the development of New England might have acted in concert to predispose West Country merchants and Newfoundland fishing crews to employ the more flexible wage agreements. This rationale would not, however, have applied to planters and by-boat-keepers. Unlike fishing masters and planter-merchants with ships going to market, they had no special interest in flexible crewing arrangements, since they sold their fish to sack ships and hired crews simply to fish.[9]

_____

and *Popular Ideology in Honour of George Rudé* (Montreal, 1985), 75–93. Cf. C. B. MacPherson, *The Political Theory of Possessive Individualism: Hobbes to Locke* (Oxford, 1962), 153; Daniel Vickers, *Farmers and Fishermen: Two Centuries of Work in Essex County, Massachusetts, 1630–1850* (Chapel Hill, N.C., 1994), 14–23; and Alan Everitt, "Farm Labourers," in Thirsk, ed., *Agrarian History*, IV, *1500–1640*, 396–465 (esp. 399), in Finberg, gen. ed., *Agrarian History*.

9. Humfrey Slanye, "A Coppy of a Clause . . . [regarding] the Luke," April 1623, Bodleian Library, Oxford University, Malone MSS, 4; Ralph Davis, "England and

The fishermen employed by planters were not, of course, the only servants in seventeenth-century Newfoundland. They were part of a larger labor pool that also included men employed by migratory fishing masters and by-boat-keepers. Unfortunately for students of the period, the employment contracts that fishermen entered into were still normally oral, so that very few fishers' contracts have survived. Much of what we know of service in the fishery is based on contemporary perceptions of those of higher status. These observations almost always relate to master-servant relations. The limited evidence we have thus tends to build a kind of economic reductionism into our understanding of service in the fishery. Some observers do, however, give us a broader sense of who fishing servants were. Seventeenth-century fisherman were not seen as wage laborers—masterless men hired on a daily basis. Fishermen had masters, so they were servants and were usually so called. If their class origins were specified, they were usually husbandmen, like most of the fishermen signing indentures to work at Robert Trelawny's fishing station at Richmond Island, Maine, in the 1640s. Husbandmen were farmers of small holdings, roughly five to fifty acres—the smallest self-sufficient peasant landholders in rural England. Lewes Roberts, who visited Newfoundland as a young man, described Newfoundland fishermen, in his *Merchants Mappe of Commerce* of 1638, as husbandmen who had adapted to a partly maritime existence. Most Newfoundland fishing servants were involved in such dual employments.[10]

------

the Mediterranean, 1570–1670," in F. J. Fisher, ed., *Essays in the Economic and Social History of Tudor and Stuart England, in Honour of R. H. Tawney* (Cambridge, 1961), 117–137 (esp. 132). On onward emigration, see Chapter 7, below.

10. Robert Robinson, "Inquiries Made . . . in Answer to Severall Heads . . . ," Oct. 11, 1680, CO 1/46 (8x), 33–34; Wheler, "Answers," Oct. 27, 1684, CO 1/55 (56i), 239–245; Patrick McGrath, "Merchant Shipping in the Seventeenth Century: The Evidence of the Bristol *Deposition Books*," pt. 2, *Mariner's Mirror*, XLI (1955), 23–37; Kenneth R. Andrews, *Ships, Money, and Politics: Seafaring and Naval Enterprise in the Reign of Charles I* (Cambridge, 1991), 73; Robert Trelawny et al., Indentures of Robert Saunders, Benjamyn Stephens, John Burridge, Nov. 20, 22, 1642, *Trelawny Papers*, 337–342; Lewes Roberts, *The Merchants Mappe of Commerce* (London, 1638), 58. "Husbandman" sometimes meant farmer, that is, yeoman or husbandman sensu stricto, but was not a synonym for farm laborer; see Keith Wrightson, *English Society, 1580–1680* (New Brunswick, N.J., 1982), 32–33; and Lorna Weatherill, *Consumer Behaviour and Material Cul-*

Full-time fishing masters, of the sort that were identified as "fisher-men" in the duke of Buckingham's maritime survey of 1619, accounted for only a few hundred of the thousands of men voyaging each year from Devon ports to Newfoundland and New England. The testimony of port officials and the inventories of fishing servants themselves indicate that the fisheries were an opportunity for dual employment no less than other rural industries like the production of cloth or the mining of tin. The occupational background of later West Country settlers in Newfound-land suggests that the fishery continued, for several centuries, to draw servants from a countywide hinterland rather than simply from the urban labor pool of the British outports that outfitted fishing voyages. In 1623, the mayor of Dartmouth reported: "There are very few mariners in these parts but are husbandmen and in winter time employ themselves in the common labours of the country and, although there be great number of mariners that usually sail out of this port to the Newfoundland, yet there are not the tenth part of them dwelling in this town." Individual fisher-men moved, from year to year, among the various fisheries along De-von's own coasts, at Ireland, Newfoundland, and New England, so that individual participation in particular fisheries was erratic. Thus, particu-lar fishing servants typically ventured to a particular overseas fishery, at Newfoundland, for example, intermittently rather than continually. This mobility was an accepted part of their struggle for a livelihood.[11]

Sir John Berry, the astute naval commodore at Newfoundland in 1675, thought servants in the fishery did relatively well by coming to New-foundland: "A poore labouringe man will gett in a summers season near £20, their dayley food comes out of the sea; which were such a person in England, he would not gett £3." Unlike Lewes Roberts or the early-seventeenth-century Dartmouth mayor, who had seen fishing servants as

---

ture in Britain, 1660–1760 (London, 1988), 174–175. There is no obvious reason to distrust the implicit assumption of seventeenth-century observers that conditions of service were generally the same in the various subregions of English Newfound-land; in the early seventeenth century, conditions of service in the fishery were common along the whole North Atlantic littoral.

11. Todd Gray, ed., *Early-Stuart Mariners and Shipping: The Maritime Sur-veys of Devon and Cornwall, 1619–35* (Exeter, 1990); Gray, "Devon's Overseas Fisheries," 121–122, 132–155; Gray, "Early Stuart Dartmouth," in Gray, Rowe, and Erskine, eds., *Tudor and Stuart Devon*, 190; Handcock, *Origins*, 258–259, table 11.3. On recruitment areas, cf. Handcock, *Origins*, 145–216; and Joyce You-ings, "Raleigh's Country and the Sea," British Academy, *Proceedings*, LXXV (1989), 267–290. For further reflections on mobility, see Chapter 7, below.

husbandmen with dual employments, Berry saw them in the context of the landless, casually employed, agricultural wage laborers at the base of the contemporary English labor market. This apparent antinomy may be resolved by recalling that, in the century between 1540 and 1640, a broad and heterogeneous class of peasant cottagers, including husbandmen, evolved into a few prosperous smallholders who hung on to their property rights and into a large class of virtually landless wage laborers. In other words, by the time Captain Berry visited Newfoundland in 1675, there were few self-sufficient husbandmen anymore, and the majority of rural folk relied on wage labor to get them through the year. Fishing servants were much better paid than farm laborers, and we might understand service in the fishery, whether at Newfoundland or New England, as one of the economic strategies that younger members of the declining class of husbandmen might adopt to keep their heads above water and to avoid slipping down into the despised pool of wage laborers.[12]

Fisherman — Socially ambiguous 11

The hierarchical social organization of the fishery meant that the designation "fisherman" was socially ambiguous. An experienced fishing master like Robert Alward, with fifty acres of land valued at forty-five pounds annually in the 1655 survey of Cockington, Devon, represented one limit of a broad social class. At the opposite boundary were lads like Nicholas, eighteen-year-old orphan of John Musique, husbandman of Southampton, apprenticed in 1631 by the local overseers of the poor for seven years—"To be instructed in the trade of a fisherman for two or three yeares and afterwards to be sent to the Newfoundland. And to have at his terme end double apparell [that is, two suits of clothes] and fortye shillings." These fishermen were separated by the social breadth of a class: the young man was something less than his late husbandman father; the retired fishing master had achieved yeoman status. They were also separated by a career, their lives documented at either end of a possible life cycle.[13]

12. John Berry to Joseph Williamson, July 24, 1675, CO 1/34 (118), 240–241; Alan Everitt, "Social Mobility in Early Modern England," *Past and Present*, no. 33 (April 1966), 56–73; Everitt, "Farm Labourers," in Thirsk, ed., *Agrarian History*, IV, *1500–1640*, 396–465 (esp. 424), in Finberg, gen. ed., *Agrarian History*.

13. Gray, "Devon's Overseas Fisheries," 133–141; "Survey of Cockington 1655," Mar. 20, 1656, DRO Exeter, 48/13/6/4/1; "Poor Child Register," Southampton, 1, Mar. 9, 1632, in Arthur J. Willis and A. L. Merson, eds., *Calendar of Southampton Apprenticeship Registers, 1609–1740*, Southampton Record Society,

In this respect, service in the fishery can be usefully compared with the early modern agricultural practice of service in husbandry. Like servants in husbandry, young fishermen hired on at markets and fairs not far from their homes, for a year or so, with the promise of remuneration at the end of employment and the understanding that in the interim they would be fed, housed, and, often, clothed. Service in the fishery differed from service in husbandry in important respects, however. Fishermen moved farther than any servant in husbandry, and not just geographically. When servants in the fishery hired on, the "household" to which they moved was different from the one in which they had grown up. It was not simply a somewhat wealthier household or one lacking hands for the familiar agricultural routines of their parents' smallholdings. The fishing ships, by-boat crews, and planters' households that servants joined in the Newfoundland fishery were a different kind of production unit than the agricultural households of rural England.[14]

Three interrelated differences characterize the contrast between service in husbandry and service in the fishery. First, the typical production unit in the fishery was much bigger. A young man, working one of the eight boats belonging to the *Olive Branch* of Barnstaple at Ferryland in 1676, was one of forty-eight fishermen employed by shipmaster Robert Neale. Not all fishing ships were as large as the 130-ton *Olive Branch*, but crews worked in groups much larger, on average, than the few servants employed on most early modern farms. Even planter and by-boat-keeper production units were relatively large. The size of the Newfoundland production unit and the physical means of production together promoted differentiation among servants in the fishery to an extent uncommon among servants in husbandry. The remuneration offered fishermen with various skills indicates considerable economic differentiation within crews, differences that contemporaries recognized as hierarchies. This sophisticated division of labor, the large size of the production unit, together with the time discipline imposed by a limited fishing

---

XII (Southampton, 1968), 770 (cf. xxxi–xxxii and the other mariners' indentures calendared). On the life cycle, see Handcock, *Origins*, 61, 190–196; Daniel Vickers and Vince Walsh, "Young Men and the Sea: The Sociology of Seafaring in Eighteenth-Century Salem, Massachusetts," *Social History*, XXIV (1998–1999), 17–38.

14. Ann Kussmaul, *Servants in Husbandry in Early Modern England* (Cambridge, 1983), 15–78 (esp. 71), 97–99.

season gave the dry fishery some of the qualities of later manufacturing industries.[15]

Finally, although servants in the fishery were generally young, they were not as young as servants in husbandry. The hierarchical social organization of service in the fishery meant that older and more experienced fishermen had an important role. Furthermore, most fishermen appear to have entered service later than most servants in husbandry. The Plymouth ship's surgeon James Yonge mentions "striplings," "boys," and even "little boys" at work in the Newfoundland fishery, but "boys" and "green men" together account for only about 15 percent of the crews he described in his journal for the 1660s. Seven older fishermen who gave depositions at Totnes in 1667 regarding their experiences at Newfoundland indicated when they had entered the fishery. Only one was as young as eleven at the time; the rest first went to Newfoundland at age fifteen to twenty-two. Most first-year servants in husbandry were younger; around 1600, they typically entered service at age fifteen, and, two centuries later, they started work even younger. Median service of about six years is probable, and most servants in husbandry would leave service to set up their own households in their early twenties, an age when many fishing servants would still be climbing the service hierarchy in the fishery.[16]

15. John Wyborn, "Accompt of the Shipps Fishing between Trepasse and Bay of Bulls," Dec. 7, 1676, CO 1/38 (79), 218-220. In 1675, fishing ships south of St. John's employed a mean of thirty-five men; see John Berry, "A List of Ships Makinge Fishinge Voyages; with Boatkeepers . . . ," Sept. 12, 1675, CO 1/35 (17i), 137-148. For differentiation among servants in husbandry, see Kussmaul, *Servants in Husbandry*, 35; for differentiation among agricultural laborers, see Everitt, "Farm Labourers," in Thirsk, ed., *Agrarian History, IV, 1500-1640,* 396-465 (esp. 433), in Finberg, gen. ed., *Agrarian History.* On wage differentials, see Yonge, *Journal,* 54-60, and below. On the fishery as industry, see André Dommergues, "La peche à la morue au XVIIe siècle d'après le témoignage de Nicholas Denys," *Études canadiennes/Canadian Studies,* XII (1982), 15-24; Jean-François Brière, *La pêche française en Amérique du nord au XVIIIe siècle* (Quebec, 1990), 58-60, 261; and Cole Harris, "European Beginnings in the Northwest Atlantic: A Comparative View," in David D. Hall and David Grayson Allen, eds., *Seventeenth-Century New England: A Conference Held by the Colonial Society of Massachusetts, June 18 and 19, 1982,* Colonial Society of Massachusetts, *Publications,* LXII, *Collections* (Boston, 1984), 119-152 (esp. 123-124).

16. Yonge, *Journal,* 54-60. Cf. Handcock, *Origins,* 61-63; John Cull et al., "Depositions of Wittnesses Taken att Totnes," Nov. 27, 1677, WDRO Plymouth,

A small proportion of fishing servants became masters of one sort or another: of fishing ships, as by-boat-keepers, or as planters. Those who managed to become fishing masters might have tended to be those unusual youths who were formally apprenticed as mariners or fishermen — a practice that was relatively rare in the West Country. Ordinary fishing servants did not normally enter formal apprenticeships. The traditional hierarchical structure of service in the ship-based fishery, involving the annual recruitment and training of green men, or "youngsters," served the whole industry, planters and by-boat-keepers included, as an informal apprenticeship mechanism. The fishery was thus able to reproduce itself: the social organization of labor not only produced fish; it also produced fishermen.[17]

Servants who decided to remain in Newfoundland were, thus, certainly not typical of the servant population. Sir David Kirke encouraged the most-skilled fishermen to remain in Newfoundland and, generally, servants encouraged to overwinter were likely recruited from the more experienced. They would therefore have been older than average, which would sometimes have permitted the accumulation of the capital needed to establish a plantation. Planters were, doubtless, normally former fishing servants, just as the masters of ships in the period were normally former seamen. Although some servants stayed in Newfoundland and became inhabitants of one sort or another, servants in the fishery did not normally become planters, in the sense of boatowners. For a few, the lowly status of fishing servant was the first stage in some such career; but most were simply poor men attracted to a relatively well-paid industry. Their temporary good fortune was, in fact, a poor indicator of their dismal prospects, at least judging by an indignant petition by the inhabitants of Marblehead, Massachusetts, to the Salem Quarterly Court in 1667:

W360/74; Kussmaul, *Servants in Husbandry*, 70–71, 80. The mean age of the Totnes deponents at entry was seventeen, and the mode was eighteen. The evidence regarding periods of service in husbandry is imperfect.

17. Keith Matthews, *Lectures on the History of Newfoundland, 1500–1830* (St. John's, 1988), 88; McGrath, "Merchant Shipping in Bristol," *Mariner's Mirror*, XLI (1955), 23–37; John Webb, "Apprenticeship in the Maritime Occupations at Ipswich, 1596–1651," *Mariner's Mirror*, XLVI (1960), 29–34; Youings, "Raleigh's Country," British Academy, *Proceedings*, LXXV (1989), 267–290 (esp. 289); Gray, "Devon's Overseas Fisheries," 133.

[Because] Marblehead hath been a place of fishing for many yeares past, on which account divers persons from England, Newfound Land, and other places have resorted thither, many of them persons undesirable, and of noe estates, butt rather indebted, yett [Marblehead] had no power to exclude them, because thay came on a fishing account soe that many of them have been burthensum to the place . . . in cases of sicknesse and lameness or other occurances that have by the providence of God befallen them.[18]

For the broken man on a Marblehead pier, the social distinctions that defined his status were inevitable, pervasive, and self-reinforcing. The average servant in the fishery, even if an experienced boatmaster, was illiterate and innumerate. Servants could rarely sign their names, which is not surprising if they were recruited among husbandmen, among whom about 80 percent were illiterate in this sense. The Acadian merchant-planter Nicholas Denys observed fishermen threading cod tongues on a line to record their catches, and fishermen on the English Shore also used such analog notations. The Marblehead perspective suggests fishermen could end their days as poor as when they began. In early-eighteenth-century Plaisance and Île Royale, the estates of fishing servants rarely amounted to more than a tenth of the value of the estates of resident fishing masters.[19]

Traditionally, a fishing crew was entitled to a specific share of the gross catch. This system of remuneration for mariners survived into the seventeenth century in fishing, whaling, and privateering, after it was abandoned in other seagoing trades. A one-third share was standard in the Newfoundland fishery, variations becoming more common as the

18. On Kirke, see Cull, "Deposition," Nov. 27, 1677, WDRO Plymouth, W360/74. On planter recruitment among servants, see Cell, *Newfoundland Discovered*, 58. The quotation is from Inhabitants of Marblehead, Petition to the Salem Court, 1667, in *RFQC Essex Co.*, V, 373 ("resorted" and "lameness" are slight emendations).

19. See the literacy rate for the diocese of Exeter, 1574–1688, in David Cressy, *Literacy and the Social Order: Reading and Writing in Tudor and Stuart England* (Cambridge, 1980), 120, table 6.2 ($N = 598$). On cod tongues, see Denys, *Histoire naturelle*, 523; and cf. the notched tally stick archaeologists recovered from the seventeenth-century Ferryland waterfront, discussed in Chapter 8, below. On Plaisance and Île Royale, see Nicolas Landry, "Culture matérielle et niveaux de richesse chez les pêcheurs de plaisance et de l'Île Royale, 1700–1758," *Material History Review*, no. 48 (Fall 1998), 101–122 (esp. 115–119).

fishing trade became more complex. Complicated arrangements among crew, master, and victualler might alter the fishermen's share to something more like 25 percent, as David Kirke observed. In some early agreements, wages supplemented the crew's third, but most share distributions reported in the later seventeenth century assign crews total earnings of one-third the gross catch. In other words, the total value of remuneration to the crew, including both fixed wages and share payments, was one-third the value of the fish and train oil taken to market. Workers with various skills were paid in different combinations of share and wage, with a wide range in their total incomes. The shares of skilled workers formed a considerable part of their pay. Less-skilled workers, on the other hand, received no share but only a small annual wage, like servants in husbandry.[20]

ৡৡ *Income Levels*

The available evidence about how much seventeenth-century New-foundland fishermen were paid is intermittent. James Yonge, who described the Newfoundland fishery in his journal, attended the seventy-man crew of the one-hundred-ton *Reformation* of Plymouth at Renews in 1663. He assessed wages and shares for that rather poor season, in which each boat crew managed to dry only 130 quintals of fish, or about two-thirds the normal catch. Captain Sir William Poole discussed wages and shares briefly in his report to the Committee of Trade and Plantations for 1677. Captain Francis Wheler's report for 1684 gives more detailed

20. Ralph Davis, *The Rise of the English Shipping Industry in the Seventeenth and Eighteenth Centuries* (1962; rpt. London, 1972), 133; Whitbourne, *Discourse*, 128, 178; Richard Breton to Francis Windebank, ca. 1640, CO 1/10 (79), 199; Cell, *English Enterprise*, 14–17; Cell, *Newfoundland Discovered*, 136n. On French share systems, see John Story, "Intelligence about the French Trade," CO 1/47 (52i), 122; and Charles de La Morandière, *Histoire de la pêche française de la morue dans l'Amérique septentrionale (des origines à 1789)*, 2 vols. (Paris, 1962) I, 109–142. Wages were not recoverable from shares in the French fishery. Thomas Newcomen, owner-victualler of the *Olive* of Dartmouth, was to have one-ninth of the crew's one-third share of the catch in 1650; see Newcomen, Interrogatory, in *Newcomen v. Johnson et al.*, ca. 1651, HCA 23/17 (137); cf. William Poole, "Answers to the Severall Heads of Inquiry . . . ," Sept. 10, 1677, CO 1/41 (62i), 149–152. Francis Wheler, "The Expence of Fitting Out Ten Boats and the Charge of a Shipp . . . ," Oct. 27, 1684, CO 1/55 (56ii), 249–250, ignores train oil.

estimates of wages and shares for the fifty-man crew of an eighty-ton ship, assuming "a good voyage" with a catch of 200 quintals per boat. "I had the account from a skillful master of a fishing shipp," Wheler reported, "which makes me give greate creditt to it." Finally, Benjamin Marston's instructions for the voyage of his small brigantine *Beginning* of Salem, Massachusetts, to the south Avalon in 1708 contain some data on wages.[21]

Several aspects of these income estimates are worth remarking upon (Table 9), particularly the gradation of remuneration. In 1663, the lowest-paid men received only a tenth of what the most-skilled workers made. These income differentials were more marked than those reported among contemporary deep-sea mariners, for whom the significant gap was between the shipmaster and his men. A comparison of the dispersion of remuneration levels in 1663 and 1684 suggests some leveling of income among fishing suboccupations over this period. The most striking shift over time is the steep rise in average remuneration between 1663 and 1677 (even after adjusting the 1663 figures upward to reflect an average catch), followed by a more gradual decline to earlier levels by 1708. The 1684 figures provoke other questions, particularly with respect to boatkeepers, that is, resident planters and migratory by-boat-men.[22]

Captain Francis Wheler's comprehensive reply to the Lords of Trade and Plantations' inquiries for 1684 includes a budget for a planter boatkeeper as well as the estimates for a ship fishing. Captain Wheler based his boatkeeper's wage costs on information received "from an intelligible planter." Although it would be amusing to imagine the Newfoundland commodore scouting the outports for a comprehensible local informant, he was doubtless familiar with the West Country dialect, given the number of Devon men in the Royal Navy, and he likely used "intelligible" in the now-obsolete sense of "intelligent." At any rate, his figures for a planter boatkeeper are thought-provoking, for at first glance they seem

21. Yonge, *Journal*, 54–60; Poole, "Answers," Sept. 10, 1677, CO 1/41 (62i), 149–152; Wheler, "Charge of a Shipp," Oct. 27, 1684, CO 1/55 (56ii), 249–250; Wheler, "Answers," Oct. 27, 1684, CO 1/55 (56i), 242 (quotation); Benjamin Marston, Instructions to Robert Holmes, Apr. 20, 1708, Essex Institute, 3530.F.14. A uniform statistical series is out of the question.

22. Kenneth R. Andrews, "The Elizabethan Seaman," *Mariner's Mirror*, LXVIII (1982), 245–262; G. V. Scammell, "Manning the English Merchant Service in the Sixteenth Century," ibid., LVI (1970), 131–154.

Table 9. *Remuneration for Fishing Crews, Newfoundland, 1663–1708*

Laborers	1663 £ s.	1677 £ s.	1684 £ s.	1708 £ s.
Boat crews				
Boatmasters	11 10	17 10	12 00	10 18
Midshipmen	6 05	15 00	9 00	4 00
Foreshipmen	3 00	4 10	6 00	2 00
Shore crews				
Splitters	8 10	—	10 00	10 00
Headers	6 00	—	8 00	—
Salters	5 00	—	—	—
Boys or green men	1 10	—	3 00	—
Ships' officers				
Master	45 00	—	40 00	20 00
Mate	12 00	—	—	—
Averages				
Boat crews	6 18	12 07	9 00	6 02
Skilled shore labor	6 10	—	9 00	—
All skilled labor	6 16	—	9 00	—
All labor	6 01	—	7 13	—
Officers and crews	6 13	—	8 06	—

Note: Remuneration includes wages and shares. The coefficient of variation for 1663 is 0.91; for 1684, 0.66. The figures for 1663 are recalculated, assuming a share of £5, which would reflect a catch of 200 quintals per boat. The figures for 1708 have been translated from colonial currency of the time to pounds sterling. All averages are weighted using the proportions of various skills suggested in the relevant document. Boatmasters, midshipmen, splitters, headers, and salters are counted as skilled labor. Foreshipmen, boys, and green men are counted as unskilled labor. Masters and mates are excluded from the "All labor" averages.

Sources: Yonge, "Journal," 55–58; William Poole, "Answers to the Severall Heads of Inquiry . . . ," Sept. 10, 1677, CO 1/41 (62i), 149–152; Francis Wheler, "The Expence of Fitting Out Ten Boats and the Charge of a Shipp . . . ," Oct. 27, 1684, CO 1/55 (56ii), 249–250; Benjamin Marston, Instructions to Richard Holmes, Apr. 20, 1708, Essex Institute, Salem, Mass., 3530.F.14.

to imply that boatkeepers paid their crews considerably better than did employers in the ship-based fishery.[23]

How did Wheler's "intelligible planter" come to spend on average between sixteen and seventeen pounds per season for skilled crewmen if the "skillful master of a fishing shipp" was paying nine pounds? How could a planter afford to budget seven pounds for green men when ships fishing paid three pounds? Part of this differential is readily explicable. Fishing ships charged passage money to carry boatkeepers' crews on the voyage out and back. Boatkeepers paid about four pounds for a crewman's passage, round-trip, or half as much for men overwintering. Deducting passage money, which Wheler appears to have included as a wage cost, reduces the income of green men working for planters or by-boat-keepers to the level of novices in the ship fishery. An income discrepancy of about three pounds a season remains between skilled ship-based workers and planter crewmen, in favor of the planter crews (Table 10). The best explanation for this discrepancy is that the income of crews on fishing ships consisted not only of the reported wages and shares but also of perquisites normally unreported in most sources. In the Newfoundland fishery, the most important of these mariners' perquisites was the custom of *portage*, the right to carry a certain amount of cargo freight-free on their own account, a right also known in the period as "privilege" or "venture."[24]

23. Francis Wheler, "The Charge for Fitting Out Two Boats . . . according to the Custome of the Inhabitants . . . ," Oct. 27, 1684, CO 1/55 (56iii), 251–252; Wheler, "Answers," Oct. 27, 1684, CO 1/55 (56i), 241; *OED*, s.v. "intelligible." Again, "boatkeeper" is used here, as it often was in the study period, to comprise both by-boat-keepers and planters.

24. Wheler's informant might have exaggerated boatkeepers' costs. Some are high compared to those cited in his ship's budget, which may reflect transatlantic differences in costs or may suggest planter pessimism. These considerations may account for a fraction of the apparent wage discrepancy. In some periods, ships' pay rates may be somewhat less than boatkeepers' rates because boatkeepers' crews were taking more risk of employer bankruptcy. Boatkeepers' high risks were sometimes reflected in interest rates on *bottomery*, roughly a combination of loan and insurance: boatkeepers could pay 28 percent per annum, whereas shipowners paid 20 percent; see CTP, Minutes, Dec. 4, 1675, CO 391/1, 25–26. Passage costs are not included in Wheler's pessimistic budget, so it is reasonable to assume that his informant included them in wage costs; compare Wheler, "Charge for Two Boats," Oct. 27, 1684, CO 1/55 (56iii), 251–252, and his "Answers," Oct. 27, 1684, CO 1/55 (56i), 242. One-way passage cost thirty shillings to two pounds; see Berry to Williamson, July 24, 1675, CO 1/34 (118), 240–241. The two pounds budgeted by

The crews in the Newfoundland trade undoubtedly took advantage of their right to portage, which included imports as well as private exports of fish. The privilege of portage long survived in the fishing trade, even as shipowners attempted to discourage the custom. When the Jersey privateer Nicholas Clause took the *Olive* of Dartmouth in October 1650, the master and crew lost not only their share of the fish laded at St. John's that September for the freighters of the vessel but also private ventures of fish "to a good value" and other goods. Portage was subject to some obvious forms of abuse; hence, private cargoes were to be kept separate from merchants' cargoes. The right to the perquisite was, however, unambiguous. Crewmen of the *Ruth* of London told the Exeter Vice Admiralty Court that in 1692 the master's mate "buyed upp a certaine quantity of dry Newfoundland fish being that proceeds of goods which he carried there upon his owne particular account." They testified that the mate's venture "was never intermixt with that fish belonging to the merchants interested in the freight of the said shipp" and, furthermore, that, when he sold the fish, it was delivered "openly and fairly att a seasonable time and not in any shuffling or clandestine manner whatsoever."[25]

From such disputes, we can get some sense of what men going to Newfoundland could expect to earn in private ventures. It cost the crewmen of the *Hopegood* £3 or more each when they lost fish shipped as their own ventures in 1650. As late as 1708, the Salem merchant Marston al-

---

Wheler in his "Charge of a Shipp," Oct. 27, 1684, CO 1/55 (56ii), 249–250, is the shipowner's profit per round-trip. Masters were free to charge more and did so; see Davis, *English Shipping Industry*, 149; and *William Kingdom et al. v. Edward Hickman and William Brooking*, July 20, 1680, in DRO Exeter, "Transcripts and Transactions" (MS transcript of Chanter 780, b–d), III, 135–157. Before the Civil War, such hidden income might have included *primage*, which was essentially a small gratuity to encourage care in lading. Primage rates were only about six pence per ton, and fishing ships carried little outbound cargo, so it probably made little difference to fishing crews when seventeenth-century masters became reluctant to share this small fee. See Davis, *English Shipping Industry*, 146. On portage, see Peter E. Pope, "The Practice of Portage in the Early Modern North Atlantic: Introduction to an Issue in Maritime Historical Anthropology," *Journal of the Canadian Historical Association*, VI (1995), 19–41.

25. Cell, *English Enterprise*, 17–18; Newcomen, Interrogatory, in *Newcomen v. Johnson et al.*, ca. 1651, HCA 23/17 (137); Michael Harding, Bill of Lading, Sept. 3, 1650 (Exhibit, in *Newcomen v. Johnson et al.*), HCA 23/17 (137); William Allday and James Andrews, Deposition, in *The* Ruth *of London v. Archer and Matthews*, Aug. 8, 1693, DRO Exeter, Moger, CC 181/18/11.

Table 10. *Remuneration for the Ship-Based and the Planter Boatkeeper Fishery, Newfoundland, 1684*

Laborers	Ship-Based Fishery £ s.	Boatkeeper Fishery £ s.
Boat crews		
Boatmasters	12 00	16 00
Midshipmen	9 00	12 00
Foreshipmen	6 00	11 00
Shore crews		
Splitters	10 00	16 00
Headers	8 00	10 00
Salters	8 00	
Boys or green men	3 00	3 00
Ships' officers		
Master	40 00	
Averages		
Boat crews	9 00	13 00
Skilled shore crews	9 00	11 07
All skilled crews	9 00	12 09
All labor	7 13	11 10
Overall	8 06	11 10

Note: An allowance of £4 for passage money has been deducted from the estimated labor costs of boatkeepers. All averages are weighted using the proportions of various skills suggested in the relevant document.

Sources: Francis Wheler, "The Expence of Fitting Out Ten Boats and the Charge of a Shipp . . . ," and Wheler, "The Charge for Fitting Out Two Boats . . . according to the Custome of the Inhabitants . . . ," Oct. 27, 1684, CO 1/55 (56ii, iii), 249–250, 251–252.

lowed portage of four barrels, that is, about six quintals of fish worth £3 10s, to his chief boatmaster, on top of a wage of £24. So it would seem that a skilled ship-based Newfoundland fisherman in the second half of the seventeenth century could make something like £3 a season on private cargo of about five quintals of fish. Portage was profitable enough for crews in the ship-based fishery to make up most of the gap between their recorded incomes and those recorded for boatkeepers' crews. Planters and by-boat-keepers had to pay more to compete with the opportunity for private venture in the ship fishery. The income of skilled Newfoundland fishermen was complex, comprising wages, shares, and private ventures; each component has its place in any estimate of average income levels. In 1675, Berry thought a man could earn £20 a summer at Newfoundland. In contemporary terms, this was excellent pay for skilled manual labor, almost three times what an experienced journeyman builder earned at the time. In isolation, Berry's claim might seem hard to accept, but, given the multiple sources of income involved, earnings by skilled fishermen as high as £20 were possible. Such levels would have been attained, however, by only the most experienced fishers and, perhaps, only in periods of international tension.[26]

Seamen's earnings fluctuated considerably in the seventeenth century and did so in counterpoint to the ebb and flow of war and peace. Daniel Defoe observed: "Whenever this kingdom is engaged in a war with any of its neighbours, two great inconveniences constantly follow, one to the king and one to the trade. 1. That to the king is, that he is forced to press seamen for the manning of his navy. . . . 2. To trade by the extravagant price set on wages for seamen, which they impose on the merchant with a sort of authority, and he is obliged to give by reason of the scarcity of men." The early modern labor markets for fishermen and able seamen overlapped; indeed, this circumstance was the basis of the contemporary cliché that the fishery was a nursery of seamen. To the extent that fishermen were seamen, fishermen's incomes would rise with seamen's wages. Meanwhile, the rise and fall of markets for cod affected the value of fishermen's shares. Since markets were strongly affected by war, the two major influences on fishermen's earnings were interdependent, although not always mutually reinforcing, since serious conflict in

26. John Heyward and Peter Philiver, Examinations, in *Hill et al. v. the* Hopegood, Aug. 17, 1654, HCA 13/71, 664-665; James Denye, Examination, Oct. 11, 1633, HCA 13/50, 412; John Pickeringe et al., Allegations, in *Pickeringe et al. v. Waringe and Grafton*, ca. 1638, HCA 30/457 (37); Marston, Instructions to Holmes, Apr. 20, 1708, Essex Institute, 3530.F.14. For wage comparisons, see E. H. Phelps Brown and Sheila V. Hopkins, "Seven Centuries of Building Wages," *Economica*, XXII (1955), 195-206. They have been criticized, among other things, for assuming that builders' incomes can be equated with wages; see Donald Woodward, "Wage Rates and Living Standards in Pre-Industrial England," *Past and Present*, no. 91 (May 1981), 28-45.

the Mediterranean could close markets for cod. Wartime inflation in seamen's wages, of the kind predicted by Defoe, is easily observed in the seventeenth century, particularly between 1650 and 1680, when Britain was more often at war than not.[27]

War was not, however, the only occasion of wage rises. Significantly, seamen's average wages in peacetime rose from about twenty to twenty-five shillings monthly in the same period. The change is important, since there was no price inflation in this period—unlike the doubling of seamen's wages between 1540 and 1640, which simply matched an equivalent rise in the cost of living. The rise in fishermen's incomes in the second half of the seventeenth century was probably not just a result of a long period of international tension. Wages of seamen in peacetime were, by 1680, almost 40 percent above their 1620 levels, but builders' wages were also up by about 50 percent—and builders' increments consistently preceded seamen's. The comparison suggests a trend even more general than the wartime pressures described by Defoe. At any rate, skilled fishermen's wages at Newfoundland followed these general trends, with a perceptible rise in incomes to about 1680.[28]

If we consider wages for skilled Newfoundland fishermen between 1620 and 1720 in the context of the wartime fluctuations of able seamen's wages and the general improvement of seamen's and builder's wages, two points are evident. Fishermen's incomes vary over time no more than the wages of seamen in general. Assuming skilled fishermen enjoyed not only wages but also shares and portage rights, there is a consistent relationship between skilled fishermen's earnings and the wages of able sea-

27. On wage fluctuations, see Davis, *English Shipping Industry*, 135-136; Andrews, *Ships, Money, and Politics*, 75-77; Daniel Defoe, "An Essay on Projects" (1697), in Henry Morley, ed., *The Earlier Life and the Chief Earlier Works of Daniel Defoe* (London, 1889), 156. On prices, see Daniel Vickers, "'A Knowen and Staple Commoditie': Codfish Prices in Essex County, Massachusetts, 1640-1775," Essex Institute, *Historical Collections*, CXXIV (1988), 186-197.

28. Davis, *English Shipping Industry*, 144; Andrews, *Ships, Money, and Politics*, 77; E. H. Phelps Brown and Sheila V. Hopkins, "Seven Centuries of the Prices of Consumables, Compared with Builders' Wage-Rates," *Economica*, XXIII (1956), 296-314; Brown and Hopkins, "Seven Centuries of Building Wages," *Economica*, XXII (1955), 195-206; F. P. Braudel and F. Spooner, "Prices in Europe from 1450 to 1750," in E. E. Rich and C. H. Wilson, eds., *Cambridge Economic History of Europe*, IV, *The Economy of Expanding Europe in the Sixteenth and Seventeenth Centuries* (Cambridge, 1967), 374-485; Andrews, "Elizabethan Seaman," *Mariner's Mirror*, LXVIII (1982), 245-262.

men as well as a looser but general relationship between the seamen's and builders' wages (Table 11). When skilled Newfoundland fishermen made "an indifferent good voyage," as Captain Berry called a catch of two hundred quintals per boat, they could expect to earn about 140–150 percent of a contemporary able seaman's wage. Newfoundland fishermen did at least as well, relative to British able seamen, as New England fishermen, who earned about 125 percent of able seamen's wages in the 1640s and late 1660s. It may be true, as some scholars have suggested, that by 1700 Massachusetts fishing incomes were relatively high, but there is little evidence that wage rates in Newfoundland were significantly lower in the seventeenth century, as is often assumed. The significant difference between these fisheries lay in the longer season possible off New England, not in rates of remuneration.[29]

Let us take Occam's razor to our discussions of seventeenth-century maritime labor. What we know of Newfoundland fishermen's incomes supports the assumption that there was, in the study period, one labor market for British seamen in the North Atlantic. Newfoundland fishermen's wages bore a consistently positive relationship with able seamen's wages, and there was no significant spread between the income fishermen of similar skills could expect, at any one time, at Newfoundland and New England. This conclusion is important for the social history of seventeenth-century Newfoundland, because it suggests that the most skilled of the island's fishermen had relatively high disposable incomes, whether or not they deteriorated in subsequent centuries. It also accords with the contemporary view that Newfoundland fishermen's wages were high, however this frequently made observation may conflict with our present-day preconceptions based on later observations of relative impoverishment.[30]

From the point of view of the naval officers and the Whitehall bureaucrats who were so inquisitive about Newfoundland in the later seven-

29. Berry to Williamson, July 24, 1675, CO 1/34 (118), 240–241; Rogers, *Historical Geography*, 119. For higher wages in New England, see Daniel Vickers, "Work and Life on the Fishing Periphery of Essex County, Massachusetts, 1630–1675," in Hall and Allen, eds., *Seventeenth-Century New England*, 83–117 (esp. 103); and Vickers, *Farmers and Fishermen*, 109. On the winter activities of Newfoundland fishermen, see Chapter 9, below.

30. Compare, for example, Poole, "Answers," Sept. 10, 1677, CO 1/41 (62i), 149, or Wheler, "Answers," Oct. 27, 1684, CO 1/55 (56i), 241, with *Historical Atlas of Canada*, I, 48.

Table 11. *Income for Skilled Fishermen, Seamen, and Builders, 1640–1684*

Years	Wages per Month Fishermen	Fishermen's Wages Relative to Wages of English	
		Seamen	Builders' Laborers
New England			
1640s	23s.	118%	100%
1666–1671	40	123	160
Newfoundland			
1625	29s.	145%	174%
1663	28	144	112
1675	57	152	228
1677	44	146	176
1684	34	139	136

Note: Seamen's wages for 1628 are the competitive rates proclaimed by Charles I in 1626. Fishermen's income for 1628 is the average of what Guy suggests for headers and splitters. Fishermen's income for 1663 is adjusted to reflect a normal catch of 200 quintals. Portage of £3 has been added to fishermen's income for 1663 and 1677; this figure for portage is assumed to be included in 1625, 1675, and 1684. Fishermen's income for 1677 is based on the average for boat crews, which was very close to the skilled average. Monthly incomes have been calculated on the basis of a 7-month season at Newfoundland and, following Vickers, a 10-month season at New England. Davis's figures for the war year 1674 are used, since Berry's 1675 estimate would have been based on the fishermen's experience of the previous year. Figures for English building laborers assume 25 working days per month, a likely parallel to employment in Newfoundland.

Sources: Nicholas Guy, "Instructions Given to John Poyntz," ca. 1628, in Cell, *Newfoundland Discovered*, 247–249; John Winter, "A Booke of Accounts . . . ," June 17, 1640, *Trelawny Papers*, 290–295; Yonge, *Journal*, 55–58; Daniel Vickers, "Work and Life on the Fishing Periphery of Essex County, Massachusetts, 1630–1675," in David D. Hall and David Grayson Allen, eds., *Seventeenth Century New England: A Conference Held by the Colonial Society of Massachusetts, June 18 and 19, 1982*, Colonial Society of Massachusetts, *Publications*, LXIII, *Collections* (Boston, 1984), 83–117; John Berry to Joseph Williamson, July 24, 1675, CO 1/34 (118), 240–241; William Poole, "Answers to the Severall Heads of Inquiry . . . ," Sept. 10, 1677, CO 1/41 (62i), 149–152; Francis Wheler, "The Charge for Fitting Out Two Boats . . . according to the Custome of the Inhabitants . . . ," Oct. 27, 1684, CO 1/55 (56iii), 251–252; Charles I, "A Proclamation Touching Mariners," 1626, NDRO Barnstaple, 913; Ralph Davis, *The Rise of the English Shipping Industry in the Seventeenth and Eighteenth Centuries* (London, 1962), 135–136; E. H. Phelps Brown and Sheila V. Hopkins, "Seven Centuries of Building Wages," *Economica*, XXII (1955), 195–206 (esp. 205, table 1).

teenth century, fishing servants remained poor men. They were, likewise, poor from the point of view of fishing merchants. Sir David Kirke's discussion of service in the fishery, with which this chapter begins, concludes with a sarcastic answer to West Country adventurers who sought to keep gentlemen, like himself, out of Newfoundland:

> It is charitably objected that it is poore men's worke and that those poore men, if they worke for noblemen or gentlemen, will eate them upp and consume them, lookinge only after their wages, without care or conscience of what they undertake. And upon this so vaine and harsh a prejudice shall some thousands of His Majesty's subjects, who have been only bredd to the skill of fishing in Newfoundland, be now neglected and cast out to seek after other trades.

For Kirke, the share system would reconcile the interests of masters and the "poore men" who worked in the fishery.[31]

ᲒᲙ Portage for Freeborn Englishmen

Shares became less important to fishermen in the later seventeenth century (Table 12). In the ship fishery, shares were less significant as a proportion of total remuneration in 1684 than they had been in 1663. Over this period, the average share component for skilled fishermen dropped from about 60 to about 40 percent of payments. A transformation in remuneration was under way in the second half of the seventeenth century, but we can hardly speak (as one account of the British fisheries does) of the replacement of an older system of fishing on shares by "the wage system," since shares were still in use in 1684 and remained so for decades, if not centuries.[32]

31. On fishers as poor, see CTP, Minutes, Dec. 4, 1675, CO 391/1, 25–26; quotation from Kirke, "Reply to Answeare," Sept. 29, 1639, CO 1/10 (38), 97–114.

32. Boys and green men do not receive shares in either period. Yonge's figures are recalculated to reflect a normative two-hundred-quintal catch. Both 1663 and 1684 were peacetime seasons, assumed fish prices were similar, and neither Yonge nor Captain Wheler had an obvious bias on the subject of shares, so the apparent decline in the significance of shares is probably real. Earlier evidence would aid assessment of whether this is a long-term trend or a variation caused by short-term factors. For the simplistic notion of "the wage system," see Lounsbury, *British Fishery*, 90.

Table 12. *Share Remuneration, Ship-Based Fishery, Newfoundland, 1663 and 1684*

	Share Proportion of Fishing Income	
Laborers	1663	1684
Boat crews		
Boatmasters	43%	33%
Midshipmen	80	44
Foreshipmen	83	33
Shore crews		
Splitters	62	40
Headers	83	50
Salters	0	
Boys or green men	0	0
Ships' officers		
Master	100	0
Mate	83	
Averages		
Boat crews	69%	37%
Skilled shore labor	48	45
All skilled labor	62	38
All labor	49	30
Overall	50%	29%

Note: Fishing income is wage plus share. The figures for 1663 are recalculated, assuming a share of £5, which would reflect a catch of 200 quintals per boat. All averages are weighted using the proportions of various skills suggested in the relevant document.

Sources: Yonge, *Journal*, 55–58; Francis Wheler, "The Expence of Fitting Out Ten Boats and the Charge of a Shipp . . . ," Oct. 27, 1684, CO 1/55 (56ii), 249–250.

The only consistent evidence of the payment of straight wages, without a share component, in the later-seventeenth-century Newfoundland fishery pertains to the youngest and least-skilled workers, who could expect payments of one or two pounds a season. These "boys and green men" formed a growing proportion of crews. In 1622, green men represented 14 percent of the crew in Richard Whitbourne's estimate, the same proportion implied by Yonge's figures for 1663. The proportion of green men then increases to 20 percent in Wheler's report for 1684 and 26 percent in the case of the Massachusetts vessel, the *Beginning*, in 1708. Since unskilled servants received straight wages, wages were becoming more important in the Newfoundland fishery in the narrow sense that those paid straight wages were better represented among crews. There is, however, no evidence that this moderate deskilling was restricted to any particular sector of the industry. The question remains of whether a particular sector of the fishery initiated the broader trend to a greater emphasis on wages in the remuneration of skilled workers.[33]

The premise that planters and migratory boatkeepers introduced the payment of straight wages in this period is one of those curious scholarly ideas with a persistent life of its own, unfettered by much in the way of relevant evidence. Boatkeepers might have been inclined to offer wages to their crews, but confirmation of that hypothesis is elusive. In 1684, Captain Wheler used the category "wages" in his boatkeeper's budget and observed that planters' servants "change from yeare to yeare, and come from England and covenant with their masters for the fishing season or the yeare at high rates." Because Wheler did not mention shares, are we to conclude that the intelligible planter paid straight wages? He seems to have used "wages" to include passage costs, and here the term might just as well have included shares. Again, the term was used through the seventeenth century to mean payments for service, including shares. In 1698, for example, Captain John Norris told the Board of Trade that fishermen's "wages . . . generally go by the shares, which is a third of the fish and train." So Captain Wheler's discussion of "wages" is not evidence that wages, in the modern sense, had displaced shares among planters, let alone that these small operators had led a transition to wages.[34]

33. Whitbourne, *Discourse*, 179; Yonge, *Journal*, 54–60; Wheler, "Charge of a Shipp," Oct. 27, 1684, CO 1/55 (56ii), 249–250; Marston, Instructions to Holmes, Apr. 20, 1708, Essex Institute, 3530.F.14.

34. Matthews, "Fisheries," 163, cites Stephens, "West Country Ports," *RT Devon*, LXXXVIII (1956), 90–101 (esp. 94); Stephens cites Lounsbury, *British Fishery*, 82–91, 110, but, despite his assurance, Lounsbury offers no documentation on this point. Matthews mentions a passage in which Wheler observed that the by-boat-men bargained with their crews "at the same price as the master[s] of shipps doe" (Wheler, "Answers," Oct. 27, 1684, CO 1/55 [56i], 242). Since shares were still in use in the ship fishery, any preference for straight wages cannot be

The idea that boatkeepers, whether planters or by-boat-men, might offer straight wages is implausible, for several reasons. First, it does not make sense from the point of view of labor discipline. Most boatkeepers did not join their boat crews' daily ventures to the fishing grounds: of the 144 by-boat-keepers and planters in 1675, only 43 percent hired fewer than the normative five men per boat. Besides, one boat or shore crew was the most one employer could supervise at a time, and most boatkeepers had more than one boat. Most crews were therefore unsupervised, so boatkeepers had a strong motive to incorporate a share component in their crew agreements in the interest of labor discipline, as emphasized by Sir David Kirke. The unpredictability of the fishery also militated against the abandonment of shares. In a bad season, small entrepreneurs would be at grave economic risk if they had promised straight wages when catches or prices or both were down.[35]

In 1675, John Parrett, a spokesman for certain West Country merchant adventurers, suggested an elegant scheme to eradicate their new competitors at Newfoundland, the migratory by-boat-keepers. He proposed to choke off their labor supply by limiting the number of servant passengers permitted to go to Newfoundland on ships fishing. This strategy would, of course, have had a serious impact on planters as well. Secretary of State Sir Joseph Williamson objected to the proposal "in behalf of the poore, that this design was to exclude them from being sharers in anything and that they would be still obliged to serve the rich as labourers." The mythic struggle between fishermen and the merchants who controlled the ship-based fishery was, as Williamson understood it, a class conflict. He saw boatkeepers and their servants as poorly capitalized "sharers" whose only alternative was labor in the well-capitalized ship fishery. There seems little reason to doubt his assumption that the fisherfolk of the West Country and Newfoundland preferred to remain "sharers," if they could, and good reason to suspect that shipmasters

---

proven. Quotations from Wheler, "Charge for Two Boats," Oct. 27, 1684, CO 1/55 (56iii), 249–250; Wheler, "Answers," Oct. 27, 1684, CO 1/55 (56i), 239 (the planters, Wheler reported, then sell fish "for their men's wages, salt, provisions, and liquour"). The 1698 quotation is from John Norris, "An Answer to the Heads . . . in Relation to Newfoundland," Nov. 13, 1698, CO 194/1 (126i), 267–268. Cf. *OED*, s.v. "wages."

35. John Berry, "A List of the Planters Names . . . ," Sept. 12, 1675, CO 1/35 (17ii), 150–156; Berry, "List of Ships," Sept. 12, 1675, CO 1/35 (17i), 137–148.

were quite ready to pay straight wages, when they could, to those who would labor for them.[36]

The only strong evidence of a straight wage arrangement, without shares, for a whole crew in the early modern period occurs in the letter of instruction the Salem merchant Marston wrote for the season of 1708; in other words, it relates to the migratory ship fishery. This was, however, an unusual case: shares were still the normal method of payment in the New England fishery. (Furthermore, the voyage ended as a financial disaster and may represent an unsuccessful experiment with wages.) The complex payments reported by Yonge and Wheler indicate that the later seventeenth century saw only a partial shift away from shares in the ship-based migratory fishery. It must be emphasized, as Commodore Norris did in 1698, that shares had not disappeared from the ship fishery; indeed, they were still in use as late as 1750. Economic logic and their continued use by Newfoundland inshore fishermen into the late twentieth century suggest that shares never ceased to be part of the pattern of remuneration in Newfoundland's resident small-boat fishery. The persistence of shares among resident crews does not necessarily illuminate the origin of wage payments, however. Boatkeepers might have been conservative—in the sense that they retained shares as a component of crew remuneration in the later seventeenth century—but might nevertheless have been the sector of the industry that originated partial payment in fixed wages earlier in the century.[37]

Some parallel evidence from Maine suggests why some fishers began to accept wages, despite the early modern aversion to wage labor. The

36. CTP, Minutes, Dec. 4, 1675, CO 391/1, 25–26.

37. Vickers, "Work and Life," in Hall and Allen, eds., *Seventeenth-Century New England*, 83–117 (esp. 92); Innis, *Cod Fisheries*, 151, 152; Glanville James Davies, "England and Newfoundland: Policy and Trade, 1660–1783" (Ph.D. diss., University of Southampton, 1980), 295. Sean Cadigan, "Seamen, Fishermen, and the Law: The Role of the Wages and Lien System in the Decline of Wage Labour in the Newfoundland Fishery," in Colin Howell and Richard J. Twomey, eds., *Jack Tar in History: Essays in the History of Maritime Life and Labour* (Fredericton, N.B., 1991), 105–131, assumes that, because Palliser's Act of 1775 required written wage agreements for fishing servants, it thereby banned share agreements. He may be reading too much into the use of the word "wage." Besides, much of the inshore fishery was carried on by inhabitants, often employing family labor without written contracts and working, effectively, on shares; cf. Rogers, *Historical Geography*, 118. Share agreements were recognized by the Judicature Act of 1824.

shift from shares to wages in the North Atlantic cod fisheries was very gradual. Patterns of remuneration in the Maine and Newfoundland fisheries of the mid-seventeenth century were similar. Indeed, early evidence from Maine is valuable from the Newfoundland perspective, for the wage agreements that have survived in John Winter's accounts for Robert Trelawny's permanent fishing station at Richmond Island, Maine, are unparalleled in the Newfoundland records for the first half of the century. In the early Maine resident fishery, lower-paid unskilled workers earned a flat rate, as they would on the English Shore. In 1639–1640, for example, junior employees in Maine were paid annually as servants, most at the rate of five pounds for a full year. Skilled workers signed on for shares plus a wage component of about a third of their total remuneration. Young, unskilled green men had a dependent status like that of a servant in husbandry and might not have had much choice about the form of their remuneration.[38]

Of the fifteen better-paid employees at Richmond Island whose incomes can be determined, only two, who might not have been fishermen, were paid straight wages (£8 and £14). Most of the rest made a share of some £9 05s., with a wage of a few pounds. Three men made simply the share, and two men a half-share plus either £2 or £3 10s. The manager, John Winter, earned £40 on top of his share, and another man a share plus £22. This pattern of payments was standard at Richmond Island in the 1630s and 1640s. Excluding the manager, Winter, earnings among those with shares averaged £11 08s., of which wages made up about one-third. The proportion of wage remuneration among skilled workers in the Newfoundland fishery of the 1660s is about the same. Why had skilled fishermen begun, by 1640, to accept employment agreements that treated them, at least in part, as wage laborers, despite contemporary cultural prejudices?[39]

The records of the Richmond Island fishery contain an interesting clue. Winter does not generally use the term "wage" for fixed annual

38. Hill, "Pottage," in Hill, *Change and Continuity*, 219; cf. Josselyn, *Voyages*, 143–144; John Winter, "Accounts for the Plantation . . . ," July 15, 1639, Winter, "A Booke of Accounts . . . ," June 17, 1640, both in *Trelawny Papers*, 183–196, 290–297.

39. Winter, "Booke of Accounts," June 17, 1640, *Trelawny Papers*, 290–295; E. A. Churchill, "A Most Ordinary Lot of Men: The Fishermen at Richmond Island, Maine, in the Early Seventeenth Century," *New England Quarterly*, LVII (1984), 184–204. Colonial currency was then at par with sterling.

payments in his accounts but instead the term "portage." His terminology strongly suggests that these fixed payments were conceptualized
by Winter and his crews as a substitute for the income from private ventures they could have expected had they been employed in the traditional
migratory fishery, rather than at a permanent station. In the end, Winter equated wages and portage. He called the fixed remuneration of forty
pounds that he received annually from May 1636 to May 1639 his "portage money," but in 1640 he referred to it as "last years wages." Such
usage seems to be the origin of the New England fishermen's term "port-
ledge bill" for wage agreement. We can glimpse here the evolution of
economic culture. The wage relationship, which self-respecting skilled
workers in this period still avoided if possible, might have been less objectionable when seen as the transmutation of a traditional right in a new
context.[40]

Workers' loss of perquisites or the transmutation of such benefits into
cash was a common phenomenon in early modern England. In the Newfoundland fishery, the development of the planter and by-boat-keeper
fisheries put the traditional privilege of portage into question. "In such
ways," as one scholar of the English working class observed, "economic
rationalization nibbled . . . through the bonds of paternalism." Wage payments became more important in the British fishery at Newfoundland,
but boatkeepers and the masters of fishing ships did not compete by dif-
ferentiating their modes of production more than the constraints of scale
and location required. The notion that the ship-based and boatkeeper
fisheries at Newfoundland represented two differentiated modes of production, structured respectively around shares and wages, has little historical basis, other than that boatkeepers could not offer their crews the
right of portage, as the masters of ships could.[41]

Some historians have seen a breakthrough from medieval conceptions
of trade to modern capitalism in seventeenth-century Newfoundland, but
this perception is implausible. By 1700, migratory fishermen certainly
resembled a working class of nominally free wage-earners as much as any
other class in any other colony, but this situation was hardly revolutionary: the Newfoundland fishery was never anything but a capitalist industry. The fluctuation of skilled fishermen's wages in the seventeenth cen-

40. Winter, "Accounts," July 15, 1639, Winter, "Booke of Accounts," June 17,
1640, both in *Trelawny Papers*, 183-196, 290-297.
41. E. P. Thompson, "Patrician Society, Plebeian Culture," *Journal of Social
History*, VII (1973-1974), 382-405 (quotation on 385).

tury, in response to conditions in a broader labor market, indicates that remuneration, however calculated, already reflected contractual and not simply customary labor relationships. The fishery was already capitalist. It was one of those early nodes of capitalism that furthered the general transformation of the world economy. The planter and by-boat sectors developed after 1640, and there followed a shift in emphasis from shares to wages, but these changes did not result in anything we would recognize as modern industrial capitalism. Despite its evolution, the Newfoundland fishery remained protoindustrial, like a combination of service in husbandry and a putting-out system.[42]

The distinctive economic culture shared by planters, by-boat-keepers, and shipmasters at Newfoundland was not sui generis. Similar piecework systems evolved elsewhere where efficient production required intensive seasonal labor, as in, for example, the contemporary hay and peat industries of the Netherlands' North Sea coast or in seasonal migratory fisheries around the Atlantic, from Maine to the Lofoten Islands of northern Norway. Newfoundland's seventeenth-century outports resembled the scattered, often newly established hamlets of Britain's own woodland settlements, which have been vividly characterized as consisting of a laboring aristocracy, on the one hand—a small core of indigenous and relatively well-off peasants—and, on the other hand, growing numbers of indigent squatters and wanderers, described by one contemporary observer, in words that might have been lifted from a West Country complaint about Newfoundland, as "given to little or no kind of labour . . . dwelling far from any church or chapel, and . . . as ignorant of God or of

42. Rogers, *Historical Geography*, 117–119, Lounsbury, *British Fishery*, 88–91, and Stephens, "West Country Ports," *RT Devon*, LXXXVIII (1956), 90–101, see a breakthrough to capitalism. Rogers, *Historical Geography*, 118–119, could make this claim about a fishing proletariat only by ignoring mariners as a class. Cf. Marcus Rediker, *Between the Devil and the Deep Blue Sea: Merchant Seamen, Pirates, and the Anglo-American Maritime World, 1700–1750* (Cambridge, 1987), who makes a similar claim for deep-sea mariners, only by ignoring fishermen. John Frederick Martin, *Profits in the Wilderness: Entrepreneurship and the Founding of New England Towns in the Seventeenth Century* (Chapel Hill, N.C., 1991), 123, 131–133, 149, sees New England town development as early capitalism. Capitalist shipping in general and fishing in particular would seem to be older; see Ralph Davis, "Earnings of Capital in the English Shipping Industry, 1670–1730," *Journal of Economic History*, XVII (1957), 409–425 (esp. 424–425); and G. V. Scammell, "Shipowning in England, circa 1450–1550," *TRHS*, 5th Ser., XII (1962), 105–122.

any civil course of life as the very savages." By the middle of the seventeenth century, several sorts of people were making a living on Newfoundland's English Shore, distinguishable by their station, by their economic relations, and also by their degree of attachment to the place.[43]

43. Jan Lucassen, "The Netherlands, the Dutch, and Long-Distance Migration in the Late Sixteenth to Early Nineteenth Centuries," in Nicholas Canny, ed., *Europeans on the Move: Studies on European Migration, 1500–1800* (Oxford, 1994), 153–191; Everitt, "Social Mobility," *Past and Present*, no. 33 (April 1966), 56–73 (esp. 58); Everitt, "Farm Labourers," in Thirsk, ed., *Agrarian History*, IV, *1500–1640*, 396–465 (esp. 411), in Finberg, gen. ed., *Agrarian History*. Other migratory fisheries are briefly discussed in Chapter 9, below.

6 ?❧ RESIDENTS

*Your petitioners ancestors being settled in the said island and haveing
lived there severall yeares under certaine lawes and orders formed to
them by patents by Your Majesties royall ancestors . . . accordingly
now are settled there with their families to the number of 1600
persons.*
—Inhabitants of Newfoundland, Petition to Charles II, Dec. 19, 1677

In 1634, King Charles I gave what came to be known as the Western Charter to the Devon and Dorset ports venturing to the Newfoundland fishery. Apart from the Grant of Newfoundland to Sir David Kirke
and his associates in 1637, the Western Charter's ground rules for an
open-access industry, amended and reinvoked in several versions, were
as close as Britain came to formally regulating the English Shore until
the very end of the seventeenth century. A clause in the Grant of 1637
required planters to live at least six miles inland, but no one paid attention to that. In fact, no planter lived more than a few minutes' walk from
the Atlantic Ocean, least of all Governor Kirke, who took up residence in
the former Mansion House of George Calvert, Lord Baltimore, at Ferryland, "within a coit-cast of the water." In 1653, the Council of State modified the 1634 Western Charter by recognizing the right of planters to
waterfront property. The second Western Charter of 1661 repeated the
first, with the addition of a clause forbidding ships going to Newfoundland from carrying passengers, except "such as are to plant and do intend
to settle there"—an exception that explicitly favored settlement. The restriction on passengers was designed to choke off labor supply to the
emerging by-boat fishery and would have done so, had it been enforced,
although complaints suggest that it was not. In 1671, Charles II and his
Privy Council amended the second Charter with several clauses, including a resuscitation of the impractical six-mile rule, which the planters
feared as a scheme for "removing them into the woods." No authority
actually tried to evict them from the coast until 1675, when a faction of
West Country merchants persuaded Whitehall to instruct the naval commodore Sir John Berry "to admonish the inhabitants either to returne
home into England or to betake them selves to other of His Majesties
plantations." After a few weeks in Newfoundland, Captain Berry could
see that this demand was neither just nor practical. Although he later

claimed to have asked the planters to go, Berry tacitly accepted their anomalous legal situation by ignoring his orders to remove them. No sooner did the Privy Council proclaim a third Western Charter early in 1676, incorporating the controversial six-mile clause, than the Lords of Trade and Plantations began to share Berry's doubts about the current antisettlement policy. Two years after the tense summer of 1675, the "Inhabitants of Newfoundland" played on these doubts when they submitted their petition for some formal recognition of their status.[1]

Thomas Dodridge was a Newfoundland planter when the late-Stuart colonial bureaucracy dealt with this defense of his rights. Dodridge would surely have supported the petition, although we have no evidence that he had even heard of it. Thanks to a series of contemporary censuses, we do know something of him, besides his Devon surname, and of his family, besides their residence on the English Shore—assuming that the

1. Charles I, "A Grant of Newfoundland," Nov. 13, 1637, CO 195/1 (2), 11-27, Council of State, "Laws, Rules, and Ordinances Whereby the Affairs and Fishery of the Newfoundland Are to Be Governed," June 3, 1653, CO 1/38 (33iii), 74-75, Charles II in Council, Western Charter, Jan. 26, 1661, CO 1/15 (3), Charles II, Order, Mar. 10, 1671, CO 1/26, 20-26, Charles II, Order, May 5, 1675, CO 1/34 (71), 151, Charles II, "A Charter Granted to the West Country Adventurers," Jan. 27, 1676, CO 1/65 (36), 128-134, all in Matthews, *Constitutional Laws*, 77-131, 139-144, 166-180; CTP, Journal, Mar. 25, 30, 1675, Apr. 6, 13, 1676, May 3, 1677, *CSP*: Colonial; James Pratt, Examination, in *Baltimore v. Kirke*, Mar. 29, 1652, HCA 13/65, n.p.; Joseph Williamson, "Newfoundland," 1675, CO 1/34 (16), 24-57, 69-73 (transcription in *CSP*: Colonial, 1675-1676, Addenda, 1574-1674, 156-163); Merchants of Dartmouth et al. to Privy Council, Nov. 27, 1663, SP 29/84 (71); John Berry to Williamson, July 24, 1675, CO 1/34 (118), 240-241; Berry to Sir Robert Southwell, Sept. 9, 1675, CO 1/35 (17), 133-134; Berry, "Observations . . . in Relation to the Trade and Inhabitants of Newfoundland," Aug. 18, 1676, CO 1/35 (81), 325-326. On planters' fears, see Captain William Davies to Mr. Wren, Sept. 9, 1675, CO 1/27 (27), 74. For a planter's permissive reading of the 1671 order, see John Downing, "A Breif Narrative concerning Newfoundland," Nov. 24, 1676, British Library, Egerton MS 2395, 560-563. For West Country pressure in 1675, see Gentry of Exeter, etc., Petition to Charles II, Mar. 25, 1675, CO 1/65 (25), 100; John Parrett, "The Great Advantages to This Kingdom . . . [of] Fishing Ships," Mar. 25, 1675, CO 1/65 (27), 102-103. *CSP*: Colonial incorrectly interprets the 1661 limitation of servants to the ship's company only. On the Council for Trade and the Council for Foreign Plantations (1660), Council for Trade and Plantations (1672), the Lords of Trade and Plantations (1675), and the Board of Trade (1696), see R. B. Pugh, *The Records of the Colonial and Dominions Offices* (London, 1964), 4-5.

Thomas "Dodridge" who fished at Brigus South with one boat in 1675 was the same Thomas "Dorderige" with one boat reported at Ferryland in 1676, the Thomas "Doderige" who operated two boats at Fermeuse in 1677, and, indeed, the Thomas "Dotterg" with two boats at Trepassey in 1681. Each census records his wife and a daughter resident with him. It would seem they were blessed with a son in the winter of 1675/6, because he, too, was enumerated in the later censuses, though unnamed, like all dependents in these early records. The Dodridges did well in this period: there were only six fishing servants in the household in 1675, but by 1677 Thomas had nine men in his service, a more practical number to handle the two boats he now owned and the sixteen to twenty tons of fish that had to be cured every summer.[2]

Yet questions remain. What are we to make of the family's repeated removal southward from Brigus South via Ferryland and Fermeuse to Trepassey? Is it best understood as residential mobility along the English Shore, or as a permanent attachment to Newfoundland? Such mobility along the Shore was not common among planters before the wars of the 1690s and 1700s, although perhaps more typical of their servants. Neither the surname Dodridge nor an obvious variant occurs in the next nominal census of 1708. What is the significance of the disappearance of this surname, given the lapse of almost thirty years, encompassing two wars, three invasions, and the exile of the inhabitants from the English Shore following the successful Franco-Canadian campaign of 1696–1697? Were people like the Dodridges never really resident? To assume so would raise other interpretative difficulties, however. How was Thomas, for example, related to the planter Trustrum Dodridge who had signed a bill of exchange on New England in 1647 and was still one of the Newfoundland debtors of a Salem merchant in 1670? Where were Thomas Dodridge and his family between 1681 and 1693, when they are documented, in Ferryland again, as customers of the Salem merchant Joseph Buckley? Some such problems are inherent in any attempt to reconstruct a population; some are issues peculiar to the English Shore, for Newfoundland was not a plantation like the others.[3]

2. For the surname "Dodridge," see Maritime History Archive, MUN, Keith Matthews, Name Files D2251. Census sources are given below. The name does not appear in E. R. Seary, *Family Names of the Island of Newfoundland*, ed. William Kirwin (St. John's, 1998).

3. Valentine Hill, Letter of Attorney, Mar. 24, 1648, *Aspinwall Records*,

⟨꽃⟩ *Comparisons with Other Colonies*

The late-seventeenth-century population history of Newfoundland is as accessible as that of almost any other European colony in North America. Just about half of early colonial censuses concern Newfoundland. Canada, the part of New France we now call Quebec, was enumerated nine times in the seventeenth century, beginning in 1666; but Virginia was the only British continental colony enumerated before 1696. On the request of a committee of the Privy Council, the naval commodores at Newfoundland filed an intermittent series of "Replies to Heads of Inquiry" from 1675 onward. The most detailed of these reports date between 1675 and 1684 and provide censuses of both the fishery and inhabitants. The Newfoundland and West Indian censuses of 1673–1684 together form a rich cluster of data, gathered for the Committee for Trade and Plantations, in its third incarnation. These remarkable sources, unparalleled in England itself until 1801, reflect the increasing interest of the Privy Council in colonial issues. Similar considerations led France's colonial bureaucracy to take repeated censuses of the recently established French settlements on Newfoundland's south coast between 1671 and 1711. The seventeenth-century English Shore lacks notarial, church, and the wide range of administrative and commercial records that make New France demographically the best-documented early modern colony in North America.[4]

127–128; Joseph Buckley, "Leager 1693," Peabody Museum, Salem, Mass., Acc,16,100; Commodore John Mitchel, "Number of the Inhabitants . . . ," Dec. 2, 1708, CO 194/4 (76ii), 252–256. The similar Irish name Doherty or Dougherty does not occur in Newfoundland until the late eighteenth century; cf. Maritime History Archive, MUN, Keith Matthews, Name Files D202. For emphasis on mobility, see Cole Harris, "European Beginnings in the Northwest Atlantic: A Comparative View," in David D. Hall and David Grayson Allen, eds., *Seventeenth-Century New England: A Conference Held by the Colonial Society of Massachusetts, June 18 and 19, 1982*, Colonial Society of Massachusetts, *Publications*, LXIII, *Collections* (Boston, 1984), 119–152 (esp. 137); Handcock, *Origins*, 43, 46; David J. Starkey, "Devonians and the Newfoundland Trade," *Maritime History of Devon*, I, 163–171.

4. Hubert Charbonneau, *Vie et mort de nos ancêtres: etude démographique* (Montreal, 1975), 28–30; Robert V. Wells, *The Population of the British Colonies in America before 1776: A Survey of Census Data* (Princeton, N.J., 1975), 7–16; Leslie Choquette, *Frenchmen into Peasants: Modernity and Tradition in*

The number of censuses taken of the residents and the fishery are a clear indication that Newfoundland was becoming an important issue for both Britain and France. The information was politically useful because the settling of the English Shore, on the one hand, and of Placentia Bay, on the other, were contested at the time. A curious little notebook kept by Secretary of State Sir Joseph Williamson provides another index of this interest. For a few years between 1674 and 1677, he summarized, in his elliptical hand, the paper and committee work he had to digest regarding British interests in the Americas. He devoted a few pages each to Surinam, Nevis, Barbados, the Leeward Islands, and New England; but his précis of the state of debate on Newfoundland takes up most of the notebook. In the larger scheme of things, colonial bureaucrats, like Secretary Williamson, were conscious of Newfoundland's strategic position as a kind of sentry post at the northern gateway to the Americas.

the Peopling of French Canada (Cambridge, Mass., 1997), 4-16. Nominal censuses survive for 1675, 1676, 1677, and 1681: John Berry, "A List of the Planters Names . . . ," Sept. 12, 1675, CO 1/35 (17ii), 150-156; John Wyborn, "The Names of the English Inhabitants . . . ," Dec. 7, 1676, CO 1/38 (89), 239-240; William Poole, "A Particular Accompt of All the Inhabitants and Planters . . . ," Sept. 10, 1677, CO 1/41 (61iv, vi, vii), 158-166; James Story, "An Account of What Fishing Shipps, Sack Shipps, Planters, etc., Boat Keepers . . . ," Sept. 1, 1681, CO 1/47 (52i), 113-121. For 1680, there are local nominal censuses in Robert Robinson, "An Account of . . . St. John's and Baye of Bulls . . . ," and Robinson, "An Account of the Inhabitants in St. John's Harbour and Quitevidi . . . ," Sept. 16, 1680, CO 1/46 (8iii, iv), 23-24. For 1682, there is a summary census for the southern Avalon as well as a nominal census of St. John's and selected outports in Daniel Jones, "Newfoundland Accompt of Inhabitants—Fishery, etc. . . . ," Sept. 12, 1682, and Jones, "An Accompt of the Planters Belonging to St. John's Harbour . . . ," Oct. 11, 1682, CO 1/49 (51v, ix), 192, 196-198. Summary data for 1680 are in ". . . Planters and Inhabitants . . . ," British Library, Add MS 15898, 133; summary data by community for 1684 is in Frances Wheler, "English Planters Inhabiting the Easterne Coast of Newfound Land . . . ," Oct. 27, 1684, CO 1/55 (56vii), 257. On West Indies censuses, see Richard Dunn, *Sugar and Slaves: The Rise of the Planter Class in the English West Indies, 1624-1713* (Chapel Hill, N.C., 1972). Censuses for Plaisance and sometimes other smaller French settlements survive for 1671, 1673, 1687, 1691, 1693, 1694, 1701, 1704, 1706, 1710, and 1711; most are nominal. Most are in France, Archives Nationales, Archives d'Outre Mer G1, CDLXVII, transcribed in NAC MG1, and published in Fernand-D. Thibodeau, "Recensements de Terreneuve et Plaisance," *Mémoires de la Société Généalogique Canadienne-Française*, X (1959), 179-188, XI (1960), 69-85, XIII (1962), 204-208, XIII (1962), 245-255.

Their great curiosity about relatively small colonies was, in this sense, simply pragmatic.[5]

At least with respect to the English Shore, the surviving "Replies to the Inquiries" of an increasingly inquisitive bureaucracy have serious statistical limitations. Many are simply head counts, providing only the number of planters, wives, children, servants, boats, fishing stages, train vats, and so on, in whatever harbors the British naval commodore or his lieutenants had managed to visit during the summer in question. Occasionally, the officers charged with collecting this information took nominal censuses, but even these omit the names of wives, children, and servants. Because the early censuses of English Newfoundland normally enumerated only those inhabitants who owned boats and fishing premises, women were named only if they were heads of households, in other words, widows. There are internal inconsistencies within the British censuses, mutual contradictions among them, and other reasons to doubt that they included all inhabitants. None of the censuses covers every known settlement. Alternative figures survive for 1674, compiled by different census takers, which show alarming variation. The most detailed data on the English Shore, for 1675 and 1677, were collected during the one period in the seventeenth century characterized by overt official hostility on the part of the London authorities to settlement in Newfoundland. In this context, some inhabitants would surely have deliberately evaded official notice. This was also a period of conflict with certain West Country migratory fishing interests and one that immediately followed the damaging Dutch raids of 1673—events likely to have dispersed the resident population, making it harder to enumerate. By way of comparison, the census of Canada for 1666, a peaceable period in a territory where colonization was actively encouraged, is thought to underestimate the actual European population by about 20 percent; the Montreal census for the war year of 1698, by 40 percent. Given these uncertainties, the British censuses of Newfoundland between 1675 and 1684 are not of much use by themselves in projecting long-term trends. They remain pivotal, nevertheless, as a mass of data for a crucial decade. Exam-

---

5. Williamson, "Newfoundland," 1675, CO 1/34 (16), 24–57, 69–73 (transcription in *CSP: Colonial*, 1675–1676, Addenda, 1574–1674, 156–163). Cf. G. A. Rawlyk and E. L. Towle, "Baron de Lahontan's Memoir," *Newfoundland Quarterly*, LXII, no. 4 (1963), 5–10; Sir Robert Robinson, "Reply to the Answer of the West Countrymen," 1670, CO 1/25 (110), 277.

ined critically, in the context of names culled from noncensus documents, they can provide a terminal benchmark for seventeenth-century English settlement. The "Recensements" of Plaisance and its outliers, particularly the nominal census of 1687, can be used in the same way for the French settlements.[6]

Until about 1640, the summer population of five thousand to six thousand on Newfoundland's English Shore was in the order of the non-Native populations of New England or Virginia—but the European overwintering population of Newfoundland did not exceed a few hundred. From 1630 to 1660, Virginia and New England experienced high immigration and rapid population growth. Newfoundland's growth in this period resembled instead that of Maryland or Canada. The number of Europeans overwintering on the English Shore was about the same as Maryland's colonial population until 1650, at which point that mid-Atlantic colony enjoyed several decades of net immigration and rapid growth, as the major continental colonies already had. Nonnative winter populations on the English Shore and in Canada grew fitfully and vir-

6. Rough censuses for 1674 were collected by fishing masters for the mayors of the West Country ports: William Arundel [of Falmouth], "Description of the . . . Portes and Harbours," Mar. 13, 1675, CO 1/34 (22i), 45, 46; Tobias Burr [of Weymouth], "An Account of the Several Harbours," Mar. 3, 1675, CO 1/34 (19i), 37; Richard Hooper and Thomas Gearing [of Barnstaple and Bideford], "Answer from the Mayors Touching the Newfoundland," Mar. 30, 1675, CO 1/34 (38), 87–88. On conflict between planters and migratory West Country crews, see John Downing, Petition to Charles II, Nov. 7, 1676, CO 1/38 (33), 69; Christopher Martin, Deposition, Jan. 29, 1678, CO 1/42 (21), 56. On the Canada census of 1666, see Charbonneau, *Vie et mort*, 42, basing his estimate on birth, death, and immigration data. For doubts about population estimates, see Peter Moogk, "Manon's Fellow Exiles: Emigration from France to North America before 1763," in Nicholas Canny, ed., *Europeans on the Move: Studies on European Migration, 1500-1800* (Oxford, 1994), 236-260 (esp. 239n). The French Newfoundland censuses of the 1690s necessarily reflect military exigencies, for example, concentration of populations in defensible harbors. There was change on the English Shore between 1675 and 1684, no doubt; what is questionable is extrapolation to the long-term. With due respect to the various scholars who have attempted the same, they may be examining the back side of a blip; see, for example, Matthews, "Fisheries," 159-161, 181; Head, *Newfoundland*, 15; Wells, *Population*, 53. This period has, however, provided a baseline for understanding the growth of eighteenth-century Newfoundland; see Head, *Newfoundland*, 1-62; Handcock, *Origins*, 33-70.

tually in parallel until 1660, by which time the English overwintering population of Newfoundland was probably approaching fifteen hundred, and Canada's, perhaps three thousand. At this point, Canada enjoyed a modest wave of immigration and a decade or two of accelerated population growth before immigration fell to a trickle and the growth rate fell back to a colonial norm. Population growth on the English Shore, on the other hand, slowed in the last decades of the century. What the naval commodore Captain Charles Talbot observed of Newfoundland in 1679 remained a fair summary: "The Colony consisteth of neare 1700 persons, viz: men, women, children, and servants." The population fell during the destructive Anglo-French wars between 1689 and 1713, enjoying only a modest recovery afterward.[7]

In this and other respects, Newfoundland's English Shore resembled the neighboring northern colonies of Acadia and Maine. By 1700, each

7. Nicholas Canny, "English Migration into and across the Atlantic during the Seventeenth and Eighteenth Centuries," in Canny, ed., *Europeans on the Move*, 39–75. The early figures for Canada given in John J. McCusker and Russell R. Menard, *The Economy of British America, 1607-1789* (Chapel Hill, N.C., 1985), 112, table 5.3, appear to be overestimates; cf. Charbonneau, *Vie et mort*, 30, table 1; Peter N. Moogk, "Reluctant Exiles: Emigrants from France in Canada before 1760," *WMQ*, 3d Ser., XLVI (1989), 425-462. On growth, see J. M. Bumsted, "The Cultural Landscape of Early Canada," in Bernard Bailyn and Philip D. Morgan, eds., *Strangers within the Realm: Cultural Margins of the First British Empire* (Chapel Hill, N.C., 1991), 363-392. Compare New England and Virginia after 1640, Maryland after 1680. Quotation from Charles Talbot, "Answers to the Enquiries . . . ," Sept. 15, 1679, CO 1/43 (121i), 216-217; cf. Samuel Pepys, "Abstract of Papers concerning Newfoundland," Dec. 6, 1676, CO 1/38 (91), 243-244; John Mannion and Gordon Handcock, "The Seventeenth Century Fishery," *Historical Atlas of Canada*, I, plate 23. Captain James Story's summary "Abstract of the Accounts Returned from Newfoundland . . . ," Dec. 31, 1681, CO 1/47 (122), *CSP*: Colonial, gives a total figure of 2,514 for the summer, which would imply overwintering by about 1,870 individuals; Wheler's figure of 2,023 (for 1684) is also for the summer and would imply 1,541 persons overwintering in the harbors enumerated, without adjustment for geographic scope. The recorded summer population of the English Shore is supposed to have fallen as low as 1,300 persons in the war year 1705, although wild fluctuations in reported population would be more significant if data were controlled for the geographic scope of each census. The figures for Newfoundland in 1690 and 1700 in Henry A. Gemery, "Emigration from the British Isles to the New World, 1630-1700: Inferences from Colonial Populations," *Research in Economic History*, V (1980), 179-231 (esp. 212, table A.2), are overestimates.

had been settled for almost a century, yet none was populous: Maine with about two thousand European inhabitants, Acadia with fourteen hundred, and the English Shore with seventeen hundred or eighteen hundred overwinterers. The English Shore and the regions it most resembled in its slow growth were not distinguished from faster-growing settlements by difficulties associated with initial efforts at colonization. Such problems were common to all early-seventeenth-century European colonies in North America. What marked development on the English Shore was the slowing of growth toward the end of the century, just when Canada, by contrast, enjoyed a period of increased immigration, essentially because of the renewed attention of the imperial government. It was no coincidence that this period also saw the foundation of a French colony in Placentia Bay, on Newfoundland's south coast.[8]

The colony at Plaisance was created by royal fiat to encourage and protect France's fishery in Newfoundland. After several false starts, colonization began inauspiciously in the winter of 1662 with a mutiny in which the governor, his chaplain, and ten others died. The colony did not really take root until the governorship of Sieur La Poippe, between 1670 and 1685. By the later 1680s, French households settled in Plaisance and outlying harbors on Newfoundland's south coast had a summer population of more than six hundred, servants included. Still, the colony could hardly be said to have flourished until Plaisance came into its own as a military base at the turn of the eighteenth century. The governors were corrupt, pretty well to a man, although perhaps no more self-serving than most officeholders elsewhere in European service at the time. Their greed represented a large cost to a small society, weakening both the local economy and, in the long run, the local authority. As one of the proponents of local government for the English fishery put it: "Such a trade will not endure tyranny or charge." Although Terre Neuve was an official colony, with its own government, in many respects its his-

8. Charles E. Clark, *The Eastern Frontier: The Settlement of Northern New England, 1610-1763* (1970; rpt. Hanover, N.H., 1983), 336; Andrew Hill Clark, *Acadia: The Geography of Early Nova Scotia to 1760* (Madison, Wis., 1968), 121-130; *Historical Atlas of Canada*, I, 49; John G. Reid, *Acadia, Maine, and New Scotland: Marginal Colonies in the Seventeenth Century* (Toronto, 1982), 184-190. On early problems, see Kenneth R. Andrews, *Trade, Plunder, and Settlement: Maritime Enterprise and the Genesis of the British Empire, 1480-1630* (Cambridge, 1984), 338; Bernard Bailyn, *The New England Merchants in the Seventeenth Century* (1955; rpt. Cambridge, Mass., 1982), 1.

tory resembled that of the English Shore in the same period. The lack of strong local authority left residents in a difficult position when conflicts arose with migratory fishing crews. As on the English Shore, New England traders came to play a crucial role in provisioning, and, as in Britain, the mercantilist economic experts of the metropolis advocated the elimination of such trade, so useful to the colony but so devoid of immediate profit to Europe. (After war broke out in 1689, Plaisance developed a similar intercolonial trade with Quebec.) Settlers in Newfoundland, French or English, were bound to be dependent on the fishery and were thus subject to the biological vagaries of catch rates, the economics of the market in cod, and, worst, in the end, the disastrous Anglo-French duel that closed the century. The settlements of French Newfoundland resembled those of the English Shore or Maine, where thousands of transient migratory fishermen swelled the population every summer. These were demographically peculiar instances of a general economic conundrum: Newfoundland, French or English, was, in the same situation, faced, in various periods, by New France and New Netherland, where dominant commercial interests had little incentive to promote continued colonization, however useful they might find limited European settlement.[9]

Such conflict has been the traditional framework of Newfoundland historiography since 1793, when the British jurist John Reeves presented his constitutional history of Newfoundland as an account of "the struggles and vicissitudes of two contending interests": "The planters and in-

9. Jean-Pierre Proulx, *The Military History of Placentia: A Study of the French Fortifications; Placentia, 1713–1811* (Ottawa, 1979); James Houblon to Sir Robert Southwell, Mar. 20, 1675, CO 1/65 (23), n.p.; John Humphreys, *Plaisance: Problems of Settlement at This Newfoundland Outpost of New France, 1660–1690* (Ottawa, 1970); Nicolas Landry, "Peuplement d'une colonie de pêche sous le régime français: Plaisance, 1671-1714," *Northern Mariner/Le Marin du nord*, XI, no. 2 (2001), 19–37. On the Anglo-French duel, see J. D. Rogers, *A Historical Geography of the British Colonies*, V, pt. 4, *Newfoundland* (Oxford, 1911), 87–108. Accounts of the early European settlement of Canada often treat merchants as if they were prima facie opponents of settlement. In the case of New France, Bruce Trigger argues that the traditional interpretation fails to recognize economic and demographic realities; see Trigger, *Natives and Newcomers: Canada's "Heroic Age" Reconsidered* (Montreal and Kingston, 1985), 298, 342; Moogk, "Reluctant Exiles," *WMQ*, 3d Ser., XLVI (1989), 425–462; cf. John Frederick Martin, *Profits in the Wilderness: Entrepreneurship and the Founding of New England Towns in the Seventeenth Century* (Chapel Hill, N.C., 1991).

habitants, on the one hand, who, being settled there, needed the protection of a government and police, with the administration of justice and the adventurers and merchants, on the other, who, originally carrying on the fishery from this country and visiting that island only for the season, needed no such protection for themselves and had various reasons for preventing its being afforded to the others." Reeves confined this analysis to the issue of local administration, and his factional analysis of opposition to what was called in the seventeenth century "settled government" makes a good deal of sense. Later historians unfortunately extended the factional analysis uncritically to the question of settlement itself. This later version of Newfoundland's most venerable historiographic tradition has so distorted the demographic history of the early English Shore that accomplished scholars specializing in adjacent regions or subsequent periods can believe that Newfoundland was not permanently settled by Europeans at this time. The ample record of late-seventeenth-century settlement in Newfoundland proves this conclusion to be unfounded. Nor is it difficult to show that the West Country opposition to Newfoundland settlement has been exaggerated to the point of myth. This is not to deny that an antisettlement lobby existed in the last third of the century, nor that migratory crews perpetrated acts of violence against specific planters, particularly in St. John's in the 1660s and 1670s, nor that the settled population in the early eighteenth century was no greater than it had been in 1680. These facts do not mean, however, that West Country fishing interests prevented effectual colonization or had ever been a significant factor in retarding the growth of a permanent population in Newfoundland. By this time, the migratory and planter fisheries were interdependent and, to a considerable degree, mutually supporting. Those who are mutually dependent are candidates for conflict, and the emergence of serious opposition to the planters in the 1660s and 1670s coincides with the continuing integration of the various sectors of the industry.[10]

10. John Reeves, *History of the Government of the Island of Newfoundland* (1793; rpt. London, 1967), 1. For classic twentieth-century versions of this position, see Charles Burnet Judah, *The North American Fisheries and British Policy to 1713* (Urbana, Ill., 1933), 78, 104-105; and Cell, *English Enterprise*, for example, 120-125. The assumption survives, for example, in Gerald M. Sider, *Culture and Class in Anthropology and History: A Newfoundland Illustration* (Cambridge, 1986), 15; and Elizabeth Mancke, "Another British America: A Canadian Model for Early Modern British Empire," *Journal of Imperial and Common-*

Between roughly 1640 and 1680, Newfoundland saw a vernacular diversification of the migratory fishery into a complex industry in which planter fisherfolk resident on the English Shore played an increasingly important part. In the last quarter of the century, however, a limit of something less than two thousand souls emerged as a ceiling on this resident population. If the English Shore failed to continue its modest growth of 1640–1680, retrenchment had less to do with government regulation than with reemigration onward to New England in the face of economic constraints on the proliferation of new fishing plantations. Newfoundland is a subarctic island; like other northern boreal regions, it has never supported human populations nearly matching those of more clement regions, where agriculture and economic diversification are less problematic. Planters were part of a long-established resource industry: their numbers were effectively determined by the economic space open for them within that industry. The Newfoundland plantation was a small colony of Europeans, dependent on a resource industry subject to crises both in production and price—a situation in which the economic effects of worst-case scenarios have a continual impact so that growth is trimmed before it is compounded. Although a whole school of historians has construed the progress of English settlement in Newfoundland as retarded in comparison with New England and some other colonies, it was closely comparable to the growth of the nearest northern colonies. The factors that constrained growth in the northern colonies in general

wealth History, XXV (1997), 1–36 (esp. 4–8). For a landmark discussion, see Keith Matthews, "Historical Fence Building: A Critique of the Historiography of Newfoundland," Newfoundland Studies, XVII (2001), 143–165. For underestimates of settlement, see N. E. S. Griffiths, The Contexts of Acadian History, 1686–1784 (Montreal and Kingston, 1992), 11; Starkey, "Devonians and the Newfoundland Trade," Maritime History of Devon, I, 163–171; David Alexander, "Newfoundland's Traditional Economy and Development to 1934," in James Hiller and Peter Neary, eds., Newfoundland in the Nineteenth and Twentieth Centuries: Essays in Interpretation (Toronto, 1980), 17–39. On the West Country lobby, see Matthews, "Fisheries," 199–239. On violence, see Planters, "Memorial concerning Newfoundland Fishing," Apr. 15, 1664, CO 1/22 (65) (in CSP: Colonial as 1668); CTP, Journal, Mar. 26, 1677, CSP: Colonial; William Downing, Petition, Apr. 2, 1679, CO 1/43 (40), 64; John Downing, "The Humble Representation . . . in Behalfe of Himselfe and Others," Feb. 11, 1680, CO 1/44 (23), 43. On antiplanter violence as a novelty, see Thomas Oxford, Petition, Apr. 4, 1679, CO 1/43 (41), 67. For a claim of long-term opposition, see Downing, "Brief Narrative," Nov. 24, 1676, British Library, Egerton MS 2395, 560–563.

and on the English Shore in particular were complex. These considerations are less dramatic, more dependent on circumatlantic context, and less flattering to Newfoundland's later sense of heroic perseverance in the face of persecution than the traditional historical mythology—but not, therefore, less plausible as explanations of the rate of development in the seventeenth century.[11]

The Newfoundland planters had the misfortune to expand their fishery in a period of crisis within the trade as a whole. They therefore suffered the real, if not entirely realistic, opposition of some migratory interests, who also objected vociferously to others who had recently expanded their activities in Newfoundland: France and New England. In the end, though, the planters won the battle of Whitehall. In 1677, the Privy Council recognized the planters' right to remain in Newfoundland by withdrawing the ineffectual expulsion order of 1675 and negating the restrictive provisions of the third Western Charter by instructing migratory masters and crews "to forbear any violence to the planters upon pretexte of the saide Westerne Charter," in particular, the six-mile clause. Early in 1680, the Committee for Trade and Plantations went even further toward normalizing the legal and economic security of the planters when it formally rescinded the six-mile rule, approved the passage of planters' servants, and even withdrew the long-standing and long-ignored ban on tippling houses and taverns. This compromise, a recognition of settlement without the settled government that the planters also sought, was the basis of King William's Act of 1699, and, hence, of the administration of Newfoundland through much of the following century. The 1699 act was, as Reeves noted, "little more than an enactment of the rules, regulations, and constitution that had mostly prevailed there for some time." A reading of the "Replies to Inquiries" makes it clear how little latitude the naval officers appointed to the Newfoundland station had in regulating settlement, whichever way the political winds blew within Privy Council committees.[12]

11. "Retarded" colonization echoes the terminology of Judah, *North American Fisheries*, 104–105. On myth, see Peter E. Pope, "Comparisons: Atlantic Canada," in Daniel Vickers, ed., *A Companion to Colonial America* (Malden, Mass., 2003), 489–507 (esp. 495–497).

12. CTP, Report to Privy Council, Mar. 28, 1677, CO 1/39 (53), 184; Privy Council, Orders, Mar. 30, May 18, 1677, CO 1/39 (56), 190, CO 1/40 (84), 180, in Matthews, *Constitutional Laws*, 185; CTP, Journal, Feb. 16, 21, 26, 1680, *CSP: Colonial*; cf. Francis Wheler, "Answers to the Heads of Inquirys . . . ," and Wheler,

Since a settlement is more than the sum of its parts and may be permanent even if few of its residents are, then in this minimum sense Ferryland and dozens of other Newfoundland communities were permanent settlements in the seventeenth century. To what extent the men and women who inhabited these hamlets were permanent residents is another question that we can resolve into a number of distinguishable issues: What proportion of the summer population were inhabitants, resident year-round? What proportion of inhabitants were economically independent planters? And to what extent were overwintering inhabitants, that is, both planters and servants, long-term residents? Answers to these questions will give us some appreciation of the context of resident-transient relations, but they will raise further issues of class and status in Newfoundland, which need to be addressed before we can move toward the underlying anthropological issue of how a small society like the English Shore held together, as it normally did, in the absence of formal political or religious institutions, despite the seasonal flux of five or six thousand migratory servants.

ᘠ Planters and Servants

As one of the most detailed and best organized of the early censuses, Sir William Poole's "Particular Accompt of All the Inhabitants and Planters Living in Every Fishing Port or Harbour on Newfoundland" can be approached as a sort of Newfoundland Domesday Book for the year 1677 (Table 13). Late that summer, Poole recorded almost nineteen hundred individuals in planter households on the English Shore.

"Observations . . . upon the . . . Articles of His Majesties Charter," Oct. 27, 1684, CO 1/55 (56, 56i), 239–246, 247–248. Quotation from Reeves, *History*, 31. The Act of 1699 is often misinterpreted as a ban on settlement; see Christopher English, "The Development of the Newfoundland Legal System to 1815," *Acadiensis*, XX, no. 1 (1990), 89–119; and Patrick O'Flaherty, "King William's Act (1699): Some Thoughts Three Hundred Years Later," *Newfoundland Quarterly*, XCII, no. 2 (2000), 21–28. For another view, minimizing the significance of the Act, see Jerry Bannister, "The Naval State in Newfoundland, 1749-1791," *Journal of the Canadian Historical Association*, N.S., XI (2000), 17–50 (esp. 21–22). The planters were willing to accept an informal ceiling on settlement; see William Downing, "Representation and Proposall of . . . the Inhabitants of Newfoundland," Feb. 21, 1680, CO 1/44 (27), 63.

Table 13. *Population by Region, Newfoundland, English Shore, September 1677*

Region (Households/ Ships)	Planters and Families	Planters' Servants	Ships' Servants	Total
South Avalon (44/44)	132	389	1,496	2,017
St. John's area (37/24)	100	213	1,358	1,671
Conception Bay (43/14)	155	395	695	1,245
Trinity Bay (39/29)	139	354	1,038	1,531
Total (163/102)	526	1,351	4,587	6,464

Note: Trinity Bay here includes the Bonavista area. Poole enumerated 628 ships' servants and 20 shipmasters for Trinity Bay, but he omitted Bonavista. Data for that area are estimated here, using Berry's 1675 figures: 410 men and 9 shipmasters. Data for 1676 are similar.

Sources: William Poole, "A Particular Accompt of All the Inhabitants and Planters . . . ," Poole, "Account of Fishing and Sackships from Trepassy to Cape Broyle," Sept. 10, 1677, CO 1/41 (62iv–x), 157–172; John Berry, "A List of Shipps Makinge Fishinge Voyages; with Boatkeepers . . . ," Sept. 12, 1675, CO 1/35 (17i), 136–146.

The planters, their wives, children, and servants lived in 163 households, slightly fewer than the average of 176 households enumerated in the census years between 1675 and 1684. But this accounting included only part of Newfoundland's summer population. Recall that migratory ships fishing and migratory by-boat-keepers as well as planters employed servants to operate their boats and to cure the catch. The naval commodores' "Replies to Inquiries" suggest that there were about forty-six hundred of these fishermen on the English Shore in 1677, for a total count in late summer of about sixty-five hundred persons—close to the average total summer population for the 1675–1684 census years. These figures would be even larger if we included the crews of sack ships. They were predominantly deep-water mariners but sometimes remained long enough in Newfoundland to engage in a certain amount of fishing. In 1677, these crews would have added more than one thousand summer visitors, although they would have been ashore for only a few weeks and not all at the same time.[13]

The censuses of French Newfoundland do not, unfortunately, enumerate migratory ships' servants, so quantifying the demographic context there is more difficult. The excellent data we do have about *habitants* and their *engagés* suggest comparable patterns and a small population in habitant households: a total of 640 in 1687, for example (Table 14, Map 10). (Note that the French term "habitant" is equivalent to the English "planter," rather than to the English "inhabitant," which often incorporated servants as well as their masters, as in the title Captain Poole gave to his census.) France's ship fishery was an enormous industry, by no means confined to the exploitation of the Grand Banks: the French Newfoundland fleet in 1664 numbered 423 vessels, averaging more than one hundred tons, and would have employed at least ten thousand men. In 1700, Captain Stafford Fairbourne estimated 61 French ships, of eighty to three hundred tons, on the south coast around Placentia Bay. He thought there were 1,010 boats in all sectors of the French inshore fishery in that area, which would imply a summer population of French fishermen on the south coast in the order of forty-five hundred. The administrative records of Plaisance confirm that migratory fishing crews were a continual and significant presence there, no less than on the English Shore.[14]

13. Poole, "Particular Accompt," Sept. 10, 1677, CO 1/41 (61iv, vi, vii), 158–166; and Poole, "Account of Fishing and Sackships from Trepassy to Cape Broyle," Sept. 10, 1677, CO 1/41 (62viii–x), 167–172; cf. Wells, *Population*, 56–59. John Berry's 1675 nominal census is also convincingly detailed; figures for servants in James Story's 1681 nominal census appear to have been back-calculated from the inventory of boats, using a five-to-one ratio. Jones's 1682 census is excluded from the household average here, because it overlooks too many communities. In other respects, 1677 might not have been typical. The number of resident households enumerated grew from 132 to 202 over the period 1675–1681. Captain Poole reported a relatively low ratio of servants to boats for some planters, particularly in the St. John's area, an estimate that suggests his count of planters' servants for some harbors may not reflect the full number employed at the height of the summer but may be closer to a count of planters' servants planning to overwinter (an issue discussed in Chapter 4, above). This data may therefore overstate the predominance of ships' servants in summer populations, although the general picture is typical.

14. Laurier G. Turgeon, "Colbert et la pêche française à Terre Neuve," in Roland Mousnier, ed., *Un nouveau Colbert: Actes du colloque pour le tricentenaire de la mort de Colbert* (Paris, 1985), 255–268; Captain Stafford Fairbourne, "Answers to

Table 14. *Population of* Habitant *Households, French Newfoundland, Summer 1687*

Area (Households)	*Habitants* and Families	Servants	Other	Total
Plaisance and area (27)	119	185	4	308
Other harbors (15)	42	289	1	332
Total (42)	161	474	5	640

Note: Other residents include priests at Plaisance and Cap Negre as well as a family of three "sauvages" at Plaisance. Servants *(engagés)* at Plaisance include 14 at the fort and 9 soldiers. The communities of Pointe Verte and Petit Plaisance are summarized here with Plaisance. The other harbors were St. Pierre, Fortune, Grand Bank, Havre Bertrand, Cap Negre, and Hermitage. The census of 1691 lists 5 *habitants* at Lissardie and Trepassey as well.

Source: Jean Auger dit Baron, Deposition, Oct. 13, 1687, in Fernand-D. Thibodeau, "Recensements de Terreneuve et Plaisance," *Mémoires de la Société Généalogique Canadienne-Française*, XIII (1962), 204–208.

Variations from harbor to harbor in the summer planter-to-servant ratio resulted, in part, from variation in the mix of ship-based and planter-based operations. To take the south Avalon as an example, there were, until late in the century, no planters in Aquafort or Cape Broyle, so migratory crews completely dominated these fishing stations. Conversely, only one ship set up a fishing room in 1677 at Brigus South, from which Thomas Dodridge and his family had recently moved, so that the summer population there consisted of the master, John Cutts, and the thirty-five men of the *Society* of Dartmouth, together with the three remaining planters—John Kent and Richard and Nicholas Coone (or Coome)—their nine dependents, and thirty-three servants. Harbors with both ship- and planter-based operations might tend to either of

the Heads of Enquirys," Sept. 11, 1700, CO 194/2, 54–57; Humphreys, *Plaisance*. My manning estimate assumes thirty men for a one-hundred-ton vessel. Robert Robinson, Proposals, ca. 1668, CO 1/22 (70), 117, estimated French employment at eighteen thousand men on four hundred ships, but he seriously overestimated British manning levels as well.

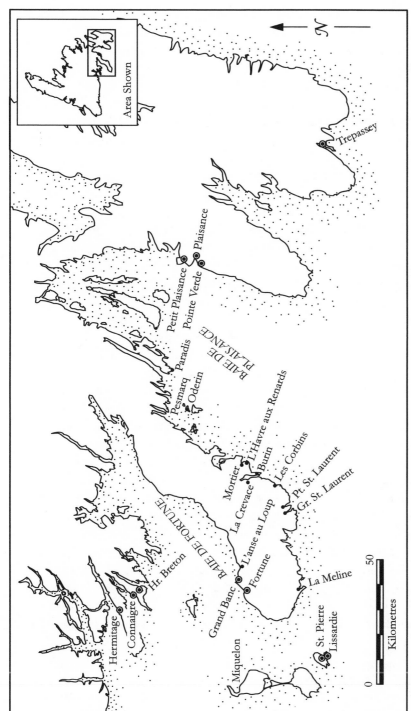

Map 10. Permanently Inhabited French Fishing Harbors in Newfoundland, 1687. Circled dots indicate winter settlements. Other harbors shown are summer fishing stations regularly used by Breton fishermen. There were additional Basque fishing stations in Placentia and St. Mary's Bays. Drawn by Ed Eastaugh

these extremes, but, in most, the migratory crews were by far the largest component of the summer population, although in Ferryland and deep in Conception Bay ships and their crews were less numerous relative to the planter fishery than elsewhere on the English Shore. Ships' servants alone accounted for slightly less than three-quarters of total summer residents in this period and together with planters' servants normally made up more than 90 percent of summer populations. Even within the average planter household, servants outnumbered family members. Like their contemporaries in Virginia, the Newfoundland planters lived in a sea of servants, at least in summer. The metaphor is less applicable to winter populations, when planters and their kin were outnumbered only two to one by those of their servants who overwintered.[15]

Newfoundland's planter households were large by the standards of early modern England. The Dodridges, with their 2 children and 9 servants, were typical. Mean household size on the English Shore was 11.5 persons in the summer of 1677, compared with 4.7 persons among households of English tradesmen, 1574–1821, or 5.9 persons among yeomen, in the same period. The demographer, if not the economist, might be more interested in the average Newfoundland planter household in winter, when parallels can be found in the West Indies, New England, and New France (Table 15). Households in both Barbados and Newfoundland were large, averaging between 7 and 9 persons. Furthermore, this size was the result of a large representation of servants, or in the Barbadian case, servants and enslaved Africans. Visiting slavers occasionally sold men in seventeenth-century Newfoundland, but slaveownership was not common. The St. John's merchant Thomas Oxford complained of the theft of his "covenant negro servant," suggesting both that a few Africans worked as servants on the English Shore and that there were those who were quite prepared to enslave them. Families constituted more than two-thirds of Newfoundland households, and these families resembled those in Bristol, Rhode Island, or Montreal more than they did those in Bridgetown, Barbados. Apart from a slightly greater proportion of families without children, the distribution of Newfoundland families by size is very close to the Rhode Island pattern and quite unlike the Barbadian pattern, in which most couples had no children. The

15. The lower proportion of servants in the summer population in Wells, *Population*, 50, table II-2, ignores the ship-based migratory fishermen. For "a sea of servants," see Darrett B. Rutman and Anita H. Rutman, *A Place in Time: Middlesex County, Virginia, 1650–1750* (New York, 1984), 71.

Table 15. *Household Structures, 1677–1693*

	English Shore 1677	Bridgetown, Barbados 1680	Montreal, Canada 1681	Bristol, R.I. 1689	French Shore 1693
Households	163	351	276	70	49
Married couples	96	231	200	67	26
Children	269	330	734	226	70
Childless couples	21	98	28	7	8
Widows and widowers	21	31	16	2	4
Single householders	53	89	60	1	19
Servants	879	402	55	56	212
Enslaved	0	1,276	0	1	0
Household Means					
Persons	8.6	7.4	4.6	6.0	7.3
Children	1.7	0.9	2.7	3.3	1.4
Servants and enslaved	5.4	4.8	0.2	0.8	4.3

Note: The figure for English Newfoundland widows and widowers represents all 12 female heads of households, 11 of whom are named as widows, plus 9 single male heads of households with children. The number of servants is an estimate based on the presumed overwintering of 65% of the 1,351 planters' servants censused during the late summer. These figures may underestimate the number overwintering, as Poole's census was taken late in the summer. It is assumed that the enslaved in Montreal are counted here as servants. Married couples in Montreal include 5 extended family households. The French Newfoundland census of 1687 is unsuitable for this analysis; it should be noted that 1693, used here, was a war year. The figures for Bridgetown are for English households.

Sources: Richard S. Dunn, "The Barbados Census of 1680: Profile of the Richest Colony in English America," *WMQ*, 3d Ser., XXVI (1969), 3–30, table 6; John Demos, "Families in Colonial Bristol, Rhode Island: An Exercise in Historical Demography," *WMQ*, 3d Ser., XXV (1968), 40–57; Louise Dechêne, *Habitants and Merchants in Seventeenth-Century Montreal*, trans. Liana Vardi (Montreal and Kingston, 1992), 239, table 4.4; William Poole, "A Particular Accompt of All the Inhabitants and Planters . . . ," Sept. 10, 1677, CO 1/41 (62iv), 157–166; Thomas Oxford, "Humble Petition," July 3, 1679, CO 1/43 (83), 153; J.-F. de Brouillan, "Ressencement de toutte la colonie establie en l'Isle de Terre Neufve pour l'année 1694," in Fernand-D. Thibodeau, "Recensements de Terreneuve et Plaisance," *Mémoires de la Société Généalogique Canadienne-Française*, XIII (1962), 245–255.

Table 16. *Families by Size, 1677–1693*

Census Area and Period (N = Families with Children)	Number of Children		
	1–3	4–6	7+
Bridgetown, Barbados, 1680 (N = 153)	86%	13%	1%
French Newfoundland, 1693 (N = 21)	67	29	5
English Shore, 1677 (N = 89)	65	29	6
Chesapeake families to 1689 (N = 386)	64	26	10
Bristol, R.I., 1689 (N = 62)	52	37	10

Note: The figures for Bridgetown are for the English households. The figures for the Chesapeake are for families of fathers born before 1689. The French census of 1687 is unsuitable for this analysis. Note that 1693, used here, was a war year.

Sources: John Demos, "Families in Colonial Bristol, Rhode Island: An Exercise in Historical Demography," *WMQ*, 3d Ser., XXV (1968), 40–57; Richard S. Dunn, "Barbados Census of 1680: Profile of the Richest Colony in English America," *WMQ*, 3d Ser., XXVI (1969), 3–30, table 7; Daniel Blake Smith, "Mortality and Family in the Colonial Chesapeake," *Journal of Interdisciplinary History*, VIII (1977–1978), 403–427, table 5; William Poole, "A Particular Accompt of All the Inhabitants and Planters . . . ," Sept. 10, 1677, CO 1/41 (62iv), 157–166; J.-F. de Brouillan, "Ressencement de toutte la colonie establie en l'Isle de Terre Neufve pour l'année 1694," in Fernand-D. Thibodeau, "Recensements de Terreneuve et Plaisance," *Mémoires de la Société Généalogique Canadienne-Française*, XIII (1962), 245–255.

distribution of families by size in Newfoundland might have been even closer to a Chesapeake pattern (Table 16). Although abnormal in English terms, both the seventeenth-century Newfoundland planter household and the Newfoundland planter family had parallels in other colonies.[16]

16. For English households, see Peter Laslett, *The World We Have Lost: Further Explored*, 3d ed. (London, 1983), 96, table 7. On enslaved people in Newfoundland, see William Douglas et al., Deposition, May 5, 1626, *Southampton Examinations*, I, 73–74; Cathy Matson, *Merchants and Empire: Trading in Colonial New York* (Baltimore, 1998), 61; and Thomas Oxford, Petition, July 3, 1679, CO 1/43 (83), 153. The cultural constructs "slave" and "servant" are more ambiguous than they may at first seem; see Hilary Beckles, "The Concept of 'White Slavery' in the English Caribbean during the Early Seventeenth Century," in John Brewer and Susan Staves, eds., *Early Modern Conceptions of Property* (London, 1995), 572–584. Of the 163 planter households enumerated in 1677, 112, or 69 percent, consisted of a couple with or without children or of a single parent with children. Compare Poole, "Particular Accompt," Sept. 10, 1677, CO 1/41 (61iv, vi, vii), with

Another fundamental demographic parallel between Newfoundland and the Chesapeake lay in the acute sexual imbalance that resulted from the preponderance of male servants in the population. Some Newfoundland planters, like Lady Sara Kirke of Ferryland and John Downing of St. John's, employed female servants, but this practice was not common. (Employers of females were typically couples or widowed with children and were relatively well-off.) The vast majority of servants employed in Newfoundland were male, and, since they outnumbered their employers, the resident population was predominantly male. In the summer of 1677, females made up only about one-eighth of planter households, and half of these females were children. Since some planters' servants did not overwinter, females were relatively better represented in the winter population, making up about one-sixth of all overwinterers. Averages in this case obscure actual household structures, and it is worth distinguishing single households from family households with a wife or at least one child present. Single heads of households in the winter of 1677 were probably outnumbered about five to one by their own exclusively male servants. These represented, however, less than one-third of planter households. In the large majority of winter households including a wife or at least one child, about one-quarter of the population was female—half adult, half children.

The low proportion of women in the population, even among overwinterers and even among conjugal households, was a sign as well as a cause of the transience of part of the population. What Captain Francis Wheler observed of ships' crews in 1684 was true of planters' servants as well: "Soe long as their comes noe women, they are not fixed." This demographic imbalance was typical of several seventeenth-century colonies, for example, Maryland, Acadia, and even Canada, where natural increase also was restricted. There were, nevertheless, some marriageable women in Newfoundland. They are particularly worth noting, because the tendency to permanent residence manifested when they married is

---

Richard S. Dunn, "The Barbados Census of 1680: Profile of the Richest Colony in English America," *WMQ*, 3d Ser., XXVI (1969), 3–30, table 6; John Demos, "Families in Colonial Bristol, Rhode Island: An Exercise in Historical Demography," *WMQ*, 3d Ser., XXV (1968), 40–57; and Louise Dechêne, *Habitants and Merchants in Seventeenth-Century Montreal*, trans. Liana Vardi (Montreal and Kingston, 1992), 238–240, table 4.4.

almost completely invisible to the study of census lists, which is the way that the permanence of early settlement on the English Shore has usually been assessed.[17]

Widows with property were very marriageable. Of the eleven widows named in the 1677 census, only one was named in 1681. The limitations of the censuses of English Newfoundland make it almost impossible to be certain of what happened to these women, for they were named in subsequent censuses only when they remained widows and were recorded otherwise only as "wife," with no indication of maiden, former, or even Christian names. Of the ten named women who disappear from the Newfoundland census lists between 1677 and 1681, we know that one (Sara Kirke) had retired, but we should not assume that the others had necessarily died or reemigrated. Normal behavior for widows in the period was to remarry within a year or two, which is likely what these women had done, surrounded as they were by economically eligible potential suitors. The contemporary censuses of the French settlements in and around Placentia Bay sometimes included better information about female habitants. In 1694, of seventeen conjugal unions with children in Plaisance, more than one-third were remarriages, and local remarriage was likely also common in the English settlements.[18]

There were other marriageable women on the English Shore. Some potential partners for single males were born on the island. A pattern of very early marriage among females is probable in Newfoundland in the seventeenth century, as it would be in newly settled parts of the island in later centuries. One eighteenth-century visitor was surprised by the early marriage of women on the English Shore and observed that some

17. Quotation from Wheler, "Answers," Oct. 27, 1684, CO 1/55 (56), 239–246 (esp. 242). The phrase quoted is used by Handcock as an appropriate title, but Wheler did not make his remark about planters (*pace* Handcock, *Origins*, 21, 32, 284). Nor was it made of by-boat crews, as in Matthews, "Fisheries," 174. Compare Lois Green Carr and Lorena S. Walsh, "The Planter's Wife: The Experience of White Women in Seventeenth-Century Maryland," *WMQ*, 3d Ser., XXXIV (1977), 542–571; and Choquette, *Frenchmen into Peasants*, 21, 46. For male persistence as an indication of permanence, see Handcock, *Origins*, 43–44.

18. Widows were the one group of women who had attained the legal and economic status normally reserved for males and therefore might choose to forgo remarriage and the consequent loss of this status. For French data, see J.-F. de Brouillan, "Ressencement de toutte la colonie establie en l'Isle de Terre Neufve pour l'année 1694," in Thibodeau, "Recensements," *Mémoires de la Société Généalogique Canadienne-Française*, XIII (1962), 204–208.

had children at the age of twelve. Clearly, this young age would have been a limit, not an average. Significantly, the French census of 1687 distinguishes "little girls" as those twelve and under, although it makes the "little boys" distinction at fifteen. Of the 130 female children resident on the English Shore in 1677, perhaps 5 or 10 would have been sixteen years old, which might have been a typical age for native-born brides. By the 1680s, there was also a steady flow of female servants into Newfoundland. In 1681, Captain James Story reported that Irish ships trading at Newfoundland "bring over a great many women passengers, which they sell for servants, and a little after theire coming they marry among the fishermen that live with the planters." This is the other side of Captain Wheler's observation that unmarried fishing servants were transient, for Story makes it clear that some fishing servants did find wives, and he goes on to emphasize that couples tended to settle permanently. Each of the 15 female servants resident on the English Shore in 1677 was likely on the marriage market, and most would be married within a year or two.[19]

All in all, we might guess that in the later seventeenth century something like twenty informal marriages took place annually on the English Shore, involving women already resident. Neither clergy nor civil servants recorded these marriages, but, in this period, marriages among countryfolk of comparable social station in the Old Country were likewise often or even normally consummated without benefit of clergy or civil registration. The chaplain of HMS *Assistance*, at Newfoundland in 1680, was struck by the absence of "holy wedlock" and made further observations suggesting that the demographic imbalance between

19. Patricia A. Thornton, "The Demographic and Mercantile Bases of Initial Permanent Settlement in the Strait of Belle Isle," in John J. Mannion, ed., *The Peopling of Newfoundland: Essays in Historical Geography* (St. John's, 1977), 152–183; *Historical Atlas of Canada*, I, 50; John Howell, ed., *The Life and Adventures of John Nicol, Mariner* (1822; rpt. London, 1937), 52; Jean Auger dit Baron, Deposition, Oct. 13, 1687, in Thibodeau, "Recensements," *Mémoires de la Société Généalogique Canadienne-Française*, XIII (1962), 204–208. Cf. Landry, "Plaisance, 1671–1714," *Northern Mariner/Le Marin du nord*, XI, no. 2 (2001), 19–37 (esp. 26). Native-born daughters in seventeenth-century Maryland married between ages sixteen and nineteen; see Lorena S. Walsh, "'Till Death Us Do Part': Marriage and Family in Seventeenth-Century Maryland," in Thad W. Tate and David L. Ammerman, eds., *The Chesapeake in the Seventeenth Century: Essays in Anglo-American Society* (Chapel Hill, N.C., 1979), 126–152. Quotation from Story, "Account," Sept. 1, 1681, CO 1/47 (52i), 113–121.

males and females resulted in a kind of promiscuity that was also reported in coastal New England: "When in their jollities with a woman, one or other of the drunken crew starts up and made some parte of the matrimony between them, soe that for a few days they call one another man and wife, until they be wearie of one another, and then change their wishe and chuse new mates." Pregnancy would likely trigger a more permanent alliance.[20]

This bald assumption ignores, of course, the personal emotional histories of the men and women who must sometimes have found themselves torn apart by the sheer momentum of a transatlantic industry. Some of the artifacts recovered by archaeologists from seventeenth-century Ferryland hint at these emotions: a delicate blue-on-white Portuguese *faiança* plate covered with floral scrolls and the single word "Amor" (Plate 9); another highly decorated plate, this one the honey-brown sgraffito slipware produced in and around Barnstaple, north Devon, with the enigmatic date "1698"; a gold ring inscribed on the inside, "Be true in hart." In hindsight, we can debate as long as we please whether unions within a particular social stratum were typically based on economic calculation, affection, or both; but these objects can be read as traces of a particularly modern sentiment: absent love. Not that lovers were never separated before; it was just that the development of a transatlantic economy created many occasions of separation. This situation may account for the sentimental treatment given the theme of parting, increasingly common on decorated pottery, for example, in the following century. The theme was particularly associated with mariners and colonists, the archetypical migrants in a world adjusting to the permanent reality of transience.[21]

20. Lawrence Stone, *The Family, Sex, and Marriage in England, 1500–1800* (London, 1977), 31; John R. Gillis, *For Better, for Worse: British Marriages, 1600 to the Present* (New York, 1985), 3–54, 190–192; John Thomas, "A True and Faithfull Accompt of the Present State of Affairs in Newfoundland," 1680, All Souls College, Oxford, Codrington Library, Wynne Collection, MS 239, 231–232, in Peter Pope, "A True and Faithful Account: Newfoundland in 1680," *Newfoundland Studies*, XII (1996), 32–49; cf. Clark, *Eastern Frontier*, 35; Kathleen M. Brown, *Good Wives, Nasty Wenches, and Anxious Patriarchs: Gender, Race, and Power in Colonial Virginia* (Chapel Hill, N.C., 1996), 34–35, 101–104.

21. Lawrence Stone, *Uncertain Unions: Marriage in England, 1660–1753* (Oxford, 1992). Cf. Eleanor Stoddart, "Seventeenth-Century Tin-Glazed Earthenware from Ferryland," *Avalon Chronicles*, V (2000), 49–100 (esp. 60–61); and *The Colonist's Departure* and *Jemmy's Farewell*, transfer-printed punch bowls of

Plate 9. Blue-on-White Portuguese Faiança *Plate, with Floral Scrolls and the Single Word* Amor. *From a midden outside the Calvert-Kirke Mansion House in Ferryland (CgAf-2), circa 1625–1650. In Portugal, plates of this type were commissioned for weddings to carry rings to the altar. Courtesy, Colony of Avalon Foundation*

⛭ Permanence and Transience

Permanence and transience are, of course, relative concepts. In the long run, we are all transient, and, in the very long run, our settlements are as well. Within a narrower postmedieval framework, we might understand permanent settlement as year-round internally regenerative

---

ca. 1775–1780, in Cyril Williams-Wood, *English Transfer-Printed Pottery and Porcelain: A History of Over-Glaze Printing* (London, 1981), 152–154, figures 83, 86; Lisa Norling, *Captain Ahab Had a Wife: New England Women and the Whalefishery, 1720–1870* (Chapel Hill, N.C., 2000), 77–79, 140–142, 165–213.

occupancy. The criterion of internal regeneration is tricky, though. Mortality rates in London, Paris, and other early modern cities were high enough to make it debatable whether these undoubtedly permanent settlements could have maintained population levels in the absence of net immigration. So internal regeneration implies a significant role for natural increase in the maintenance of population, but it must be compatible with a dependence on migration. As we have seen, about two-thirds of Newfoundland planter households were families, and about a fifth of overwinterers were children. Clearly, then, the south Avalon, the St. John's area, and Conception, Trinity, and Placentia Bays were permanently settled by Europeans in the seventeenth century in a sense that would not apply to other parts of Newfoundland until later: the eighteenth century in the case of the northeast and southwest coasts or the nineteenth century for the Great Northern Peninsula and Strait of Belle Isle.[22]

Permanent settlement in the sense defined was already part of the complex residential behavior of the European population of seventeenth-century Newfoundland—but residence was often qualified. Some planters left Newfoundland, dependents sometimes returned to the Old Country for a season or two at a time, and many overwintering servants did not intend to spend more than a few years on the island. Yet, if the Perriman brothers of Trepassey retired to England sometime after 1677, they were not necessarily transients when they occupied their plantations on the English Shore. If the younger David Kirke's wife, Mary, was in Bideford, Devon, in 1676–1677, we are hardly constrained to deny that she was a permanent resident—particularly given that she returned to live and work in Newfoundland well into the following century and that her descendants can be found today in the local telephone book. The typical mobility of servants does not prove that they were invariably tran-

22. Thornton, "Strait of Belle Isle," and John J. Mannion, "Settlers and Traders in Western Newfoundland," both in Mannion, ed., *Peopling of Newfoundland*, 152–183 (esp. 157), 234–277; Olaf Uwe Janzen, "'Une Petite Republique' in Southwestern Newfoundland: The Limits of Imperial Authority in a Remote Maritime Environment," in Lewis R. Fischer and Walter E. Minchinton, eds., *People of the Northern Seas* (St. John's, 1992), 1–33. On urban natural decrease, see E. A. Wrigley, "A Simple Model of London's Importance in Changing English Society and Economy, 1650–1750," *Past and Present*, no. 37 (July 1967), 44–70; Wrigley, *Population and History* (New York, 1969), 96–98; and, for a critical discussion, Jan de Vries, *European Urbanization, 1500–1800* (London, 1984), 179–182.

sients, and it certainly does not show that the households they served were impermanent. Such indications of mobility disconfirm permanent residence only by narrow and ahistorical standards. The sense of permanence historical archaeologists have in examining the material remains of seventeenth-century Newfoundland is probably justified. Archaeologists researching the William Hefford plantation in the Trinity Bay community of New Perlican found his descendants living there still, 325 years after the family was first recorded there in the census of 1675. This is an example of unusual stability, certainly by North American standards. Neither planters nor even their servants were as transient as implied in the twentieth-century literature on Newfoundland settlement. Furthermore, comparable populations elsewhere were as mobile.[23]

Transience in Newfoundland is best understood in the context of circumatlantic levels of mobility. There is little doubt that planters' servants were mobile. They contracted to work for a few years at a time, and the fishery was typically an occupation of persons at a mobile stage of their life cycle. Neither of these characteristics of service in the fishery was unique, however. In the later seventeenth century, something like thirty thousand seasonal migrants worked in the coastal agricultural and peat industries of the Netherlands. In rural England itself, many young people were servants in husbandry, who annually bound themselves in service to farm families. These servants, who made up about 10 percent of the rural population, were transient in much the same sense that the fishing servants of Newfoundland's planters were transient: their resi-

23. For emphasis on transience, see Keith Matthews, *Lectures on the History of Newfoundland, 1500–1830* (St. John's, 1988), 83–88; Handcock, *Origins*, 23–32; John Mannion and Gordon Handcock, "Seventeenth Century Fishery," in *Historical Atlas of Canada*, I, 48–49; Starkey, "Devonians and the Newfoundland Trade," *Maritime History of Devon*, I, 163–171; Sean T. Cadigan, *Hope and Deception in Conception Bay: Merchant-Settler Relations in Newfoundland, 1785–1855* (Toronto, 1995), 20. On Mary Kirke's descendants, see Seary, *Family Names*, "Benger." On circumatlantic mobility, see David Souden, "English Indentured Servants and the Transatlantic Colonial Economy," in Shula Marks and Peter Richardson, eds., *International Labour Migration: Historical Perspectives* (London, 1984), 19–33; J. P. P. Horn, "Moving on in the New World: Migration and Out-Migration in the Seventeenth-Century Chesapeake," in Peter Clark and David Souden, eds., *Migration and Society in Early Modern England* (London, 1988), 172–212; Moogk, "Reluctant Exiles," *WMQ*, 3d Ser., XLVI (1989), 425–462. On the Hefford plantation, see William Gilbert, *Journeys through Time: Ten Years of Archaeology on the Baccalieu Trail* (Carbonear, 2003), 27.

dence was fixed a year at a time. They were labor migrants, who had left home for at least a year, rather than migrant laborers, like the ship fishermen, who migrated seasonally. Servants in husbandry rarely remained in one household for more than a year or two. No one has seriously proposed excluding them from regional population estimates, and to exclude planters' servants from the population of Newfoundland makes no more sense. This kind of life cycle subsistence migration was a widespread implication of their social class and age grade, not something peculiar to Newfoundland. It is harder to assess comparatively the mobility of Newfoundland planters' servants at the end of their youth, when their peers, the servants in husbandry or the indentured servants of the Chesapeake, would settle down and attempt to raise their own families. Exit from service in husbandry typically meant a longer move than those made during service. Servants in the Chesapeake almost invariably moved when their service indentures expired. Newfoundland servants had reasons to return to the West Country or move on to New England; among the most likely was a desire to meet marriageable women. Similar demographic imbalance had similar results in Canada. There were, on the other hand, counterbalancing considerations, among these the financial and physical costs of passage back across the North Atlantic on a crowded fishing ship.[24]

24. Matthews, "Fisheries," 173–175, and Matthews, *Lectures*, 85, discount servants as part of the Newfoundland population. On life-cycle migration, see Jan Lucassen, "The Netherlands, the Dutch, and Long-Distance Migration in the Late Sixteenth to Early Nineteenth Centuries," in Canny, ed., *Europeans on the Move*, 153–191 (esp. 155); Ann Kussmaul, *Servants in Husbandry in Early Modern England* (Cambridge, 1981), 12 (table 2.1), 31–93 (esp. table 4.3); David Souden, "'Rogues, Whores, and Vagabonds'? Indentured Servant Emigrants to North America, and the Case of Mid-Seventeenth-Century Bristol," *Social History*, III (1978–1979), 19–33; Ilana Krausman Ben-Amos, *Adolescence and Youth in Early Modern England* (New Haven, Conn., 1994), 69–83; Choquette, *Frenchmen into Peasants*, 21, 127–128, 188–194; Lois Green Carr and Russell R. Menard, "Immigration and Opportunity: The Freedman in Early Colonial Maryland," in Tate and Ammerman, eds., *The Chesapeake in the Seventeenth Century*, 206–242. On subsistence migration, see Peter Clark, "The Migrant in Kentish Towns, 1580–1640," in Clark and Paul Slack, eds., *Crisis and Order in English Towns, 1500–1700* (London, 1972), 57–90. On the goal of marriage, compare Wheler, "Answers," Oct. 27, 1684, CO 1/55 (56), 239–246; Moogk, "Reluctant Exiles," *WMQ*, 3d Ser., XLVI (1989), 425–462; and Moogk, "Fellow Exiles," in Canny, ed., *Europeans on the Move*, 236–260 (esp. 250).

Servants in Newfoundland have not usually been considered in discussions of permanence, the assumption being that they were, by definition, not permanent residents. Captain Story's observation that servant girls "marry among the fishermen that live with the planters" suggests, however, that both male and female servants in the Newfoundland planter fishery sometimes became permanent residents. Furthermore, planters might become servants, without leaving the island. After the notoriously corrupt Major Thomas Lloyd beat the St. John's planter John Adams in 1703 "and made severall holes in his head," Adams was forced, as a result of his injuries, "to be a servant who was before a master." Loss of capital could have the same effect. John Kent was one of the planters of Ferryland whose boats and stages were destroyed by the Dutch in 1673. He was later a planter, in a small way, at Brigus South in 1676 and 1677 but was not mentioned in Berry's census of 1675. His absence from that census is as likely to indicate a loss of status as removal from Newfoundland. The danger of confusing geographical and status mobility must be recognized, or assessments of permanence based on nominal censuses of planters will go astray.[25]

These scattered examples are not the only evidence that social status is a hidden factor in estimates of mobility. Consider, for example, Captain Sir Robert Robinson's census of St. John's for 1680, which records how long twenty-eight "planters and inhabitants" had been resident. Residency ranged from two weeks, for the most recent arrival, to the thirty-nine years reported by Elizabeth Matthews, who indicated that she was born in St. John's, as were the thirty-four-year-old William Kines (Cains) and the twenty-seven-year-old Richard Horton. Only four residents had been in St. John's for less than four years, and the mean duration of residence was just under fifteen years. Although sixteen of the people enumerated in 1680 said they were resident in 1669, only two had been listed as planters at that time by the Plymouth surgeon James

25. On Lloyd, see Inhabitants of Newfoundland, Deposition, 1704, CO 194/3 (31iii), 101; and Prowse, *History*, 241–270. On Kent, see Dudley Lovelace, ". . . The Duch Fleet upon the Coast . . . ," Mar. 29, 1675, CO 1/34 (37), 85. Cf. the case of Richard Lee, a sometime planter of Ferryland and Fermeuse, 1675–1677. Linda Auwers Bissell, "From One Generation to Another: Mobility in Seventeenth-Century Windsor, Connecticut," *WMQ*, 3d Ser., XXXI (1974), 79–110, and Keith Wrightson and David Levine, *Poverty and Piety in an English Village: Terling, 1525–1700* (New York, 1979), 107, suggest that social mobility may sometimes require geographic mobility.

Yonge. Of the twenty-three persons in the 1680 census who indicated they had been resident in 1675, only twelve had been named then by Sir John Berry as planters. It would seem that the social scope of Robinson's twenty-eight "planters and inhabitants" was somewhat wider than that of Berry's twenty "planters." Perhaps the mayor of Falmouth's contemporary report that "about 50 or 60 Familyes, all English," lived at St. John's was based on an even broader sense of who was worth enumerating. Clearly, persistence of a surname in censuses is affected not only by geographical and social mobility but also by variation in the socioeconomic scope of enumeration.[26]

Low estimates of persistence in Newfoundland have been used as evidence that migration was much more important than natural increase and succession in the early settlements. One study of the planters and by-boat-keepers of St. John's in 1669, listed by the surgeon James Yonge, finds only five in John Berry's 1675 census of planters. This kind of name-sieving, the computation of how many names in an earlier census recur in a later one, must be done critically, allowing for the impressionistic spelling of surnames that followed from the frequent illiteracy of the census population and the passing character of the relationship between naval officers and the populace they enumerated. If we allow for vagaries of spelling, at least ten and probably twelve of the 1669 St. John's surnames recur six years later—a very different picture. Even the apparently impressive turnover of nine of twenty-seven individuals between 1677 and 1681 at St. John's is not, when closely examined, persuasive evidence that migration was more important, let alone much more important, than mortality, remarriage, and status mobility. Name-sieving does not mea-

26. Robinson, "St. John's and Baye of Bulls," Sept. 16, 1680, CO 1/46 (8iv), 23–24. Yonge's 1669 planters were John Downing II and Philip Roberts (Rogers). (There is evidence for the latter identification in the 1680 census.) Rosemary Loeney (Loney), another of those claiming long residence in 1680, was probably the widow of a 1669 planter. See Yonge, *Journal*, 119–120. The count of John Berry's 1675 planters even includes two presumed husbands of later widows. Robinson provided similar information for six inhabitants of Bay Bulls. One had recently arrived, but Robert Dench had been in Newfoundland since 1650, and the others had been there for periods of four to twelve years, yet Berry listed only two of them as planters in 1675. Compare Arundel, "A Description of the . . . Portes and Harbours . . . ," Mar. 13, 1675, CO 1/34 (22i), 45, 46; and the estimate of "a good colony of 400 or 500 people" at St. John's, in Williamson, "Newfoundland," 1675, CO 1/34 (16), 24–57, 69–73.

sure geographical mobility alone. A person named in an earlier census and missing from a later one might have moved on to New England but might also have fallen out of the class surveyed, remarried, or simply gone to a final reward. Thomas Barnes and William Matthews had died, since Widow Barnes and Widow Matthews occur among female heads of households in 1680 or 1681. Andrew Exon was another likely decedent, survived by John. Widows Loney, Sertall, and Haman (Holeman) might well have remarried. Robert Warren and John Peirce turn up again as planters in 1682 and might simply have been missed (the 1681 census is a fairly sloppy job) or might have suffered temporary economic setbacks. George Peircill (Piercey) owned no boat in 1677, so quite possibly he had become a servant. Only one of the 1677 planters, Thomas Oxford, would then be left as a possible out-migrant—hardly an ebb tide. This version of the fate of these early Newfoundland planters is speculative, but no more so than the assumption that they migrated elsewhere. In the end, evaluating turnover and persistence for an area like the English Shore is impossible, except when done comparatively. When such a comparative approach is taken, it becomes clear that the transience of Newfoundland planters fell within the normal circumatlantic range.[27]

ᴓ᥉ *Persistence and Turnover*

Censuses were rare in seventeenth-century England, and instances when a second census was taken of the same settlement were even rarer. One of the most surprising implications of such records, when they do occur, is the mobility of early modern populations. In the ten years be-

27. Handcock, *Origins*, 43–44, lists Furze, Bennet, Loony, Hopkings, and Downing as surnames occuring in 1669 and 1675. Yonge's "Goodman Bennet" may be Berry's "William Bennet" and not a relative, as Handcock suggests, since "Goodman" is an honorific, not a name; see Laslett, *World We Have Lost*, 74. We must add Woods, Cullen (Collins), and Doddle (Durdell) and ask whether "Coke" in Poynters edition of Yonge's *Journal* is a misreading for "Cole" and whether Yonge's "Rogers," a misremembered "Roberts." "Holeman" recurs as "Holman" in 1676. If by-boat-keepers are considered for 1675, as included by Yonge in the 1669 list, two names are added: "Andrews" and "Bickford." See John Berry, "A List of Ships Makinge Fishinge Voyages; with Boatkeepers . . . ," Sept. 12, 1675, CO 1/35 (17i), 136–148. "And. Exon" may be misidentified in 1681, replaced by "Jno. Exton."

tween the censuses of Cogenhoe, Northamptonshire, of 1618 and 1628, 52 percent of the 185 persons resident vanished from the records; at Clayworth, Nottinghamshire, among 401 persons resident in 1676, 61 percent were gone twelve years later, in 1688. Other kinds of evidence indicate that such levels of population turnover were common in seventeenth-century England, where the great mass of the national population was physically mobile. The demographic history of colonial America suggests that the transatlantic situation was more variable. In the late seventeenth century, some communities, particularly inland New England townships, seem to have been very stable, whereas the colonial port town of Boston and most of the Chesapeake counties were much less so.[28]

To compare residential persistence in various regions, annual turnover rates are more useful than impressionistic evaluation of change over arbitrary intercensal periods, determined simply by documentary happenstance. Calculation of an annual rate from population turnover over several years yields higher annual turnover rates than a simple arithmetic fraction, since after the first year the mobile group will include some persons who have already moved. For example, the annual turnover rate for Clayworth between 1676 and 1688 was 7.5 percent, not the 5 percent one might expect at first glance, given a 60 percent turnover in twelve years. These figures applied to the whole population of Clayworth, servants included. Mobility among heads of households was, predictably,

28. Peter Laslett and John Harrison, "Clayworth and Cogenhoe," in H. E. Bell and R. L. Ollard, eds., *Historical Essays, 1600-1750, Presented to David Ogg* (London, 1963), 157-184 (esp. 176, 183); Peter Clark, "Migration in England during the Late Seventeenth and Early Eighteenth Centuries," *Past and Present*, no. 83 (May 1979), 57-90; Peter Clark and David Souden, "Introduction," in Clark and Souden, eds., *Migration and Society*, 11-48; Julian Cornwall, "Evidence of Population Mobility in the Seventeenth Century," *Bulletin of the Institute of Historical Research*, XL (1967), 143-152; Laslett, *World We Have Lost*, 75-77; Paul A. Slack, "Vagrants and Vagrancy in England, 1598-1664," *EHR*, 2d Ser., XXVII (1974), 360-379; Keith Wrightson, *English Society, 1580-1680* (New Brunswick, N.J., 1982), 42. Regarding America, see Douglas Lamar Jones, "The Strolling Poor: Transiency in Eighteenth-Century Massachusetts," *Journal of Social History*, VIII (1974-1975), 28-54 (esp. 30, table 1); Horn, "Migration in the Chesapeake," in Clark and Souden, eds., *Migration and Society*, 172-212; and Kevin P. Kelly, "'In Dispers'd Country Plantations': Settlement Patterns in Seventeenth-Century Surry County, Virginia," in Tate and Ammerman, eds., *The Chesapeake in the Seventeenth Century*, 183-205 (esp. 193).

lower, and turnover rates for householders in England, New England, and the Chesapeake provide the most useful statistical background for the evaluation of turnover and persistence in the Newfoundland planter censuses (Table 17).[29]

Although the turnover rate among planters on the English Shore was above average, it was by no means the highest rate for householders in the regions examined. If Cogenhoe (1618/1628) and Clayworth (1676/1688) in England, Windsor, Connecticut (1676/1686), or Charles County, Maryland (1675/1690), represent modal annual rates of turnover at about 5.5 percent, then communities like Dedham, Massachusetts, after 1660 were exceptionally stable communities, with only half of this annual turnover. Newfoundland's annual turnover of 7.9 percent of all householders was, without question, relatively high, but it was exceeded in Lancaster County, Virginia, in two periods (1669/1679 and 1678/1688) and was closely approached in Boston, Massa-

---

29. Cf. Kussmaul, *Servants in Husbandry*, 53. An annual turnover rate (Rt) can be calculated from the equation:

$$R_t = 1-(P_p/P_o)^{1/n} \qquad \text{that is, } R_t = 1-(1-P_t/P_o)^{1/n}$$

Where $P_t = P_o-P_p$ = turnover in n years; P_p = persistent population over n years; P_o = original population; and n = number of years elapsed between censuses.

The comparative data are based on two English villages with initial populations of fewer than 100 households, three New England townships, each with 50–165 households, the colonial city of Boston, with more than 1,200 households, and three Chesapeake counties, each with several hundred tithable households. Most of these populations are in the same order of magnitude as the 163 Newfoundland householders used here as the 1675 baseline. The Newfoundland planters were, like their fellows in the Chesapeake counties, scattered over a much larger area than the populace of the English village of Clayworth and over a somewhat larger area than the extensive Massachusetts townships. In comparing rates of turnover, it is well to keep in mind that these populations were differently distributed within the administrative units typical of the various regions in question. Thus, a householder like Thomas Dodridge, who remained on the English Shore between 1675 and 1681 but moved from Brigus South via Ferryland and Fermeuse to Trepassey, exemplified a different kind of residential persistence than a householder of Dedham, Massachusetts, who remained in the same township from, say, 1660 to 1670. Mobility like the Dodridges' along the English Shore was, in fact, rare—at least among planters. In any event, Dodridge is excluded from our analysis because Trepassey, his harbor of residence in 1681, was not part of the 1675 census.

Table 17. *Turnover Rates for Householders, 1618–1698*

Place (N = Initial Population)	Residential Interval	Gross Turnover Rate	Annual Rate
England			
Cogenhoe, N. Hants (N = 154)	1618–1628	43%	5.5%
Clayworth, Notts (N = 98)	1676–1688	48	5.3
Orby, Lincs (N = 59)	1692–1694	15	7.9
Mean	5.4%		
New England			
Rowley, Mass. (N = 54)	1643–1653	41%	5.1%
Dedham, Mass. (N = 98)	1648–1660	48	5.3
Dedham, Mass. (N = 91)	1660–1670	22	2.5
Dedham, Mass. (N = 113)	1680–1690	27	3.1
Windsor, Conn. (N = 165)	1676–1686	43	5.5
Mean for townships	4.3%		
Boston, Mass. (N = 1,224)	1687–1695	47	7.6
Chesapeake			
Charles Co., Md.	1660–1675	53%	4.9%
Charles Co., Md.	1675–1690	58	5.6
Surry Co., Md.	1668–1678	54	7.5
Lancaster Co., Va.	1669–1679	61	9.0
Lancaster Co., Va.	1678–1688	57	8.1
Lancaster Co., Va.	1688–1698	55	7.7
Mean	7.1%		
Newfoundland			
English Shore (N = 89)	1675–1681	39%	7.9%
South Avalon (N = 21)	1675–1681	33	6.5
Outports (N = 41)	1675–1682	32	5.3

Table 17 (*continued*)

Note: The figures for Cogenhoe are for "nonservants," a broader class than house-holders. Initial population *(N)* is not given in the source for the Chesapeake, but it would have been in the order of several hundred. Figures for Newfoundland exclude Brigus South, Bauline South, Bonaventure, and English Harbour, which were not censused in 1681, and Keels, Barrow Harbour, Salvage, and Fair Island, which were not censused in 1675. Duplicate surnames in the same household in 1675 have also been excluded, since the 1681 census lists only one name per household. With these exclusions, there were 132 heads of households in 1675, of which 81 recur in 1681. The slovenliness of the 1681 report suggests it is more likely to contain errors and omissions than the better-organized 1675 census. The persistence level of 81 individuals of 132 is probably, therefore, a minimum figure. The outports reported in 1675 and 1682 were Witless Bay, Bay Bulls, Petty Harbour, Bay de Verde, Old Perlican, New Perlican, Scilly Cove, and Trinity.

Sources: Peter Laslett and John Harrison, "Clayworth and Cogenhoe," in H. E. Bell and R. L. Ollard, eds., *Historical Essays, 1600–1750, Presented to David Ogg* (London, 1963), 157–184, addendum III; Douglas Lamar Jones, "The Strolling Poor: Transiency in Eighteenth-Century Massachusetts," *Journal of Social History*, VIII, no. 3 (1974–1975), 28–54, table 1; James P. P. Horn, "Moving on in the New World: Migration and Out-Migration in the Seventeenth-Century Chesapeake," in Peter Clark and David Souden, eds., *Migration and Society in Early Modern England* (London, 1988), 172–212, table 22; John Berry, "A List of the Planters Names . . . ," Sept. 12, 1675, CO 1/35 (17ii), 149–156; James Story, "An Account of What Fishing Shipps, Sack Shipps, Planters, etc., Boat Keepers . . . ," Sept. 1, 1681, CO 1/47 (52i), 113–121; Daniel Jones, "An Accompt of the Planters Belonging to St. John's Harbour . . . ," Oct. 11, 1682, CO 1/49 (51ix), 196–198.

chusetts (1687/1695), Surry County, Virginia (1668/1678), and Lancaster County, Virginia (1688/1698). Turnover in these areas exceeded that among south Avalon planters (1675/1681). The low incidence of geographical mobility within English Newfoundland in the 1670s and 1680s means that the mobility rate for the whole colony is not too far off average mobility rates for particular communities. One stretch of the English Shore, the south Avalon, exhibited lower mobility than the colony as a whole. Analysis of a smaller sample of communities enumerated in 1675 and 1682 indicates that the outport population was decidedly less transient than St. John's, with an annual turnover rate (1675/1682) of only 5.3 percent, almost exactly the English norm and only a percentage point higher than the New England township average. Discussions of residence in Newfoundland often presume a standard of permanence matched historically only in certain periods, in some places. This sample of published figures should put Newfoundland transience in perspective.[30]

Again, a crucial consideration in making sense of such data is that turnover is not equivalent to geographical mobility; it is a sum of geographical mobility and two other elements: downward social mobility and mortality. Seventeenth-century Chesapeake records suggest that more than 3 percent of householders there died each year. This high death rate, also typical in the Caribbean colonies, often accounted for much of observed turnover. On the other hand, variation in turnover rates from county to county and decade to decade was determined by variation in levels of physical mobility, which might be more than 25 percent of the population of householders over a decade in areas with high turnover rates. Mortality decreased to the north, at least from the West Indies to New England, and there is no reason to assume Newfoundland was a significantly less-healthy environment than, say, Salem, Massachusetts, where the mortality rate among adults was about two-thirds the Chesapeake rate. Turnover on the English Shore (1675/1681) thus reflected somewhat greater geographical mobility than in contemporary Chesapeake counties with similar gross turnover. It was death that called most Chesapeake residents away; if they moved on, Newfoundlanders were as likely to go to New England.[31]

Contemporary maritime populations are the obvious comparative context for understanding mobility in seventeenth-century Newfoundland. In the absence of appropriate census data for maritime communities, we can turn to other longitudinal studies. Maritime folk often escaped offi-

30. In the absence of information about the month of enumeration, it would be unwise to trust these turnover rates much further than one significant digit.

31. Horn, "Migration in the Chesapeake," in Clark and Souden, eds., *Migration and Society*, 172–212 (esp. 196, table 23); Walsh, "'Till Death Us Do Part,'" in Tate and Ammerman, eds., *The Chesapeake in the Seventeenth Century*, 126–152; Dunn, *Sugar and Slaves*, 300–334; Daniel Blake Smith, "Mortality and Family in the Colonial Chesapeake," *Journal of Interdisciplinary History*, VIII (1977–1978), 403–427. Death rates among taxpayers in eighteenth-century Beverly, Massachusetts, were about 2 percent per annum; see Douglas Lamar Jones, *Village and Seaport: Migration and Society in Eighteenth-Century Massachusetts* (Hanover, N.H., 1981), 31, table 2.4. Cf. John Thomas to Richard[?], Sept. 15, 1680, in Pope, *"True and Faithful Account," Newfoundland Studies*, XII (1996), 32–49 (esp. 41); Peter Edward Pope, "Ceramics from Seventeenth Century Ferryland, Newfoundland (CgAf-2, Locus B)" (master's thesis, MUN, 1986), 241. For another view, see Handcock, *Origins*, 44.

cial notice, but their names were carefully recorded in the account books of the merchants who provisioned them on credit. George Corwin, of Salem, Massachusetts, was one of these merchants. A search for individuals named in his account book for 1658–1664 in other New England records yielded dates for first and last appearance in the region and therefore is another index of population turnover.[32]

What is immediately striking about this Salem population is that levels of long-term persistence were substantial: 57 percent of those in Corwin's accounts persisted in the region for at least ten years. Yet there was also a strong transient element: 36 percent persisted for less than five years—at least in the records surveyed. Only 6 percent of Corwin's customers disappeared from the records after persisting for an intermediate period. Thus, the breakdown of individuals by periods of persistence has a marked bipolar distribution, strongly suggesting that the Corwin accounts consisted of two subpopulations with different demographic characteristics: one very mobile, one relatively stable. Turnover rates calculated from such data cannot be compared with rates based on censuses. However, a comparison of Salem rates for two different periods suggests a subtle but important point. The turnover level among all individuals five years after entry into the records was high, although turnover among all individuals a decade after their first entry into these records was unremarkable. These disparate results are reconcilable if we recognize that in maritime communities those most likely to move were those who were already mobile. Almost a tenth of the population might move each year, but this fraction was not equally distributed over the whole population (the assumption normally made in analysis of transience, as in Table 17). In the maritime context, most emigrants consisted of recent immigrants, who themselves had displaced earlier emigrants, who were themselves

32. Total turnover between 1731 and 1741 for Beverly, Massachusetts, was 50 percent, indicating an annual turnover rate of 6.7 percent, but this population lived a half-century later in a town that was only in part a maritime community. See Jones, "Strolling Poor," *Jour. Soc. Hist.*, VIII (1974–1975), 28–54 (esp. 30, table 1). Corwin data courtesy of Daniel Vickers, Department of History, University of California at San Diego, who had the imaginative idea of treating as a population individuals named in the George Corwin (Curwen), Account Book, 1658–1664, Essex Institute, Salem, Mass., MS 45. Using *RFQC Essex Co.*, I–IX, *Suffolk Records*, pts. 1, 2, *Baxter MSS*, IV, VI, and Sidney Perley, *The History of Salem, Massachusetts*, 3 vols. (Salem, Mass., 1924–1928), Vickers calculated years elapsed between the first and last indication, in these records, of the presence on the New England littoral of each of the individuals in the Corwin population.

only slightly earlier immigrants, and so on. Because maritime communities had a socioeconomic niche for highly mobile individuals, high rates of turnover in short periods were consistent with much lower rates of turnover over longer periods.[33]

Seventeenth-century Newfoundland had room for the highly mobile, even among those who kept boats and employed others. The by-boat-keepers, who generally migrated annually, were a good example of this mobile population, and there were others, often recorded in a gray area in which small fishing masters or even servants were not clearly distinguished from small-scale single planters. The annual turnover rate reported above for the English Shore is based on an intercensal interval of only six years, or about half the interval used for the comparative data. Thus, in light of the Salem figures, a rate of 7.9 percent likely overstates turnover on the English Shore, because it is based on a relatively short intercensal interval. The Salem evidence suggests that such a level of transience over the limited period of six years may well be compatible with a significantly lower level over a decade or so—implying that the Newfoundland planters were no more mobile than their peers in other parts of the English-speaking world.[34]

We should not misconstrue conditions in seventeenth-century Newfoundland as unique; they were part of a larger picture. Long-distance mobility was a typical aspect of English life between about 1540 and 1660. Shorter distance, seasonal subsistence migration was increasingly common in post-Restoration England until about 1700, when such mobility was confined to a rump of ex-soldiers and sailors, gypsies, and the Irish. The parallels with Newfoundland's population history are apparent. Internal mobility was somewhat lower in the West Country than in the rest of England, but this estimate ignores movement from other ports, and Devon ranks third among English counties in emigrants to America. The ebb and flow of migrants to Newfoundland were part of a much larger scene. It is not the transience of a relatively unremarkable percentage of Newfoundland planters that requires a regional expla-

33. Cf. Keith Wrightson, "Aspects of Social Differentiation in Rural England, c. 1580–1660," *Journal of Peasant Studies*, V (1977), 33–47; Jones, "Strolling Poor," *Jour. Soc. Hist.*, VIII (1974–1975), 28–54; Christine Leigh Heyrman, *Commerce and Culture: The Maritime Communities of Colonial Massachusetts, 1690–1750* (New York, 1984), 213; Corwin data, Vickers, personal communication.

34. Cf. Handcock, *Origins*, 25–26.

nation but rather the quickly achieved stability of inland New England populations.[35]

If we see Newfoundland's population history in this light, it will not be necessary to invoke the demographic turbulence of frontier areas to explain the turnover characteristic of the English Shore around 1675. Neither Boston, Massachusetts, nor Virginia's Surry and Lancaster Counties were frontier areas at that time, yet they shared with the English Shore annual turnover rates about higher by half than the average rate in England and Anglo-America. Parts of the English Shore, in particular the south Avalon, St. John's, and Conception Bay, had already passed the frontier stage when the first generation of settlers had made the area their permanent home. Many planters were native-born, as Father Jean Baudoin observed in 1697 during the French invasion of the Shore, when he noted the recent death of a native-born planter, at the age of eighty-four. Although there was a broad niche for transients, a core of about two thousand residents was well established in Newfoundland by the end of the seventeenth century.[36]

35. Peter Clark, "Migration in England during the Late Seventeenth and Early Eighteenth Centuries," *Past and Present*, no. 83 (May 1979), 57–90 (esp. 76); Slack, "Vagrants and Vagrancy," *EHR*, 2d Ser., XXVII (1974), 360–379 (esp. 366, 371); Souden, "Indentured Servant Immigrants," *Social History*, III (1978–1979), 19–33 (esp. 21); R. D. Brown, "Devonians and New England Settlement before 1650," *RT Devon*, XCV (1964), 219–243. Cf. David Rollison, "Exploding England: The Dialectics of Mobility and Settlement in Early Modern England," *Social History*, XXIV (1998–1999), 1–16.

36. Handcock, *Origins*, 44; Horn, "Migration in the Chesapeake," in Clark and Souden, eds., *Migration and Society*, 172–212 (esp. 180, map 8); Kelly, "Seventeenth-Century Surry County," in Tate and Ammerman, eds., *The Chesapeake in the Seventeenth Century*, 183–205; Thornton, "Strait of Belle Isle," in Mannion, ed., *Peopling of Newfoundland*, 152–183 (esp. 163); Abbé Jean Baudoin, "Journal," Jan. 28, 1697, in Alan F. Williams, *Father Baudoin's War: d'Iberville's Campaigns in Acadia and Newfoundland, 1696, 1697* (St. John's, 1987), 173–191 (esp. 184). The planter was, perhaps, the child born to Nicholas Guy at Cupids about 1611.

7 ⟨⟩ TRANSIENTS

*Five hundred sayle great and small doe from England yearly sayle to
this coast . . . and, arriving there about the middle of Aprill, unrigge
their shippes, set up boothes and cabanets on the shore in divers
creekes and harbours, and there, with fishing provisions and salt,
begin their fishing in shallops and boates, continue it till September
. . . and this fishing ended and the cold beginning, they leave their
stations and booths and, repairing aboord their shippes, lade their fish
and, rigging their vessels, returne to their native homes, where these
fishermen winter and then become husbandmen, so their lives may be
compared to the otter, which is spent halfe on land and halfe in sea.*
—*Lewes Roberts,* The Merchants Mappe of Commerce, *1638*

The maritime world is fluid. The thousands of men and the handful
of women who served in the Newfoundland fishery moved as easily as
the ships that worked their way seasonally across the North Atlantic.
In the seventeenth century, most British fishing voyages to Newfoundland fitted out at Barnstaple, Bideford, Plymouth, Dartmouth, Topsham,
or Poole (Map 7). Fishing masters or their agents recruited servants
for Newfoundland in the hinterland of these towns: the pasturelands of
north Devon, Dartmoor, Exmoor, south Somerset, and Dorset.[1]

Toward the end of the century, ships venturing from north Devon
began to call in the nearby ports of southeast Ireland to take on provisions. By 1680, Englishmen were increasingly able to find alternatives to long-distance seasonal subsistence migration, and so it was only
a matter of time before fishing masters took on servants as well when

1. John Berry, "A List of Ships Makinge Fishinge Voyages; with Boatkeep-
ers . . . ," Sept. 12, 1675, CO 1/35 (17i), 137-148; William Poole, "Account of
Fishing and Sackships from Trepassy to Cape Broyle," Sept. 10, 1677, CO 1/41
(62viii-x), 167-172; James Story, "An Account of What Fishing Shipps, Sack
Shipps, Planters, etc., Boat Keepers . . . ," Sept. 1, 1681, CO 1/47 (52i), 113-121;
Francis Wheler, "Ships, Men, Boats, Stages, Fish," Oct. 27, 1684, CO 1/55 (56vi),
256. They also report occasional participation in at least one fishing expedition by
Dublin, Bristol, Fowey, Teignmouth, Brixham, Exeter, Weymouth, Lyme Regis,
Southampton, Shoreham, London, Jersey, and Guernsey. On catchment areas, see
Handcock, *Origins,* 55-70.

they called in the Irish ports of Waterford and Wexford for butter and salt meat. In a similar way, earlier in the century the Irish provisions trade to the Caribbean had facilitated migration to the island colonies there. Irish recruitment for the Newfoundland fishery began later, in the closing decades of the seventeenth century. Some Irish merchants were themselves involved in the Newfoundland trade, notably the Waterford master John Aylward. Most of the merchants trading in Irish goods at Newfoundland were originally from Devon—like Peter Fewings, who traded in north Devon, Ireland, and Ferryland. Irish ports mounted a few fishing voyages to Newfoundland: the *Sea Horse* of Dublin, for example, fished at Harbour Grace in 1681; the *Aron*, also of Dublin, at Old Perlican in 1682. Although Captain James Story noted the arrival of Irish servant girls in the early 1680s, male fishing servants from Ireland would have been rarer, given that the Irish were engaged primarily in the sack trade. During the French campaign on the English Shore in the winter of 1697, Father Jean Baudoin noted a few Irish servants in Conception Bay, "who the English here treat like slaves." Ireland remained a minor reservoir of servants recruited to the Newfoundland fishery in this period, and Irish names were, as yet, rare in the planter censuses.[2]

2. John Mannion, "Victualling a Fishery: Newfoundland Diet and the Origins of the Irish Provisions Trade, 1675-1700," *IJMH*, XII (2000), 1-57 (on Aylward [Aylred], see 17-20; on Fewings, 48-49); Nicholas Canny, "English Migration into and across the Atlantic during the Seventeenth and Eighteenth Centuries," in Nicholas Canny, ed., *Europeans on the Move: Studies on European Migration, 1500-1800* (Oxford, 1994), 39-75. Audrey Lockhart, *Some Aspects of Emigration from Ireland to the North American Colonies between 1660 and 1775* (New York, 1976), exaggerates Irish immigration to Newfoundland before 1700. The sources she cites do not support her interpretation. On Irish trade, see John Downing, "A Breif Narrative concerning Newfoundland," Nov. 24, 1676, British Library, Egerton MS 2395, 560-563; Lawrence Wright, "A List of Sack Ships," August 1679, CO 1/43 (112), 202; Story, "Account," Sept. 1, 1681, CO 1/47 (52i), 113-121; Daniel Jones, "Sacke Ships . . . ," Oct. 11, 1682, CO 1/49 (51vii), 194. A few ships from Limerick and Youghal also traded at Newfoundland between 1675 and 1684. On Irish servants, see Abbé Jean Baudoin, Journal, Jan. 25, 1697, in Alan F. Williams, *Father Baudoin's War: d'Iberville's Campaigns in Acadia and Newfoundland, 1696, 1697* (St. John's, 1987), 173-191 (my translation). Arthur Moone (Mooney, Mahone?), a resident of Witless Bay in the 1670s, might have been Irish or might have been a reemigrant from north Devon, which had absorbed many Irish immigrants earlier in the century. Williams, 168, mentions an

Significant Irish migration, seasonal and otherwise, did not reach Newfoundland until after 1713, the real boom coming in the 1760s and sustained into the following century. This was the beginning of a wave of migration that by 1840 had profoundly changed the ethnic and religious makeup of the island. That is another story, although one with historiographic relevance here. Most historical mythologies have some basis in fact: events with serious impact are, of course, those most likely to leave a trace on collective memory, whether remembered or misremembered. From the time of his appointment in 1763, immediately following the Seven Years' War, the influential and aggressively Protestant governor, Admiral Sir Hugh Palliser, mounted a very real opposition to Irish, or, more precisely, to Catholic, immigration into Newfoundland, which was continued by his immediate successors. This opposition was, likely, the effective historical seed of the later mythology of illegal settlement, of which Irish Newfoundlanders have certainly been among the most vehement proponents.[3]

Irish mercenary, John Bermony, at Plaisance in the 1690s, married to a refugee from the sack of St. John's.

3. J. D. Rogers, *A Historical Geography of the British Colonies*, V, pt. 4, *Newfoundland* (Oxford, 1911), 120–121; Thomas F. Nemec, "Trepassey 1505–1840 A.D.: The Emergence of an Anglo-Irish Newfoundland Outport," *Newfoundland Quarterly*, LXIX, no. 4 (1973), 17–28; Nemec, "St. Shotts in Historical Perspective," ibid., LXXI, no. 3 (1975), 17–22; Head, *Newfoundland*, 86–99; Handcock, *Origins*, 30–31; L. M. Cullen, "The Irish Diaspora of the Seventeenth and Eighteenth Centuries," in Canny, ed., *Europeans on the Move*, 113–149; John Mannion, "Irish Migration and Settlement in Newfoundland: The Formative Phase, 1697–1732," *Newfoundland Studies*, XVII (2001), 257–293; John P. Greene, *Between Damnation and Starvation: Priests and Merchants in Newfoundland Politics, 1745–1855* (Montreal, 1999); Kirsten Hastrup, "Worlds Apart: Comprehending Each Other across Time and Space," *Acta Borealia*, I (1990), 14–24; Sir Hugh Palliser, "Order to Preserve the Peace," Oct. 31, 1764, PANL, GN 2/1/a, III, 272; Sir John Byron, "Order concerning Irish Papists," Oct. 11, 1771, PANL, GN 2/1/a, V, n.p.; Patrick Morris, *A Short Review of the History, Government, Constitution, Fishery, and Agriculture of Newfoundland . . .* (St. John's, 1847); Shane O'Dea, "Newfoundland: The Development of Culture on the Margin," *Newfoundland Studies*, X (1994), 73–81; Patrick O'Flaherty, *Old Newfoundland: A History to 1843* (St. John's, 1999), 38–48.

Whatever the origins of migrants and however imperial administrators regarded their migrations, we know that Newfoundland's population grew slowly in the late seventeenth century—hence, the inward flow of migrants, seasonal and otherwise, must have been roughly equaled by the flow out. This balance was very desirable from the metropolitan point of view, since the Newfoundland fishery was traditionally valued as a "nursery of seamen"—a training ground for a population of mariners from which the Royal Navy could draw in time of war. Secretary of State Sir Joseph Williamson expressed the theory clearly in his private notes: "*N.B.*—Three voyages make a landsman a good seaman." The amendments to the Western Charter of 1671 and 1676 formalized the practice by requiring that at least one in five fishers setting sail for Newfoundland be green men. Increasingly, however, there were problems in the nursery. Unlike ships, crews and passengers were not necessarily inclined to a return voyage: the outflow of newly engaged servants from the British Isles was not quite matched by the inflow of experienced seamen returning from the Newfoundland fishery. Some remained in Newfoundland; some moved on, sooner or later, to New England. If we think of the seventeenth-century English Shore as a rather inelastic vessel, subjected to a net inflow of young men from the Old World, we will not be surprised to learn that it leaked. Imagine a roughly built, open, wooden boat, beached on the shore, filled a little more each time it rains—the pressure of water within it will soon cause seepage along the keel, at the garboard strakes. The metaphor is crude, though, and does not fully elucidate the net inflow of servants to Newfoundland, despite the regular return of most fishing servants to the West Country.[4]

Although the fishery on the English Shore was not a closed system, the interdependent resident and migrant fisheries constrained, in vary-

<hr />

4. For a skeptical view of the "nursery of seamen," see David J. Starkey, "The West Country–Newfoundland Fishery and the Manning of the Royal Navy," in Robert Higham, ed., *Security and Defence in South-West England before 1800* (Exeter, 1987), 93–101. Quotation from Joseph Williamson, "Newfoundland," 1675, CO 1/34 (16), 24–57, 69–73 (transcription in *CSP*: Colonial, 1675–1676, Addenda, 1574–1674, 156–163). For "green men," note clause 7 in Charles II, Order in Council, Mar. 10, 1671, CO 1/26, 20–26, and cf. additional clause 7 in Charles II, "A Charter Granted to the West Country Adventurers," Jan. 27, 1676, CO 1/65 (36), 128–134, both in Matthews, *Constitutional Laws*, 139–144, 167–180.

ing degrees, entrance to and exit from Newfoundland. A young man living in the hinterland of one of the West Country ports or, later, in the alternative recruitment area of Waterford and Wexford could easily sign on as a fishing servant and thereby get passage to Newfoundland for the fishery. The Western Charter of 1661 did attempt to limit servants' passage to those serving the fishing ship itself, that is, those most likely to make a return voyage. The regulation was widely ignored, however, for ships fishing went out lightly laden or even in ballast, and fishing masters had economic incentive to carry not only their own crews but also paying passengers who were going to Newfoundland to serve independent by-boat-keepers and planters. Passage back across the Atlantic did not come so easily. Space was at a premium, since ships returned with cargoes of fish and train oil, not to mention equipment and crewmen from other fishing ships, laden at Newfoundland as sacks for southern Europe. Migratory fishing masters had little incentive to bring back every man who had shipped out with them, a context that favored net migration from the British Isles. In fact, they had incentive to leave some men behind, for ships could easily be handled at sea by crews much smaller than those needed for the summer's work ashore, and every servant left in "the Land" saved space, victuals, or even passage money for the master and his business partners. By-boat-keepers had a direct disincentive to return their crews to home, that is, the cost for passage, and they were often blamed for impeding the orderly flow of trained men back across the Atlantic. Similar criticisms were sometimes leveled at planters, but, in the end, blame fell elsewhere.[5]

The St. John's merchant John Downing explained the situation: "As for any men wee inhabitants have out of fishing ships, wee have the masters good will to have them . . . it saving the owners the victualls they should eate homewards, and many times they carry [paying] passengers in their places." The naval commodores verified Downing's observations. Captain John Berry told the Committee for Trade and Plantations that seamen would "tarry" in Newfoundland because shipmasters "doe persuade the planters to receive them" and estimated the savings at thirty to forty shillings per man. Not every ship left men behind: Captain Francis Wheler reported that, in the normal run of things, migratory ships' crews

5. Mayors of Dartmouth, Totnes, etc., Petition to Privy Council, Dec. 4, 1662, SP 29/84 (71, 71i); Mayors of West Country Ports, Petition to Charles II, Dec. 23, 1669, CO 389/5, 18–19; Charles Talbot, "Answers to the Enquiries . . . ," Sept. 15, 1679, CO 1/43 (121i), 216–217. Hiring practices are discussed in Chapter 5, above.

were "upon bargaine to be payd in England, which keeps them from staying here." He added that some ship fishermen nevertheless did stay on, for several reasons: "Good husbandry to take two voyages [that is, to work two fishing seasons], sometimes out of drunkeness—haveing spent theire summer voyage, butt chiefly when their masters are not able to pay them. However, this is very uncertaine, the last winter in the whole country there stayed but 120, but for want of a markett their will be many more this." The annual rate of net servant migration into Newfoundland from England might have varied, but the fundamental differential that drove it remained: the economics of the seasonal fish trade made return from the Newfoundland fishery to the British Isles more difficult than entrance into it, at least for some people, some of the time.[6]

The migratory fishery thus created population pressure in Newfoundland—a pressure that was not easily relieved. As a result, a market in maritime labor developed in Newfoundland itself from a surprisingly early date. In the 1630s, the *Castle* (of London?) shipped eight or ten men at Newfoundland for a sack voyage to Malaga. In 1669, a New York master took it for granted that men, no less than fishing supplies, could be easily obtained at Newfoundland. The planters, of course, needed a certain amount of labor, but one doubts that they preferred to hire in the fall. Some older servants might become planters and enter the fishery on their own account, but only with capital accumulation in the form of a boat and fishing stage—a modest requirement from the point of view of a merchant but a significant challenge for a fishing servant. Fishing rooms in the older parts of the English Shore were already enclosed, and migratory crews still expected access to rooms seasonally, even in long-established harbors like Ferryland and St. John's. Possibilities for growth in the number of planter households in the older communities were therefore economically limited, at least until the introduction of offshore fishing techniques and potato cultivation in the following century.[7]

6. Downing, "Breif Narrative," Nov. 24, 1676, British Library, Egerton MS 2395, 560-563; Privy Council, Order to Admiralty, Apr. 19, 1676, CO 389/3, 32-33; William Poole, "Answers to the Severall Heads of Inquiry . . . ," Sept. 10, 1677, CO 1/41 (62i), 149-152, noting some current control; Francis Wheler, "Answers to the Heads of Inquirys . . . ," Oct. 27, 1684, CO 1/55 (56), 239-246; John Berry to Joseph Williamson, July 24, 1675, CO 1/34 (118), 240-241.

7. William Clarke, Examination, Apr. 3, 1638, HCA 13/53 (594), in Dorothy O. Shilton and Richard Holworthy, eds., *High Court of Admiralty Examinations (MS Volume 53), 1637-1638* (London, 1932), 274-275; Samuel Mavericke to Colonel

The seventeenth-century outport niche was narrow. Except around St. John's, the number of households in the older parts of the English Shore did not change rapidly in the later seventeenth century. Significant growth in the number of planter households depended on the extension of the limits of English settlement to Trepassey, Trinity Bay, and Bonavista. Thomas Dodridge's drift southward, with his boats, his wife, and his family, might have made economic sense within this context. English planters were also settling in French Newfoundland. Isaac Dethick was an eyewitness to the original fortification of Plaisance in 1662, and twenty years later a pair of Plaisance residents, including Stephen Dethick, passed similar intelligence to the British. A French census recorded Tom Pic, Jean Bardet, and Louis de Beaufet as "anglois" at Plaisance in 1671. Captain William Poole noted some of the same families there in 1677: "Mr Jackson, his wife, and family, all English; the other three, viz. Thomas Peck, William Buffitt, and Phillip Leymer were his servants but are now married to French women." Pick and Leymer (Lemard) were still at Plaisance in 1696 with their French wives. Elsewhere, especially on the boundaries of English settlement, the scarcity of women remained a serious constraint on the establishment of new households. Unfortunately for Newfoundland, New England enjoyed a better demographic balance between the sexes. Thus, as the quotable Captain Wheler observed, the flow of men from England to Newfoundland was often only the first stage of a longer migration that brought men from the West Country to the fishing communities of Maine and Massachusetts: "This I find very inconvenient for the kings service, that the New England men constantly carry away abundance of the fishermen and seamen, who presently marry and then that is there home."[8]

Nichols, April 1669, *CSP*: Colonial. Nicolas Landry, "Culture matérielle et niveaux de richesse chez les pêcheurs de Plaisance et de l'Île Royale, 1700–1758," *Material History Review*, no. 48 (Fall 1998), 101–122, has evidence that at death the estates of French fishing servants were rarely worth a tenth of the estates of habitants.

8. John Rayner, "Deposition," Jan. 2, 1668, CO 1/22 (66), 109; James Story, "Intelligence about the French Trade," Sept. 1, 1681, CO 1/47 (52i), 122; "Rolle des gens de l'habitation de Plaisance 1671," in Fernand-D. Thibodeau, "Recensements de Terreneuve et Plaisance," *Mémoires de la Société Généalogique Canadienne-Française*, X (1959), 179–188; Poole, "Answers," Sept. 10, 1677, CO 1/41 (62i), 149–152; cf. Thomas Farr to CTP, Mar. 21, 1675, *CSP*: Colonial; Williams, *Father Baudoin's War*, 161–168. Dethick ended his days in Trinity Bay, at Heart's Content; see John Knight, Deposition, Apr. 17, 1704, CO 194/3, 74. The other English

For servants without a passage home, or with some incentive to forgo it, New England was not merely an attractive destination; it was the cheapest exit from Newfoundland. Passage to England cost up to £3 sterling, whereas passage to New England might be had for only £2 Massachusetts tenor, or about £1 12s. sterling. Economic realities on the English Shore restricted the escape of servants through social mobility, although the subsidy the French offered to English immigrants facilitated servant migration to Plaisance. For those unwilling to plunge into another milieu, economic constraints on social mobility limited geographical mobility at the boundaries of English settlement. Apart from seasonal exploitation of the interior, there was only one significant relief valve for the population pressure created by the net inflow of servants: migration onward to New England.[9]

?§ Onward Migration

The well-established trade between Newfoundland and the colonies to the south created a rear exit from Britain's nursery of seamen. This trade was not limited to Maine and Massachusetts: the naval commodores reported sacks from New York and Barbados as well, and an intermittent tobacco trade continued with Maryland and Virginia. However, most of the colonial vessels trading at Newfoundland were from New England, which had a special relationship with the island from the beginnings of European settlement in the region. The fishermen of early Stuart Devon set up shore stations in both places, and the migratory fishery in northern New England was, originally, a kind of imitation of

spy in 1681 was John Molum. Another Englishman, Amus Trotel, and Nicolas Aubin, from Jersey, were also at Plaisance in 1696. Quotation from Wheler, "Answers," Oct. 27, 1684, CO 1/55 (56), 241. On demographic balance, see David Cressy, *Coming Over: Migration and Communication between England and New England in the Seventeenth Century* (Cambridge, 1987), 37–73. Todd Gray, "Devon's Coastal and Overseas Fisheries and New England Migration, 1597–1642" (Ph.D. diss., University of Exeter, 1988), emphasizes mobility among all the fisheries, inshore and offshore.

9. Williamson, "Newfoundland," 1675, CO 1/34 (16), 24–57, 69–73; Samuell Aburne, Administration of Henry Ball, June 1679, *RFQC Essex Co.*, VII, 225; William Davies to Mr. Wren, Sept. 9, 1675, CO 1/27 (27), 74; [Sir Robert Robinson?], "Reasons for the Settlement of Newfoundland . . . under Government," 1671 or after, CO 1/22 (69), 115–116. On use of the interior, see Chapter 9, below.

the Newfoundland fishery. Early visitors to coastal Maine spoke of the application of "Newfoundland law" there, by which they meant the traditions of the established fishery to the north, later codified in the Western Charters. In its earliest days, ships from New England sometimes fished at Newfoundland, but in the 1670s and 1680s, New Englanders rarely came to fish along the island's coasts, as they had once done and would do again in the eighteenth century. (This trend perhaps reflected declining catches in the north, in the context of a booming offshore industry on fishing banks closer to New England itself: Brown's, Sable Island, Banquereau, Green, Canso, and St. Pierre.) The connection between Newfoundland and New England was now primarily commercial, as the St. John's merchant Downing noted, in 1676: "From New England one year with the other comes commonly eight saile of vessels, burthens from 16 tonns to 50, their commodities a little bread, pease, flower, beef, pork, butter, tarr, boards, tobacco, black sugar, mollasses, the produce of which they invest here in brandy, cloathing, apparells for their vessels, peeces of eight if they can gett them, some French and Spanish wines, and some red stinking fish for the negroes of Barbadoes." Within a decade or two, Newfoundland was also importing quantities of rum from New England and even Canary and Fayal wines, reversing the earlier pattern of trade, in which Newfoundland supplied drink to New England.[10]

10. Francis Wheler, "An Account of Sack Shipps . . . ," Oct. 27, 1684, CO 1/55 (56v), 255; Ralph Greenlee Lounsbury, *The British Fishery at Newfoundland, 1634–1763* (1934; rpt. Hamden, Conn., 1969), 190–203; Head, *Newfoundland*, 100–137; Todd Gray, "Devon's Fisheries and Early-Stuart Northern New England," *Maritime History of Devon*, I, 139–144; Charles E. Clark, *The Eastern Frontier: The Settlement of Northern New England, 1610–1763* (1970; rpt. Hanover, N.H., 1983), 29–30; Poole, "Answers," Sept. 10, 1677, CO 1/41 (62i), 149–152; Wheler, "Answers," Oct. 27, 1684, CO 1/55 (56), 239–246; Vickers, *Farmers and Fishermen*, 148–153; Downing, "Breif Narrative," Nov. 24, 1676, British Library, Egerton MS 2395, 560–563. For a New England fishing voyage to Ferryland in 1708, see Benjamin Marston to Robert Holmes, Apr. 20, 1708, and Robert Holmes, master of the *Beginning* of Salem, "A True Copy of an Account," Nov. 20, 1720, both in Essex Institute, Salem, Mass., Essex Co. Court of Common Pleas, 3530, 14. In 1720, sixty thousand gallons of rum went from Boston to Newfoundland, most of Boston's rum exports in this period; see John J. McCusker, *Rum and the American Revolution: The Rum Trade and the Balance of Payments of the Thirteen Continental Colonies* (New York, 1989), II, 498, 518; Peter Pope, "Adventures in the Sack Trade: London Merchants in the Canada and Newfoundland

Besides "refuse or decayed fish . . . sold att half price," Newfoundland sent fishing servants to New England, a diversion of servant migrants that had been going on for decades. Captain Charles Talbot, the naval commodore in 1679, reported that New England masters "steale fishermen" and attributed this practice to the contemporary growth of New England's own fishery. Captain Daniel Jones saw things in much the same light in 1682, when he attempted to effect some kind of control on this flow:

> The traders from New England . . . yearly make voyages, by spiriting away His Majesty's subjects to the utter ruin of both merchants adventurers and planters and the decay of the fishing trade. I was an eye witness to one at St Johns harbour, whoe came in with 11 hands and was sayling away with an addition of twenty men, had hee not been brought to an anchor againe by my pinnace and forc'd to turne ashoare att butt his complyment. To prevent such disorders for the future, I tooke bonds from the New England vessels there.

These bonds are interesting in themselves as indoctrination in the principles of mercantilism. The document signed by William Pepperill of Portsmouth, New Hampshire, for example, reiterates Jones's improbable hysterics about "the great damage" caused by the transportation of servants.[11]

Neither bonds nor mercantilist propaganda were effective in controlling the onward migration of servants: New England ships traded at Newfoundland and carried men away until the American Revolution. At the turn of the eighteenth century, Captain John Graydon told the Board of Trade, "The New England traders seldom depart the countrey till men

Trades, 1627–1648," *Northern Mariner*, VI (1996), 1–19; Mannion, "Victualling a Fishery," *IJMH*, XII (2000), 1–57 (esp. 41–44).

11. On servants as exports, see Wheler, "Answers," Oct. 27, 1684, CO 1/55 (56), 239–246. Downing follows his list of exports with a discussion of servant migration; cf. Inhabitants of Marblehead, Petition, 1667, *RFQC Essex Co.*, V, 373; Mavericke to Nichols, April 1669, *CSP: Colonial*; Davies to Wren, Sept. 9, 1675, CO 1/27 (27), 74. On remigration as theft, see Talbot, "Answers," Sept. 15, 1679, CO 1/43 (121i), 216–217; and Captain Daniel Jones to William Blathwayt, Sept. 12, 1682, CO 1/49 (51), 187; William Pepperill, Bond, Sept. 7, 1682, CO 1/49 (51iii), 188. George Snell, Thomas Harvey, and John Sawley posted similar bonds.

of warr are first sail'd, and then they carry with them numbers of handicraftsmen, seamen, and fishermen, which they inveagle thither by telling them what vast wages are given there." In 1701, Captain George Larkin heard that New England vessels had taken "upwards of five hundred men" from Conception Bay the year preceding, some of them "headed up in casks" to avoid detection. Perhaps Larkin did not expect the Board to take this statement literally, for he added ambiguously: "Of what consequences this is to England your Lordships are the most proper judges." The occasional tall tale aside, the naval commodores and others paint a fairly consistent picture of the number of onward migrants, the terms on which they moved, their destination, and their reception.[12]

Newfoundland planters were not nearly as mobile as their servants, but some did move on to New England. John Slaughter, a planter of Ferryland between 1628 and 1652, appears in Salem records around 1663 as a married fisherman. An apprenticeship indenture of 1673 made in Fermeuse, on the south Avalon, provides an example of out-migration in a long-established planter family. With the consent of his stepfather Richard Lee and his mother Elizabeth, George Lowry bound himself for five years as apprentice to Nicholas Chatwill of Salem, mariner. A defense of settlement, written about this time, claimed that one result of the 1671 amendment to the Western Charter "for turning the planters six miles into the country from the seaside" was that "the chiefest of them have transported themselves into New-England." This statement was, likely, an exaggeration, but periods of crisis probably did provoke planter emigration, particularly of wealthier merchant planters. We should not be surprised to find one of the third-generation Newfoundland Kirkes, Sarah, born about 1685, married in Charlestown, Massachusetts, in 1708. Planter turnover was consistent with onward migration of about three families a year, that is, a total of ten or twelve men, women, and children.[13]

12. [John Graydon], "Answers to the Heads of Enquiries," Sept. 20, 1701, CO 194/2, 176–178; George Larkin to CTP, Aug. 20, 1701, CO 194/2, 131–132.

13. George Curwen [Corwin], Account Book, 1661, 1663, 1664, Essex Institute, MS 45, IV, 193, 221, VI, 3, 6; George Lowry, Indenture, Aug. 7, 1673, *RFQC Essex Co.*, VIII, 205; "Reasons for the Settlement of Newfoundland . . . under Government," after 1670, CO 1/22 (69), 115–116. Sarah Kirke, ca. 1685–1722 (likely a child of George, Jarvis, or Phillip Kirke), married Joseph Gorham (1681–1742), Nov. 9, 1708: Charlestown Wills, Edward Chafe, personal communication, 1999. The reemigration estimate assumes long-term turnover of 6–8 percent annually,

The great majority of migrants to New England from Newfoundland were, not planters, but servants. Since only a few New England vessels fished at Newfoundland in the later seventeenth century, most migrants onward in this period were not hired on the English Shore. Instead, most went as passengers on New England traders, who carried "as many seamen as they can pack them in." Early-eighteenth-century lists of passengers arriving at the Port of Boston are instructive. Of three sloops arriving with passengers from Newfoundland in 1715 and 1716, the *Friends Adventure* might have been fishing, for it came in with three Newfoundland mariners as well as three passengers. The *Adventure* and the *Eliza* brought passengers only, numbering respectively twenty-seven and twenty-two, almost all men, but including one married couple (with an Irish surname). If six to eight New England sloops were trading annually at Newfoundland in the late seventeenth century, each carrying twenty or thirty onward migrants, then the annual flow was normally no more than one hundred or two hundred men. In 1718, the appropriately named Captain Passenger claimed that "1100 went to New England"—but, as usual with such high estimates, this was hearsay about "the year before." The New England masters facilitated onward migration—in whatever numbers and whether immigrants were packed in casks or not—by extending credit for passage. We know from the administration of his estate that Henry Ball, who died in New England in 1678, had borrowed forty shillings from Samuell Aburne of Salem "in money to pay his passage from Newfoundland." The *Beginning* of Salem, which fished at Ferryland in 1708, brought home five men from Newfoundland, one as a mate and one who had promised to work off his debt; the rest, apparently, were paying passengers. There are other references to Newfoundland servants in the Salem records, but this community was not the only one into which migrants flowed. The home ports of New England vessels trading at Newfoundland between 1675 and 1684 include New London, Boston, and Portsmouth as well. Servant migrants would be likely to settle, to the degree that they did settle, either in these ports or in nearby fishing communities.[14]

death or retirement accounting for half of turnover and retirement to England accounting for half of geographical mobility.

14. Story, "Account," Sept. 1, 1681, CO 1/47 (52i), 113–121; Edward V. Chafe, "Passengers Arriving in the Port of Boston from the Island of Newfoundland, 1715–1716 and 1762–1769," research file (1982), Centre for Newfoundland Studies, MUN; Handcock, *Origins*, 29; Samuell Aburne, Administration of Henry Ball,

Servant arrivals from Newfoundland were not necessarily welcome. In 1667, the inhabitants of Marblehead complained to the Salem Quarterly Court that fishermen arriving from Newfoundland were often "persons undesirable, and of noe estates, butt rather indebted," who became burdens to the community if they were sick or lame. Marblehead therefore asked "that we may either have power putt into our hands to kepe outt such persons from coming into our plantation as are like to be burthens to us, or that we may be eased of the charge . . . by the countie." The attempt to control such in-migration was no more successful than the many attempts to control onward migration at Newfoundland itself. Since the very beginnings of New England, a migrant stream had flowed in from the British Isles via Newfoundland. This flow continued through most of the eighteenth and nineteenth centuries, by which time many of the arrivals from Newfoundland were of Irish extraction. Immigration from Newfoundland did not dry up until confederation with Canada in 1949, although by then Newfoundlanders were more likely to end up elsewhere in the United States, even if these were known generically as "the Boston States." If several generations of residence in Newfoundland were easily forgotten by the descendants of eighteenth- and nineteenth-century Newfoundland immigrants, there was less reason for seventeenth-century servants to pass on memories of a season or two on the English Shore.[15]

The Newfoundland fishery was effectively a pump—a somewhat inefficient and leaky pump, which year after year drove a seasonal flow of five or six thousand migrant laborers back and forth across the Atlantic. The successful operation of this ramshackle commercial machine came to involve a sump of about fifteen hundred fishing servants overwintering on the English Shore with their employers, the Newfoundland planters. One of the inefficiencies of this complex economic pump was a continual, if erratic, leakage of labor migrants onward to New England every fall, just when most migratory servants set sail once more for Europe. In the seventeenth and eighteenth centuries, Newfoundland was a place where seasonal subsistence migration was easily transformed into transatlantic

June 1679, *RFQC Essex Co.*, VII, 225; Edward Pell, Deposition, in *Marston v. Holmes*, June 28, 1709, Essex Institute, Essex Co. Court of Common Pleas, 3530, 14; Wheler, "Account of Sack Shipps," Oct. 27, 1684, CO 1/55 (56v), 255.

15. Inhabitants of Marblehead, Petition, 1667, *RFQC Essex Co.*, V, 373; Edward V. Chafe, "A New Life on 'Uncle Sam's Farm': Newfoundlanders in Massachusetts, 1846–1859" (master's thesis, MUN, 1982).

life-cycle migration. Or, to recall a useful threefold distinction, it was a place where seasonal migrant labor, typical of ship fishermen, verged on the multiyear, life-cycle, labor migration typical of planters' servants, and even on permanent transatlantic migration for those who shipped onward to New England. Assuming that the figures collected by the naval commodores were typical, the net outflow was, perhaps, two hundred men per year, that is, 3 percent of the normal transatlantic seasonal flow. This estimate is, of course, just an educated guess; but it raises the question of why the Committee for Trade and Plantations treated this limited amount of onward migration as an issue of consequence.[16]

The tone and content of both Whitehall's inquiries and the naval commodores' replies suggest that mercantilist fears of New England's growing fishery and its associated export trade worried colonial bureaucrats at least as much as leakage from the vaunted nursery of seamen. Secretary of State Williamson might have filled his copybook with notes on Newfoundland—but his apparent obsession with this small colony reflected, to a considerable degree, his worries about New England. This mercantilist perspective goes some way to explaining the apparently paradoxical attitude struck by British administrators like Williamson in the early 1670s when, on the one hand, they pressured Newfoundland's planters to leave for other colonies, while, on the other, they pressured fishing servants to stay. The Committee for Trade and Plantations' fantasies about replantation involved Barbados, where the reemigrants might be useful to British interests, rather than the more plausible destinations of coastal Maine or Massachusetts, where experienced fishing masters were more likely to be of use to New, rather than to Old, England. It was, however, fishing servants rather than Newfoundland planters who reemigrated in serious numbers. In a period when immigration to New England had slowed to a trickle, the inflow from Newfoundland, relentless and concentrated in a few coastal communities, was a testament to the migratory momentum of the fishery. A few hundred onward migrants a year were not many, compared to the continued inflow of thousands directly from Britain to the mid-Atlantic colonies. But a few hundred a year were, after all, a few thousand every decade, and, between 1660 and 1776, prob-

16. Jan Lucassen, "The Netherlands, the Dutch, and Long-Distance Migration in the Late Sixteenth to Early Nineteenth Centuries," in Canny, ed., *Europeans on the Move*, 153–191 (esp. 154); Leslie Choquette, *Frenchmen into Peasants: Modernity and Tradition in the Peopling of French Canada* (Cambridge, Mass., 1997), 18–20.

ably something like twenty thousand immigrants, predominantly young males, many in debt, entered New England from Newfoundland.[17]

🐟 Transhumance

Although seventeenth-century Newfoundland planters were much more rooted in their outports than their servants and not much more prone to migration than most of their peers elsewhere in the Anglo-American world, they, too, were transients, to the degree that they participated in the distinctive, local, residential practice of *winter-housing*. In the eighteenth and nineteenth centuries, particularly north of St. John's, coastal fisherfolk abandoned their summer fishing stations for winter houses built in less-exposed locations, farther inland, closer to supplies of firewood. The practice was documented as early as 1708, when John Oldmixon observed: "The English in the northern parts are forc'd to remove from the harbours into the woods, during that [winter] season, for the convenience of [wood] firing. There they build themselves cabbins and burn up all that part of the woods where they sit down." Winter-housing is usefully understood as a form of transhumance. This pattern of locational flexibility is (or was) unusual in a Euramerican context, and both the origins and "evolutionary trajectory" of Newfoundland winter-housing remain in question. Late-seventeenth-century winter expeditions by fishing servants into the woods to hunt and to collect furs and fuel are certainly part of this story. For men employed to fish on a seasonal basis, a winter in the woods was an alternative to the long trip back to the West of England. In this sense, fishing servants were already adapted to an unsettled life.[18]

17. Charles II in Council to Jonathan Aitkins, governor of Barbados, June 1675, CO 1/34 (106), 217. Lounsbury, *British Fishery*, 202, observes: "Newfoundland was a great hole in the wall of national self-sufficiency that the mercantilists sought to erect around the mother country and her colonies." On the context, see Canny, "English Migration," in Canny, ed., *Europeans on the Move*, 39–75, for example, 64, table 4.1; on the inertia of migratory flows, cf. Choquette, *Frenchman into Peasants*, 181. On reemigration to New England, cf. Vickers, *Farmers and Fishermen*, 156–157.

18. John Oldmixon, *The British Empire in America, Containing the History of the Discovery, Settlement, Progress, and Present State of All the British Colonies, on the Continent and Islands of America* (London, 1708), I, 109; Philip E. L. Smith,

The concept of transhumance is not simply a synonym for mobility. The drifting of the dispossessed rural poor sometimes took on a nomadic quality in the early modern period, but the surprising and widespread mobility of populations at this time is not itself evidence of transhumance, for much of this mobility took the form of migration, from country to town and from Old World to New. On the other hand, seasonal movements by rural folk, in search of farm and other employments, can be seen as transhumance, a coping strategy of middle-distance mobility that reduced vulnerability to fluctuations in resources. In the historical literature, the term "transhumance" has this wide sense, implying residential mobility in the interests of logistic advantage, whether or not only one gender or age grade is implicated. Thus, the classic pastoral transhumance of the Mediterranean involved bands of men leaving their homes for months at a time to herd sheep and other livestock. Such transhumance was still practiced in early modern times by the Basques of northern Spain and also in the English West Country. Pastoral transhumance in these regions may be particularly relevant here, for they were also deeply involved in the early exploitation of Newfoundland.[19]

"Européens transhumants non pastoraux de la période récente sur la côte atlantique du Canada," *Recherches Amérindiennes au Québec*, XXIII, no. 4 (1993), 5–21 (esp. 10, 20); Smith, "In Winter Quarters," *Newfoundland Studies*, III (1987), 1–36 (esp. 33); Smith, "Transhumant Europeans Overseas: The Newfoundland Case," *Current Anthropology*, XXVIII (1987), 241–250 (esp. 245). For early winter expeditions, see Story, "Account," Sept. 1, 1681, CO 1/47 (52i), 113–121; and Chapter 9, below.

19. Peter Clark, "Migration in England during the Late Seventeenth and Early Eighteenth Centuries," *Past and Present*, no. 83 (May 1979), 57–90; Clark, "The Migrant in Kentish Towns, 1580-1640," in Peter Clark and Paul Slack, eds., *Crisis and Order in English Towns, 1500-1700* (London, 1972), 117-163; Choquette, *Frenchmen into Peasants*, 184-194; Fernand Braudel, *The Mediterranean and the Mediterranean World in the Age of Philip II*, trans. Sian Reynolds (New York, 1972), I, 85-102. One can attempt a distinction between logistic mobility and residential mobility: the former refers to the search by male producers for resources, the latter, to the movement of whole families. At times, Philip E. L. Smith seems tempted to make residential mobility by families the defining characteristic of transhumance; see Smith, "In Winter Quarters," *Newfoundland Studies*, III (1987), 1-36 (esp. 21); Smith, "Transhumant Europeans Overseas," *Current Anthropology*, XXVIII (1987), 241-250 (esp. 246). Transhumance is sometimes defined as regular seasonal movement by a whole people but is more often defined

However the category "transhumance" might be confined conceptually, it is the history of winter-housing that is at issue. This practice arose within a particular historical context, the informal permanent European settlement of Newfoundland between roughly 1640 and 1680. The settlement of seventeenth-century Newfoundland was based on a planter fishery, which grew within the matrix of the larger and older migratory fishery. The migratory fishery was itself a residential practice and, in this sense, a form of transhumance. The fishermen who came to Newfoundland, summer after summer, were rural West Country lads who every winter became husbandmen, as Lewes Roberts put it, "so their lives may be compared to the otter, which is spent halfe on land, and halfe in sea." Roberts exaggerated, slightly, by implying that to be at Newfoundland was to be at sea, but his point is clear: this population practiced seasonal transatlantic mobility as a way of improving its access to resources. Fishing servants hired on at annual markets and fairs, with the promise of remuneration at the end of their seasonal employment. To observe that this logistic and residential mobility was itself a form of transhumance is not to claim that the transhumance of the migratory fishery was the same thing as winter-housing. The practices were different—but the latter emerged in the context of the former, with informal settlement as a kind of middle term. The anthropological question is, How did the practices of the migratory fishery and winter-housing compare, from the point of view of participants, and how, therefore, did the earlier practice prepare early Newfoundland fisherfolk for the later one?[20]

Seventeenth-century fishers alternated between maritime and agricultural employments, and the cycle of these dual employments was, inevitably, seasonal. The temporal structure of the migratory fishery on the

---

to imply movement by a segment of a community rather than the whole. If anything, the mobility of whole families is often taken as a defining characteristic of nomadism rather than of transhumance. See Julius Gould and William L. Kolb, *A Dictionary of the Social Sciences* (New York, 1964); and Hugo F. Reading, *Dictionary of the Social Sciences* (London, 1977), 222.

20. Lewes Roberts, *Merchants Mappe of Commerce* (London, 1638), 57–58; cf. Chapter 5, above; and Gray, "Devon's Coastal and Overseas Fisheries," 141. Migratory fishers were, to use a word now widely proscribed, exclusively fisher*men*. One could find females in Newfoundland in this period only within nonmigratory, resident, planter households; see Chapter 6, above. The Canadian *coureurs de bois* were another instance of young men seasonally on the move; see Louise Dechêne, *Habitants and Merchants in Seventeenth-Century Montreal*, trans. Liana Vardi (Montreal and Kingston, 1992), 119.

coast of Newfoundland was very close to that of winter-housing. In both cases, men devoted their energy to the fishery from April to September or October and were elsewhere from October to March. In the early seventeenth century, they returned to their Devon or Dorset smallholdings to undertake late harvests, hedging, or animal husbandry—the seasonal agricultural tasks of a region that enjoys mild winters. In the later seventeenth century, some instead stayed in Newfoundland. If it occurred to some overwinterers to abandon their summer fishing stations, this was hardly an innovation. It was, in fact, already a normal practice. What was innovative in seventeenth-century Newfoundland was the idea of staying in one place. In this context, winter-housing looks less like a surprising and unprecedented aberration in the direction of mobility and more like a local adaptation in the direction of a more sedentary life.[21]

As a species of transhumance, the early modern practice of a transatlantic migratory fishery might itself be thought to replicate earlier pastoral practices. The traditional custom of summer transhumance, well established in Basque shepherding communities by the early sixteenth century, has striking parallels to the organization of the early modern fishing voyage. Males went to cabins in the mountains, with a few possessions, from May until September to tend flocks of sheep owned by a formal cooperative syndicate, the *olha*, an exclusively male society in which individuals participated by shares, half-shares, and so on. From the point of view of their exclusively male crews, the early modern fishing voyage involved a trip to *Terra Nova*, with a few possessions, from March until October to catch and dry fish for a formal syndicate consisting of the shipowners, victuallers, and crew, who agreed by charter party to participate in the voyage by shares, half-shares, and so on. The historical anthropology of these practices suggests that they may be connected in ways that go beyond experience in one industry's adapting young men for work in another. A New World echo of European pastoral transhumance is perhaps audible in one version of the name sixteenth-century Basque whaling crews used for Red Bay, the largest of their seasonal whaling stations on the coast of Labrador. Breton fishermen had called this station "Buttes," but the Basques sometimes called it "Buitres"— their name for a migratory bird, the "white lady of the cattle trail," traditionally considered companion to men and herds as they migrated to

21. Gray, "Devon's Coastal and Overseas Fisheries," 141–155; Chapter 2, above. Archaeologists call the tendency to stay in one place "sedentism," although this technical term is not recorded in dictionaries.

their summer pastures. Similar connections might be traceable between the late medieval pastoral transhumance practiced in the uplands of rural Devon and the seasonal migratory fisheries that developed in the West Country after 1400.[22]

Site seasonality, whether in inner-bay winter-housing territory or on outer-headland summer fishing grounds, is an indispensable key to understanding early modern Newfoundland, not just to locate winter-houses but also to pick out informal permanent settlements contained within the larger migratory context. The chronological overlap of more than a century between the migratory fishery and the practice of winter-housing poses a difficult analytic challenge for historical archaeology, for there may be little discernible difference between the remains of summer fishing rooms operated by migratory fishermen and those occupied seasonally by planters. Planter occupations are distinguishable to the extent that we can reliably detect the presence of women and children or, perhaps, by analysis of the status associations of artifact assemblages. Archaeologists working at the bottom of Conception Bay might have already identified an early case of winter-housing. Despite having been an early proprietary colony, Cupids was usually not reported in the later-seventeenth-century censuses, except in 1675, when Captain Berry recorded Stephen Atkins as the "keeper of Mr Buttlers cattle." Yet ceramics and other archaeological materials recovered from the site suggest a

---

22. Sandra Ott, *The Circle of Mountains: A Basque Shepherding Community* (Oxford, 1981), 131–170; Peter E. Pope, "The Sixteenth-Century Fishing Voyage," in James E. Candow and Carol Corbin, eds., *How Deep Is the Ocean? Historical Essays on Canada's Atlantic Fishery* (Sidney, N.S., 1997), 15–30; E. G. Fogwill, "Pastoralism on Dartmoor," Devonshire Association, *Reports and Transactions*, LXXXVI (1954), 89–114; Joan Thirsk, "The Farming Regions of England," in Joan Thirsk, ed., *The Agrarian History of England and Wales*, IV, *1500–1640* (London, 1967–), 1–112 (esp. 6–7), in H. P. R. Finberg, gen. ed., *The Agrarian History of England and Wales*; Maryanne Kowaleski, "The Expansion of the South-Western Fisheries in Late Medieval England," *EHR*, LIII (2000), 429–454. On "Buitres," see Brad Loewen, "Les barriques de Red Bay et l'espace Atlantique septentrional, vers 1565" (Ph.D. diss., Université Laval, 1999), I, 3–4; and Claude Dendaloxte, "El isolte vasco," ed. Xabi Otero, in Jesús Altura et al., eds., *Euskal Herria, Esentziak* (Arraiotz, Spain, 1997), 16–25. Selma Barkham finds this Basque etymology implausible and suggests that the Breton *Buttes* became *Buetes* (*Buytes, Boytus*, or, rarely, *Butus*), which, pronounced by a Basque, could sound like *Buitres* (personal communication, August 2001).

more permanent occupation in this period. Since Thomas Butler was the major planter at nearby Port de Grave, a notoriously exposed headland conveniently close to excellent fishing grounds, Cupids itself may well have become, for the relatively well-off Butlers, a place to overwinter near the woods, whereas in summer, when the Royal Navy commodores took their censuses, it was merely a convenient place for cattle. The 1677 census records Butler as possessing two houses, as did several of the more substantial planters in Trinity Bay. The closer we consider the archaeology of early Newfoundland settlements, the clearer it is that questions of seasonality are intertwined with questions of gender and class.[23]

Some socioeconomic distinctions are needed before accurate generalizations about residence and transience are possible. Fishing servants were relatively mobile, most engaged in seasonal transatlantic transhumance, and many eventually took advantage of the option of permanent migration to New England. Planters, on the other hand, exhibited real attachment to Newfoundland's English Shore, even if they came to express this attachment paradoxically, by engaging in winter-housing, their own form of residential mobility. Even though this subsistence strategy mimicked the seasonal transhumance of poorer folk and although some planters' servants were inevitably involved in the practice, seventeenth-century instances suggest that winter-housing was only within the means of substantial planters. This adaptation to local climate and geography apart, planter mobility was not, however, abnormal in colonial terms. One interesting example of colonial mobility, and a symptom of the commercial energy of New England so mistrusted by British administrators, was reemigration from New England to Newfoundland. In the 1690s and early 1700s, a number of second- and third-generation New England merchants set up sons and nephews in Newfoundland, usually at St. John's. These immigrants included Joseph Buckley, John Ruck (Rooke), and William Keen. The various vectors of mobility visible in Newfoundland are another indication that there were three distinguishable populations here: servants, who were typically very mobile at a circumatlantic level; planters, typically attached to a particu-

23. John Berry, "A List of the Planters Names . . . ," Sept. 12, 1675, CO 1/35 (17ii), 150-156; William Gilbert, "Finding Cupers Cove: Archaeological Excavations at Cupids, 1995-1999," report on file, Centre for Newfoundland Studies, MUN, 2000, 33; William Poole, "A Particular Accompt of All the Inhabitants and Planters . . . ," Sept. 10, 1677, CO 1/41 (62iv, vi, vii), 157-166.

lar part of the English Shore, even if they moved seasonally within it; and merchants, arriving or departing to and from Newfoundland according to commercial considerations. We cannot hope to understand the lives of merchants, planters, or their servants without understanding something of class differences.[24]

24. John Buckley and Joseph Ruck et al. to Bishop [?], July 30, 1699, British Library, Add MSS 9747, 27. On Keen, see his journal, in Prowse, *History*, 269–270; cf. Vickers, *Farmers and Fishermen*, 158.

8 🎋 PLANTERS AND GENTRY

Sir Davy Kirke . . . exersiseth greate tyranny, especially amongst the
planters, so as hee is seldome spoken of without a curse.
— John Harrison to John Winthrop, Fermeuse, June 11, 1639

In 1639, Newfoundland's English Shore was a simple society. It was
small, and it was, in effect, a part-society: the social structure could take
the form it did only because more complex societies existed elsewhere.
Newfoundland lacked kings and parliaments, but not the authority of
kings or parliaments; it lacked vagrants and beggars, but not the threat
of being returned to a life of vagrancy and beggary. The English Shore
lacked a gentry in the strict sense, for land was not the basis of wealth,
but it did not lack a class of merchants who behaved like gentry. A half-
century later, at the outbreak of the French wars that would challenge the
existence of this society, the English Shore was not much more complex
than it had been in Sir David Kirke's day. Yet this simple society was not
without structure. In the later seventeenth century, English Newfoundland lacked local government, but never masters and servants; priests,
but not religion; marriage, but not women and children; a state, but not
a social contract.[1]

Early in the century, John Guy and his successor, John Mason, had
exercised limited authority in Conception Bay. From 1638 to 1651, civil
power was represented on the south Avalon by the governor, Sir David
Kirke — de jure among the planters and de facto among West Country
migratory crews within his sphere of operations. Kirke held courts and
was capable of enforcing his decisions, executive or judicial, by force
majeure. One planter later recalled that when differences arose among
the inhabitants Kirke would "judge and determine the same," whereby
the land was "quietly governed." In the ecclesiastical realm, no autho-
rized representative of God resided on the English Shore after the departure from Ferryland of the Roman Catholic priests Anthony Smith,

---

1. A "part-society" is a vertical or horizontal segment or formal institution of
a complex society; see Hugo F. Reading, *Dictionary of the Social Sciences* (London, 1977), 187. On paupers, see, for example, Overseers for the Poor of Barnstaple
et al. and Symon Amoree, Apprenticeship Indenture of Richard Verchill, July 24,
1637, NDRO Barnstaple, 1185.

Thomas Longville, and Anthony Hacket in the late 1620s, following their squabbles with the Puritan divine Erasmus Stourton, whose stay was also brief. The Western Charter of 1634, reiterated in 1661 and 1676, required ships' companies to assemble on Sundays "in meete places and have devine service to bee said by some of the masters of the shippes or some others, which prayers shal be such as are in the Booke of Comon Prayer." In the absence of churchmen, the religious tendency of such services, whether held by a shipmaster or a devout planter, was beyond the control of the hierarchy.[2]

During the early 1650s, successive commissions to Newfoundland represented the Commonwealth, and one of the commissioners, the Puritan merchant from Maine, John Treworgy, acted for the Protectorate government from 1653 to 1659. His administration was said to have been weak, as it must have been, given that it was partly financed out of his own pocket. Charles II restored Cecil Calvert, second Lord Baltimore, to proprietorship of the Province of Avalon in 1661, but Calvert's ineffectual deputies represented "only the picture but not the effects of . . . government," as one West Country merchant put it, and did little more than collect rents. With increasing stridency, the Newfoundland planters bewailed the absence of an effective local government. Their problems culminated in the 1670s, when some West Country interests took it upon

2. Prowse, *History*, 99-108. Charles I, "A Grant of Newfoundland," Nov. 13, 1637, CO 195/1 (2), 11-27, in Matthews, *Constitutional Laws*, 82-116 (esp. 95), permitted the Newfoundland patentees "to execute all acts of justice" regarding planters. Quotation on Kirke's court from John Mathews, "Concerning the French in Newfoundland," Jan. 27, 1671, British Library, Egerton MS 2395, 471; cf. John Shawe (of Boston), Power of Attorney to Robert Love (of Ferryland) ". . . to appeare before the Governor etc: to sue etc.," Mar. 23, 1648, *Aspinwall Records*, 130. If these courts kept written records, they have not survived. On the use of force, see Nicholas Luce, Deposition, Nov. 27, 1667, WDRO Plymouth, W360/74. On churchmen, see R. J. Lahey, "The Role of Religion in Lord Baltimore's Colonial Enterprise," *Avalon Chronicles*, III (1998), 19-48; Luca Codignola, *The Coldest Harbour of the Land: Simon Stock and Lord Baltimore's Colony in Newfoundland, 1621-1649*, trans. Anita Weston (Montreal and Kingston, 1988), 43-45. Smith was also known as "Anthony Pole." Hacket's first name is uncertain. On the Western Charter, see Charles I in Council, Order, Jan. 24, 1634, CO 1/8 (1), Charles II in Council, Order, Jan. 26, 1661, CO 1/15 (3), cf. Council of State, "Laws, Rules, and Ordinances Whereby the Affairs and Fishery of the Newfoundland Are to Be Governed . . . ," June 3, 1653, CO 1/38 (33iii), 74-75, all in Matthews, *Constitutional Laws*, 71-75, 131, 171-180.

themselves to attempt to drive residents from the island. From the Puritan point of view, Newfoundland was an unruly society of fisherfolk, bereft of government, civil or ecclesiastical—particularly compared to New England. For several decades, at least until the gradual establishment of naval government after 1680, the state was only distantly present. Is it any wonder that social relations occasionally threatened to degenerate into a Hobbesian war of every man against every man?[3]

To the extent that Newfoundland was governed in the second half of the century, it was governed by merchants; but these men did not have the wealth or power of either Sir David Kirke or Sir George Calvert, first Lord Baltimore. Crucially, they lacked the clout necessary to regulate disputes between planters and ship fishermen. Under the terms of the Western Charters, migratory fishing crews were supposed to be self-governing, to stretch a phrase, using a traditional delegation of administrative powers to the "admiral," or fishing master first arriving at each harbor. Newfoundland-based merchants thus lacked legal authority over migratory crews, let alone the police power necessary to regulate their behavior. The Royal Navy eventually filled this administrative vacuum. Even after the appointment of local justices of the peace in 1729 and the establishment of an annual criminal court at St. John's in 1751, the navy

3. Gillian T. Cell, "Treworgie, John," *DCB*; Lewis Kirke, Petition to Charles II, 1660, CO 1/14 (8), 12; John Treworgie, Petition to the Council of State, April 1660, British Library, Egerton MS 2395, 262. Trewogy did manage to collect some taxes; see John Downing, "A Breif Narrative concerning Newfoundland," Nov. 24, 1676, British Library, Egerton MS 2395, 560-563. On the Restoration, see Orlando Bridgeman and Heneage Finche to Charles II, Feb. 28, 1661, CO 1/14 (10i), 19. Quotation from Robert Prowse et al. to George Kirke, Mar. 18, 1667, British Library, Egerton MS 2395, 447. See also Matthews, "Fisheries," 197-239. Christopher English, "The Development of the Newfoundland Legal System to 1815," *Acadiensis*, XX, no. 1 (1990), 89-119, underestimates Kirke's legal authority but gives an accurate impression of post-Restoration anarchy; cf. Captain William Poole, "Answers to the Severall Heads of Inquiry . . . ," Sept. 10, 1677, CO 1/41 (62i), 149-152; Christopher Martin, Deposition, Jan. 1, 1678, CO 1/42 (20), 54; "An Account of His Majesties Plantations in America," ca. 1680, British Library, Add MS 15898, 129-131. The English Shore was a state society in the anthropological sense that it was controlled ultimately by a permanent, literate, hierarchical bureaucracy; cf. Elman R. Service, *Origins of the State and Civilization: The Process of Cultural Evolution* (New York, 1975), 4, 14-15. For a contemporary view of a stateless society, see Thomas Hobbes, *Leviathan* (1651), ed. C. B. Macpherson (Harmondsworth, 1968), 183-188.

acted as a police force. By this time, Newfoundland was more closely regulated than sparsely populated regions in Britain itself. Eighteenth-century Newfoundland can therefore fairly be called a naval state, even allowing that it was governed in the interest of the merchants, resident or semiresident, who dominated the society.[4]

Elusive as it may be, the social structure of seventeenth-century Newfoundland is worth trying to pin down, the better to understand the protopolitics implicit in colonial relations with Britain, before these relations came to be mediated by the Royal Navy. What distinguished the social structure of the seventeenth-century English Shore was a class of plantation owners, just as plantation owners of a different sort came to typify other colonies. Who were these planters?[5]

⁊ꜗ Planters

The social distinction most obvious to contemporary visitors to seventeenth-century Newfoundland was that between masters and servants. This distinction was fundamental because it marked the economic divide between those who owned means of production and those who did not: control over a means of production was the key to independent comfort or competency. The social landscape of the British Isles might well have consisted of a number of independent status hierarchies set like towers

4. Charles I in Council, Order, Jan. 24, 1634, CO 1/8 (1), 65–75, Charles II in Council, Orders, Jan. 26, 1661, CO 1/15 (3), Jan. 27, 1676, CO 1/65 (36), in Matthews, *Constitutional Laws*, 167–180; Jerry Bannister, "The Fishing Admirals in Eighteenth Century Newfoundland," *Newfoundland Studies*, XVII (2001), 166–219; Bannister, "The Naval State in Newfoundland, 1749–1791," *Journal of the Canadian Historical Association*, N.S., XI (2000), 17–50; Bannister, *The Rule of the Admirals: Law, Custom, and Naval Government of Newfoundland, 1699–1832* (Toronto, 2003).

5. On the application of the concept "class" in the seventeenth century, see Keith Wrightson, "The Social Order of Early Modern England: Three Approaches," in Lloyd Bonfield, Richard M. Smith, and Wrightson, eds., *The World We Have Gained: Histories of Population and Social Structure: Essays Presented to Peter Laslett on His Seventieth Birthday* (Oxford, 1986), 177–201; and Wrightson, "Estates, Degrees, and Sorts: Changing Perceptions of Society in Tudor and Stuart England," in Penelope J. Corfield, ed., *Language, History, and Class* (Oxford, 1991), 30–52. Cf. *OED*, s.v. "class," used in the sense of a rank or grade of society, from 1656.

on a broad hill of the poor and humble, but seventeenth-century Newfoundland had only one social edifice, and its economic foundation was
the fishery. Those who owned boats were in a very different position
from those who did not. Nor was there much in the way of intermediate
status. Some planters owned smaller two-man boats, but all boatkeepers were employers, and almost all employers were boatkeepers. Thus,
the Newfoundland planters can be described as a class of resident boatkeepers who were the masters (or mistresses) of household production
units. Their servants made up the other broad class of residents. These
servants were predominantly male, usually young, and relatively mobile
fishermen, who contracted to work for particular planters. The resident
fishery was thus at the same time a family and a servant fishery: all boatkeeping planter families in 1675 employed at least one servant, and most
families, many more. In later centuries, servant and family fisheries can
be distinguished; but, in the seventeenth-century planter fishery, residents employed servants within a household production unit. This practice was no aberration, but a typical early modern phenomenon—one of
the extinct large reptiles of economic history, to borrow a suggestive description of the contemporary practice of service in husbandry. Both sub-
species of service began to die out after 1815, a coincidence that suggests
that the evolution of class relations in Newfoundland was part of a larger
transition.[6]

6. On competency, see Vickers, *Farmers and Fishermen*, 14–23. On the "San
Gimignano model," see Lawrence Stone, "Social Mobility in England, 1500–1700:
Conference Paper," *Past and Present*, no. 33 (April 1966), 16–55. Note that the
present study uses "boatkeeper" in the common seventeenth-century sense, which
comprises planters as well as by-boat-keepers *(DNE)*, and not as a synonym for
the latter, as in, for example, Innis, *Cod Fisheries*. On planter and servant fisheries,
see John Berry, "A List of the Planters Names . . . ," Sept. 12, 1675, CO 1/35 (17ii),
150–156; Gerald M. Sider, "Christmas Mumming and the New Year in Outport
Newfoundland," *Past and Present*, no. 71 (May 1976), 102–125; and Sider, *Culture
and Class in Anthropology and History: A Newfoundland Illustration* (Cambridge,
1986), 15, 22, 55; cf. Ann Kussmaul, *Servants in Husbandry in Early Modern England* (Cambridge, 1983), 125, 134. In conceptually marginalizing the seventeenth-
and eighteenth-century planter fishery, Sider artificially minimizes the extent and
permanence of early Newfoundland settlement, which suits his version of the venerable hypothesis that the British government successfully opposed settlement in
the interests of a West Country merchant class. A planter fishery survived into
the twentieth century in Labrador; see Robert M. Lewis, "The Survival of the
Planters' Fishery in Nineteenth and Twentieth Century Newfoundland," in Rose-

The definition of planters as resident boatkeepers omits a few who in fact owned no vessel, like Lawrence Hilliard of Fermeuse. Hilliard had two servants in 1677 but no "dwelling house," boat, fishing room, stage, or train vat. How did men like Hilliard survive? Probably as their equivalents in the Old Country did: by using their limited holdings, in Hilliard's case a "lodging for servants," as a means of production. Since most of his fellow planters also kept such establishments and since migratory ships' crews were only seasonally present, this economic strategy cannot have provided much of a living. The few nonboatkeeping inhabitants in the census records show every sign of having been transitory in status between planter and servant. Those so listed invariably became boatkeepers, as Hilliard did in 1681, or disappeared from the records into the anonymous pool of servants.[7]

Fundamental as the master/servant distinction might have been, it is too simple, even for the seventeenth-century English Shore. Contemporaries distinguished "big planters" from their fellows. These big planters differed not merely in the scale of their operations but commercially, as merchants with transatlantic connections, and politically, because they acted as a sort of gentry. For such reasons, John Josselyn divided the contemporary inhabitants of coastal Maine into three classes: magistrates, planters, and servants. A similar social structure emerged in the late seventeenth-century French settlement of Plaisance. Servants, however, also fell into two categories. Again, this distinction was recognized by contemporaries: fishermen skilled as boatmasters, boatswains, headers, splitters, or salters enjoyed a different status from unskilled "boys," or "youngsters." Since servants were introduced to the fishery through unspecialized service, this lesser category was, in effect, an age grade of the class of servants—one stage in a normative life cycle. These two grades of servants are, nevertheless, distinguishable, for they were not hired on the same terms. In brief, the early inhabitants of Newfoundland can be placed in three classes and one subclass: planter gentry, ordinary planters, and servants—the latter skilled and unskilled.[8]

mary E. Ommer, ed., *Merchant Credit and Labour Strategies in Historical Perspective* (Fredricton, N.B., 1990), 102–113.

7. William Poole, "A Particular Accompt of All the Inhabitants and Planters ... ," Sept. 10, 1677, CO 1/41 (62iv, vi, vii), 157–166; James Story, "An Account of What Fishing Shipps, Sack Shipps, Planters, etc., Boat Keepers ... ," Sept. 1, 1681, CO 1/47 (52i), 113–121.

8. William Swanley et al., "An Act Made by the Tenants of Avalon," July 30,

Planters were the most distinctive residents. They exhibited, at the same time, characteristics of the increasingly prosperous and "competent" yeomen of England's agricultural landscape, their more marginal rural neighbors the husbandmen, and the citizen-tradesmen of towns. As in England itself, those involved in nonagricultural trades seem often to have had an ambiguous status somewhere between that of yeomen and husbandmen, the latter being increasingly marginalized smallholders. Like yeomen or citizen-tradesmen, planters were independent but market-oriented, and, like their fellow immigrants to New France, they were essentially artisans rather than peasants. They owned their own boats and plantations. A planter who kept two boats in the late 1670s, Henry Codner of Renews, for example, would have been worth something like £150, assuming he had few debts not balanced by credits and cash on hand. This figure can be compared with a mean probate of almost £200 for a cross-section of early modern English yeomen, or with the estates of craftsmen, ranging between £30 for bricklayers to about £280 for mercers. The average planter probably ranked in wealth with contemporary butchers and innkeepers, whose average net worth was also in the vicinity of £150. In 1688, Gregory King thought average family income for yeomen freeholders of the lesser sort to be £55 and the incomes of artisans and craftsmen to average about £40 per family. Planter family incomes probably often fell in this range. Planters corresponded to the yeomen, artisans, and smaller merchants of the Old Country who were beginning to think of themselves as "the people," distinct from the gentry above and the poor, without property, below.[9]

1663, Md. HS, Calvert MSS 174/210; [John Thomas], "A Briefe Relation How the Peopl in Newfound Land, Stand as to Religion," ca. 1680, Codrington Library, All Souls College, Oxford University, MS 239, 231–232, in Peter Pope, *"A True and Faithful Account*: Newfoundland in 1680," *Newfoundland Studies*, XII (1996), 32–49; cf. Matthews, "Fisheries," 175. Poole, "Particular Accompt," Sept. 10, 1677, CO 1/41 (61iv, vi, vii), 158–166, seems to list the St. John's planters in order of status. On Maine, see Josselyn, *Voyages*, 142; cf. Head, *Newfoundland*, 142–143; and Robert Brenner, *Merchants and Revolution: Commercial Change, Political Conflict, and London's Overseas Traders, 1550–1653* (Princeton, N.J., 1993), 105. On French Newfoundland, see Nicolas Landry, "Culture matérielle et niveaux de richesse chez les pêcheurs de Plaisance et de l'Île Royale, 1700–1758," *Material History Review*, no. 48 (Fall 1998), 101–122. On terms of service, see Chapter 5, above.

9. David Cressy, "Describing the Social Order of Elizabethan and Stuart England," *Literature and History*, III (1976), 29–44 (esp. 38); Keith Wrightson, *En-*

Planter production units were larger than those of English yeomen or tradesmen. An average early-seventeenth-century yeoman employed, perhaps, four servants. Most tradesmen and craftsmen of the period employed neither servants nor apprentices, and few of those employing servants had more than one. Newfoundland's planters, on the other hand, almost always employed at least three men, and the average planter had nine or ten servants. As a production unit, the Newfoundland planter household resembled the average Barbadian planter household, with its four or five servants and enslaved laborers, more than any common production unit in England itself.[10]

Of course, not all planters operated on the same scale, something evident if we chart the distribution of plantations by number of boats (Table 18). The planter fishery in the mid-1670s can be broken into three ranks: operations based on one, two, and three or more boats each constituted roughly a third of this fishery. In 1681, the proportion of larger

glish Society, 1580-1680 (New Brunswick, N.J., 1982), 17-38; Lorna Weatherill, Consumer Behaviour and Material Culture in Britain, 1660-1760 (London, 1988), 208-214; and Weatherill, "Consumer Behaviour and Social Status in England, 1660-1750," Continuity and Change, I (1986), 191-216; David Underdown, Revel, Riot, and Rebellion: Popular Politics and Culture in England, 1603-1660 (Oxford, 1987), 24; Leslie Choquette, Frenchmen into Peasants: Modernity and Tradition in the Peopling of French Canada (Cambridge, Mass., 1997), 127-128. Planter valuation is based on replacement costs of the dwelling, outbuildings, boats, stage, and train vat and the control of rooms. Cf. probate valuations in David Cressy, Literacy and the Social Order: Reading and Writing in Tudor and Stuart England (Cambridge, 1980), 139-140, tables 6.9, 6.10 (in 1640 values); and Gregory King, "Scheme of the . . . Several Families of England" (1688), in Peter Laslett, The World We Have Lost: Futher Explored, 3d ed. (London, 1983), 32-33. Inflation in the period 1640-1680 was about 8 percent; see E. H. Phelps Brown and Sheila V. Hopkins, "Seven Centuries of the Prices of Consumables, Compared with Builders' Wage-Rates," Economica, XXIII (1956), 296-314. On social distinctions, see Christopher Hill, "The Poor and the People in Seventeenth-Century England," in Frederick Krantz, ed., History from Below: Studies in Popular Protest and Popular Ideology in Honour of George Rudé (Montreal, 1985), 75-93. These distinctions crystallize into the concept of class in the eighteenth century; see Penelope J. Corfield, "Class by Name and Number in Eighteenth-Century Britain," in Corfield, ed., Language, History, and Class, 101-130.

10. A. J. Tawney and R. H. Tawney, "An Occupational Census of the Seventeenth Century," EHR, V (1934), 25-64 (based on a Gloucestershire muster roll for 1608); cf. Berry, "Planters," Sept. 12, 1675, CO 1/35 (17ii), 150-156. See Chapter 6, above, particularly Table 15.

Table 18. *Distribution of Planters by Number of Boats, Newfoundland,*
1675–1681

	Proportion of Planters		
Number of Boats	1675 (N = 131)	1677 (N = 163)	1681 (N = 202)
0	5%	3%	5%
1	28	35	33
2	39	34	45
3	14	16	10
4	9	7	3
5	5	4	2
6	1	2	0
7	0	0	1
3 or more	29	29	16

Note: Percentages total 101 in 1675 and 1677 and 99 in 1681 owing to rounding errors.

Sources: John Berry, "A List of the Planters Names . . . ," Sept. 12, 1675, CO 1/35 (17ii), 149–156; William Poole, "A Particular Accompt of All the Inhabitants and Planters . . . ," Sept. 10, 1677, CO 1/41 (62iv, vi, vii), 157–166; James Story, "An Account of What Fishing Shipps, Sack Shipps, Planters, etc., Boat Keepers . . . ," Sept. 1, 1681, CO 1/47 (52i), 113–121.

planters dropped to about 15 percent. These 1681 census figures reflect, in part, a sharp increase in planters operating two boats but also an absolute decline in planters operating three or more boats. On the south Avalon, at least, this trend was long-term, since the early major planters, George Calvert and David Kirke, had operated at a much larger scale than the largest planter in the census period, Jonathan Hooper of Renews, who kept seven boats in 1681. Why the number of large planters dropped, just when plantations with two boats became even more common, is difficult to say. The increasing predominance of smaller plantations does suggest some significant differences between smaller and larger plantations.

One important difference among planters might have been the degree of their own physical participation in fishing or processing activities. The census data suggest that big planters did not work with their crews. This generalization is supported by the recorded ratio of servants to boats.

Table 19. *Servants in Newfoundland, 1675, by Number of Boats per Planter*

Number of Boats per Planter	Mean Number of Servants per Planter (N = 277)	Mean Number of Servants per Boat (N = 1,250)
0	0.0	
1	3.9	3.9
2	8.5	4.2
3	14.7	4.9
4	18.8	4.7
5	25.7	5.1
6	32.0	5.3

Source: John Berry, "A List of the Planters Names . . . ," Sept. 12, 1675, CO 1/35 (17ii), 149–156.

In 1675, for example, Lady Kirke employed a crew of twenty-five fishing servants in Ferryland—exactly the number necessary to handle the five boats she kept and to cure the fish her crews would catch. Quite apart from her advanced years, there is no reason to think that she herself fished or cut bait. Richard Poole of Renews and his son, on the other hand, probably helped their eight servants to man their two-boat operation. Owners of one or two boats employed only about four servants per boat, on the average, suggesting that the smaller planters often worked with their crews (Table 19). Given that most planters operating more than two boats employed something like five servants per boat, these employers were likely busy with other matters.[11]

The capacity to tend to commercial administration was, in part, what distinguished the larger planters. Literacy, defined as the ability to sign rather than merely mark documents, correlates closely with both status and wealth in seventeenth-century England. Evidence from business records and depositions suggests that the literacy rate among male south Avalon planters from 1647 to 1707 was about 50 percent. Evidence regarding the literacy of female planters and servants is rare. None of the women giving depositions in Ferryland in 1652 could sign her name, nor could either of the servants accused of theft and vandalism in a 1680

11. Berry, "Planters," Sept. 12, 1675, CO 1/35 (17ii), 150–156.

Table 20. *Male Literacy Rates, 1647-1715*

Population	Period	Proportion of Sample Signing
Newfoundland		
Ferryland planters ($N = 17$)	1647-1707	47%
Conception Bay planters ($N = 40$)	1706	48
St. John's area planters ($N = 99$)	1706	59
West Country		
Devon parishioners declaring for Parliament ($N = 4{,}903$)	1641-1644	28%
Exeter tradesmen and craftsmen ($N = 889$)	1574-1680	53
Exeter yeomen ($N = 367$)	1574-1680	73
New England		
Testators ($N = 700$)	1650-1670	60%
Testators ($N = 1{,}000$)	1705-1715	65

Sources: Aspinwall Records, 126, 308-309, 388-389; Depositions in Scisco, "Testimony," 240-251; Papers Relating to *John Ducarrett v. Samuel Wood et al.*, 1680, CO 1/45 (68i-iv), 252-256; Affidavits regarding Mr. Campbell's Allegations about Major Lloyd, 1708, CO 194/4 (50-52), 186-189; Her Majesty's Subjects Inhabiting Conception Bay, Petition to Queen Anne, ca. September 1706, CO 194/4 (9), 15; Traders and Inhabitants of St. John's and Places Adjacent, Petition to Queen Anne, Sept. 24, 1706, CO 194/4 (6), 10; David Cressy, *Literacy and Social Order: Reading and Writing in Tudor and Stuart England* (Cambridge, 1980), 120, table 6.2 (and cf. 73, table 4.1, 163, graph 7.15); Kenneth A. Lockridge, *Literacy in Colonial New England: An Enquiry into the Social Context of Literacy in the Early Modern West* (New York, 1974), 19, graph 1 (but see 142n).

case. Literacy rates for male planters in St. John's are well documented because of controversies regarding the peculations of the commander of the British garrison, Major Thomas Lloyd, and the need for a Christian minister. Petitions by a cross-section of this planter population between 1704 and 1708 suggest a literacy rate of about 60 percent. Because the precise degree of literacy indicated by signing is debatable, literacy rates so defined are best seen in comparative context (Table 20). With rates of about 50 percent, the planters of later-seventeenth-century Ferryland and early-eighteenth-century Conception Bay were much more likely to be literate than Devonshire parishioners in the 1640s, somewhat less likely to be literate than New England males who made wills between 1650 and 1670, and about as likely to be literate as early modern Exeter tradesmen and craftsmen. Since the contemporary English curriculum produced readers before it produced writers, signing ability significantly underestimates the proportion of people able to read print. Widespread print literacy would imply that most Newfoundland planters could participate in the contemporary popular printed culture of the Bible, chapbooks, and broadside ballads. On the other hand, only some of those signing documents were fluent writers, so that signing rates for the south Avalon of roughly 50 percent suggest that only a minority of planters were actually able to write.[12]

In this period, many people were numerate without being fully literate, in the sense of reading and writing script fluently. Newfoundland planters not only had to keep rudimentary accounts; they had to confirm these accounts with fishing servants, most of whom were illiterate. Many must therefore have used systems of analog notation involving notches, bundles of sticks, counters, or the like. Archaeologists working in Ferryland contexts of 1620 to 1650 have recovered several jetons, or counting pieces, both mass-produced in brass and homemade in slate, for use in simple calculations as well as a notched tally stick of a type used by Western Europeans well into the nineteenth century (Plate 10). These objects give some sense of how a semiliterate planter could manage com-

12. Cressy, *Literacy*, 20, 118–141 (esp. 136, table 6.8); cf. Kenneth A. Lockridge, *Literacy in Colonial New England: An Enquiry into the Social Context of Literacy in the Early Modern West* (New York, 1974), 4–5, 25–26, 109; Anne Love, "Examination and Deposition . . . ," and "The Answers . . . upon the Interrogatories . . . ," both Aug. 31, 1652, Amy Taylor, "The Examinations and Depositions . . . ," Aug. 24, 1652, and "The Answere . . . to . . . the Interrogatories . . . ," Aug. 29, 1652, Philis Davies, "The Examination and Deposition . . . ," Aug. 24, 1652, and "The Answere . . . upon the Interrogatoryes . . . ," Aug. 31, 1652, all in Md. HS, Calvert MSS 174/200, in Scisco, "Testimony"; Samuel Wood and John Wallis, Examinations, in *Ducarrett v. Wood et al.*, Aug. 22, 24, 1680, CO 1/45 (68i), 252–253. The Ducarrett case is discussed in detail in Chapter 9, below. On print literacy, see Keith Thomas, "The Meaning of Literacy in Early Modern England," in Gerd Baumann, ed., *The Written Word: Literacy in Transition* (Oxford, 1986), 97–131; Peter Burke, *Popular Culture in Early Modern Europe* (London, 1978), 250–259.

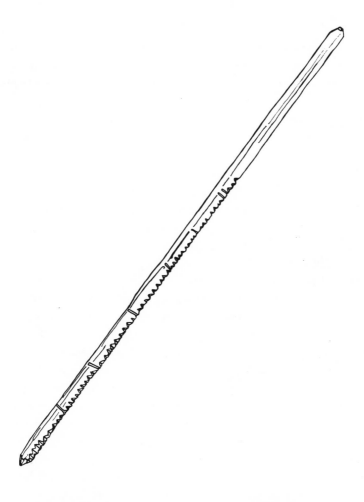

Plate 10. Top, *Notched Wooden Tally Stick. Probably spruce, used for recording counts, in this case likely of quintals of fish, from the Ferryland waterfront (CgAf-2), circa 1620–1650;* bottom, *Brass Jeton or Counter. Struck by Hans Crauwinckel of Nuremburg. Used for simple calculations, from midden deposits near the Calvert-Kirke Mansion House, Ferryland (CgAf-2), circa 1620–1650. Excavators found a similar jeton at the Ferryland smithy. Tally stick drawn by Talva Jacobson. Computer image of jeton, courtesy, Colony of Avalon Foundation*

plex share payments to crews of five or ten men in proportion to the value of forty or fifty thousand pounds of fish, sold to two or three passing sack ships, over several months. Full numeracy, in the sense of confidence in manipulating the new Arabic notation, was a much less widely distributed skill. Along with full literacy, it was probably more or less restricted to merchant planters.[13]

𝔢🙋 *Planter Merchants as Provincial Gentry*

The idea of a "merchant gentry" would have struck many contemporaries as an oxymoron, not so much because planters might lack landed property but, as one mid-seventeenth-century commentator put it, because "tradesmen in all ages and nations have been reputed ignoble in regard of the doubleness of their tongue, without which they hardly grow rich." Sir David Kirke, who is an excellent example of someone who qualified as both merchant and gentleman, took this bull by the horns in an essay he wrote in Ferryland in 1639. Here he refutes the argument made by some of his competitors that the gentry ought not to be involved in the fish trade: "Hath noe man ever heard of the noblemen and gentlemen of Italy? Have they noe hand in marchandize? Nay, are not the greatest of their princes some way or other engaged in a constant course of traffique? But not to send you soe farr for examples, it is very well knowne that divers gentlemen of the West of England have for many yeares past, and doe yet to their great proffit continue ever this trade of fishing." Merchants might not be archetypical gentlemen, but in early modern England some merchants became gentlemen, and, increasingly, merchants behaved like gentlemen. A pair of cavalier cufflinks, recovered by archaeologists from the floor of one of the

13. Thomas, "Literacy," in Baumann, ed., *Literacy in Transition*, 97–131 (esp. 109); Karl Menninger, *Number Words and Number Symbols: A Cultural History of Numbers* (Cambridge, Mass., 1969), 223–256; Matthew Carter, "A Seventeenth-Century Smithy at Ferryland, Newfoundland," *Avalon Chronicles*, II (1997), 73–106; Jean-Jacques Hémardinquer, "À propos d'une enquête sur la taille: tour d'horizon européen," *Annales*, XVIII, no. 1 (1963), 141–148; Roman K. Kovalev, "Counting in the New World: Two Early Modern Tallies from Newfoundland and Labrador," *Avalon Chronicles*, VIII (2003), 73–81. On analog computation and on the new Arabic numeracy, see Keith Thomas, "Numeracy in Early Modern England," *TRHS*, 5th Ser., XXXVII (1987), 103–132.

Plate 11. Cavalier Cufflinks. From the floor of a planter's house, Ferryland. Drawn by Talva Jacobson

larger planter houses at Ferryland, exemplifies such pretension to gentle status (Plate 11).[14]

Newfoundland's major planters were a "pseudogentry": they behaved like gentry but were not supported by landed estates. Unlike others to whom this term applies, however, the planters of the English Shore were not urban, nor were they leisured, although they might occasionally have been rentiers. David Kirke II leased out the Ferryland Pool Plantation for several years in the 1680s or 1690s, and his widow, Mary Benger, received sixteen pounds as rent for it in 1704. Some of the wealthiest planters even held property in England. Although such arrangements were not very common, the planter elite had a gentrylike position. In effect, their status lay somewhere between the lesser, or parish, gentry of the Old Country and the county elites of squires and knights—just as Newfoundland had a population somewhere between that of a parish and that of a county. The four "able men of estates," John Pinn of Harbour Grace, John Downing of Quidi Vidi, Thomas Oxford of St. John's, and George Kirke of Renews, proposed as potential tax farmers in 1680 were merchants, no doubt, but they were also something more. Other

14. Edward Chamberlayne, *Angliae Notitia; or, The Present State of England: Together with Divers Reflections upon the Antient State Thereof*, 2d ed. (London, 1669), 344, in Stone, "Social Mobility," *Past and Present*, no. 33 (April 1966), 18; Sir David Kirke, "Reply to the Answeare to the Description of Newfoundland," Sept. 29, 1639, CO 1/10 (38), 97–114. For parallels, see Richard Grassby, "Social Mobility and Business Enterprise in Seventeenth-Century England," in Donald Pennington and Keith Thomas, eds., *Puritans and Revolutionaries: Essays in Seventeenth-Century History Presented to Christopher Hill* (Oxford, 1978), 355–381; Theodore K. Rabb, *Enterprise and Empire: Merchant and Gentry Investment in the Expansion of England, 1575–1630* (Cambridge, Mass., 1967), 171–172; Alan Everitt, "Social Mobility in Early Modern England," *Past and Present*, no. 33 (April 1966), 56–73; Wrightson, "Estates, Degrees, and Sorts," in Corfield, ed., *Language, History, and Class*, 30–52.

well-established planter families, the Taverners and the Baileys in Bay de Verde, the Guys in Carbonear, and the Butlers in Port de Grave, probably played similar roles. In 1697, the French chaplain Jean Baudoin thought some of these families might have been worth as much as two thousand pounds. Since their wealth, literacy, and political activities were those of a gentry, let us call them such. To invent some other name for them on the grounds that they lacked acreage on the scale of their social equals in the Old Country is to insist on too fine a distinction.[15]

If the possession of political rights was a defining characteristic of the seventeenth-century gentry, then the circumstances of Newfoundland's planter gentry required full literacy, in a sense that was not so in England itself. The lack of a state apparatus on the English Shore after 1660 meant that only those with the ability to contact a transatlantic bureaucracy could exercise political power. Before the Restoration, a precondition for governorship was the ability to deal at a distance with the imperial state. The literary remains of the Kirke family consist, essentially, of a series of transatlantic petitions. In their turn, Sir David, Lady Sara, their son George, nephew John, daughter-in-law Mary, and grandson Phillip rap at the portals of Whitehall. The petitions of the early St. John's merchants, like John Downing's "Humble Representation . . . in Behalfe of Himselfe and Others," are a more edifying example of that combination of public service and self-interest, also visible in the founding of New England towns, which is perhaps the most that can be expected of a class of political representatives. The hereditary character of membership in the Newfoundland planter gentry is apparent in both examples; as in England itself, class membership in successive generations depended on the inheritance of wealth and the transmission of skills like literacy. That in Newfoundland even female gentry were usually able to write underlines the prevalence there of full literacy among that class. In

15. On pseudogentry, see Everitt, "Social Mobility," *Past and Present*, no. 33 (April 1966), 56–73 (esp. 70–71). On leases, see William Healle, Deposition, Aug. 14, 1707, CO 194/4 (50), 186; and John Bridge, Court Order, Oct. 5, 1704, CO 194/4 (55), 194. On property in England, see Probate of Will of James Kirke, Nov. 25, 1656, PROB 11/259, 88; and cf. Bannister, *Rule of the Admirals*, 8–9, 85–86, 156–158. On "able men of estates," see William Downing and Thomas Oxford, Proposals to CTP, Mar. 2, 1680, CO 1/44 (34), 85; Abbé Jean Baudoin, "Journal," Feb. 11, 1698, in Alan F. Williams, *Father Baudoin's War: d'Iberville's Campaigns in Acadia and Newfoundland, 1696, 1697* (St. John's, 1987), 173–191 (esp. 186). Cf. Gordon Handcock, "Settlers on the English Shore" (paper presented to the Newfoundland Historical Society, St. John's, March 2001).

the mid-seventeenth century, only about a tenth of women of the status of planters could read. Even among gentry ladies and merchants' wives, full literacy was not widespread. So Sara Kirke and Frances Hopkins were not merely unusual women; they were unusual ladies, insofar as they could communicate the views of their kin and clients. In Newfoundland, given the political context, this ability would have been a defining characteristic of the local gentry and not simply a close correlate, as in England itself.[16]

Among the Newfoundland planter elite, full numeracy was likely also common, although rare among the English gentry. Mathematics was still often looked upon as a mechanical skill suitable for merchants, seamen, carpenters, and the like. It was taught outside the educational system, with the consequence that "a barre-boy at an alehouse will reckon better and readier than a master of arts," as John Aubrey observed. Full numeracy fitted big planters to administer commercial enterprises, which is what a large plantation was. Two aspects of full numeracy were crucial to the Newfoundland planters because they were merchants and despite their otherwise gentrylike behavior: fluency in reckoning with Arabic numerals and the ability to draw up and read accounts. Just as those unable to read script ran the risk of being defrauded when they entered commercial contracts, so those not fully numerate ran similar risks in verifying accounts.[17]

16. John Downing, "The Humble Representation . . . in Behalfe of Himselfe and Others," Feb. 11, 1680, CO 1/44 (23), 43; cf. John Frederick Martin, *Profits in the Wilderness: Entrepreneurship and the Founding of New England Towns in the Seventeenth Century* (Chapel Hill, N.C., 1991), 27. Recall that the elder John Downing originally came to Newfoundland as a representative of the proprietors; cf. Hill, "The Poor and the People," in Krantz, ed., *History from Below*, 75–93 (esp. 82). On female literacy and status, see Cressy, *Literacy*, 113–116, 120 (table 6.2), 128, 143; and Nigel Wheale, *Writing and Society: Literacy, Print, and Politics in Britain, 1590–1660* (London, 1999), 22–32. Wheale thinks female literacy was more widespread, but his limited evidence is ambiguous. For examples, see Sara Kirke to Charles II, 1660, British Library, Egerton MS 2395, 258; Thomas Povey, "Report concerning Newfoundland upon Lady Hopkins Information," May 11, 1660, and Frances Hopkings, "The Information and Relation of the Lady Hopkings," ca. 1670, both in British Library, Egerton MS 2395, 263, 266. For a Chesapeake parallel, see Linda L. Sturtz, *Within Her Power: Propertied Women in Colonial Virginia* (New York, 2002), 156.

17. Thomas, "Numeracy," *TRHS*, 5th Ser., XXXVII (1987), 103–132 (esp. 105, 109–111); and Thomas, "Literacy," in Baumann, ed., *Literacy in Transition*, 97–131

Pen-and-paper computation and accounts in Arabic numerals were just beginning to replace analog computation and recordkeeping with Roman numerals around 1650. In the maritime world, however, this process was well advanced, and Arabic numerals are much more frequently seen in merchants' ledgers than previously. The Kirke brothers were quite up-to-date in this respect. About the only surviving example of seventeenth-century planter bookkeeping is David Kirke's bill of lading for Nicholas Shapley's shipment from Ferryland in 1648. Quantities, rates, and totals are worked out in Arabic numerals and, unlike many contemporary commercial computations, without obvious error. Lady Hopkins used Arabic numerals exclusively in her report on the French colonization of Placentia Bay around 1670, which would be consistent with the full numeracy expected of the operator of a large plantation. John Downing used Arabic numerals exclusively in his 1676 account of the fishery, a common practice by this time.[18]

Today there is little social cachet in being able to write a letter or in recognizing one's own name. This was not always so. When neither the literate nor the illiterate formed a vast majority of the population and when literacy was even more closely associated with social status than it is today, small affirmations of literacy seem to have been common. In this and related social emotions lies one of the motivations to mark possessions with names and initials. The material culture of the south Avalon

---

(esp. 110); Grassby, "Social Mobility," in Pennington and Thomas, eds., *Puritans and Revolutionaries*, 355–381 (esp. 369–370). On accounts, see B. S. Yamey, H. C. Edey, and Hugh W. Thomson, *Accounting in England and Scotland, 1543–1800: Double Entry in Exposition and Practice* (London, 1963). Complete innumeracy was much rarer than full illiteracy.

18. Thomas, "Numeracy," *TRHS*, 5th Ser., XXXVII (1987), 103–132 (on errors, see 118; on Arabic numerals, 121). For examples, see John Rashleigh, "Account Book," 1608–1630, Cornwall Record Office, MSS DDR 4546; Sir David Kirke and Nicholas Shapley, "Invoyce of Goods Shipped Abord the *David* of Ferryland . . . ," Sept. 8, 1648, *Baxter MSS*, VI, 2–4, summarized in Chapter 10, below; Hopkings, "Information and Relation," ca. 1670, British Library, Egerton MS 2395, 266; John Downing, "Newfoundland, an Account concerning the Following Perticulars . . . ," Dec. 14, 1676, British Library, Egerton MS 2395, 564. Sir David used Arabic numerals exclusively in his "Reply to the Answeare" of 1639, as did his brother John in Admiralty Court libels; see John Kirke, Libel, in *Kirke v. Fletcher and Tylor*, Feb. 19, 1644, HCA 24/106 (67). It would be interesting to know if Sara Kirke was also fully numerate; unfortunately, her only surviving letter contains no numerals, Arabic or otherwise—like many letters of the period, it is undated.

provides many examples, including an earwax spoon marked with Lady Kirke's initials, "SK," pipe bowls decorated with Sir David's monogram, "DK," a brass seal with the monogram "KK," presumably for one of the Kirkes, and numerous initialed wine bottle seals, almost all of which can be identified with planters or shipmasters, for example, the second-generation Ferryland planter Phillip Kirke or Peter Fewings, a Bideford master who traded at Waterford and Ferryland in the late seventeenth century. Each of these monograms (Plate 12) served to assert ownership. Did they not also serve to proclaim, "I am literate," and, therefore, in the context of the time and place, "I have power"?[19]

✺ Social and Political Relations

The three classes distinguished among the inhabitants of the English Shore—planter gentry, planters, and servants—were ranked in a hierarchy of status and wealth. Although planter and servant lived in proximity, their relationship was, in the last analysis, contractual. Relationships among planters are more difficult to pin down.[20]

Horizontal relationships among ordinary planters are largely undocumented. We know that Sir David Kirke settled differences between planters in the 1640s, but, because the records of these early civil courts have not survived, we can only guess at the issues that divided one neighbor from another. Planters managed competing household production

19. Michael F. Howley, *Ecclesiastical History of Newfoundland* (1888; rpt. Belleville, Ont., 1976), 124, reports the excavation, near the Ferryland Pool, of a silver snuff spoon, bearing the initials "GK." He supposes these initials to refer to George Kirke, although the drawing he published shows the inscription clearly as "SK." Was the idea that Lady Sara Kirke might have taken snuff too distasteful for Bishop Howley to contemplate? In fact, this spoon was more likely for collecting earwax. Snuff was common in Spain and Ireland by 1650 but was not known in England until about 1665 and not fashionable until 1700. See Jordan Goodman, *Tobacco in History: The Cultures of Dependence* (London, 1993), 69–75. On the wine bottle seals, see John Wicks, "Seventeenth- and Eighteenth-Century Bottle Seals from Ferryland, Newfoundland," *Avalon Chronicles*, III (1998), 99–108. On Peter Fewings, see Keith M. Matthews, "Name Files," Maritime History Archive, MUN; and John Mannion, "Victualling a Fishery: Newfoundland Diet and the Origins of the Irish Provisions Trade, 1675-1700," *IJMH*, XII (2000), 1–57 (esp. 48–49).

20. On service in the fishery, see Chapter 5, above.

Plate 12. Monogrammed Objects from Seventeenth-Century Ferryland (CgAf-2):
top, *Earwax Spoon. Marked with Lady Sara Kirke's initials* SK; *center,*
Chesapeake Clay Tobacco Pipe Bowl. 1640–1650, with Sir David Kirke's monogram
DK; *bottom left, Glass Wine Bottle Seal. Marked* Peter Fewings, *a Bideford master*
trading at Waterford and Ferryland in the late seventeenth century; bottom right,
Glass Wine Bottle Seal. Monogrammed PK, *for the second-generation planter*
Phillip Kirke. Spoon drawn by Peter E. Pope, after Michael F. Howley,
Ecclesiastical History of Newfoundland *(Boston, 1888), 124. Pipe bowl drawn by*
Talva Jacobson. Bottle seals drawn by Talva Jacobson and Peter E. Pope

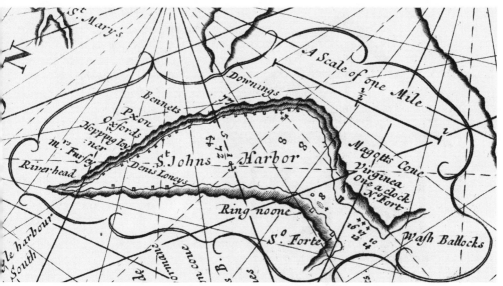

Map 11. St. John's. By Henry Southwood. Showing the harbor in 1677. From William Fisher and John Thornton, The English Pilot, *bk. 4 (London, 1689). Note the names of the planters' establishments along part of the harborside where Water Street is today. Courtesy, Centre for Newfoundland Studies, Memorial University of Newfoundland, St. John's*

units within the salt fish industry. Records of later legal conflicts among fishing families suggest that those resources most difficult to enclose were most often in dispute: fishing spots, woodland, and even topsoil itself, which neighbors were sometimes accused of stealing. Planters had, at the same time, a common interest in maintaining unambiguous claims to their fishing rooms in the face of competition from migratory crews. The oldest surviving map of St. John's, showing the harbor in 1677, suggests that they managed to do so by designating one stretch of shore for planters and another for fishing ships (Map 11). Marking properties well would certainly have facilitated neighborly relations. The inscription on a glacial erratic boulder, set back from the waterfront at King-man's, Fermeuse, may be an indication of how boundaries were fixed in the absence of a land registry or a civil court (Plate 13). It reads, "I.K. 1684," which could be John or Jarvis Kirke, both of whom were planters of the period. Archaeologists working at Ferryland have found that seventeenth-century property boundaries there coincide with modern boundaries more often than not, which speaks volumes about the

Plate 13. Inscription on a Boulder at Kingman's, Fermeuse (CfAf-25). I.K. 1684, could refer to John or Jarvis Kirke, both of whom were planters of the period. Drawn by Peter E. Pope

socioeconomic stability of that community and strongly suggests that a social contract has been continuously observed, at least with respect to property.[21]

The relationship between planter gentry and ordinary planters raises other questions. Was it true, as John Harrison reported to John Winthrop, that Sir David Kirke exercised "great tyranny" among ordinary planters? If they cursed him behind his back, what did they say to his face? Or did Kirke simply match, for Harrison, a Puritan stereotype of the swaggering, popish, plundering, and tyrannical cavalier? Did the planters defer to Kirke's gentle status, however ruthless his administra-

21. Sean T. Cadigan, *Hope and Deception in Conception Bay: Merchant-Settler Relations in Newfoundland, 1785–1855* (Toronto, 1995), 64–65. There are other "I.K." inscriptions on the Fermeuse boulder, dated 1727 and 1729; see Peter E. Pope, "Fermeuse Area Survey, 2002," report on file, Culture and Heritage Division, Newfoundland, 2003, figs. 11, 12, 13.

tion? What sort of relations developed between his successors, like his son George, and the smaller planters of the English Shore?[22]

David Kirke took control of the south Avalon with a firm hand. In 1638, he evicted the Calverts' deputy, William Hill, from the Pool Plantation at Ferryland and seized other "fishing harbours, defences, and stages." Kirke embarked defensible ships to collect his 5 percent "imposition of fish" from foreign ships and sent armed crews to control fishing rooms and collect rents. This policy not only affected migratory crews but undercut the role of planters as caretakers. The former Bay Bulls planter, Thomas Cruse, voiced further complaints retrospectively:

> After Sir David Kirke arrived there . . . he imposed taxes on all the inhabitants to pay a greate fine and yearly rents for theire houses and ground by the water side in several harbors and fishing places, as this deponent did for a house and some ground graunted to him by the said Sir David Kirke as by a writing made in the yeare 1640, for which he paid the yearly rent of £3.6s.8d. and a fatt hogg or 20 shillings in lew thereof. And the said Sir David Kirke did summon the inhabitants of several harbors in the Newfoundland to repaire att Ferriland and compelled them to take estates in land in several harbors for erecting of houses and fishing places by the waterside and to pay greate fines and rents for the same, and in case of refusal threttned to expell them out of the land. And alsoe enticed them to take licences of him for the selling of wine and other liqors and made them pay greate rents yearly for the same—And made this deponent take and pay for such a licence £15 per annum. . . . And Sir David Kirkes constant practice was to ingrosse salt and other necessary provitions brought thither for sale for suply of the fishing ships which he sould againe . . . att exessive rates.

Cruse's complaints were essentially three. He was forced to pay an annual rent or tax for his house and fishing rooms; he was "enticed" to operate a tavern and then charged excessively for a license; and, if he wanted salt or other provisions (for example, wine?), he had to deal with a monopolist. How serious were such conditions for ordinary planters?[23]

22. John Harrison to John Winthrop, June 11, 1638, *Winthrop Papers*, IV, 138; Underdown, *Revel, Riot, and Rebellion*, 164.

23. James Pratt, Examination, in *Baltimore v. Kirke*, Mar. 12, 1652, HCA 13/65, n.p.; Richard Parker and Thomas Cruse, Depositions, Nov. 27, 1667, WDRO Plymouth, W360/74; cf. Cell, *English Enterprise*, 122.

Cruse's uncertainty about whether the fee he paid Kirke for his premises at Bay Bulls was a rent or a tax expressed the ambiguity of the proprietorship. Whatever the legal niceties, the fee was in effect both rent and tax, for Kirke was both proprietor and governor. The annual payment of £3 6s. 8d. is not the odd sum it looks, but 10 nobles, a traditional unit of value. The fee thus has a seigneurial flavor, as does the payment in kind and the general summons of planters "to take estates in land." This flavor suits the ambiguity of the imposition. Considered as a rent charged by a proprietor in an isolated North American territory, the amount was not particularly high. Fourteen "tenants of Avalon" agreed in 1663 to pay Cecil Calvert's deputies £1 per household plus a quintal of fish per boat and 5s. per fishing room—an annual cost of about £2 10s. to the average planter. Even Lady Kirke agreed to "attourne tenant" in this period "and pay the adknowledgement due to the Lord Baltimore." Sir David Kirke had demanded somewhat more than an acknowledgment; but then he probably offered something more in return.[24]

Kirke's property "fines" were not challenged by Cecil Calvert in his suit of 1651. Like the Council of State, Baltimore saw the tax on foreign fishermen as a more important source of profits. For the planters, the tavern license fees and Kirke's manipulation of the market in salt and other provisions were, probably, more significant than the "fines and rents." A fee of fifteen pounds for a tippling house license was far in excess of the few shillings required to license an English alehouse. Even the inns licensed by the monopolist Sir Giles Mompesson under his 1620s patent paid only five pounds down and ten shillings annually. The size of the fee imposed by Kirke suggests that the imposition was intended to restrict the market in alcohol. Cruse tells us that Kirke himself kept "a common taverne in his owne house." As with salt, Kirke's manipulation of the market would have most affected the planters while also offering serious offense to the principles of his Puritan critics.[25]

24. On the noble, see Thomas, "Numeracy," *TRHS*, 5th Ser., XXXVII (1987), 103–132 (esp. 117); and *OED*, s.v. "noble." On rents, see Stephen Innes, *Labor in a New Land: Economy and Society in Seventeenth-Century Springfield* (Princeton, N.J., 1983), 56, 59; William Swanley et al., "Act," July 30, 1663, Md. HS, Calvert MSS 174/210. Quotation from Charles Hill to John Kirke, Sept. 12, 1661, British Library, Egerton MS 2395, 308.

25. Cecil Calvert, Interrogatories, in *Baltimore v. Kirke*, ca. 1651, HCA 23/16 (79); Peter Clark, *The English Alehouse: A Social History, 1200–1800* (London, 1983), 170–178; Cruse, Deposition, Nov. 27, 1667, WDRO Plymouth, W360/74.

Cruse's hostility cannot, however, be taken at face value. His is one of eight depositions collected in 1667 to oppose appointment of a new governor. When a more random group of planters had been cross-examined in 1652, in Cecil Calvert's action against Kirke, the tone was different, although not precisely warm. Kirke had posed interrogatories that asked witnesses how the outcome would affect them, which party they personally preferred, and to whom they would "give the victorye unto." Another interrogatory asked whether witnesses had suits or claims against Kirke. These questions were designed to expose witnesses biased in favor of Calvert, but the deponents actually exhibited considerable deference to Kirke.[26]

Not that these planters expected much from either Sir David Kirke or the second Baron Baltimore. John Stevens of Renews said that he "affects Sir David best" but added that he had not met Calvert and, with sly wit, acknowledged that "as far as hee knows my Lord Baltimore may be as bad." Anne Love, who had come to Ferryland in George Calvert's time, liked Calvert better, although she knew Kirke well. Nevertheless, "she careth not which . . . prevails." Philis Davies, another colonist from Calvert's time, had a similar attitude: "Shee knowes Sir David Kirke a little too well and wisheth she had not knowne him." Despite her feelings, she expressed indifference to the outcome. John Slaughter of Caplin Bay was indifferent to the litigants and did not care which prevailed. Amy Taylor of Fermeuse, on the other hand, "loves Sir David Kirke best and would give the victory to Sir David." William Poole of Renews likewise answered that he preferred victory to go to Kirke, despite that "he had a suite against Sir David if he could meete him."[27]

Allowing for the pressures ordinary planters felt to hedge their bets

---

At least Newfoundland tipplers did not pay the excise introduced on beer in 1643. On markets, cf. Brenner, *Merchants and Revolution*, 118; and Stephen Innes, *Creating the Commonwealth: The Economic Culture of Puritan New England* (New York, 1995), 160–191.

26. Sir David Kirke, Interrogatories, in *Baltimore v. Kirke*, ca. 1651, HCA 23/16 (393), n.p.

27. John Stevens, "The Answeares . . . uppon the Interrogatories . . . ," Aug. 26, 1652, Love, "Answers," Aug. 31, 1652, Taylor, "Answere," Aug. 29, 1652, Davies, "Answere," Aug. 31, 1652, John Slaughter, "The Answere . . . upon Interrogatories . . . ," Aug. 30, 1652, William Poole, "The Answere . . . upon the Interrogatories . . . ," Aug. 24, 1652, all in Md. HS, Calvert MSS 174/200, in Scisco, "Testimony."

in a period of political uncertainty, these depositions leave, nevertheless, an impression both of profound ambivalence about Kirke and of strong personal relationships with him. Such relationships are only hinted at, in Philis Davies's comment that she knew him "a little too well" and in a remark of John Stevens, who said he had no suit against Kirke but that "if Sir David would be pleased to forgive him hee will forgive Sir David with all his heart." Kirke had the unqualified support of only one of the six planters. On the other hand, neither of the two planters who personally liked Calvert better preferred him to win political control. Even the two Renews planters, with their unspecified grievances against Kirke, expressed neutrality or supported him politically. The one planter totally indifferent to the litigants was in a distinct minority. Most of the planters either supported Kirke or expressed neutrality despite personal affection for the Calverts. How can this deference be explained in the context of what appears to have been intense, personal, but ambivalent relationships between Sir David Kirke and ordinary planters?[28]

The deference shown Kirke in these depositions, even after his recall to London, is best understood in terms of an important social relationship not quite captured in our modern notions of class but better reflected by the complementary concepts of patronage and clientage. Studies of seventeenth-century Massachusetts communities suggest that these forms of social behavior were important in both maritime-oriented Essex County and in the Connecticut River valley. Paradoxically, inland Springfield might have resembled Newfoundland's English Shore more closely in this respect. Both were isolated regions in which one family was able to dominate relations with the outside world. Patron-client relationships flourished elsewhere at the time and continue to flourish today in such isolated conditions. First William Pynchon and later John Pynchon dominated Springfield from the position of mediator, or gatekeeper, a position based on economic, family, and political connections elsewhere. The Kirkes, as we have seen, had precisely such connections, and Sir David Kirke had the same kind of extraordinary local administrative powers and property rights, close family links with London merchants, and personal relationships with gentry leaders elsewhere that the Pynchons enjoyed in the Connecticut Valley. Like Springfield, Ferryland was essentially a commercial enterprise, oriented to the market, developed through exploitation of a single important staple. It was depen-

28. For interpretation of these examinations as "almost uniformly hostile," see Cell, *English Enterprise*, 121.

dent on the recruitment of servants in the Old Country and was neither an intentional sectarian community nor, in fact, particularly religious. There is even an eerie and perhaps not entirely accidental coincidence in chronology. William Pynchon founded Springfield as a fur-trading post in 1636, returned to London because of trouble with Puritan leaders in 1652, and turned over control of the community to his son John, who dominated it until the 1690s. David Kirke appropriated the Ferryland fishing station in 1638, returned to London because of trouble with the Commonwealth in 1651, and turned over control of the community to his wife and sons, particularly George and David II, who dominated it until the 1690s. How are we to understand the modus operandi of these influential colonial families, who managed to maintain patronage relations over several generations? And what is it about resource peripheries, like the Connecticut Valley or the English Shore, that encouraged patron-client relationships to flourish, even when they were abandoned in Essex County?[29]

Patron-client relationships can be characterized in several ways. They are particularistic, long-range but diffuse in aim, voluntary but personally binding, though not in a legal or contractual sense. Clientage depends on interpersonal loyalty, albeit sometimes ambivalent, and on vertical relations between persons with very different degrees of access to the means of production, markets, and centers of the society. Patron-client relations are characterized by simultaneous exchange of different types of resources in a package deal; they depend on what anthropologists call "generalized exchange," that is, exchange that creates social obligation. Such relations therefore act as insurance against uncertainties in the open market. They arise, typically, in societies with export-oriented extractive economies and low internal specialization, in which trade is regulated by external groups, impeding access to resources. What clients get from their patrons is protection from the market, for which they give up autonomous convertibility of resources and accept the patron's control of access both to private markets and to public goods as well.[30]

29. Vickers, *Farmers and Fishermen*, 103–116, 141, 153–167; Wrightson, "Social Order," in Bonfield, Smith, and Wrightson, eds., *World We Have Gained*, 177–201; Martin, *Profits in the Wilderness*, 30–37, 58, 105, 126, 294–296; Robert Paine, ed., *Patrons and Brokers in the East Arctic* (St. John's, 1971); Innes, *Labor in a New Land*, xix–xx, 3, 9, 12, 16, 20–21, 28–29, 124, 151, 171, 180.

30. S. N. Eisenstadt and Louis Roniger, "Patron-Client Relations as a Model of

The informal and oral nature of patron-client relationships makes them difficult to observe. They often do not leave traces so much as perturbations in the expected course of affairs. The ambivalent deference to Sir David Kirke in the planters' testimony of 1652 may be an example of such perturbation. Only one deponent actually liked Kirke, and several had grievances with him, yet most either stood by him or at least refused to stand against him. Since the Kirkes' account books have not survived, we have no hard evidence that the smaller planters were indebted to them, as John Pynchon's tenants often were to him, and as fishermen were to merchants in Salem, Gloucester, and Marblehead. We know that credit relationships pervaded early modern life and that in the later seventeenth century the Newfoundland planters were often chronically indebted to merchants, so an aspect of the Kirkes' clientage must have been quantified into ledger debits and credits. Debt and informal expectations of factional support in return for favors typify the asymmetry of the relationships that develop when one individual in a small community is much more powerful than the others.[31]

Patron-client credit relations became known in Newfoundland as the *truck system*. "Truck" simply meant barter in the seventeenth century, taking on the narrower sense in the eighteenth century of a system of payment in kind in lieu of wages. In nineteenth-century Newfoundland, "truck" referred to a system in which merchants advanced provisions to nominally independent producers on credit against the expected catch of the ensuing season. Its distinguishing feature was not that it was a credit relationship, for these were pervasive in early modern times, but that it was a credit relationship with an annual rhythm in which creditors had first claim on the seasonal product of debtors. Such arrangements were widespread, whether the product on which credit was based was tobacco, as in the Chesapeake, fur, as on the Canadian Shield, or fish, as in Newfoundland or New England in its early decades. Although the term "truck" was not used in its modern Newfoundland sense until the

Structuring Social Exchange," *Comparative Studies in Society and History*, XXII (1980), 42–77 (esp. 52, 62–64, 71). Cf. Rosemary E. Ommer, *From Outpost to Outport: A Structural Analysis of the Jersey-Gaspé Cod Fishery, 1767–1886* (Montreal and Kingston, 1991), 24–47.

31. Innes, *Labor in a New Land*, 40, 64–71; Vickers, *Farmers and Fishermen*, 100–116; Matthews, "Fisheries," 160–161, 176; Eisenstadt and Roniger, "Patron-Client Relations," *Comparative Studies in Soc. and Hist.*, XXII (1980), 42–77 (esp. 50, 73).

1800s, many of its essential features were already in place in the seventeenth century. During a crisis in the fish trade in 1684, Captain Francis Wheler noted: "By certaine experience there is hardly a planter in the country but is a greate deale worse then nothing and although they are allmost sure to loose, yett they must goe on, or else the marchants wont sell them provisions to live in the winter, which they [the merchants] part with at greate profit, and soe are able to beare some losses." What was most distinctive about Newfoundland's version of the once-widespread practice of patron-client credit was its persistence well into the twentieth century.[32]

The credit terms that later became locally known as the truck system were first legally recognized in Newfoundland in the 1680s, though evidently in use before that time. In 1681, the London merchant William Miles petitioned the Committee for Trade and Plantations to instruct the Royal Navy to send a ship into Trinity Bay to enforce collection of fish worth eight hundred pounds from planters in New Perlican, Heart's Content, and Scilly Cove. The fish was due in exchange for salt and salt meat, supplied on credit in 1679 by John Vallet, master of the *Pembrooke* of London. When Vallet returned to Trinity Bay on behalf of Miles in the *Elizabeth* of London in 1680, these planters had offered him fish worth only fifty pounds. The Lords of Trade and Plantations agreed, on consideration of the "encouragement it will be to such as carry on that trade that they bee not defrauded of their just rights," to enforce the debt. The

32. *OED*, s.v. "truck"; *DNE*, s.v. "truck system." On credit, see Jacob M. Price, "Conclusion," in Ommer, ed., *Merchant Credit*, 360–373 (and cf. the other essays in the volume); B. A. Holderness, "Credit in English Rural Society before the Nineteenth Century, with Special Reference to the Period 1650-1720," *Agricultural History Review*, XXIV (1976), 97–109; Craig Muldrew, *The Economy of Obligation: The Culture of Credit and Social Relations in Early Modern England* (New York, 1998), 95–119; Sturtz, *Within Her Power*, 132–138. On the key role of credit in the fur trade, see Louise Dechêne, *Habitants and Merchants in Seventeenth-Century Montreal*, trans. Liana Vardi (Montreal and Kingston, 1992), 97–107. On credit in Newfoundland, see Steven Antler, "The Capitalist Underdevelopment of Nineteenth-Century Newfoundland," in Robert J. Brym and R. James Sacouman, eds., *Underdevelopment and Social Movements in Atlantic Canada* (Toronto, 1979), 179–202; Handcock, *Origins*, 232–235; Sider, *Culture and Class*, 46–57; James K. Hiller, "The Newfoundland Credit System: An Interpretation," in Ommer, *Merchant Credit*, 86–102; Cadigan, *Hope and Deception*, 100–120. Quotation from Francis Wheler, "Answers to the Heads of Inquirys . . . ," Oct. 27, 1684, CO 1/55 (56), 239–246 (esp. 241).

settlement imposed by the British government through the Royal Navy enforced the custom that indebted planters were to supply "merchantable Newfoundland fish" to their creditors, an essential feature of what later generations of Newfoundlanders would know as the truck system, and, we may suppose, of patron-client relations on the English Shore since the development of a planter fishery. Pastour de Costebelle, governor of Plaisance, recognized the distinctive features of this system of credit in a report of 1699:

> The English have a precaution in the truck trade [la commerce de la troque] which cannot be costly for them, nor for those whom they supply, which is that each planter marries his merchant. This term, which [the English] use and which is rather significant, amounts to saying that they do not trade except with one another. One side undertakes to give all his catch and the other to furnish all the commodities and equipment necessary for his support. The merchant involved in such an account never risks a loss, the catch being ordinarily abundant enough to account for what the work consumes, when it is done with a bit of economy. If it works out to the profit of the planter, [the merchant] pays him, as one might expect, for the surplus of fish at the current price.[33]

Various intimations of clientage and patronage, in their broader senses, echo in the records of later-seventeenth-century Newfoundland. An affidavit of 1661, signed by the planters William and Amy Wrixon and Anne Love, countering claims that the Calverts had maintained continual possession of the south Avalon in the 1630s, looks very much like political support by clients of the Kirkes at a time when the Kirkes were trying to reassert their proprietorship. One suspects patron-client relations were somehow involved, in part because the Wrixons were not replying to a specific interrogatory and in part because the letter is in Lady Sara Kirke's own hand. Although the Kirkes failed to reestablish their proprietorship, both fishing masters and naval officers continued to defer to Sir David Kirke's son George, in particular, as a broker and media-

33. William Miles, Petition to CTP, May 10, 1681, John Vallet, "Accompt of Debts . . . ," May 10, 1681, CTP, "Report Touching an Account of William Miles . . . ," May 17, 1681, all in CO 1/46 (154i–iii), 359, 360, 361–362; Pastour de Costabelle, Report, Oct. 20, 1699, France, Archives des Colonies, C¹¹C, II, 239–246 (my translation).

tor. By the last quarter of the seventeenth century, there were a number of such regional patrons in Newfoundland—certainly the "four able men of estates" of 1680. The petitions of Thomas Oxford, William Downing, and John Downing to London in the late 1670s can be seen as the efforts of patrons to mediate effectively for their clients regarding common adversaries, in this case troublemakers among West Country fishing crews, just as patrons in the Connecticut Valley turned to governments to intercede with unruly Native people.[34]

Although patron-client relationships disappeared from coastal New England and, eventually, the Connecticut River valley as their economies developed, the extinction of such relationships is not inevitable. Patron-client relationships serve to mediate between international capitalist markets and a particular kind of dependent society in which some individuals have monopolistic control. The entrepreneurial early modern patron maximized returns by relying on the precapitalist deferential behavior of his clients; he or she depended on the continued existence of others less fully adapted to a market economy. Although this social relationship was transitory in some regions, it continued to flourish, under the right circumstances, in other peripheries, as it certainly did in Newfoundland, for several centuries.[35]

The asymmetrical dependence of clients on their patrons is not a complete picture of planter-merchant relations, any more than endemic violence among fishing crews that were competing for the same unenclosed resource represents all that can be said about relationships among fishing masters, migratory or resident. Another form of social relation was becoming more prevalent, one that emphasized commercial cooperation and mutual trust between putative economic peers: the contract. In the

34. William Wrixon, Anne Love, and Amy Wrixon, "Concerning the Lord Baltemores Possession of Newfoundland," Sept. 13, 1661, British Library, Egerton MS 2395, 309; cf. Kirke to Charles II, 1660, British Library, Egerton MS 2395, 258; cf. Innes, *Labor in a New Land*, 25.

35. Eisenstadt and Roniger, "Patron-Client Relations," *Comparative Studies in Soc. and Hist.*, XXII (1980), 42–77 (esp. 46, 73). Innes, *Labor in a New Land*, 18, 42, interprets patron-client relations as transitory, succeeding the master-servant relations of the feudal manor and preceding the contractual wage-labor relations of capitalism. He sees them as harking back to the personal social relations of the premodern period and, at the same time, anticipating the cash nexus in the predominance accorded economic considerations. For Essex County, see Vickers, *Farmers and Fishermen*, 158–167.

seventeenth century, the Anglo-American maritime world definitively adopted the ideology of the willing seller and the willing buyer.[36]

Such shifts in *mentalité* reached Newfoundland's English Shore promptly—a fact nicely illustrated by the changing constellation of names given the ships that linked Newfoundland with the emerging capitalist world system. A comparison of the names of Plymouth and Dartmouth ships in 1619, many of which were in the Newfoundland trade, and of ships fishing and trading at Newfoundland in 1675, many of which were based in Plymouth or Dartmouth, suggests that early ships' names fall into surprisingly few categories (Table 21). Certain themes remained popular through the century. About one-third of the ships in 1619 bore personal names, like the *Priscilla* or the *William and Jane*, as they did in 1675. Other types of names became less common. Names referring to service, like *Handmaid*, virtually disappeared. Names with a Christian reference, such as *Blessing, Grace*, or *Phoenix* (a symbol of Resurrection), were proportionately much less frequent in 1675, as were names like *Success, Hopewell*, and *Nonsuch*, invoking good luck.

Shipowners came to prefer other kinds of names. Those invoking commercial virtues, like *Endeavour, Patience*, and *Willing Mind*, or commercial results, like *Prosperous*, became twice as common in the later Newfoundland sample. In fact, a new form of commercial name is apparent in 1675, one that advertised the trade, like the *Malaga Merchant* or John Downing's sack ship, the *St. John's Merchant*. A whole lesson in ideology might be read into names that evoked a contract, which were much more common in 1675: *Consent, Exchange, Friends' Agreement, Loyalty, Fidelity, True Dealing*, and *True Intent*. In 1619, names evoking cooperation were already more prevalent than the few referring to contract and occurred even more frequently in 1675, for example, the *Amity, Society, True Love, Unity*, the *Olive Branch*, and the *Real Friend*. Two minor name types became more common, too: male names, like *Batchelor* and *Young Men's Delight*, and maritime names, like *Neptune* or *Mermaid*. The increasing popularity of names alluding to commerce, contract, and cooperation and the decline of names invoking Christianity, good luck, and service reflect, surely, important shifts in the outlook of shipowners. (It might be noted that Christianity and good luck had also been major motifs in French shipping nomenclature in the sixteenth century.)[37]

36. Cf. Jean-Christophe Agnew, *Worlds Apart: The Market and the Theater in Anglo-American Thought, 1550-1750* (Cambridge, 1986), esp. 57–100.

37. On Downing's ship, see CTP, Minutes, Apr. 26, 1677, CO 391/2, 11. For

Table 21. *Ships' Names in Plymouth and Dartmouth, 1619, and Newfoundland, 1675*

Name Types	Sample Name	1619 ($N = 130$)	1675 ($N = 119$)
Consistently popular			
Animal or bird	Eagle	5%	8%
Flower or fruit	Mayflower	4	3
Personal	Marye	37	34
Place	Chudleigh	1	1
Less popular			
Christian	Providence	17	11
Classical	Hercules	2	0
Good luck	Hopewell	17	9
Service	Handmaid	3	1
Other nature	Sunn	1	0
More popular			
Commercial	Prosperous	6	12
Contract	True Intent	2	8
Cooperation	Unity	4	7
Male	Batchelor	0	3
Maritime	Neptune	1	3
Total		100%	100%

Note: Thematic analysis preceded analysis by date. Each name was assigned to what was taken to be the single relevant category. The "Christian" category includes symbols, like "Pelican." "Good luck" includes abstractions like "Desire" as well as desirable objects like "Pearl" and names such as "John Bonadventure." "Commercial" includes virtues like "Patience" as well as names like "Newfoundland Merchant." "Contract" includes virtues like "Fidelity" and names like "Friends Agreement." "Cooperation" includes names like "Real Friend" and "Olive Branch."

Sources: Edward Seymour et al., "A Booke of All the Shippinge . . . Belonginge to All the Ports Harbours and Sea-Townes within the Vice-Admiralty of the South-Part of Devon," Feb. 28, 1619, in Todd Gray, ed., *Early-Stuart Mariners and Shipping: The Maritime Surveys of Devon and Cornwall, 1619–35* (Exeter, 1990), 1–57; John Berry, "A List of the Ships Makinge Fishinge Voyages; with Boatkeepers . . . ," Sept. 12, 1675, CO 1/35 (17i), 136–148.

Ships' names do not reflect all aspects of social reality, of course. Some are likely just whimsical: the late-seventeenth-century *Francis Duck*, for example. In the last analysis, ships' names present a shipowners' view of the world — vide the ill-fated twentieth-century English Channel ferry, *Herald of Free Enterprise*. The names used in the later-seventeenth-century Newfoundland trade do remind us that some aspects of early modern maritime social behavior are not captured by the concepts of service, clientage, or competition. The declining use of names connoting Christianity and service raises other complex issues concerning religious controversy and changing political cultures.[38]

ᎧᎦ *The Complications of Religion*

Between about 1630 and the turn of the eighteenth century, the absence of churches, or at least of resident churchmen, limited the religious culture of the English Shore. Visitors reported that services were not observed and that the inhabitants "lived more like heathens then Christians." The Reverend John Thomas, chaplain of HMS *Assistance*, visited Newfoundland in the summer of 1680 and wrote of the planters:

> They have not the means of grace, neither do they generally mind eternall glory; noe ordinances nor templ of God in all the land. Nor sign of religion, as if that part of the world were exempted from the first tabl of the ten commandments they make them noe show of duty towards God. Noe publicke prayers, nor sermons, noe sacraments, noe holy wedlock, noe worshipp, nor praise to God all the year long, unless a chaplain in a man of warr comes in and happily marryes, and baptizeth a very few in that harbour only when he resides. Neither did I here of any sectarie [Dissenter] amongst them.

There were, however, exceptions to these generalizations, exceptions that illuminate significant cultural tensions.[39]

---

sixteenth-century Bordeaux, see Jacques Bernard, *Navires et gens de mer à Bordeaux (vers 1400–vers 1550)* (Paris, 1968), II, 733, 736–741.

38. *Alexander Dawes v. the Francis Duck*, ca. 1690, HCA 23/22 (225), n.p.

39. Robert Robinson, "Certaine Arguments or Reasons for a Settled Government . . . ," 1670, CO 1/68 (99), 288; Colonel Gibson to CTP, June 28, 1697, CO 194/1 (81), 159; [John Thomas], "A True and Faithfull Accompt of the Present State of Affairs in Newfoundland," 1680, Codrington Library, All Souls College,

Regional religious culture was affected by the presence of Roman Catholics, who were implicitly tolerated by Sir George Calvert's 1623 charter for the Province of Avalon. Calvert's charter omitted any requirement that settlers would take the oath of supremacy acknowledging the monarch as the head of the Church of England—a condition that had been included in the Newfoundland Company's Charter of 1610. By 1630, the Catholic priests Smith, Longville, and Hacket had departed Newfoundland, but some of Lord Baltimore's coreligionists remained. After 1662, the presence of Roman priests and even a monastery, at the French settlement of Plaisance, revived the specter of Catholicism among the Protestants of the English Shore. The beginnings of Irish immigration in the late seventeenth century aroused similar prejudices. Roman Catholicism was thus a more tangible political position for the early inhabitants of English Newfoundland than it was in many districts of England itself, where Catholics were rare and accusations of Catholicism were often just verbal abuse. Even High Church Anglicans like Sir David Kirke could think of themselves as occupying a virtuous middle ground between two fanatical extremes, as in his quip to Archbishop William Laud that no one complained about the weather in Newfoundland "except Jesuits and Schismatics."[40]

One south Avalon planter, William Poole of Renews, verbalized something of his religious opinions. He supported Kirke in his legal struggle

Oxford University, Wynne Collection, MS 239, 231–232, in Pope, *"True and Faithful Account," Newfoundland Studies*, XII (1996), 32–49; cf. Thomas Bray, *A Memorial, Representing the Present State of Religion, on the Continent of North-America* (London, 1700), 16–19. For an early case of baptism by a passing man of the cloth, see N. E. S. Griffiths and John G. Reid, "New Evidence on New Scotland, 1629," *WMQ*, 3d Ser., XLIX (1992), 492–508 (esp. 502). There was a church in St. John's in the 1690s and an army chaplain from 1701. See Joseph Buckley et al., Letter, July 30, 1699, and William III to John Jackson, 1701, British Library, Add MS 9747, 27, 30. An excellent undergraduate paper by Victoria Netten at MUN (1995) presents evidence for an Anglican Church at St. John's before 1696.

40. James I in Council, Charter of Avalon, Apr. 7, 1623, CO 1/2 (23), in Cell, *Newfoundland Discovered*, 258–269 (discussion on 49); James Story, "Intelligence about the French Trade," Sept. 1, 1681, CO 1/47 (52i), 122; Michael Richards, "Att a Hearing at Fort William . . . upon the Takeing Up of Severall French and Irish Papists Dissafected to His Majesties Service," Mar. 9, 1702, British Library, Stowe MS 464, 66; Sir David Kirke to Archbishop Laud, Oct. 2, 1639, CO 1/10 (40), 119; Victoria Taylor-Hood, "Religious Life in French Newfoundland to 1714" (master's thesis, MUN, 1999).

with Cecil Calvert, "by reason Sir David is a Protestant and my Lord of Boltomore a Papist." Poole had strong personal reasons for his prejudice. In 1628, the priests Anthony Smith and Hacket had baptized Poole's child into the Roman Church "by the procurement" of George Calvert and contrary to Poole's own wishes. Calvert and the priests might have had their own reasons for the baptism (perhaps the child was seriously ill), but the event raises the question of whether Calvert's religious tolerance was not simply the current political tactic of English recusants, rather than a deeply held conviction. Poole's resentment a quarter of a century later indicates that Newfoundland was not immune to the religious factionalism that divided England, and New England, too. Although controversy in much of the English-speaking world was now typically situated elsewhere on the spectrum of religious belief, the English Shore was one of those regions in which the older Catholic-Protestant tension survived as an element of internal politics rather than being externalized, as in British policy after the Glorious Revolution of 1688 replaced the crypto-Catholic James II with the aggressively Protestant William III.[41]

In past centuries, people did not distinguish religious from political issues in the way we commonly do, or at least pretend that we do, in our more secular societies. For most ordinary people, politics was religion; that is, they committed themselves in some way politically because a perceived religious issue was at stake. In mid-seventeenth-century England, there were many religious tendencies but, broadly speaking, only two major "parties" within an increasingly sharply divided Anglican Church: on the one hand, traditionalists who accepted the existing hierarchy or even wanted to reinforce it and, on the other hand, the reformist Puritans. From this point of view, the Civil War of 1642 can be understood, among other things, as the outbreak of conflict between those nostalgic for a harmonious and vertically integrated society against those who would reform society according to principles of order and godliness. The former were willing to defend traditional hierarchies with political innovation, like the personal rule of Charles I (1629–1640), and even with

41. Poole, "Answers," Sept. 10, 1677, CO 1/41 (62i), 149–152; Erasmus Stourton, "Examination," Oct. 9, 1628, CO 1/4 (59), 144. Lahey, "Role of Religion," *Avalon Chronicles*, III (1998), 19–48, argues for Calvert's sincere belief in tolerance. For another example of late-seventeenth-century Protestant-Catholic political tensions, see Ronald Hoffman in collaboration with Sally D. Mason, *Princes of Ireland, Planters of Maryland: A Carroll Saga, 1500–1782* (Chapel Hill, N.C., 2000), 41–46, 61–97.

the religious innovations of Archbishop Laud's Arminianism and Carolism. This party nevertheless emphasized traditional religious and social rituals, whether Communion or church ales, because they expressed important aspects of traditional political culture: paternalism, deference, and neighborliness. Sir David Kirke's alliance with Laud and Charles I is no more surprising than the virulent attacks on Kirke expressed by West Country merchant elites in the 1640s. These merchants were Puritan in outlook and strongly supported Parliament, hence their political opposition to Kirke was a predictable outcome of their cultural and religious views, quite apart from any regional resentment they might have felt toward a London interloper.[42]

Whether ordinary Newfoundland planters shared the typical outlook of these West Country elites is another question. The record of popular politics in Dorset, Somerset, and Devon through the Civil War indicates that allegiances were strongly affected by local cultures, perhaps, in turn, by local economies, and, certainly, by political tensions raised over issues like ship money during the period of Charles I's personal rule. Based on the popular politics of Barnstaple, Plymouth, Dartmouth, and Poole, we might guess that planters from Devon and Dorset would tend to have a Puritan outlook. The south Avalon had close links with Devon, particu-

---

42. Christopher Hill, "The English Revolution and the Brotherhood of Man," in Hill, *Puritanism and Revolution: Studies in Interpretation of the English Revolution of the Seventeenth Century* (London, 1968), 126–153; Hill, "The Many-Headed Monster," in Hill, *Change and Continuity in Seventeenth-Century England* (London, 1974), 181–204; Brenner, *Merchants and Revolution*, 460–462, 484, 494, 641–643, 650; Underdown, *Revel, Riot, and Rebellion*, 40, 108, 290; Mark Stoyle, *Loyalty and Locality: Popular Allegiance in Devon during the English Civil War* (Exeter, 1994), 180–226. The term "Anglican" was not often used in this period, but *OED* finds it in use in 1638. Meanwhile, many "Puritans" considered themselves to be good members of the Church of England, undermining the emic character of this label too. We can usefully consider traditionalists and Puritans as "parties," because they frequently proposed organized political action, coherent with their religious doctrines; cf. Susan Dwyer Amussen, *An Ordered Society: Gender and Class in Early Modern England* (Oxford, 1988), 184–185. There were third parties, for example, the Clubmen, which were not religious in the same sense. Meanwhile, some individuals adhered to other religious positions, Roman Catholicism, for example, that had no significant political voice in England itself. For Puritan criticism of Kirke, see Exeter Justices, Petition to Privy Council, Jan. 10, 1640, CO 1/10 (28), 46; Robert Gabbes [mayor of Plymouth] et al., Petition to Archbishop Laud and the Privy Council, Jan. 22, 1640, SP 16/442 (77).

larly north Devon. Devon was generally pro-Parliament; north Devon was a hotbed of Puritanism; and the mariners of Dartmouth, Plymouth, and Barnstaple were among the occupational groups most actively anti-royalist. Many Newfoundland planters must have been inclined by religious preference or political experience to sympathize with Parliament. Yet some planters might have been inclined, as Kirke was, to a more hierarchical point of view.[43]

The transplantation of traditional Anglican sentiments, to the south Avalon at least, is probable on several grounds. First, the fifteen years of Sir David Kirke's personal proprietorship between 1638 and 1652 were relatively important in the permanent occupation of this part of the English Shore. Insofar as Kirke promoted settlement, he had the opportunity to encourage planters who would defer to his political outlook. Furthermore, after 1639, Laud's administration attempted to control emigration by the politically suspect. In general, the fisherfolk of the Atlantic littoral did not originate in the same strongly Puritan milieu from which the Pilgrims emigrated to the northern colonies. Maine, a fisheries-based colony, was more Anglican than Massachusetts, and there were strong anti-Puritan factions among the fishing families of Gloucester and Marblehead. If Anglicans were well represented among the fishermen of Puritan New England, the same was probably true of Newfoundland. Finally, we have the testimony of the Puritan oligarchy of Devon itself. About 1650, the merchants of Plymouth called the south Avalon planters "atheistical," which in the contemporary jargon was a label for false belief. They were not saying that the planters had no faith; they were saying, roughly, that they were not Puritans and that they let fishermen drink on Sundays.[44]

43. Stoyle, *Loyalty and Locality*, 22, 37–42, 89–91, 158–161, 174–175; Underdown, *Revel, Riot, and Rebellion*, 197.

44. Chapter 2, above; Privy Council, Order regarding Petition of Walter Barret et al., Jan. 4, 1639, CO 1/10 (2), 2; Daniel Vickers, "Work and Life on the Fishing Periphery of Essex County, Massachusetts, 1630–1675," in David D. Hall and David Grayson Allen, eds., *Seventeenth-Century New England: A Conference Held by the Colonial Society of Massachusetts, June 18 and 19, 1982*, Colonial Society of Massachusetts, *Publications*, LXIII, *Collections* (Boston, 1984), 83–117; Josselyn, *Voyages*, 142; Charles E. Clark, *The Eastern Frontier: The Settlement of Northern New England, 1610–1763* (1970; rpt. Hanover, N.H., 1983), 36–51; Christine Leigh Heyrman, *Commerce and Culture: The Maritime Communities of Colonial Massachusetts, 1690–1750* (New York, 1984), 39–51, 209–230; Petition of the Merchant Adventurers of Plymouth, England, to the Council of State, ca. 1650,

In 1639, Sir David Kirke had boasted to Archbishop Laud of "our strict observance and use of the rites and service of the Church of England." In carrying on such private services, planters would only be doing what was required of ships' crews by the Western Charters. In 1680, the Reverend John Thomas, of HMS *Assistance*, noting exceptions to what he perceived as a general absence of religious practice among the settlers of the English Shore, emphasized an adherence to Anglican ritual: "Some of them, not withstanding, who are honest loyal Protestants and housekeepers [that is, householders] are of a more sober temper then the generalitie be, who doe usually read the lyturgy of the Church of England in their own houses every Lords day." Again, the absence of resident churchmen did not, in fact, imply the absence of religious practice. Thomas reported that the most serious problem created by the absence of churchmen, as far as the planters were concerned, was that their children remained unbaptized for years. Otherwise, how the absence of church institutions affected the beliefs of ordinary planters is hard to estimate. Certainly, Newfoundland did not escape the religious tensions experienced within the Church of England during the Civil War and Interregnum.[45]

The popular politics of the West Country is better seen as an object lesson for understanding Newfoundland, rather than as an opinion poll of the outlook of likely emigrants from particular counties. Popular allegiances in the Old Country were based not only on class, deference to local magnates, or a calculating neutralism but also on local social structure and economic development. The pattern of patron-client relationships between Sir David Kirke and ordinary planters on the south Avalon as well as the relatively limited scope of class differentiation suggest a generally Anglican polity. Yet Devon maritime folk, of the kind who were settling the south Avalon in this period, were strongly Puritan and pro-Parliament in outlook. Furthermore, Puritans were planted elsewhere on the English Shore, for example in Trinity and Conception Bays, where the Taverners represented an extended Dissenting family, founded at Bay de Verde in the 1650s. Finally, Puritans did preach in

Winthrop Papers, VI, 4-6; cf. G. E. Almyer, "Unbelief in Seventeenth-Century England," in Pennington and Thomas, eds., *Puritans and Revolutionaries*, 22-46.

45. Kirke to Laude, Oct. 2, 1639, CO 1/10 (40), 119; [Thomas], "True and Faithfull Accompt," 1680, Codrington Library, All Souls College, Oxford University, Wynne Collection, MS 239, 231-232, in Pope, *"True and Faithful Account,"* *Newfoundland Studies*, XII (1996), 32-49.

Newfoundland and were well received, even by members of Kirke's own family.[46]

Puritan preachers, en route to or from New England, offered divine service when vessels called at Newfoundland. The Reverend Hugh Peter, the Salem minister who became chaplain to Cromwell's New Model Army and eventually one of the convicted regicides executed after the Restoration, preached in the south Avalon in 1641, as did Thomas Welde, a Dissenting minister of Roxbury. George Downing of Salem preached at Newfoundland in 1645, and the Reverend Richard Blinman spent some time preaching at Ferryland in 1659. In a letter to his friend John Winthrop, Blinman reported that he had been welcomed to Ferryland by two Dissenting New London fishing masters and Lady Kirke herself. He told Winthrop, "People flock from neighbouring harbors to heare the word of God, and attend diligently." Blinman also reported Quaker missionaries at St. John's in 1659, in the persons of Hester Biddle and Mary Fisher. These Quaker women had managed to convert several shipmasters, which provoked others to invite Blinman to come from Ferryland to preach in St. John's as well. There had been an earlier Quaker mission in 1656, and these missions continued into the 1660s. A competition for souls existed in Newfoundland, despite the absence of permanent religious institutions. Furthermore, this sectarian competition occurred among Dissenting factions on the left of the religious spectrum.[47]

Evidence for Anglican-Puritan sectarian conflict on the mid-seventeenth-century English Shore has survived in the archaeological record of the south Avalon. One of the most striking objects recovered from the smithy at Ferryland is a gilded baroque cross, found in a context of the 1650s (Plate 14). Although unique in construction (it appears to have been manufactured by someone skilled in gun repair) the cross was, of course, a common religious symbol, like others proscribed by Parliament during the Civil War as "popish." Indeed, it bears some resemblance to the ornate cross on Lord Baltimore's coat of arms, now used on the flag of Maryland. It was not necessarily made or used by Roman Catholics,

46. Underdown, *Revel, Riot, and Rebellion*, 4, 104; Stoyle, *Loyalty and Locality*, 17, 20, 89–92 (but note 149–161); Handcock, "Settlers"; cf. Handcock, *Origins*, 47–52.

47. Hans Rollman, "Anglicans, Puritans, and Quakers in Seventeenth-Century Newfoundland," *Avalon Chronicles*, II (1997), 44–72 (esp. 60–64). On the Reverend Hugh Peter, see Raymond Phineas Stearns, *The Strenuous Puritan: Hugh Peter, 1598–1660* (Urbana, Ill., 1954).

Plate 14. Gilded Baroque Cross from Ferryland. X-ray image. About twenty-four centimeters tall, from the smithy (CgAf-2), buried in the roof-fall when the building collapsed in the 1650s. Iron, except for the decorative open finial orbs, which are bimetallic strips of brass and steel, with the brass on the interior to sustain the illusion created by the gilding. Courtesy, Colony of Avalon Foundation

however. If the Ferryland cross was used there in the 1640s, it would have been, as David Kirke boasted to Laud, within "the rites and service of the Church of England." Because it was ornate and because it was a visual symbol, it would have been, to Dissenters, evidence of the Romish tendencies of Anglicans and therefore a target of censure when Puritans took power in Newfoundland in 1652. The value of the cross, its apparent date of deposition, and its archaeological context within the roof structure of the smithy together suggest that this potent royalist symbol was hidden or deliberately discarded, for such objects are rarely lost. The Ferryland cross survives as mute witness to the fact that the absence of churches from the English Shore between 1630 and 1700 does not imply an absence of religion. In light of Sara Kirke's enthusiastic reception of the Puritan divine Richard Blinman, the caching of the cross just about the time her husband was recalled to London must raise a question about her own religious beliefs and whether they might have come to differ from her husband's ostentatious high Anglican commitments.[48]

Questions concerning belief and personal behavior are often difficult to answer about seventeenth-century women, particularly seventeenth-century Newfoundland women, whose lives are poorly documented at best. The relative obscurity of these women cannot, however, be taken as a reliable index of their importance within planter society.

⟨⟩ "Women Would Bee Necessary Heere"

In a letter from Ferryland in 1621, Edward Wynne told his patron, Sir George Calvert, that "women would bee necessary heere for many

48. The cross is of iron, once gilded, except for the decorative open finial orbs, which are bimetallic strips of brass and steel—the brass on the interior to sustain the illusion created by the gilding (Judith Logan, Canadian Conservation Institute, Ottawa, personal communication, 1989). It was found in the roof fall, that is, it was in the building, but not in the floor debris (James A. Tuck, personal communication, 1990). The styles of clay tobacco pipes found in the youngest smithy deposits indicate that the cross must still have been in use into the late 1640s or early 1650s; see Pope, "South Avalon," 520, appendix A.1. On the excavations, see Carter, "Smithy at Ferryland," *Avalon Chronicles*, II (1997), 73–106. It is worth noting that Calvert left his daughters and their husbands gold crosses in his will; see George Calvert, Will, Apr. 14, 1632, John Wesley Murray Lee and Andrew White, eds., *The Calvert Papers*, 3 vols. (Baltimore, 1888–1889), I, 48–50. On iconoclasm, cf. Underdown, *Revel, Riot, and Rebellion*, 256.

respects." In 1622, he asked for "a couple of strong maids that (besides other worke) can both brew and bake" to join the seven women already there. The "other worke" probably included traditionally female tasks, such as livestock husbandry. The economic responsibilities of women on the English Shore expanded; planters' wives and daughters became economically significant participants in the fishery, while they continued to fulfill their traditional household roles. Several women were planters in their own right, and, curiously, some of the largest plantations were operated by women. Although women in early modern England were subordinates in a male-dominated society, many participated actively in economic life, either as partners in household production units or, occasionally, in their own right as a single head of such an enterprise. Women thus had a degree of power, which housewives in subsequent generations lacked. Newfoundland planters' wives participated at least as fully in economic power as women anywhere in the seventeenth century. In other words, they were powerful relative to their sisters elsewhere in a century in which women were powerful relative to some of their great-granddaughters. How was this so?[49]

First, planter women were more than housewives. Evidence that women participated in the seventeenth-century planter fishery is particularly clear in Captain John Berry's 1675 census. Married and unmarried planters both averaged 1.9 boats; unmarried planters employed a mean of 9.1 servants, but married planters, only 8.0. For an average planter, a wife could shoulder the responsibilities of a servant. Like their more recent counterparts, who often made up much of the "shore crowd," women

49. Edward Winne to George Calvert, Aug. 28, 1621, Aug. 17, 1622, in Cell, *Newfoundland Discovered*, 200-204, 257-258; B. A. Holderness, "Widows in Pre-Industrial Society: An Essay upon Their Economic Functions," in Richard M. Smith, ed., *Land, Kinship, and Life-Cycle* (Cambridge, 1984), 423-442 (esp. 424); Michael Roberts, "Women and Work in Sixteenth-Century English Towns," in Penelope J. Corfield and Derek Keene, eds., *Work in Towns, 850-1850* (Leicester, 1990), 86-102. On seventeenth-century women, see Lois Green Carr and Lorena S. Walsh, "The Planter's Wife: The Experience of White Women in Seventeenth-Century Maryland," *WMQ*, 3d Ser., XXXIV (1977), 542-571; Laurel Thatcher Ulrich, *Good Wives: Image and Reality in the Lives of Women in Northern New England, 1650-1750* (New York, 1982); Amy Louise Erickson, *Women and Property in Early Modern England* (London, 1993); Underdown, *Revel, Riot, and Rebellion*, 287; Kathleen M. Brown, *Good Wives, Nasty Wenches, and Anxious Patriarchs: Gender, Race, and Power in Colonial Virginia* (Chapel Hill, N.C., 1996), 287-291; Sturtz, *Within Her Power*, 8-12, 29, 41, 66-67.

would have worked at fish processing and marketing rather than on the water. New England fishermen's wives kept accounts, supervised servants as they culled fish, protected fishing rooms from encroachment, and dealt with suppliers and buyers. Newfoundland planters' wives must have acted in similar capacities.[50]

Women did not, however, abandon their traditional contribution to household production in brewing, baking, dairying, and the care of poultry and pigs. Judging by the agricultural activities of households reported in Sir William Poole's census for 1677, Newfoundland households that included at least one female were much more likely to keep pigs than all-male households (Table 22). Furthermore, among households keeping swine, households with a female kept somewhat more, on the average, than all-male households. Less than a quarter of all-male households kept cattle; households with a female were much more likely to do so and were likely to keep considerably larger herds. Not many planters kept sheep, but, again, households with a female were much more likely to do so and, if they did, were likely to keep more animals than all-male households. On the other hand, there is no evidence that women were particularly active as gardeners.[51]

A surprising number of Newfoundland planter households were headed by women. The censuses almost always identify these female heads of households as widows. The plantations maintained by these widows were, generally, significantly larger than the average plantation. In both 1675 and 1681, for example, widows employed a mean of about thirteen servants, rather than the nine or so employed on the average plantation. (In 1677, however, a number of impoverished widows appear in the records, including two with no boats and five with only one.)

---

50. Berry, "Planters," Sept. 12, 1675, CO 1/35 (17ii), 150–156. The figures for 1677 in Poole, "Particular Accompt," Sept. 10, 1677, CO 1/41 (61iv, vi, vii), 158–166, appear to run against the hypothesis that a wife was the equivalent of a servant, owing to a positive correlation between married status and the size of plantations. That is, married planters were likely to have more servants because they were likely to have more boats. If, however, planters are grouped by number of boats, the married planters in almost all cases employed fewer servants. Cf. Cadigan, *Hope and Deception*, 64–80; James C. Faris, *Cat Harbour: A Newfoundland Fishing Settlement* (St. John's, 1972), 67; Ulrich, *Good Wives*, 41.

51. Ulrich, *Good Wives*, 13–34; Weatherill, *Material Culture*, 137–165; Amussen, *Ordered Society*, 43, 68; Brown, *Good Wives, Nasty Wenches*, 24–26. Poole, "Particular Accompt," Sept. 10, 1677, CO 1/41 (52i), 113–121, omits poultry and goats, two additional components of early Newfoundland agriculture.

Table 22. *Agricultural Activities of Households, Newfoundland, 1677*

Agricultural Effort	Proportion of All Households		Average Kept by Households	
	All Male (*N* = 51)	Female Present (*N* = 112)	All Male (*N* = 51)	Female Present (*N* = 112)
Hogs	47%	74%	7.7	8.3
Cattle	20	38	5.7	10.3
Sheep	8	13	5.0	7.2
Gardens	76	77	1.4	1.4

Note: The figures for gardens relate only to the English Shore from St. John's north, since data for gardens are not reported for the south Avalon in Poole's account. For all male households in this region, *N* = 33, and for households with a female, *N* = 78.

Source: William Poole, "A Particular Accompt of All the Inhabitants and Planters . . . ," Sept. 10, 1677, CO 1/41 (62iv, vi, vii), 157–166.

By becoming planters themselves, Newfoundland widows were adopting a male role, a situation not as anomalous as it may seem within the context of the patriarchal society of the period. Women's economic functions were not completely distinguished from men's in Newfoundland any more than they were in preindustrial Europe; furthermore, English women had an acknowledged right to assume male roles under certain circumstances.[52]

In the English-speaking world of the seventeenth century, a husband had patriarchal authority, but, if circumstances prevented him from attending to family interests, then his wife acted in his stead. This situation was particularly apparent during wartime: in the Ferryland census of 1709, the number of wives (twenty-eight) exceeds the number of planters (twenty-two). Widowhood was a limiting case of this principle, in which the widow took complete control of the family enterprise until such time as she remarried. Widowers and widows normally remarried, unless they were elderly, although women who lost their husbands were less prone to rush into a new marriage than men who lost their wives. Some women, particularly those with a livelihood, might have preferred to retain the

52. Holderness, "Widows," in Smith, ed., *Land, Kinship, and Life-Cycle*, 423–442 (esp. 425).

status of widow, precisely because it was the only possible way a woman could attain independent status as a householder.[53]

Survival in Newfoundland as feme sole was certainly possible, as the case of the Bay Roberts planter Joan Clay illustrates. She owned a single boat and employed four men in 1675; two years later, she owned two boats and employed eight men. Her success was probably based, in part, on her herd of sixteen cattle. She is not visible, however, in the census of 1681, and one suspects that she had remarried. Other widows remained heads of households for decades, like Mary Weymouth of Carbonear, who ran a plantation there in the 1630s and 1640s. This strategy had serious drawbacks, however, in Newfoundland as in most colonial settings. A couple was more likely to be a successful economic unit than an individual. In most census years, married planters maintained larger-than-average plantations—a local illustration of this home truth. So widowed female planters likely remarried rapidly, as they did in French Newfoundland. For example, Mary, the widow of David Kirke II, married the St. John's merchant James Benger within a year or two of Kirke's death in 1697. Among widows who chose not to remarry were those controlling the largest plantations.[54]

Sara Kirke and her sister, Frances Hopkins, were among the widows who retained control of their own large plantations. Why did these planter gentry women forgo remarriage? Probably because they had the least to gain and the most to lose from a new alliance. These were merchants' wives (Plate 15). Their high social status left them relatively isolated, for virtually the only males in Newfoundland with equivalent status were their own kin. Lady Frances traveled as far as Boston to find an appropriate partner in the Acadian merchant Alexandre Le Borgne de Belle-Isle, whom she married there in 1656. She later appears in the

53. Ulrich, *Good Wives*, 36–38; Joseph Taylor, "An Account of the Fishery of Newfoundland," 1709, CO 194/4 (101), 421; Holderness, "Widows," in Smith, ed., *Land, Kinship, and Life-Cycle*, 423–442 (esp. 431); Vivien Brodsky, "Widows in Late Elizabethan London: Remarriage, Economic Opportunity, and Family Orientations," in Bonfield, Smith, and Wrightson, eds., *World We Have Gained*, 122–176 (esp. 122–123); Laslett, *World We Have Lost*, 113; Sturtz, *Within Her Power*, 21–24, 66–68, 71–79, 144–151; Lisa Norling, *Captain Ahab Had a Wife: New England Women and the Whalefishery, 1720–1870* (Chapel Hill, N.C., 2000), 36–42, 148–153.

54. Gabriell Viddomas, Deposition, Nov. 27, 1667, WDRO Plymouth, W360/74. On remarriage in French Newfoundland, see Chapter 6, above. On Mary Kirke, see Thomas Cleasby, Deposition, Mar. 23, 1707, CO 194/4 (63), 212.

Plate 15. Marchants Wife of London. *By Wenceslaus Holler, 1643.*
Permission of the Museum of London

Newfoundland records under her first husband's name, presumably after the marriage with her second husband dissolved, and she did not bother to find a third. Even the children of planter gentry might have trouble finding suitable partners. Thus, Mary Kirke, the wife of Lady Kirke's son David, had been Lady Hopkins's servant girl and was married to David over family protest. Mary herself had status only by marriage, which may explain, in part, her willingness to form a new alliance after her first husband's death. The independence of the two ladies of Ferryland might also have been related to their living through the Civil War—not so much because women's rights were then occasionally mooted but because women had opportunities to act on their beliefs and because the dislocations of war left them alone with responsibilities. Lady Hopkins's role in harboring Charles I on the Isle of Wight and Lady Kirke's management of her husband's estate in Ferryland after his recall to London in 1651 are excellent examples of these passing phenomena.[55]

Although Frances Hopkins was a political refugee when she arrived in Newfoundland around 1650, and, although Sara Kirke could be seen as a political exile during the Interregnum, it does not follow that these women were stranded in Newfoundland. After the Restoration, Lady Kirke told Charles II that she and her children "have lived but in a poor and sad condition," but poverty is relative, especially in correspondence

55. "American Marriage Records before 1699," in *http://homepages.rootsweb .com/ahopkins/colonial3.htm*, had (as of September 2001) "Hopkins, Lady Frances and Monsieur Belvele, 9 April 1656, Boston." (My thanks to Barry Gaulton for this reference.) Despite his youth, this reference is likely to Alexandre Le Borgne de Belle-Isle, son of Emmanuel Le Borgne, who was sent to deal with the occupation of Acadia by Thomas Temple and William Crowne at this time; see Mason Wade, "Le Borgne, Emmanuel," *DCB*. Belle-Isle's exploits in the mid-1650s call into question the approximate date of birth given in Clément Cormier, "Le Borgne de Belle-Isle, Alexandre," *DCB*. On Mary Kirke, see Richard Hartnoll et al., Deposition, Sept. 15, 1707, CO 194/4 (77ix), 316. There is a traditional belief (in, for example, Handcock, *Origins*, 35) that Mary was Irish. This conclusion seems to be one of Agnes Field's imaginative contributions to Newfoundland history. See her racist interpretation of David's "mésalliance" in Agnes M. Field, "The Development of Government in Newfoundland, 1638–1713" (master's thesis, University of London, 1924), 173. That Mary Kirke took her children to Barnstaple for baptism in 1677 suggests that she was of Devon origin. The Kirkes were a family of strong women: Elizabeth, Sir David Kirke's mother, had traded on her own account as a London wine merchant after the death of her husband Gervaise in 1629; see Chapter 3, above.

with royalty. The two ladies of Ferryland were among the wealthiest planters on the English Shore, according to the censuses of the 1670s. As literate gentry, they retained contact with their kin in the Old Country. If either had liquidated her assets, she could have returned to England, where kin would have offered shelter. To return to England, however, would have been to return to the status of a dependent. In Newfoundland, these women were independent heads of planter households, of very high status as well as the matriarchs of important planter lineages. They played an important and visible role in Newfoundland as elder stateswomen. Like substantial widows elsewhere, they also would have played an important but less-visible role financially by extending credit to a clientage of kin and neighbors, possibly with the expectation of interest, certainly with the hope of future goodwill. Despite their gender, they, too, were patrons of development.[56]

ॐ Social Evolution

No single aspect of the socioeconomic organization of Newfoundland's seventeenth-century English Shore was unknown in other colonies or counties, although the mix of elements was closely paralleled only in French Newfoundland and northern New England. Newfoundland was settled and its economy developed within the context of an early capitalist industry, the European migratory fishery. The English Shore became a society of merchants, planters, and fishing servants in which women of the propertied classes played a significant role. The politics of religion might have divided this society, at times, but bonds of patronage and service tied it together. Patronage on the English Shore was a more complex and, perhaps, more balanced phenomenon than it was in midcentury New England. Sir David Kirke's clients were other planters, themselves employers, not his own employees, as was often the case for the Pynchons in the Connecticut Valley or the merchants of Essex County, Mas-

56. Kirke to Charles II, 1660, British Library, Egerton MS 2395, 258; Hill to Kirke, Sept. 12, 1661, British Library, Egerton MS 2395, 308; Hopkings, "Information and Relation," ca. 1670, British Library, Egerton MS 2395, 266; Holderness, "Credit," *Agricultural History Review*, XXIV (1976), 97–109 (esp. 105); Holderness, "Widows," in Smith, ed., *Land, Kinship, and Life-Cycle*, 423–442 (esp. 435–442); Alice Clark, *Working Life of Women in the Seventeenth Century* (London, 1982), 28–34. For another view, see Handcock, *Origins*, 35.

sachusetts, and it was in Kirke's own interest for his planter clientele to prosper. He protected the planters of the south Avalon as entrepreneurs in a competitive industry by leasing them fishing rooms, which he defended from migratory West Country crews. The planters deferred to Kirke, permitting him not merely the seigneurial perquisites of a proprietor ("ten nobles and a fat hog") but also allowing him to exploit the local market in certain key imports, particularly salt and wine.[57]

In Newfoundland, at least, clientage turned out to be a more durable social relationship than service. In the seventeenth century, servants in the fishery far outnumbered planters. The most common socioeconomic relationship was therefore that between servant and planter, however important the intricate exchange of deference and favor that bound planter and merchant. Through the later eighteenth and early nineteenth centuries, as the population grew, resident fish producers depended less and less on seasonally migratory servants. This shift in the socioeconomic organization of the English Newfoundland fishery is captured only crudely by the notion of a transition from a servant fishery to a family fishery, for the family had always been the predominant unit of production in the resident fishery. By 1850, however, the typical family production unit was smaller and differently organized than it had been in 1750 or 1650. Just as the very word "family" evolved from a concept encompassing the members of a household, servants included, so the traditional family fishery evolved to gradually exclude servants. What did endure was the dependence of fisher families on merchant patronage: Newfoundland's fisherfolk were "married" to their merchants for a very long time. If service in the fishery is, like service in husbandry, one of the forgotten dinosaurs of economic history, we might think of the merchant-planter patron-client relationship as a more adaptable creature that flourished within several successive economic faunas. Though no longer locally extant, this beast is by no means forgotten in Newfoundland.[58]

There is no society without exchange, as Rousseau put it, and one of the ways we can understand a society is by understanding which goods

57. Landry, "Culture matérielle chez les pêcheurs," *Material Hist. Rev.*, no. 48 (Fall 1998), 101–122; Heyrman, *Commerce and Culture*, 269–271; Clark, *Eastern Frontier*, 13–35; Innes, *Labor in a New Land*, 73–122; Vickers, *Farmers and Fishermen*, 103–116.

58. Sider, *Culture and Class*, 15, 22, 55; *OED*, s.v. "family"; Hiller, "Newfoundland Credit System," in Ommer, *Merchant Credit*, 86–102.

change hands and how. The staple economy of seventeenth-century Newfoundland, year in and year out, was simple enough: the island exported salt cod in exchange for whatever was necessary to produce fish. This oversimplification obscures, however, the reality of everyday life on the English Shore and the degree to which the familiar material culture of the seventeenth-century Anglo-American world functioned somewhat differently there.

9 ⟨⟨ OUTPORT ECONOMICS

*The planters hogs and cattle . . . sometimes breake out to [fishers']
stages and spoile some of their fish, but this is not great prejudice to
them in that the custom of the country obligeth the proprietors of the
cattle to returne to them soe many fish as they have spoyled.*
—*Captain William Poole to the Committee for Trade
and Plantations, Sept. 10, 1677*

The Royal Navy commodores who visited the English Shore toward
the end of the seventeenth century saw much of planter life. Sir William
Poole was particularly inquisitive about the planter economy and had,
as well, a kind of anthropological curiosity about the interrelationship
between migratory fishing crews, whose interests were concentrated on
one industry, and the planters, who had developed a range of economic
interests that reached beyond the fishery to other concerns, like cattle
and hogs, for example. The assumption that there was little economic life
outside the fishery is a tempting simplification, particularly for analysis
of staple production, but it is not necessarily an accurate assessment of
the economic realities of later-seventeenth-century Newfoundland. Nor
were the landward activities of the planters significant only for their own
households. In fact, as Captain Poole understood, the economic activities
of those who overwintered on the English Shore were inevitably connected to the migratory fishery. A pair of civil and criminal cases, arising
from an English expedition into Placentia Bay in the fall of 1679, illustrates this entanglement and makes an apt introduction to the complex
theme of outport economics.[1]

⟨⟨ *The Case of the Furriers' Boats*

In mid-September 1679, John Wallis, a fishing servant of Fermeuse,
traveled northward along the English Shore to John Roulston's plantation at Toad's Cove. There he met four old friends, and they talked "about

---

1. Captain William Poole to CTP, Sept. 10, 1677, CO 1/41 (62), 147–148. For
the simplistic view, see Kenneth H. Norrie and Douglas Owram, *A History of the
Canadian Economy* (Toronto, 1991), 58.

going to the westward . . . a furring . . . as most years tis usuall for some of the English to goe that way in the winter and have made good voyages of itt and turn to good profitt." Roulston provisioned Wallis and his mates on credit and agreed to equip a sixth man, his own servant Samuel Wood, with provisions and ammunition for the expedition, "upon hopes of a good voyage" and a share of any proceeds. The men then traveled south to Caplin Bay and obtained "an old French shalloway" from Christopher Pollard, the planter there. (A shalloway was a decked sailing vessel a bit larger than an open fishing shallop.) Later, they claimed to have rented the shalloway for five pounds; at any rate, they agreed that if they lost Pollard's boat they would pay him fifteen pounds or find him a replacement. Subsequent events suggest that this last option, a search for a new boat in French territory, was the actual intent of the agreement.[2]

The case sheds light on several aspects of the planter economy. Successful planters, like John Roulston and Christopher Pollard, did more than fish. On the other hand, fishing clearly structured other activities, like furring: the whole expedition was conceived as a "voyage," and the servants were provisioned and supplied as a boat crew would be. The theft and vandalism of fishing equipment were common enough occurrences. What was unusual was that both the civil and criminal issues came to trial. The expedition itself and its legal consequences fell naturally into the accentuated annual rhythm of the early modern North Atlantic. The case can serve, at once, as an entrée to both the spatial and the temporal structures of the English Shore.[3]

After ten days coasting around the Avalon Peninsula in Pollard's shalloway, the six fishing servants arrived in St. Mary's Bay, "where the French fish." They were reluctant to meet these competitors, for reasons Wallis frankly admitted under examination: "Being in a French shalloway, they would not put in there, least [the French] should take theire

2. Samuel Wood, Examination, Aug. 22, 1680, John Wallis, Examination, Aug. 24, 1680, John Ducarrett, Power of Attorney to George Perriman, July 31, 1680, George Perriman, "Paper concerning Damage," Aug. 31, 1680, Christopher Pollard and John Rolson, Bond, Sept. 30, 1680, Aaron Browning and Robert Fishley, "Declaraton," Sept. 27, 1680, Robert Robinson et al., Sentence of Francis Knapman, John Wallis, William Couch, and Samuel Wood, Sept. 30, 1680, all in CO 1/45 (68i–iv), 252–256. On shalloways, see Head, *Newfoundland*, 80.

3. Records of either a civil or a criminal complaint tried in Newfoundland are rare before 1750; see Jerry Bannister, "The Fishing Admirals in Eighteenth-Century Newfoundland," *Newfoundland Studies*, XVII (2001), 166–219.

boat from them, itt being usuall for the English that went that way a furring, if the boat they carried out with them proved defective, to take a better of the Frenches shalloways . . . and supposing [their own vessel] had formerly been taken upon that account, they would not put in there." So, instead, they went to Colinet, "a place likewise where the French fish."[4]

Landing at Colinet, they "staved their boat," which was quite a coincidence, since the French had left four shalloways and ten shallops at that very spot. They launched one of these French shalloways, put their remaining provisions into it, and anchored it with *killicks*, or stone anchors. The next day, four of them took one of the French shallops and headed up a creek to hunt. They shot a few birds and an otter and found more French fishing gear, hidden in a pond. A gale came up, and it was days before the hunters could return to camp, where their mates had not been able to prevent the shalloway (and their provisions in it) from destruction in the storm. So they launched yet another French shalloway and left the smaller shallop they had used for hunting to the mercy of the waves. After a month at Colinet, they headed from the bay to St. Mary's, taking with them about twenty fir rinds, probably from the roof of a cabin. Jean Ducarret, the Frenchman whose premises they had looted, would accuse them of burning his cabin, but they swore they had done "no other mischief" besides the theft of the rinds and vessels.[5]

At St. Mary's, they covered a train vat with the rinds "to make themselves a little shelter in the dead time of winter." (It was mid-December by the modern calendar.) They lived in this box impregnated with cod-liver oil for three weeks, subsisting on shorebirds. Wood and Wallis later swore that they "did noe dammage to anything of the French concerns" but admitted that they took four hundred to five hundred pounds of iron spikes and nails. These, they claimed, they had "cut out of drift timber which came from stages." After a difficult voyage, they arrived back in Caplin Bay, where they delivered the new shalloway to Christopher Pollard on December 31, 1679. They shared out the scavenged iron; their backer, John Roulston, took Wood's share as well as the furs the men

4. Wallis, Examination, Aug. 24, 1680, CO 1/45 (68i), 252–253.
5. Wood, Examination, Aug. 22, 1680, Wallis, Examination, Aug. 24, 1680, Ducarrett, Power of Attorney to Perriman, July 31, 1680, all in CO 1/45 (68, 68i), 251–253. A *killick* is an elongated stone in a frame of sticks *(DNE)*. This is an early use of the term.

had managed to bag on their fifteen-week expedition: thirteen fox, seven otter, and four beaver.[6]

Late the following July, the aggrieved French fishing master, Jean Ducarret, came to Trepassey, the English settlement closest to St. Mary's Bay, to complain that an English crew had destroyed two new shalloways, three shallops, and his cabin. Aaron Browning and Robert Fishly, masters of the *Exchange* of Bideford and the *Standerbay* of Barnstaple, were the fishing admirals there; that is, they were the masters who had arrived first in Trepassey that year and were therefore empowered by the Western Charter to settle such disputes. They agreed to look into the case. Meanwhile, Ducarret gave power of attorney to George Perriman, a major planter in Trepassey, to retrieve the stolen vessel from the Caplin Bay planter, Christopher Pollard. In late August, Perriman wrote George Kirke of Renews, then the major planter on the south Avalon, delegating power of attorney to retrieve the stolen shalloway. Before acting, Kirke awaited the legal decision of the two fishing admirals. By late September, the decision had been made. The English planters, Pollard and Roulston, bound themselves to repay Ducarret for his damages, estimated at fifty to sixty pounds. The exact figure was to be negotiated, with the fishing admiral at Trepassey acting as "umpire." This bond was probably signed at Trepassey; at any rate, it was witnessed by a Frenchman, Daniel Darmelly, as well as by George Kirke. The Trepassey fishing admirals, Browning and Fishly, filed a report with the Royal Navy commodore, Sir Robert Robinson, at Bay Bulls, as did Kirke. On September 29, 1680, a year after the whole affair began, the English fishing masters Browning and Fishly with Captain Robinson and another naval officer held criminal court on board HMS *Assistance* and passed sentence on four of the furriers to be "duck att the maine yard arme of the shipp."[7]

The case of the furriers' boats is full of suggestive details. As the weather began to close in and migratory fishermen prepared to return across the Atlantic, some hid their gear in ponds. Others, who had decided to overwinter, had seasonal strategies for making a little extra cash,

6. Wallis, Examination, Aug. 24, 1680, Wood, Examination, Aug. 22, 1680, both in CO 1/45 (68i), 252–253.

7. Ducarrett, Power of Attorney, July 31, 1680, Perriman, "Damage," Aug. 31, 1680, Pollard and Rolson, Bond, Sept. 30, 1680, Browning and Fishley, "Declaration," Sept. 27, 1680, Robinson et al., Sentence, all in CO 1/45 (68, 68ii–iv), 251, 254–256.

and these strategies could require mobility along the English Shore or even beyond its somewhat permeable bounds. It says something about fishing servants' usual room and board that they were willing to live in an oily wooden box on a diet of shorebirds. The repeated thefts and casual vandalism highlight the extralegal conflicts that were not simply an internal problem between the migratory and resident sectors of the English fishery but part of a larger pattern of physical competition among all participants in the cod fishery. The St. John's merchant John Downing acknowledged that in the early years of settlement "some English inhabitants would burne the Frenchmans boates, carry away some, carry away their salt, break open their houses, and riffle them." Wallis's frank testimony strongly suggests that the planned theft of French boats was still common. The scavenging of iron from French stages, even supposing these had already been damaged by weather, was or at least became an important goal of the expedition. Given that the limited bag of furs would have been worth about fifteen pounds, whereas the iron was worth something like ten pounds and the new shalloway was at least fifteen pounds, the plan to go "a furring" was, evidently, little more than a cover for a scavenging expedition.[8]

The eventual resolution of the case is instructive too. Although the crimes occurred in early winter, no one thought to deal with them until after the busy spring and well into the middle of the following summer, when the fishing season was beginning to shape up and when those with the power to respond might be expected to have time to deal with such issues. That the English acted on Ducarret's complaint is politically significant. The sentence calls the punishment "a publick example to all others in this Island." This sentence might have been an attempt to remedy a previous, more tenuous, rule of law: Wallis's testimony indicates that scavenging, at least on French rooms, was considered a legitimate winter activity by the English inhabitants. George Kirke's func-

---

8. Quotation from John Downing, "A Breif Narrative concerning Newfoundland," Nov. 24, 1676, British Library, Egerton MS 2395, 560–563. The English appear to have been stealing French boats for almost a century. See "The Voyage of Charles Leigh" (1597), in Quinn, *New American World*, IV, 68–75. Furs estimated from Arthur J. Ray and David B. Freeman, *"Give Us Good Measure": An Economic Analysis of Relations between the Indians and the Hudson's Bay Company before 1763* (Toronto, 1978), 64 (table 1), 88 (fig. 3), 149 (fig. 25). On ironwork, see John Downing, "Newfoundland, an Account concerning the Following Perticulars . . . ," Dec. 14, 1676, British Library, Egerton MS 2395, 564.

tion in this case as a sort of justice of the peace, or at least as a notary and representative of south Avalon planter interests, suggests that the Kirke family continued to function as local patrons a quarter of a century after the death of Sir David Kirke. His role was very much that of the gatekeeper-mediator: it was to him that the Trepassey planter turned for recovery of the shalloway, he witnessed the bonds that the receivers of the stolen goods were asked to sign, and he provided the naval officers with an assessment of the Frenchman's losses. The younger Kirke was the one person involved in the episode who dealt with the French, the officers who passed sentence, and the planters who made reparations. Finally, that Ducarret took his complaint to Trepassey suggests that this southernmost harbor functioned as an interface between French and English Newfoundland.[9]

Because the settlements of the seventeenth-century English Shore were small and closely linked to particular West Country ports, overlooking the relationships they had among themselves is all too easy. Such Eurocentrism rests, in part, on the notion that Newfoundland was nothing but a permanent fishing station, moored conveniently near the banks. As the scene in which migratory crews played out the annual drama of the fishery, Newfoundland was not much more homogeneous than the West Country that manned and provisioned the industry. Nor did time stand still for planters and their servants as they faced seasonal tasks driven but not exclusively determined by the production of salt cod.[10]

₰ Outport Geography

The convoluted and deeply embayed coast, known in the seventeenth century as the English Shore, stretches roughly 150 miles (or 230 kilometers) as the crow flies from Salvage, a few leagues north of Bonavista, to Trepassey in the south (Map 5). In the fairest of winds, this distance would be far more than 200 sea miles and, on foot, many times that distance. (How many times depends on one's commitment to trac-

9. On Wallis's testimony, cf. Prowse, *History*, 174, although the quotation is inaccurate, even as an abstract.

10. Glanville James Davies, "England and Newfoundland: Policy and Trade, 1660–1783" (Ph.D. diss., University of Southampton, 1980), 40; David J. Starkey, "Devonians and the Newfoundland Trade," in *Maritime History of Devon*, I, 163–171.

ing the fractal geometry of Newfoundland's rocky coast.) By the second half of the seventeenth century, the English Shore had developed a regional structure, despite the limited size of the twenty or thirty scattered hamlets that were home to an anomalous colony of folk, supposed to "live by catching fish." Crews fished in every outport, but not every outport devoted itself to the fishery in the same way. There were still fishing stations without planters: Aquaforte, just south of Ferryland; the Isles of Spear, off Toad's Cove; Bell Island, in Conception Bay; and Heart's Ease and English Harbour, on opposite sides of Trinity Bay. There were even a few settled outharbors that ships fishing usually bypassed: Brigus South and Harbour Main, for example. Practically speaking, though, resident and planter crews worked side by side in most of the fishing harbors then regularly in use.[11]

At the southern limits of the English Shore, Trepassey and Renews had become an interface with "our friends the enemy," the French who fished in St. Mary's and Placentia Bay, just to the west. In 1621, Sir George Calvert's manager, Edward Wynne, sought salt (commonly a French good) in these southern harbors for the Avalon colony. In 1684, Captain Francis Wheler reported French families settled at Trepassey, "where our nation and theirs fish without disagreeing." The censuses of the 1670s and 1680s suggest that several planters in this area, particularly the Perriman brothers and Jonathan Hooper in Renews, employed French servants, for the number of English servants reported was not nearly sufficient for the number of boats operated. After war broke out between France and England in 1689, some complained that at least one planter in Renews continued to employ French servants.[12]

The average size of plantations varied considerably from place to place. Ferryland represented a cluster of large plantations, strongly com-

11. For another view, see Keith Matthews, *Lectures on the History of Newfoundland, 1500–1830* (St. John's, 1988), 19, 46.

12. Edward Wynne to George Calvert, Aug. 17, 1622, in Whitbourne, *Discourse*, 200–204; Francis Wheler, "Answers to the Heads of Inquirys . . . ," Oct. 17, 1684, CO 1/55 (56), 239–246; Downing, "Breif Narrative," Nov. 24, 1676, British Library, Egerton MS 2395, 560–563; William Poole, "A Particular Accompt of All the Inhabitants and Planters . . . ," Sept. 10, 1677, CO 1/41 (62iv, vi, vii), 157–166; William Roberts and Thomas Dibble, Depositions, Dec. 2, 1703, CO 194/3 (22i), 70. Cf. Jean Daigle, "Nos amis les ennemis: les marchands Acadiens et le Massachusetts à la fin du 17e siècle," *Les Cahiers de la Société Historique Acadienne*, VII, no. 4 (1976), 161–170.

mitted to agricultural activity: in 1677, the average Ferryland planter owned more boats and employed more servants than the typical Newfoundland planter, by a factor of about 50 percent. In the south Avalon, only Caplin Bay and Toad's Cove, each with a single large plantation, matched Ferryland in plantation size. Nor did this merely result from the existence of one or two very large plantations: Ferryland had more large plantations in 1677 than any other harbor in Newfoundland, the much more populous St. John's included. The aptly named Petty Harbour, just to the south of St. John's, was a kind of counterfoil to Ferryland. It was a haven for small operators: in 1677, its eight planters operated only ten boats among them. The average scale of operation was not much more in St. John's itself, despite the existence of several large plantations, or in Torbay just to the north, so that the St. John's region as a whole was one of small plantations, in contrast to the south Avalon in general and Ferryland in particular. Ferryland clearly functioned as a central place. Sir David Kirke held courts there, as Cecil Calvert's deputies continued to do in the early 1660s. Planters from smaller settlements would sometimes trade there, like Henry Cooke of Renews, who in 1646 obtained six jars of olive oil and twenty yards of linen from the *Hopton* of Bristol.[13]

Other outports filled other functions. Fishing and sack ships used the large naturally protected harbor of Bay Bulls to assemble transatlantic convoys—something done more and more frequently under naval protection as the century wore on. Captain Sir Robert Robinson had John Wallis and his mates ducked at the yard arm in Bay Bulls when the Royal Navy squadron assembled the autumn convoy in late September 1680. Centuries later, during the Second World War, convoys would assemble there in much the same fashion. Military investment has often had a strong impact on Newfoundland. In the seventeenth century, the use of Bay Bulls as a rendezvous no doubt helped support the tippling houses that planters operated there.[14]

13. Poole, "Particular Accompt," Sept. 10, 1677, CO 1/41 (62iv, vi, vii), 157–166; John Shawe (of Boston), Power of Attorney to Robert Love (of Ferryland), 1648, *Aspinwall Records*, 130; John Mathews, "Concerning the French in Newfoundland," Jan. 27, 1671, British Library, Egerton MS 2395, 471; Samuel Hartnall, Deposition, Mar. 3, 1648, *Bristol Depositions*, I, *1643–1647*, 190–191.

14. James Denye, Examination, in *Delabarre v. Crew of the* William and Jane, Oct. 11, 1633, HCA 13/50, 412; Thomas Newcomen, Interrogatories, in *Newcomen v. Johnson and Goodsonne*, 1651, HCA 23/17 (137), n.p.; Robert Plumleigh to Admiralty, Nov. 12, 1657, SP 18/172 (72), 134; Thomas Cruse, Deposi-

St. John's became increasingly important after the Restoration of 1660, an instance of the general rule that British colonial administrators favored the development of a centrally located port in each colony. After 1675, when the Royal Navy's commodores began to remain in Newfoundland for weeks or even months, St. John's was where they established themselves, even if they might issue orders, late in the season, from Bay Bulls. By 1677, it had long since become the largest settlement in Newfoundland, with about two hundred fisherfolk regularly overwintering, settled in twenty-seven plantations, with their houses, eighty storehouses and lodgings for servants, forty-six fishing rooms for salting and drying cod, with twenty-nine fishing stages and forty-five fishing boats. These figures were roughly twice those of second-rank settlements like Ferryland, Carbonear, Bay de Verde, Old Perlican, and Bonavista, with eight to sixteen plantations each in 1677. Only the French settlement of Plaisance approached St. John's in size, at least by 1687, when it, too, had twenty-seven resident households.[15]

Because St. John's was very oriented to the migratory fishery, these figures understate its importance. In the summer of 1677, 38 ships with crews were fishing at St. John's, which meant an additional 384 boats, moored at 118 additional fishing stages, on an additional 175 fishing rooms, manned by 1,973 men, lodged in 88 additional servants' lodgings. The ships fishing ranged in size from the 40-ton *Samuell*, with its single boat and crew of 6, to the 200-ton *Darius*, with its 19 fishing boats and its crew of 95. By August, the 2,000 or so fisherfolk catching and processing fish at St. John's were joined by more than 400 deep-sea mariners, who crewed the 45 sack ships that called there in the summer of 1677. Many were small, like the 25-ton *Adventure Sloop* of Boston, which arrived with provisions en route to Plaisance, or the 40-ton *Endeavour*

tion, Nov. 27, 1667, WDRO Plymouth, W360/74; and the Royal Navy captains' journals cited below.

15. Leonard Harris, "Journall" (HMS *Sucess*), 1674, Admiralty, ADM 51/3981 (6); John Berry, "Captain's Log" (HMS *Bristoll*), 1675, ADM 51/134, pt. 2; William Poole, "Journall" (HMS *Leopard*), 1677, Magdalene College, Cambridge, Pepys Library, PL 2813; Lawrence Wright, "Journal" (HMS *Reserve*), 1679, ADM 51/4119; "Journal" (HMS *Assurance*), 1680, ADM 51/4119; Poole, "Particular Accompt," Sept. 10, 1677, CO 1/41 (61iv, vi, vii), 158–166; Jean Auger dit Baron, Deposition, Oct. 13, 1687, in Fernand-D. Thibodeau, "Recensements de Terreneuve et Plaisance," *Mémoires de la Société Généalogique Canadienne-Française*, XIII (1962), 204–208.

Katch of Dartmouth, with wine from Fayal in the Azores; some were larger, like the 150-ton *Hopewell* of Dartmouth, which arrived with salt and was bound for Alicante, Spain, with fish. St. John's was not just a fishing station; it was already a busy port. Large or small, each of these ships and all of their boats needed moorings, so the St. John's waterfront must have been very crowded. Ships' boats outnumbered planters' boats by a factor of almost 9 to 1. Little wonder that, as far as Captain Poole was concerned, "this particular harbour of St John's makes more trouble then all the country besides." The relative importance of St. John's grew with fortification and the stationing of troops in 1689. Until 1713, the turmoil of the French wars resulted in the centralization of some south Avalon planters at St. John's during the conflicts, but also at Ferryland and Carbonear. Although St. John's role as administrative capital of the colony was still technically in doubt in this period, the die was cast: the second-tier settlements would remain regional centers at best. The human geography of the English Shore was, inevitably, subject to the pressures of imperial policy and international conflict.[16]

The inner Conception Bay settlements of Carbonear, Mosquito, Bay Roberts, Port de Grave, and Harbour Main resembled the south Avalon settlements in the local importance of large or at least moderately large plantations: nine plantations in these harbors had three or more boats in 1677. These outports resembled Ferryland and differed strongly from St. John's in the sense that migratory crews would not have overwhelmed these communities each summer, the number of planters' and ships' boats being in a ratio of roughly one to one. At this time, plantations in Harbour Grace were small, almost all with only one boat each. Ships' crews were relatively more numerous at Harbour Grace, and for every planter's boat here there were two or three ships' boats, just as there were in the south Avalon outports of Renews, Fermeuse, and Bay Bulls. Some of the

16. William Poole, "Account of Fishing and Sackships from Balene to St. John's Harbour . . . ," Sept. 10, 1677, CO 1/41 (62ix), 168–170; quotation from Poole to CTP, Sept. 10, 1677, CO 1/41 (62), 147–148. On garrisons and population movements, see CTP, "Order for a Governor of Newfoundland, etc.," May 18, 1689, CO 324/5, 51–52; Board of Ordnance, "Instructions for Martin Skinner," July 27, 1689, CO 1/65 (79), 285; Christopher Desborow, Deposition, May 18, 1695, CO 194/1 (78), 150–152; Richard Amiss et al., Address to Governor Dudley, May 1709, Boston Public Library, MSS Acc.468 (1); Abbé Jean Baudoin, "Journal," Jan. 24, 1698, in Alan F. Williams, *Father Baudoin's War: d'Iberville's Campaigns in Acadia and Newfoundland 1696, 1697* (St. John's, 1987), 173–191 (esp. 183).

inner-bay settlements not far from Harbour Grace had excellent access to good timber, and, in the eighteenth century, the latter developed a ship-building industry, no doubt rooted in earlier experience with lumbering and boatbuilding. Carbonear was somewhat larger, with an overwinter-ing population of about one hundred in 1677, and could function as a central place for Conception Bay. John Pinn, one of the four "able men of estates" nominated in 1680 as administrators of a proposed tax scheme, belonged to a successful Carbonear planter family. Most of these inner-bay communities, including Port de Grave, Bay Roberts, Mosquito, Har-bour Grace, and Carbonear, consisted largely of family-based plantations with at least one woman present. Most had well-developed livestock agriculture by this time: Carbonear planters owned seventy-nine head of cattle in 1677, besides twenty-two sheep and forty-eight hogs. At the end of the century, Pierre Le Moyne d'Iberville's chaplain, Father Jean Baudoin, found the north shore of Conception Bay to be "much better established and more populated" than the coast between Renews and St. John's. He was impressed by the wealth of some of the Conception Bay plantations: "Harbour Grace has fourteen planters and Carbonear twenty-two, very well established, the best built in all of Newfoundland . . . these two places supply all the other English settlements with what they need, which attracts considerable business: there are people here worth one hundred thousand *livres* [about a quarter of a million dollars today]."[17]

Northward, the long-established outer-bay communities of Bay de Verde, on the northern side of the mouth of Conception Bay, and Old Perlican, nearby on the south side of the mouth of Trinity Bay, resembled Ferryland in several respects. They were relatively large, with eight and thirteen plantations respectively in 1677, with a number of middling or large plantations in both places. Bay de Verde was not very agricultural, but Old Perlican certainly was, thanks, perhaps, to the number of family-based plantations there. Both outports matched the old-settlement pat-tern of Ferryland, in terms of the moderate importance of the migra-tory fishery. As in Ferryland, planters' and ships' boats were balanced in a ratio of roughly one to one, and planters were not seasonally over-whelmed by migratory crews as they were at St. John's. Like Ferryland,

17. Alan D. Cass, "The Schooner *Jenny*," *Mariner's Mirror*, LXXXII (1996), 325–335; William Downing and Thomas Oxford, Proposals to CTP, Mar. 2, 1680, CO 1/44 (34), 85; Abbé Jean Baudoin, "Journal," Jan. 29, Feb. 11, 1698 (transla-tions are mine), in Williams, *Father Baudoin's War*, 173–191 (esp. 184, 186).

these were essentially resident fishing stations, not primarily service centers for the migratory fishery.[18]

Northern Trinity Bay was still Beothuk territory in the 1620s, and French Basque fishermen still frequented this shore in the 1640s, but, by the later seventeenth century, the English had begun to settle here as well. The community of Trinity would become an important central place in the eighteenth century, with a strong commitment to agriculture, lumbering, and boatbuilding, but, as late as 1677, it was still a scattered settlement of just three plantations, only one of which was a family-based household, although there were also plantations at nearby Bonaventure and Trouty. The tiny fleet of twelve resident fishing boats in this area was overshadowed by migratory crews, who worked seventy-one boats that summer in the Trinity area, between Bonaventure and English Harbour. Bonavista, on the headland between Trinity Bay to the south and Bonavista Bay to the north, was already considerably more developed as a community than Trinity. It was relatively large, with sixteen plantations in 1677, and resembled some of the older, smaller outharbors of the south Avalon. Although one planter, James Shambler, operated six boats, the average plantation there was not particularly large. As in Renews, Fermeuse, and Bay Bulls, the migratory fishery was important, without completely swamping the resident effort—the ratio of planters' to ships' boats being about 1 to 2.5.[19]

Bonavista Bay remained a frontier in the late seventeenth century, like inner Trinity Bay. Captain James Story's 1681 census lists twenty plantations, including some families in Keels and Salvage, with a handful of single planters in Barrow Harbour and Fair Island. Given Bonavista's position near what was then the northern limit of permanent European settlement, it inevitably became an interface both with the aboriginal Beothuk people and also with the Bretons and Basques, who had fished seasonally for almost two centuries on these coasts. Permanent English settlement threatened Native people, for it immediately reduced possibilities for scavenging iron on seasonally abandoned fishing posts. It also

18. For Old Perlican, the ratio was 1.0 to 0.7, planters' boats to ships' boats. Torbay represented the other extreme at 1 to 18.5 in favor of ships' boats.

19. G. William Gilbert, "Russell's Point (CiAj-1): A Little Passage/Beothuk Site at the Bottom of Trinity Bay" (master's thesis, MUN, 2001), 43; Handcock, *Origins*, 222–232; Jerry Bannister, "Citizen of the Atlantic: Benjamin Lester's Social World in England, 1768–69," *Newfoundland Quarterly*, XCVI, no. 3 (2003), 32–37.

tended, in the longer term, to exclude Natives completely from access to the coast. In the second half of the seventeenth century, migratory Basque fishermen experienced similar pressure to withdraw from Trinity Bay, still an open-access resource, into Bonavista Bay and, eventually, even farther northward. Bonavista occasionally suffered retaliation for its central role in English expansion in the area, although it also benefited from opportunities for trade.[20]

The late-seventeenth-century English Shore was structured both by its geography and by its history. The long-settled communities, Ferryland, St. John's, Carbonear, and Old Perlican, were relatively large and shared a commitment to livestock agriculture. Bonavista was beginning to play a similar role in the north. All had a core of substantial family-based plantations, though the St. John's area had also attracted many smaller plantations. Women were proportionately best represented in these traditional settlements. Like St. John's and the old south Avalon outport of Trepassey, the newer outer-bay settlements of Torbay and Trinity were strongly oriented to servicing the seasonal migratory fishery. The central ports of St. John's, Carbonear, and Ferryland served as provisioning links with Ireland and New England, whose small trading vessels, in turn, linked these English Newfoundland ports with the French Newfoundland capital of Plaisance. Communities near the limits of the English Shore naturally functioned, in part, as interfaces with the other peoples who inhabited or regularly used Newfoundland: the Normans, the Bretons, and the Basques on the south coast and the Beothuks, Bretons, and Basques on the northeast coast. Although Newfoundland communities differed in such ways, they also had much in common.[21]

20. James Story, "An Account of What Fishing Shipps, Sack Shipps, Planters, etc., Boat Keepers . . . ," Sept. 1, 1681, CO 1/47 (52i), 113-121. Settlements north of Bonavista were not mentioned in the censuses of 1675 and 1677, but that does not really establish when they were founded, since the naval commodores making these censuses did not get that far north. On the Beothuk, see Ralph T. Pastore, "Fishermen, Furriers, and Beothuks: The Economy of Extinction," *Man in the Northeast*, XXXIII (1987), 47-62. Downing, "Breif Narative," Nov. 24, 1676, British Library, Egerton MS 2395, 560-563, and Wheler, "Answers," Oct. 27, 1684, CO 1/55 (56), 239-246, report "Basques" fishing to the north. On trade, see Thomas Farr to CTP, Mar. 21, 1675, CO 1/34 (28), *CSP: Colonial*.

21. Downing, "Breif Narrative," Nov. 24, 1676, British Library, Egerton MS 2395, 560-563; John Mannion, "Victualling a Fishery: Newfoundland Diet and the Origins of the Irish Provisions Trade, 1675-1700," *IJMH*, XII (2000), 1-57. Downing reports that the Waterford merchant John Aylred had been in Plaisance.

Newfoundland's outports in the seventeenth century were more than seasonal fishing camps; but almost every harbor on the English Shore became a seasonal camp each spring, as migratory crews returned to claim their fishing rooms and pass the summer, fishing side by side with planter boatkeepers who had overwintered in these hamlets. How did fisherfolk, migratory and resident, share this economic space? And what exactly was that space? What did a seventeenth-century Newfoundland outport look like?

The youthful Plymouth surgeon James Yonge sketched the key elements of the industry when he worked as a kind of one-man medical service for crews fishing at Fermeuse and Renews in the summer of 1663 (Plate 16). Yonge's little drawing shows a *fishing room*, with a *shallop* returning to a large, covered, *fishing stage*, where the day's catch will be unloaded and then dried on a nearby *flake*, on a hill overlooking a convenient *cookroom*, where crews could be fed. Of these structures, the stage was the largest and most costly. This stage was, essentially, a wharf projecting up to sixty meters from shore, with a one-story enclosure at its seaward end, used for the initial processing of fish. Yonge described stages as "built out into the sea, a floor of round timber, supported with posts and shores of great timber" (Plate 17). Cabins, cookrooms, and the work space on the stage head were constructed of wattle: fir posts woven with what he called poetically "a frythe of boughs," sealed on the inside with bark rinds from balsam fir and roofed with rinds and turf or a sail. Accommodations for crews were small, and the Western Charter limited cookrooms to sixteen feet in length. For lodging, crews often made do with a *tilt*, a tent of fir poles under a canvas sail; or they might careen their ship itself and use it as the centerpiece of an extended tilt. In 1620, the Dutch shipmaster David de Vries saw ships at St. John's "without any men in them while the latter are fishing," adding that the fishing crews covered their ships with sails and "placing them on the land, build from them." The Basque master Jean de Castmayle careened his ship at Trinity in 1638, and two New England vessels, the *Hobline Galley* and the brigantine *Beginning*, were still doing the same thing at Caplin Bay, near Ferryland, in 1708.[22]

22. Denys, *Histoire naturelle*, 531–534; Gerald L. Pocius, "The House That Poor-Jack Built: Architectural Stages in the Newfoundland Fishery," in Larry McCann and Carrie MacMillan, eds., *The Sea and Culture of Atlantic Canada:*

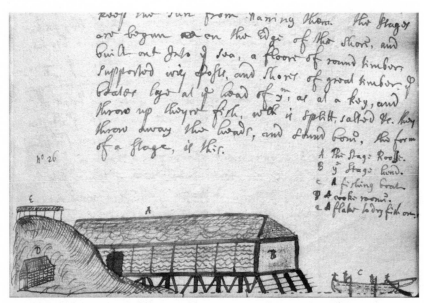

Plate 16. Fishing Stage, Shallop, and Cookroom, circa 1663. By James Yonge.
Pen-and-ink sketch. Courtesy, Plymouth Athenaeum

The flakes used to dry the fish were ramshackle platforms of fir boughs, erratically supported on posts (Plate 18). Where cobble beaches existed, as at Ferryland, shore crews simply spread boughs on the clean and convenient surface. When additional space was needed, the English were inclined to build flakes, whereas French fishermen usually chose to pave grassy areas with cobbles to prepare an artificial beach or *galet*, perhaps for lack of accessible wood. Yonge's sketch omits the *train vat*,

---

A Multidisciplinary Sampler (Sackville, N.B., 1992), 63–105; Mark Eliot Ferguson, "Making Fish: Salt-Cod Processing on the East Coast of Newfoundland: A Study in Historic Occupational Folklife" (master's thesis, MUN, 1996), 62–63; Yonge, *Journal*, 56; Downing, "Breif Narrative," Nov. 24, 1676, British Library, Egerton MS 2395, 560–563; Charles I in Council, Order, Jan. 24, 1634, CO 1/8 (1), clause 7, in Matthews, *Constitutional Laws*, 67–75; David Peterszoon de Vries, *Short Historical and Journal Notes of Several Voyages Made in the Four Parts of the World, Namely, Europe, Africa, Asia, and America* (1655), trans. Henry C. Murphy, New-York Historical Society, *Collections*, 2d Ser., III, pt. 1 (New York, 1857), 6; William Hill, Examination, in *Castemayle v. [Lewis] Kirke*, Apr. 18, 1642, HCA 13/58, 9–10; Benjamin Pickering, Deposition, in *Marston v. Holmes*, Jan. 29, 1709, Essex Institute, Salem, Mass., Court of Common Pleas, 3530, 14. On italicized terms in this section, see *DNE*. *OED* defines "fruz" as a collection of small branches.

Plate 17. Fish Flakes and Fishing Stages at Quidi Vidi, near St. John's. Circa 1900. Photograph C27881. Courtesy, National Archives of Canada

needed for rendering cod-liver oil, which might be a purpose-built box—as in the case of the furriers' boats—sometimes just a cask, or even an aging shallop.[23]

The scarcity of safe landings for small boats acted to concentrate summer populations in good harbors where stages could be easily built. Ordinary human sociability and the shared need for access to fresh water must have amplified this effect. The need for space to dry fish, whether on cobbles or on flakes, acted in the opposite direction, however, spreading fishing rooms apart from one another, since each boat crew had irreducible requirements. Archaeological reconnaissance around Fermeuse Bay and at Crouse on the Petit Nord, in the traditional French zone in northern Newfoundland, suggests that migratory fishing rooms and early plantations might be a kilometer or two apart, scattered around a suitable harbor. On the other hand, plantations and ships' rooms were already pressing one against another, every few hundred meters, in seventeenth-century St. John's, promoting the construction of flakes over

23. There is an excellent example of a cobble pavement, or *galet*, at Ferolle Island, near present-day Plum Point, and remnants of others are in the Trinity area.

Plate 18. A View of the Upper End of the Harbour . . . (St. John's),
Newfoundland. *[By Nicholas Pocock?], eighteenth century. NMC 003372.
Courtesy, National Archives of Canada*

otherwise unusable coastal fens. Like early St. John's, twentieth-century
Newfoundland fishing villages were often relatively nucleated. Closely
examined, though, even these later settlements turn out to extend flexibly
across the landscape, as did many of their early predecessors.[24]

Early North American fishing shallops were often double-enders and
probably closely resembled later Newfoundland boats or the similar
Hampton, Block Island, and Isle of Shoals boats of northern New En-

24. Peter E. Pope, "Fermeuse Area Survey, 2002," report on file, Culture and
Heritage Division, Newfoundland, 2003; Pope, "The Waterfront Archaeology of
Early Modern St. John's, Newfoundland," in Marinella Pasquinucci and Timm
Weski, eds., *Close Encounters: Sea- and Riverbourne Trade, Ports and Hinter-
lands, Ship Construction and Navigation (Antiquity, Middle Ages, Modern Times)*,
British Archaeological Reports (Oxford, forthcoming); Gerald L. Pocius, *A Place
to Belong: Community Order and Everyday Space in Calvert, Newfoundland* (Mon-
treal and Kingston, 1991); Robert Mellin, *Tilting: House Launching, Slide Hauling, Potato Trenching, and Other Tales from a Newfoundland Fishing Village* (New
York, 2003).

Plate 19. Fishing Boats Outside the Harbour Mouth, St. John's, Newfoundland. *By William Notman and son, 1909. Photograph C37556. Courtesy, National Archives of Canada*

gland (Plate 19). Shallops were also built with transom sterns, and one such is badly illustrated in the most widely copied depiction of the early Newfoundland fishery (compare Plate 20 and Plate 21). The hulls were probably planked in smooth carvel style over sawn frames, rather than with overlapping lapstrakes, although lapstrakes were sometimes used above the waterline. According to Nicholas Witsen's 1671 treatise on Dutch shipbuilding, "Shallops which go to the Greenland fishery are long, lightly constructed, narrow and sleek," and "on the bottom they are smoothed and painted white." Colonial boatbuilders likely still made do with pitch, and, in Newfoundland, train oil would have been an obvious vehicle for such tarry concoctions. A typical Newfoundland boat was about twenty-four feet long on the keel, hence thirty to thirty-five feet overall (ten meters), displacing about five tons, the size of its lineal descendants, the nineteenth-century western boat and the twentieth-century trap-skiff (the standard open boat of the inshore cod-trap fishery, powered by a simple inboard engine but still often carrying a stay sail).

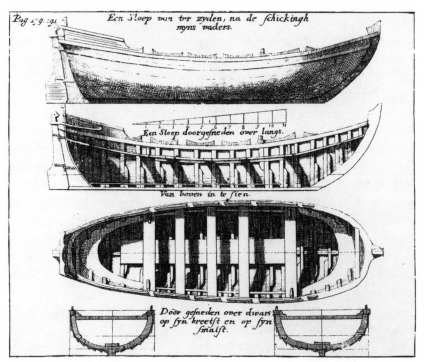

Plate 20. Dutch Shallop of 1671. By Nicholas Witsen. From Architectura Navalis et Regimen Nauticum *(Amsterdam, 1690). Note transom stern. Courtesy, Queen Elizabeth II Library, Memorial University of Newfoundland, St. John's*

The bare hull of a fishing shallop was worth six to eight pounds, completely fitted out, twenty to twenty-five pounds. Shallops could carry square sails on two masts or a single spritsail, but, as Yonge pointed out, fishing crews often had to rely on their oars.[25]

25. William A. Baker, *Colonial Vessels: Some Seventeenth-Century Sailing Craft* (Barre, Mass., 1962), 36–44; Joseph M. Herbert, "Descriptions of the Shallop in Western Europe and the New World, 1597–1671," *American Neptune*, LII (1992), 167–179 (esp. 169, 178–179); Howard Irving Chapelle, *American Small Sailing Craft, Their Design, Development, and Construction* (New York, 1951), 20–22, 136–177; Nicolaas Witsen, *Architectura Navalis et Regimen Nauticum* (1690; rpt. Amsterdam, 1972), 191 (translation from the 1671 edition adapted from Herbert, "Descriptions," *American Neptune*, LII [1992], 167–179); Downing, "Concerning Perticulars," Dec. 14, 1676, British Library, Egerton MS 2395, 564; *Historical Atlas of Canada*, I, 47; Nehemiah Trout, Deposition, Feb. 1, 1678, CO 1/42 (22), 58–59; Alexander Wood, "A True Account of the Vallue of the Shallop Hopewell," Deposition, in *Wood v. Chantrell*, Oct. 30, 1672, in *Suffolk Records*, pt. 1,

Plate 21. A View of a Stage and Also of the Manner of Fishing for, Curing, and Drying Cod at New Found Land. *By Herman Moll, 1720.*
With a badly illustrated transom-sterned shallop. NMC 24613.
Courtesy, National Archives of Canada

The material culture of settled communities was, of course, somewhat more complex. The Dutch artist Gerard Edema visited Newfoundland in the 1690s, and his painting of a permanent fishing room is the earliest surviving detailed representation of settlement on the Avalon Peninsula (Plate 22). Captain William Poole also provided a glimpse of this little world, even in the very headings he used to record his "Particular Accompt" of Newfoundland in 1677: "Dwelling Houses, Store Houses, Lodgings for Servants, Boats, Stages, Trainfats, Roomes . . . Garden, Pasture Land." Henry Codner's plantation in Renews was fairly typical, consisting of a dwelling house, where he lived with his wife, sons, and

160–161; cf. William Burley, Examination, in *Castmayle v. Kirke*, Apr. 16, 1642, HCA 13/58, 15–16; Yonge, *Journal*, 57. On twentieth-century inshore boats, see David A. Taylor, *Boat Building in Winterton, Trinity Bay, Newfoundland* (Ottawa, 1982), 56–82.

Plate 22. Newfoundland Fishing Station, circa 1690. By Gerard Edema. Detail. Permission of Royal Ontario Museum, Toronto

daughters; two storehouses for the fishing equipment needed for his two boats; a lodging for his nine servants; a fishing stage; and a train vat. Captain Poole does not report Codner's garden or pasturelands, but he records two "rooms," that is, the shore space needed to put two boats to sea every day and to process the fish that they caught. In Poole's census, the number of rooms recorded per planter is almost invariably the number of boats, but most planters with several boats managed to do with a single stage and train vat, although a few of the wealthier planters in 1677 had two stages, and John Downing, in St. John's, had three. Downing is also one of the handful of men in the 1677 census with two "dwelling houses," but he is less likely than the others, who lived in Conception and Trinity Bays, to have been practicing some form of winter-housing.[26]

26. D. W. Meinig, *The Shaping of America: A Geographical Perspective on Five Hundred Years of History*, I, *Atlantic America, 1492–1800* (New Haven, Conn., 1986), 88, follows the Royal Ontario Museum identification of this landscape as Placentia Bay. The museum's accession records indicate that the painting was originally identified simply as "A Fishing Station in Newfoundland" and that specific connection with Placentia Bay derives from an assumption made, on the basis of rocks and trees depicted, by the London dealer who supplied the picture. The

Most planters had but one house, and it was not large. Archaeological examples range in size from a small cabin in Renews, a little more than 14 by 21 feet (4.4 by 6 meters), inhabited around 1660, to the more substantial house built by the Newfoundland Company at Cupids after 1610 for John Guy's original colony and in use until about 1665, which was about 13 by 36.5 feet with an adjoining wing that was 12 by 30 feet (3.9 by 11.1 meters and 3.7 by 9.1 meters). A dwelling of about 18 by 39 feet (5.4 by 12 meters) overlooked the Ferryland Pool from about 1670 to 1696, and a less sturdily built contemporary house nearby measured 15 by 30 feet (4.6 by 9 meters). The Ferryland Mansion House, built by Edward Wynne for George Calvert in 1622 and later occupied by the Kirkes, was a bit larger: 15 by 44 feet with an adjoining kitchen 12 by 18 feet (4.6 by 12.4 meters and 3.4 by 5.1 meters). A new mansion, built by the Kirkes in the early 1650s, measured 21 by 64 feet (6.4 by 19.5 meters), with massive stone fireplaces in both gable walls. Augustine Fitzhugh's map of Newfoundland in 1693 has an inset of Ferryland, showing a gabled structure that just might be a depiction of the Kirkes' mansion, although displaced from its actual position near the Pool (Map 12). Except for the Calvert and Kirke mansions and the Cupids house built for John Guy, there is no evidence of partitions in these dwellings. Second-story lofts probably provided some separate sleeping and storage space, but the simpler planter houses seem to have functioned flexibly like Elizabethan open-hall houses, in which one open space served many functions.[27]

---

landscape is, in fact, reminiscent of the protected harbors of the south Avalon or the bottom of Conception Bay, regions much more accessible than Placentia Bay for a friendly visit by an English crew in the 1690s. Poole, "Particular Accompt," Sept. 10, 1677, CO 1/41 (61riv, vi, vii), 158–166, unfortunately did not gather information on gardens or pasturelands on the south Avalon, and he drops "pasture lands" as a category north of Ferryland and combines "Store Houses and Lodging Houses." In most of his census, Poole records shore space as "rooms or flakes." Downing's second house was probably either in the Virginia Water area, where he had a farm, or in Quidi Vidi, where he had property; see Paul O'Neill, *The Oldest City: The Story of St. John's, Newfoundland* (Erin, Ont., 1975), 45.

27. Stephen F. Mills, "The House That Yonge Drew? An Example of Seventeenth-Century Vernacular Housing at Renews," *Avalon Chronicles*, I (1996), 43–66; William Gilbert, "Finding Cupers Cove: Archaeological Excavations at Cupids, 1995–1999," report on file, Centre for Newfoundland Studies, MUN, 2000; Amanda Crompton, "A Planter's House at Ferryland, Newfoundland," *Avalon Chronicles*, V (2000), 1–48; Douglas Nixon, "A Seventeenth-Century

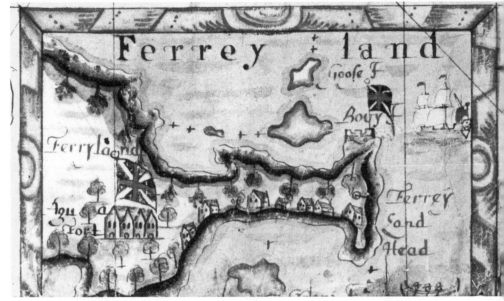

Map 12. Ferreyland. Detail from New Found Land, *by Augustine Fitzhugh, 1693. Add MSS 5415, 30. Permission of British Library, London*

The plan of these early Newfoundland dwellings resembled simple West Country houses, with a large stone fireplace at one gable end (Figure 3). In construction they are more typical of the New World, stone being limited to the hearth and sometimes a partial foundation, whereas the walls themselves were timber-framed with close studs, insulated perhaps with moss, and clad with clapboards, cut locally or imported from New England. A visitor in the 1680s described planters' houses as small, "low, and simply built, the best sort with sawd plancks from the foundation up, roof and all, others with the whol timber joyned together, standing stable wise and the roof covered with the rinde or bark of tress,

Planter's House at Ferryland, Newfoundland," *Avalon Chronicles*, IV (1999), 57–95; Wynne to Calvert, July 28, 1622, in Whitbourne, *Discourse*, 195–198; Peter Child, "Farmhouse Building Traditions," in Peter Beacham, *Devon Building: An Introduction to Local Traditions* (Tiverton, U.K., 1995), 33–46. Archaeological excavations support Wynne's description of the Calvert Mansion House and have uncovered the Kirke mansion (James Tuck, personal communication, October 2001). On use of space, cf. the Newfoundland kitchen in Pocius, *A Place to Belong*, 228–238.

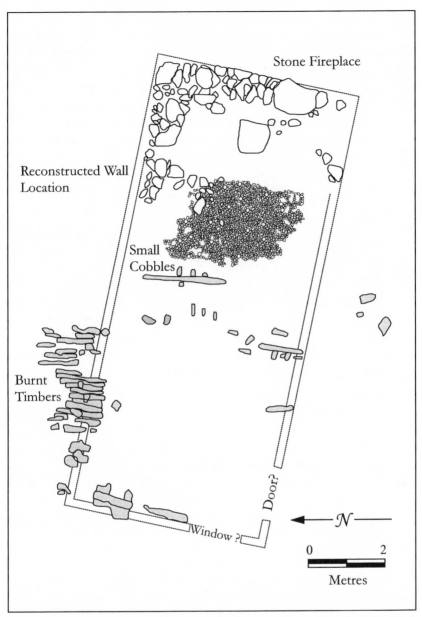

Figure 3. Plan of a Middling Newfoundland Planter's House, Ferryland (CgAf-2). In use circa 1670–1697. About fifteen by thirty feet. Drawn by Amanda Crompton and Ed Eastaugh

with green turfs cast over them." The small Renews house was roofed in this way; the larger houses probably had board roofs. Only the better-off could afford glazing: absolutely no window glass survives from the Renews house or the smaller Ferryland house, although finds of hinge hardware suggest some form of fenestration, even if only shuttered openings. Floors were generally earthen, sometimes over beach cobble, but the Cupids house and both the Ferryland mansion houses had wooden floors, and even the small Renews house might have had planks over a damp area near the hearth.[28]

Substantial hearths were, not surprisingly, a key feature of every planter house. Those excavated to date take up most of a gable wall. Housebuilders paved or floored a relatively large area in front of the hearth; in the Renews house, this area took up a third of the floor space. Fragments of ceramic dishes and wine cups, cutlery, bottle glass, clay tobacco pipes, and coins, excavated in these hearthside spaces, hint at their social function. Storage vessels tend to be found away from the hearths, on the other hand. These containers are very well represented in Newfoundland sites, reflecting the high priority that planters had to give to adequate food stocks. Agricultural and boatbuilding tools, fishhooks, netting needles, lead shot, and line weights, dispersed throughout these dwellings, attest to the functional flexibility that followed from their generally open plan. Although planters' houses were no smaller than ordinary dwellings elsewhere in colonial North America, they must often

28. M. W. Barley, "Rural Housing in England," in Joan Thirsk, ed., *The Agrarian History of England and Wales*, IV, *1500-1640* (London, 1967-), 696-766 (esp. 764-766), in H. P. R. Finberg, gen. ed., *The Agrarian History of England and Wales*; Nixon, "Planter's House," *Avalon Chronicles*, IV (1999), 57-95 (esp. 65-66); Downing, "Breif Narrative," Nov. 24, 1676, British Library, Egerton MS 2395, 560-563; Gerald L. Pocius, "Architecture on Newfoundland's Southern Shore: Diversity and the Emergence of New World Forms," Society for the Study of Architecture in Canada, *Bulletin*, VIII, no. 2 (1983), 12-19, 23; James P. P. Horn, "'The Bare Necessities': Standards of Living in England and the Chesapeake, 1650-1700," *Historical Archaeology*, XXII, no. 2 (1988), 74-91 (esp. 77-79). Quotation from John Thomas to Sir Richard [?], Codrington Library, All Souls College, Oxford University, Wynne Collection, MS 239, 229-230, in Peter Pope, "*A True and Faithful Account*: Newfoundland in 1680," *Newfoundland Studies*, XII (1996), 32-49. For finds of window hardware, see Matthew Carter, "A Seventeenth-Century Smithy at Ferryland, Newfoundland," *Avalon Chronicles*, II (1997), 73-106 (esp. 96).

have been more crowded, since Newfoundland households typically incorporated a significant number of servants, and those who overwintered could not stay in the simple wattle or canvas structures used for summer lodgings. The impressive size of early modern Newfoundland hearths is, among other things, an index of the socioeconomic role planters came to play as hosts and as the heads of extended households.[29]

Archaeologists have yet to identify a servants' lodging, so the arrangement and use of these structures remains speculative. Captain Poole's census does provide some information. Servants' lodgings were small and ordinarily provided accommodation for four or five men, that is, roughly a boat crew. Smaller planters generally dispensed with separate lodgings, presumably sharing space in their own houses with their servants. The number of servants employed is not always a good predictor of the number of lodgings for servants, however. Thomas Dodridge, for example, employed nine men at Fermeuse in 1677 yet kept four "lodgings for servants," which would seem to be more than he needed. Henry Cornish and William Bowden also invested heavily in lodgings there, and two other Fermeuse planters owned lodgings but no boats. In St. John's, Richard Hoppings had four servants to help prosecute the fishery with his single boat, yet he owned five "storehouses and lodgings houses." Three or four other St. John's planters seem likewise to have overinvested in outbuildings. Fermeuse was one of the older settlements in which migratory crews continued to dominate the fishery, and St. John's was even more strongly oriented to the migratory fishery, so it is a safe bet that these apparently surplus lodgings were hired out to migratory crews, as storehouses were. Such outbuildings would cluster closely around the planter's house, none of them very far from the water, arrayed intermittently with other plantations and seasonal fishing rooms along preferred stretches of protected shoreline. Petty Harbour was another settlement in which the migratory fishery was very dominant, and it was here that Captain Poole found "one poore woman which cannot follow the fishery but lets out her house and stage for yearly rent." Although the planter economy was based on the fishery, economic activity was not limited to fishing.[30]

29. On food storage, see Crompton, "Planter's House," *Avalon Chronicles*, V (2000), 1–48 (esp. 19–20).

30. Poole, "Particular Accompt," Sept. 10, 1677, CO 1/41 (61iv, vi, vii), 158–166. The boatless Fermeuse planters were Lawrence Hilliard and Abraham King.

Other significant, if less distinctive, features marked the economic landscape of the English Shore. The early settlers at Cupids built themselves a stone-lined cellar, and most planters would have had some such structure for winter storage of turnips, carrots, and other root vegetables. In the 1670s, the complex of buildings on the Ferryland waterfront was reconstructed, in part as a cow byre and storage shed of 35 by 37.5 feet (10.5 by 11.3 meters), partially paved in cobble, with a slate drain and a thatched roof. This agricultural investment, which almost certainly belonged to one of the Kirkes, was more substantial than most of the cowsheds, pigsties, or sheepfolds on the English Shore, but it was surely not the only one. The same might be said of the Ferryland smithy, which has a parallel at Cupids, the only other outport that has been intensively investigated archaeologically. Not every harbor had a full-time blacksmith; nor was almost every farmer-fisherman his own smith, as in medieval Iceland or Greenland. But every harbor needed a smithy, and someone in almost every harbor must have been capable of the ad hoc manufacture and repair of boat fittings.[31]

The impressive quay and warehouse, on which the Ferryland byre was later built, are more unusual (Plate 7). The work of Calvert's first site manager, Edward Wynne, these structures would have done a small West Country port proud. They would compare in size, for example, with the quay and customhouse of seventeenth-century Exeter. Ferryland's masonry seawall stands well over 3 feet high and runs at least 165 feet along the Pool (1 meter by 50 meters). The slate-roofed stone warehouse standing on this waterfront enclosed a 16-by-56-foot interior space (4.8 by 16.8 meters), partially floored in flagstones. A lead weight, for use on a balance scale, surviving in this archaeological context speaks of the commercial uses to which this substantial and secure structure was

---

Amanda Crompton, "A Seventeenth-Century Planter's House at Area D, Ferryland, Newfoundland" (master's thesis, MUN, 2001), 276, observes that planters employing fewer than twenty servants usually kept no separate lodgings. When smaller planters did keep separate lodgings, these were, likely, for rental to migratory crews. On storehouses, see Wheler, "Answers," Oct. 27, 1684, CO 1/55 (56), 239–246.

31. Gilbert, "Finding Cupers Cove," 15–17. Potatoes were not commonly grown in Newfoundland until about 1750. On the byre, see Barry Gaulton, "Seventeenth-Century Stone Construction at Ferryland, Newfoundland (Area C)," *Avalon Chronicles*, II (1997), 1–43 (esp. 16–18); on a smithy, see Carter, "Smithy at Ferryland," *Avalon Chronicles*, II (1997), 73–106.

put first by Calvert and later by the Kirkes, until it was demolished in a hail of cannonballs during the Dutch raid of 1673, which destroyed "commodities, cattle, household goods, and other stores" at Ferryland, though not, apparently, dwellings.[32]

St. John's, Carbonear, and Plaisance, the other seventeenth-century Newfoundland harbors that regularly functioned as ports, might have seen similar investment in permanent wharves and warehouses. An archaeological site on Water Street in St. John's, possibly part of Thomas Oxford's plantation, shows evidence of investment in waterfront improvement about 1665 in the cutting and filling of the steep natural shoreline, but the only early structures uncovered at this site are wooden. Such structures may in part reflect lower investment in St. John's when it was a proprietorship, or the continued dominance of migratory fishing interests there, or simply the difficulty of finding good building stone, in comparison with Ferryland. A 1751 map of St. John's harbor shows eight wharves, carefully distinguished from fishing stages. Where there are wharves, there must be warehouses, but, as yet, the archaeological evidence does not establish whether either were stone-built.[33]

James Yonge's sketch maps of several south Avalon outharbors in the 1660s are the earliest known plans of settlements on the English Shore. His map of Renews (Map 13) shows planters' and ships' fishing rooms interleaved along the north side of the harbor, in a zone where the for-

32. Robert Sherwood, Exeter Quay, ca. 1620, in C. G. Henderson, J. A. Dunkley, and J. Z. Juddery, "Archaeological Investigations at Exeter Quay," in S. R. Blaylock and C. G. Henderson, eds., *Exeter Archaeology 1985/6* (Exeter, 1987), 1–20; Gaulton, "Stone Construction at Ferryland," *Avalon Chronicles*, II (1997), 1–43 (esp. 10, 13–14, 25–27). Note that Exeter traded through Topsham and Exemouth and was itself only a small postmedieval port. On the Dutch attack, see Dudley Lovelace, "An Accompt of the Duch Fleet . . . ," Mar. 29, 1675, CO 1/34 (37), 85. A slightly confused account appears in Donald G. Shomette and Robert D. Haslach, *Raid on America: The Dutch Naval Campaign of 1672–1674* (Columbia, S.C., 1988), 197–205. Many cannon shot of various bores were uncovered in archaeological strata related to the 1673 destruction of the Ferryland waterfront.

33. Peter E. Pope, "1998 Excavations at 327 Water Street, St. John's, CjAe-08," 1999, and Pope, "Summer 2000 Excavations at 327 Water Street, St John's, CjAe-08," 2003, reports on file, Culture and Heritage Division, Newfoundland; James Bramham and Edmond Scott Hylton, "Plan of St. John's Harbour in Newfoundland," 1751, British Library, K Top. CXIX 104, copy in NAC, NMC 18046.

Map 13. Renooze Harbor. *By James Yonge, circa 1663.*
Courtesy, Plymouth Athenaeum

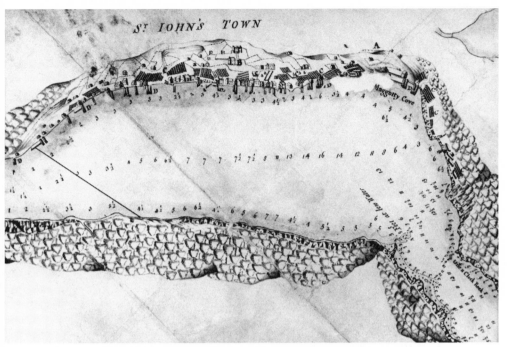

Map 14. A Plan of St. John's Harbour in Newfoundland, *circa 1728.*
War Office, WO 78/307. Detail. Permission of Public Record Office, London

est has been cut back, well away from the shore. "Biscayn Cove" hints at
earlier migratory fishers, by then displaced. The wildlife at "Bever Pond"
had probably changed by this time, too. The first detailed depiction of the
geography of settlement is an anonymous bird's-eye view of St. John's
in 1728. Construction details apart, it provides a clear sense of the arrangement of economic infrastructure in the landscape (Map 14). Fishing rooms are squeezed along the gentler northern slope of the harbor,
and, clearly, planters and migratory crews must have lived and worked
cheek by jowl. Late-seventeenth-century Plaisance was also crowded: a
contemporary map shows a stretch of protected shoreline densely occupied by habitants, while the nearby cobble beach is left for seasonal crews
(Map 15). Like Captain Poole's census, Edema's painting, or Yonge's
sketches, this map represents a moment in time: settlement in summer.
What of the rest of the year?[34]

34. Yonge also mapped Ferryland and Fermeuse; see *Journal*, plates 4, 7, 8.

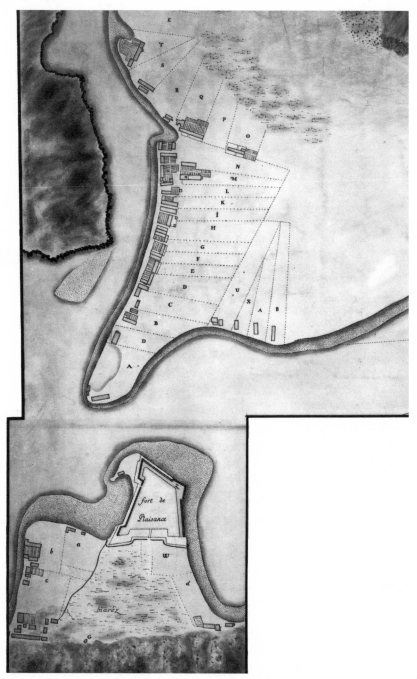

Map 15. Plan particulier du fort et des graves et habitations de Plaisance.
*By Jacques L'Hermitte, circa 1697. France, Dépôt de Fortification de Colonies,
carton 2, piece 109. Detail. NMC 113511-2. Courtesy, National Archives of
Canada*

The annual cycle of the European settlements in Newfoundland inevitably paralleled the seasonal cycle of the migratory fishery. In a sense, the latter drove the former. But the nine months between August and June were not the period of indolence that seventeenth-century opponents of settlement feared or that historians have sometimes, too hastily, assumed. Like seasonal workers in other new trades, Newfoundland planters soon devised dual employments. They included lumbering, boatbuilding or scavenging for French boats, agriculture, and what today would be called the "hospitality industry." These secondary sectors had a close relationship to the fishery. Even the trade in furs and skins, which was not directly linked to the fishery, was structured by the staple industry. Although overshadowed by the fishery, the other components of the nascent Newfoundland economy were critically important to the inhabitants, for they could not live by fish alone.[35]

The nine-month inshore fishery envisaged by some proponents of settlement was not possible on the English Shore, since cod did not appear in abundance on the east coast of the Avalon Peninsula much be-

35. Merchants of West Country Ports, "Reply . . . to the Allegations of Capt. Robert Robinson," ca. 1668, CO 1/22 (71); CTP, Report, Apr. 15, 1675, CO 1/65 (32i), 114–119; Josiah Child, *A New Discourse of Trade* . . . (London, 1693), 201; Gillian T. Cell, "The Cupids Cove Settlement: A Case Study of the Problems of Early Colonisation," in G. M. Story, ed., *Early European Settlement and Exploitation in Atlantic Canada* (St. John's, 1982), 97–114; Cell, *English Enterprise*, 79, 96. On dual employments, cf. Joan Thirsk, *Economic Policy and Projects: The Development of a Consumer Society in Early Modern England* (Oxford, 1978), 110, 155; John J. McCusker and Russell R. Menard, *The Economy of British America, 1607–1789* (Chapel Hill, N.C., 1985), 23–34. Some nascent industries are examples of backward linkage, that is, local production of inputs used to produce the staple export; others exhibit final demand linkage, investment in domestic production of consumer goods; see Melville H. Watkins, "A Staple Theory of Economic Growth," *Canadian Journal of Economics and Political Science*, XXIX (1963), 141–158. There are no obvious cases in seventeenth-century Newfoundland of forward linkage to industries using the staple product as an input and adding value by further processing. Watkins (153) proposes a shift from the wet, or green, cure to the dry cure as an example of forward linkage. This questionable idea probably arises from the mistaken theory that the dry fishery displaced an existing green fishery in Innis, *Cod Fisheries*, 21. Besides, the wet and dry cures are alternatives; neither wet nor dry fish is ready for the pan.

fore June and were gone by November (although French settlers based in Placentia Bay, which opens onto Newfoundland's south coast, were able to fish in the spring). The resident fishing season on the English Shore did extend into the fall, according to Captain Poole: "After the fishers are returned home, which is about the midst of September, the planters begin to fish againe and carry on the trade to the fine of October following (longer or sooner as the season permitts). The fish then catcht if well cured proves the best of all the yeares and is called winter fish." The eighteenth century would see some diversification from cod to other species, particularly salmon and, later, seals. Newfoundland exported some salmon in the seventeenth century (to Venice, among other markets), but this trade was not, as yet, significant. In any event, the salmon fishery takes place in midsummer. It would become, in some northern districts, an alternative to the cod fishery, but it could not provide a living in the off-season. How, then, did planters occupy themselves through the fall, winter, and spring, year after year, as they waited for the fish and the ships fishing to return?[36]

In late summer and early fall, Newfoundland is, for a month or two, a relatively rich environment. The early promoter of settlement, Richard Whitbourne, emphasized the plenty of berries and their health benefits. Berries are everywhere: particularly raspberries, blueberries, and partridge berries, an even tastier cranberry, equally easy to preserve. No one survived on berries, of course, but they were a healthy addition to a traditional maritime diet, which lacked good sources of vitamin C, besides the turnip. Fall is a good time, too, for hunting. Early accounts of Newfoundland stressed the availability of "deer," that is, woodland caribou, *Rangifer tarandus*. This emphasis reflected, in part, release from the class-based legal restrictions on the hunt in the home country. Although caribou were common in the south Avalon and on the Bay de Verde peninsula between Conception and Trinity Bays in the early seventeenth century, they became scarcer as the century wore on. They re-

36. "Some Modest Observations and Queries upon . . . Newfoundland," Mar. 25, 1675, CO 1/34 (32), 69–72; Wilfred Templeman, *Marine Resources of Newfoundland* (Ottawa, 1966), 40; cf. Ian K. Steele, *The English Atlantic, 1675–1740: An Exploration of Communication and Community* (New York, 1986), 83; William Poole, "Answers to the Severall Heads of Inquiry . . . ," Sept. 10, 1677, CO 1/41 (62i), 149–152; Head, *Newfoundland*, 176. On salmon exports, see [James] Hubland [Houblon] and [John] Gold [Gould], "Paper in Answer Mr. Dodington's . . . ," Nov. 28, 1673, CO 388/1, 80–82.

mained part of the subsistence economy, with catches in various seasons of trout, salmon, eel, bear, beaver, arctic hare, otter, seal, duck, goose, pigeon, and ptarmigan, not to mention the seabirds, like murre, auk, loon, puffin, and eider duck on which the servant scavengers in the case of the furriers' boat dined for more than a month in the late fall of 1679.[37]

Such expeditions had aims that went beyond subsistence. Beaver and otter were also hunted commercially for furs, as were muskrat, fox, ermine, marten, and lynx. Sixteenth-century fishermen had traded with Beothuks for skins: in 1598, the thirty-ton *Grace* of Bristol came home from Newfoundland with sixty "deer skins." Early residents were certainly aware of the potential value of furs and skins, and by the 1640s they were involved in furring. The emergence of *furriers*, or fur trappers of European origin, in the seventeenth century tended to isolate the Beothuks economically. Overwinterers went "with their trapps and gunns a furring," promoting European settlement and therefore increasing competition for coastal resources, although in the short term Beothuks gained further opportunities for scavenging iron in the form of trap parts. References to beaver in the south Avalon suggest that furring was common there as late as the 1660s, and the case of the furriers' boats

37. Whitbourne, *Discourse*, 120; J. K. Crellin, "'The Aire in Newfoundland Is Wholesome Good': The Medical Landscape of Newfoundland in the Seventeenth Century," *Avalon Chronicles*, IV (1999), 1–24; D. Dodds, "Terrestrial Mammals," in G. Robin South, ed., *Biogeography and Ecology of the Island of Newfoundland* (The Hague, 1983), 509–549; P. B. Munsche, "The Gamekeeper and English Rural Society, 1660–1830," *Journal of British Studies*, XX (1981), 82–105; Roger B. Manning, *Hunters and Poachers: A Social and Cultural History of Unlawful Hunting in England, 1485–1640* (Oxford, 1993), 232–236; John Guy to John Slaney, May 16, 1611, in Prowse, *History*, 125–127; Henry Crout to Percival Willoughby, Apr. 13, 1613, in Cell, *Newfoundland Discovered*, 79–89; Poole, "Answers," Sept. 10, 1677, CO 1/41 (62i), 149; [John] Graydon, "Answers to the Heads of Enquiry," Sept. 20, 1701, CO 194/2 (20), 176–178; Yonge, *Journal*, 60. For archaeological analysis of faunal remains, see Lisa Hodgetts, "Seventeenth-Century English Colonial Diet at Ferryland, Newfoundland," postdoctoral report on file, Archaeology Unit, MUN, 2003; for plant remains, see Michael Deal and Aaron Butt, "The Great Want: Current Research in Beothuk Paleoethnobotany," in Sarah L. R. Mason and Jon G. Hather, eds., *Hunter-Gatherer Archaeobotany: Perspectives from the Northern Temperate Zone* (London, 2002), 15–27. For a fine discussion of local subsistence, see Gilbert, "Russell's Point," 20–36. On seabirds, see William Threlfall, "Seabirds," in South, ed., *Biogeography of Newfoundland*, 467–496.

makes plain that in the 1670s it was still "usuall for some of the English" from that region to go furring in St. Mary's Bay. Fishing ships sometimes arrived in England with respectable cargoes of furs: Mark Bickford imported twenty-five "catts skinns" (that is, lynx), twenty beaver, sixty-nine otter, and thirteen "ordinary fox skinns" on the *Unity* of Dartmouth in October 1666. Contemporary estimates of the annual value of the trade toward the end of the seventeenth century ranged as high as two thousand pounds. In the 1680s, Captain Francis Wheler found the fur trade "not inconsiderable," at least regionally, and Captain James Story put it at about five hundred pounds, "most att Bonavista and farther northerly." According to Story: "The planters go out a furring about the middle of September and live in the woods but carry with them no provisions only bread and salt, for they find food bevers, otters, and seales enough to feed on which they kill with gunns they alwayes carry with them and likewise they kill a great deale of veneson, which they salt upp, and it serves them for their winter provision and then turne back to theire habitations by the first of May." In fact, the "gangs of men" who went to "stay in the woods all the winter" were more often fishing servants, as in the case of the furriers' boats, rather than planters themselves.[38]

38. Bristol Port Books, 1598, E 190/1132/9, in J. Vanes, ed., *Documents Illustrating the Overseas Trade of Bristol in the Sixteenth Century* (Bristol, 1979), 161; John Poyntz, Instructions Given to Sir Henry Salusbury, 1626, in Cell, *Newfoundland Discovered*, 246-249; David Kirke, "A Narrative Made by the Latt Governor," ca. 1652, British Library, Egerton MS 2395, 259-261; Ralph Pastore, "The Collapse of the Beothuk World," *Acadiensis*, XIX, no. 1 (1989), 52-71 (esp. 57); "Modest Observations," Mar. 25, 1675, CO 1/34 (32), 69-72; Yonge, *Journal*, 60; Mathews, "Concerning the French," Jan. 27, 1671, British Library, Egerton MS 2395, 471; Dartmouth Customer, Port Books 1666, E 190/954/10; cf. Todd Gray, "Fishing and the Commercial World of Early Stuart Dartmouth," in Todd Gray, Margery Rowe, and Audrey Erskine, eds., *Tudor and Stuart Devon: The Common Estate and Government: Essays Presented to Joyce Youings* (Exeter, 1992), 173-199 (esp. 182). The *Grace* encountered Beothuks in a 1594 expedition; see Ingeborg Marshall, *A History and Ethnography of the Beothuk* (Montreal and Kingston, 1996), 21-24. Calvert's men took furs; see George Calvert [to Francis Cottington], Aug. 18, 1629, in Cell, *Newfoundland Discovered*, 292-294. On the value of the trade around 1700, see Marshall, *Beothuk*, 80-83, table 5.1. Davies, "Policy and Trade," 245-247, provides eighteenth-century evidence for significant imports of skins from Newfoundland to the West Country—but this could be misleading if sealskins, for example, are not distinguished from other "skins." Quotes from Wallis, Examination, Aug. 24, 1680, CO 1/45 (68i), 252-253; Wheler, "An-

Planters were more likely to remain close to salt water, where they could invest time working on the infrastructure of the fishery, particularly fishing boats. John Downing boasted that Newfoundland fishing shallops were "built in the country . . . of the country wood." Migratory crews took it for granted that they would be able to buy boats or the lumber to build them in Newfoundland. These industries were of long standing: John Guy and George Calvert both had boats built locally for their fishing operations in the early seventeenth century. Captain Poole explained why this industry made the planters particularly useful to the fishers: "All the winter they employ their people in the woods to fell trees to saw into boards to build boats and make oars against the next season, that the fishers may be accommodated to begin their fishing as soone as they arrive." In his 1678 defense of settlement, Nehemiah Troute emphasized that lumbering by the inhabitants made possible the building of boats, a "privillege" the English enjoyed in Newfoundland, whereas the French brought their boats from France, "they having not the advantage of his Majesties forest." On the English Shore, two local industries, lumbering and boatbuilding, were thus linked serially to the requirements of staple production.[39]

By the later seventeenth century, these related wood industries had become important off-season activities for the planters. Consider the construction of fishing shallops: these were made of softwoods, had little

swers," Oct. 27, 1684, CO 1/55 (56), 239-246; and Story, "Account," Sept. 1, 1681, CO 1/47 (52i), 113-121 (esp. 116).

39. Downing, "Concerning Perticulars," Dec. 14, 1676, British Library, Egerton MS 2395, 564; John Scantlebury, "John Rashleigh of Fowey and the Newfoundland Cod Fishery, 1608-20," *Royal Institution of Cornwall Journal*, N.S., VIII (1978-1981), 61-71 (esp. 66); Benjamin Marston, Instructions to Robert Holmes, Apr. 20, 1708, Essex Institute, Essex Co. Court of Common Pleas, 3530, 14. Merchants did not supply planters with boats (pace Matthews, *Lectures*, 21), nor were they even regularly imported for English migratory fishermen (pace Norrie and Owram, *History of the Canadian Economy*, 58). On Guy and Calvert, see Cell, *English Enterprise*, 64; Anne Love, "Examination and Deposition . . . ," Aug. 31, 1652, Amy Taylor, "Examinations and Depositions . . . ," Aug. 24, 1652, John Slaughter, "The Examination and Deposition . . . ," Aug. 31, 1652, all in Md. HS, Calvert MSS 174/200, in Scisco, "Testimony." Quotations from Poole to CTP, Sept. 10, 1677, CO 1/41 (62), 147-148; and Troute, Deposition, Feb. 1, 1678, CO 1/42 (22), 58-59. Transport systems for staple collection are, historically, the prime example of backward linkage; see Watkins, "Staple Theory," *Canadian Jour. Econ. Pol. Science*, XXIX (1963), 141-158 (esp. 145).

protection from the elements, and were given hard use. Their average working life was no more than five to eight years. The planters were operating about three hundred boats in the 1670s, the migratory fishermen about nine hundred. These figures imply a demand for about two hundred boats a year in a period when there were only about that many planter households. Boatbuilding must have been an important activity for many of these households for several months every year. Although boatbuilding was worth less than 5 percent of the wholesale value of fish produced by the planters, it probably accounted for roughly 20 percent of their net income. Similar conjectural estimates could be made for the production of oars or the cutting of timber for stages, cookrooms, train vats, and flakes. Ships fishing exported significant cargoes of timber to the West Country in the early eighteenth century, and as early as 1684 Captain Wheler thought Newfoundland's forests were overexploited. Wood industries were a significant part of the planter economy. One of their advantages was the timing of these occupations, which are conveniently carried on in late winter and early spring, when there is still some snow in the woods and before mosquitoes and black flies have hatched. During this time of year, Newfoundland fisherfolk also had to turn their minds to agricultural pursuits, for which there would be less time once the fishing season was under way.[40]

Newfoundland's agricultural limitations impress visitors from geologically better-favored regions, and seventeenth-century visitors were no exception. As Captain Wheler put it, cynically, "The colony is not able to support itselfe, the earth, or rather the rock, producing nothing

40. Some biased estimates in the 1640s put the useful life of a Newfoundland fishing boat at three years, but rental rates in the 1680s suggest greater durability; see William Hill, Examination, in *Baltimore v. Kirke*, Feb. 15, 1653, HCA 13/67, n.p.; Francis Wheler, "The Charge for Fitting Out Two Boats . . . according to the Custome of the Inhabitants . . . ," Oct. 27, 1684, CO 1/55 (56iii), 251–252. About 1800, Lloyds classified Newfoundland ships of spruce and juniper as first-class risks for seven years and those of fir and black birch, for four years; see "Rules Adopted by the Committee of the New Register-Book of Shipping," in [Lloyds], *New Register Book of Shipping for the Year 1800* (London, n.d.), n.p. Total recorded value of planter fish production in 1680 was £42,087; see "Abstract of the Newfoundland Fishery . . . ," 1680, CO 1/46 (78), 152–153. The boatbuilding industry was probably worth something between £1,500 and £2,000. Poole, "Answers," Sept. 10, 1677, CO 1/41 (62i), 149–152, emphasizes the role of woods industries, including exports; on the eighteenth century, see Davies, "Policy and Trade," 244–246.

for the life of man." In fact, hardy vegetables and grains and the suite of domestic animals that have followed northern Europeans since the Bronze Age could be raised on the English Shore without much difficulty. Seventeenth-century settlements in Newfoundland were situated to access marine resources, but, where good soil was available, this resource was exploited as well. Although the commercial value of agricultural products was not high, they answered specific local needs. Most historians have admitted as much, even if some have exhibited an unreflective skepticism about agriculture in early Newfoundland. The quasi-Marxist claim that West Country fishing interests discouraged agriculture, as part of a strategy of class domination, is even more implausible. The evidence for this interpretation is scant, and it depends on ignoring the agriculture that did exist on the English Shore. There is no need for a complex explanation of why Newfoundland's agricultural development was constrained in the early modern period: it could not compete with the fishery. As Sir Robert Robinson put it in 1680, more arable land and pastureland could be created, "but tis not done by reason the fishing trade is more profitable." Labor was not available for agriculture in the English mode. "Servants wages are soe excessive, that clearinge ground and sewinge corne will not be to profitt," Captain Charles Talbot argued in 1679. The point is well taken: Newfoundland fishermen could earn much more than contemporary farm laborers. These reports somewhat exaggerated, however, the preponderance of the fishery.[41]

41. For visitors' views, see Handcock, *Origins*, 39. Quotations from Wheler, "Answers," Oct. 27, 1684, CO 1/55 (56), 239–246; Robert Robinson, "Inquiries Made . . . in Answer to Severall Heads . . . ," Oct. 11, 1680, CO 1/46 (8x), 33–34; Charles Talbot, "Answers to the Enquiries . . . ," Sept. 15, 1679, CO 1/43 (121), 214–217; and cf. Colonel Gibson to CTP, June 28, 1697, CO 194/1 (81), 159–160. On agriculture as a response to local needs, see Head, *Newfoundland*, 45; Sean Cadigan, "The Staple Model Reconsidered: The Case of Agricultural Policy in Northeast Newfoundland, 1785–1855," *Acadiensis*, XXI, no. 2 (1992), 48–71. See Cell, *English Enterprise*, 79, 96, and Mannion, "Victualling a Fishery," *IJMH*, XII (2000), 1–57 (esp. 6), for doubts about horticulture. Even the best discussion of early Newfoundland agriculture dates its beginnings a half-century too late; see Robert MacKinnon, "Farming the Rock: The Evolution of Commercial Agriculture around St. John's, Newfoundland, to 1945," *Acadiensis*, XX, no. 2 (1991), 32–61. For a theory about repression of agriculture, see Gerald M. Sider, "The Ties That Bind: Culture and Agriculture, Property and Propriety in the Newfoundland Village Fishery," *Social History*, V (1980), 1–39; and Sider, *Culture and Class in Anthropology and History: A Newfoundland Illustration* (Cambridge, 1986), 112–

Newfoundland planters were, in fact, active gardeners who had, as John Downing boasted, "cleansed the wilderness" and kept livestock, in particular pigs and cattle. In 1677, 80 percent of the planter households in St. John's, for example, had gardens, some of them more than one garden, so that there were even more gardens than households. Crops included peas, beans, lettuce, radishes, carrots, turnips, cabbages, and, occasionally, oats, rye, and barley. Since grains ship well and could be produced more cheaply in England itself, vegetables took precedence, as the experienced Conception Bay planter Nicholas Guy indicated in 1626 when he recommended, to those intending to settle, "seede for all sortes of garden herbes and rootes for the kitchen." Early colonists realized that vegetables were important to control scurvy. Although they had no clear idea of what it was that antiscorbutics provided, contemporaries with an interest in settlement understood that a staple diet of bread, peas, and salt meat put health at risk. Gardens therefore filled an important health function in the seventeenth-century Newfoundland subsistence economy.[42]

Livestock played a larger role in the commercial economy. In the Conception Bay, St. John's, and south Avalon areas, most planters kept swine. That this practice was already taken to be the norm in the 1640s is suggested by the annual rent Sir David Kirke imposed on planters: £3 6s. 8d. "and a fatt hogg." Swine husbandry is an efficient sideline for fish processors, since swine can be fed on fish offal. More than half the planters in 1677 kept more than five hogs. Keeping five hogs might, conceiv-

---

115. On lack of evidence for Sider's theory, see Cadigan, "The Moral Economy of the Commons: Ecology and Equity in the Newfoundland Cod Fishery, 1815-1855," *Labour/Le Travail*, XLIII (Spring 1999), 9-42 (esp. 13-14). For wage rates, see Chapter 5, above.

42. John Downing, Petition to Charles I, Nov. 7, 1676, CO 1/38 (33), 69. There were twenty-eight gardens and twenty-seven households in St. John's in 1677; see Poole, "Particular Accompt," Sept. 10, 1677, CO 1/41 (61iv, vi, vii), 158-166. On crops, see Wynne to Calvert, July 28, Aug. 17, 1622, in Whitbourne, *Discourse*, 195-198, 200-204; Poole, "Answers," Sept. 10, 1677, CO 1/41 (62i), 150; Poyntz, Instructions Given to Sir Henry Salusbury, 1626, in Cell, *Newfoundland Discovered*, 246-249. On antiscorbutics, see William Colston to John Slany, July 29, 1612, in Samuel Purchas, *Hakluytus Posthumus; or, Purchas His Pilgrims: Contayning a History of the World in Sea Voyages and Lande Travells by Englishmen and Others* (1625) (Glasgow, 1905-1907), XIX, 417-424; Crout to Willoughby, Apr. 13, 1613, in Cell, *Newfoundland Discovered*, 79-86; William Vaughan, *The Newlanders Cure . . .* , 7th ed. (London, 1630), 51, 67-74.

ably, be construed as a subsistence activity, but the thirty swine Edward Haine kept at Petty Harbour or the twenty the younger David Kirke kept at Ferryland were clearly commercial ventures. In 1677, about a quarter of Conception Bay, St. John's, and south Avalon planters kept more than ten hogs. Cattle were even more clustered in distribution. Most planters did not keep cows, but, of the 30 percent who did, only a few kept one or two. Not all herds were as large as John Downing's, with thirty-five head, at St. John's, but the average herd consisted of eight cattle there, and herds were even larger in Conception Bay. Such figures suggest something verging on commercial agriculture, in which context we might note the export of hides to the West Country, for example, to Barnstaple in 1664 as well as the large byre excavated at Ferryland, with its impressive archaeological assemblage of north Devon and south Somerset coarse earthenware milk pans.[43]

Cattle and swine were probably both kept primarily as sources of fat, a key nutritional requirement, lacking in a diet based on fish taken from the sea and on the import of peas, bread, and malt. Butter could be imported from the British Isles, of course, and was: the baluster-shaped tall pots produced in North Devon for the shipment of butter are the most common ceramic form recovered from seventeenth-century archaeological contexts at Ferryland. On the other hand, commercial butter was "under a bad repute" in the mid-seventeenth century because of abuses in packing, oversalting, and weighing—a situation that particularly affected maritime victualing. There was an incentive, then, in seventeenth-century Newfoundland, to keep cattle for dairy products, as they were generally kept at this time in England itself. Although early modern swine were certainly valued for roasting when they were small, "great pigges" or "fatt hoggs" were, essentially, ambulatory stores of fat. Like the cattle of the bigger planters, the hogs that the great majority of planter households raised were animal mechanisms for transforming available resources into fat, something that was otherwise an expensive import.[44]

43. Poole, "Particular Accompt," Sept. 10, 1677, CO 1/41 (61iv, vi, vii), 158–166; Cruse, Deposition, Nov. 27, 1667, WDRO Plymouth, W360/74; Barnstaple Customer, Port Books, 1664, E 190/954/2. Cf. Mannion, "Victualling a Fishery," *IJMH*, XII (2000), 1–57 (esp. 6–7).

44. Alison Grant, *North Devon Pottery: The Seventeenth Century* (Exeter, 1983), 91–96; Peter Edward Pope, "Ceramics from Seventeenth Century Ferryland, Newfoundland (CgAf-2, locus B)" (master's thesis, MUN, 1986), 188, table

The livestock agriculture practiced by most planters might be seen as subsistence, since the produce would have been consumed largely within their own households. On the other hand, the numbers of cattle and pigs owned were, on average, far in excess of numbers kept by most rural households in the West of England, and livestock products, like butter, inevitably found a market among crews visiting Newfoundland. Planter households were themselves commercial operations, one of the functions of which was to serve the migratory fishery.[45]

This early hospitality industry was the most important of the secondary economic sectors driven by the economic pump of the migratory fishery. Proponents of settlement emphasized the aid inhabitants gave to fishermen separated from their ships early in the season or to those sick or injured. Captain Poole told the Committee for Trade and Plantations that, when ships bound for the fishery encountered ice or unfavorable winds, "they usually dispatch away their boates to take possession of the harbour (for first come, first served) whilst they get upp with their ships, which sometimes they cannot doe in ten or 12 days tyme." Poole asked the Committee to consider "what would become of such poore men at such a cold season, if they were not releeved by the planters?" He also pointed out that migratory fishers, once they reached their fishing rooms, were dependent on Newfoundlanders should they fall sick: "Heere are no other nurseries for them but the planters houses, which are allways at their service, and their wifes to attend them."[46]

Opponents of the Newfoundland Plantation stressed a different aspect of planter hospitality: almost every home in Newfoundland functioned as a tippling house, providing fishermen with their preferred luxuries, tobacco and alcohol. In seventeenth-century England, working people found temporary accommodation and alcohol in a single institution, the

11; John Collins, *Salt and Fishery* . . . (London, 1682), 137; C. Anne Wilson, *Food and Drink in Britain: From the Stone Age to Recent Times* (Harmondsworth, 1984), 150; cf. Crout to Willoughby, Apr. 13, 1613, in Cell, *Newfoundland Discovered*, 79–86.

45. Alan Everitt, "Farm Labourers," in Thirsk, ed., *Agrarian History*, IV, *1500–1640*, 396–465 (esp. 415, table 7), in Finberg, gen. ed., *Agrarian History*; Thomas Bushrode, Debit Account regarding the *Susan*, Mar. 18, 1648, *Aspinwall Records*, 205.

46. James Houblon to Robert Southwell, Mar. 20, 1675, CO 1/65 (23), 97; Troute, Deposition, Feb. 1, 1678, CO 1/42 (22), 58–59; John Carter et al., "Severall Reasons Offered for Not Removing the Planters," ca. 1680, CO 1/46 (77), 151; Poole to CTP, Sept. 10, 1677, CO 1/41 (62), 147–148.

alehouse. So it was nothing out of the ordinary to find Newfoundland planters operating tippling houses that combined the functions of the modern boardinghouse and tavern. The boarding function came to seem more important in the eighteenth century, and the term *dieter* evolved to describe fishermen who overwintered with planters who were not their masters. The retailing of wine and tobacco were relatively more important earlier.[47]

That certain investors in the migratory fishery took a puritanically dim view of the commercial hospitality that planters regularly extended to fishermen does not, of course, diminish the value of these services to those who worked day in and day out, lodged in rough accommodations, in what could be a cold and damp environment. Tippling houses were part of the infrastructure of home ports like Dartmouth—why not of fishing stations? Once cod arrived inshore, practical constraints on the timing of commercially viable operations condemned both shore and boat crews to a rigid schedule and intensive labor. Sometimes this regimen meant going with little sleep. As Yonge observed: "Sometimes the boys are so tired with labour they will steal off and hide under the flakes, or get into the woods and sleep 3 or 4 hours, so hearty that they feel not the muscetoes, who by the time he wakes shall have swoln him blind." Downing wrote that crews might work "from Sunday night to Saturday night resting onlie in ther beds onlie Saturday night." "Some rest not it: the dayes except Sundayes they atend codd catching." Since Sundays were the sole regular break enjoyed by crews on the English Shore, it is not surprising that tension developed around the issue of whether those days were to be passed in prayer or with a bottle of wine. Nor is it hard to understand why planters came to be identified with what we might think of as the consumer option.[48]

47. Petition of the Merchant Adventurers of Plymouth, England, to the Council of State, ca. 1650, *Winthrop Papers*, VI, 4-6; Gentry of Exeter, Dartmouth, Totnes, etc., Petition, Mar. 25, 1675, CO 1/65 (25), 100; Peter Clark, *The English Alehouse: A Social History, 1200-1800* (London, 1983), esp. 128-139; *DNE*, s.v. "dieter."

48. Gray, "Early Stuart Dartmouth," in Gray, Rowe, and Erskine, eds., *Tudor and Stuart Devon*, 173-199 (esp. 176). On schedules, cf. Jean-François Brière, *La pêche française en Amérique du nord au XVIIIe siècle* (Saint-Laurent, Quebec, 1990), 59, 261-262. Quotations from Yonge, *Journal*, 60; and John Downing, "The Maner of Catching and Makeing Drie Fishe in Newland," 1676, British Library, Egerton MS 2395, 565-566.

In such matters, the English Shore closely resembled regions else-where in which migratory fisheries depended, in part, on the presence of a certain number of permanent residents, who were in turn dependent on their seasonal visitors. In the seventeenth century, these similar regional economies included Maine, then seasonally exploited by fishermen from southern New England; southern Iceland, then exploited by both English and French fishers; western Ireland, still an important fishery for West Country crews, who had used the region since the preceding century; the Lofoten Islands, off northwestern Norway, used by fishermen from other parts of the Norwegian coast; and the Novgorod coast of Russia's White Sea, where Dutch fishermen arrived every summer to set up fishing camps in an environment remarkably similar to Newfoundland. To varying degrees, these were all places outside regular political administration, where the rule of law was reputed to be problematic. In each, a similar symbiosis emerged between transient seamen and hospitable residents who were willing to turn fish into wine.[49]

49. Charles E. Clark, *The Eastern Frontier: The Settlement of Northern New England, 1610-1763* (1970; rpt. Hanover, N.H., 1983); Evan Jones, "England's Icelandic Fisheries in the Early Modern Period," in David J. Starkey, Chris Reid, and Neil Ashcroft, eds., *England's Sea Fisheries: The Commercial Sea Fisheries of England and Wales since 1300* (London, 2000), 36–45; John C. Appleby, "A Nursery of Pirates: The English Pirate Community in Ireland in the Early Seventeenth Century," *IJMH*, II (1990), 1–27; Pal Christensen and Alf Ragnar Nielssen, "Norwegian Fisheries, 1100-1970: Main Developments," in Poul Holm, David J. Starkey, and Jón Th. Thór, eds., *The North Atlantic Fisheries, 1100-1976: National Perspectives on a Common Resource* (Reykjavik, 1996), 145–167 (esp. 152–153); J. W. Veluwenkamp, "The Murman Coast and the Northern Dvina Delta as English and Dutch Commercial Destinations in the Sixteenth and Seventeenth Centuries," *Arctic*, XLVIII (1995), 257–266.

10 🐟 FISH INTO WINE

*The inhabitants . . . have ben very distructive and prejudiciall to the
said fishing trade . . . and by keepeing of tipling houses and selling of
brandy and other strong waters, wine, beere, and tobacco, deboist the
fishermen sent thither in fishing voyadges and thareby hinder them
and detaine them from theire imployments to the greate losse in the
voyadges . . . and cause them to expend and waste a greate part of
theire wages.*
—Christopher Selman, Deposition, Nov. 27, 1667

Since the early 1650s, Christopher Selman had sailed from Dartmouth
"to use Newfoundland," as he put it. His testimony, taken at nearby
Totnes, was intended to discredit the planters. We might be inclined,
therefore, to discount his inflammatory language, or at least to suspend
judgment on whether planters did, in fact, debauch crews with alcohol and tobacco, provoking a "waste" of earnings. Selman's opinion depended on a particular ideological view of the consumer demands working persons might properly make. Such views are part of the history of
early modern Newfoundland, indeed, of the whole North Atlantic world,
but are best set aside, for the nonce, in the interests of answering simpler
and more fundamental questions: What did fisherfolk exchange for fish?
And why?[1]

Others, less biased than Selman, were struck by the quantities of alcohol and tobacco imported into seventeenth-century Newfoundland. Several impartial observers suggest such sales were, essentially, how the
planters balanced their books. Surviving inventories, cargo manifests,
and archaeological remains confirm these reports. Making sense of this
pattern of demand requires a broader strategy, however. To answer the
more complex question of what the consumption of little luxuries like
wine and tobacco meant to the men and women who lived and worked in
the early modern fishery, we must put consumption at the fishing periphery within a wider North Atlantic cultural context. To the extent that
we can interpret demand in this manner, we will be better able to re-

1. Christopher Selman, Deposition, Nov. 27, 1667, WDRO Plymouth, W360/
74.

turn to the issue of social control implicit in Selman's prejudices about appropriate forms of consumption.[2]

To ask why the early European inhabitants of Newfoundland turned fish into wine is to raise wider issues. These issues pertain to customs of use as much as to problems of abuse. Although alcoholism has attracted a great deal more scholarly attention than the normal use of alcohol, cross-cultural studies suggest that few societies treat alcohol as a problem, even if drinking is customary or drunkenness common. From the external point of view of a migratory fishing master, the abuse of alcohol was problematic, but it does not seem to have been a significant cultural issue within the English Shore itself, where the consumption of alcohol had other meanings. For fishing servants, drinking and smoking were social activities that helped them to deal with the difficulties of living in crowded conditions, close to the scene of production, and far from their own homes. For both planters and crews, the sharing of drink facilitated or reinforced social transactions, while the consumption of specific drinks satisfied perceived metabolic needs. Whatever the significance of alcohol to fisherfolk, the pattern of demand epitomized in the exchange of fish for wine exemplifies the strategic role played by maritime communities in the development of a consumer society.[3]

⁊ᵹ Consumer Revolution

Many years ago, Eric Hobsbawm posed a fundamental question about the rise of capitalism: Why was the economic expansion of the fifteenth and sixteenth centuries interrupted by a protracted seventeenth-century economic crisis, which delayed a decisive industrial revolution until the

2. Cf. Sara Pennell, "Consumption and Consumerism in Early Modern England," *Historical Journal*, XLII (1999), 549–564.

3. Mary Douglas, "A Distinctive Anthropological Perspective," in Douglas, ed., *Constructive Drinking: Perspectives on Drink from Anthropology* (Cambridge, 1987), 3–15; Peter Weston Black, "The Anthropology of Tobacco Use: Tobian Data and Theoretical Issues," *Journal of Anthropological Research*, XL (1984), 475–503; Dwight Heath, "A Decade of Development in the Anthropological Study of Alcohol Use, 1970–1980," in Douglas, ed., *Constructive Drinking*, 16–69; Peter E. Pope, "Fish into Wine: The Historical Anthropology of Demand for Alcohol in Seventeenth-Century Newfoundland," in Jack S. Blocker, Jr., and Cheryl Krasnick Warsh, eds., *The Changing Face of Drink: Substance, Imagery, and Behaviour* (Ottawa, 1997), 43–64.

following centuries? He argued that wage laborers were not numerous before 1720 and that this economic situation restricted development of a mass market and therefore limited incentives to invest in mass production. Expansion was possible within the limits of a largely rural society, but, when the requirements of its fragmented markets were met, the European economy faltered, recovering only when demand expanded. The development of a mass market and of a large and available free labor force were two aspects of a single process, spread over several centuries.[4]

Although scholars recognized the significance of rising levels of aggregate demand, the postmedieval expansion was not very comprehensible as long as it remained abstracted from qualitative changes in consumption. In early modern times, goods formerly socially restricted in distribution, like distilled alcohol and glass, found their way into a wider range of households. Substitute goods, ceramic serving vessels, for example, replaced their medieval counterparts (in the case of food service, wooden *treen*). The history of sugar, perhaps the archetypical modern good, suggests that more was going on culturally than substitution for a medieval equivalent, in this case, honey. The industrialization of sugar production had enormous socioeconomic implications, not only for Europe but for Africa and the Americas as well. At least one unprecedented good, tobacco, appeared on the market, and the spread of the habit of smoking inevitably implied cultural innovation. The modern world economy differs qualitatively, not simply quantitatively, from the economy (or economies) that preceded it.[5]

4. E. J. Hobsbawm, "The General Crisis of the European Economy in the Seventeenth Century," *Past and Present*, no. 5 (May 1954), 33–53; Hobsbawm, "The Crisis of the Seventeenth Century—II," ibid., no. 6 (November 1954), 44–65; Hobsbawm, "The Seventeenth Century in the Development of Capitalism," *Science and Society*, XXIV (1960), 97–112.

5. On the quantitative issue, see Elizabeth Waterman Gilboy, "Demand as a Factor in the Industrial Revolution" (1932), in R. M. Hartwell, ed., *The Causes of the Industrial Revolution in England* (London, 1967), 121–138. On qualitative changes, see Fernand Braudel, *Civilization and Capitalism, Fifteenth-Eighteenth Century*, I, *The Structures of Everyday Life: The Limits of the Possible*, trans. Siân Reynolds (New York, 1981), 183–333; Walter Minchinton, "Patterns and Structure of Demand, 1500-1750," in Carlo M. Cipolla, gen. ed., *Fontana Economic History of Europe*, II, *The Sixteenth and Seventeenth Centuries* (London, 1974), 83–176; Sidney W. Mintz, *Sweetness and Power: The Place of Sugar in Modern History* (New York, 1986); Jordan Goodman, *Tobacco in History: The Cultures of Dependence* (London, 1993), 59–89.

Identification of a consumer revolution, to parallel the industrial revolution on the other side of the coin, has become a tempting goal for historians, who have identified a number of important shifts in demand in early modern times. Depending on whether emphasis is put on mass consumption and the growth of markets, on specifically modern consumption practices, or on the manipulation of mass culture to shift patterns of demand, a plausible case can be made for several consumer revolutions, breaking out here and there, before and after the one originally proposed for late-eighteenth-century Britain. The consumer revolution, like its obverse the industrial revolution, might be better termed an evolution. It has unfolded over at least four centuries in a surprisingly wide area.[6]

Mass demand developed early in specific regions. Whatever the relative merits of self-sufficiency and consumerism as alternative models of colonial American rural life, by the later eighteenth century something like a modern consumer society had developed in England and the Netherlands and, perhaps to some limited degree, in France. London's great size and predominance within the British economy decisively influenced England's home and colonial markets. In no other nation, except the Netherlands, was 10 percent of the population concentrated in one urban region by 1700. The regions exhibiting early mass demand can be characterized in another way: they were maritime areas. Maritime trade made international markets possible, of course. Seamen, like the soldiers, small rentiers, minor civil servants, and personal dependents who formed the rest of the early modern mass market, enjoyed cash incomes and had no aversion to standardized goods. Furthermore, maritime communities were in a position to tap international flows of goods, even when these were directed elsewhere, geographically or socially.[7]

6. Lorna Weatherill, *Consumer Behaviour and Material Culture in Britain, 1660-1760* (London, 1988), 16-21; Jean-Christophe Agnew, "Coming Up for Air: Consumer Culture in Historical Perspective," in John Brewer and Roy Porter, eds., *Consumption and the World of Goods* (London, 1993), 19-39; Paul Glennie, "Consumption within Historical Studies," in Daniel Miller, ed., *Acknowledging Consumption: A Review of New Studies* (London, 1995), 164-203 (esp. 165-166); Craig Clunas, "Modernity Global and Local: Consumption and the Rise of the West," *American Historical Review*, CIV (1999), 1497-1511.

7. Joan Thirsk, *Economic Policy and Projects: The Development of a Consumer Society in Early Modern England* (Oxford, 1978); Neil McKendrick, John Brewer, and J. H. Plumb, *The Birth of a Consumer Society: The Commercialization of Eighteenth-Century England* (Bloomington, Ind., 1985); Simon Schama, *The Embarrassment of Riches: An Interpretation of Dutch Culture in the Golden Age* (New

Some early modern consumption patterns of considerable social depth date from the later sixteenth century. In his well-known *Description of England* of 1587, William Harrison remarks that hopped beer had displaced traditional ale and notes the introduction of tobacco and pipes, the replacement of open fires with "the multitude of chimneys lately erected," the frequent, "although not general," replacement of straw pallets or rough mats by feather bedding on a framed bedstead, and what he calls "the exchange of vessel" of pewter for treen platters and silver or tin for wooden spoons. Harrison did not claim that tobacco, beds, chimneys, or pewter became universal in his time, but by 1650 tobacco was widespread, pewter and feather beds were common, and cottages without chimneys were rare. By the early seventeenth century, large sectors of the English population were consuming goods for which there had been only a restricted market in late-medieval times. Among these increasingly cheap and common goods, besides those mentioned by Harrison, were earthenware, metal pots and frying pans, knives and other edge tools, nails, pins, glass bottles, vinegar, distilled alcohol, knitted wool stockings and caps, felt hats, gloves, the new draperies (that is, cheaper and lighter fabrics), linens, ribbons, and even lace as well as starch and soap for the latter. The new consumer goods of the early seventeenth century are often the "small things forgotten" in the documentary record, but their being taken for granted does not detract from their economic significance at the time, when late Tudor and early Stuart administrations

---

York, 1987); Daniel Roche, *A History of Everyday Things: The Birth of Consumption in France, 1600–1800*, trans. Brian Pearce (Cambridge, 2000); Carole Shammas, *The Pre-Industrial Consumer in England and America* (Oxford, 1990), esp. 291, 294, on timing; and Jan de Vries, "Between Purchasing Power and the World of Goods: Understanding the Household Economy in Early Modern Europe," in Brewer and Porter, eds., *Consumption and the World of Goods*, 85–132. On eighteenth-century America, see T. H. Breen, "An Empire of Goods: The Anglicization of Colonial America, 1690–1776," *Journal of British Studies*, XXV (1986), 467–499; Cary Carson, "The Consumer Revolution in Colonial British America: Why Demand?" in Carson, Ronald Hoffman, and Peter J. Albert, eds., *Of Consuming Interests: The Style of Life in the Eighteenth Century* (Charlottesville, Va., 1994), 483–697; Dennis J. Pogue, "The Transformation of America: Georgian Sensibility, Capitalist Conspiracy, or Consumer Revolution?" *Historical Archaeology*, XXXV, no. 2 (2001), 41–57. On London, see Nuala Zahedieh, "London and the Colonial Consumer in the Late Seventeenth Century," *EHR*, 2d Ser., XLVII (1994), 239–261; John Styles, "Product Innovation in Early Modern London," *Past and Present*, no. 168 (August 2000), 124–169.

supported industrial and agricultural projects to produce such goods because they promised import substitution. Although only some of the import substitutes produced in England reached a mass market, some at least began to do so.[8]

Consider the North Devon coarse earthenwares, widely distributed geographically in the seventeenth century and now found in archaeological contexts in the south Devon towns of Plymouth and Exeter, south Wales, southwest Ireland, and along the Atlantic littoral of North America. Ordinary North Devon ceramic vessels were widely distributed socially as well and occur in a range of archaeological contexts. At Ferryland, for example, North Devon storage pots and pipkins are the most common vessel forms, whether in a smithy used as a warm retreat by fishing crews or in a better-off planter's kitchen. The North Devon kilns also produced slip-decorated sgraffito dishes, mugs, and other service vessels. The sgraffito ware was also widely distributed geographically and is well represented in certain contexts at Ferryland (Plate 23). These products were, originally, imitations of similarly decorated Italian, French, and Dutch wares. Although North Devon sgraffito was cheaper than these "outlandish" ceramics, it did not reach anything resembling a mass market. It is, typically, excavated in association with other up-market wares, like delft, majolica, or faience tin-glazed earthenwares. The success of the North Devon potteries in the seventeenth century depended partly

8. William Harrison, *The Description of England* (1587), ed. Georges Edelen (Ithaca, N.Y., 1968), 135–138, 195–204, 266. On tobacco, see Ralph Davis, "English Foreign Trade, 1660–1700," *EHR*, 2d Ser., VII (1954), 150–166. On hops, see Peter Clark, *The English Alehouse: A Social History, 1200–1800* (London, 1983), 31, 96. On pewter and bedsteads, see Shammas, *Pre-Industrial Consumer*, 169, 172. On chimneys, see C. A. Hewett, "The Development of the Post-Medieval House," *Post-Medieval Archaeology*, VII (1973), 60–78. On clothes, see Margaret Spufford, *The Great Reclothing of Rural England: Petty Chapmen and Their Wares in the Seventeenth Century* (London, 1984). On small goods, see Thirsk, *Economic Policy and Projects*, 2, 6, 23, 44, 106, 125–127; cf. James Deetz, *In Small Things Forgotten: The Archaeology of Early American Life* (Garden City, N.Y., 1977), 4. Metal cooking pots and earthenware had already deeply penetrated the English market in late-medieval times; see G. G. Astill, "Economic Change in Later Medieval England: An Archaeological Review," in T. H. Aston et al., eds., *Social Relations and Ideas: Essays in Honour of R. H. Hilton* (Cambridge, 1983), 217–247. For a bibliography, see Beverly Lemire, "Popular Consumption and the Mass Market in Early Modern England: A Selected Bibliography," *Material History Bulletin*, no. 31 (Spring 1990), 71–73.

Plate 23. North Devon Earthenware, Slip-Decorated Sgraffito Dish. Excavated at Ferryland (CjAf-2). Courtesy, Colony of Avalon Foundation

on the social expansion of their markets with imitations of luxurious, foreign serving vessels but also on the geographical expansion of their traditional market for cheap, sturdy, storage and cooking vessels. This was still a vernacular industry, distributing its products within a restricted commercial network, but it had reached across the Atlantic and in doing so had made a step in the direction of mass distribution. The potters of north Devon had expanded their maritime market, which permitted them to benefit from a wider geographic distribution of all their wares and, at the same time, to test the social limits on distribution of their new decorated wares.[9]

9. Alison Grant, *North Devon Pottery: The Seventeenth Century* (Exeter, 1983), esp. 83–130; Carson, "Why Demand?" in Carson, Hoffman, and Albert, eds., *Of Consuming Interests*, 483–697 (esp. 540–541, fig. 4); Anne Yentsch, "Minimum Vessel Lists as Evidence of Change in Folk and Courtly Traditions of Food Use," *Historical Archaeology*, XXIV, no. 3 (1990), 24–53; John P. Allan, *Medieval and Post-Medieval Finds from Exeter, 1971–1980* (Exeter, 1984), 131; Amanda Crompton, "A Planter's House at Ferryland, Newfoundland," *Avalon Chronicles*, V (2000), 1–48 (esp. 19); Peter Edward Pope, "Ceramics from Seventeenth Century Ferryland, Newfoundland (CgAf-2, Locus B)" (master's thesis, MUN, 1986), 84–90. On the European wares, see John G. Hurst et al., *Pottery Produced and Traded in North-West Europe, 1350–1650* (The Hague, 1986), 30–33, 108–116, 150–153. Ceramic variation among socially distinguishable contexts is minimal at medieval English sites, although the typical modern social contrasts are apparent at some Italian medieval sites; see Astill, "Economic Change," in Aston et al., eds., *Social Relations and Ideas*, 217–247 (esp. 222).

Probate inventories attest to the limits that still existed on the consumer society of late-seventeenth- and early-eighteenth-century England. These inventories indicate that the social depth of the developing market for decorated ceramics, books, clocks, pictures, mirrors, table utensils, or table linen was still not great. Independent craftsmen, for example, were often participants in the new market; husbandmen, on the other hand, rarely so. The social limitation of demand for such goods meant that the gentry and the middle class continued to play a predominant role in home demand, even after 1700. A consumer mass market in the modern sense was not fully formed. Most people did aspire to own books and clocks, and for these goods wealth was therefore closely correlated with rates of ownership across the whole society. Apart from these widely shared tastes, though, there were few socially widespread patterns of demand: different parts of the market were likely to spend an extra shilling on completely different goods. Consumption patterns for most of the new middle-class decencies thus mirrored only part of the socioeconomic hierarchy. Social emulation turns out to be an incomplete explanation of the development of mass demand.[10]

The postmedieval expansion of demand was not simply a trickling down of consumption habits from social superior to social inferior. Consumption habits spread (they are, after all, learned behavior), but they do not necessarily spread from the top down. To take a concrete example, we might reevaluate the identification of Walter Raleigh as the vector by which tobacco arrived in England. Supposing this cliché to be true, at

10. Lorna Weatherill, "Consumer Behaviour and Social Status in England, 1660–1750," *Continuity and Change*, I (1986), 191–216; Weatherill, *Material Culture*, esp. 185, 192–193; D. E. C. Eversley, "The Home Market and Economic Growth in England, 1750–1780," in E. L. Jones and G. E. Mingay, eds., *Land, Labour, and Population in the Industrial Revolution: Essays Presented to J. D. Chambers* (New York, 1967), 206–259; Thirsk, *Economic Policy and Projects*, 179; Shammas, *Pre-Industrial Consumer*, 78–79, 110, 180, 284. On "consumption hierarchies," see Mary Douglas and Baron Isherwood, *The World of Goods* (New York, 1979), 176–194. Weatherill's care to avoid conflation of evidence about patterns of demand among distinct social classes makes her critique of emulation as an analysis very convincing. Compare Eric L. Jones, "The Fashion Manipulators: Consumer Tastes and British Industries, 1660–1800," in Louis P. Cain and Paul J. Uselding, eds., *Business Enterprise and Economic Change: Essays in Honor of Harold F. Williamson* (Kent, Ohio, 1973), 198–226; H. J. Perkin, "The Social Causes of the British Industrial Revolution," *TRHS*, 5th Ser., XVIII (1968), 123–143.

some level of approximation, we can consider Raleigh as a gentleman, among a circle of gentle friends who adopted his habit of smoking, as is done by those who prefer social emulation as an explanation for shifts in consumption patterns. Alternatively, we might reconsider Raleigh as one of a number of mariners who first took up the habit and helped to bring it ashore to their circle of acquaintances, whatever their social status. By 1650, ordinary mariners were not only consuming goods previously unknown among persons of their humble status; they were also consuming goods that were essentially new to the market. The most notable expanded market was in wine; the important new good was tobacco; the case of spirits lay in between. Tobacco was a complete novelty, in English use from about 1585. Consumption of distilled alcohol for nonmedicinal purposes was rare before the late sixteenth century and expanded rapidly in the following century, as did consumption of wines. In each case, mariners constituted a significant part of the new market. Production of spirits for nonmedicinal purposes in early-seventeenth-century England was largely devoted to maritime victualing. Licenses for tobacco retailers in the 1630s were strongly concentrated in London and the counties most involved in the early Atlantic trades: Devon, Cornwall, and Somerset.[11]

11. Rudi Matthee, "Exotic Substances: The Introduction and Global Spread of Tobacco, Coffee, Cocoa, Tea, and Distilled Liquor, Sixteenth to Eighteenth Centuries," in Roy Porter and Mikuláš Teich, eds., *Drugs and Narcotics in History* (Cambridge, 1995), 24–51; George Latimer Apperson, *The Social History of Smoking* (London, 1914), 4–23; Jan Craeybeckx, *Un grand commerce d'importation: les vins de France aux anciens Pays-Bas, XIIIe–XVIe siècle* (Paris, 1958), 4, 6, 42–43, 254; C. Anne Wilson, "Burnt Wine and Cordial Waters," *Folklife*, XIII (1975), 54–65; Christopher Dyer, "English Diet in the Later Middle Ages," in T. H. Aston et al., eds., *Social Relations and Ideas*, 191–216; Clark, *English Alehouse*, 106, 209–211, 239; Davis, "English Foreign Trade," *EHR*, 2d Ser., VII (1954), 150–166, table 2; Alfred Rive, "The Consumption of Tobacco since 1600," *Economic History*, I (1926), 57–75; Adrian Oswald, "The Clay Pipes," in Allan, ed., *Finds from Exeter*, 279–293; Tim Unwin, *Wine and the Vine: An Historical Geography of Viticulture and the Wine Trade* (London, 1991), 239. On maritime populations, see Peter Pope, Roundtable on Marcus Rediker, *Between the Devil and the Deep Blue Sea, IJMH*, I (1989), 330–334; and Steven R. Pendery, "Consumer Behavior in Colonial Charlestown, Massachusetts, 1630–1760," *Historical Archaeology*, XXVI, no. 3 (1992), 57–72 (esp. 64). Apperson, *Smoking*, 25, notes elite demand for tobacco in late-sixteenth-century England but admits that tobacco use spread rapidly among all classes. Goodman, *Tobacco in History*, 43, 47–48, 51, 63–64, emphasizes the maritime market.

Table 23. *Earthenware in Inventories of English Husbandmen, Yeomen, Craftsmen, and Mariners, 1675–1725*

Occupation	Mean Value of Inventory	Proportion of Estates with Earthenware
Yeomen	£165	33%
Craftsmen	96	43
Mariners	85	60
Husbandmen	32	28

Source: Lorna Weatherill, *Consumer Behaviour and Material Culture in Britain, 1660–1760* (London, 1988).

A similar pattern of early demand within the maritime market is apparent at the end of the century. English mariners' inventories of 1675–1725 were much more likely to include earthenware than the inventories of husbandmen, yeomen, or even craftsmen. Books, clocks, pictures, mirrors, table linen, china, utensils for hot drinks, and silverware were also considerably better represented among mariners. Thus, the novel lower-middle-class consumer goods of the early eighteenth century were already common among mariners whose estates were probated. Inventoried mariners were, no doubt, of higher status than the average mariner, but this bias equally affected the inventories of other occupations sampled. The mariners in question were, in fact, somewhat less wealthy than the craftsmen and barely half as wealthy as the yeomen for whom we have comparative data—making the frequent occurrence of the new decencies in the mariners' inventories even more remarkable (Table 23). Maritime communities often had the opportunity to express demand for novel goods before their landlubber social peers. This circumstance would have been true for different classes of seamen, over several centuries, vis-à-vis succeeding suites of goods.[12]

Seventeenth-century England was a consumer society, then, only in a restricted sense. A mass market existed for a limited range of goods, but the goods produced for this market were not standardized nor was distri-

12. Carole Shammas, "Changes in English and Anglo-American Consumption from 1550 to 1800," in Brewer and Porter, eds., *Consumption and the World of Goods*, 177–205 (esp. 199–201), concludes that occupational status did not affect the level of demand for consumer goods, but she does not distinguish the maritime trades as an occupational group.

bution commercialized in the eighteenth-century manner. Furthermore, the seventeenth-century market was bifurcated in a way that we do not associate with modern mass markets. Probate inventories suggest there were still two major patterns of demand at the end of the seventeenth century. Among craftsmen and others of like or superior status, a then-novel suite of goods was beginning to become standard. The new decencies included table linen, earthenware, books, clocks, and silverware. Among husbandmen and laborers, on the other hand, only earthenware and linen, among these goods, occur in more than one in ten inventories. Like their economic betters, most laborers and husbandmen owned tables, cooking pots, and pewter, but, if they had a little ready money, they did not generally spend it on the other goods in demand among those further up the consumption hierarchy, even if a few chose to buy a book or a clock. They chose cheaper and already familiar goods, including, particularly, warm clothes, tobacco, and alcohol. In later centuries, a ratchet effect developed in which initial wage gains were first taken in leisure and drink but were soon absorbed into expanded demand for domestic comforts. This modern pattern of demand for goods to ameliorate the domestic environment developed very slowly, however, and was not socially widespread in the seventeenth century.[13]

The history of demand suggests, then, that we should expect at least two distinct consumption patterns in seventeenth-century Newfoundland. Planters had a status comparable to tradesmen or the less-affluent

13. Thirsk, *Economic Policy and Projects*, 173; Weatherill, *Material Culture*, 168, 191, 199; Beverley Lemire, "Consumerism in Preindustrial and Early Industrial England: The Trade in Secondhand Clothes," *Journal of British Studies*, XXVII (1988), 1–24; Peter Mathias, "Leisure and Wages in Theory and Practice," in Mathias, *The Transformation of England: Essays in the Economic and Social History of England in the Eighteenth Century* (New York, 1979), 148–167; Carole Shammas, "The Domestic Environment in Early Modern England and America," *Journal of Social History*, XIV (1980–1981), 3–24; and Shammas, *Pre-Industrial Consumer*, 172, 186–187; Roche, *History of Everyday Things*, 107–108. The bimodal structure of demand has parallels in earlier periods. Consider the two patterns of demand reported in sixteenth-century mining camps. Some miners worked full-time in order to maximize incomes and maintain a relatively high standard of living, particularly in food and drink. Other "cottar" miners were more interested in limiting labor intensity and, like the farmer-miners of the fifteenth century, sought only paltry incomes to satisfy irreducible cash requirements. See Ian Blanchard, "Labour Productivity and Work Psychology in the English Mining Industry, 1400–1600," *EHR*, 2d Ser., XXXI (1978), 1–24.

yeomen of the Old Country, so we should expect household demand for the suite of consumer durables typical of lower-middle-class inventories of the time, including, for example, sgraffito plates, even if Chesapeake probate records indicate that North American colonists often made do with simpler or older possessions than people with similar incomes enjoyed in the home country. Earlier in the century, planters' lives were doubtless simpler, but we should expect demand for the early consumer goods of that time. Newfoundland fishing servants, on the other hand, were recruited among husbandmen and laborers and had similar status, although they were generally better paid. We should not expect demand among this class of working men for the kind of consumer goods that were still middle-class novelties in the seventeenth century. On the other hand, we should not be surprised that fishing crews were part of the early maritime mass market for small metal goods like knives, cheap warm clothes like knitted stockings and caps, not to mention coarse earthenware cooking pots, alcohol, and tobacco. Fishing servants considerably outnumbered planters, particularly during the season of commercial activity, with the result that servant demand had a great impact on imports to the island. Inevitably, wine, spirits, and tobacco made up the bulk of cargoes bound for Newfoundland.[14]

ℰ Imports to Newfoundland

The geographical isolation of the English Shore facilitated monopoly, although the dispersion of settlement eventually limited its scale. In the early days of the proprietary colonies, economic control was a deliberate exercise of political power. Sir George Calvert's patent granted him exclusive authority over ports. Kirke's grant gave the Newfoundland patentees "the sole trade, and traffique . . . for all manner of commodities" and banned other merchants, forbidding them to "haunt or frequent" the island, "except for fishing." Although Calvert's rights were limited to the south Avalon and Sir David Kirke would have had difficulty enforcing his monopoly of imports in Conception or Trinity Bays, the control these early proprietors had over trade, even in a limited area, was a

14. James P. P. Horn, "'The Bare Necessities': Standards of Living in England and the Chesapeake, 1650–1700," *Historical Archaeology*, XXII, no. 2 (1988), 74–91; John E. Crowley, *The Invention of Comfort: Sensibilities and Design in Early Modern Britain and Early America* (Baltimore, 2000), 79–140.

valuable right. Migratory fishing masters testified that Kirke engrossed salt and other provisions and sold them at "excessive rates," which would have particularly offended contemporary Puritan concepts of a just price. In reaction to Kirke's monopoly, the south Avalon planters attempted to control their own terms of trade in 1663 by requiring vessels bringing in provisions or merchandise to refrain from unloading or selling goods until the importing master or merchant had given "inhabitants the refusall in buieing such goods or provision, if they have occasion of it." Ordinary planters cared about this issue not simply because they wished to minimize their own expenditures but also because virtually all were themselves petty traders. Of about thirty planters at St. John's in the 1670s, for example, all but one kept a tippling house. Only a few, however, would have been merchants financially able to organize imports. There were two distinguishable levels of exchange at Newfoundland: retail exchange between planters and their crews and wholesale exchange between merchants and planters. Some merchants were resident, but this was also the province of West Country businesses, with a growing admixture of New England enterprises. Control over Newfoundland supply was somewhat less concentrated than it had been in Sir David Kirke's day, but it was markedly more external.[15]

Both levels of exchange operated as systems of credit, a normal feature of commerce at all levels in this period, particularly in North America, where specie was scarce. A few commercial records of such debts exist, exemplifying merchant supply to planters on the English Shore, but

15. James I, "Grant of the Province of Avalon," Apr. 7, 1623, CO 195/1 (1), 1–10, Charles I, "Grant of Newfoundland," Nov. 13, 1637, CO 195/1 (2), 11–27, both in Matthews, *Constitutional Laws*, 39–75 (esp. 59), 82–116 (esp. 111); Thomas Cruse, Deposition, Nov. 27, 1667, WDRO Plymouth, W360/74; William Swanley et al., "An Act Made by the Tenants of Avalon," Aug. 30, 1663, Md. HS, Calvert MSS 174/210; William Poole, "Answers to the Severall Heads of Inquiry . . . ," Sept. 10, 1677, CO 1/41 (62i), 149–152; Robert Robinson, "Certaine Arguments or Reasons for a Settled Government . . . ," 1670, CO 1/68 (99), 288; Francis Wheler, "Answers to the Heads of Inquirys . . . ," and Wheler, "Observations . . . upon the . . . Articles of His Majesties Charter," Oct. 27, 1684, CO 1/55 (56, 56i), 239–248; David Kirke and Nicholas Shapley, "Invoyce of Goods Shipped Abord the *David* of Ferryland . . . ," Sept. 8, 1648, *Baxter MSS*, VI, 2–4; William Downing and Thomas Oxford, Proposals to CTP, Mar. 2, 1680, CO 1/44 (34), 85; John Benger et al., Petition to Lord Nottingham, Mar. 28, 1706, CO 194/3 (148), 474–476. On Puritan ideas about just price, see Stephen Innes, *Creating the Commonwealth: The Economic Culture of Puritan New England* (New York, 1995), 160–191.

Table 24. *Accounts of William Lucas, Richmond Island, Maine, 1638–1639*

	£	s.	d.
Debtor for			
Commodities		12	8
Wine	1	2	
Aqua vitae		5	6
Tobacco		10	
Money paid him by Mr. Trelawney			
with adventure	7	3	
Cider and oil		4	1
Aqua vitae at his first coming		1	6
More paid him in full to balance			
this account	1	17	$3\frac{3}{4}$
Total	11	16	$\frac{3}{4}$
Creditor for			
His share of the first fishing	1	16	5
His portage money	1	15	
His share this year	8	4	$7\frac{3}{4}$
Total	11	16	$\frac{3}{4}$

Note: Colonial New England currency was still on par with sterling at this time.

Source: John Winter, "His Accounts for the Plantation . . . ," July 15, 1639, *Trelawny Papers*, 181–198.

there are no known surviving records of planter supply to servants. The closest parallel information comes from the seventeenth-century fishing stations of Maine, which of all early European settlements in the New World most closely resembled Newfoundland. The relations between John Winter and his fishing crews at Richmond Island about 1640 are a plausible model of servant supply. The accounts of "necessaries" supplied to William Lucas and John Vivion provide a clear picture of fishing servants' material needs in this period (Tables 24 and 25). Winter paid his crews in early summer, after deducting the cost of aqua vitae, wine, tobacco, and other "commodities" (probably clothing, soap, and knives) supplied on credit in the course of the previous work year. Newfoundland's planters paid crews at the end of the fishing season; settlement with servants overwintering would await the end of the following fish-

Table 25. *Account of John Vivion, Richmond Island, Maine, 1639–1640*

Quantity	Item
2 pair	shoes
3 pair	stockings
1	suit of canvas
1	suit of kersey
1	waistcoat
1	calfskin for a barvel
1 pair	boots
400	sparables
300	brads
8	thongs (for 2 pair of hauling hands
1 pound, 6 ounces	leather and list to line them)
—	cape cloth to make a pair of mittens
$\frac{1}{4}$ pounds	thread
1	coverlet
2 $\frac{1}{4}$ yards	cape cloth to make a pair of breeches
2	shirts
1	knife
1	lock for a chest . . .
1 pound, 12 $\frac{1}{2}$ ounces	soap

Note: Kersey was a coarse, narrow, woven wool cloth, usually ribbed. A barvel was an apron worn when catching or processing fish. A hauling hand was a glove covering the palm, with the fingers protruding, used in handling fishing lines. Sparables were small, wedge-shaped iron nails, used in the soles and heels of shoes and boots, and a list was a strip of cloth.

Source: John Winter, "A Booke of Accounts for the Plantation at Richmon Island," June 17, 1640, *Trelawny Papers*, 289–303.

ing season. Sometimes servants ventured to Newfoundland to work off such obligations, like Seymour Dolberye, who sailed about 1630 with the Southampton master William Ayles to clear a debt for advances of food, beer, and clothes. Others ran up debts in Newfoundland.[16]

16. Jacob M. Price, "Conclusion," in Rosemary E. Ommer, ed., *Merchant Credit and Labour Strategies in Historical Perspective* (Fredricton, N.B., 1990), 350–363; Charles E. Clark, *The Eastern Frontier: The Settlement of Northern New England, 1610–1763* (1970; rpt. Hanover, N.H., 1983), 29; John Winter, "His Accounts for the Plantation . . . ," July 15, 1639, Winter, "A Booke of Accounts for the Planta-

Dependent servants were often young men, and, in this sense, consumption patterns were linked to life cycle and, in turn, to mobility. Young servants working away from home in an industry that provided a disposable income were, naturally, among those most likely to smoke and drink, even if they had to do so on credit. In the seventeenth century, prodigal servants whose earnings did not balance their debit accounts sometimes escaped their debts in Newfoundland by returning with Yankee traders to the prosperous New England colonies. The Committee for Trade and Plantations gradually tightened control on reemigration and the consequent loophole in the collection of servant debts. This restriction on mobility would simplify control of labor through credit relationships and was, perhaps, a precondition of the alcohol-debt nexus that seems to have become more important in eighteenth-century master-servant relations in Newfoundland.

Bills held by the Salem merchant John Croad when he died in 1670 indicate that some Newfoundland planters already depended on New England for annual supply and remind us that it was normal for planters to be indebted to merchants. In 1693, another Salem merchant, Joseph Buckley, sent four vessels to Newfoundland, and a ledger with details of his accounts with planters there has survived. These planter accounts resemble the earlier employee accounts at Richmond Island, although the sums involved are larger, of course. Thirteen of Buckley's Newfoundland accounts were for more than one hundred pounds. Debits for the New England goods were generally offset by credits for fish, although in a few cases supplies were balanced by cash or a bill of exchange. Thus, Thomas Bishop paid for victuals, sundries, and a chest of drawers and bought the bark *Endeavour* with a seventy-two-pound bill of exchange drawn on his wife in Poole. John Way, on the other hand, settled his account of twenty-nine pounds "by cash." Perhaps he did not fish: the two hundred gallons of molasses and 840 pounds of hops debited to him in the ledger would

tion at Richmon Island," June 17, 1640, Winter, "A Booke of Account," May 31, 1642, all in *Trelawny Papers*, 181–198, 289–303, 323–336; Charles Talbot, "Answers to the Enquiries . . . ," Sept. 15, 1679, CO 1/43 (121), 216–217; Robert Alward, Libel, in *Allward v. Kirke and Gutenville*, 1650, HCA 24/111 (4); Henry Temple, Deposition, June 12, 1634, *Southampton Examinations*, III, 9–10. There are better records surviving for the French Newfoundland settlement of Plaisance; see Nicholas Landry, "'Qu'il sera fait droit à qui il appartiendra': la société de Lasson-Daccarrette à Plaisance, 1700–1715," *Newfoundland Studies*, XVII (2001), 220–256.

have brewed enough beer, of an unusual sort, to supply a busy tippling house. Generally, however, Buckley's vessels took payment in fish.[17]

Because Buckley often recorded his 1693 sales as "sundries," assessing proportions of the various goods he brought from Salem is difficult. Besides molasses and hops, he recorded several large sales of rum, by the hogshead or the puncheon. He sold large quantities of tobacco, flour, salt, and pork to David Kirke II and to Thomas Dodridge, who by this time was resettled in Ferryland after his migration down the coast. Besides further sales of tobacco in quantities up to three hundred pounds, Buckley also sold cider, beer, bread, flour, cornmeal, pork, beef, oil, turnips, salt, sugar, lumber, empty hogsheads, "wooden ware," earthenware pitchers and milk pans, chairs, a chest of drawers, nails, leather aprons and suits, a quire of paper, window glass, two vessels (the bark *Endeavour* and the ketch *Hope*), and "halfe of a pair curtaines." His ledger suggests that the Newfoundland planters of the late seventeenth century consumed goods typical of craftsmen and mariners in the Old Country; but it also supports the contemporary consensus that a strong demand for alcohol and tobacco existed among the planters and their servants.[18]

The demand for these little luxuries is best seen in the context of overall consumption patterns. English visitors to Newfoundland stressed the imports required by the fishery. Fishing ships and plantations needed boats, nails and other ironwork, pitch, oakum, canvas, cordage, hooks, lines, lead, nets, knives, barrels, pans, funnels, flasks, breadboxes, kettles, platters, bowls, and so on. Those involved sometimes compiled inventories, in greater or lesser detail, of this equipment, and these changed remarkably little over time. This material has, of course, a cultural meaning; however, demand for goods beyond those necessary for the fishery bears more complex cultural implications, if only because such demands expressed matters of choice. Much of the documentary evidence for imports to the early modern English Shore results from British export controls (Tables 26, 27, and 28). The diet of wheat, peas, oatmeal, cheese, butter, oil, and salt meat suggested by these records is unexceptional. The remaining material falls within the range of goods that characterizes the seventeenth-century consumer society, including ready-made clothing, shoes, iron tools, soap, candles, and pewter as well as wine and

17. Veren Hilliard, Henry Skerry, and John Price, Inventory of John Croad, June 1671, *RFQC Essex Co.*, IV, 401–403; Joseph Buckley, "Leager 1693," Peabody Museum, Salem, Mass., Acc,16,100, 55, 96.

18. Buckley, "Leager 1693," Peabody Museum, Acc,16,100, 55, 96.

Table 26. *Imports to Newfoundland by the Adventurers for the Plantation of Newfoundland, 1639*

Quantity	Item
312 bushels	wheat
224 bushels	malt
59 bushels	peas
39 bushels	oatmeal
672 pounds	cheese
27 [wine?] gallons	sweet oil
2 firkins (18 gallons)	ordinary soap
1 rundlet (8–27 gallons)	Castille soap
1 firkin (27 gallons)	butter
2 bushels	mustard seed
312	candles
2 hogsheads (126 wine gallons)	wine vinegar
2 firkins (18 gallons)	small nails

Note: Some units have been converted to modern measures. A bushel of grain weighs about 25 kilograms, or 55 pounds. The gallons here are probably beer gallons of about 4.6 liters, except for the wine vinegar and perhaps the oil, which are expressed in wine gallons of 3.8 liters.

Source: Privy Council, Pass for Export, June 14, 1639, *APC*: Colonial.

spirits. The Dutch also carried on a trade on the English Shore until the 1660s. Cargoes outbound from the Netherlands to Newfoundland were only occasionally specified, although we know that two large Enkhuizen ships, the *Eenhorn* and the *de Coninck David*, carried coal, salt, and victuals to Newfoundland in the mid-1620s. If Dutch manifests resembled English ones, then "victuals" would often have included alcohol. Consider, for example, the cargo of the *Unicorne* of London, which went to Newfoundland in 1640 with forty barrels of Irish beef and a ton of sea biscuit as well as three tuns of French aqua vitae and one and a half tons of tobacco. In 1660, the *St. Laurens* of Amsterdam took a cargo of salt and brandy from France to St. John's for London merchants. Like wine and tobacco, spirits were readily available on the English Shore.[19]

19. Nehemiah Trout, Deposition, Feb. 1, 1678, CO 1/42 (22), 58–59; "The Inventorie of Thinges Remayning in Newfoundland," Aug. 26, 1611, and John Poyntz, Instructions Given to Sir Henry Salusbury, ca. 1625, both in Cell, *New-*

Table 27. *Imports to New England and Newfoundland, 1640,*
on the Charles *of Bristol*

Quantity	Item
300 barrels (30 tons)	beef
100 barrels (10 tons)	butter
200 quintals (10 tons)	cheese
80 hogsheads (630 bushels)	malt
3,600	stockings
3,600	shirts
3,600	suits of clothes
3,600	drawers
600	shoes
480	Monmouth caps
400 ells (500 yards)	cloth for shirts
— (worth 100 pounds)	iron tools
1 ton	candles
1,000 gallons	wine
200 gallons	oil
20,000	nails
40	muskets
750 gallons	spirits
240	hats
8 barrels (32 bushels)	gunpowder
600	boots
40 hogsheads (315 bushels)	peas
40 hogsheads (315 bushels)	oatmeal
500 gallons	vinegar
320 bushels	grain
1,100 pounds	small shot
12 tons	sheet lead

Note: Some units have been converted to familiar measurements. "Ton" here is the British long ton, which is almost a metric tonne. A bushel of grain weighs about 25 kilograms, or 55 pounds. The gallons here are probably wine gallons of about 3.8 liters.

Source: Privy Council, Pass for Export, Apr. 10, 1640, *APC*: Colonial.

Because legal authority in seventeenth-century Newfoundland was disputed and intermittent, probate inventories, of the sort used so effectively to investigate material life elsewhere, are rare. At least three such records have survived, however, and fortunately represent planters who had accumulated various degrees of wealth. Robert Dench was an important planter of Bay Bulls, who had been in Newfoundland since about 1650 and who already owned five boats, a dwelling house, and four outbuildings in 1677, employing a couple dozen fishers. When he died in September 1687, he left £145 in "goods, chattles, and credit," exclusive of real estate. His major moveable assets were provisions of salt meat, biscuit, peas, brandy, wine, molasses, and so on, in quantities sufficient to feed a sizable household of overwintering servants. He also possessed valuable ropes, nets, and six boats, "some old and some worn"—but some, by implication, new (Table 29). Dench left none of the consumer

foundland Discovered, 65–67, 246–249; Whitbourne, *Discourse*, 173–175; Inventory of 1619, Cornwall Record Office, Rashleigh MSS, DDR 4546, in John Scantlebury, "John Rashleigh of Fowey and the Newfoundland Cod Fishery, 1608–20," *Royal Institution of Cornwall Journal*, N.S., VIII (1978–1981), 66–67; Ambrose Gibbins and Thomas Wannerton, "An Inventory of . . . the Plantation at Piscataway," July 1635, in Nathaniel Adams, *Annals of Portsmouth* (Portsmouth, N.H., 1825), appendix 1; John Winter, "An Inveltory . . . ," July 15, 1639, *Trelawny Papers*, 177–179; Francis Wheler, "The Expence of Fitting Out Ten Boats and the Charge of a Shipp . . . ," and "The Charge for Fitting Out Two Boats . . . according to the Custome of the Inhabitants . . . ," Oct. 27, 1684, CO 1/55 (56ii, iii), 249–252. For discussion, see Alaric Faulkner, "Archaeology of the Cod Fishery: Damariscove Island," *Historical Archaeology*, XIX, no. 2 (1985), 57–86; and Nicolas Landry, "Culture matérielle et niveaux de richesse chez les pêcheurs de Plaisance et de l'Île Royale, 1700–1758," *Material History Review*, no. 48 (Fall 1998), 101–122. On Dutch supplies, see Pieter Wiltraet and Jan t'Herdt, Charter Party for *'t Swerte Herdt*, June 19, 1601, GA Amsterdam NA 90, 4–5, Claes Backer and Pieter Evertsz, Charter Party for *Coninck Davith*, May 9, 1651, Rotterdam City Archives, Notarial (V. Mustelius), Cornelius van Goor and Thys de Gilde, Charter Party for *de Trouw*, Apr. 30, 1658, GA Amsterdam NA 2711, 963–965, Jan Oort and Hendrick Schram, Charter Party, Apr. 1, 1624, GA Amsterdam NA 631, 135–140, Jan Kuijsten and Gerriot Schuijt, Charter Party, Apr. 30, 1624, GA Amsterdam NA 631, 145–149, all in NAC MG 18, 012/38, /69, /95, /205, /328; London Searcher, Port Books, 1640, E 190/44/1, 90; Jan Frederickson and Thomas Thompson, Deposition, Sept. 5, 1662, GA Amsterdam NA 2213, 527–531, NAC MG 18 012/517. Wine was an important export to the Caribbean as well; see Zahedieh, "London and the Colonial Consumer," *EHR*, 2d Ser., XLVII (1994), 239–261 (esp. 247–248).

Table 28. *Dutiable Goods Exported to Newfoundland in the*
Red Lyon *of Dartmouth, 1679*

Quantity	Item
3	short cloths
6 pieces	linen
2 pieces	coarse Barnstaple baize
2 pieces	fine single Barnstaple baize
336 pounds	coarse haberdashery
336 pounds	woolen stuff
40 pounds	other stuffs and silk manufactures
60 yards	dimity
52 pounds	shoes
43 pounds	pewter
6 dozen	men's and women's woolen stockings
12 dozen	children's woolen stockings
52 pairs	men's and women's worsted stockings
88 pounds	sugar
336 pounds	nails

Note: The goods were exported to Newfoundland by Andrew Neale, master of the *Red Lyon*, for Richard Newman of Dartmouth, June 22, 1679. Baize was a woolen fabric with a long nap, suitable for clothing. Dimity was a stout cotton fabric, woven with raised stripes or fancy figures, for bed hangings, etc.

Sources: Dartmouth Controller, Port Book, 1679, E 190/954/8; Dartmouth Customer, Port Book, 1679, E 190/954/18.

goods that would become common among the English lower middle class around 1700. He lived in frugal comfort, his personal possessions confined to clothing and a kettle, iron pots, feather beds, "old chests," and "old chairs," the simple household equipment of the period. When Dench had time or money to spend, he apparently preferred productive goods, like new boats, rather than the replacement of household goods, like old chairs.[20]

20. George Prouse, Walter Rowe, and Samuell May, "A True and Perfect Inventary of All and Singular the Goods, Chattles, and Credit of Robert Deinch Late of Newfoundland in the Parts beyond the Sea: Ordered Left in the Custody of Joshua Stoon," Sept. 20, 1687, PROB 4/3154. On Dench, see William Poole, "A Particular Accompt of All the Inhabitants and Planters . . . ," Sept. 10, 1677, CO

Table 29. *Probate Inventory of Robert Dench of Bay Bulls, 1687*

Item	£	s.	d.
17 barrels of beef	15	6	
5 barrels of pork	7	10	
7 barrels of brandy	10	10	
8,000 of bread [ship biscuit]	26		
3 hogsheads of molasses	11		
1 parcel of wine	9		
1 parcel of tobacco	2		
1 puncheon and 2 barrels of rum	6		
1 piece of brandy	1	2	
8 hogsheads of peas	10		
5 hogsheads of pork	7		
500 pounds of malt	5		
2 barrels of flour	2	4	
80 pounds of hops	1	6	4
6 boats, some old and some worn	12		
1 half [size] shallop	1	2	
7 roads [heavy ropes]	3		
5 old sails for the boats		10	
7 nets	4	10	
5 hogsheads of salt	1	10	
1 kettle	1		
3 iron pots	1		
2 feather beds	2	10	
5 old chests		5	
6 old chairs		6	
Wearing apparel	2		
Lumber and things forgotten	2		
Total	145	11	4

Note: This inventory omits real estate. The arithmetic is poor and is corrected here. The source gives, in error, £159 12s. 2d. as the total valuation. The major error was valuation of five hogsheads of salt at 6s. each as £15, rather than the correct £1 10s. The figures for "bread" likely represent 8,000 ship biscuits rather than 8,000 pounds of biscuit. "Lumber" had a broader meaning than we would give it today: things stored.

Source: George Prouse, Walter Rowe, and Samuell May, "A True and Perfect Inventory of All and Singular the Goods, Chattles, and Credit of Robert Deinch Late of Newfoundland in the Parts beyond the Sea: Ordered Left in the Custody of Joshua Stoon," Sept. 20, 1687, PROB 4/3154.

Table 30. *Probate Inventory of Thomas Anger of Bauline, 1674*

Item	£	s.
2 feather beds	7	
1 feather bolster and 3 feather pillows	1	
1 rug [coverlet]		18
3 chests and 3 pillows	1	
3 pewter platters		6
1 small silver cup and 1 dram cup		15
2 iron pots		5
1 shallop	4	
1 boat	2	10
1 skiff	1	10
1 dwelling house and 1 fishing stage	10	
Total	29	4

Source: Peter White and Emanuel Youland, "An Inventorie of the Goods and Chattells of Thomas Anger, Who Dyed att Balleen in the Newfoundland, the Seaventh October 1674," Oct. 10, 1674, PROB 4/725.

His plentiful stock of provisions aside, Dench's possessions parallel those of Thomas Anger, a Bauline planter who died in October 1674, leaving an estate worth £29, and even those of John Collins (Cullings), who died in St. John's in November 1673, leaving only £8 9s. (Tables 30 and 31). Anger's major assets were his dwelling house, fishing stage, shallop, and two feather mattresses. Collins left a similar, even smaller estate, consisting notably of old houses, old casks, old nets, old shallops, and "old frayed clothes." Perhaps Collins himself was old and no longer fishing. Apparently, he owned no fishing stage and, although he left be-

1/41 (62iv, vi, vii), 157–166; Robert Robinson, "An Account of . . . St. John's and Baye of Bulls . . . ," Sept. 16, 1680, CO 1/46 (8iii), 23–24; and James Story, "An Account of What Fishing Shipps, Sack Shipps, Planters, etc., Boat Keepers . . . ," Sept. 1, 1681, CO 1/47 (52i), 113–121. On colonial "frugal comfort," see Nicholas Canny, "English Migration into and across the Atlantic during the Seventeenth and Eighteenth Centuries," in Canny, *Europeans on the Move: Studies on European Migration, 1500–1800* (Oxford, 1994), 39–75 (esp. 70–73); cf. Henry Waddocke and James Gibbines, "A True Inventory of the Reall Estate of Ambrose Berry," Nov. 4, 1661, in Charles T. Libby, ed., *Province and Court Records of Maine*, II, *York County Court Records (1653–1679)* (Portland, Maine, 1931), 124.

Table 31. *Probate Inventory of John Collins of St. John's, 1673*

Item	£	s.
A parcel of old houses, about 6 old casks, 6 old nets, and 1 old road [heavy rope] and a piece	2	5
1 rug [coverlet] and bed ticky [mattress] of old canvas		10
2 old shallops and a train vat		15
Kitchen stuff—what was left		10
100 pounds beef and pork	1	10
1 parcel of wine taken off by William Furse		9
1 piece of plate taken off by Richard	1	
1 pair of sheets and 1 empty bolster		10
Lumber and old frayed clothes of all sorts, supposed	1	
Total	8	9

Note: The "piece" in the first item is likely another piece of rope cable. It might, conceivably, be a musket, but the valuation seems too low.

Source: Christopher Martin, Denis Luony, and William Bennett, "An Inventory of All Singular the Goods and Chattles Which Late Were of John Cullings of the Newfoundland, Deceased," Nov. 29, 1673, PROB 4/18476.

hind "houses," their low value suggests they were no more than huts. Perhaps he died in debt—a situation that would explain the wine "taken off by William Furse [Fursey]" (another St. John's planter) and the "piece of plate" taken by an otherwise unidentified Richard. Perhaps some of his estate was already in the hands of an heir: from 1675, a second John Collins managed a small plantation at St. John's. Suppose that Thomas Anger or the elder Collins had survived to see another year and that settlement of their accounts had left them a little cash not earmarked for retirement. Would they have invested in household decencies, even chests and chairs, like Robert Dench? Their inventories suggest not. Anger limited himself to a few pewter platters and some drinking equipment, including "a dram cup." Collins contented himself with his "piece of plate" and "parcel of wine." These minor extravagances apart, when small planters spent money they bought clothing, the minor tools of their trade, or consumables like wine that usually leave no trace in probate. As consumers, their demands resembled those of their own servants: warm clothes, a drink, and a place to sleep. They differed from their young employees in possessing their own gear for fishing, cooking, and keeping warm through the long Newfoundland winter. To the extent that they differentiated themselves with material possessions, they made do with a few pieces of eating or drinking paraphernalia, along the lines of pewter platters and silver cups.[21]

The presence of a merchant gentry on the English Shore drawing handsome profits on the trade in fish and wine meant that Newfoundland's material culture was not restricted to the "necessary provisions" imported for ordinary planters and their servants. Archaeological finds of luxury ceramics at the Pool Plantation in Ferryland hint at the complex material life major planters like the Kirkes enjoyed. Two of the most unusual wares are Portuguese. Excavators have recovered many examples of faiança, often hand-painted in blue, with floral and similar motifs (for example, Plate 9). These are not the only tin-glazed earthenwares uncovered at the site. There is a good representation of English plates, bowls, cups, mugs, and posset pots, and even some Spanish lusterware, but Portuguese vessels are unusually well represented here, in comparison to other English sites on either side of the North Atlantic. These beautiful plates, porringers, and dishes occur particularly in contexts dating between 1640 and 1670, bespeaking a strong trading connection with Portugal as well as a taste for exotic ceramics, both during Sir David Kirke's life and for several succeeding decades, when his widow Sara controlled

21. Peter White and Emanuel Youland, "An Inventorie of the Goods and Chattells of Thomas Anger, Who Dyed att Balleen in the Newfoundland, the Seaventh October 1674," Oct. 10, 1674, PROB 4/725; Christopher Martin, Denis Luony, and William Bennett, "An Inventory of All Singular the Goods and Chattles Which Late Were of John Cullings of the Newfound-Land, Deceased," Nov. 29, 1673, PROB 4/18476. Richard, who took Collins's piece of plate, is not further identified here, but Richard Hopkins, Matthews, and England were planters of St. John's in 1675. On these men, Denis Luony (Loney), William Bennett, widow Mary Furse, and the later John Collins, see John Berry, "St. Johns Harbor," in Berry, "A List of the Planters Names . . . ," Sept. 12, 1675, CO 1/35 (17ii), 150–156. Compare the standards of these small planters with the farm laborer's possessions (straw bedding, a blanket, a wooden bowl, and a pan or two), cited in Alan Everitt, "Farm Labourers," in Joan Thirsk, ed., *The Agrarian History of England and Wales, IV, 1500–1640* (London, 1967), 396–465 (esp. 448), in H. P. R. Finberg, gen. ed., *The Agrarian History of England and Wales*; cf. John Amerideth, "True Inventory of the Estate of John Tucker," Apr. 26, 1671, in Libby, ed., *York County Court Records (1653–1679)*, 124. For similar evidence from French Newfoundland, see Landry, "Culture matérielle," *Material Hist. Rev.*, no. 48 (Fall 1998), 101–122 (esp. 107).

Plate 24. Portuguese
Earthenware Terra Sigillata
Jar, Incised and Inlayed with
Fine White Clay. Excavated at
Ferryland (CjAf-2). Courtesy,
Colony of Avalon Foundation

the family plantation. Archaeological contexts of the same period have
also yielded examples of Portuguese terra sigillata, an even more luxurious ware, produced in Estremoz, upriver from Lisbon. These pieces
were baroque imitations of similar Roman products, incised and often
decorated with inlays of fine white clay (Plate 24). There was a fashion for terra sigillata among the Spanish and Portuguese elite at the turn
of the seventeenth century, and later archaeological examples have been
recovered from the homes of wealthy merchants in Amsterdam and Ant-
werp, but the ware is hitherto unknown archaeologically in the English-
speaking Atlantic world. Although these exquisite ceramics might have
reached Newfoundland from Amsterdam, with which the Kirkes had
continuing commercial regulations, they are more likely a trace of direct trade with Portugal, a great market for salt fish and an excellent

place to buy wine. The bowls, chalices, and handled jars found at Ferryland are delicate decorative pieces, obviously intended for display rather than table use. The provenance and pseudoclassical style of these pieces suggest that they might have represented a self-conscious celebration of Western Europe as the new Rome, on the threshold of empire, a thought that would certainly have appealed to Sir David.[22]

Kirke, Barkeley, and company had built their business on the wine trade, only gradually moving into the Canada and Newfoundland trades after 1627. As their business evolved, they tried to extend their market in alcohol. Depositions made in the dispute with the Quebec merchant Emery de Caen indicate that they imported wines and aqua vitae to Quebec in the early 1630s for truck with the Indians, although the French or at least Champlain had refrained from this trade. Sir David Kirke established himself in Newfoundland, in part, by dealing in alcohol, and certain West Country merchants saw this trade, at least in retrospect, as a key factor in the growth of settlement: "The many tippling houses and taverns . . . were first created by Sir David Kirke whoe made it his advantage (as governor) which was the first cause of debauching our seamen and the principall occasion of the inhabitants' increase, whoe before were inconsiderable." He and his sons continued to deal in wines, as is evident in the lading of the *David* of Ferryland, bound for New England, in 1648 (Table 32). This shipment is telling, not only because it appears to consist largely of continental European rather than English goods nor simply as an example of early intercolonial trade but also because of the specific products shipped. Of goods valued at £548, 46 percent consisted of eighteen butts (more than eight thousand liters) of Canary and Madeira wines worth £252. These wines were by far the major component of the cargo, followed by 2,743 pounds

22. Eleanor Stoddart, "Seventeenth-Century Tin-Glazed Earthenware from Ferryland," *Avalon Chronicles*, V (2000), 49–100; Steven R. Pendery, "Portuguese Tin-Glazed Earthenware in Seventeenth-Century New England: A Preliminary Study," *Historical Archaeology*, XXXIII, no. 4 (1999), 58–77; Charlotte Wilcoxen, "Seventeenth-Century Portuguese *Faiança* and Its Presence in Colonial America," *Northeast Historical Archaeology*, XXVIII (1999), 1–20; Barry Gaulton and Cathy Mathias, "Portuguese Terra Sigillata Earthenware Discovered at a Seventeenth-Century Colonial Site in Ferryland, Newfoundland," *Avalon Chronicles*, III (1998), 1–18; Jan M. Baart, "*Terra Sigillata* from Estremoz, Portugal," in David Gaimster and Mark Redknap, eds., *Everyday and Exotic Pottery from Europe, c. 650–1900: Studies in Honour of John G. Hurst* (Oxford, 1992), 273–278.

Table 32. *Goods Shipped to New England on the* David *of Ferryland, September 1648*

Goods	Value	Proportion of Goods
18 butts of Canary and Madeira wine	£252	46%
2,743 pounds of sugar	137	25
787 yards of vitry	59	11
2,200 pounds of $\frac{1}{4}$, 10-pound cordage	44	8
200 pounds of wool	20	4
10 hogsheads of salt	5	1
hogsheads [empty]	3	1
128 yards of dowlas	10	2
120 pieces of "Virginia"	18	3
Total goods	£548	101%

Credits	Value	Proportion of Goods and Credits
Bill by Richard Right	£20	3%
Bond of Derby Feild	41	7
[Bill] of Mr. Brewster for stockings, shoes and "semakes"	5	1
Total debts	£66	11
Grand total	£614	100%

Note: Figures are given to the nearest pound sterling. Percentage of goods totals 101 owing to rounding errors. Vitry was a light, durable canvas, suitable for clothing; dowlas was a coarse linen cloth. Both fabrics originated in Brittany. "Virginia" is probably tobacco, although the unit, "pieces," is odd. "Semakes" is probably a misreading for "hemakes" (hammocks), as in Privy Council, Permit to Richard Long et al., Nov. 22, 1639, *APC*: Colonial.

Source: Sir David Kirke and Nicholas Shapley, "Invoyce of Goods Shipped Abord the *David* of Ferryland . . . ," Sept. 8, 1648, *Baxter MSS*, VI, 2–4.

of sugar, valued at £137, or 25 percent of the total. Sugar was likely used in seventeenth-century Newfoundland primarily for the preservation of berries and for the sweetened and spiced alcoholic drinks that were popular in the period.[23]

The importance at midcentury of the Atlantic islands in the trans-atlantic trade in alcohol is obvious, although West Country ships carried French and Spanish wines as well. Kirke's import of Madeira and Canary wines in 1648 was not an isolated transaction. In 1650, William Fishman brought fifteen pipes (6,900 liters) of wine from the Canaries on the *Adventure* of London and "sold or trucked" this shipment with Sir David. The Canary wine merchant John Paige saw Newfoundland as a better market for wine than New England, although he realized that even a strong market could be oversupplied. When he failed to interest the Kirkes in additional wines that season, he noted that Newfoundland "is every year overlaid, and, as I am informed, there goes from Madiera 100 pipes [460,000 liters] this year." About this time, Fayal in the Azores began to supply wine and brandy to the fisherfolk of Newfoundland and New England. The *Jonathan* of Minehead took a pipe (460 liters) of Fayal wine from Barnstaple for the Newfoundland fisheries in March 1647. John Bass, master of the forty-five-ton sack ship *John* of Topsham, took his ship first to Fayal for wine before calling at Caplin Bay for fish in 1677.[24]

The naval commodores' reports of the 1670s confirm that alcohol,

23. John Grosthwaite and Thomas Kirke, Examinations, in *Merchants Trading to Canada v. de Caen*, Sept. 22, 1632, Feb. 1, 1636, HCA 13/50, 91, HCA 13/52, 250–251; Merchants of the Western Ports, "Reply . . . to the Allegations of Captain Robert Robinson," ca. 1671, CO 1/22 (71), 118. On Champlain's attitude to the liquor trade, see Bruce G. Trigger, *Natives and Newcomers: Canada's "Heroic Age" Reconsidered* (Montreal and Kingston, 1985), 205, 318.

24. John Bewley, Answer to Allegations, in *Fishman et al. v. Bewley*, July 25, 1651, HCA 13/124, n.p.; Hugh Oldreday, Examination, ibid., July 16, 1651, HCA 13/65, n.p.; John Paige to George Paynter and William Clerke, Jan. 16, Feb. 6, 1650, in Paige, *Letters*, documents 11b, 13; Barnstaple Searcher, Port Books, 1647, E 190/952/4; William Poole, "Account of Fishing and Sackships from Trepassy to Cape Broyle," Sept. 10, 1677, CO 1/41 (62viii), 167–168. On Fayal, see T. Bentley Duncan, *Atlantic Islands: Madeira, the Azores, and the Cape Verdes in Seventeenth-Century Commerce and Navigation* (Chicago, 1972), 137–157, 248–250; on the Canaries, see George F. Steckley, "The Wine Economy of Tenerife in the Seventeenth Century: Anglo-Spanish Partnership in a Luxury Trade," *EHR*, 2d Ser., XXXIII (1980), 335–350.

particularly in the form of wine and brandy, was an important import into Newfoundland. Of fifty vessels arriving with cargoes at harbors between Trepassey and St. John's in Captain William Poole's list of sack ships for 1677, about sixteen, or one in three, imported alcohol. Captain John Berry's 1675 list of those supplying inhabitants and ships' crews with "Brandy, wines, etc." indicates that fishing ships also imported such goods to Newfoundland, although the vessels by far most likely to bring in alcohol were ships on mixed sacklike voyages employing only one or two boats. Berry also named five West Country merchants as alcohol importers. Of the six vessels carrying dutiable exports from Barnstaple to Newfoundland in 1664, five carried wines, including Malaga, sherry, and French vintages (Table 33). The exception, the *Hopewell*, carried one thousand pounds of white sugar. Captain Poole's 1677 list, "Severall Sorts of Wynes and Provisions Imported This Yeare Only in St. Johns Harbour," confirms that alcohol was a significant proportion of imports (Table 34). The beverages brought into St. John's would have exceeded the value of all other imports listed. The wine alone must have outweighed most other commodities, except flour and peas. Rum accounted for only 8,000 of the 68,000 gallons of wines and spirits imported in 1677, but by 1770 the continental colonies would send 274,000 gallons of rum to Newfoundland, making the island the largest New World market for this product at that time. Such demand reflected not only population growth but also a shift in taste from wine to rum, which was only beginning to be known in the northwest Atlantic in the 1660s and 1670s.[25]

25. Poole, "Trepassy to Cape Broyle," and William Poole, "Account of Fishing and Sackships from Balene to St. John's Harbour . . . ," Sept. 10, 1677, CO 1/41 (62 ix), 168–170. These figures assume that "Barbados goods" included rum and that imports from the Canary Islands included wine. "Provisions" from New England are not assumed here to have included rum, which they probably often did. John Berry, "A List of Ships Makinge Fishinge Voyages; with Boatkeepers . . . ," and Berry, "A List of Those That Have Furnisht . . . Brandy, Wines, etc. . . . ," Sept. 12, 1675, CO 1/35 (17i, 17iii), 136–148, 157, name as wine importers: Thomas Tucker of Teignmouth, James Lake of Dartmouth, Christopher Hayle and Mr. Woodsale of Topsham, and John Morrish of Plymouth. R. Cole Harris and Geoffrey J. Matthews, in *Historical Atlas of Canada*, I, 49, are in error in assuming that rum was the normal alcoholic drink in seventeenth-century Newfoundland; cf. David W. Conroy, *In Public Houses: Drink and the Revolution of Authority in Colonial Massachusetts* (Chapel Hill, N.C., 1995), 61–62; John J. McCusker, *Rum and the American Revolution: The Rum Trade and the Balance of Payments of the Thirteen Continental Colonies* (New York, 1989), II, 481–482, 497 (table VIII-3).

Table 33. *Dutiable Exports to Newfoundland from Barnstaple, 1664*

George Frigott of Barnstaple, 50 tons, February 24, 1664
Edward Rowe, master, for . . . Dolson, merchant
   2 hogsheads French wine

Guift of Bideford, 50 tons, March 4, 1664
Henry Cornish, master, for John Roberts, merchant
   1 tun French wine

Willing Minde, 50 tons, March 11, 1664
George Lake, master, for John Darracott, merchant
   1 butt sherry wine

Providence of Barnstaple, 140 tons, March 18, 1664
William Rowe, master, for John Seldon, merchant
   2 hogsheads French wine
   2 small casks Malaga wine

Hopewell of Bideford, 120 tons, April 1, 1664
John Loveringe, master, for John Boole and company, merchants
   100 yards Irish cloth
   6 dozen Irish stockings
   250 [Spanish] reals, in pieces of eight
   180 calf skins, worth £120
   1,000 pounds white sugar in ten little casks
   48 pieces Barnstaple single baize

Chesnutt of Barnstaple, 30 tons, May 10, 1664
Nicholas Taylor, master, for Jonathan Hooper, merchant
   1 butt French wine
   2 butts Malaga

Note: A tun is 252 wine gallons of 3.8 liters; a butt is 126; and a hogshead is 63.
   Sources: Barnstaple Customer, Port Book, 1664, E 190/954/2; Barnstaple Controller, Port Book, 1664, E 190/954/4.

The other important little luxury, tobacco, is a more elusive commodity in the documentary record of the English Shore (even if the stems and bowls of clay pipes are among the most prevalent material remains of the seventeenth century). The tobacco trade into Newfoundland was of long standing. The Dutch shipmaster David de Vries met a 120-ton

Table 34. *Imports of Provisions by Origin into St. John's,*
Newfoundland, 1677

Item (Unit)	England	France	America	West Indies	Atlantic Islands
Bread (pounds)	50,000	20,000	6,000		
Flour (pounds)	25,000	8,000	4,000		5,000
Pork (pounds)	41,000	10,000	2,600		5,000
Beef (pounds)	3,400				
Peas (pounds)	83,000		28,000		
Sugar (pounds)	13,000			11,000	2,200
Oil (small jars)					500
Hops (pounds)	2,000				
Malt (pounds)	28,000				
Molasses (pounds)				32,000	

Virginia ship trading tobacco for cod at Ferryland in 1620. Devon merchants with interests in Newfoundland and the Chesapeake kept this trade alive. In the late 1630s, the Dartmouth merchant Alexander Shapley sent the 80-ton *Susan* from Virginia to Newfoundland to pick up fish and to deliver tobacco there, en route to the British Isles. William Davis of Ferryland imported eighty pounds of tobacco on credit from the Boston merchant Charles Dobson in 1647, and others bought more on similar terms in the 1640s and 1650s. Tobacco also came roundabout, crossing the Atlantic twice, like the "Providence tobacco" on the *Unicorne* in 1640, the "Virginia" on the *David* of Ferryland in 1648, or the hogsheads of Virginia tobacco Thomas Chope took to Newfoundland on the 24-ton *Pleasure* of Bideford in 1665. Curiously, tobacco was imported into England from Newfoundland in the same period: in 1666, Mark Bickford

Table 34 (*continued*)

Item (Unit)	England	France	America	West Indies	Atlantic Islands
Rum (gallons)	4,000			4,000	
Wine (gallons)	28,000	3,800			24,000
Brandy (gallons)		4,500			
Salt (tons)		7,500			
Nets	150				
Lines	600				
Boat canvas (yards)		2,000			

Note: Some quantities have been converted to familiar measurements. Conversions for pork, sugar, and molasses required some estimates. Figures are rounded to 2 significant digits. For a slightly different reading of these data, see Head, *Newfoundland*, 101 (table 6.1).

Source: William Poole, "Severall Sorts of Wynes and Provisions Imported This Yeare Only in St. Johns Harbour," in Poole, "The Whole Account of All the Inhabitants in Newfoundland with All the Fishshipps, and Boats, and All Sackshipps for the Yeare 1677," Sept. 10, 1677, CO 1/41 (62x), 171–172.

brought five hundred pounds on the 40-ton *Unity* of Dartmouth back to his home port for the influential merchant Ambrose Mudd. Levels of tobacco imports are harder to fix than levels of alcohol imports. Surviving statistics leave no doubt that seventeenth-century Newfoundland was well supplied with wines and spirits, but, as a colonial good, tobacco easily escaped the wide mesh of British navigation regulations until the stricter interpretation of the 1680s.[26]

26. David Peterszoon de Vries, *Short Historical and Journal Notes of Several Voyages Made in the Four Parts of the World, Namely, Europe, Africa, Asia, and America* (1655), trans. Henry C. Murphy, New-York Historical Society, *Collections*, 2d Ser., III, pt. 1 (New York, 1857), 7; cf. Dicky Glerum-Laurentius, "A History of Dutch Activity in the Newfoundland Fish Trade from about 1590 till about 1680" (master's thesis, MUN, 1960), 22–25; Dartmouth Controller, Port Books, 1641, E 190/951/8; Thomas Bushrode, Statement of Account regarding

Anecdotes of alcohol and tobacco use in Newfoundland, and even the well-documented statistical data for the import of wines and brandy, require some evaluation. One difficulty is that Newfoundland was an entrepôt: British and New England merchants exchanged goods there. What the former supplied the latter was often wine and brandy. The Canary and Madeira wines David Kirke had entrusted to Nicholas Shapley in 1648 were eventually sold at Boston. The transatlantic current of alcohol that washed the shore of Newfoundland gave the planters and their servants access to wine and brandy in wholesale quantities but does not itself prove Newfoundland fisherfolk were wholesale consumers. The problem is broader. Fisherfolk were a major part of the New England market for alcohol, so the question raised by wine supply to Newfoundland is not what made island residents such consumers but why fisherfolk, including those of Newfoundland, were such a good market. This question has two aspects: quantity and quality. Visitors to the fishing periphery were impressed not simply by the amounts consumed but also that ordinary working people regularly drank "good liquor." Wines were, in seventeenth-century England, a middle-class luxury. Yet, along the Atlantic littoral, fishing men and women consumed wines and spirits in quantities considered unusual, given their modest social standing.[27]

The issue of class raises an additional problem in interpreting social

the *Susan*, Mar. 18, 1647, William Davies, Receipt, Sept. 26, 1647, William Preston, Receipt, Aug. 27, 1649, all in *Aspinwall Records*, 126, 205–206, 309; William Hudson, Deposition, Jan. 12, 1654, *RFQC Essex Co.*, I, 415; James Story, "An Account of What Fishing Shipps, Sack Shipps, Planters, etc., Boat Keepers . . . ," Sept. 1, 1681, CO 1/47 (52i), 113–121; Barnstaple Customer, Port Books, 1665, E 190/954/6; Dartmouth Customer, Port Books, 1666, E 190/954/10; Robert Robinson, "Inquiries Made . . . in Answer to Severall Heads . . . ," Oct. 11, 1680, CO 1/46 (8x), 33–34.

27. Ralph Greenlee Lounsbury, "Yankee Trade at Newfoundland," *New England Quarterly*, III (1930), 607–626; John Wyborn, "An Accompt of His Majesties . . . Subjects in Newfoundland," Dec. 7, 1676, CO 1/38 (83), 226; cf. John Berry, "Observations . . . in Relation to the Trade and Inhabitants of Newfoundland," Aug. 18, 1676, CO 1/35 (81), 325–326; Wheler, "Answers," Oct. 27, 1684, CO 1/55 (56), 239; James Kirke, Protest, Nov. 8, 1650, *Aspinwall Records*, 388–389; Poole, "Answers," Sept. 10, 1677, CO 1/41 (62i), 149; Clark, *English Alehouse*, 8, 96, 125; A. D. Francis, *The Wine Trade* (London, 1972), 26.

comment about the fishing stations of the Atlantic littoral. Middle-class Englishmen, like the merchants and naval officers who left observations of Newfoundland, were beginning to question levels of drinking by their social inferiors. Contemporary criticism of the alehouse can be seen as an early salvo in the effort to exert the kind of class-based cultural hegemony that resulted in eighteenth-century England in the "closed parish" and in New England in a significant reduction in the number of alehouses and taverns. The first and most vociferous criticisms of the Newfoundland tippling house coincided with a wave of similar disapproval of workers' drinking establishments on both sides of the Atlantic. Furthermore, this spate of criticisms was voiced by merchants of the same social background as those concerned with the maintenance, or establishment, of social order elsewhere. Contemporary accounts of drinking and smoking by Newfoundland fishermen express in part a class bias against working-class "waste" on luxuries like tobacco and alcohol or, in the case of the latter, against working-class consumption of inappropriately expensive forms of alcohol, like wine and spirits.[28]

If we discount class prejudices, were the fishermen of the early mod-

28. "Reasons for the Settlement of Newfoundland . . . under Government," ca. 1668, CO 1/22 (69), 115-116; CTP, Minutes, Feb. 2, Apr. 8, May 5, 1675, CO 391/1; Clark, *Eastern Frontier*, 22-23; Christine Leigh Heyrman, *Commerce and Culture: The Maritime Communities of Colonial Massachusetts, 1690-1750* (New York, 1984), 35, 218; cf. Duncan, *Atlantic Islands*, 154-156; Keith Wrightson, "Alehouses, Order, and Reformation in Rural England, 1590-1660," in Eileen Yeo and Stephen Yeo, eds., *Popular Culture and Class Conflict, 1590-1914: Explorations in the History of Labour and Leisure* (Sussex, N.J., 1981), 1-27; Peter Clark, "The Alehouse and the Alternative Society," in Donald Pennington and Keith Thomas, eds., *Puritans and Revolutionaries: Essays in Seventeenth-Century History Presented to Christopher Hill* (Oxford, 1978), 47-72; Clark, *English Alehouse*, 40, 166-187; Exeter Justices, Petition to Privy Council, Jan. 10, 1640, CO 1/10 (28), 46; Robert Gabbes [mayor of Plymouth] et al., Petition to Archbishop Laud, Jan. 22, 1640, SP 16/442, 77; Bartholomew Nicholl [mayor of Plymouth] et al., Petition, Mar. 24, 1646, in Stock, *Debates*, I, 177; Petition of the Merchant Adventurers of Plymouth, England, to the Council of State, ca. 1650, *Winthrop Papers*, VI, 4-6; cf. David Underdown, *Revel, Riot, and Rebellion: Popular Politics and Culture in England, 1603-1660* (Oxford, 1987), 84-88, 239-246. For doubts that such attempts at social control were novelties of the early modern period, see Margaret Spufford, "Puritanism and Social Control?" in Anthony Fletcher and John Stevenson, eds., *Order and Disorder in Early Modern England* (Cambridge, 1985), 41-57.

ern Atlantic littoral in fact just an ordinary lot of men, at least as far as the consumption of alcohol went? This conclusion is implausible. Contemporary observers with no motive to exaggerate the situation have left unambiguous testimony of an anomalous pattern of demand. John Winter, manager of the fishing station at Richmond Island, Maine, in the late 1630s, observed, "Great store of sacke and stronge waters comes in all the shippes." He himself regularly sold wines and spirits. For example, alcohol supplied to his fishing servant Nicholas Mathew made up 23 percent of his total account of £11 15s. 2.5d. in 1639, and Mathew's workmate Richard Cummings spent 41 percent of his £11 7s. 6d. account in the same way. Alcohol was, in fact, the most important consumer good among fishermen, and much of it was wine and spirits.[29]

The fisherfolk of the Atlantic littoral were atypical of working people in the Anglophone world, insofar as they consumed wines and spirits rather than beer. Fermented malt-based drinks were part of the daily diet of our ancestors. Laborers and their families could often afford only small beer, the weak product of a second fermentation of the wort that had already produced a stronger brew. In a period when water supplies were often suspect, home-brewed beers and ales of low alcohol content functioned in part simply as a healthier substitute for water. (Recall that brewing required preliminary boiling.) On the fishing littoral, from the English Shore to the coast of New England, the choice between thirst-quenching and pharmacological recreation was a choice between water or weaker ales, on the one hand, and, on the other hand, stronger ales or beers, French, Iberian, or island wines, French, Dutch, or island brandy, and, after 1660, American rum. The relatively new alco-

29. For New England parallels, see Richard P. Gildrie, "Taverns and Popular Culture in Essex County, Massachusetts, 1678–1686," Essex Institute, *Historical Collections*, CXXIV (1988), 158–185; Conroy, *In Public Houses*, 8, 12–59; Innes, *Creating the Commonwealth*, 135. E. A. Churchill, "A Most Ordinary Lot of Men: The Fishermen at Richmond Island, Maine, in the Early Seventeenth Century," *NEQ*, LVII (1984), 184–204, argues that the image of early New England fishermen as drinkers and brawlers is overdrawn. "The reality of leisure time activities" offered by way of an alternative is, however, based on secondary accounts and conjecture, and it ignores the testimony discussed here: John Winter to Robert Trewlawney, July 18, 1639, and "Monnyes Owing to the Plantation," Nov. 29, 1639, *Trelawny Papers*, 174, 184–187. This debate is of long standing; cf. John Scribner Jenness, *The Isles of Shoals: An Historical Sketch* (New York, 1873), 123–124; and Clark, *Eastern Frontier*, 13–35.

hols—brandy, grain spirits or aqua vitae, and the strong sweet wines of Iberia and the Atlantic islands—shipped better than weaker, drier wines or beer. The traditional, unhopped English ale did not store, let alone ship well, and the new, stronger hopped beers shipped only somewhat better. Until the development of bottled porter in the eighteenth century, Newfoundland generally imported malt, not beer. Without denying that Newfoundland beers might sometimes have been brewed for strength, imported malt or molasses would normally have been stretched to produce as much as possible, given the contemporary mistrust of water as a regular drink. But, when planters and fishermen wanted alcohol, Newfoundland's isolation and the shipping qualities of the various available beverages meant that they were likely to tap a cask of wine, brandy, or, eventually, rum—a pattern that middle-class visitors to the island would find remarkable.[30]

Archaeological analysis confirms the tendency of most of those living and working at Newfoundland to seek the immediate satisfaction of the jug, the pipe, or a warm suit of clothes, rather than the longer-term gratifications of consumer durables, whether decorative pottery or better housing. Excavators at Ferryland have uncovered, among other features, the smithy constructed for Sir George Calvert's original colony in 1622 and in use until the 1650s. The thousands of artifacts recovered include a surprisingly wide range of pottery and clay tobacco pipes, within a deposit of slag, scale, cinders, iron concretions, and coal, which had accumulated around the forge. Comparison with assemblages excavated elsewhere makes it clear that fishermen often shared a mess of pottage, a pipe, or a jug of wine in the Ferryland smithy (Table 35). Beverage vessels are strongly represented in the assemblage, composing about 30 per-

30. Clark, *English Alehouse*, 24, 95, 103; Josselyn, *Voyages*, 13, 15, 145; McCusker, *Rum Trade*, I, 55–58; Duncan, *Atlantic Islands*, 38–39; James E. McWilliams, "Brewing Beer in Massachusetts Bay, 1640–1690," *NEQ*, LXXI (1998), 543–569. Exemption from Customs, Sept. 14, 1629, in Cell, *Newfoundland Discovered*, 291; John Berry to Joseph Williamson, July 24, 1675, CO 1/34 (118), 240–241. E. S., *Britaines Busse; or, A Computation as Well of the Charge of a Busse or Herring-Fishing Ship; as Also of the Gaine and Profit Thereby* (London, 1615), an anonymous proposal for an improved fishery, assumes a daily beer ration of one gallon, in addition to a shipboard supply of aqua vitae. For a balanced discussion of the range of beverages available, see John Burnett, *Liquid Pleasures: A Social History of Drinks in Modern Britain* (London, 1999), 7–11, 111–115, 141–147, 160–166.

Table 35. *Ceramic Beverage Vessels at Ferryland and Comparative Contexts, Seventeenth Century*

Context	Date	Beverage Vessels	All Vessels	Beverage as Proportion of All Vessels
Ferryland Smithy				
3b, smithy debris	1640–1660	19	60	32%
2b, household fill	1660–1700	23	77	30
Martin's Hundred, Virginia				
Site H, dwelling	1620–1622	15	95	16%
Site B, dwelling	1620–1640	25	194	13
Site A, governor's(?)	1625–1645	20	126	16
Place Royale, Quebec City				
Place Royale II	1627–1632	2	15	13%
Habitation II	1627–1632	4	25	16
Place Royale III	1633–1688	9	43	21
Habitation III	1633–1688	6	32	19
St. Mary's City, Maryland				
Lewgar house	1638–1660	16	86	19%
Smith's ordinary	1667–1680	18	51	35
Exeter, Devon				
Urban sites	1600–1660	51	197	26%
Urban sites	1660–1700	149	559	27
Pentagoet, Maine				
French fort	1635–1674	22	108	20%

Table 35 (*continued*)

Context	Date	Beverage Vessels	All Vessels	Beverage as Proportion of All Vessels
		Bay Bulls, Newfoundland		
HMS *Saphire*	1696	49	196	25%

Note: All assemblages are stratigraphic, except those from the Lewgar residence at St. Mary's City and Exeter. The former is Phase I, that is, artifacts typologically classified as predating 1660. The Exeter data reflect totals for sites ascribed to the seventeenth century. At Quebec City, "Habitation" is the main interior space of Samuel de Champlain's habitation, including the towers. "Place Royale" refers to the open public space nearby. Minimum numbers of individual ceramic vessels were assessed taking into account both ware and form. Beverage vessels include cups, mugs, drinking pots, jugs, bottles, ewers, pitchers, punch bowls, and very small bowls suitable for drinking.

Sources: Peter Edward Pope, "Ceramics from Seventeenth-Century Ferryland, Newfoundland (CgAf-2, Locus B)" (master's thesis, MUN, 1986). For Ferryland, Martin's Hundred, Quebec, St. Mary's City, and HMS *Saphire*, counts are based on artifact inspection, guided by the inventories of the repositories: MUN Archaeology Unit, St. John's, Newfoundland; Colonial Williamsburg Foundation, Williamsburg, Va.; Ministère des Affaires Culturelles, Quebec City; Historic St. Mary's, Maryland; and Archaeological Service, National Historic Parks and Sites Canada, Ottawa. Comparison was based in part on William Pittman, "Vessel Count for Martin's Hundred Sites," Colonial Williamsburg Foundation, n.d.; and Gérard Gusset, "Interim Report on the Ceramics Found in Bay Bulls in 1977," National Historic Parks and Sites Canada, Ottawa, 1978. The investigations at St. Mary's City, Quebec City, and Ottawa were made with the guidance of Dr. Henry Miller, François Neillon, and Gérard Gusset, respectively. The Exeter data are from John P. Allan, *Medieval and Post-Medieval Finds from Exeter, 1971-1980* (Exeter, 1984), microfiche 43. The Pentagoet data are from Alaric Faulkner and Gretchen Fearon Faulkner, *The French at Pentagoet, 1635-1674* (St. John, N.B., 1987), 184-185. On the comparison sites, see also Ivor Noël Hume, *Martin's Hundred: The Discovery of a Lost Colonial Virginia Settlement* (New York, 1982); Henry M. Miller, *Discovering Maryland's First City: A Summary Report on the 1981-1984 Archaeological Excavations in St. Mary's City, Maryland* (St. Mary's City, Md., 1986); and François Neillon and Marcel Moussette, *Le site de l'Habitation de Champlain à Québec: étude de la collection archéologique (1976-1980)* (Quebec, 1985).

cent of all vessels, which is about twice the proportion at contemporary colonial residential sites and matched only at a Maryland tavern, among a range of contemporary comparison sites. The forms of ceramic vessels used at the Ferryland smithy make it look like a cookroom or tippling house. Since a tippling house needed a warm fire, blacksmiths were among the tradesmen most likely to branch into the hospitality industry. The Ferryland smithy certainly had some such secondary function. This analysis does not, however, do much more than prove that Ferryland fishermen had at least one warm place to drink and smoke.[31]

The problem of differential rates of consumption of alcohol and tobacco remains. A broader comparison of four seventeenth-century assemblages from Ferryland with assemblages from contemporary contexts elsewhere can be used to address this issue. The Ferryland contexts include the late smithy deposits of the 1640s and 1650s, the working floor at a waterfront structure of about 1640–1670, household refuse dating between 1660 and 1700, and fill of around 1670 in the waterfront privy. The artifacts best suited to comparative statistical analysis of early modern assemblages are ceramics, glass, clay tobacco pipes, and gun flints. Table glass in the seventeenth century was, however, a very status-sensitive good, not much used by people like fishermen, and gun flints are absent from most urban sites. So, in the end, what we have to work with are ceramics, bottles, and pipes. This methodological limitation places a heavy interpretative burden on ceramics, particularly nonbeverage vessels, for these are made to stand for all goods not related to the pastimes of drinking and smoking. For the purposes of statistical comparison, the minimum numbers of individual ceramic vessels, ceramic beverage vessels, bottles, and clay tobacco pipe bowls were translated into three indexes. The first, reflecting tobacco use, counts clay tobacco pipes and expresses this number as a percentage of all ceramics, glass bottles, and pipes. The second, reflecting drink, counts beverage ceramics and glass bottles and expresses these figures as a percentage in the same way. The third index, for pastimes, combines pipes with beverage ceramics and glass bottles and expresses these numbers together as a percentage of all the relevant artifacts (Table 36).[32]

31. Matthew Carter, "A Seventeenth-Century Smithy at Ferryland, Newfoundland," *Avalon Chronicles*, II (1997), 73–106; Pope, "Ceramics from Ferryland," 223–244; Pope, "South Avalon," 416–417; Mary C. Beaudry et al., "A Vessel Typology for Early Chesapeake Ceramics: The Potomac Typological System," *Historical Archaeology*, XVII, no. 1 (1983), 18–43; Clark, *English Alehouse*, 66, 75.

32. This may be too heavy an interpretative burden for a stack of dishes, especially given that even earthenwares were moderately status-sensitive in the period in question, and tin-glazed ceramics and stonewares were markedly so. The attempt to rest interpretation on this fragile basis is made here faute de mieux. Comparative analysis of assemblages is necessarily limited to artifacts not subject to marked differences of preservation in different soils. Attempts made to identify

Between about 1630 and 1660, there appears to have been a modal pattern in the English-speaking world in which drinking and smoking artifacts made up about 25 and 35 percent, respectively, of artifacts analyzed; pastimes together, then, are about 60 percent of all artifacts. This pattern appears at the Ferryland waterfront and at the Lewgar mansion, St. John's, an early administrative center, and the gentry residence at St. Mary's City, Maryland. The Ferryland smithy, on the other hand, exhibits a pattern much more like that at Pope's Fort, an English Civil War defense of 1645 at St. Mary's City. War, it has been said, is 90 percent boredom and 10 percent terror. The archaeological remains here tell us as much about the months passed in waiting by the Virginian mercenaries who manned the fort as they do about the soldiers' brief hour of battle. The artifact pattern at Ferryland probably also reflects periods in which groups of men passed time smoking and sharing an occasional drink. In this case, the archaeological remains would relate to periods of a day or two, while crews waited for better weather, rather than a single wait of several months, but the resulting deposits would be archaeologically similar. The artifacts reported from Fort Pentagoet suggest drinking and smoking indexes of about 10 and 60 percent, which are close to the indexes for Pope's Fort and the Ferryland smithy. The proposed modal pattern disguises important differences between artifact patterns in Anglo-colonial contexts and lower-middle- or middle-class residential contexts excavated in Exeter, Devon. Mid-seventeenth-century artifact patterns in Exeter resemble those at Quebec, rather than in the English colonies: in each case, drink-related artifacts are three to four times as frequent as pipes. If the pastime indexes for Anglo-colonial sites are much higher than for Exeter or Quebec, that is primarily because of the relatively high frequencies of pipes in the former. Thus, in the early and mid-seventeenth century, smoking was less common in Quebec or even in English county centers like Exeter than it was in the English colonies, where it had already found a mass market.[33]

---

statistical patterns including ferrous metal objects like nails are therefore unconvincing. Another problem with such comparisons is the conflation of architectural materials with artifacts from within the structure, although these are stratigraphically distinct. On glass, see Shammas, *Pre-Industrial Consumer*, 182–185.

33. Alaric Faulkner and Gretchen Fearon Faulkner, *The French at Pentagoet, 1635–1674* (St. John, N.B., 1987), 184–185 (table 7.1), 232, 297; cf. Goodman, *Tobacco in History*, 63.

Table 36. *Artifacts Related to Drink and Tobacco in Seventeenth-Century Assemblages from Ferryland and Comparative Contexts*

Assemblage (Date)	Artifacts (N)	Proportion of Assemblage		
		Drink	Tobacco	Pastime
ca. 1630–1660				
Ferryland				
Smithy 3b (1640–1660)	165	13%	62%	75%
Waterfront 3 (1640–1670)	87	25	36	61
St. Mary's City				
Pope's Fort (ca. 1645)	142	21	66	87
Lewgar res. I (1638–1660)	165	25	32	58
Colonial average		21	49	70
Exeter, Devon				
Valiant Soldier 61, 63 (1620–1645)	57	32	4	35
Trichay St. 316 (ca. 1660)	146	24	16	40
Exeter average		28	10	38
British Atlantic average		23	36	59
Quebec City				
Place Royale (1627–1632)	23	35	9	43
Habitation (1627–1632)	40	33	15	48
Place Royale (1633–1688)	64	44	3	47
Habitation (1633–1688)	43	33	7	40
Quebec average		36	8	44
Overall average		35%	31%	67%

Table 36 (*continued*)

Assemblage (Date)	Artifacts (N)	Proportion of Assemblage		
		Drink	Tobacco	Pastime

<table>
<tr><td colspan="5" align="center">ca. 1660–1700</td></tr>
</table>

Assemblage (Date)	Artifacts (N)	Drink	Tobacco	Pastime
Ferryland				
Smithy fill 2b				
(1660–1700)	159	24%	42%	66%
Privy fill				
(ca. 1670)	127	13	44	57
St. Mary's City				
Smith's ordinary				
(1666–1677)	76	32	25	57
Lawyer's cellar				
(ca. 1670?)	163	31	7	37
Colonial average		25	29	54
Exeter, Devon				
Goldsmith St. 96				
(1660–1680)	103	17	12	28
Goldsmith St. 98				
(1660–1680)	65	28	19	46
Goldsmith St. 80				
(1670–1700)	160	18	24	41
North Street 150				
(1680–1690)	117	26	11	37
Exeter average		22	16	38
Overall average		23%	23%	46%

Note: Percentages for "Pastime" are derived from raw data. The size of assemblages given *(N)* is the minimum count of ceramic vessels, clay tobacco pipes, and bottles. "Drink" artifacts include both ceramic beverage vessels and bottles. "Tobacco" artifacts are clay tobacco pipe bowls. "Pastime" artifacts are drink and tobacco artifacts together. Minimum numbers of individual ceramic vessels take into account both ware and form. Beverage vessels include cups, mugs, drink pots, jugs, bottles, ewers, pitchers, punch bowls, and very small bowls, suitable for drinking. The count of tobacco pipe bowls includes pipe heels distinct from bowls already counted, but pipes were not distinguished by stem decoration or by clay fabric, because this method of analysis was not possible at

Table 36 (*continued*)

all sites. Bottle glass represents counts based on mouths and bases, taking into account shades of glass, but excludes small vials and urinals. All assemblages are stratigraphic, except the sample from the Lewgar residence, St. John's, at St. Mary's City, which is Phase I, that is, artifacts typologically classified as predating 1660. The Pope's Fort sample is from the preliminary excavation, that is, units 1221, 1222, and 1280–1283. At Quebec City, "Habitation" is the main interior space of Champlain's Habitation, excluding the towers. "Place Royale" refers to the open public space nearby.

Sources: Counts are based on artifact inspection, guided by the inventories of relevant repositories. These are the Archaeology Unit at MUN, St. John's, Newfoundland; Historic St. Mary's, Maryland; the Royal Albert Museum, Exeter, Devon; and the Quebec Ministère des Affaires Culturelles, Quebec City. The comparative investigations were made with the guidance of Dr. Henry Miller, John Allan, and François Neillon, respectively. On the comparison sites, see Henry M. Miller, *Discovering Maryland's First City: A Summary Report on the 1981–1984 Archaeological Excavations in St. Mary's City Maryland* (St. Mary's City, Md., 1986); John P. Allan, *Medieval and Post-Medieval Finds from Exeter, 1971–1980* (Exeter, 1984), microfiche 43; François Neillon and Marcel Moussette, *Le site de l'Habitation de Champlain à Québec: étude de la collection archéologique (1976–1980)* (Quebec, 1985).

The Ferryland assemblages of 1660–1700 exhibit high pastime indexes, in the order of 60 percent, a level matched only by Smith's "ordinary," or tavern, at St. Mary's City. Drink-related artifacts are relatively less common at the Ferryland waterfront than in the household fill, whereas pipes are well represented in both assemblages, suggesting that drink was primarily a leisure activity, but smoking also went on in the workplace. (Recall that planter households were almost always tippling houses as well.) Again, the colonial contexts exhibit high tobacco indexes compared to Exeter contexts. The Goldsmith Street contexts in Exeter are mixed assemblages, reflecting disparate aspects of seventeenth-century urban life. The ceramics from Goldsmith Street 80 include some sugar-refining wares, suggesting that part of the assemblage relates to a workplace, which may explain the relatively high smoking index for this context. Pipes are more common in later samples at Exeter, indicating that the habit of smoking was still spreading in the closing decades of the seventeenth century. The merchant's house at North Street 1501 exhibits a low smoking index combined with a high drinking index, a pattern also apparent in refuse from a St. Mary's City lawyer's office of about 1670. The archaeological evidence thus confirms the suspicion that in the late seventeenth century smoking was "out of vogue among those most amenable to the dictates of fashion," who by this time were using snuff.[34]

Both earlier- and later-seventeenth-century assemblages from Ferryland suggest strong demand for alcohol and tobacco relative to demand for nonbeverage ceramics. Among comparison contexts, only a fort and a tavern were occupied by people so strongly inclined to immediate gratification. At Exeter, Devon, only one site bears much of a similarity in the functional distribution of artifacts. Finds at Quebec indicate that early French colonists there were just as inclined to drink, but much less likely to smoke. The archaeological evidence from one site cannot prove that fishermen were abnormally inclined to consume alcohol and tobacco any more than one document could establish such a point. Taken together, however, the documentary and the archaeological evidence suggest, consistently, that fisherfolk preferred alcohol and tobacco among the goods on which they might have spent their discretionary income. The archaeological evidence has the virtue of being firsthand: the many jugs, bottles, and clay pipes at Ferryland must be explained because they were there, not because a West Country fishing master complained about them. The evidence from commercial and customs papers has the virtue of putting tobacco and alcohol in context, or at least in social and economic context. The consumption of alcohol and tobacco surely also has a cultural significance.

ⳛ The Cultural Significance of Alcohol and Tobacco

Robert Hitchcock's late Elizabethan vision of Englishmen exchanging fish for European wines (Plate 4) became a seventeenth-century

---

34. Valiant Soldier 63 became the site of a tippling house after the English Civil War, hence the name. Despite the relatively high drinking index, its very low smoking index suggests that such an establishment did not exist on the site before being slighted during the defense of the city in 1643. There is an extraordinary assemblage of 160 pipe bowls and twenty-two bottles from the northwest tower of the Quebec Habitation, phase II (1627–1632), but, since the pipes are almost all of one form and are all unsmoked, the assemblage is likely goods stored—probably by the Kirke brothers, who controlled Quebec at this time. Quotation from Apperson, *Social History of Smoking*, 57. On snuff, see Goodman, *Tobacco in History*, 69–75.

reality, although Hitchcock had not foreseen the extent to which English demand for wine would be expressed at the second vertex of his proposed triangle of trade, the fishing periphery itself. The economy of the cod fishery and the economy of the wine trade interconnected at the Iberian, Mediterranean, and Atlantic island ports, where London and West Country ships delivered Newfoundland and New England fish. The tobacco and cod economies meshed at tobacco-distributing Devon ports like Barnstaple, which had close ties with the Chesapeake, as well as Newfoundland. These macroeconomic structures did not, however, preclude exchange at Newfoundland itself, and, in a sense, they required it. In the situation of chronic specie scarcity, typical of the early modern world, merchants were under great pressure to develop returns for the goods whose export they organized: they could not hope to pay for fish entirely in coin, for coin was too scarce. The reasonably high unit value and portability of sweet wines, spirits, and tobacco made them useful commodities in this respect. Fish itself was a quasi currency on the Atlantic littoral, and alcohol sometimes played the same role. Divisibility is an important economic property of such quasi currencies, which has been noted in other contexts, from the Australian outback to the twentieth-century St. John's waterfront. Divisibility also made it possible to tap the passing flow of these goods.[35]

Demand for a good, whether alcohol or tobacco, earthenware or Barnstaple baize, represents some combination of taste and disposable income. However much the inhabitants of seventeenth-century Ferryland might have wanted a cup of wine or a pipe of tobacco, they could not enjoy these little luxuries unless they could afford them. Newfoundland fishing crews made good money compared to what they could expect in

35. Grant, *North Devon Pottery*, 116–125; W. T. Baxter, *The House of Hancock: Business in Boston, 1724–1775* (1945; rpt. New York, 1965), 16, 295; Jacob Price, *Capital and Credit in British Overseas Trade: The View from the Chesapeake, 1700–1776* (Cambridge, Mass., 1980), 121; Price, "Conclusion," in Ommer, *Merchant Credit*, 368; McCusker, *Rum Trade*, 552; Adam Smith, *An Inquiry into the Nature and Causes of the Wealth of Nations* (1776) (Harmondsworth, Eng., 1970), 127; Heath, "Alcohol Use," and Gerald Mars, "Longshore Drinking, Economic Security, and Union Politics in Newfoundland," both in Douglas, ed., *Constructive Drinking*, 16–69 (esp. 33), 91–101; Black, "Anthropology of Tobacco Use," *Jour. Anthro. Research*, XL (1984), 475–503 (esp. 486); Jeff Collman, "Social Order and the Exchange of Liquor: A Theory of Drinking among the Australian Aborigines," ibid., XXXV (1979), 208–224.

the Old Country, and they spent freely on their preferred goods, tobacco and alcohol. This apparently feckless attitude is like one observed among deep-sea mariners of the period in which gratification and consumption are the norm rather than deferral and saving. To observe that fishermen are mariners is, however, only to broaden a difficult question. Why did this particular culture of consumption flourish among maritime folk? At one level, fishermen used alcohol and tobacco just as young, mobile, erratically employed males did in the home country, as an occasion for socializing. The *Young Men's Delight*, which brought wines from Plymouth to Ferryland in 1675, was well named. The recreational nature of early modern drinking, with its shift from the home to the tippling house and the concomitant exclusion of wives and children, distinguished it from medieval patterns of consumption. For most people, home was a place to work, or to sleep, or to pray, but not a place for relaxation. What the typical fishing servant temporarily called home in Newfoundland was at best a pallet in a planter's loft, at worst a few spruce boughs in the corner of a flimsy wattle and canvas shack, shared with a dozen of his mates. The seventeenth-century worker normally found social life outside the home, either in a religious congregation or in a tippling house, but, as Captain Wheler observed of the English Shore, "if the people doe assemble 'tis not to heare divine service." Why did fishermen choose the tippling house? What was it that made tobacco and alcohol sociable? Did these goods have a special role in Newfoundland or at the fishing periphery in general?[36]

36. Marcus Rediker, *Between the Devil and the Deep Blue Sea: Merchant Seamen, Pirates, and the Anglo-American Maritime World, 1700–1750* (Cambridge, 1987), 149; Clark, *English Alehouse*, 49, 114, 139, 148; Berry, "List of Ships," Sept. 12, 1675, CO 1/35 (17i), 136–148; Berry, "Brandy, Wines, etc.," Sept. 12, 1675, CO 1/35 (17iii), 157; Jessica Warner, "Before There Was 'Alcoholism': Lessons from the Medieval Experience with Alcohol," *Contemporary Drug Problems*, XIX (1992), 409–429; Shammas, "Domestic Environment," *Jour. Soc. Hist.*, XIV (1980–1981), 3–24 (esp. 10); Clark, *English Alehouse*, 123–132; Weatherill, *Material Culture*, 158; Wheler, "Observations," Oct. 27, 1684, CO 1/55 (56i), 247–248. Daniel Vickers, "Work and Life on the Fishing Periphery of Essex County, Massachusetts, 1630–1675," in David D. Hall and David Grayson Allen, eds., *Seventeenth Century New England: A Conference Held by the Colonial Society of Massachusetts, June 18 and 19, 1982*, Colonial Society of Massachusetts, *Publications*, LXIII, *Collections* (Boston, 1984), 83–117, suggests that high rates of alcohol consumption on the resource periphery resulted from social and political marginality. Newfoundland was certainly politically marginal, but fisherfolk were not

To ask why people enjoy alcohol or tobacco may seem willfully obtuse, but the question needs to be posed. Nor is the answer straightforward. Anthropological literature supports the consensus of psychologists and sociologists that the cardinal value of alcohol is pharmacological, as a cheap, easy-to-administer tranquilizer. The value of tobacco is also rooted in its psychopharmacological properties, although these are more complex. Nicotine sharpens responses, but it is also highly addictive, to the extent that deprivation provokes irritability among chronic smokers. So, in a sense, tobacco is also a cheap and simple tranquilizer, although, unlike alcohol, this potential depends on its addictiveness in small dosages. The physiological and pharmacokinetic effects of both drugs are socially processed: interpreted and expressed in terms of familiar attitudes and expectations. If the use of alcohol can be seen in three distinct aspects — as a component of economic activity, as a manifestation of the structure of social reality, and as a ceremonial construction of an ideal world — then these aspects apply, surely, to tobacco as well. Although it is not easy to pin down the sociocultural construction seventeenth-century mariners put on the pharmacological effects of their drugs, we have enough evidence to try.[37]

Alcohol and tobacco both functioned as "little hearths," for each satisfied the need for warmth. Dr. Giles Everard's early-seventeenth-century defense of tobacco argued that those proposing a ban should take into account users' needs: "Sea-men will be supplied with it for their long voyages; souldiers cannot want it when they keep guards all night, or are upon other hard duties in cold and tempestuous weather." Half a century later, Captain Francis Wheler contended that the "intolerable cold" at Newfoundland "would make it hard liveing with out strong drink." The perceived warmth of either tobacco or alcohol as a real physiological effect is difficult to see. Although nicotine briefly increases heart rate and blood pressure, it reduces peripheral blood flow and, therefore, warms

---

much more marginal than most of the working population of England itself; cf. Keith Wrightson, *English Society, 1580–1680* (New Brunswick, N.J., 1982), 149–182.

37. Heath, "Alcohol Use," and Douglas, "A Distinctive Anthropological Perspective," in Douglas, ed., *Constructive Drinking*, 3–15 (esp. 4, 8), 16–69 (esp. 39, 46); Black, "Anthropology of Tobacco Use," *Jour. Anthro. Research*, XL (1984), 475–503 (esp. 486, 494). Even drunkenness is a learned comportment, varying from culture to culture; see Craig MacAndrew and Robert B. Edgerton, *Drunken Comportment: A Social Explanation* (Chicago, 1969), 83–99.

your body only at the expense of cooling your hands and feet. Smoking a pipe of tobacco did involve a cheery glow, but any consequent warming probably had less to do with the combustion of a few grams of dried leaves than with the need to enter a building like the Ferryland smithy for an ember to light the pipe. The warmth ascribed to tobacco is, in effect, a social warmth, since the good is often shared. Mariners also thought of alcohol as a source of warmth, but, in fact, it contributes to cooling the body by dilating surface blood vessels. It provides physiological warmth only as a concentrated and surprisingly inexpensive source of calories. Otherwise, the association of alcohol and heat was also primarily symbolic.[38]

This symbolism is rooted in ancient humoral theories about the four elements, earth, water, air, and fire, and the four primary properties, cold, moisture, dryness, and heat. The association of dryness and heat with alcohol in general and with red wines and spirits in particular is explicit in a tract of 1622 on "divers kindes of drinke." Tobias Venner argues that one of the "commodities of wine" is that it "mightily strengtheneth the naturall heat." Ale, beer, even white and Rhenish wines he dismisses as cold, like water. Sack, on the other hand, is "compleatly hot," as are Canary wine and the wines of western France. Predictably, he treats distilled aqua vitae as hot and cautiously suggests moderate consumption "be permitted unto cold and phlegmaticke bodies, especially in colde and moyst seasons," as does William Vaughan, the Newfoundland promoter, who calls aqua vitae "the most dry and fiery of all liquids" in his *Di-*

38. [Giles] Everard, *Panacea; or, The Universal Medicine, Being a Discovery of the Wonderfull Vertues of Tobacco* . . . (London, 1659), A [3]; Wheler, "Observations," Oct. 27, 1684, CO 1/55 (56i), 247–248; G. L. Mangan and J. F. Golding, *The Psychopharmacology of Smoking* (Cambridge, 1984), 100, 116; Leslie O. Simpson and Robin J. Olds, "Ethanol and the Flow Properties of Blood," in Kathryn E. Crow and Richard D. Batt, eds., *Human Metabolism of Alcohol*, III, *Metabolic and Physiological Effects of Alcohol* (Boca Raton, Fla., 1989), 62–75. Distilled alcohol provided the cheapest available calories for the eighteenth-century Polish peasantry, according to F. P. Braudel and F. Spooner, "Prices in Europe from 1450 to 1750," in E. E. Rich and C. H. Wilson, eds., *Cambridge Economic History of Europe*, IV, *The Economy of Expanding Europe in the Sixteenth and Seventeenth Centuries* (Cambridge, 1967), 415–416; cf. McCusker, *Rum Trade*, 478. "Little hearths" is my late colleague Ralph Pastore's felicitous phrase. Coffee, tea, and chocolate raise similar issues; see Ross W. Jamieson, "The Essence of Commodification: Caffeine Dependencies in the Early Modern World," *Jour. Soc. Hist.*, XXXV (2001–2002), 269–294.

rections for Health, Naturall and Artificiall of 1626. In 1639, the Privy Council referred to spirits simply as "hot waters" in a permit for export to Newfoundland. Venner and Vaughan could hardly have written more explicit prescriptions for those facing the rigors of the North Atlantic fishery. What would new arrivals face? Cold and moisture. How could they deal with these discomforts? With drinks that were conceptually hot and dry. Venner identifies precisely those most in demand at Newfoundland: spirits, sack, Bordeaux, and the red wines of the Atlantic islands. From this point of view, tobacco was also entirely appropriate for the North Atlantic environment, for smoke is hot and dry. When early modern Europeans brought this exotic commodity into their philosophical systems, they conceptualized it as possessing the appropriate humoral properties to "expell moisture." The ideal world that wine, brandy, and tobacco constructed for the planters and crews of the English Shore might well have been simply a warmer and drier one.[39]

The question of how the use of tobacco and alcohol manifests the structure of social reality remains. Desirable, portable, divisible little luxuries, like alcohol and tobacco, are well suited as prestations, that is, gifts that create social obligations. Prestation may be horizontal, among peers, or vertical, from employer to employee or from patron to client. For planter or servant, no less than for the merchant, alcohol and tobacco were valuables, appropriate for exchange and short-term storage of capital. They had high unit value and were reasonably durable, although not so durable as to encourage long-term accumulation. Binges dispersed such short-term savings in a neighborly way. The valuables in question were then transformed into social capital, that is, the distributor of little luxuries could expect favorable treatment by those with whom the gifts were shared.[40]

39. For a brief summary, see E. M. W. Tillyard, *The Elizabethan World Picture* (Harmondsworth, Eng., 1963), 77–83; cf. Beverly Ann Tlusty, "Gender and Alcohol Use in Early Modern Augsburg," and Pope, "Fish into Wine," both in Blocker and Warsh, eds., *Changing Face of Drink*, 21–42, 43–64; [Tobias Venner], *Via Recta ad Vitam Longam* . . . (London, 1622), 23–36; William Vaughan, *Directions for Health, Naturall and Artificiall* . . . , 6th ed. (London, 1626), 81–82; cf. Richard Short, *Of Drinking Water, against Our Novelists, That Prescribed It in England* (London, 1656); Privy Council, Permit to Richard Long et al., Nov. 22, 1639, *APC*: Colonial; Goodman, *Tobacco in History*, 41–43, 46, 61, 76, 85.

40. Hugo F. Reading, *Dictionary of the Social Sciences* (London, 1977), 160; Marcel Mauss, *The Gift: Forms and Functions of Exchange in Archaic Societies,*

The consumable nature of tobacco and alcohol is important here, for small gifts of such goods can hardly be passed down the line. The distribution of drink sometimes took on the very traditional character of a work feast, a celebration designed to discharge the social obligations undertaken by accepting volunteer help with a large task. In 1680, Captain Sir Robert Robinson thought the fortifications at St. John's could be improved at little cost, "except some small gratuity to the seamen in time of laboring, in brandy or the like." The use of alcohol to seal bargains is, surely, a similar kind of generalized exchange in the sense that an economic relationship is cemented by strengthening its social dimension. Within the context of a dispute, a shared drink might have even more significance, as in an attempted mutiny on a Newfoundland sack ship in 1672, when "the master and marchant profered [the mutineers] that if thay would . . . take a drame of the botell and set doune and drinke friends and that all things should be forgoting." Insofar as economic relationships on the fishing periphery were a continuous succession of mutual favors, payment without prestation of drink, in particular, was likely the exception, not the rule. Captain Wheler's "intelligible planter," for example, had "given away for incouragment: In liquour £6." Such verti-

trans. Ian Cunnison (London, 1970); Heath, "Alcohol Use," in Douglas, ed., *Constructive Drinking*, 16–69 (esp. 40); Black, "Anthropology of Tobacco Use," *Jour. Anthro. Research*, XL (1984), 475–503 (esp. 481, 488–490); Wheler, "Charge for Two Boats," Oct. 27, 1684, CO 1/55 (56iii), 251–252; Robert Robinson to [William Blathwayt?], Apr. 5, 1680, CO 1/44 (50), 383. On drinking binges, see Clark, *English Alehouse*, 114; and Michael Dietler, "Consumption, Agency, and Cultural Entanglement: Theoretical Implications of a Mediterranean Colonial Encounter," in James G. Cusick, ed., *Studies in Culture Contact: Interaction, Culture Change, and Archaeology* (Carbondale, Ill., 1998), 288–315 (esp. 302, on the work feast). On social capital and prestation, see Collman, "Exchange of Liquor," *Jour. Anthro. Research*, XXXV (1979), 208–224 (esp. 216); Mars, "Longshore Drinking," in Douglas, ed., *Constructive Drinking*, 91–101; James R. Barrett, "Why Paddy Drank: The Social Importance of Whiskey in Pre-Famine Ireland," *Journal of Popular Culture*, XI (1977), 155–166; Felicity Heal, "The Idea of Hospitality in Early Modern England," *Past and Present*, no. 102 (February 1984), 66–93; Tlusty, "Gender and Alcohol Use," in Blocker and Warsh, eds., *Changing Face of Drink*, 21–42; Asa D. Hauken, "Gift-Exchange in Early Iron Age Norse Society," and Elizabeth Vestergaard, "Gift-Giving, Hoarding, and Outdoings," both in Ross Samson, ed., *Social Approaches to Viking Studies* (Glasgow, 1991), 97–104, 105–112.

cal prestation is typical of societies structured by patron-client relation-ships.[41]

Because the little luxuries have the power, when presented, to say, "We are friends here, we share more than just the cash nexus," they are markers of sociability. John Josselyn noted of coastal Maine in the study period, "If a man of quality chance to come where [the fishermen] are roystering and gulling in wine with a dear felicity, he must be sociable and roly-poly with them, taking off their liberal cups as freely, or else be gone." In a similar vein, James I complained in his famous *Counterblaste to Tobacco* that the herb had become a symbol of fellowship. As proof of sociability, alcohol has become, in modern Western societies, a boundary marker for periods of leisure. Likewise, the exchange of cigarettes or of cups of coffee often marks short breaks from labor. In the task-oriented world of the early modern fishery, alcohol and tobacco served similar functions.[42]

Drink reflects social reality in another sense, insofar as various forms of alcohol can be distinguished, ranked, and read symbolically. Consumer choice of distinguishable inebriants not only permits the commu-

41. Robert Robinson to [William Blathwayt?], Apr. 5, 1680, CO 1/44 (50), 383. The mutiny quotation is from John Tooley, Examination, June 11, 1673, in John F. Cronin, ed., *Records of the Court of Assistants of the Colony of the Massachusetts Bay, 1630-1692*, III (Boston, 1928), 236-238; Wheler, "Charge for Two Boats," Oct. 27, 1684, CO 1/55 (56iii), 251-252. My terminology here assumes what economic anthropologists will recognize as a formalist analysis, that is, cost/benefit economics are extended to concepts like "social capital." The argument can be reformulated to emphasize the substantivist view that exchange is embedded in social relations and is concerned as much with creating relationships as it is with procurement. For a brief discussion, see Ross Samson, "Economic Anthropology and Vikings," in Samson, ed., *Viking Studies*, 87-96.

42. Josselyn, *Voyages*, 144-145; James I, *A Counterblaste to Tobacco* (1604), in Edward Arber, ed., *The Essayes of a Prentise, in the Divine Art of Poesie, Edinburgh, 1585; A Counterblaste to Tobacco, London, 1604* (London, 1895); Conroy, *In Public Houses*, 22-23; Goodman, *Tobacco in History*, 66; Joseph R. Gusfield, "Passage to Play: Rituals of Drinking Time in American Society," in Douglas, ed., *Constructive Drinking*, 73-90. Tobacco is a symbol of sociability and sharing in Micronesia; see Black, "Anthropology of Tobacco Use," *Jour. Anthro. Research*, XL (1984), 475-503 (esp. 478, 487, 492); compare the gift of cigarettes among smoking acquaintances, in Richard Klein, *Cigarettes Are Sublime* (1993; rpt. London, 1995), 86, 137.

nity to rank the drinker; it also permits the drinker pretensions to connoisseurship. If only a single form of alcohol is available, claims to be drinking for anything but pharmacological effect are difficult to make. Such considerations probably affected the market for alcohol in early modern Newfoundland, where different kinds of alcohol remained available, despite cost differentials. Seventeenth-century consumers ranked beer, wine, and spirits in social prestige as well as in alcoholic content, a ranking that was emphasized in England and Massachusetts by the proscription of wines and spirits in alehouses. In *Wine, Beere, Ale, and Tobacco Contending for Superiority*, an early-seventeenth-century burlesque, drinks appear as social labels: Wine, Beer, Ale, and Water are, respectively, a gentleman, citizen, countryman, and parson. When visitors brought such perceptions to Newfoundland, there arose a fundamental contradiction between social norms (working men drink beer, gentlemen wine) and what was simply common sense (cold wet men should have "hot" "dry" drinks). The evidence suggests that common sense prevailed.[43]

ᚦᚱ *Consumption and Social Control*

The quantity and quality of alcohol consumed by the planters and fishing crews of the English Shore were, in the last analysis, determined by what made sense to them. Since goods like wine, brandy, and tobacco were socially and culturally useful, demand was strong, and thus criticism by those living elsewhere about inappropriate consumption was almost inevitable, certainly among Puritans, who found strong alcohols particularly objectionable. The merchants of Exeter and Plymouth leveled such criticism at their competitor Sir David Kirke in the 1640s and 1650s. They told the Council of State that Kirke, besides being "a man of corrupt and scandalouse lyfe, in respect of his knowne drunkennesse, swearinge, and prophanesse," injured the Commonwealth at Newfoundland "especially by his continuall support of rude, prophane, and athisticall planters, whome hee not only licenceth to keepe tavernes att severall yearly rents in most of the choysest fishinge portes and harbors, butt

43. Collman, "Exchange of Liquor," *Jour. Anthro. Research*, XXXV (1979), 208–224 (esp. 219); Clark, *English Alehouse*, 8, 125; Gallobelgicus [pseud.], *Wine, Beere, Ale, and Tobacco Contending for Superiority* (London, 1630).

furnisheth them with wynes, att his owne rates and prises, to the debauchinge of the seamen, who are thereby taken off from theyre labors." The West Country Merchant Adventurers managed to obtain a ban on tippling houses in the Western Charters and ordinances of 1634, 1653, 1661, and 1676, each of which provided (complete with socioeconomic rationale)

> that noe person doe set up any taverne for sellinge of wyne, beere, or stronge waters, cyder, or tobacco to entertayne the fishermen, because it is found that by such meanes they are debauched, neglecting thar labors, and poore illgoverned men not only spend most part of their shares before they come home, upon which the life and mayntenance of their wife and children depende, but are likewise hurtfull in divers other waies, as by neglectinge and makinge themselves unfit for their labour, by purloyninge and stealinge.

The ban was dropped in William III's "Act to Encourage the Trade to Newfoundland" of 1699, reflecting that legislation's tacit acceptance of the planters' right to a livelihood.[44]

The repetition of complaints about the sale of alcohol and tobacco, like the one made by the Dartmouth master Christopher Selman at Totnes in 1667, indicates that the paper regulation of taverns had no more practical effect than the later rule that technically excluded planters from the coast. Governments enforced neither ban, their inaction thus protecting planters and a major trade, despite the notional threat to both. Notice that no one, not even the Western Adventurers, proposed to forbid tobacco, wine, or even spirits on the English Shore. Any such ban would have flown in the face of common sense. Despite repeated protestations of an aim only to eliminate the "debauching" of "poor ungoverned men," West Country insistence on the banning of taverns probably had less to do with control of drink and tobacco than it did with control of the

44. Petition of the Merchant Adventurers of Plymouth, England, to the Council of State, ca. 1650, *Winthrop Papers*, VI, 4–6; and cf. Exeter Justices, Petition, Jan. 10, 1640, CO 1/10 (28), 46. See also Charles I in Council, Western Charter, Feb. 10, 1634, DRO Exeter, DO 62571, Council of State, "Laws, Rules, and Ordinances . . . ," June 16, 1652, SP 25/29, 15–18, 10 and 11 Will. III, c. 25, "An Act to Encourage the Trade to Newfoundland," 1699, all in Matthews, *Constitutional Laws*, 71–75, 123–126, 202–218. On New England Puritan objections to strong liquor, see Conroy, *In Public Houses*, 38; on attempts at control in this period, see 53–59.

market in these goods. Nothing about the behavior of the West Country merchants, least of all their cargoes on the westward voyage to Newfoundland, suggests that they would have eliminated supplies of the little luxuries to the English Shore. What they wanted, it would seem, was a legal monopoly of supply to their own crews, like that maintained by the eighteenth-century fishing proprietors at Isle Royale.[45]

If the pivotal role of wine and tobacco in the local social economy goes some way to explaining why levels of consumption were high in Newfoundland, it may also help to explain why control of distribution was so often in question there. The middle-class puritanical attempt to limit working-class conviviality through absolute control was, at most, a debating point with respect to the English Shore. Other, more practical management issues were in question and likely in Plaisance as well. Employers at Newfoundland, particularly planters, could hope to recover some part of their wage costs through the sale of tobacco and alcohol. In this period, Polish landowners used an alcohol monopoly to siphon off excess peasant income that might otherwise result in savings and the growth of competing production units. As employers, fishing masters and planters might have been tempted to use the supply of alcohol and tobacco in a similar way, as a form of labor control, to encourage fishermen to fall into debt and thus to remain in service.[46]

The demand for alcohol was elastic: if the price of wine fell or fishermen's incomes rose, consumption expanded. Elasticity of demand was once less common than it is today. Workers used to have a tendency to choose increased leisure over consumption, or at least this was a common perception of employers. The middle class often exaggerated the leisure-preference of their employees and, with blithe lack of logic, combined moral condemnation of what they conceived as laziness with complaints about indulgence in extravagances like drink and tobacco. Any good with an elastic demand, luxurious or not, short-circuits leisure preference and therefore benefits the employer. Alcohol frequently fulfilled this function in the early modern period, particularly at the resource periphery. The

45. Captain Wheler thought a ban would not work; see Wheler, "Answers," Oct. 27, 1684, CO 1/55 (56), 240. On monopoly, see B. A. Balcom, *The Cod Fishery of Isle Royale, 1713–58* (Ottawa, 1984), 63.

46. Hillel Levine, "Alcohol Monopoly to Protect the Non-Commercial Sector of Eighteenth-Century Poland," in Douglas, ed., *Constructive Drinking*, 250–269; cf. A. J. B. Johnson, "Alcohol Consumption in Eighteenth-Century Louisbourg and the Vain Attempts to Control It," *French Colonial History*, II (2002), 61–76.

Hudson's Bay Company, for example, used brandy in this way in its fur trade with the Indians. (Tobacco, on the other hand, tended to be price inelastic—a reflection, perhaps, of its addictiveness.)[47]

At the turn of the eighteenth century, Captain Stafford Fairbourne argued that consumption patterns kept Newfoundland crews in service: "Considerable quantity's of rumm and molasses are brought hither from New-England, with which the fishers grow debauch't and run in debt, so that they are oblig'd to hire themselves to the planters, for payment thereof." Captain George Larkin expressed similar views in 1701, as had the judicious Captain Wheler in 1684. Josselyn found a similar economic world in late-seventeenth-century Maine:

> [Shares] doth some of them little good, for the merchant . . . comes in with a walking tavern, a bark laden with the legitimate bloud of the rich grape . . . from Phial, Madera, Canaries, with brandy, rhum, the Barbadoes strong-water, and tobacco, coming ashore he gives them a taster or two, which so charms them that for no perswasions that their imployers can use will they go out to sea. . . . When the day of payment comes . . . their shares will do no more than pay the reckoning; if they save a kental or two to buy shooes and stockins, shirts and wastcoats with, 'tis well, otherwayes they must enter into the merchants

47. Robert C. Nash, "The English and Scottish Tobacco Trades in the Seventeenth and Eighteenth Centuries: Legal and Illegal Trade," *EHR*, 2d Ser., XXXV (1982), 354–372; D. C. Coleman, "Labour in the English Economy of the Seventeenth Century," ibid., VII (1956), 280–295; E. P. Thompson, "Time, Work-Discipline, and Industrial Capitalism," *Past and Present*, no. 38 (December 1967), 56–97; Maxine Berg, Pat Hudson, and Michael Sonenscher, eds., *Manufacture in Town and Country before the Factory* (Cambridge, 1983), 3, 29; Mathias, "Leisure and Wages," in Mathias, *Transformation of England*, 148–167; de Vries, "Between Purchasing Power and the World of Goods," in Brewer and Porter, eds., *Consumption and the World of Goods*, 85–132 (esp. 110–114); Carole Shammas, "Consumer Behavior in Colonial America," *Social Science History*, VI (1982), 67–86; Arthur J. Ray and Donald B. Freeman, *"Give Us Good Measure": An Economic Analysis of Relations between the Indians and the Hudson's Bay Company before 1763* (Toronto, 1978), 128–130; Ann M. Carlos and Frank D. Lewis, "Trade, Consumption, and the Native Economy: Lessons from York Factory, Hudson Bay," *Journal of Economic History*, LXI (2001), 1037–1064. On theories of motivation, see M. G. Marshall, "Luxury, Economic Development, and Work Motivation: David Hume, Adam Smith, and J. R. McCulloch," *History of Political Economy*, XXXII (2000), 631–648.

books for such things as they stand in need off, becoming thereby the merchants slaves.

Josselyn was not describing the fate of fishing servants, however, but of "shore men," the New England equivalent of small planters. These small employers often ended up mortgaging their own plantations for drink. Seventeenth-century visitors to Newfoundland were, likewise, chiefly concerned that "planters and boate keepers drink out all they are worth," as Wheler put it. In 1679, Captain Charles Talbot denied that servants were "debauched by the colony" or "forced to hire themselves for satisfaction of theyr debts," and Berry had found the same in 1675. Wheler saw planters' sale of alcohol to servants as a means for the former to balance their books, despite the high wages they paid, but he emphasized that this strategy was merely a potential: "The liquor they sell at a very deare rate does something help them—But it is very uncertaine, for that most of the servants they hire comes from England, and, having famielys there, some of them are nott very prodigal." Perhaps credit sales of the little luxuries became an integral part of the social control of labor in eighteenth-century Newfoundland, but chronic indebtedness for advances of drink was not perceived as a common behavior pattern among fishing servants before the turn of the century.[48]

The consumer habits of seventeenth-century fisherfolk were situated in a cultural context much more complex than the accepted custom of extending credit to servants. Drink was part of the generalized exchange that characterized patron-client and employer-employee relationships and was, therefore, often a perquisite, like the six pounds "given away for incouragement: in liquor" by Wheler's intelligible planter. Seventeenth-century fishing servants did not necessarily drink less than their successors. They consumed a great deal of alcohol, usually wine and brandy

48. Stafford Fairborne, "Answers to the Heads of Enquirys," Sept. 11, 1700, CO 194/2 (16), 54–57; George Larkin, Report to CTP, Aug. 20, 1701, CO 194/2 (44); Wheler, "Answers," Wheler, "Observations," and Wheler, "Charge for Two Boats," Oct. 27, 1684, CO 1/55 (56, i, iii), 239–246 (esp. 239, 241), 247–248, 249–252; Josselyn, *Voyages*, 144–145; Talbot, "Answers," Sept. 15, 1679, CO 1/43 (121i), 216–217; Berry, "Observations," Aug. 18, 1676, CO 1/35 (81), 325–326; cf. Heal, "The Idea of Hospitality," *Past and Present*, no. 102 (February 1984), 66–93. For the later period, see John E. Crowley, "Empire versus Truck: The Official Interpretation of Debt and Labour in the Eighteenth-Century Newfoundland Fishery," *CHR*, LXX (1989), 311–336.

rather than beer. Like the taste for tobacco, this pattern of demand was determined, even overdetermined, by a range of factors. Newfoundland fishermen lived and worked thousands of cold sea miles away from the bonfire of consumption that had been kindled in Europe. They had cash or credit and, not surprisingly, they expected a share of that warmth.

Nothing escaped the barborous fury of the enemy, but Bonavista and the little island of Carbonera. . . . To the southward of this, there is not an inhabitant left but two or three in the Bay of Bulls and two at Brigos by South, and from that to Trepasse, which is the southmost of the English plantations, there is not a liveing soule left, yea not at Feryland which was allwayes look'd upon, as I am told, to be the best harbour and the pleasantest place in the whole Island. However, I intend when ever wee have secured [St. John's] to goe to Feryland . . . to secure that allso, which possibly may incouradge the people to come and settle there againe.
—*Colonel John Gibson to the Board of Trade, June 28, 1697*

Biogeographers are fond of islands, for they are natural experiments in controlled circumstances. Isolated communities have some of the same appeal for anthropologists, historical or otherwise, who want to understand how people belong to their societies and how each culture belongs to the wider world. In islands they find a plausible metonymy—the part will somehow represent the whole. Individual interactions can represent a small society more completely than they might a larger one. Or, alternatively, the relatively self-contained tensions of an island society can be an index of wider cultural issues. In this spirit, we might use the small-scale society of seventeenth-century Newfoundland analytically in one of two ways. We can ponder the historical process in which this culture was constructed, or we can take such processes for granted, at least for a moment, and consider the island and its society as an image of the Atlantic world of the time.[1]

In 1689, Louis XIV declared war on Britain. Within a year, English privateers took Plaisance, which was then looted by planters from Ferryland. The French soon revenged themselves on Bay Bulls, after an attempt at Ferryland, to which they returned in 1694, when the planters managed to hold them off again with ad hoc coastal defenses.

---

1. Marshall Sahlins, *Islands of History* (Chicago, 1985), for example, 138; Kirsten Hastrup, *Island of Anthropology: Studies in Past and Present Iceland* (Odense, 1990), esp. 13–21, 123–136, 218–233; Gerald M. Sider, *Culture and Class in Anthropology and History: A Newfoundland Illustration* (Cambridge, 1986), 12–33.

Plate 25. Canadian Soldier on Snowshoes during Pierre Le Moyne d'Iberville's 1697 Campaign in Newfoundland. From [Claude-Charles] Bacqueville de La Potherie, Histoire de l'Amérique septentrionale *(Paris, 1722), 39, 50–51. Courtesy, Centre for Newfoundland Studies, Memorial University of Newfoundland, St. John's. The image is well known in Quebec as an iconic* habitant; *the context of ethnic cleansing of Newfoundland's English Shore is usually ignored. After describing offensives in Torbay and Portugal Cove, de La Potherie commented: "It was time to use snowshoes for the trip [into Conception Bay], without which it would be impossible to advance"*

Saint-Ovide de Brouillon, nephew of the governor of Plaisance, finally captured Ferryland in the fall of 1696 with a fleet of privateers from the traditional Breton fishing port of Saint-Malo. Thus he began the systematic devastation of the English Shore, executed over the ensuing winter by Canadian and Abenaki troops commanded by the celebrated Pierre Le Moyne d'Iberville (Plate 25). The planters watched their homes and fishing craft burn as they embarked on crowded ships to an uncertain future on distant shores. In the south Avalon, the war destroyed the native planter gentry: Sir David Kirke's surviving sons, George, David, and Phillip, died, after being taken as prisoners of war to Plaisance in the terrible winter of 1697, the coldest of the century and, for the planters of the English Shore, the saddest. Further attacks followed in 1705 and 1708. Economic and social destruction wrought in the northern colonies between 1689 and 1713 has much to do with what later seemed like delayed development or retarded colonization. After the protracted war between Britain and France, Maine lay bleeding, scarred and desolate, and Newfoundland was not much better off.[2]

Although settlement on the English Shore was briefly all but extinguished, Colonel John Gibson's hopes were fulfilled. Planters, in particular the "Constant Inhabitants of Ferryland," petitioned for help in returning home. Settlement was quickly restored: the census of 1698 reported 370 persons overwintering in the south Avalon, compared to 431 in 1692, and by 1710 the population had surpassed prewar levels. In the end, the English settlements in Newfoundland were surprisingly resilient. Rapid recovery from military devastation was possible, despite the serious loss of infrastructure, precisely because the fishery was decentralized. Resettlement did not require a massive coordinated effort, like that proposed by the refugee Caplin Bay planter Christopher Pollard; it was something that could happen through uncoordinated efforts to pursue the traditional fishery. If settlement flowed in channels worn by the migratory industry, then resettlement was inevitable. Surname continuities suggest that Newfoundland was reoccupied, at least in part, by its own refugees, even if substantial mixing of populations occurred in the war period among St. John's, the south Avalon, and Conception Bay. Wartime devastation makes the early English Shore look impermanent: it was, after all, suddenly eclipsed in 1697, as the French settlements of Placentia Bay would be in 1713. We should not, however, let the destruction of communities and the displacement of populations at the turn of the eighteenth century distort our view of seventeenth-century Newfoundland, where European fisherfolk created dozens of viable settlements between 1630 and 1697. The intensity of competition over the

2. Charles Hawkins, "Answers to the Several Heads of Enquirys," Dec. 16, 1691, CO 1/68 (92i), 259–262; John Cleer et al., "An Account of an Action . . . ," May 18, 1695, CO 194/1 (78vi), 152; William Holman to Privy Council, July 1696, CO 194/1 (5), 12; Richard Hartnoll et al., Deposition, Sept. 15, 1707, CO 194/4 (77ix), 316; [Claude-Charles] Bacqueville de La Potherie, *Histoire de l'Amérique septentrionale* (Paris, 1722), 22–55; Prowse, *History*, 235–276; Alan F. Williams, *Father Baudoin's War: d'Iberville's Campaigns in Acadia and Newfoundland, 1696, 1697* (St. John's, 1987), 32–33; James Pritchard, "'Le Profit et la Gloire': The French Navy's Alliance with Private Enterprise in the Defense of Newfoundland, 1691-1697," *Newfoundland Studies*, XV (1999), 161–175; Charles E. Clark, *The Eastern Frontier: The Settlement of Northern New England, 1610-1763* (1970; rpt. Hanover, N.H., 1983), 68–72, 111.

coast of Newfoundland is itself a testament to the value it had for France and Britain.[3]

✆ Circumstance

In the late sixteenth century, a handful of West Country ports developed a transatlantic migratory fishery at Newfoundland that became, in the seventeenth century, the matrix for permanent occupation of the English Shore. The intersection of this open-access industry with the coastal range of the Natives of the island created an economic incentive for settlement. Scavenging for iron at seasonally abandoned fishing stations by Beothuks and rival European fishing crews prompted overwintering by caretakers in various parts of the English Shore in successive decades. Because crews could not enclose the resource itself, they competed by attempting to control shore space. Once European overwintering occurred in a particular harbor, it therefore tended to spread. Other factors then promoted intensive settlement.

3. Christopher Pollard, "Reasons Offerd for Inhabiting the Newland . . . ," Apr. 12, 1697, CO 194/1 (25ii), 58; John Clappe et al., Petition to William III, 1697, CO 194/1 (6), 14; Colonel Gibson to CTP, June 28, 1697, CO 194/1 (81), 159–160; John Norris, "Abstract of the Planters . . . ," Sept. 27, 1698, CO 194/1 (125i), 262; Thomas Crawley, "An Accoumpt of the Number of the Inhabitants . . . ," Oct. 15, 1692, CO 1/68 (94iii), 272; Archibald Cumings, "A Scheem of the Fishery . . . ," Dec. 15, 1710, CO 194/4 (145i), 579. Bacqueville de La Potherie, *Histoire de l'Amérique*, 52, thought it would take the English in Newfoundland "many years before they have returned to their previous situation" (my translation). Curiously, R. Cole Harris and Geoffrey J. Matthews, in *Historical Atlas of Canada*, I, 49, report the resettlement of English *"fishermen"* but of French *"planter families"* after these wars (emphasis mine). Handcock, *Origins*, 46, finds only a single surname (Dibble) spanning the thirty-four years between 1675 and 1708 in the Ferryland area—but White, Roberts, and Pearce (Pass) were established south Avalon planter families before 1675, who recur in John Mitchel, "A List of Inhabitants . . . ," Dec. 2, 1708, CO 194/4 (76ii), 252–256. The patronym Webber, at Aquaforte in 1681, and Lang, Short, Tucker, and Fletcher, all in the area before 1696, also recur in 1708. About 120 surnames of the period before 1696 in the whole area south of Conception Bay recur between 1700 and 1710, and almost 100 of these date to 1681 or earlier. The case of Mary Kirke, who married James Benger soon after she lost her husband, should remind us that most female continuities will elude surname studies.

The early proprietorships played a significant role in establishing a permanent European presence on the island. The Newfoundland Company eventually wrote off the first colony of 1610, but its patent rights passed to other investors, and some of the Cupids colonists moved on to informal settlements elsewhere in Conception Bay. Sir George Calvert, who organized the first effective colonization of the south Avalon, made a huge investment, as did his successor, Sir David Kirke, who with his associates preempted control of the region in 1638. Calvert did not recoup his Newfoundland investment, but Kirke, Barkeley, and company probably did. They devised a proprietorship that paid profits by concentrating on trade and, by so doing, greatly improved prospects for ordinary English fisherfolk planted in this new territory. The Kirkes were already involved in the Newfoundland trade as owners of ships let to freight cargoes of cod on sack voyages to southern ports. These London wine merchants took up the fish trade to subsidize their attempts to break into the fur trade in the Gulf of St. Lawrence and to round out their growing business in Spain and the Atlantic islands as these producing regions replaced France as sources of wine for Kirke, Barkeley, and company's expanding markets.

The sack ship, an innovation of the fishery boom of the early 1600s, signaled the development of an efficient market in fish at Newfoundland itself and was a key factor in facilitating European settlement. The Dutch dominated the sack trade until about 1640, by which time Kirke, Barkeley, and other London shipowners had forced their way into the business. Many later-seventeenth-century sack ships, however, were small- or medium-sized West Country vessels of 20–130 tons. Together, these smaller vessels carried considerably more fish than the imposing Dutch and London sacks of 200–300 tons as well as played a key role in bringing wine and other goods to the fishery. They also ensured that the seventeenth-century Newfoundland carrying trade was competitive, so that even the grander sack ship merchants could not extract the very high profits that world-system theory hypothesizes. Kirke, Barkeley, and company's objective was at once more practical and somewhat more modest: to make extraction from the periphery a single integrated process. Substantial profits were possible, but they required secure sources, a powerful rationale for investment in permanent fishing stations.[4]

4. Immanuel Wallerstein, *The Modern World System*, II, *Mercantilism and the Consolidation of the European World-Economy, 1600–1750* (New York, 1980), 120–122; Wallerstein, "European Economic Development: A Commentary on

In the 1640s, David Kirke developed a thriving trade in fish and wines based in Newfoundland itself, at Ferryland. Although his brothers, James and John, managed the European terminus of the business in London, their transatlantic operations depended on an existing West Country commercial network linking Dartmouth, Ferryland, Piscataqua, and Boston. When Kirke's patron, Charles Stuart, lost the second Civil War, his kingdom, and soon his head, the Newfoundland Plantation was finished as a commercial enterprise, but it was hardly a failure. Ferryland and Kirke's family endured and even flourished. Commercial ties with New England intensified during the Interregnum and after the Restoration, but they were not innovations of the 1650s or 1660s. David Kirke had already developed an intercolonial trade in wines and other goods in the 1640s by co-opting Dartmouth's transatlantic commercial network.

The older parts of the English Shore, in Conception Bay and on the south Avalon, had ceased to be a frontier by 1660, in the sense that the planter population had begun to reproduce itself. By this time, the over-wintering English population of Newfoundland had reached about fifteen hundred souls but grew only fitfully for the rest of the century. From 1680, there were normally no more than seventeen hundred or eighteen hundred planters, wives, children, and servants resident—with a transient summer population of an additional six thousand or so fishing servants. The French settlements in Placentia Bay were still growing in this period, but the total overwintering population was likely only something like four hundred persons. The European population resident in late-seventeenth-century Newfoundland was about the same as in Acadia, a very different settlement area, or in Maine, a rather similar one. Although conventional historical wisdom considers the population of the English Shore to have been transient, the mobility of the planters was not, in fact, significantly different from the mobility of heads of households in many other parts of the Anglo-American world. There was, certainly, a wide socioeconomic niche for propertyless and transient servants, but this situation was true elsewhere, particularly in the maritime world.[5]

O'Brien," *EHR*, 2d Ser., XXXVI (1983), 580–583. Cf. Louise Dechêne, *Habitants and Merchants in Seventeenth-Century Montreal* (1974), trans. Liana Vardi (Montreal and Kingston, 1992), 280–282.

5. Daniel Vickers and Vince Walsh, "Young Men and the Sea: The Sociology of Seafaring in Eighteenth-Century Salem, Massachusetts," *Social History*, XXIV (1998–1999), 17–38 (esp. 35).

This was a society of three social classes: servants, planters, and a provincial merchant gentry. Servants in the fishery were, predominantly, young husbandmen, in a period when husbandmen were being relegated to the status of wage laborers. The planters were boatkeeping proprietors of permanent fishing stations, with the approximate literacy, wealth, and social status of yeomen or tradesmen. Women were outnumbered by men on the English Shore, but most households consisted of a planter couple, their children, and servants. Planter merchants were effectively a provincial gentry, that is, a small class of relatively wealthy and literate persons who dominated transatlantic economic connections and monopolized political power. The existence of a small, literate, and numerate elite within a larger, isolated, and only partly literate population encouraged the development of patron-client relations on the English Shore within the context of the increasingly pervasive ideology of contract. Sir David Kirke was one of the original merchant-entrepreneur patrons of development who flourished in the isolated peripheries of seventeenth-century North America. This gentry of merchants found in clientage a useful form of economic control. The relative poverty of their fellow settlers created relations of personal dependency on these men, without whom these isolated regions would have remained resource-rich but capital-poor. When they passed from the scene, their sons and widows were in a position to pick up the reins of patronage.[6]

As long as Kirke was governor, to 1651, and even under the Commonwealth and Protectorate commissioners, to 1660, ordinary planters could depend on a local authority to maintain order, even if a kind of personal allegiance was required of them. Ordinary planters were, of necessity, competitors in an open-access resource, but conflict between planters and migratory crews was institutionalized and limited, essentially, to the collection of rents and fees by the governor's men. The migratory fishing fleet was decimated in the wars of the 1640s and 1650s. When the West Country attempted to rebuild its fishery in the 1660s, it was plagued by poor catches. Some migratory interests saw the planters as the cause of their woes, and tension increased on the English Shore.

6. Stephen Innes, *Labor in a New Land: Economy and Society in Seventeenth-Century Springfield* (Princeton, N.J., 1983), 150–172; John Frederick Martin, *Profits in the Wilderness: Entrepreneurship and the Founding of New England Towns in the Seventeenth Century* (Chapel Hill, N.C., 1991), 10, 45, 58; Robert Brenner, *Merchants and Revolution: Commercial Change, Political Conflict, and London's Overseas Traders, 1550–1653* (Princeton, N.J., 1993), 118.

In the early 1670s, the situation deteriorated to anarchy, at least in St. John's, where the well-established planters Thomas Oxford and John Downing had their premises vandalized. In 1675, the Committee for Trade and Plantations ordered the planters removed, but two years later, after several policy flip-flops, Whitehall recognized their legitimacy. The imperial government did not, however, accept planter proposals for local government and chose to continue to depend on the vernacular custom of the fishery, codified and occasionally amended in the Western Charters. The government then superimposed the jurisdiction of the naval commodores, a reinforcement of authority that had only recently become possible with the institution of regular naval convoys in the 1660s. The second generation of Newfoundland planters thus weathered a serious economic crisis, the hostility of competing fishing interests, and the ponderous indecision of their own imperial bureaucracy before facing the military challenge of the French and their colonial guerrillas in the 1690s.

?৯ Economic Culture

The early planter fishery at Newfoundland can usefully be seen as another vernacular industry, like its migratory predecessor. This terminology emphasizes the local and traditional nature of such industries, in which labor and capital markets were narrowly circumscribed and the operation of the industry depended on collective community experience. Low entry cost is a significant characteristic of vernacular industry. The capital resources required by merchants trading the products of the new regional industries of the period were not needed by producers, who were often men of relatively modest means. Low entry cost was typical of the planter and by-boat-keeping sectors of the Newfoundland fishery. The technique of raising necessary capital by shares—for ships, provisions, and labor costs—made it possible for these early industrial enterprises to be completely financed within a restricted region. Robert Hitchcock had described vernacular finances in 1580: "In the West countrey . . . the fishermen conferres with the money man, who furnisheth them with money to provide victualls, salte, and all other needefull thinges, to be paied twentie five pounde at the shippes returne upon the hundreth pound." Some of these money men were themselves borrowers, all part of a great chain of credit. A century later, boatkeepers raised capital in exactly the same fashion, if at slightly higher rates, as did the merchants who owned and provisioned fishing ships.[7]

Like other successful early modern fisheries, English enterprise at Newfoundland in this period was financed, organized, and manned in atomistic vernacular modules. At first glance, the activities of Kirke and his fellow Newfoundland patentees of 1637 look like an exception to this generalization: as sack ship merchants, they were managers and major shareholders of a project for a directed commercial monopoly. To the extent that they became involved in fish production, however, the Kirkes relied on a distinctly vernacular development in mid-seventeenth-century Newfoundland, the settlement of resident producers. As these *Settlement of resident producers* vernacular production units formed in an isolated resource periphery, they were inevitably enmeshed in patron-client relationships, which are above all a way of mediating unspecialized, weakly developed, and disorganized producers with wider markets. A particular economic culture favored a particular social relationship.[8]

7. Joan Thirsk, *Economic Policy and Projects: The Development of a Consumer Society in Early Modern England* (Oxford, 1978), 111, 120, 169; A. R. Michell, "The European Fisheries in Early Modern History," in E. E. Rich and C. H. Wilson, eds., *Cambridge Economic History of Europe*, V, *Economic Organization of Early Modern Europe* (Cambridge, 1977), 132–184 (esp. 140, 158); Cell, *Newfoundland Discovered*, 2; David J. Starkey, "Devonians and the Newfoundland Trade," *Maritime History of Devon*, I, 163–171 (esp. 168); CTP, Minutes, Dec. 2, 1675, CO 391/1, 25–26; Robert Hitchcock, *A Pollitique Platt for the Honour of the Prince* . . . (1580), in R. H. Tawney and Eileen Power, eds., *Tudor Economic Documents* (1924; rpt. London, 1953), III, 239–256 (esp. 253). Recall that bottomry had an insurance component, so Hitchcock's 25 percent return does not reflect profit rates. Cf. B. A. Holderness, "Credit in a Rural Community, 1660–1800: Some Neglected Aspects of Probate Inventories," *Midland History*, III (1975), 97–109 (esp. 99); and George Shute, Bond to R. Land, Aug. 7, 1641, NDRO Barnstaple, 4116. On shared provisioning, see *Robert Hichins et al. v. John Parre and George Tremblett*, Vice Admiralty Court of Devon, Apr. 12, 1677, in DRO Exeter, "Transcripts and Transactions," III, 24. "A great chain of credit" is borrowed from Jacob M. Price, "Conclusion," in Rosemary E. Ommer, ed., *Merchant Credit and Labour Strategies in Historical Perspective* (Fredericton, N.B., 1990), 360–373 (esp. 360).

8. For the term "atomistic," see Innis, *The Cod Fisheries*, 91. On producers and markets, see S. N. Eisenstadt and Louis Roniger, "Patron-Client Relations as a Model of Structuring Social Exchange," *Comparative Studies in Society and History*, XXII (1980), 42–77.

The mode of production that emerged among the planter inhabitants of the seventeenth-century English Shore bears a close resemblance to the protoindustrial "putting-out" system. This system, in which raw materials were advanced to household production units and finished goods were returned to the entrepreneur, had developed in late-medieval textile industries. The system began to spread to other crafts industries in the late sixteenth century and first became well established in the mid-seventeenth century. Producers in the Newfoundland putting-out industry made fish, not cloth, or nails. To do this, they accepted advances from merchants for outfitting their boats and provisioning themselves and their servants. Even if they were smaller than the migratory ships fishing, Newfoundland planter production units were large, relative to the households of yeomen and craftsmen in the Old Country. Fishing plantations were, nevertheless, extended households, at least within the contemporary perspective, expressed unambiguously in the naval censuses of the later seventeenth century. Merchants must have begun supplying Newfoundland planter producers on credit as soon as the original colonial proprietors, like George Calvert, withdrew their support for colonization. The credit system meshed perfectly with the kind of patron-client network developed by David Kirke. He was criticized for supplying the planters in the 1640s and had, likely, introduced this mode of production to the south Avalon. At any rate, something like it was certainly widespread in Newfoundland by 1670 and probably decades before.[9]

In many respects, the seventeenth-century English Shore resembled England's new regional concentrations of industry, which were often located in woodland districts in areas of uncertain jurisdiction. The Newfoundland planter fishery was typical of these protoindustrial regions in several ways. It came into being with the extension of an international market for a mass-produced good: England's southern markets for fish had expanded rapidly in the late sixteenth century. The protoindustrial specialization of the English Shore promoted the symbiotic development of adjacent agricultural regions: successively, the West Country, southeastern Ireland, New England, and, eventually, Lower Canada. It was organized by merchants in nearby towns: successively, the West Country ports—particularly Dartmouth, Plymouth, and Barnstaple—later in Salem, Massachusetts, and St. John's in Newfoundland itself. Finally,

9. E. J. Hobsbawm, "The Crisis of the Seventeenth Century—II," *Past and Present*, no. 6 (November 1954), 44–65; Petition of the Merchant Adventurers of Plymouth, England, to the Council of State, ca. 1650, *Winthrop Papers*, VI, 4–6.

the protoindustrial household combined production with other subsistence activities in a seasonal cycle. On the English Shore, woods industries, including, particularly, boatbuilding, and pastoral agriculture played key roles. The development of a rural planter fishery in a region previously dominated by a migratory fishery based in towns was typical of the marked seventeenth-century shift in favor of rural production. As elsewhere, the development of protoindustrial household production units in Newfoundland probably has much to do with demand for cheaper labor in a period of economic crisis.[10]

Late-seventeenth-century visitors to the English Shore often commented on the chronic indebtedness of planters to merchants. The credit system they were noticing was not a novelty of this period; what had changed was the ability of the average planter to keep accounts in balance from year to year. As Captain James Story noted in 1681, the influx of Irish servant girls encouraged fishing servants to marry and remain in Newfoundland, swelling the ranks of the smallest production units and least financially secure inhabitants, who "being extreamly poor contract such debts as they are not able to pay." Only a few years later, Captain Francis Wheler observed: "There is hardly a planter in the country but is a greate deale worse then nothing and, although they are allmost sure to loose, yett they must goe on." Debts had, apparently, reached crisis levels. In 1701, Captain George Larkin thought the inhabitants a "poor, indigent, and withall a profuse sort of people," who did not care how fast or far they went into debt.[11]

10. Laurier Turgeon, "Le temps des pêches lointaines: permanences et transformations (vers 1500–vers 1850)," in Michel Mollat, ed., *Histoire des pêches maritimes en France* (Toulouse, 1987), 134–181, calls the transatlantic migratory fisheries themselves "protoindustrial," and one can see a general sense to this understanding of what Harris and Matthews, in *Historical Atlas of Canada*, I, 48, call, aptly enough, "unmechanized seasonal factories." The planter fishery was, however, closer to what most historians mean by protoindustry, in which household production units depended on alternative seasonal subsistence activities in the industrial region itself. See Hans Medick, "The Proto-Industrial Family Economy: The Structural Function of Household and Family during the Transition from Peasant Society to Industrial Capitalism," *Social History*, I (1976–1977), 291–315; Maxine Berg, Pat Hudson, and Michael Sonenscher, eds., *Manufacture in Town and Country before the Factory* (Cambridge, 1983), 1–32; and Berg, "Markets, Trade, and European Manufacture," in Berg, ed., *Markets and Manufacture in Early Industrial Europe* (London, 1991), 3–25.

11. James Story, "An Account of What Fishing Shipps, Sack Shipps, Planters,

Seventeenth-century Newfoundland was, nevertheless, not a capital-intensive, low-wage plantation economy, like the West Indies or the Chesapeake. Newfoundland merchants made substantial profits, not by the superexploitation of labor kept at a subsistence minimum, but by cultivation of profitable trade with a clientele of reasonably successful, creditworthy small producers. Fishers are, almost by definition, poor men, as they were often called (who else would risk life and limb for an unpredictable livelihood?), but they were not the poorest men. Contemporary visitors to the English Shore repeatedly commented on the high wages that were common there, and small planters did well enough to attract further settlement, at least until the 1680s. Skilled Newfoundland fishermen could expect incomes in the order of 150 percent of those paid ordinary Atlantic seamen. Both planters and ships fishing expanded their use of unskilled crewmen who were paid fixed wages rather than shares between 1660 and 1680; and, late in the century, unskilled Irish labor began to be drawn into the Newfoundland fishery. These trends suggest that the long-term increase in fishermen's pay put pressure on small producers that could be ignored only as long as fish prices continued to rise. Planters paid their skilled crewmen an even better fixed wage, to which shares were added, than did the masters of fishing ships —but this differential just offset the seaman's perquisite of portage, the freight-free carriage of private ventures that ship fishermen could expect to carry and that planters' servants had to forgo. Even if costs for wages were relatively high for planters, their capital investment was small compared to that needed in the ship fishery and certainly safer from the marine risks of storm, decay, and piracy. These relatively small production units participated efficiently in the Newfoundland cod fishery in the 1660s and 1670s.[12]

In the first half of the seventeenth century, the English Shore had close

etc., Boat Keepers . . . ," Sept. 1, 1681, CO 1/47 (52i), 113–121; George Larkin to CTP, Aug. 20, 1701, CO 194/2 (44), 181–182; Francis Wheler, "Answers to the Heads of Inquirys . . . ," Oct. 27, 1684, CO 1/55 (56), 239–246 (esp. 241).

12. Robert E. Baldwin, "Patterns of Development in Newly Settled Regions," *Manchester School of Economics and Social Studies*, XXIX (1956), 161–179; Andre Gunder Frank, *World Accumulation, 1492–1789* (New York, 1978), 240; Handcock, *Origins*, 30, 88; John Mannion, "Irish Migration and Settlement in Newfoundland: The Formative Phase, 1697–1732," *Newfoundland Studies*, XVII (2001), 257–293.

economic parallels with coastal New England, but these regional economies diverged before the century was out. Until the closing decades of the century, merchants involved with the inshore shallop fishery of Massachusetts outfitted a clientele of quasi-independent producers using a system of credit similar to Newfoundland's. When fish prices began to sag after 1675, the merchants of Salem and Marblehead tightened the credit they gave boat fishermen and began to use their capital, instead, to invest seriously in their own larger vessels to pursue the new, offshore bank fishery. To the extent that capital previously buried in long-term credit relations between merchants and a clientele of small producers was freed up, and to the extent that a labor market no longer constrained by personal dependency could function with increased efficiency, this shift represented a kind of regional economic development for New England. Although there were some limited parallel developments on the English Shore after 1713, when small ships began to exploit offshore banks, such economic modernization was long delayed in Newfoundland and in Atlantic Canada generally. This delay was not, however, necessarily inefficient, given France's stake in the Grand Banks fishery, which was jealously defended; the magnitude of the inshore fish stocks around Newfoundland, which were easily accessible by boat; and the continued demand in southern Europe for traditionally cured dry fish, which could be produced only by an inshore fishery. Ships are not, simply by definition, more efficient than boats, which are much cheaper to build, after all. A ship fishery certainly creates an occasion for respectable accumulations of profit by shipowners, but profit is not the same thing as efficiency, unless social costs and ecological constraints are ignored.[13]

The natural environment into which the Newfoundland fishery had intruded, productive as it was, had its own limits. When fishers approached or exceeded the maximum sustainable catch for specific species, they inevitably had to face the consequences of human impact on stocks. The large marine mammals were affected first: by 1600, Europeans had depleted the walrus and the right whale in Newfoundland waters. Although the whole northern cod stock was not at risk in the seventeenth

13. Vickers, *Farmers and Fishermen*, 153–158; Rosemary E. Ommer, "What's Wrong with Canadian Fish?" *Journal of Canadian Studies*, XX, no. 3 (1986), 122–142; Sean Cadigan, "The Moral Economy of the Commons: Ecology and Equity in the Newfoundland Cod Fishery, 1815–1855," *Labour/Le Travail*, XLIII (Spring 1999), 9–41.

century, in the sense that it would be in the twentieth, fishing effort in some periods already reached levels that affected local stocks.[14]

Another natural limit on the traditional inshore fishery lay in the geography of the English Shore itself, with its shortage of useful land. The oversupply of land in most of colonial North America, relative to the contemporary scarcity of labor, has provided economic historians with an explanatory Swiss Army knife, useful on many occasions, to explain why wages were high, agricultural improvements slow, or credit limited. This analysis is not very applicable to Newfoundland, despite its vast tracts of forest and taiga. For an inshore fishing master, the only land that really mattered was his fishing room, that is, a place close to fishing grounds where a small boat could be safely brought to shore. Although there are many productive fishing rooms on the east coast of the Avalon Peninsula, their numbers are limited, and, by the 1640s, fishing crews were in conflict over them. Planter boatkeepers, with their interests in livestock husbandry and woods industries, had an interest in a wider range of land. Still, good land for gardens and pastures was in short supply in Newfoundland, and even forestland was not always easily accessible. In a sense, the scarcity of useful land resulted in a surplus of labor every fall, but the fluid Atlantic labor market drained fishing servants from Newfoundland with the rhythm of an annual ebb tide. The shortage of productive fishing rooms limited the growth of the old English Shore, or at least this was a perception of the time.[15]

The economic culture of the English Shore itself perhaps limited the adaptability of the resident fishery. The tendency of planters to disperse disposable income on imported consumables would have acted as a restraint on economic diversification. The fisherfolk of the seventeenth-century North American littoral were particularly prone to high levels of consumption of wine, brandy, and tobacco. These goods were easily

14. Jeremy B. C. Jackson et al., "Historical Overfishing and the Recent Collapse of Coastal Ecosystems," *Science*, CCXCIII (2001), 629–638; Johanna J. (Sheila) Heymans and Tony J. Pitcher, "A Picasso-Esque View of the Marine Ecosystem of Newfoundland and Southern Labrador: Models for the Time Periods 1450 and 1900," Fisheries Centre, University of British Columbia, *Research Reports*, X, no. 5 (2002), 44–74; Peter Pope, "Early Estimates: Assessment of Catches in the Newfoundland Cod Fishery, 1660–1690," in *Maritime Resources and Human Societies in the North Atlantic since 1500*, ISER Conference Paper, no. 5 (St. John's, 1997), 9–40.

15. Head, *Newfoundland*, 66–68.

available; economically attractive because of their portability, divisibility, and high unit value; and culturally useful in a number of ways, particularly as symbols of warmth and sociability. Consumption of such imported luxuries was, in aggregate, a drain on the regional economy. Indeed, had Newfoundland planters and their crews spent more of their earnings on a locally produced good, for example, housing, the economic development of the English Shore might have been advanced—but only in the counterfactual world without context of the thought experiment. In the seventeenth century that we know from documents and archaeological remains, fisherfolk exhibited an irreducible demand for alcohol and tobacco and appear to have had limited ambitions for better housing. They were a significant part of the market for wine, the export of which permitted regions like the Mediterranean and the Atlantic islands to import salt fish, among other goods. This exchange furthered development of the European world economy if, by the same token, it furthered a dependence on staple production in peripheries like Newfoundland and semiperipheries like southern Europe.[16]

Undesirable as these outcomes might be for such regional economies in the long run, the consumption of luxuries, like wine and tobacco, on

16. Staple theorists concerned with a single periphery, who greatly influenced Canadian economic history, stressed expense on luxury imports as an obstacle to economic development through linkages in productions: see Baldwin, "Patterns of Development," *Manchester School of Economics and Social Studies*, XXIX (1956), 161-179 (esp. 172); and Melville H. Watkins, "A Staple Theory of Economic Growth," *Canadian Journal of Economics and Political Science*, XXIX (1963), 141-158 (esp. 146). For a more positive view of luxuries, see, for example, Ralph Davis, "England and the Mediterranean, 1570-1670," in F. J. Fisher, ed., *Essays in the Economic and Social History of Tudor and Stuart England, in Honour of R. H. Tawney* (Cambridge, 1961), 117-137; and Nuala Zahedieh, "London and the Colonial Consumer in the Late Seventeenth Century," *EHR*, 2d Ser., XLVII (1994), 239-261. Although staple theory is not completely forgotten, it was displaced by world systems theory, which (significantly) has revived the staple theorists' interest in linkages, now conceived of as "commodity chains." See Sean Cadigan, "The Staple Model Reconsidered: The Case of Agricultural Policy in Northeast Newfoundland, 1785-1855," *Acadiensis*, XXI, no. 2 (1992), 48-71; and Immanuel Wallerstein, "Introduction," *Commodity Chains in the World-Economy, 1590-1790*, Fernand Braudel Center, *Review*, XXIII, no. 1 (2000), 1-13. On housing, see Gregory Clark, "Shelter from the Storm: Housing and the Industrial Revolution, 1550-1909," *Journal of Economic History*, LXII (2002), 489-511.

the English Shore indicates that the center of the world economy was already partly extended to its own periphery. That is to say, the extraction of riches by Europe was not absolute. One of the wonders of capitalism is that it concentrates riches by sharing them, if only a little. Those who lived and worked in Newfoundland and similar resource peripheries were willing to do so precisely because they could thereby obtain the goods that they found desirable. The celebrated triangular trade that linked England, Newfoundland, and the Iberian Peninsula might have consisted of two steady flows and one trickle, but the trickle is worth noting. It might have been relatively small. It might have consisted of the wrong goods from the point of view of improvers of that period or ours. But it also represented, in a small way, a share in the new wealth of Europe. The sack trade turned fish into wine and did so, in part, by returning some of that wine to Newfoundland and turning it back into fish.[17]

ও৯ Crisis

However smooth the exchange of fish and wine had become, the economic expansion of the English Shore collapsed in the 1680s. What obstacle to growth had Newfoundland encountered? The explanation lies in the very way its economy had previously grown. Newfoundland was settled as the international division of labor intensified. It was a classic case of economic adaptation to production of a single staple: a subarctic island that could barely support a medieval level of self-sufficiency was instead put to its most efficient use, the production of salt fish, with the result that wealthier households there could live well enough to raise the eyebrows of European visitors. An instructive comparison might be made with Iceland, where a colony of isolated Europeans spent centuries of cultural anguish before they admitted to themselves, in the nineteenth century, that they were fishermen as well as farmers. Icelandic law and custom took a dim view of permanent fishing stations and put difficulties in the way of those who moved seasonally to work in the fishery. The English Shore was a society with no such doubts about its economic function in the wider scheme of things, certainly not in the seventeenth century. When the fish trade did well, so did the fisherfolk of the

17. Cf. Gordon S. Wood, "Inventing American Capitalism," *New York Review of Books*, June 9, 1994, 44–49.

English Shore. A crisis in the trade, on the other hand, spelled serious trouble. The terrible economic truth was that the planter fishery was part of an international economy and could be threatened in distant markets, or by shifts in fish stocks, as seriously as by a determined invasion. Further development of the English Shore might have been limited, in some sense, by the confinement of capital and labor within traditional credit clientage, by coastal geography, or even by the character of its imports, but the Newfoundland plantation's very existence was continually at risk because the isolated local economy depended on production of a single staple, subject to significant fluctuations in availability and price. Like their Native predecessors, Europeans in seventeenth-century Newfoundland were limited by worst cases in an unstable environment.[18]

[handwritten margin note: Part of international economy]

[handwritten margin note: Subject to market fluctuations]

The reports of the naval commodores, from 1684 to the turn of the century, suggest that Newfoundland experienced a tightening of credit in this period, which eliminated or impoverished the larger planters and left the typical indebted smaller planter "a kind of servant to the merchant men," as Captain John Norris put it in 1698. The case of Ferryland/Caplin Bay is instructive. An important settlement through most of the seventeenth century, it consisted of a dozen or so plantations in the 1670s, most of them larger than average. Many big planters, including Ferryland's, suffered setbacks in the 1680s, and only eight plantations, each only about half the previous typical size, are reported there in the early 1690s, before a recovery by the time of the French attack of 1696. In other words, an economic crisis in the 1680s had just as great an impact on growth as the war of the ensuing decade.[19]

18. Kirsten Hastrup, *Nature and Policy in Iceland, 1400–1800: An Anthropological Analysis of History and Mentality* (Oxford, 1990), 45–79, 280–281; William Poole, "Answers to the Severall Heads of Inquiry . . . ," Sept. 10, 1677, CO 1/41 (62i), 149–152.

19. John Norris to CTP, Mar. 17, 1698, CO 194/1 (96), 196–197. Matthews, "Fisheries," 160, suggests that chronic indebtedness trapped planters in Newfoundland from about 1660 to 1690; cf. Handcock, *Origins*, 35. There are few reasons, however, to date this credit crisis to the 1660s or 1670s. Planters were certainly enmeshed in the kind of debt relations that were pervasive in the study period and apparent, for example, in the 1671 list of creditors of the Salem merchant John Croad. Only a few of those debts amount to the net worth of even a small planter, however. Nor do observers suggest that debt was out of control before 1680. Berry, for example, an acute and sympathetic observer, makes no reference to chronic debt in 1675: John Berry to John Williamson, July 24, Sept. 12, 1675, CO 1/34 (118), 240–241, CO 1/35 (16), 109–110; Berry, "Observations . . . in

The seriousness of this crisis is thrown into relief by the recovery of the Newfoundland fishery from the doldrums of the 1660s and early 1670s. The English fishery grew significantly between 1675 and 1682, with the planters expanding a bit more rapidly than the migratory sector (Table 37). The Newfoundland censuses of the last quarter of the seventeenth century, adjusted for their variable scope, indicate a steady growth in effort during peacetime until about 1684, when participation in the migratory fishery dropped by more than half from the level of roughly eight hundred boats, typical of the early 1680s, to about three hundred. Even the planters, who had no real alternative to participation in the fishery, reduced their commitment of boats by 10 or 20 percent at this time. This serious decline in fishing effort in the mid-1680s resulted in part from a renewed scarcity of fish. Catch rates had fallen in the early 1680s, so that by 1682 the area south of St. John's reported catches of only about 150 quintals a boat, three-quarters of the catch that fishing masters normally expected. In February 1683, Captain Charles Talbot reported that investors in the migratory fishery were

> so discouraged by the ill success they have had of late Yeares, that many of them have laid upp their ships by the Wall and more threaten. Theyre being limitted to fish betwixt the Capes de Ray [Cape Race] and Bonavista is the reason of their ill success, for though there be Harbours and convenience on shoare for the making of Fish, there is not fishing ground or can constantly be fish enough for so many Boates as they have kept . . . whereas were there but half so many Boates fisht there, they could not make so great Destruction One yeare as to prejudice the next yeares fishing.

Poor catches might simply have driven up the price of fish, but, in fact, the price of cod fell at this time, in both Newfoundland and New England, to the lowest peacetime level recorded since 1639 (Table 2).[20]

The ill-timed collapse in demand resulted, no doubt, from economic crisis in Spain, one of the most important markets for Newfoundland fish. Following a currency crisis in New Castile in 1680, prices fell al-

---

Relation to the Trade and Inhabitants of Newfoundland," Aug. 18, 1676, CO 1/35 (81), 325–326.

20. Talbot to Charles II, Feb. 14, 1683, CO 1/51 (29), 67–68 (quotation). Pope, "Early Estimates," in *Maritime Resources and Human Societies*, 9–40, suggests that British fishing effort in Newfoundland did not vary wildly in the way suggested by some historical summaries.

Table 37. *Planter and Migratory Fishing Effort and Dried Catch,*
Newfoundland, 1675–1698

	Planters		Migratory Fishers		Total	
Year	Boats	Catch (Quintals)	Boats	Catch (Quintals)	Boats	Catch (Quintals)
1675	277		669		896	170,000
1676	281	42,000	888	179,000	1,169	221,000
1677	337	62,000	892	177,000	1,229	238,000
1680	361	67,000	793	134,000	1,154	201,000
1681	365		806		1,171	213,000
1682	408	62,000	792	120,000	1,200	182,000
1684	335	65,000	304	60,000	639	125,000
1692	299	104,000	693	243,000	992	347,000
1698	397	101,000	532	164,000	929	265,000

Note: The numbers for catches are given to the nearest 1,000 quintals.

1675: Catch based on estimated rate, 1676/1677 average.

1676: The addition errors have been corrected. John Rich's account of St. John's varies slightly from Captain Russell's; the latter is followed here.

1677: The migratory catch from Torbay to Trinity is estimated. The Bonavista area boats and catch are estimated. The St. John's planter catch is estimated.

1680: The relatively high planter catch rate may be explained by a reported very good early season. Detailed data exists only for St. John's and Bay Bulls, although the total data reported are coherent. It is assumed here that reported totals are for the whole English Shore.

1681: The overall catch rate is extrapolated from the regionally adjusted migratory rate, based on a few ships at Trinity and Bonavista.

1682: Participation is extrapolated from St. John's and Bay de Verde areas using 1677 ratios. Catch is based on a rate of 152 quintals per boat, the mean catch rate in the southern shore harbors reported. If there were better catches to the north, as often happened, then these figures are somewhat too low.

1684: For planters, the Petty Harbour catch is estimated, and the Trepassey and Bonavista participation and catch rate is estimated. For the migratory fishery, Trepassey, Bay Bulls, Trinity North, and Bonavista are estimated.

1692: Bonavista and Trepassey are estimated. Ship fishery catches are extrapolated from accounts of fish shipped from the southern shore, using 1681 catch ratios. Participation is calculated assuming the catch rate.

Sources: 1675: John Berry, "A List of Ships Makinge Fishinge Voyages; with Boat-keepers . . . ," and Berry, "A List of the Planters Names . . . ," Sept. 12, 1675, CO 1/35 (17i, ii), 136–156.

1676: John Rich [captain of the *Blackmore* of Dartmouth], ". . . List of the Whole . . . ," Dec. 7, 1676, CO 1/39 (29), 60; John Russell, "An Accompt of the En-

Table 37 (*continued*)

glish Inhabitants in Newfoundland betweene Boniventure and Petty Harbour . . . ,"
and Russell, "From Salvadge to Petit Harbour; an Accompt of What Ships Have Made
Fishing Voyages . . . ," with an annotation by John Wyborne, Dec. 7, 1676, CO 1/38
(81), 223–224, (88) 237–238; John Wyborn, "Accompt of the Shipps Fishing between Trepasse and Bay of Bulls," and Wyborn, "A Totall Accompt of the Inhabitants,
Their Boates, Fish, Traine, etc. . . . ," Dec. 7, 1676, CO 1/38 (79), 218–220, and (80),
239–242 (esp. 242).

1677: William Poole, "A Particular Accompt of All the Inhabitants and Planters . . . ," Poole "Account of Fishing and Sackships from Trepassy to Cape Broyle,"
Poole, "Account of Fishing and Sackships from Balene to St. John's Harbour . . . ,"
Poole, "Sack Shipps . . . Fishing Ships . . . ," Sept. 10, 1677, CO 1/41 (62iv, vi, vii),
157–166, (62viii), 167–168, (62ix), 168–170, (62x), 171–172.

1680: "A List of All the Planters and Inhabitants . . . ," "An Account of Shipps . . . ,"
and "A List of Ships Which Goes for Sacks . . . ," 1680, CO 1/46 (79), 154–155.

1681: James Story, "An Account of What Fishing Shipps, Sack Shipps, Planters,
etc., Boat Keepers . . . ," Sept. 1, 1681, CO 1/47 (52i), 113–121.

1682: Daniel Jones, "Newfoundland Acc of Inhabitants—Fishery etc.," Jones, "An
Accompt of the Fishing Ships in the Harbour of St. John's . . . ," Jones, "An Accompt
of the Boatkeepers Belong to St. Johns Harbour," Jones, "An Accompt of the Planters
Belonging to St. Johns Harbour . . . ," and Jones, ". . . An Abstract of an Accompt of
the Fishery," Sept. 12, 1682, CO 1/49 (51v), 192, (51vi), 193, (51viii), 195, (51ix),
196–198, (51x), 199.

1684: Francis Wheler, "An Account of the Fishing Shipps . . . ," Wheler, "Ships,
Men, Boats, Stages, Fish," and Wheler, ". . . English Planters Inhabiting the Easterne
Coast of Newfoundland . . . ," Oct. 27, 1684, CO 1/55 (56iv), 254, (56vi), 256, (56vii),
257.

1692: Thomas Crawley, "An Accompt of the Number of the Inhabitants . . . ," Oct.
15, 1692, CO 1/68 (94iii), 272.

1698: John Norris, Report to Council of Trade and Plantations, Nov. 13, 1698, CO
194/3 (126).

most 50 percent over the next few years in Andulasia, New Castile, and
Old Castile-León. This crisis, compounded by plague and a severe earth-
quake, triggered a spate of bankruptcies and widespread unemployment,
which did not end until a successful currency revaluation in 1686. In
New Castile, the price of twenty-five pounds of dried cod fell from about
2,000 maravedis (about 30 shillings), the average between 1676 and
1680, to a low of 982 in 1682. Prices remained miserably low until 1687.
The Newfoundland fishery began to recover in the early 1690s, when
Spanish prices recovered somewhat, to the levels that would be typical
during the first half of the eighteenth century, ranging between 60 and

75 percent of their seventeenth-century highs. At least fish became more plentiful, after the sharp reduction in fishing effort of the mid-1680s, and, in the following decade, both the migratory and planter sectors made extraordinary catches, as high as 350 quintals per boat. After 1689, however, both resident and migratory fishers faced the looming dangers of the war with France.[21]

Under such circumstances, the planters naturally intensified their reliance on local resources. Economic innovations that tended to diversify subsistence brought some stability to a precarious situation. The spread of transhumant winter-housing, which was common in the northern bays by 1700, manifested the trend toward diversification. The inclusion of seal meat into the planters' diet was another innovation of this period, "which they and none but they could eat," Commodore John Graydon sniffed in 1701, adding, dismissively, "Such people such stomachs." The new salmon, seal, and offshore banks fisheries of the eighteenth century, the practice of winter-housing, and the introduction of the potato all materially increased the carrying capacity of the island. Following the Treaty of Utrecht in 1713 and another failure in the fishery between 1714 and 1720, the broader economic base permitted population growth on the old English Shore, the beginnings of serious Irish immigration, and the extension of settlement into Placentia Bay to the south and, despite treaty provisions, into Bonavista and Notre Dame Bays to the north. By the later eighteenth century, Newfoundland's traditional culture had emerged, in a form still remembered, strongly shaped by these developments in subsistence and migration. The form this traditional culture took in the eighteenth and nineteenth centuries is, naturally enough, what persists in Newfoundland's historical memory. On the other hand, some elements of a distinctive culture had already emerged by 1680.[22]

Treaty of Utrecht 1713

Traditional culture

21. On the crisis in Castile, see Earl J. Hamilton, *War and Prices in Spain, 1651–1800* (Cambridge, Mass., 1947), 120, chart II, 126–127, and appendix I, table A, 236–237, 242–245. For a more general explanation of the crisis, see Vickers, *Farmers and Fishermen*, 155–167.

22. [John] Graydon, "Answers to the Heads of Enquiry," Sept. 20, 1701, CO 194/2 (46xii), 175–178. Archaeologists recovered seal bones from a late-seventeenth-century kitchen context at Ferryland in their excavations; see Lisa Hodgetts, "Seventeenth-Century English Colonial Diet at Ferryland, Newfoundland," postdoctoral report on file, Archaeology Unit, MUN, 2003. On the eighteenth century, see Handcock, *Origins*, 91–120; and Head, *Newfoundland*, 83–94.

Without questioning the changes that Newfoundland would undergo in later centuries, we might ask to what extent the small-scale society of the late-seventeenth-century English Shore already constituted a distinguishable culture. The inhabitants of the island were certainly treated as an identifiable interest. When William Downing and Thomas Oxford went to London in 1679 to plead for local government, or at least a church and the fortification of St. John's, the Committee for Trade and Plantations received them as appearing "on behalf of the inhabitants." Distinguishable cultural practices were remarked, not only by Welsh chaplains upset by female promiscuity or Royal Navy officers repelled by flipper pie. How seriously can we take the ethnographic implications of such comments? Newfoundlanders were not yet, of course, the people they would become, but, to use the jargon of the social sciences, the inhabitants of the English Shore were already refashioning their ethnicity.[23]

Key aspects of the economic culture of the English Shore, entrenched by 1680, would endure for several centuries. The fishery was and would remain, well into the twentieth century, a vernacular industry, organized in local modules. Merchants had a clientele of planter families to whom they extended credit and from whom they expected fish. Planter clients depended on their merchant patrons for supplies, on the one hand, and on unpropertied fishing servants for labor, on the other. In the later eighteenth century, migratory service in the fishery declined as local recruitment of labor became increasingly feasible—but this shift left the system of patron-client credit in place. The Newfoundland fishery continued to be predominantly an inshore industry: cod were present along the coasts of the island in huge quantities until the 1960s. The inshore orientation of the traditional fishery suited the size of vessels easily built locally and induced an annual summer-winter rhythm in the local economy that persisted in rural areas into the late twentieth century. The local cuisine of fish, dried peas, salt meat, game, and seabirds, supplemented by cabbage, root vegetables, and preserved berries, has subsequently admitted only two significant innovations: the potato and the pot of tea, typical eighteenth-century novelties in most of the North Atlantic world. The

23. *CSP*: Colonial reports the Downing-Oxford lobby "on behalf of the Newfoundland people," a promising turn of phrase from the anthropological point of view, but CTP, Journal, Apr. 5, 1679, CO 391/2, 159, reads "inhabitants," as quoted.

1970s and 1980s saw the development of large, all-season, deep-water trawler fleets; electronic fish-finding equipment; the decline and collapse of fish stocks; and, finally, a moratorium on North America's oldest industry. Outmigration or economic diversification into lumbering and the hospitality industry remain the first responses of Newfoundland fisherfolk in time of crisis.[24]

Some aspects of public life on the early modern English Shore likewise endured for centuries, or at least have parallels in more recent times. In the absence of a legally constituted local government, personal patron-client relationships played a crucial role in seventeenth-century Newfoundland. Virtually the only political process was the petition, an instrument that forges the general will in the absence of representative institutions and is another practice that has endured in Newfoundland. Since the social contract was often enforced only by consensus, personal behavior was not closely regulated, except for matters affecting the staple industry. (No one cared where you kept your cows as long as you were willing to make good for damaged fish.) Distant and intermittent government authority fostered personal liberty, sometimes almost to the point of anarchy.[25]

It should not be surprising that Newfoundlanders were among the first of Britain's North American colonists to attempt to constitute their own government or that they were among the last to do so. In 1723, a committee of St. John's merchant planters, disturbed by the lack of local authority, invoked John Locke's second treatise and set up their own court to protect their property from their more anarchic neighbors. Planter pretensions to even this limited form of self-government were, in the end, unacceptable to the Board of Trade, although the attempt to establish a Lockean civil society doubtless helped to pressure the naval commodore into appointing a winter justice in 1727 and the Board of Trade into finally recognizing the broad legal authority of the annual naval commodore by appointing Captain Henry Osbourne as gov-

24. Sean T. Cadigan, *Hope and Deception in Conception Bay: Merchant-Settler Relations in Newfoundland, 1785–1855* (Toronto, 1995), 37–50, 100–120; Jeffrey A. Hutchings and Ransom A. Myers, "The Biological Collapse of Atlantic Cod off Newfoundland and Labrador: An Exploration of Historical Changes in Exploitation, Harvesting Technology, and Management," in Ragnor Arnason and Lawrence Felt, eds., *The North Atlantic Fisheries: Successes, Failures, and Challenges* (Charlottetown, P.E.I., 1995), 37–83.

25. Sider, *Culture and Class*, 26–29.

Aspects of public life
• Personal patron-client relationship
• Political process of petition
• personal behavior not regulated

ernor as well as commander of the Newfoundland Squadron in 1729. Through the eighteenth century, the Royal Navy policed Newfoundland, its administration eventually displacing the fishing admirals' traditional authority over the declining migratory industry. This "naval state" involved an increasingly complex system of local surrogate courts, justices of the peace, and constables, all thrown into question in the 1790s by a British court of appeal. This peculiar mix of naval authority with local constables and courts suited the overlapping interests of the interrelated merchant gentries of Newfoundland and the West Country—a circumstance that probably explains the survival of this ad hoc government well into the nineteenth century. Britain did not grant representative government until 1832, following a decade of local lobbying for reform.[26]

The inhabitants of the seventeenth-century English Shore had, inevitably, a mid-Atlantic point of view: they were Britons with a special relationship to New England, on the one hand, and to New France, on the other. Despite their frequently demonstrated loyalty to British interests, late-seventeenth-century Newfoundlanders already exhibited a sense of being shortchanged by Britain, another reaction that is not hard to fathom. Newfoundland was a cosmopolitan place, which also traded with Spain, Portugal, and their island possessions. At home, planters rubbed shoulders with the Dutch until the 1660s and with Basques, Normans, and Bretons through the century. The Beothuk had withdrawn from trading contacts with the English about 1620, so that Newfoundland planters experienced Native people only as a threat to property. At the same time, English overwinterers were in the habit themselves of looting seasonally abandoned French fishing stations for boats and other equipment. Although cooperation and trade were not unknown among English and French settlers, the English became increasingly suspicious of their competitors as the French settlements in Placentia Bay grew. By 1680, they had worked themselves into a frenzy of apprehension, in

26. Jeff A. Webb, "Leaving the State of Nature: A Locke-Inspired Political Community in St. John's, Newfoundland, 1723," *Acadiensis*, XXI, no. 1 (1991), 156-165; Jerry Bannister, "The Naval State in Newfoundland, 1749-1791," *Journal of the Canadian Historical Association*, N.S., XI (2000), 17-50; and, for an extended analysis, Bannister, *The Rule of the Admirals: Law, Custom, and Naval Government in Newfoundland, 1699-1832* (Toronto, 2003); Keith Matthews, "The Class of '32: St. John's Reformers on the Eve of Representative Government," in P. A. Buckner and David Frank, eds., *Atlantic Canada before Confederation* (Fredericton, N.B., 1985), 212-226.

part, no doubt, through consciousness of their own unchristian behavior. Native participation in the rout of the English Shore in 1696/7 was over-perceived, and average planters did not likely distinguish very clearly between the Abenaki invaders and the local Beothuks, although they might have been aware that many of the French forces arrayed against them came from Canada. If Newfoundlanders of the eighteenth and nineteenth centuries were intensely suspicious of "Indians" and Canadians, these cultural reactions were understandable. *Métissage* with Native peoples and cultural mediation by missionaries were unheard of until a much later period and, even then, were more typical of Labrador than of the island itself. In such respects, the planters of the English Shore still faced the Atlantic rather than the continent behind them.[27]

The transatlantic trade in alcohol remained a central element of Newfoundland's connection with the rest of the world, because wine and spirits played an essential role for this insular society as social and commercial lubricants. Valuables like alcohol and tobacco had two aspects: to the consumer, whether planter or servant, they represented culturally useful goods; to the supplying merchant, they were economically efficient returns for fish. These little luxuries were, in some sense, the cultural face of local systems of credit and clientage. In the absence of more regular forms of commerce and government, these goods were more critical and relatively more common on the English Shore than in England itself. In such small societies, where patron-client relationships and credit are more significant than legally constituted governance and a ready cash market, social drinking plays an important role in the socio-economic life of the community. The institution of the tavern becomes a key scene of economic relations, as a free space for negotiation and as a market for the limited range of goods and services, some doubtless embezzled, available outside the normal credit relations of the society. St. John's, in particular, was known for centuries for its many snugs or small taverns—a characteristic that was not a historical accident but one facet of a coherent economic culture.[28]

27. On fear of the French, see John Thomas to Sir Richard[?], Sept. 15, 1680, Codrington Library, All Souls College, Oxford University, Wynne Collection, MS 239, 229–230, in Peter Pope, *"A True and Faithful Account*: Newfoundland in 1680," *Newfoundland Studies*, XII (1996), 32–49 (esp. 42).

28. Lars Magnusson, "Markets in Context: Artisans, Putting Out, and Social Drinking in Eskilstuna, Sweden, 1800–50," in Berg, ed., *Markets and Manufacture*, 292–320.

Culture is a process

Ethnonym

Since culture is a process, there is no single moment when a particular ethnicity comes into existence. On the other hand, cultures have history, and events mark the progress of ethnogenesis. One of these events is the introduction of an *ethnonym*, that is, a name used by the *ethnos* for itself. The use of an ethnonym bespeaks a conceptual differentiation from others who do not share the same history, or law, or customs. Thus, Ari the Learned's *Book of the Icelanders*, a history written about 1120, marks not only the first use of that ethnonym but also suggests that by this time Icelanders could see themselves as sharing a common past that distinguished them from others, particularly Norwegians. In New France, a shift in the connotation of the word *Canadien*, from Aboriginal to French-speaking native of Canada, was first recorded in 1664 and by 1700 was well established in use, primarily by officials from metropolitan France to describe native-born troops. The French historian Chrestien Le Clercq used Canadien for the people in 1691, and the ethnonym was probably in popular use by this time. In the same period, under very different circumstances, the Dutch of New York City began to accentuate their own ethnicity.[29]

The case of Acadia provides, as it often does, a closer parallel to Newfoundland. Distinctive social, economic, political, religious, and cultural traditions, including the pervasive ethic of mutual aid, date from the seventeenth century, but Acadians do not seem to have had a concept of themselves as a distinct people until the 1730s. They achieved this understanding, at least in part, through negotiation of the neutrality that came to define them in this period among their neighbors. The *dérangement*, or expulsion, of 1755 and the eventual return of many of the exiles became a founding myth for the Acadians, but the very tenacity with which the refugees held on to their memory of Acadia is clear evidence that they had already developed a strong ethnic identity before they were dispersed by the tragedy of war. Newfoundland planter families had suffered the same kind of tragedy in 1697. Surviving petitions speak movingly of their desire "to againe be possest of our places for rebuilding our houses and stages and rooms for carrying on of our fisherye trade,"

29. Kirsten Hastrup, "Establishing an Ethnicity: The Emergence of the 'Icelanders' in the Early Middle Ages," in Hastrup, *Island of Anthropology*, 69–82 (esp. 76–77); Gervais Carpin, *Histoire d'un mot: l'ethnonyme "Canadien" de 1535 à 1691* (Sillery, Quebec, 1995), 144–157, 167–187 (annexe III); Joyce D. Goodfriend, *Before the Melting Pot: Society and Culture in Colonial New York City, 1664–1730* (Princeton, N.J., 1992), 217–221.

but they bespeak identification with particular outharbors, on the one hand, or with Britain, on the other, rather than with Newfoundland as an abstraction. The "Inhabitants of Ferryland" called themselves "Constant" to emphasize their loyalty to Britain in the person of the Protestant monarch, William III, and to win his support for their return to their "places" and for the military protection to do so safely—but with little indication that they hoped to reconstitute an intermediate sociocultural entity. In fact, lexicographers have not found the ethnonym "Newfoundlander" in use before 1765. This period, following the Seven Years' War (1756–1763), was one of rapid population growth, when Newfoundland's boundaries were renegotiated and the island assimilated a large number of outsiders, just as Acadia had done in the 1730s. As in Acadia, the select ingredients of this ethnic stew had been on the boil in a small pot for a long time, which is a good recipe for a distinctive dish, when the time comes to serve it up. In 1697, however, English Newfoundland was still a part-society, a congeries of plantations, in the narrow sense, not yet able to imagine themselves as anything more than a plantation, in the wider sense. Newfoundland's distinctive culture has roots in the seventeenth century, but a consciousness of cultural distinctiveness did not emerge in that period.[30]

Roots of a distinctive culture in 17th c but not a consciousness

Although the inhabitants of seventeenth-century Newfoundland had not yet developed a conception of themselves as a political collectivity or even as an ethnos, the English, paradoxically, had already constructed an identity for Newfoundland and, by implication, Newfoundlanders. By 1700, Newfoundland played a problematic metaphorical role for Britain, or for literate middle-class Britons, at any rate, which would bedevil perceptions of the island for a very long time. Certain oppositions were frequently repeated (Table 38). Many of these oppositions had some basis

Paradoxically the English did construct an identity

30. Peter E. Pope, "Comparisons: Atlantic Canada," in Daniel Vickers, ed., *A Companion to Colonial America* (Malden, Mass., 2003), 489–507; N. E. S. Griffiths, *The Contexts of Acadian History, 1686–1784* (Montreal and Kingston, 1992), 33–61; Clappe et al., Petition to William III, 1697, CO 194/1 (6), 14; *DNE*, s.v. "Newfoundlander"; Mannion, "Irish Migration, 1697–1732," *Newfoundland Studies*, XVII (2001), 257–293. Sider, *Culture and Class*, 32, argues that Newfoundland culture could not emerge until after the collapse of the servant fishery permitted the growth of "the village and family-based fishery." Since I reject Sider's apparent assumption that the early servant fishery was not family-based, his analysis of limits on the emergence of a local culture does not make much sense within my analytic framework, though the chronology roughly coincides.

Table 38. *Seventeenth-Century British Middle-Class Conceptions of England and Newfoundland*

England	Newfoundland
Warm	Cold
Land	Sea
Soil	Rock
Culture	Nature
Harvest	Hunt
Cattle	Cod
Rich	Poor
Social	Solitary
Residence	Transience
Order	Disorder
Enclosed	Unenclosed
Competent	Dependent
Credit	Debt
Lawful	Lawless
Civilized	Wild
Farm	Forest
Fertile	Infertile
Family	Young males
Marriage	Sex
Church	Tavern
Christian	Godless
Good	Wicked

Sources: These oppositions occur in sources quoted throughout this book, particularly the naval commodores' "Replies to the Heads of Inquiry" and John Thomas to Sir Richard[?], Sept. 15, 1680, Codrington Library, All Souls College, Oxford University, Wynne Collection, MS 239, 229–230, in Peter Pope, *"A True and Faithful Account*: Newfoundland in 1680," *Newfoundland Studies*, XII (1996), 32–49.

in geographical or sociological reality, of course. Others are the common currency of perceptions of the other, particularly by the richer of the poorer. (As the Quebecois put it, "Everyone is someone else's Newfie.") What is of more interest, culturally speaking, is the extent to which these preconceptions could disguise the economic geography of the eastern coast of Newfoundland and the sociology of the colony of English there, without government ecclesiastical or civil, who lived by catch-ing fish.[31]

An example will suggest the power of metaphor to muffle an other-wise competent observer. Captain Sir William Poole was the author of the planter census of 1677, the most detailed of the century. He enumer-ated gardens and pastures, swine, cattle, and sheep, besides the usual infrastructure of the staple industry. Yet, in his "Answers to the Sever-all Heads of Inquiry," he told the Committee for Trade and Plantations, "The planters and all others conclude the country not able to support itselfe, affording nothing but wood, except what is hooked out of the sea." Just as farming was overperceived in late-medieval Iceland, fish-ing was overperceived in early modern Newfoundland. The invisibility of fishing in Iceland is the inverse of the invisibility of farming in New-foundland. In Iceland, only outsiders valued fishing, which the inhabi-tants themselves disregarded; in Newfoundland, it was the outsiders who discounted the underperceived category, farming. This difference marks, perhaps, the extent to which late-medieval Icelanders had devel-oped their own ability to deceive themselves, as good an indication of having developed their own culture as any, whereas seventeenth-century Newfoundlanders still relied on others.[32]

The characteristics ascribed to Newfoundland in the later seventeenth century, in opposition to English values and virtues, constituted a kind of cultural impediment to the development of settlement. Medieval Norwe-gians had ascribed to Iceland a similar cluster of unattractive attributes, with a similar implication: there was something fishy about the place; it was so cold, unattractive, infertile, and wicked that it could not be seri-ously considered as a possible place to emigrate. Icelanders themselves projected similarly negative preconceptions on their own fishery. Ice-landic law permitted men to make the long trek to seasonal fishing camps

31. Yvon Dulude and Jean-Claude Trait, *Dictionnaire des injures québécoises* (Montreal, 1996), 295, quotes Sylvain Lelièvre: "On est toujours le newfie d'un autre." In his song, *Le chanteur indigène*, Lelièvre puts the idea more elegantly: "On est toujours un peu l'Iroquois de quelqu'un." ("You're always sort of some-body's Indian") (translation is mine, as in the text). The characterization of New-foundland from "An Account of His Majesties Plantations in America," ca. 1680, British Library, Add MS 15898, 129–131, is in the Introduction, above.

32. William Poole, "A Particular Accompt of All the Inhabitants and Plant-ers . . . ," and Poole, "Answers," Sept. 10, 1677, CO 1/41 (62i, iv), 149–152, 157–166; Hastrup, *Island of Anthropology*, 218–232.

in the southeast every spring but required them to return in the summer to man the social world of the farm households scattered along the valleys of the north and west. It was culturally acceptable for young men to move into the natural world to fish, but it was not acceptable for them to reside there, outside the social world of the farm. These prejudices present an obvious parallel with English policy in the second half of the seventeenth century, to the extent that the latter was designed to corner fishing servants into returning to the West Country from the English Shore. The underlying, profoundly negative cultural attitude to Newfoundland was probably far more effective in retarding the development of "settled government" than the occasional cabal of West Country merchants or the intermittent and erratically enforced legal regulations of the period. The English Shore might not yet have developed a consciousness of itself, but it already played a cultural role for England, tolerated as a nursery of seamen but scorned as an exemplar of the wretched life of those beyond a properly ordered agricultural society.[33]

Conclusion

Despite the optimism of the early proprietary projectors, late-seventeenth-century Newfoundland was neither a true plantation, in the original broad sense, nor England's county farthest west; it had become something literally in between, a forest encroachment, en route to the American enclosure. The informal unsponsored settlement of the English Shore, between 1630 and 1700, is comprehensible only within the context of the West Country migratory fishery and the international trade in cod. Conversely, these important ventures cannot be properly understood without considering the planters, who by 1675 were shipping a third of the total British catch. As one of the extinct large creatures of the early modern North Atlantic economy, the cod fishery is part of European history. But the island's history also faces west. From its beginnings, Newfoundland had close links with the North American Atlantic seaboard, particularly greater New England and the Gulf of St. Lawrence.[34]

33. Kirsten Hastrup, *Culture and History in Medieval Iceland: An Anthropological Analysis of Structure and Change* (Oxford, 1985), 160–161; Hastrup, *Nature and Policy*, 69–79; Hastrup, *Island of Anthropology*, 218–232.

34. Cf. Cole Harris, "European Beginnings in the Northwest Atlantic: A Com-

The North American context of Newfoundland history is epitomized in the seventeenth century by the adventures of the Kirke family. They seized Champlain's *comptoir* in Quebec in 1627, traded in "The River of Canada" in the 1620s and 1630s, expanded England's share of the New-foundland fish trade in the 1630s, backed settlement after 1638, turned the commercial disruption of the Civil War into an opportunity to pro-mote intercolonial trade in the 1640s, maintained successful fishing plan-tations through the political and economic crises of the 1650s, invested in the original stock of the Hudson's Bay Company in 1666, and survived boom and bust in the Newfoundland fishery of the 1670s and 1680s, managing to remain preeminent planter gentry on the English Shore through the better part of a century. The pivotal characters in this family saga, at least from the Newfoundland perspective, were Sir David and Lady Sara Kirke.

[handwritten margin note: Adventures of the Kirke family summarized]

On her deathbed, in the early 1680s, Lady Sara could look back on four decades at Ferryland. Outside her window lay the Pool Plantation, which she had managed for thirty years, since her husband's imprison-ment in 1651. Three sons and her refugee sister were well established as substantial planters in their own right in nearby Renews or Ferryland itself. If the latter was still one of the best harbors in the land, it was be-cause her family had rebuilt it after the Dutch raid of 1673. Her eldest son, George, was now the major planter on the south Avalon. These were Lady Kirke's accomplishments, despite the ominous situation that had faced her and her family after Sir David's death in prison in 1654, "a knowne malignant, and an inveterate enemye to this present state and government." Of course, she had relied on the help and advice of her brother-in-law John in London and, no doubt, on whatever capital her late husband had managed to cache, under the prying eyes of the parlia-mentary commissioners. In the end, though, Ferryland, "the pleasantest place in the whole Island," was as much her monument as theirs.[35]

Sir David's expedient discretion about commercial success leaves his own accomplishments less tangible. With the perspective of three and a half centuries, the substantial remains of stone and mortar laid bare

---

parative View," in David D. Hall and David Grayson Allen, eds., *Seventeenth-Century New England: A Conference Held by the Colonial Society of Massachusetts, June 18 and 19, 1982*, Colonial Society of Massachusetts, *Publications*, LXIII, *Collections* (Boston, 1984), 119–152.

35. Characterization of Kirke, in Petition of the Merchant Adventurers of Plym-outh, England, to the Council of State, ca. 1650, *Winthrop Papers*, VI, 4–6.

on the Ferryland waterfront make more of an impression than a terse bill of lading or an allusive reference to favors done and others expected in a moldering bundle of court papers. Yet David Kirke was a big fish in what was then a very big pond. He had his own genius: he grasped possibilities in a period of rapid change. When he and his brothers devised a way to break into the Newfoundland sack trade, they were only imitating competitors like John Delabarre and the Dutch innovators in this business. But David Kirke also recognized the potential value of fishing plantations to sack merchants and understood that the profitable transformation of fish into wine could service something broader than the essentially middle-class home market if wines and spirits could be brought back to the fisherfolk of the North American littoral. Making these goods available to ordinary working people was a novelty and, with the new markets in tobacco and sugar, was one of the ways resource peripheries like Newfoundland were modern places. To put it differently, this was one of the ways seventeenth-century maritime populations were modern people. The Newfoundland plantation was, from Kirke's time at least, deeply implicated in long-distance exchange and thus, inevitably, part of a wider, transatlantic cultural system.[36]

36. Cf. Leslie Choquette, *Frenchmen into Peasants: Modernity and Tradition in the Peopling of French Canada* (Cambridge, Mass., 1997), esp. 178, 302.

GLOSSARY

Newfoundland has its own English. The language of the fishery is even more esoteric, and to venture into the seventeenth century is itself to cross a kind of conceptual frontier. This glossary does not deal with technical topics treated in a single chapter; it is meant, rather, as a guide to the recurring jargon of a specialist historiography. Some key terms have a challenging resemblance to nested Russian *matriuschka* dolls: every reexamination reveals a finer level of qualification. In the interests of brevity, only the surface is glossed here. For refinement of traditional terms, please consult the invaluable *Dictionary of Newfoundland English*, 2d ed., with supplement, ed. G. M. Story, W. J. Kirwin, and J. D. A. Widdowson (Toronto, 1990).

Admiral. *See* Fishing admiral

Admiralty Court: the English court system that enforced the traditional law of the sea, or Law of Admiralty, in the High Court of Admiralty in London and in Vice Courts of Admiralty in regional centers

Atlantic islands: Madeira, the Canaries, and the Azores

Banks. *See* Fishing banks

Beothuk: the aboriginal Amerindian Native people of the island of Newfoundland at the time of European contact, circa 1500

Boatkeeper: the owner of a boat used in the *inshore fishery*, whether a *planter* or a *by-boat-keeper*

By-boat: a fishing boat kept in Newfoundland and used in the *inshore fishery* during the summer fishing season by a migratory *by-boat-keeper*

By-boat-keeper: a migratory boatmaster, owning a *by-boat* kept in Newfoundland and seasonally employing other men

By-boat-men: migratory fishers employed in the *by-boat* fishery

Charter of Avalon: proprietary grant in 1623 by James I to Sir George Calvert of the Avalon Peninsula between Aquaforte and Petty Harbour

Common-property resource: an unenclosed open-access resource. Before the introduction of licenses and quotas, the *inshore fishery* was a common-property resource

Cookroom: a temporary, wooden, wattle structure used to prepare and serve meals to seasonal fishing crews

Corporate colony: a community founded, subsidized, and directed in its activities by a proprietor or proprietors

Court of Admiralty. *See* Admiralty Court

Dry fish: lightly salted, air-dried cod

English Shore: the east coast of Newfoundland from Trepassey in the south to Bonavista Bay in the north, after 1565 seasonally frequented by *West Country* fishing crews and settled by fisherfolk after 1610

Fish: in Newfoundland, cod

Fishing admiral: the *fishing master* arriving first in a particular Newfoundland harbor in spring, thus claiming first choice of *fishing rooms* and the right to enforce the traditional custom of the fishery during the ensuing fishing season. The term was sometimes used, in a similar sense, to mean the first fishing ship arriving. Fishing admirals were not naval officers

Fishing banks: fishing grounds, well offshore, where cod were once prolific, for example, the Grand Banks, exploited by French ships since the mid-sixteenth century and by English and colonial ships after 1713. Properly speaking, inshore fishing grounds are not *banks*

Fishing master: person in charge of a *fishing ship*

Fishing room: the shore space from which fishers, whether resident *planters* or migratory *ship fishermen*, seasonally prosecuted a coastal *inshore fishery*

Fishing ship: a ship coming to Newfoundland for the summer fishing season, carrying fishermen and provisions for an *inshore fishery* prosecuted in open boats. Although the vessels involved in this fishery were called *fishing ships* in the seventeenth century, before 1713 the English at Newfoundland did not, in fact, fish from ships. Ships fishing, in the seventeenth-century sense, often also carried fish to market

Flake: a rough wooden scaffold of poles, supporting a roughly horizontal surface of evergreen boughs, used especially by English fishers to dry salt cod

Freight, to: to hire the services of a ship and its crew

French Shore: in the seventeenth century, loosely the area where the French fished, especially between Trepassey and Port aux Basques on the south coast of Newfoundland. In the eighteenth and nineteenth centuries, a French fishing zone on the northeast and west coasts of the island, including the Petit Nord, was formally delimited by treaty as the French Shore

Furriers: European overwinterers in Newfoundland, who spent time inland hunting and trapping

Furring: in Newfoundland, the hunting and trapping of fur-bearing animals

Grant of Newfoundland: patent granted in 1637 by Charles I to Sir David
Kirke and three courtiers for a trading monopoly, with powers to tax
foreign fishers and traders, and restricted rights to property in
Newfoundland. The patentees invited *Kirke, Barkeley, and company* to
manage the project

Green fish: synonym for *wet fish*, heavily salted in a brine

Green man: a novice in the fishery; synonym for youngster

Inhabitant: a person resident in Newfoundland, who could be either a
planter or a servant

Inshore fishery: the fishery prosecuted from shore stations in open boats
venturing to sea daily

Kirke, Barkeley, and company: the London-based trading house, active in
the 1630s and 1640s. It was a partnership of three of the Kirke
brothers—James, John, and David—with William Barkeley

Make fish, to: producing dry salt cod from fresh fish

Master: the person in charge of a ship or boat

Migratory fishery: the seasonal *inshore fishery* prosecuted along the coasts
of Newfoundland by transient fishers from England and continental
Europe and the seasonal *offshore fishery* prosecuted on the Grand Banks
and other *fishing banks*, notably by ships from Normandy

Newfoundland commissioners: representatives of the Commonwealth
(1649–1653) appointed by the Council of State to look into Sir David
Kirke's administration of Newfoundland and to attend to the
Commonwealth's affairs

Newfoundland Company: a chartered limited-stock company set up by
London and Bristol merchants to establish a colony in Newfoundland at
Cupids in 1610

Newfoundland Plantation: a project for commercial exploitation of the
Newfoundland fishery under a patent granted in 1637 by Charles I to Sir
David Kirke and a syndicate of courtiers

Offshore fishery: the fishery prosecuted from ships venturing to the Grand
Banks and other *fishing banks* for weeks at a time, in the seventeenth
century by French ships

Outport: in England, a port other than London; in Newfoundland, a port
other than St. John's

Passengers: persons other than a ship's crew carried to and from the British
Isles and Newfoundland, whether they were *by-boat-men*, intended
planters, or their servants

Petit Nord: the French term for the east coast of Newfoundland's Great

Northern Peninsula, together with the Bay Verte Peninsula, where the Bretons, in particular, prosecuted a productive migratory *inshore fishery* from the sixteenth century until 1904

Plantation: the waterfront property from which a Newfoundland *planter* prosecuted the fishery

Planter: a resident of Newfoundland owning property, normally a fishing plantation

Portage: among ships' crews, the perquisite of carrying private cargo for profit, free of freight charges

Proprietary colony: one of the early colonies owned outright by a proprietor, for example, Lord Baltimore, or proprietors, for example, the *Newfoundland Company*

Province of Avalon: a territory within Newfoundland's Avalon Peninsula, granted in 1621 by James I to Sir George Calvert, later first Baron Baltimore

Quintal: a traditional unit of weight for *salt fish* of 112 pounds (pronounced and sometimes spelled "kental")

Room. *See* Fishing room

Sack ship: a ship coming to Newfoundland to buy a cargo of fish to carry to market. Sometimes the term was used loosely to mean any ship carrying fish to market

Salt fish: unless otherwise specified, *dry fish*

Shallop: an open wooden boat about ten meters long (thirty to thirty-five feet)

Ship fishermen: fishers arriving in Newfoundland on so-called *fishing ships* to prosecute an *inshore fishery* in boats

Ship fishing. *See* Fishing ship

Stage: a rough wooden wharf with an enclosed space for unloading and processing fish

Ton: a traditional unit of weight for *salt fish* of 20 *quintals*, or 2,240 pounds. A ton is also a traditional estimate of the displacement of a ship, originally the space taken to stow a *tun* of wine. Since *salt fish* is a light cargo, a ton of fish would take up more space than a tun of wine. Hence, a 100-ton ship could not carry 100 tons of salt cod. Furthermore, before 1700, actual cargo tonnage was less than measured tonnage (that is, cubic capacity), so a discount was made on the latter for registered tonnage. Impressionistic estimating procedures often leave it unclear whether "tons burthen" reflected measured tonnage, actual cargo tonnage, or registered tonnage. Differing figures are often given for the same ship; hence, ships' tonnage figures are not precise

Tonne: a metric ton, about 2,205 pounds, used here in estimates of the live
weight or biomass of fish caught

Train oil: an industrial oil rendered from cod livers and shipped to Europe
in barrels

Train vat: a large wooden container used to collect *train oil*, as it was
rendered

Truck system: in Newfoundland historiography, a system of payments in
kind by which fish merchants advanced provisions to nominally
independent households, on credit, against the expected catch of the
ensuing season

Tun: a large wooden staved container for the shipment of wine, equivalent
to 8 barrels, or 252 imperial gallons, or about 925 liters

West Country: traditionally, the English counties of Somerset, Dorset,
Devon, and Cornwall, with an emphasis here on Devon and Dorset,
which were most heavily involved in the Newfoundland trade

Western Adventurers: English investors in the *West Country* migratory
fishery at Newfoundland

Western Charters: royal patents granted in 1634, 1661, and 1676 to the
West Country ports seasonally involved in the fishery on the *English
Shore*, prescribing how migratory *fishing masters* could claim *fishing
rooms* and reiterating the traditional customs of the fishery, including the
power of *fishing admirals* to settle disputes

Wet fish: cod heavily salted in a brine

Winter-housing: the practice of seasonal residence inland, close to supplies
of firewood

Youngster: a novice in the fishery; a synonym for *green man*

INDEX

235, 265–266; economy of, 315–316, 344–345, 360

Conflict: between planters and migratory crews, 50, 65, 71, 77, 199, 203–206, 257, 285, 310, 413; among fishing crews, 68, 71, 310, 420; between English and French crews, 72–73, 306–311; between fishing and sack ships, 111; among ports, 111, 147; between fishers and merchants, 188, 203–204; among planters, 275

Connecticut, 227–228

Connecticut Valley, 280–282, 285, 303

Consumer revolution, 31, 350–360

Consumption: by mariners, 218, 356–358, 383–395; criticism of, 349–350, 382–383; by servants, 349, 360–367, 383–406, 438; and hierarchies, 355 n. 9, 356–360, 382–385, 388, 400–401, 422; by planters, 359–360, 368–373, 400–406, 438; by merchant gentry, 373–375. *See also* Demand

Contracts: for fish, 100; for employment, 161–163, 168, 192, 239, 251, 273; economic culture of, 285–287, 399–400

Convoys, 29, 313, 414

Cookrooms, 22, 319–320, 439

Cooperation. *See* Interdependence

Corfish, 27–28

Cornwall, 12, 33, 105

Corwin, George, 231

Credit: letters of, 98, 100, 112–113, 144; and New England merchants, 157, 196, 231, 245, 362–365, 380, 404–405; and wages, 165–166, 403–406; by patrons, 282–284, 303, 415–416, 428; and planters, 284, 361, 364, 368, 404–406, 414–419, 423, 428. *See also* Debt

Crews. *See* Servants

Croad, John, 157, 364

Cromwell, Oliver, 142, 154, 294

Crouse, 321

Crout, Henry, 51, 145

Cruse, Thomas, 57, 59, 277–279

Cufflinks, 268–269

Cupids: as colony, 32, 48–52, 55–56, 73, 79, 122, 158, 233 n. 36, 411; archaeology of, 51, 252–253, 327, 330, 332; and trade, 100, 158, 441

Customs duties, 119, 155

Cutlery, 330, 356, 358–359

Dairies, 298, 332, 345

Dartmouth (Devon): and fishery, 12, 32, 41, 111, 145–148, 161–163, 169, 210, 234, 349, 416; Atlantic links of, 41, 126, 144–149, 152–158, 315, 412; trade of, 93–94, 97, 100, 111, 315, 340, 369, 381; merchants of, 111, 152, 155, 380–381; ships of, 111, 286–287, 369; as port, 129–131, 145–148, 347; politics in, 291–292

David of Ferryland, 90, 153–155, 159, 375–376, 380

Davies, Philis, 57, 279–280

Davis, William, 157, 380

Debt: for passage, 174, 245–248; to patrons, 282–284, 303–304, 417–418; for supply, 283, 361–365, 417, 423; and alcohol, 364, 403–406. *See also* Credit

Delabarre, John, 88–90, 112–118, 120

Demand: for fish, 12, 14, 31; for alcohol, 351, 353, 357, 359, 377–378, 384–406, 421, 431, 438; for tobacco, 351, 353, 356–360, 385–406, 421, 431, 438. *See also* Consumption

Dench, Robert, 60, 368–372

Denys, Nicolas, 25, 174

Desire, 105, 112–113, 151

Devon: fisheries of, 12, 17, 169, 241; and navy, 176; politics in, 194, 291–292; and migration, 232, 234, 251–252; literacy in, 265–266; and tobacco, 357, 380–381

Disease. *See* Health

91–92, 242, 378–381, 384, 397–
398; Spanish, 88–97, 110, 242, 377,
384; Malaga, 88, 95, 239, 378–379;
sack, 95, 384, 397–398; Fayal, 96,
242, 315, 377, 404; Canary, 96, 242,
375–377, 382, 397, 404; Madeira,
375–377, 382, 404; sherry, 378–379
Winter, John, 190–191, 362, 384
Winter-housing, 248–253, 326, 427,
443
Winthrop, John, 79, 255, 276, 294
Witless Bay, 41, 100, 235 n. 2
Wives: of migratory fishers, 166, 215–
217; of planters, 196, 208, 213–218,
297–300, 346; and taverns, 395
Women: among early colonists, 50, 54;
as planters, 56, 215–219, 240, 252,
264, 296–303, 316, 318, 413; and

demographic balance, 56, 213–218,
222, 240; and censuses, 199, 223–
225; as servants, 217, 222, 235; as
merchant gentry, 270–274, 300–303
Woods, 128, 342 n. 40; birch, 28; balsam fir, 28, 308, 319–320, 328, 341;
spruce, 70 n. 30, 267, 341, 395. *See
also* Firewood; Forest industries;
Lumber
Wrixon, Amy, 59, 284
Wrixon, William, 59, 284
Wynne, Edward, 6, 54, 128, 137, 296–
297, 312, 327, 332

Yarmouth, 94, 111
Yonge, James, 8, 24–25, 42, 56, 70,
175, 224, 319–320, 333–334
Youngsters. *See* Green men